The Handbook of Latin American and Caribbean Intelligence Cultures

SECURITY AND PROFESSIONAL INTELLIGENCE EDUCATION SERIES (SPIES)

Series Editor: Jan Goldman

In this post–September 11, 2001, era there has been rapid growth in the number of professional intelligence training and educational programs across the United States and abroad. Colleges and universities, as well as high schools, are developing programs and courses in homeland security, intelligence analysis, and law enforcement, in support of national security.

The Security and Professional Intelligence Education Series (SPIES) was first designed for individuals studying for careers in intelligence and to help improve the skills of those already in the profession; however, it was also developed to educate the public on how intelligence work is conducted and should be conducted in this important and vital profession.

1. *Communicating with Intelligence: Writing and Briefing in the Intelligence and National Security Communities*, by James S. Major. 2008.
2. *A Spy's Résumé: Confessions of a Maverick Intelligence Professional and Misadventure Capitalist*, by Marc Anthony Viola. 2008.
3. *An Introduction to Intelligence Research and Analysis*, by Jerome Clauser, revised and edited by Jan Goldman. 2008.
4. *Writing Classified and Unclassified Papers for National Security*, by James S. Major. 2009.
5. *Strategic Intelligence: A Handbook for Practitioners, Managers, and Users*, revised edition by Don McDowell. 2009.
6. *Partly Cloudy: Ethics in War, Espionage, Covert Action, and Interrogation*, by David L. Perry. 2009.
7. *Tokyo Rose / An American Patriot: A Dual Biography*, by Frederick P. Close. 2010.
8. *Ethics of Spying: A Reader for the Intelligence Professional*, edited by Jan Goldman. 2006.
9. *Ethics of Spying: A Reader for the Intelligence Professional*, Volume 2, edited by Jan Goldman. 2010.
10. *A Woman's War: The Professional and Personal Journey of the Navy's First African American Female Intelligence Officer*, by Gail Harris. 2010.
11. *Handbook of Scientific Methods of Inquiry for Intelligence Analysis*, by Hank Prunckun. 2010.
12. *Handbook of Warning Intelligence: Assessing the Threat to National Security*, by Cynthia Grabo. 2010.

To view the books on our website, please visit https://rowman.com/Action/SERIES/RL/SPIES or scan the QR code below.

The Handbook of Latin American and Caribbean Intelligence Cultures

Edited by
Florina Cristiana Matei
Carolyn Halladay
Eduardo E. Estévez

ROWMAN & LITTLEFIELD
Lanham • Boulder • New York • London

Published by Rowman & Littlefield
An imprint of The Rowman & Littlefield Publishing Group, Inc.
4501 Forbes Boulevard, Suite 200, Lanham, Maryland 20706
www.rowman.com

86-90 Paul Street, London EC2A 4NE, United Kingdom

British Library Cataloguing in Publication Information Available

Library of Congress Cataloging-in-Publication Data

Names: Matei, Florina Cristiana, editor. | Halladay, Carolyn, editor. | Estévez, Eduardo E., editor.
Title: The handbook of Latin American and Caribbean intelligence cultures / Edited by Florina Cristiana Matei, Carolyn Halladay, Eduardo E. Estévez.
Other titles: Latin American and Caribbean intelligence cultures
Description: Lanham : Rowman & Littlefield Publishing Group, [2022] | Series: Security and professional intelligence education series | Includes bibliographical references. | Summary: "The Handbook of Latin American and Caribbean Intelligence Cultures provides a comprehensive analysis of the contemporary efforts of Latin American and Caribbean nations to develop an intelligence culture that converts the former military regimes' repressive security apparatuses into democratic intelligence communities"— Provided by publisher.
Identifiers: LCCN 2022003972 (print) | LCCN 2022003973 (ebook) | ISBN 9781538160817 (cloth) | ISBN 9781538197691 (paper) | ISBN 9781538160824 (epub)
Subjects: LCSH: Intelligence service—Latin America. | Intelligence service—Caribbean Area. | Democracy—Latin America. | Democracy—Carribean Area.
Classification: LCC JL959.5.I6 H36 2022 (print) | LCC JL959.5.I6 (ebook) | DDC 327.128—dc23/eng/20220412
LC record available at https://lccn.loc.gov/2022003972
LC ebook record available at https://lccn.loc.gov/2022003973

Contents

PART III: NON-DEMOCRATIC REGIMES

Preface

Peter Gill

While there has been significant growth in intelligence studies since the 1990s, viewed globally, this field has been very uneven—with the greatest preponderance of studies concerning intelligence agencies within the "Anglosphere," especially the United States and the United Kingdom. Scholarly interest in intelligence studies owes to several factors including the broadening of perceived non-state threats, the "war on terror," the rise of surveillance society, and an increasing number of intelligence organizations in the corporate sector and civil society. Thus, there are many more students of intelligence studies but also a clear need to increase the coverage of areas hitherto neglected.

The editors' introduction notes that coverage of Latin America and the Caribbean, especially in English, is still relatively sparse, and they have set out to provide some much-needed correction. Intelligence studies in the UK/US started with examinations of history, especially the use of intelligence in the major twentieth-century wars, and only later developed into more contemporary concerns with governance, especially the related issues of the control and oversight of intelligence. The contrasting histories and political cultures of the countries analyzed here provide important context—for example, the precise institutional form of the authoritarian repression perpetrated by domestic security, intelligence, and police agencies during the second half of the twentieth century varied, but human rights violations were widespread. Therefore, it is entirely appropriate that the central theme of *The Handbook of Latin American and Caribbean Intelligence Cultures* is democratization—how intelligence must be governed so that it enhances rather than diminishes human security.

The so-called Third Wave[1] of democratization starting in 1974 raised multiple challenges for countries, which were also often struggling with such serious economic and social challenges as corruption, poverty, and violence and, in many cases, these perils continue to prevent any consolidation of liberal democracy. Furthermore, while democratic progress can be identified through the first decade of the twenty-first century, a resurgence of authoritarian populism more recently has stalled this momentum—not only in Latin America—and with it, progress in democratic reform of intelligence.[2]

An essential precondition, some would say synonym, for democracy is rule *of* law rather than the rule *by* law that is common in what might be termed "defective democracies." But even if the former is established so that laws are made by legislatures chosen in essentially free and fair elections, are enforced impartially by responsible ministers, and interpreted by independent judges, a very specific challenge remains as to whether intelligence agencies remain in a "reserved domain of power,"[3] where they continue to operate according to authoritarian norms. The many Latin American regimes that have passed specific intelligence laws, purporting to increase the control and oversight of reformed—or at least renamed—agencies, fulfill one necessary condition for democracy. But this initial step is not sufficient. The central question is whether the law brings about real rather than just symbolic change.

Democratization is not an *event*; it is a *process*, and it requires constant vigilance and effort. As can be seen in even the older democracies—and as is well documented here in many chapters—there are many challenges to first establishing and then maintaining democratic control and oversight of intelligence. A legislative mandate for the agencies must clarify the rules of operation and determine that elected officials will establish national security policies, appoint agency heads, and in agreement with legislatures, determine their budgets. A key element of this process is to curtail the practice of many authoritarian agencies of maintaining their own (often illegal) sources of finance. The legislation must also determine which combination of legislative, judicial, and/or expert bodies will monitor the effectiveness and propriety of the agencies.

The challenges facing those people elected or chosen for these tasks are great: fundamentally, they must manifest the political *will* to carry out their tasks. In countries where there is (for very good reasons) such a historic lack of trust in security, intelligence, and police agencies, this step requires very strong personalities. They have two audiences for their work: first, policy makers and executives who may just not be interested in developing security and intelligence policies or who may lack any expertise as to how they might do so. Second, they (along with academics and researchers) must get involved in trying to educate a fearful or skeptical public into the realities of intelligence. This process may involve some necessary accounting for past abuses but must also include patient explanation of how current policies and practices, not just the law (including intelligence law), are different from previous periods of repression.

The context for this work is now dramatically different from that of the 1990s with almost complete governmental secrecy having been at least modified by the free-for-all that is the Internet. To be sure, intelligence agencies still seek, quite properly, to maintain secrecy of their "sources and methods," but in other respects—access to historical archives, greater journalistic interest, and civil society research—it is possible to understand a great deal more now than before about what intelligence does and whether it enhances or degrades security. On the other hand, because of endemic secrecy and its reflexive tendency to act repressively, intelligence agencies have always been a focus of conspiracy theorizing; the Internet and the current prevalence of "fake news" has only worsened this tendency. Therefore, such collections of scholarly research articles as the present volume are so important in that their wide promulgation can possibly counteract the growth of misinformation.

Finally, these country studies provide a solid basis for the further development of comparative analysis in an increasingly uncertain world—in terms of both security and democracy—and thus constitute an important contribution to the study of intelligence not only in Latin America and the Caribbean but globally. Ultimately, this global perspective on intelligence democratization is a key part of the intelligence studies field.

NOTES

1. Samuel P. Huntington, *The Third Wave: Democratization in the Late Twentieth Century* (Norman: University of Oklahoma Press, 1991).

2. Intelligence agencies have been either vilified by populist leaders or used by these leaders for political gain and consolidation of power.

3. Larry Diamond, *Developing Democracy: Towards Consolidation* (Baltimore MD: Johns Hopkins University Press, 1999).

Acknowledgments

There are many people who helped bring this volume to fruition, and we are grateful to all of them. We are very grateful to the Naval Postgraduate School's School of International and Defense Studies (IDS), the National Security Affairs Department (NSA), the Center for Homeland Defense and Security (CHDS), and the former Center for Civil-Military Relations (CCMR)—now the Institute for Security Governance (ISG)—for providing an environment that fosters academic and curriculum development. As always, we gratefully acknowledge the research support of Ms. Greta Marlatt at the Dudley Knox Library. Our profound gratitude also goes to those who stimulated and mentored us to build a trajectory in intelligence studies—Thomas C. Bruneau, Peter Gill, Richard Valcourt, Kenneth R. Dombroski, Jan Goldman, Dante Giadone, Holger Bunning, Jesús Rodríguez, León Arslanian, and the late Michael Hermann. We are also grateful to the Intelligence Studies Section of the International Studies Association for providing an annual forum for discussion of intelligence culture trends.

Our deep appreciation goes to our students—military officers, intelligence professionals, and civilians from the United States and Latin America and the Caribbean Basin—whose expertise and experience in the field of intelligence and democracy in the region helped us understand the challenges and opportunities of institutionalizing effective and accountable intelligence agencies in this region of the world that we hold dear.

In the same vein, we highly appreciate the relationship with, and support from, our American and Foreign Service National colleagues in the U.S. embassies in Latin America and the Caribbean Basin. While we cannot thank you by name, all of you have brought an enormous contribution to the completion of this book.

Editing of the chapters and the preparation of the manuscript for submission was done by Major Richard Elmore, U.S. Air Force, and NPS graduate. We also relied on his regional expertise—as a foreign area officer and contributor to U.S. security cooperation efforts in the Latin America region—throughout the process. We are grateful for his professional commitment to assist us in all phases in the development and completion of this volume. We would also like to thank Captain Alex Wilson, U.S. Air Force, and NPS graduate, for his initial assistance with the index for this volume.

We would like to express our gratitude to the Roman & Littlefield editorial team, led by Ms. April Snider, acquisitions editor for Career Guides, Significant Figures in World History Encyclopedias, and Historical Dictionaries, who have been outstanding in guiding us and supporting us throughout the publication process. We are also grateful to Ms. Dhara Snowden, former senior acquisitions editor at Rowman & Littlefield, who had enthusiastically supported us since the manuscript proposal submission until her departure from Roman & Littlefield in 2021.

Our families deserve tremendous appreciation and gratitude for their support throughout this process. Cris would like to thank her husband, Eugen C. Matei, her parents, Victoria and Nicolae Vâjdea, and children, Claire and Albert Matei, for their understanding of the long hours she dedicated to the completion of this volume.

Carolyn would like to thank Penny for her forthrightness, Leelah for her companionship, Gitta because she expects it—and Jim for wrangling them all.

Eduardo would like to thank his wife, Mónica; his daughter Emilce; late feline Luna, who—together with Cris's cat Kenny—incidentally inspired this project.

Latin America

Los Angeles
San Diego
El Paso
United States
Houston
New Orleans
Bermuda (U.K.)
Monterrey
Gulf of Mexico
Miami
Nassau
The Bahamas
North Atlantic Ocean
Mexico
Guadalajara
Mérida
Havana
Cuba
Dominican Republic
Santo Domingo
Puerto Rico (U.S.)
Mexico
Jamaica
Haiti
Kingston
Port-au-Prince
St. Kitts and Nevis
Antigua and Barbuda
Belize
Belmopan
Honduras
Dominica
Guatemala
Guatemala
San Salvador
Tegucigalpa
Nicaragua
St. Vincent and the Grenadines
St. Lucia
Barbados
El Salvador
Managua
Grenada
Trinidad and Tobago
Port-of-Spain
North Pacific Ocean
Costa Rica
San José
Panama
Maracaibo
Caracas
Panama
Medellín
Venezuela
Guyana
Georgetown
Suriname
Paramaribo
Bogotá
Cayenne
French Guiana (Fr.)
Colombia
Cali
Ecuador
Quito
Guayaquil
Galápagos Islands (Ecuador)
Belém
Manaus
Fortaleza
Trujillo
Peru
Recife
Lima
Brazil
Salvador
La Paz
Bolivia
Brasília
Sucre
South Pacific Ocean
Antofagasta
Paraguay
São Paulo
Rio de Janeiro
Asunción
Easter Island (Chile)
Chile
Pôrto Alegre
Córdoba
Archipiélago Juan Fernández (Chile)
Rosario
Valparaíso
Uruguay
Santiago
Buenos Aires
Montevideo
Concepción
Argentina
South Atlantic Ocean
Scale 1:50,000,000
0   1000 Kilometers
0   1000 Miles
Azimuthal Equal-Area Projection
Falkland Islands (Islas Malvinas) (administered by U.K. claimed by Argentina)
South Georgia and the South Sandwich Islands (administered by U.K. claimed by Argentina)
Cape Horn
Boundary representation is not necessarily authoritative.

801490 (644170) 3-90

Map of Latin America
Courtesy of the Perry-Castañeda Library Map Collection at the University of Texas

Introduction

Florina Cristiana Matei, Eduardo Estévez, Carolyn Halladay, with Richard Elmore

This volume[1] explores the contemporary efforts of Latin American and Caribbean nations to develop an intelligence culture. Specifically, it analyzes these countries' efforts to democratize their intelligence agencies[2] (i.e., to develop intelligence services that are both transparent and effective) to convert the former military regimes' repressive security apparatuses into democratic intelligence communities—a rather paradoxical task, considering that democracy calls for political neutrality, transparency, and accountability, while effective intelligence services must operate in secrecy.[3] Indeed, even the most successful democracies face this conundrum of democracy and intelligence; the Latin America and the Caribbean region is not alone in facing this challenge.[4] The legacy of the repressive military regimes or brutal civil wars—which have inspired in the public a general disdain toward intelligence services due to the grave human rights abuses—coupled with politicians' persistent lack of interest or expertise in intelligence matters complicate the region's quest for a proper balance between the competing demands of democracy and intelligence. This volume details the attempts of the region's countries to overcome these obstacles and pursue democratic intelligence institution building—transforming the legal basis for intelligence; establishing democratic control and oversight mechanisms; and fostering intelligence openness, transparency, and outreach.

This handbook aspires to complement the emerging, yet meager, literature—in Spanish, Portuguese,[5] and English—that confers comparative analyses on intelligence and democracy in the region. Among the first of the very few academic works in English, two volumes stand out: *Intelligence Professionalism in the Americas*, and *Democratization of Intelligence*—both edited by Russell G. Swenson, and Susana C. Lemozy.[6] These excellent works provide an overview of the intelligence profession in different national political regimes in Latin America.

Equally important is the contribution to the development of the field of intelligence and democracy by Hans Born, Loch Johnson, and Ian Leigh whose edited volume titled *Who's Watching the Spies? Establishing Intelligence Service Accountability* discusses the challenges encountered by new democracies in bringing intelligence agencies under democratic control and oversight and includes one chapter dedicated to Latin America—Argentina—written by Eduardo Estévez.[7] In his chapter, Estévez concludes that enacting intelligence legislation is not a panacea for intelligence democratization, unless robust oversight mechanisms are also institutionalized.[8]

Similarly, the volume edited by Thomas C. Bruneau and Steven C. Boraz titled *Reforming Intelligence: Obstacles to Democratic Control and Effectiveness* collectively outlines the best practices for intelligence services in the United States and other democratic states. The authors examine intelligence practices in the United States, United Kingdom, and France, as well as such developing democracies as Brazil, Romania, South Africa, and Argentina. While rich in case studies, this volume only evaluates two Latin American intelligence reform cases—Argentina, written by Priscila Antunes, and Brazil, authored by Marco Cepik. Both authors agree with Estévez that the legacy of the past—the stigma that the intelligence agencies have to carry due to their non-democratic-regime-era human rights violations—has challenged intelligence democratization in Brazil and Argentina, enormously.[9]

Another exquisite contribution to intelligence democratization literature is Philip H. J. Davies and Kristian C. Gustafson's *Intelligence Elsewhere: Spies and Espionage Outside the Anglosphere*,[10] an edited book that provides a comparative study of national intelligence agencies outside of the Five Eyes countries (Australia, Canada, New Zealand, United Kingdom, and United States), including one case study from Latin America and the Caribbean Basin—Argentina—again authored by Estévez. In his chapter, Estévez asserts that policymakers in Argentina have failed to develop accountable and effective intelligence agencies, and thereby creating several security crises.[11] Likewise, noteworthy is the book edited by Peter Gill and Michael Andregg, *Democratization of Intelligence*. This seven-chapter volume examines intelligence democratization efforts around the globe, including both single-country studies (Romania, Bosnia and Herzegovina, and Brazil) and comparative ones (East Central European and the Balkan states; Brazil, Colombia, South Africa, and India; Argentina, Peru, and Ecuador). Notwithstanding the range of these case studies, this volume only includes three Latin America–related chapters.[12]

Of great relevance to the field of intelligence and democracy in Latin America and the Caribbean is the edited volume by Russell Swenson and Carolina Sancho titled *Intelligence Management in the Americas*, which provides a thorough examination of the current policies and practices of democratic governance in the region. The chapter authors reveal that most countries in the region have passed new legislation aimed at addressing intelligence democratization, identified management challenges, explored best practices, and highlighted issues yet to be addressed, aware, as well, that internal controls and judicial reviews have been flawed.[13]

Notably, a special European-based academic journal, dedicated to intelligence transformations in Latin America and the Caribbean, included articles on Argentina, Venezuela, Uruguay, Colombia, and El Salvador, to name a few. The authors reveal that the current status of the region's intelligence democratization is precarious, with democratic civilian control remaining weak due to lack of expertise and interest in intelligence reform by policy makers.[14]

Finally, one of the most recent contributions to the literature worth mentioning here is the book edited by Florina Cristiana Matei and Carolyn Halladay—*The Conduct of Intelligence in Democracies. Processes, Practices, Cultures*—which provides detailed analysis of the role, place, and conduct of intelligence in democratic societies, with numerous empirical examples from all over the world, including Latin America and the Caribbean. The editors find that democracies around the world have encountered similar challenges to intelligence democratization—the multifariousness of reform, resistance to reform by the intelligence agencies, reluctance to reform by civilian elites, and legacies of the past.[15] Despite these efforts, Latin America and the Caribbean Basin remains largely understudied.[16]

AN OVERVIEW OF THE GEOPOLITICAL AND GEOSTRATEGIC CONTEXT IN THE REGION AND THE EVOLUTION OF INTELLIGENCE

Since the end of the colonization era (1500s–1800s), the Latin American and the Caribbean geopolitical and geostrategic landscape has been in perpetual change. Then the Cold War began in the 1940s, which polarized the region, thereby allowing the Soviet Union and more particularly the United States a pretense to exercise their prerogatives in the name, purportedly, of a grander scheme of global security. The superpowers utilized a combined approach: installing tame dictators in some states, making other countries' access to resources and training conditional on a commitment to U.S.-inflected anti-communism, and promoting counter-insurgency efforts to keep loyal, if illiberal, governments in power. This interplay of superpower politics in Latin America and the Caribbean artificially froze the region's ability to independently advance intelligence reforms and democratic consolidation. With U.S. support, military dictatorships in the second half of the twentieth century implemented the so-called national security doctrines that granted the Latin American armed forces carte blanche to counter subversion—real or imagined—violently.[17] Indeed, enabled by their intelligence apparatuses, these nations practiced state terrorism—using the rule of force and fear against their own citizens.[18] Unsurprisingly, then, the intelligence services' repressive practices led to dire, *en-masse*, human rights violations, illegal detentions, and torture of their fellow citizens, which in turn resulted in the deaths and disappearances of tens of thousands of people throughout the region.[19]

At the height of the Cold War in the region, authoritarianism—characterized by ruthless military or military-backed regimes and repressive security forces, including the intelligence agencies—Chile, 1973–1989; Paraguay, 1940–1989—coincided paradoxically with several successful transitions to democracy during the so-called Third Wave of democratization (Brazil in 1975, Argentina in 1983, and Uruguay in 1985) to shape the political life of many Latin American and Caribbean countries.[20] Prolonged intrastate conflicts (for example, in Guatemala, 1960–1996; El Salvador, 1979–1992; and Suriname, 1986–1992) as well as border disputes (Ecuador and Peru in 1980, for instance) negatively affected regional security above and beyond the deformities of the Cold War.[21]

Since the end of the Cold War the region was marked by a decade of democratic progress (1990 to the mid-2010s)—though with a few exceptions, most notably Cuba, which remained a non-democratic regime, and Peru, which became an authoritarian regime under Alberto Fujimori (1990-2000)—followed by a period of democratic decline (mid-2010s to the present).[22] Indeed, while the struggle between democracies and military dictatorships ended, with the democracies well ahead, at the turn of the millennium, a new struggle—this time between liberal democracy and populism—emerged, founded on recurring economic, social, and political crises: Bolivia's debt woes, Argentina's debt calamity, and Venezuela's coup and eventual hyperinflation—which the region's weak, corrupt government institutions have not been able to overcome effectively. This situation has led to a decline in the quality of democracy (Brazil) or, in some cases, overall democratic regression (Venezuela).[23] As Power and Hunter note when talking about Brazil, the election of Bolsonaro was a "perfect storm" for the advent of populism and democratic decline in Brazil—as a result of "at least four simultaneous crises: an economic crisis caused by a prolonged recession, a political crisis of rising polarization and falling trust in established parties, a corruption crisis brought to the fore by the *"Lava Jato"* investigation, and the deterioration of an already dismal public-security environment."[24] At the same time, the security landscape has become increasingly unstable and violent in the region, characterized by a mix of traditional security threats—both intrastate (civil wars, insurgencies, political violence, military coups) and interstate (border disputes)—and non-traditional human security challenges (economic, food, health, environmental, individual, community, and political security).[25] Taken together, these sources of insecurity have resulted in increased violence throughout the region, promulgated by criminal gangs, transnational organized criminal groups, or even by the governments against their own citizens. No government in the region has yet tackled this entrenched problem effectively, resulting in a dilution of legitimacy of democracy and democratic institutions in the region.[26]

This era has been dominated by a few trends in intelligence: the continuation of intelligence agencies as the political police of non-democratic regimes (for example in Peru during the Fujimori reign);[27] attempts by the new democracies in the region to remove the military intelligence services from domestic security in parallel with democratic reform of intelligence organizations—including establishing legislation for intelligence agencies that provides for roles and missions of the intelligence services, developing mechanisms of democratic civilian control in all branches of government over intelligence (Brazil, Chile, and Argentina);[28] endeavors to strengthen intelligence cooperation and sharing among countries in the region;[29] and the use of military intelligence agencies domestically, for such public security purposes as fighting drug-related crime (Colombia, Mexico, and Central America),[30] which has led to corruption and human rights violations (for example, in 2006, forty-five thousand Mexican soldiers deployed by Mexican President Felipe Calderón domestically to combat drug trafficking and drug-related violence resulted in abuses against the population).[31]

Unfortunately, as the authors in this volume note, democratic reforms of intelligence have been less than perfect, plagued by weak, uninterested, inexperienced, or corrupt politicians, who are unable to exercise de facto and de jure democratic civilian control over their intelligence agencies, and who more often than not revert to using intelligence for political and personal gain.[32] Indeed, well-publicized scandals of intelligence, cases of corruption and violations of human rights, political espionage, illegal surveillance, and misuse of secret funds, have resulted in intelligence crises in Argentina, Colombia, Ecuador, Mexico, Peru, Trinidad and Tobago.[33] Furthermore, reforming intelligence has equated to one or more of the following precarious endeavors: defunding intelligence agencies, and creating new ones on the ruins of the defunct services, with no real transformation (Peru and Colombia);

policy and practice swinging wildly between supporting the government of the day—either rightist or leftist—to the detriment of the democratization of intelligence (Ecuador and Peru); arrested development of intelligence reforms due to undercooked oversight-related legislation, which enables politicization and abuses (Honduras, Paraguay,[34] Brazil,[35] Venezuela, and Nicaragua); granting intelligence agencies arrest powers—a practice that is usually associated with non-democratic regimes (Venezuela, and Nicaragua); and the militarization of intelligence (Argentina).[36] Some of these issues—for reasons previously detailed—are specific to the Latin American region; some are global challenges of democratizing states; some are just an ongoing struggle. In sum, the nebulous, sometimes incomplete, superficial, or elusive intelligence reforms in Latin America, appear to speak to the broken promises of democracy that Norberto Bobbio stresses.[37]

THE FRAMEWORK OF ANALYSIS

Ultimately, this book seeks to provide the reader with a current and comprehensive assessment of the role and place of effective intelligence in the Latin American and Caribbean democratic *milieu*. To this end, it uses a framework of analysis of democratic intelligence governance and accountability that combines the Democratic Governance of Intelligence Matrix (GDI), originally developed by Alejandra Otamendi and Eduardo Estévez, based on Peter Gill's work,[38] and a framework developed by Bruneau and Matei.[39]

This framework includes the following dimensions: First is *legislation*, which implies that as a good practice, a publicly available law should govern the intelligence sector to maintain accountability. Such a comprehensive legal framework should include the protection of human rights, particularly regarding intrusive special powers, and use of public funds. The second dimension refers to *democratic civilian control and oversight*, which includes some or all of the following mechanisms: *financial resources*, aimed at controlling secret budgets, an important tool to prevent the intelligence bureaucracies from becoming a powerful and unchecked shadow actor in politics, even under democracy; *political control*, a key aspect of the democratic governance of intelligence, with elected leaders playing a pivotal role in fostering intelligence practices and cultural change; *legislative oversight*, referring to the powers, resources, and access to information that the legislature requires to exert democratic control; *judicial review*, namely ensuring that the intelligence agencies carry out their intrusive activities in line with the law; and *public oversight*, which deals with the role of civil society and the media in overseeing intelligence activities and transparency. The third dimension includes *professionalism and effectiveness*, which involves one of all of the following mechanisms: clear guidelines for the *collection of information* (which requires secrecy, intrusive measures, and control of sensitive information) on when and how to perform such actions to respect human rights; *recruitment*, namely staffing the intelligence agencies with new personnel, free of associations with the non-democratic, abusive, past; *education* and *training*, namely teaching the new recruits the intelligence tradecraft within a democratic context. All these dimensions aim at reducing the risk of politicization and corruption of intelligence bureaucracies.

THE REST OF THE BOOK

This volume is divided into three parts. Part I starts with a preface by Peter Gill. The next section includes chapters that evaluate intelligence reforms in two old democracies (Colombia and Mexico). Part II assesses intelligence democratization in fourteen developing democracies (Argentina, Uruguay, Brazil, Chile, Peru, Ecuador, Costa Rica, Bahamas, Trinidad and Tobago, Jamaica, Paraguay, Bolivia, El Salvador, and Guatemala). Part III examines intelligence reforms in non-democracies (Venezuela and Cuba). The volume ends with a concluding essay by Thomas C. Bruneau.

Chapter 1 explores the progress of Colombia's democratic reform of intelligence. It finds that corruption and human rights violations have plagued Colombia's intelligence reform. Chapter 2 discusses intelligence democratization in Mexico. It finds that the intelligence agencies have not achieved a proper transparency-effectiveness tradeoff. The Mexican intelligence community remains politicized and outside of de facto and de jure democratic civilian control. At the same time, it is incapable of combatting the nefarious organized crime activities and violence that dominate the country's security context.

Chapter 3 provides a review of Argentina's attempts since the end of military rule to democratize intelligence. It finds that despite significant legal, institutional, and organizational transformations, the culture, practices, and uses of intelligence remain obscure and highly politicized. Chapter 4 explores Bolivia's intelligence reform attempts. It finds that although the Morales administration appointed scholars with expertise in security affairs in key areas, these endeavors were not successful in promoting intelligence democratization.

Chapter 5 analyzes Brazil's post-authoritarian regime democratic reform of intelligence. It finds that while Brazil has endeavored to create new agencies, removed from the military regime's human rights abuses, it has not achieved a proper tradeoff between effectiveness and transparency, because of the legacy of the past—the stigma associated with intelligence—coupled with a lack of expertise in intelligence on the part of policy makers.

Chapter 6 assesses Chile's post-Pinochet democratic reform of intelligence. It finds that the legacy of the past—lack of trust in intelligence organizations and the influence of the military in intelligence reform-related decision making—has challenged intelligence democratization in the country. Chapter 7 assesses Ecuador's democratic reform of intelligence since 2009. It finds that despite attempts at intelligence modernization and reform, including the new legislation adopted, the historic opportunity to establish a modern democratic governance of intelligence was missed.

Chapter 8 provides an assessment of the democratic reform of intelligence in post-Fujimori Peru. It finds that despite legal, institutional, and organizational changes, the intelligence sector in Peru is neither effective nor fully accountable, due to repeated and far-reaching corruption scandals. Chapter 9 analyzes Uruguay's intelligence democratization endeavors after the fall of military dictatorship. It finds that despite this achievement, democratic management of intelligence remains challenging due to over-powerful intelligence agencies.

Chapter 10 analyzes the challenges to intelligence democratization in Costa Rica. It finds that while Costa Rica has established democratic civilian control over the intelligence services, these mechanisms have not been entirely effective. The challenge of balancing a national identity associated with peace, disarmament, human rights, and a robust democracy contrasts diametrically to public perception of intelligence agencies, creating an endemically weak intelligence culture and crippling debate about the role of the institution in the twenty-first century.

Chapter 11 explores the post-conflict transition to democracy in Guatemala since the 1980s, which had limited impact on an intelligence community controlled by the military. Indeed, only in 2005 was the civil intelligence agency that the peace agreements of 1996 detailed finally created. It finds that intelligence democratization is challenged by weak democratic institutions, corruption, impunity, and the presence of clandestine and illegal security apparatuses.

Chapter 12 evaluates the intelligence reforms in three Caribbean countries: the Bahamas, Jamaica, and Trinidad and Tobago. It finds that achieving a tradeoff between transparency and effectiveness is constantly challenged by lack of interest and expertise by policy makers in intelligence. Chapter 13 discusses intelligence democratization in Paraguay, after the fall of Stroessner's regime. It finds that despite some progress, the intelligence system is limited to analytical rather than operational capabilities, and it is still vulnerable to politicization.

Chapter 14 assesses El Salvador's endeavors to democratize its intelligence sector after the end of the civil war in 1992. It finds that the intelligence agencies in the country are politicized and ineffective, because a law that promotes the transformation of the entire intelligence community is still pending.

Chapter 15 discusses intelligence reform in Venezuela. It finds that Venezuela's intelligence agencies act as political police of the government, used by Chavez and Maduro to oppress citizens. Chapter 16 discusses intelligence transformation in Cuba since the installment of the Castro regime in 1959. It finds that the intelligence agencies are the chief prop of the communist regime, developed to fight real or imaginary enemies of the regime, with egregious human rights abuses.

The contributing authors are all academic and practitioners, subject-matter experts on intelligence and democracy and on the region and countries about which they are writing. The three editors of the handbook are well versed in conceptual issues in both their writing and teaching; they are also regional and country experts. Matei and Halladay are the coeditors of *The Conduct of Intelligence in Democracies: Processes, Practices, Cultures*, published in 2019, in which Estévez contributed a chapter on counterinsurgency and intelligence. All editors are teaching courses related to intelligence transformation in democracies, for U.S. and international military officers and civilian counterparts, both in the United States and abroad.

NOTES

1. Disclaimer: The views expressed in this volume are those of the authors and do not reflect the official policy or position of the Department of Defense, Department of the Navy, Naval Postgraduate School, or the U.S. government, or of any other entity.

2. In general, American scholars of intelligence use the word "agency" when referring to an institution that carries out intelligence roles, while academics from other parts of the world prefer to use the word "service." We use both in this volume.

3. Florina Cristiana Matei and Carolyn Halladay, "The Role and Purpose of Intelligence in a Democracy," in *The Conduct of Intelligence in Democracies: Processes, Practices, Cultures*, eds. Florina Cristiana Matei and Carolyn Halladay (Boulder: Lynne Rienner Publishers, 2019), 1–23.

4. Matei and Halladay, "The Role and Purpose of Intelligence in a Democracy," 10–16. See also Florina Cristiana Matei and Thomas C. Bruneau, "Intelligence Reform in New Democracies: Factors Supporting or Arresting Progress," *Democratization* 18, no. 3 (2011): 602–30.

5. It is worth mentioning the following main academic works in Spanish, or Portuguese, on intelligence democratization: Andrés Gómez de la Torre, "Institucionalización y Crisis de Inteligencia: Perú en el Contexto Andino," in *Los Macro y Micro Desafíos de la Seguridad en Democracia. Contradicciones y Vulnerabilidades en*

América Latina, eds. Bertha García Gallegos and José M. Ugarte (Quito: Pontificia Universidad Católica del Ecuador, 2018), 238–39; Priscila Carlos Brandão, *Serviços Secretos e Democracia no Cone Sul: Premissas para uma Convivência Legítima, Eficiente e Profissional* (Niterói: *Impetus*, 2010); José M. Ugarte, "Actividad de Inteligencia en América Latina: Características, Fortalezas, Debilidades, Perspectivas de Futuro," *Revista Política y Estrategia* 127 (2016): 37–74; Juan Rial, "Organismos de Inteligencia en América Latina," *Inteligencia y Seguridad, Revista de Análisis y Prospectiva 5* (2008–2009): 83–84; Katalina Barreiro Santana and Fredy Rivera Vélez, "Rendición de Cuentas, Democracia e Inteligencia," in *Inteligencia Estratégica y Prospectiva*, ed. Fredy Rivera Vélez (Quito: FLACSO-Sede Ecuador / Secretaría Nacional de Inteligencia del Ecuador, 2011); José M. Ugarte, "Un Gran Reto Democrático: Controlar la Inteligencia," in *Los Macro y Micro Desafíos de la Seguridad en Democracia*; Mariano Bartolomé et al., *Inteligencia Estratégica Contemporánea: Perspectivas desde la Región Suramericana* (Quito: Universidad de las Fuerzas Armadas, ESPE, 2016); José Gabriel Paz, ed., and Roberto Román, coord., *Inteligencia Estratégica Latinoamericana: Perspectivas y Ejes Predominantes para la Toma de Decisiones Estratégicas ante un Mundo en Cambio, Antología* (Ciudad Autónoma de Buenos Aires: Ministerio de Defensa, 2015); Héctor Luis Saint Pierre et al., *Amenazas Globales Consecuencias Locales: Retos para la Inteligencia Estratégica Actual* (Sangolquí, Ecuador: Universidad de las Fuerzas Armadas ESPE, 2017); Manuel Ignacio Balcazar Villareal, "Modernización del Sistema de Inteligencia Estratégica para la Seguridad Nacional en México," *Revista de Estudios en Seguridad Internacional*, vol. 5, no. 1 (2019): 71–81; Arturo Cabrera, "Diferencias entre la Cooperación Norte y Sur en Inteligencia: Apuntes sobre la Definición de Cooperación en Inteligencia," *Líneasur*, vol. 3, no. 12 (May–August 2016): 3–116. Waldo Ansaldi and Mariana Alberto, "Muchos Hablan de Ella, Pocos Piensan en Ella. Una Agenda Posible para Explicar la Apelación a la Violencia Política en América Latina," in *América Latina: Tiempos de Violencias*, eds. Waldo Ansaldi and Verónica Giordano (Buenos Aires: Ariel, 2014), 31–32.

   6. Russell G. Swenson and Susana C. Lemozy, eds., *Intelligence Professionalism in the Americas* (Washington, DC: Joint Military Intelligence College, 2004); Russell G. Swenson and Susana C. Lemozy, eds., *Democratization of Intelligence* (English excerpts) (Washington, DC: National Defense Intelligence College, 2009).

   7. Hans Born, Loch Johnson, and Ian Leigh, eds., *Who's Watching the Spies? Establishing Intelligence Service Accountability* (Washington, DC: Potomac Books 2005).

   8. Eduardo E. Estévez, "Executive and Legislative Oversight of the Intelligence System in Argentina," in *Who's Watching the Spies? Establishing Intelligence Service Accountability*, Hans Born, Loch Johnson, and Ian Leigh, eds. (Washington, DC: Potomac Books 2005), 177.

   9. Thomas C. Bruneau and Steven Boraz, eds., *Reforming Intelligence. Obstacles to Democratic Control and Effectiveness* (Austin, TX: University of Texas Press, 2007).

   10. Philip Davies, and Kristian Gustafson, eds., *Intelligence Elsewhere: Spies and Espionage outside the Anglosphere* (Washington, DC: Georgetown University Press, 2013).

11. Eduardo E. Estévez, "Intelligence Community Reforms: The Case of Argentina," in *Intelligence Elsewhere: Spies and Espionage outside the Anglosphere*, Philip Davies and Kristian Gustafson, eds. (Washington, DC: Georgetown University Press, 2013), 232.

12. Peter Gill and Michael Andregg, eds., *Democratization of Intelligence* (Oxford/New York: Routledge, 2015).

13. Russell Swenson and Carolina Sancho, *Intelligence Management in the Americas* (Washington, DC: National Intelligence University, 2015).

14. Florina Cristiana Matei and Andres de Castro Garcia, eds., *Journal of Mediterranean and Balkan Intelligence* 7, no. 1 (2016).

15. Matei and Halladay, "The Role and Purpose of Intelligence in a Democracy."

16. Several journal articles have covered intelligence transformation in select countries in the region, including, among others, Florina Cristiana Matei and Andrés de Castro García, "Chilean Intelligence after Pinochet: Painstaking Reform of an Inauspicious Legacy," *International Journal of Intelligence and CounterIntelligence* 30, no. 2 (2017): 340–67; Marco Vinicio Méndez-Coto and Fredy Rivera Vélez, "The Intelligence Service in Costa Rica: Between the New and the Old Paradigm," *The International Journal of Intelligence, Security, and Public Affairs* 20, no. 1 (2018): 6–19; Iduvina Hernández, "A Long Road: Progress and Challenges in Guatemala's Intelligence Reform," WOLA Special Report (Washington, DC: Washington Office on Latin America, October 2005); David J. Myers. "The Institutions of Intelligence in Venezuela: Lessons from 45 Years of Democracy," *Iberoamericana: Nordic Journal of Latin American and Caribbean Studies* 33, no. 1 (2003): 85–95; Kevin Ginter, "Latin American Intelligence Services and the Transition to Democracy," *Journal of Intelligence History* 8, no. 1 (2008): 69–93; Zakia Shiraz and John Kasuku, "Intelligence Culture and the Global South: China, Africa and Latin America," in *Secret Intelligence*, eds. Christopher Andrew, Richard J. Aldrich, and Wesley K. Wark (London: Routledge, 2019); Marco Cepik, "Bosses and Gatekeepers: A Network Analysis of South America's Intelligence Systems," *International Journal of Intelligence and CounterIntelligence* 30, no. 4 (2017): 713. Also see Eduardo E. Estévez and Paula di Domenico, "Contemporary Dares of Strategic Intelligence in Latin America. An IR Perspective," *Journal of European and American Intelligence Studies* 1, no. 1 (2018): 171–94; Thomas C. Bruneau and Florina Cristiana (Cris) Matei, "Intelligence in the Developing Democracies: The Quest for Transparency and Effectiveness," in Loch K. Johnson, ed., *The Oxford Handbook of National Security Intelligence* (Oxford University Press, 2010); Marco Vinicio Méndez-Coto and Fredy Rivera Vélez, "The Intelligence Service in Costa Rica: Between the New and the Old Paradigm," *The International Journal of Intelligence, Security, and Public Affairs* 20, no. 1 (2018): 6–19.

17. For more information, see Bill Mc Sweeney, *Security, Identity, and Interests: A Sociology of International Relations* (Cambridge: Cambridge University Press 1999), 20; David Pion-Berlin, "Latin American National Security Doctrines: Hard- and Softline Themes," *Armed Forces and Society* 15, no. 3 (1989): 411–29; Francisco Leal Buitrago, "La Doctrina de Seguridad Nacional: Materialización de la Guerra Fría en América del Sur," *Revista de Estudios Sociales*, no. 15 (2003): 74–87; David R. Mares, "The National Security State," in *Blackwell Companion to Latin American*

History, ed. Thomas H. Holloway (London: Blackwell, 2007), 386–405; Daniel Feierstein, "National Security Doctrine in Latin America: The Genocide Question," in *The Oxford Handbook of Genocide Studies*, eds. Donald Bloxham and A. Dirk Moses (Oxford: Oxford University Press, 2010), 489–508; Daniel M. Goldstein, "Citizen Security and Human Security in Latin America," in *Routledge Handbook of Latin American Security*, eds. David R. Mares and Arie M. Kacowicz (New York: Routledge, 2016), 138–48.

18. See Andrés Gómez de la Torre, "Institucionalización y Crisis de Inteligencia: Perú en el Contexto Andino," in *Los Macro y Micro Desafíos de la Seguridad en Democracia*, 238–39; Waldo Ansaldi and Mariana Alberto, "Muchos Hablan de Ella, Pocos Piensan en Ella: Una Agenda Posible para Explicar la Apelación a la Violencia Política en América Latina," in *América Latina: Tiempos de Violencias*, eds. Waldo Ansaldi and Verónica Giordano (Buenos Aires: Ariel, 2014), 31–32. Intelligence services became the political police of their governments. Matei and Halladay, "The Role and Purpose of Intelligence in a Democracy."

19. In fact, it was because of these egregious human rights abuses that the verb "disappear" became a transitive verb in the region. For more, see Wolfgang S. Heinz and Hugo Frühling, eds., *Determinants of Gross Human Rights Violations by State and State-Sponsored Actors in Brazil, Uruguay, Chile, and Argentina (1960–1990)* (Den Haag: Kluwer Law International, 1999); Marcia Esparza, Henry R. Ruttenbach, and Daniel Feierstein, eds., *State Violence and Genocide in Latin America. The Cold War Years* (Abingdon: Routledge, 2010).

20. For a definition of authoritarianism, see Juan J. Linz and Alfred Stepan, *Problems of Democratic Transition and Consolidation* (Baltimore: Johns Hopkins University Press, 1996). The Third Wave of democratization started in Portugal on April 25, 1974, with a military coup that resulted in a democratic transition, and ultimately with the installment of democracy in the country; and continued with Southern Europe, Latin America, Africa, Asia, Eastern and Central Europe, and the Arab Spring. Samuel P. Huntington, *The Third Wave: Democratization in the Late Twentieth Century* (Norman: University of Oklahoma Press, 1991). In general, the literature on democracy divides democratic systems into two ideal types: *electoral democracies*, which are characterized by free and fair elections, and *liberal democracies*, which involve free and fair elections, as well as the protection of individual, civil, and political rights and freedoms of the citizenry. See Andreas Schedler, "What Is Democratic Consolidation?" in *The Global Divergence of Democracies*, eds. Larry Diamond and Marc F. Plattner (Baltimore and London: Johns Hopkins University Press, 2001), 149–64. Schedler notes that the liberal democracy includes an ideal subtype—the advanced democracy.

21. On civil wars, see Caroline A. Hartzell, "Relative Peace and Emerging Fault Lines: Accounting for Trends in Intrastate Conflict in Latin America," in *Routledge Handbook of Latin American Security*, eds. David R. Mares and Arie M. Kacowicz (New York: Routledge, 2016), 187–96. On border disputes, see Rodrigo Tavares, *Security in South America: The Role of States and Regional Organizations* (Boulder, CO: Lynne Rienner Publishers, 2014).

22. "Freedom in the World: Latin America Report Card," March 10, 2020, https://theglobalamericans.org/2020/03/freedom-in-the-world-latin-america-report-card/#:~:text=In%20its%20recently%20released%20Freedom,world%2C37%20 countries%20reported%20improvements.

23. The region has known an increase in both right-wing populism, as in the case of the Jair Bolsonaro administration in Brazil, and left-wing populism, as in the case of the Cristina Fernandez de Kirchner administration in Argentina (2007–2014). See Pía Riggirozzi and Christopher Wylde, "Governance in South America," in *Handbook of South American Governance*, eds. Pía Riggirozzi and Christopher Wylde (London: Routledge, 2018), 1–2; Mitchell A. Seligson, "The Rise of Populism and the Left in Latin America," *Journal of Democracy* 18, no. 3 (2007): 81–95; Chantal Mouffe, *For a Left Populism* (London: Verso Books, 2018), 32–39; Timothy J. Power and Wendy Hunter, "Bolsonaro and Brazil's Illiberal Backlash," *Journal of Democracy* 30, no. 1 (2019): 68–82; Aníbal Pérez-Liñán and Scott Mainwaring, "Regime Legacies and Levels of Democracy: Evidence from Latin America," *Comparative Politics* 45, no. 4 (2013): 380; to illustrate this, see the statement by the former intelligence chief: "En carta abierta, el jefe del SEBIN, la policía secreta, critica "corrupción desproporcio nada" en Venezuela" (2019), CNN, May 2, accessed June 21, 2019, https://cnn espanol.cnn.com/2019/05/02/el-jefe-del-sebin-la-policia-secreta-venezolana-rompe -con-maduro/; José Antonio Sanahuja, "América Latina: Malestar democrático y retos de la crisis de la globalización," in *Panorama Estratégico 2019*, Instituto Español de Estudios Estratégicos (España: Ministerio de Defensa, 2019), 226–41, and 241–44, respectively; Rodrigo Tavares, *Security in South America: The Role of States and Regional Organizations* (Boulder, CO: Lynne Rienner Publishers, 2014).

24. Timothy J. Power and Wendy Hunter, "Bolsonaro and Brazil's Illiberal Backlash," *Journal of Democracy* 30, no. 1 (2019): 68–82. There are significant cases of corruption (e.g., Odebrecht) investigations involving the payment of bribes to officials of several Latin American countries related to infrastructure or energy projects. See Astrid Puentes Riaño (2017), "Tsunami de Odebrecht: ¿a recuperar el interés público o sólo el dinero?" *El País* (España), February 16, accessed June 13, 2019. https://elpais.com/internacional/2017/02/16/actualidad/1487272037_782885 .html. On corruption in Latin America, see this special issue: "Corruption Wars: New Narratives of Graft, Influence, and Power in the Americas," *NACLA Report on the Americas* 51, vol. 2 (2019).

25. José Antonio Sanahuja, "América Latina: Malestar democrático y retos de la crisis de la globalización," in *Panorama Estratégico 2019*, Instituto Español de Estudios Estratégicos (España: Ministerio de Defensa, 2019), 241; Rodrigo Tavares, *Security in South America: The Role of States and Regional Organizations* (Boulder, CO: Lynne Rienner Publishers, 2014).

26. Waldo Ansaldi and Mariana Alberto, "Muchos Hablan de Ella, Pocos Piensan en Ella: Una Agenda Posible para Explicar la Apelación a la Violencia Política en América Latina," in *América Latina: Tiempos de Violencias*, eds. Waldo Ansaldi and Verónica Giordano (Buenos Aires: Ariel, 2014), 42, 45; Brett J. Kyle and Andrew G. Reiter, "A New Dawn for Latin American Militaries," *NACLA Report on the*

Americas 51, no. 1 (2019): 18–28; Rodrigo Tavares, *Security in South America: The Role of States and Regional Organizations* (Boulder, CO: Lynne Rienner Publishers, 2014); David R. Mares and Arie M. Kacowicz, eds., *Routledge Handbook of Latin American Security* (New York: Routledge, 2016); José Antonio Sanahuja, "América Latina: Malestar democrático y retos de la crisis de la globalización," in *Panorama Estratégico 2019*, Instituto Español de Estudios Estratégicos (España: Ministerio de Defensa, 2019), 212–16; Ana Arjona and Luis de la Calle, "Conflict, Violence and Democracy in Latin America," *Política y Gobierno* 23, no. 1 (2016): 5; Graciela de Conti Pagliari and Milton Carlos Bragatti, "Surveying Contemporary Latin American International Security Approaches and Themes," *Revista da Escola de Guerra Naval* 24, no. 2 (2018): 424; Marta Lucía Ramírez de Rincón, "Drug Trafficking: A National Security Threat—Similarities between Colombia and Mexico," in *One Goal, Two Struggles*, eds. Cynthia J. Arnson and Eric L. Olson, with Christine Zaino (Washington, DC: Woodrow Wilson International Center for Scholars, 2014), 77–78; Juan Carlos Garzón and Eric L. Olson, eds., "The Criminal Diaspora: The Spread of Transnational Organized Crime and How to Contain Its Expansion" (Washington, DC: Woodrow Wilson International Center for Scholars, 2013), 15; Andrés Gómez de la Torre, "Institucionalización y Crisis de Inteligencia: Perú en el Contexto Andino," in *Los Macro y Micro Desafíos de la Seguridad en Democracia*, 260–61.

27. SIN, the Peruvian intelligence agency under Fujimori was dubbed the "Andean Stasi." Andrés Gómez de la Torre, "Institucionalización y Crisis de Inteligencia: Perú en el Contexto Andino," in *Los Macro y Micro Desafíos de la Seguridad en Democracia*, 243–44.

28. Brazil was the first country that passed an intelligence law in 1999. On the delay, see Priscila Carlos Brandão, *Serviços Secretos e Democracia no Cone Sul: Premissas para uma Convivência Legítima, Eficiente e Profissional* (Niterói: Editora Impetus, 2010). See José M. Ugarte, "Actividad de Inteligencia en América Latina: Características, Fortalezas, Debilidades, Perspectivas de Futuro," *Revista Política y Estrategia*, no. 127 (2016): 37–74. Several countries have endeavored to develop criminal intelligence capabilities within their intelligence communities to combat criminal activities emerging from drug trafficking and narcoterrorism. Eduardo E. Estévez, "Criminal Intelligence and the Challenge of Transnational Organized Crime in Latin America," *Journal of Mediterranean and Balkan Intelligence* 9, no. 1 (2017): 100–101; Daniel Sansó-Rubert Pascual, "Analysis of Criminal Intelligence from a Criminological Perspective: The Future of the Fight against Organized Crime," *Journal of Law and Criminal Justice* 3, no.1 (2015): 46–47.

29. Zakia Shiraz and John Kasuku, "Intelligence Culture and the Global South: China, Africa and Latin America," in *Secret Intelligence*, eds. Christopher Andrew, Richard J. Aldrich, and Wesley K. Wark (London: Routledge, 2019). They mention the intelligence-sharing agreement between Colombia and México of 2012. See also Javier Pérez, "Presidente respalda unión contra el crimen en Guatemala," *Deguate*, October 8, 2018, accessed June 20, 2019, https://www.deguate.com/artman/publish/noticias-guatemala/presidente-respalda-union-contra-el-crimen-en-guatemala.shtml. See Henry Cancelado, "Intelligence Systems in Latin America: The Colombia and

Venezuela Cases," *Journal of Mediterranean and Balkan Intelligence* 7, no. 1 (2016): 169–84.

30. Marcos Pablo Moloeznik, "Hacia una Interpretación del Proceso de Militarización de la Seguridad Pública en América Latina," in *Contextualizaciones Latinoamericanas: Proceso de Militarización de la Seguridad Pública en América Latina*, eds. Marcos Pablo Moloeznik and Ignacio Medina Núñez (Guadalajara: CUCSH, Universidad de Guadalajara, 2019), 16–17, accessed May 27, 2019, https://www .editorialjuris.com/administracion/frm-libros/pdf/1557928056_Contextualizacio nes%20Latinoamericanas.pdf. See also Sonia Alda Mejías, "Políticas y Fuerzas de Seguridad Alternativas ante los Retos de la Seguridad Regional," in *Desafíos Estratégicos del Regionalismo Contemporáneo: CELAC e Iberoamérica*, eds. Adrián Bonilla Soria and Isabel Álvarez Echandi (San José, C.R.: FLACSO, 2013), 243–82; Brett J. Kyle and Andrew G. Reiter, "A New Dawn for Latin American Militaries," *NACLA Report on the Americas* 51, vol. 1 (2019): 18–19. See Lester Cabrera Toledo, "Entre el Cambio y la Inercia Histórica: El Contexto Actual de la Inteligencia Militar en Suramérica," *URVIO, Revista Latinoamericana de Estudios de Seguridad* 21 (2017): 8–21; Daniel Sansó-Rubert Pascual, "Inteligencia Militar y Criminalidad Organizada. Retos a Debatir en América Latina," *URVIO, Revista Latinoamericana de Estudios de Seguridad* 21 (2017): 22–38.

31. David Pion-Berlin, *Military Missions in Democratic Latin America (Politics, Economics, and Inclusive Development)* (New York: Palgrave Macmillan, 2016), 88.

32. See Carlos Maldonado, "Dilemas Antiguos y Modernos en la Inteligencia Estratégica en Sudamérica," *Interdisciplinary Journal of the Center for Hemispheric Defense Studies* 9, no. 1 (2009): 49–66.

33. See Zakia Shiraz, "Intelligence Governance in Colombia: Lessons Learnt and Challenges for the Future," paper presented at the 57th ISA (International Studies Association) Annual Convention, Atlanta, Georgia, USA, March 16–19, 2016; Privacy International, "Shadow State: Surveillance, Law and Order in Colombia," Special Report (Privacy International, 2015), accessed September 6, 2015, http://privacy international.org/sites/default/files/2017-12/ShadowState_English.pdf; "Gobierno cerrará la DINI por 180 días para su reestructuración" (2015), *El Comercio*, Lima, February 9, accessed June 23, 2019, http://elcomercio.pe/politica/gobierno/ollanta -humala-dijo-que-analizara-cierredini-noticia-1790387?ref=nota_politica&ft=mod _leatambien&e=titulo. Some scandals have resulted in firings of intelligence directors (Brazil, Argentina) or dismantling of agencies altogether and replacing them with new ones (Colombia, Argentina). Nevertheless, these changes have only been *pro forma*, as these agencies have continued to be manned with the defunct services' personnel, who kept at their non-democratic, unethical, and illegal practices. On the other hand, recurring shift from left to right populism—known in the literature as "pendularism" (e.g., Argentina, Bolivia, Ecuador y Venezuela)—has had deleterious effects on the professional development of intelligence agencies in the region as strategic priorities are changed and intelligence activity is even politicized. On democratic pendularity in the region, see María Matilde Ollier, "Liderazgos Políticos y Democracia en América Latina," *SocietàMutamentoPolitica* 9, no. 17 (2018): 87–106.

34. These two countries passed intelligence laws lacking in external control mechanisms. See José M. Ugarte, "Un Gran Reto Democrático: Controlar la Inteligencia," in *Los Macro y Micro Desafíos de la Seguridad en Democracia*, 229.

35. Thomas C. Bruneau, "Democratic Politics in Brazil. Advances in Accountability Mechanisms and Regression in Civil–Military Relations," unpublished manuscript, 2019.

36. For example, military intelligence budget increases in Argentina during the Cristina Fernández de Kirchner administration. See Mariano De Vedia, "Aumentan 31,8% los fondos que Milani destina a tareas de inteligencia," *La Nación*, October 7, 2014, accessed October 9, 2014, http://www.lanacion.com.ar/1733456-aumentan -318-los-fondos-que-milani-destina-a-tareas-de-inteligencia.

37. See Jan-Werner Müller, *What Is Populism?* (Philadelphia: University of Pennsylvania Press, 2016), 95–98.

38. Peter Gill, *Intelligence Governance and Democratisation. A Comparative Analysis of the Limits of Reform* (London: Routledge, 2016). Sources include Hans Born and Fairlie Jensen, "Intelligence Services: Strengthening Democratic Accountability," in *Democratic Control of Intelligence Services: Containing Rogue Elephants*, eds. Hans Born and Marina Caparini (Aldershot: Ashgate, 2007), 257–69; Marina Caparini, "Controlling and Overseeing Intelligence Services in Democratic States," in *Democratic Control of Intelligence Services: Containing Rogue Elephants*, eds. Hans Born and Marina Caparini (Aldershot: Ashgate, 2007), 3–24; Andrés Gómez de la Torre, *Política y Legislación de Inteligencia en el Perú e Iberoamérica: Tendencias y Perspectivas*, Documento 1 (Lima: Instituto de Estudios Internacionales, 2013); Juan Carlos Morales Peña, "Hacia una Revisión Estratégica del Sector de Inteligencia en El Salvador," *Revista Policía y Seguridad Pública* 5, no. 2 (2016): 209–84; Fred Schreier, "The Need for Efficient and Legitimate Intelligence," in *Democratic Control of Intelligence Services: Containing Rogue Elephants*, eds. Hans Born and Marina Caparini (Aldershot: Ashgate, 2007), 25–44, among others.

39. Alejandra Otamendi and Eduardo Estévez, "Intelligence Challenges in Latin America: A Comparative Matrix on Democratic Governance," in *¿Nuevos Paradigmas de Vigilancia? Miradas desde América Latina. Memorias del IV Simposio Internacional Lavits, Buenos Aires*, ed. Camilo Ríos (Córdoba: Fundación Vía Libre, 2017), 277–94. The matrix is based on Peter Gill, *Intelligence Governance and Democratisation. A Comparative Analysis of the Limits of Reform* (London: Routledge, 2016). It draws on the findings of major intelligence reform studies; see Florina Cristiana Matei and Thomas C. Bruneau, "Intelligence Reform in New Democracies: Factors Supporting or Arresting Progress," *Democratization* 18, no. 3 (2011): 602–30; Florina Cristiana Matei and Thomas C. Bruneau, "Policymakers and Intelligence Reform in the New Democracies," *International Journal of Intelligence and CounterIntelligence* 24, no. 4 (2011): 656–91.

Part I

ESTABLISHED DEMOCRACIES

Chapter One

Colombia

Jason M. Blazakis

Colombia's intelligence community has slowly transformed from an inchoate structure and at times undemocratic set of entities to one of greater transparency. This shift mirrored the country's larger democratic transformation. Colombia's internally focused security challenges called for highly effective coordination of intelligence agencies, which has been absent until recently. The intelligence evolution was ultimately catalyzed through legal reforms, responses to domestic scandals, conflicts, and threats leading to some notable successes. Colombia reacted to its governance challenges with a series of iterative laws and decrees that over time, led to a more comprehensive intelligence system, accompanied by lower levels of corruption. These improvements have enabled Colombia to function more consistently according to its democratic ideals and further democratic consolidation of its intelligence agencies.

South America's oldest democracy, Colombia became an independent state in 1810 after breaking away from Spanish control. Colombia's realization of democratic ideals has been marked by a turbulent cycle of ebbs and flows. Since its founding, Colombia witnessed three occasions where the military interceded and took control from civilian power brokers. In 1830, 1854, and between 1953 and 1957, the Colombian military exerted control over all aspects of Colombia society. In the third instance, General Gustavo Rojas Pinilla took the reins during a particularly dangerous time in Colombia's history known as *La Violencia*.[1] Aside from this one glaring exception in the 1950s, however, Colombia's military has been subordinated to civilian institutions. Colombia's Intelligence Community (CIC) generally reported to senior civilian officials, and the Colombian military intelligence system has primarily been used to deal with internal threats, to include terrorist groups and drug cartels. It is important to keep in mind that there is a legal mandate for these intelligence entities to project their capabilities against domestic threats (which may seem anathema to U.S.-based readers who understand that the deployment of U.S. military assets, intelligence or otherwise, could profoundly alter the shape of U.S. democracy). However, the possible waning of Colombia's drug cartels and terrorist groups' capabilities may liberate the full capacity of Colombia's military apparatus, including its intelligence capability, to reorient toward looming external threats.

COLOMBIA'S INTELLIGENCE EVOLUTION

Colombia was one of the last democracies in South America to clearly define its intelligence structure within an analytical framework appropriate for a flourishing democracy. The modern beginnings of Colombia's intelligence community commenced in 1953 with the formation of the Colombian Intelligence Service (SIC). The SIC later evolved into the Administrative Department of Security (DAS) in 1960, and on October 31, 2011, Colombian President Juan Manuel Santos (2010–2018) dissolved the DAS through Decree 4057. Formed in the wake of DAS's dissolution in November 2011 was the National Intelligence Directorate (DNI). Since 1953 these three entities constituted the Colombian government's primary civilian intelligence agencies.

Colombia has seven intelligence agencies (see figure 1.1) in total, five are centralized within the Ministry of Defense (MOD) and two are civilian agencies. The DNI is controlled by the president, and the Financial Information and Analysis Unit (UIAF) is a specialized unit within the Ministry of Finance and Public Credit. Both civilian agencies play important roles in collecting, analyzing, and disseminating intelligence information.

The Ministry of Defense oversees the Armed Forces D-2, the Army's E-2, the Air Force's EMA-2, Naval Intelligence, and the Police Intelligence Directorate (DIPOL) under the National Police of Colombia (CNP). Greater analysis of the DNI and its predecessor agencies (SIC and DAS) will occur within the success stories and failures that ultimately formed the organizational basis of today's CIC.

Military Intelligence

The Colombian Ministry of Defense (MOD) has long been a focal point within Colombia's intelligence apparatus. Since the 1990s, Colombia's military intelligence has been under the management and purview of the Armed Forces Joint General Staff Intelligence Section (D-2). According to a heavily redacted and partially declassified U.S. Army Intelligence Agency threat

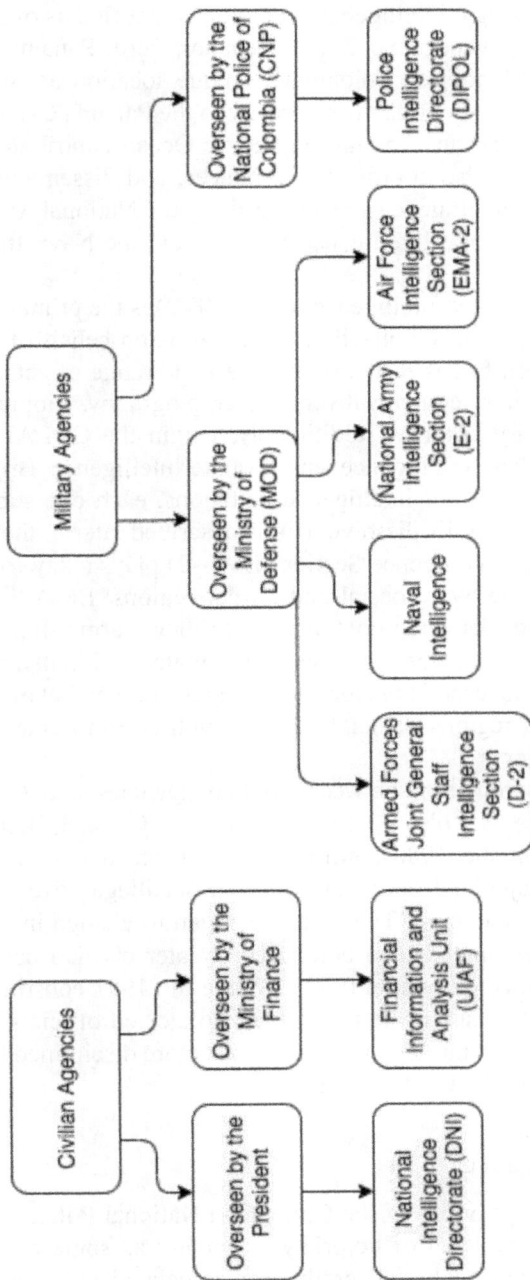

Colombian Intelligence Community

- Civilian Agencies
  - Overseen by the President
    - National Intelligence Directorate (DNI)
  - Overseen by the Ministry of Finance
    - Financial Information and Analysis Unit (UIAF)
- Military Agencies
  - Overseen by the Ministry of Defense (MOD)
    - Armed Forces Joint General Staff Intelligence Section (D-2)
    - Naval Intelligence
    - National Army Intelligence Section (E-2)
    - Air Force Intelligence Section (EMA-2)
  - Overseen by the National Police of Colombia (CNP)
    - Police Intelligence Directorate (DIPOL)

Figure 1.1.

analysis from 1990, the D-2 collects external intelligence and is responsible for collating strategic intelligence on nations identified as of particular interest to Colombia: Venezuela, Brazil, Ecuador, Peru, Panama, Nicaragua, El Salvador, and Honduras. Colombia's unique location as South America's gateway to Central America, its proximity to the Panama Canal, and its coastlines on the Caribbean Sea and the Pacific Ocean contribute to its security outlook. The D-2 also coordinates, produces, and disseminates intelligence to three military intelligence service entities—the National Army Intelligence Section; the Air Force Intelligence Section; and the Navy Intelligence Section.[2]

The National Army Intelligence Section (E-2) is the primary military organization for intelligence collection and analysis on behalf of the Colombian Army (COLAR). E-2 is responsible for a wide range of activities including counterintelligence, countersubversion, cryptography, biometric identification, and military security. Additionally, within the COLAR infrastructure was the twentieth Intelligence and Counterintelligence Brigade (BRICI), which consisted of four intelligence battalions, each one supporting a COLAR division.[3] BRICI's dissolvement is described later in the chapter.

The Air Force Intelligence Section (EMA-2) plays a key role in providing aerial surveillance over coastal and border regions. EMA-2 also maintains responsibility for detecting contraband and illegal arms shipments, and providing security to Air Force personnel and material. Finally, the Navy Intelligence Section is responsible for countering the movement of contraband and arms from port regions of neighboring countries from entering Colombian sovereign territory.[4]

Effective coordination between civilian agencies and Colombian military intelligence has historically been anemic. Colonel Humberto Castillo reflected that in the 1980s, military intelligence had free rein and often conducted extrajudicial operations, carried out illegal arrests, and committed human rights abuses.[5] This practice began to change in 1991, when the constitution was amended to emphasize greater civilian control and place greater importance on human rights.[6] While the 1991 constitutional reforms did not completely subjugate the military to elected officials, it is clear that Colombia's military intelligence system was more disciplined than its civilian counterparts, particularly the DAS.

Police Intelligence

Historically the activities of the Colombian National Police (CNP) have not received the same level of notoriety or infamy as some of its intelligence counterparts. The CNP has generally been associated and credited with legitimate human intelligence collection capabilities. It was created in 1891 under the Ministry of Government but disbanded in 1948 following the assassination of Liberal Party politician Jorge Gaitan—the event that triggered the *La Violencia* turmoil. Although the CNP was quickly reconstituted in 1953, it was placed under the Ministry of War in an effort to remove it from partisan political control. In 1960, the CNP was granted a status independent of the armed forces under the minister of war.[7]

Early organizational charts of the CNP demonstrate that its various components were organized as departments, and at both the headquarter level and department levels, the organization had a functional designation—denoted as "F-2"—for intelligence and counterintelligence responsibilities.[8] This functional designation is of particular note, because early in the CNP's existence, it did not have clear-cut legal authorities to conduct investigations. A 1957 presidential decree (Decree Number 0696) specified that the CNP would have intelligence and counterintelligence responsibilities and that F-2 would be responsible for collection, collation, analysis, and dissemination of information in criminal and subversive fields.[9] Beginning in the 1950s, the CNP was led by a brigadier general who reported directly to the minister of war.[10] Today, as in the past, the CNP's director general reports to the minister of defense.[11]

As of November 2019, Brigadier General Jesus Alejandro Barrera Pena heads the CNP's DIPOL. According to the CNP's website and mission statement, intelligence remains a core competency in the organization's efforts to counter a diverse array of threats. DIPOL touts that it generates strategic, operational, and tactical intelligence to prevent harm to Colombian citizens and property.[12] The effectiveness of DIPOL was lauded by a former U.S. Army officer who said that police human intelligence was superior to military intelligence because, "the police are good at intelligence collection because he is a policeman first. The police culture is to show initiative, talk to people, find out what's going on. The army is locked down in their bases. If they get an informer, they can't tell if he's talking BS, whereas police can look the guy in the eye and know if he's lying."[13]

DIPOL Functional Organizational Structure

The effectiveness of DIPOL may also be attributable to its organizational reach and structure. Within the police intelligence subdirectorate, there are six focus areas (figure 1.2). First, there is a counterintelligence arm comprised of five groups that analyze and evaluate the credibility of internally based counterintelligence threats. Second, an intelligence operations group exists that collects intelligence and manages human sources. Third, there is an intelligence production unit that carries out signal intelligence analysis. Fourth,

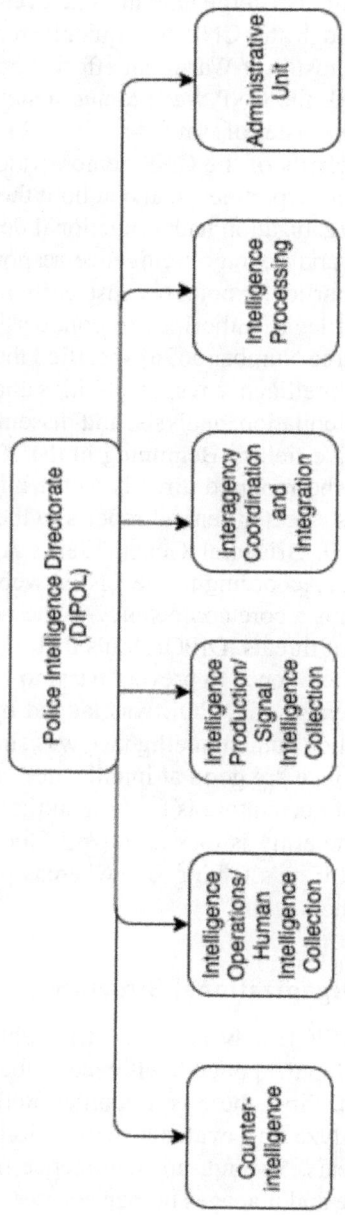

Six Functional Areas of DIPOL

Police Intelligence Directorate (DIPOL)

- Counter-intelligence
- Intelligence Operations/ Human Intelligence Collection
- Intelligence Production/ Signal Intelligence Collection
- Interagency Coordination and Integration
- Intelligence Processing
- Administrative Unit

Figure 1.2.

there is a coordination and intelligence integration unit that is responsible for leading the DIPOL's working-level interaction with interagency counterparts. This unit is also responsible for ensuring that information derived from other agencies is appropriately disseminated to the relevant DIPOL officiate. Fifth, there is a unit responsible for the processing of intelligence information. Finally, there is an administrative unit that handles logistics, contracts, finance, and real estate maintenance and acquisition for DIPOL.[14] The CNP's scope of intelligence activities requires a robust infrastructure and bureaucratic organization due to the immense amount of territory in which the CNP is responsible for enforcing law and order.

Other Intelligence Bodies

Like the CNP, the Financial Information and Analysis Unit (UIAF) within the Ministry of Finance has avoided public attention. The UIAF, created in 1999[15] and fully operational by February 2000,[16] is the Colombian government's financial intelligence mechanism. Specifically, the UIAF's mission is to analyze financial and economic intelligence provided by financial institutions and other open sources to prevent and detect money laundering, terrorism financing, and other financial crimes.[17] The UIAF disseminates financial intelligence reports to a range of national and international authorities to counter illicit financial activity. The mission of the UIAF is important not least because the primary motivation of the drug cartels is monetary.

Intelligence-Coordination Bodies

In addition to the intelligence agencies noted above, Colombia has a number of intelligence-coordination bodies. In 2003, President Alvaro Uribe (2002–2010) created in his Security and Democracy Plan an interagency coordinating body called the Joint Intelligence Board (JIB).[18] The JIB is composed of the directors of Colombia's intelligence community and reports directly to the president and minister of defense. The JIB translates policy directives into intelligence requirements and deconflicts the activities of Colombia's intelligence community agencies.[19] The JIB is also responsible for producing consolidated strategic intelligence analysis,[20] similar to the U.S. National Intelligence Council's intelligence products. Uribe's strategy also resulted in the creation of regional intelligence boards,[21] which report to the JIB. This structure is not unlike the U.S. joint terrorism task forces (JTTFs) that facilitates cooperation between federal, state, and local agencies to share threat-related information.

The structure of the CIC has been fundamentally shaped by Colombia's national experiences. Threats to Colombian civil society have primarily manifested as narco-terrorist and right-wing paramilitary groups making it incumbent upon Colombia's senior leadership to create an intelligence community postured for greater collaboration. Moreover, internal political turmoil—that often manifested in political scandals—guaranteed that policy makers would ensure that as the CIC evolved it would embrace the importance of democratic ideals, such as the preservation of privacy and civil rights.

DOMESTIC THREATS, CONFLICTS, AND SCANDALS

Since its infancy, Colombia has been beset by a range of internally driven national security challenges that made an effective intelligence apparatus both necessary and difficult to effectuate. Economic and political turmoil fomented political polarization and violence that has been exacerbated by Colombia's infamous cocaine trade. More recently, it was the short military rule (1953–1957)[22] that emerged in the aftermath of *La Violencia*, which served as the incubator for one of the world's most protracted insurgencies. Military rule—and its fight against agrarian peasant communist groups—set the backdrop for the creation of the Revolutionary Armed Forces of Colombia (FARC). The FARC was an agrarian communist organization that operated from 1966 to 2016, wreaking havoc and destruction throughout the Colombian state. While the fifty-year conflict between the Colombian government and the FARC officially culminated in an agreement in June 2016, FARC splinter cells continue to engage in violence and every aspect of the illicit narcotics life cycle. More worrisome, as of August 29, 2019, one of the FARC's most influential senior personnel, Ivan Marquez, called for a return to violence.[23] Even if Marquez's call is heeded, it is very unlikely that the FARC will be anything more than a national security irritant rather than the formidable threat it was when the group was at its zenith in the late 1980s and 1990s. In the lead-up to the 2016 peace process, the FARC was already reeling from a number of successful Colombian government initiatives designed to erode the group's capabilities, which manifested in massive defections, loss of territory, destruction of the FARC Secretariat, toppling senior leaders, and exploitation of the FARC's communications (including computer) networks.[24] While resentment regarding sufficient implementation of the peace process has frustrated some FARC hard-liners, such as Marquez, the majority have remained resistant to returning to violence. This resistance toward violence, combined with Colombia's advancements, including the restructuring of its intelligence community, may mean the FARC will never project the power it once did during its heyday.

In addition to the FARC, Colombia has dealt with a wide array of other internal threats. Another left-leaning group founded in 1964, the National Liberation Army (ELN), continues to fight the Colombian government and has claimed that the "conflict is going to last."[25] This originally Catholic, Marxist-Leninist revolutionary group continues to violently advocate for reforms that would benefit the poor.[26] M19, a guerilla group that formed in the wake of the 1970 presidential elections, became infamous for seizing the Palacio de Justicia and holding the Colombian Supreme Court hostage in 1985. In the aftermath of the Colombian government's raid, eleven of the twenty-five Supreme Court justices were dead.[27] M19 demobilized in 1990 and transitioned into a recognized political party.[28]

In addition to the threat posed by left-wing groups, Colombia has also been afflicted by an assortment of right-wing paramilitary groups, often created to counter the FARC, ELN, and M-19, not least because of the Colombian government's perceived inability to counter such organizations. The most well known of these groups, the United Self-Defense Forces of Colombia (AUC) founded by Carlos Castaño in 1997, became synonymous with extrajudicial killings, indiscriminate massacres, torture, and leveraging government contacts—especially civilian intelligence contacts to operate outside democratic civil society norms. The AUC officially disbanded in 2006; however, there were allegations that AUC continued extralegal activities for several more years.[29]

With record cocaine production in recent years, there is no clear solution to resolving the security challenges caused by Colombia's cocaine trade.[30] Colombia's challenge of curbing the processing and illicit trade of cocaine is a national security problem that is so well known that it has been dramatized by Hollywood in the form of blockbuster movies and television.[31] In the 1980s and 1990s, Colombia was approaching the level of a failed state because large criminal drug-profiting syndicates like the Cali and Medellín cartels corrupted public officials, killed innocent civilians, and harmed the economy.[32] In fact, the Medellín cartel's infamous leader Pablo Escobar was slotted in *Forbes Magazine*'s billionaires list for seven straight years, starting in 1987 until his violent death in 1993.[33] The Colombian drug trade and its effects on drug addiction in the United States was the motivation for the creation of Plan Colombia—an effort largely designed to curb coca cultivation. In fact, U.S. congressional appropriations under Plan Colombia made the country the third-largest recipient of U.S. aid in the early 2000s, following Israel and Egypt.[34] Colombia's crippling cocaine dilemma and U.S. expenditures to counteract this complex dilemma placed the government of Colombia's national security apparatus under what was often an uncomfortable spotlight.

A tendency to blur the distinction between combatants and non-combatants was an attribute that afflicted the CIC. This trend created an environment of uncertainty within Colombian civil society, thereby creating an atmosphere of suffocating fear. The state did not serve as the protector and preserver of human rights. In fact, it created a permissive environment where internationally accepted human rights were trodden on by state actors—especially by Colombia's early civilian intelligence agencies.

In 1998, the BRICI—previously within the E-2—was disbanded because of its role in carrying out abuses attributable to right-wing paramilitary groups. Two members of the brigade were implicated in the murder of a Colombian politician, Alvaro Gomez Hurtado. In announcing the dissolution of the BRICI, General Manuel Jose Bonett argued, "Intelligence operations were really the root of the problem because they could suddenly provoke somebody to commit or become involved in criminal activity."[35]

Corruption within the DAS

One of the greatest intelligence scandals and periods of difficulty occurred between 2002 and 2010. This notorious parapolitical scandal led to the arrest of high-level DAS officials. Jorge Noguera Cotes, director of the DAS from 2002 to 2006,[36] was sentenced to more than twenty-five years in prison for providing information to right-wing paramilitary groups who later leveraged the information to carry out attacks against political enemies.[37] Among them was university professor Alfredo Correa de Andreis, who was murdered in 2004 by paramilitaries.[38] Noguera's sentence was modified in September 2017 when the Supreme Court of Justice added seven years and ten months to his sentence upon discovering his involvement in overseeing illegal DAS communication interceptions of journalists, politicians, and businessmen.[39] Noguera was not the only DAS official enveloped in scandal. His deputy, Maria del Pilar Hurtado, was charged and sentenced for abuse of power and intercepting phone calls.[40] Her prison sentence was 168 months.[41]

The ensuing institutional crisis that engulfed the DAS would not be the first nor would it be the last to afflict Colombia's intelligence community. Nearly fifty years prior, the SIC was dissolved because it had been associated with abuses and repression during *La Violencia*.[42] The death knell for the DAS arrived less than five years (August 2009) following Noguera's ousting, precipitated by a wiretapping scandal. The DAS spied on human rights activists, members of congress, judges, state prosecutors, and presidential candidates who were perceived as a political threat to President Alvaro Uribe.[43] The DAS's transgressions ultimately culminated in the passage of Presidential Decree 4179 of 2011, which dissolved the organization.

Oversight of such a powerful intelligence body is difficult at best and this challenge, coupled with its exploitation by multiple presidents for personal gain, partially explains the DAS's failures. These indiscretions were amplified by a deadly combination of terrorism, drug cartels, and insurgency violence that led to DAS overreach and inappropriate use of intelligence resources to target innocent civilians and political enemies. DAS's egregious corruption led to the abolishment of the agency and creation of the DNI.

Domestic threats continue to plague the CIC. As of July 2020, guerrilla and paramilitary groups, along with drug cartels, are exploiting the COVID-19 crisis and its associated curfews to assert their power, inflicting violence upon civilians and exacerbating existing intelligence challenges.[44]

LEGAL REFORMS THAT
TRANSFORMED THE INTELLIGENCE SYSTEM

Colombia's intelligence agencies, especially its civilian components, naturally formed and evolved in tandem with the creation of new laws and decrees. This chapter focuses predominantly on laws and decrees that have transformed Colombia's civilian intelligence agency. The underlying legal reforms that created the SIC—and then successor agencies like the DAS and DNI—also correlate either to important inflection points in Colombia's history or myriad Colombian government scandals.

The Colombian Constitution is the origin of all Colombian laws, and since its inception as an independent country in 1830, there have been multiple constitutions and reforms adopted—the most recent being in 1991.[45] The 1886 Constitution, and later iterations, featured a strong executive branch—one that allowed the president to declare a state of siege and an ability to govern by decree. Presidential decrees played an outsized role in establishing and altering Colombia's intelligence agencies. This power was wielded frequently during times of turmoil in Colombia's history. This situation changed, however, with Colombia's 1991 Constitution, which scaled back the president's emergency powers by providing greater powers to the legislative and judiciary branches.[46] Analysis by Donald A. Fox and Anne Stetson makes clear that the change was meant to foster democratic participation, rule of law, and human rights, as well as to dismantle a system susceptible to corruption.

On November 10, 1953, the SIC was created by Decree 2872.[47] The SIC formed amid one of Colombia's most turbulent times with a mission of serving as an autonomous technical intelligence body. Article II of the decree lays out the SIC's three core functions: (1) prevent the commission of violent acts that would threaten Colombia's internal and external security; (2) provide direct support to the criminal justice system, particularly the courts; and (3) investigate internal government officials who may be abusing their power.[48]

Notably, the SIC reported directly to the president. The decree makes multiple references to internal security and criminal investigations. Very early on, it became clear that the SIC's mission was more of a law enforcement and internal intelligence investigative body, as opposed to an impartial and non-interventionist intelligence agency. SIC's creation during a precarious point in Colombia's history led to hastily devised mission sets and authority levels—as a stop-gap measure—that contributed to future democratic deficiencies.

The SIC's shelf-life was short. Seven years after its formation, it was dissolved. In its wake, the DAS was formed in 1960 through Decree 1717.[49] Decree 1717 cites Law 19 of 1958 as the statutory impetus behind the formation of the DAS. Article I of Decree 1717 lays out the scope of the DAS mission. Again, like the SIC, it was threefold: (1) to exercise powers to assist the judicial police, Ministry of Police, and judicial branch with their criminal investigations; (2) maintain public order in close collaboration with the national police; and (3) keep a registry of foreign nationals on Colombian soil. Article II mandated DAS coordination with various government ministries to include Foreign Affairs, Justice, War, and National Police. Article III outlined the structure of the DAS. Like the SIC, the DAS reported directly to the president. The decree forming the DAS was significantly more detailed than the decree forming the SIC. In total, Decree 1717 had more than sixty articles that spoke to a wide array of personnel, budgetary, investigative, and administrative tasks.[50] The legal authorities establishing the DAS also make clear that the organization was responsible for several issues. The vast breadth of DAS's responsibilities and the apparent justification for it to be an intelligence and judicial panacea may have eroded its ability to function appropriately as a custodian of intelligence within a functioning democracy. The legal underpinnings may have very well been a significant contributing factor to the DAS's eventual unraveling in 2011.

The DNI was established in 2011 by Presidential Decree 4179. The DNI, like the SIC and DAS before it, reports directly to the president. The DNI formed in the aftermath of a scandal, which explains the decree's emphasis on "adhering to the law in a democracy that guarantees the fundamental rights and freedoms of citizens."[51] The decree, pursuant to Article I, also limits the scale of DNI activities to strategic intelligence and counterintelligence. This measure represented an important and significant change in Colombia's intelligence system. Finally, the decree is clearly enumerated in Articles III, VII, VIII, XIV, and XV that the DNI will uphold human rights, collaborate with interagency partners, fall under the purview of an inspector general, and put into place data privacy protection protocols.[52]

In April 2013, Law 1621 was passed by congress with the aim of strengthening the legal framework that allows agencies carrying out intelligence and counterintelligence activities to fulfill their constitutional and legal mission. This regulation has been positively received because of well-defined parameters delineating intelligence activities as they relate to the potential restriction of civil rights. Additionally, the law mandates oversight (political control) and created the Congressional Legal Commission to Monitor Intelligence and Counterintelligence.

Turmoil and persistent security threats distorted Colombia's national security structure, necessitating adjustments that considered important legal norms. The evolution of the CIC, especially the transition from DAS to the DNI, led to important legal modifications that were more in tune with Colombia's democratic ideals. These shifts within the intelligence community, including those that fostered greater civil-military intelligence cooperation examined in prior sections, took into account vitally important human rights and also coincided with some of Colombia's most important intelligence successes.

INTELLIGENCE SUCCESSES

Despite some of the previously mentioned infamous missteps, Colombia's intelligence system had a number of successes worthy of examination. The CIC's ability to use intelligence to augment operations against high-value targets is of particular note. In 2010, Colombia successfully eliminated FARC senior leader Mono Jojoy in La Macarena by means of a human intelligence source that placed a tracking device in Jojoy's boot. The GPS tracker provided the intelligence needed for Colombia's Joint Special Operations Command to carry out an airstrike that terminated Jojoy.[53] Earlier operations against other FARC senior leaders like Gustavo Rueda Diaz, Milton Sierra Gomez, and Raul Reyes were all effective because the Colombian military was able to utilize intelligence collected from a wide range of CIC partners—both civilian and military.[54]

There is no better intelligence and military success than that of *Operation Jacque*, which used a combination of human and signals intelligence to carry out one of the most successful hostage rescues in recent memory. Using a FARC defector[55] to infiltrate the organization, coupled with signal intelligence penetration of the FARC's secretariat-level communications and the deployment of a savvy deception operation, fifteen hostages were rescued.[56] Without a shot fired, Colombian Army Intelligence rescued the hostages, including former presidential candidate Ingrid Betancourt, three Americans, and Colombian military and police officials, some of whom had been held for more than a decade. As recounted by the American hostages, Colombian special forces had posed as non-governmental workers doing a medical check and, in this guise, loaded all of the hostages, plus two FARC members, without much commotion, onto a helicopter for exfiltration.[57] These notable successes of the CIC are indicative of a system that can harness intelligence in a manner that allows for positive operational outcomes.

While anecdotal and unscientific, there are indicators that the transition from the DAS to the DNI has enhanced South America's oldest democracy. The DNI appears to be less the media pariah than the DAS. The DAS's indiscretions were routinely reported by Colombian newspapers like *El Tiempo* and *Semana*. In contrast, the DNI makes fewer headlines. More concretely, in the 2017/2018 Amnesty International country report on Colombia, neither civilian nor military intelligence agencies were implicated in human rights abuses.[58] In stark contrast, Amnesty International's 2010 Colombia Report took Colombia to task by highlighting DAS abuses.[59]

Over time, the structural and legal reforms made within both Colombia's military and civilian-led intelligence agencies resulted in enhanced inter-agency joint activity that decreased the capabilities of some of Colombia's oldest threats, most notably the FARC, which was pushed to the negotiating table because of the deleterious impact the coordinated Colombian action had on the narco-terrorist group.

CONCLUSION

Colombia's intelligence culture has intrinsically been linked to the country's threat environment. While domestic security threats will likely continue to consume some of the CIC's attention and resources, the promising changes that have occurred within the intelligence system, along with important cease-fires and peace deals with violent groups, provide the promise of a more stable CIC. It can possibly be expected that Colombia's allies will continue to play a role in both controlling cocaine trade and addressing the urgent needs of the rural poor who rely upon coca production as their livelihood, as this dual approach is likely to quell economic and political instability, along with the violence that characterizes that instability.

There are at least two other internal challenges that may present difficulties for the CIC to maintain its course. First, as noted previously, the COVID-19 situation has resulted in non-state actors imposing their parochial versions of martial law against the public and thus have subverted the security domain of the state. This challenge is particularly acute in rural areas. Furthermore, if this non-state actor vigilantism remains unchecked, it will call into question whether the current security sector reforms are sufficient. Second, just as the COVID-19 pandemic has challenged the state apparatus, historical political divides possibly forbode future instability. In August 2020, Colombia's Supreme Court ordered the arrest of former Colombian president Alvaro Uribe for alleged fraud, bribery, and witness tampering.[60] Uribe's arrest has triggered denouncements from the political right and delight from the left. Uribe's arrest underscored Colombia's polarization and within this political calamity the CIC must remain an impartial entity that respects and protects all citizens irrespective of political affiliation. The CIC's reforms, especially those stemming from the series of DAS scandals, has created safeguards that hopefully will inoculate the intelligence system from becoming enmeshed in politics. The risk of CIC partaking in democratic backsliding would not only undo previous progress but could reopen old wounds that Colombia's most repugnant enemies, the cartels and terrorist groups, would no doubt exploit.

NOTES

1. This period locked the Conservative and Liberal parties in extreme political violence between 1948 and 1958, because it resulted in the deaths of thousands of civilians, especially those living outside major city centers in rural Colombia. The result of *La Violencia* was a short period of military rule in Colombia (1953–1957). Foreign Relations of the United States, 1955–1957, Volume VII, American Republics: Central and South America, Document 467, accessed on July 25, 2020, https://history .state.gov/historicaldocuments/frus1955-57v07/d467.

2. United States Army Intelligence Agency, "Colombia Army Country Profile," August 9, 1990, 89.

3. United States Army Intelligence Agency, "Colombia Army Country Profile," 89.

4. United States Army Intelligence Agency, "Colombia Army Country Profile," 89.

5. Douglas Porch and Jorge Delgado, "Masters of Today: Military Intelligence and Counterinsurgency in Colombia, 1990–2009," 280.

6. Porch and Delgado, "Masters of Today," 280.

7. United States Department of State Agency for International Development Office of Public Safety, "Report on the Republic of Colombia: National Police and the Administrative Department of Security," December 1962, 12.

8. United States Department of State Agency for International Development Office of Public Safety, "Report on the Republic of Colombia," 15, 19.

9. United States Department of State Agency for International Development Office of Public Safety, "Report on the Republic of Colombia," 29.

10. United States Department of State Agency for International Development Office of Public Safety, "Report on the Republic of Colombia," 13.

11. See Organization Chart from Rex A. Hudson, ed., *Colombia: A Country Study* (Library of Congress Federal Research Division, 2010), 292. https://www.loc.gov/item/2010009203. The Colombian National Police Website clearly indicates that it falls under the purview of the defense minister.

12. "Dirección de Inteligencia Policial de la Policía Nacional – DIPOL," Policía Nacional de Colombia, accessed November 12, 2019, https://www.policia.gov.co/direccion/inteligencia.

13. Porch and Delgado, "Masters of Today," 280.

14. "Estructura organica Dirección de Inteligencia Policial," Policía Nacional de Colombia, accessed November 12, 2019, https://www.policia.gov.co/unidades/organigrama/3901.

15. "Unidad de Información y Análisis Financiero," República de Colombia, accessed on November 13, 2019, https://www.uiaf.gov.co/nuestra_entidad/mision_vision/ley_creacion_526_1999.

16. "Colombia – Unidad de Informacion y Analisis Financiero (UIAF)," Egmont Group, accessed November 13, 2019, https://egmontgroup.org/en/content/colombia-unidad-de-informacion-y-analisis-financiero.

17. "Unidad de Información y Análisis Financiero," República de Colombia, accessed on November 13, 2019, https://www.uiaf.gov.co.

18. Porch and Delgado, "Masters of Today," 281.

19. República de Colombia, *Política de Defensa y Seguridad Democrática.* (2003): 35, 40.

20. República de Colombia, *Política de Defensa y Seguridad Democrática,* 35.

21. República de Colombia, *Política de Defensa y Seguridad Democrática,* 40.

22. Foreign Relations of the United States, 1955–1957, Volume VII, American Republics: Central and South America, Document 467, accessed on July 25, 2020, https://history.state.gov/historicaldocuments/frus1955-57v07/d467.

23. Nicholas Casey and Lara Jakes, "Colombia's Former FARC Guerilla Leader Calls for Return to War," *New York Times*, August 29, 2019.

24. Javiar Martin Merchan, "Unmasking the Colombian Peace Accord," April 1, 2018, E-International Relations, accessed on August 5, 2020, https://www.e-ir.info/2018/04/01/unmasking-the-colombian-peace-accord-farc-strategy-in-a-never-ending-conflict/.

25. Héctor Velasco, Agence France-Presse, "ELN Say Will Keep Fighting in Colombia's Out-of-Sight War," June 22, 2019, https://www.france24.com/en/20190622-eln-say-will-keep-fighting-colombias-out-sight-war.

26. Mapping Militant Organizations, "National Liberation Army," Stanford University, last modified July 2019, accessed on July 25, 2020, https://cisac.fsi.stanford.edu/mappingmilitants/profiles/national-liberation-army-eln.

27. Harvey F. Kline, *Historical Dictionary of Colombia* (Lanham, MD: Scarecrow Press, 2012), 322.

28. Mauricio García Durán, Vera Grabe Loewenherz, and Otty Patiño Hormaza, *The M-19's Journey from Armed Struggle to Democratic Politics* (Berlin: Berghof

Research Center for Constructive Conflict Management, 2008), accessed on July 25, 2020, https://www.berghof-foundation.org/fileadmin/redaktion/Publications/Papers/Transitions_Series/transitions_m19.pdf.

29. Mapping Militant Organizations, "United Self-Defense Forces of Colombia," Stanford University, last modified August 28, 2015, accessed on July 25, 2020, https://stanford.edu/group/mappingmilitants/cgi-bin/groups/print_view/85.

30. Adriaan Alsema, "Colombia's Cocaine Production Reaches All-Time High: US," *Colombia Reports*, March 7, 2020, accessed on July 31, 2020, https://colombia reports.com/colombias-cocaine-production-reaches-all-time-high-us/.

31. Notable films such as *Scarface* (1983 drama by Universal Pictures) and *Blow* (2001 drama by New Line Cinema) and Netflix television series *Narcos* (2015–2017) depict the Colombian drug cartel.

32. Richard Rocha García, "Drug Trafficking and Its Impact on Colombia: An Economic Overview," *Canadian Journal of Latin American and Caribbean Studies* 28, no. 55/56 (2003): 277.

33. Corrine Jurney, "Netflix's Narcos Kingpin Pablo Escobar: A Look Back at His 7 Years on Forbes' Billionaires List," *Forbes*. September 18, 2015.

34. Dickie Davis et al., *A Great Perhaps? Colombia: Conflict and Convergence* (London: Hurst Publishers, 2016), 112.

35. Associated Press, "Colombia: Military Announce Closure of 20th Intelligence Brigade," May 20, 1998.

36. "Jorge Noguera, de próspero abogado a condenado," *El País*, September 18, 2011, accessed on November 25, 2019, https://www.elpais.com.co/colombia/jorge -noguera-de-prospero-abogado-a-condenado.html.

37. "Jorge Noguera pidió la libertad con 11 de 25 años de pena cumplida," *El Tiempo*, February 7, 2019, accessed on November 25, 2019, https://www.eltiempo .com/justicia/investigacion/exdirector-del-das-jorge-noguera-pide-su-libertad-por -pena-cumplida-179996.

38. Rafael Pérez Becerra, "Niegan Libertad Condicional al Exdirector del DAS, Jorge Noguera." RCN Radio, February 28, 2019, accessed on November 25, 2019, https://www.rcnradio.com/judicial/niegan-libertad-condicional-al-exdirector-del-das -jorge-noguera.

39. "Jorge Noguera," *El Tiempo*, February 7, 2019.

40. Rafael Pérez Becerra, "Juez pregunta por María del Pilar Hurtado y su lugar de reclusion," LAFM.COM, August 12, 2019, accessed on November 25, 2019, https:// www.lafm.com.co/judicial/juez-pregunta-por-maria-del-pilar-hurtado-y-su-lugar-de -reclusion; BBC "Ex-Colombia Spy Chief Maria del Pilar Hurtado Jailed for 14 Years," May 1, 2015, accessed on July 26, 2020, https://www.bbc.com/news/world-latin -america-32544248.

41. Johana Rodríguez, "Permiso de 72 Horas Sin Vigilancia a Exdirectora del DAS, María del Pilar Hurtado." RCN Radio, November 21, 2018, accessed on November 25, 2019, https://www.rcnradio.com/judicial/permiso-de-72-horas-sin -vigilancia-exdirectora-del-das-maria-del-pilar-hurtado.

42. Hudson, ed., *Colombia*, 318.

43. Oxford Research Daily Brief Service, "Colombia: Intelligence Reform Would Be Incomplete," November 3, 2009.

44. Megan Janetsky and Anthony Faiola, "Colombian Guerrillas Are Using Coronavirus Curfews to Expand Their Control. Violators Have Been Killed," *The Washington Post*, July 26, 2020, accessed on July 26, 2020, https://www.washingtonpost.com/world/the_americas/colombia-coronavirus-farc-eln-guerrillas/2020/07/25/927d3c06-cb64-11ea-bc6a-6841b28d9093_story.html.

45. Antonio Ramirez, "An Introduction to Colombian Governmental Institutions and Primary Legal Sources," Hauser Global Law School Program – New York University, May 2007, 1, https://www.nyulawglobal.org/globalex/Colombia.html.

46. Donald T. Fox and Anne Stetson, "The 1991 Constitutional Reform: Prospects for Democracy and the Rule of Law in Colombia," *Case Western Reserve Journal of International Law* 24, no. 2 (1992): 146–47.

47. The SIC's legal authorities are derived from article 121 of the 1946 Constitution and also made reference to Decree 3518 from 1949. Decree 3518 was issued in response to *La Violencia*. Official Diary of Colombia, Number 28343, November 10, 1953, 594, http://www.suin-juriscol.gov.co/viewDocument.asp?id=1778201.

48. Official Diary of Colombia, Number 28343, 594.

49. Official Diary of Colombia, Number 30307, August 18, 1960, 1, http://www.suin-juriscol.gov.co/clp/contenidos.dll/Decretos/1801084?fn=document-frame.htm$f=templates$3.0.

50. Official Diary of Colombia, Number 30307, 1.

51. http://wsPagepresidencia.gov.co/Normativa/Decretos/2011/Documents/Noviembre/03/dec417903112011.pdf

52. Republic of Colombia, Presidential Decree 4170, November 3, 2011, http://wsp.presidencia.gov.co/Normativa/Decretos/2011/Documents/Noviembre/03/dec417903112011.pdf.

53. Davis et al., *A Great Perhaps?*, 49.

54. Davis et al., *A Great Perhaps?*, XXIX.

55. Alexander Grenoble and William Rose, "David Galula's Counterinsurgency: Occam Razor and Colombia," *Civil Wars* 13, no. 3 (2011): 302.

56. John A. Gentry and David E. Spencer, "Colombia's FARC: A Portrait of Insurgent Intelligence," *Intelligence and National Security* 25, no. 4. (2010): 476.

57. Mark Gonsalves, Keith Stansell, and Tom Howes, *Out of Captivity* (New York: Harper, 2009), 413–29.

58. Amnesty International. *Annual Report: Colombia 2017/2018*, accessed on November 26, 2019, https://www.amnesty.org/en/countries/americas/colombia/report-colombia/.

59. Amnesty International. *Annual Report: Colombia 2010*, accessed on November 26, 2019, https://www.amnestyusa.org/reports/annual-report-colombia-2010/.

60. Julie Terkewitz, "Colombia Supreme Court Orders Ex-President Álvaro Uribe Detained," *The New York Times*, August 4, 2020, https://www.nytimes.com/2020/08/04/world/americas/colombia-president-uribe-charged.html.

Chapter Two

Mexico

Marcos Pablo Moloeznik

Mexico is a country that has not enjoyed a long democratic tradition; for seventy-one years, the nation was governed by the Institutional Revolutionary Party (PRI), before transitioning to democracy in 2000. In its day—and those days lasted for decades—the PRI controlled the entire state apparatus, hence controlling public life in the country.[1] In 1939, a right-wing party, the National Action Party (PAN), was founded; for many decades it stood as Mexico's only opposition party. However, it did not present any real obstacle to the PRI's domination until, surprisingly, PAN won the 2000 presidential election.[2]

From 1947 to 1985, the Federal Security Directorate (DFS) was the main intelligence agency at the service of the PRI's authoritarian political regime that aimed to control dissent by force. However, the governments of the transitional period lacked the interest, incentive, and expertise required to transform the intelligence institutions, mechanisms, and practices inherited from the past PRI administrations, with their authoritarian bent. Two decades after the peaceful transfer of political power, a fragmented Mexican intelligence community continues to respond more to the government *du jour* than to the needs of Mexican democracy and the citizens it is meant to serve. This chapter reviews the incomplete democratic reforms of Mexico's intelligence services.

THE RPI REGIME AND THE ROLE OF INTELLIGENCE

The Mexican Revolution (1910–1920) gave birth to an authoritarian regime without real political opposition. Additionally, all controversies were solved with violence. Under the PRI's "sexennial monarchy," there was a strong centralization of power, and decision making was concentrated in the hands of the president. For instance, the president had the power to appoint judges to the supreme court and exercise influence in determining governor and mayor positions.[3] Furthermore, the PRI also exerted full political and social control by using the military for public security activities, including domestic intelligence gathering on the civilian population. These intrusive practices were carried out without the necessary declaration of a state of emergency, as stipulated in the Mexican constitution[4]—in other words, while the population was nominally protected by the rule of law, in practice the ruling party exercised unlimited power and used the armed forces within national boundaries. Ultimately, the DFS became the PRI's and especially the president's political police.[5] The PRI violently controlled dissent and conducted political espionage—committing egregious human rights violations—which were not investigated because such inquiries would be counterproductive to the regime and call into question the legitimacy of the state both domestically and internationally.

President Miguel Alemán Valdés (1946–1952) created DFS in 1947; in 1952 the agency was transferred to the Ministry of Interior, as a bureaucratic branch that reported directly to the president.[6] Between 1950 and the 1980s, the DFS was characterized by corruption, unlawful practices, and collaboration with criminal enterprises. The most illustrative examples were the killing of journalist Manuel Buendía in May 1984 and a U.S. Drug Enforcement Agency (DEA) agent Enrique Camarena in February 1985, which uncovered the endemic corruption of the DFS and its links with drug trafficking.[7] These events led to the replacement of the DFS with the Directorate of Investigation and National Security (DISEN) in November 29, 1985; this institution was formed to cleanse the civil intelligence services of corrupted staff and paved the way for the establishment of the Investigation and National Security Center (CISEN), tasked with national security intelligence—which involved more than just a name change.[8]

Indeed, this change prompted a sweeping reimaging of the civil intelligence institution, especially to entice professional and qualified personnel, based on the principle of civil service, to join CISEN. Hence, there was a reform of the Internal Regulations of the Ministry of Interior issued on February 13, 1989, by President Carlos Salinas de Gortari (1988–1994), establishing CISEN.[9] CISEN was a civilian agency, decentralized from the Ministry of Interior, with technical and operative autonomy. However, CISEN directly reported to the head of the agency while being responsible for the execution of Mexico's interior policy under the prerogative of the Ministry of Interior.[10] Therefore, CISEN had relative autonomy but remained under the Minister of Interior, which, in turn, received directives from the president. This management structure led to a perceived superficial reform, but the basic structure of the former system remained. Moreover, CISEN was tasked with providing intelligence to policy makers on risks and threats—most notably drug trafficking—to national security.

Notwithstanding these developments, CISEN was not always effective in preventing national security threats. For example, it failed to anticipate the January 1, 1994, armed insurgency movement perpetrated by the Zapatista Army of National Liberation (EZLN). After eleven days of fighting against the Mexican Army, the EZLN took five municipalities in the state of Chiapas: San Cristóbal de las Casa, Altamirano, Las Margaritas, Ocosingo y Chanal, forcing the government to negotiate a cease-fire and better conditions for the indigenous communities of the mentioned localities.[11] The differentiated treatment of these communities persists until today and remains a historic shortcoming of CISEN in dealing with or anticipating threats.

TRANSITION TO DEMOCRACY AND DEMOCRATIC REFORM ATTEMPTS

The democratic transition in Mexico began in 2000, when Vicente Fox Quezada (2000–2006) became the first non-PRI president. As part of this process, the Fox administration introduced a new national security concept, described in his National Development Plan and founded on democracy. It does not foresee prominent risks to Mexican sovereignty from traditional external threats (e.g., invasion by another state); rather, it emphasizes the existence of risks and threats of an internal nature that combine with transnational pressures from drug trafficking, organized crime, terrorism, and environmental crises.[12] The resulting violence and insecurity to society pose a clear threat to the state's institutions because of corruption, issues of negative perception, and citizens' mistrust of the government. The strategy and the transition reveal that Mexico was ready for change.

Under President Fox, the military endorsed the transition and, thus, respected the democratic election. Nonetheless, the new administration had to concede to keeping the traditional civil-military pact, which still exists today, that guarantees the armed forces' autonomy in legal, organizational, and budgetary matters.[13] Still, the new doctrine sought to protect national interests by separating the security apparatus and institutions from political parties' parochial interests.[14]

The Fox administration also embarked upon a few intelligence-related changes. His National Development Plan, and Law on National Security of 2005, for example, included provisions related to the role of national security intelligence.[15] Nonetheless, the Fox administration did not seem interested in de facto and de jure democratic and intelligence reform than one might expect of democratizers. For instance, neither the plan nor the law provided stipulations related to any checks and balances against intelligence activities, which in turn enabled intelligence politicization.[16] This situation led to the misuse of the intelligence apparatus, further discrediting competent institutions, and appropriating government tasks necessary to effectively protect national security.[17]

Several additional reforms occurred during the administration of Felipe Calderón (2006–2012)—who was a member of the National Action Party—most notably: the creation of an intelligence organization within the revenue (tax) sector, specifically, the Financial Intelligence Unit (FIU), established on May 7, 2004, to combat money laundering, terrorist financing, and tax evasion; the creation of the Naval Intelligence Unit of the Secretary of the Navy on February 1, 2008, charged with providing intelligence to support national security decision making; the intensification of bilateral cooperation with the United States, especially through the Merida Plan of June 30, 2008; and the creation of the School of Intelligence for National Security in 2009, entrusted with imparting specific national security civil intelligence training and knowledge. In addition, the national security strategy—based on aggressively combating drug trafficking, focused on neutralizing the primary leaders of these criminal organizations, and increased information collaboration between Mexican and U.S. intelligence organizations—was President Calderón's most impactful achievement.

Intelligence reform attempts continued during President Enrique Peña Nieto's administration (2012–2018). The Peña government initiated the Program for National Security 2014–2018, which underscored the need for an effective interagency process in Mexico aimed at combating national security threats.[18] This program aimed to develop an extensive national intelligence system, composed of federal agencies and predicated on intelligence cooperation and sharing, interoperability, and linking processes and tools to generate actionable intelligence. The objective of connecting these organizations' resources and efforts was to enable the national security system to fulfill the mission of fighting domestic and transnational security threats successfully.[19]

A corollary of President Peña Nieto's national intelligence system was an attempt to rectify Mexican strategic intelligence components systemic resistance to sharing and collaboration among themselves and civil authorities.[20] The first step to consolidate this system was the creation of the National Center for Intelligence Fusion (CENFI)[21] to facilitate the exchange of strategic information and the planning of joint operations involving members of the Ministry of Interior, Ministry of Defense, Ministry of Navy, General Prosecutor, National Security Commission, CISEN, and Federal Police.[22]

During the administration of President Andrés Manuel López Obrador (2018–2024), the intelligence system has also gone through several foundational reform iterations related to its hierarchy, structure, and function. For example, in 2018, the president decided to dismantle CISEN and replace it with the National Center for Intelligence (CNI), placing it under the umbrella of the Ministry of Public Security and Civilian Protection, however, retaining almost the entire CISEN personnel and leadership positions.[23]

The decision to place CNI under the Ministry of Public Security allegedly changes CNI's focus from strategic intelligence to law enforcement (public security) and criminal investigations,[24] underscoring the president's lack of expertise—and interest—in strategic intelligence and security matters.[25] In 2019, President López developed the National Development Plan 2019–2024 that aims to establish a National Intelligence System, promote the concept of a National Security culture dictated by informed elected governmental officials, and lay the basis for the creation of a biometric National Identity document.[26] In addition, to align with the National Plan on Peace and Security 2018–2024, the Mexican government will establish strategic intelligence sharing protocols between domestic and international security intelligence organizations, the National Institute of Migration, and the Intelligence Unit of the Ministry of Finance.[27] These actions were President Lopez Obrador's attempt to put his personal "imprint" on the intelligence and security systems, as a gesture to assert power opposed to democratic reform. Currently, limited information on the implementation and prospects of success of the plans and provisions exists yet mounting concerns about possible intelligence failures are materializing.[28]

ANALYSIS

Mexico's intelligence democratization has been incomplete. Indeed, an imperfect legal framework, coupled with civilian decision makers' limited interest and expertise in intelligence matters and intelligence reform, has resulted in weak oversight over a fragmented, politicized, and ineffective intelligence community.

Legal Framework

The Law on National Security is the only piece of legislation that stipulates the organization and function of CISEN. The law regulated the activities of CISEN (now CNI); established the personnel structure (Chapter III); defined the coordination of national security activities (Chapter IV); and detailed the protection of classified information (Chapter V).[29] The manner in which the Law on National Security was created has produced much consternation and confusion because it mingles national security and intelligence terms, unnecessarily obfuscating the ideal scenario of proper regulations for each subsection. The lack of clear delineation of agencies' roles and missions, relationship with consumers of intelligence, and oversight process mechanisms producing an incomplete intelligence legal framework has stunted intelligence reform progress.[30]

Regarding CISEN staffing, the Law on National Security (Chapter III) specified personnel allocations, individual responsibilities to safeguard classified information, and stipulated that employees would only be compelled to provide written testimony when requested by the federal judicial authorities under exceptional circumstances.[31] In late 2006, a formalized qualification requirements list for CISEN members was enacted that established regulations and procedures for CISEN's professionalization through recruitment, selection, education, training, evaluation, promotion, removal, and accountability of all CISEN personnel.[32] According to the Labor Code, which also specifies rules of confidentiality (Articles 8 and 26), all personnel are prohibited from disseminating or sharing information to which they have or had access due to their position; information should only be released to authorized individuals or entities.[33]

CISEN—throughout its short history—has been able to attract young, university-educated professionals; on the other hand, the organization has not been able to retain its valuable personnel due to unusually high and continuous turnover, caused either by resignation of the staff (due to corruption) or the general director's decision to separate a person under the pretense of loss of confidence.[34] Additionally, as indicated by Jorge Torres, another sensitive issue is CISEN's leadership.[35] Torres clarifies that generally an appointed individual does not possess the requisite knowledge or ideal skill sets to execute the position; rather CISEN leadership is determined based on loyalty or repayment of a political favor.[36] Furthermore, Torres asserts that the decay occurring in CISEN since 2000 can only be attributed to political weakness. Moreover, CISEN leadership, different ministers of interior, and directors of the center are unable to influence and enact fundamental intelligence reform.[37] Torres elaborates on this politically charged dynamic that has encumbered consolidated democratic intelligence progress:

> [P]olitical espionage was still part of CISEN's operations. Hundreds of public officials, politicians of the official party and opposition were victims of the work of agents and analysts of CISEN. These went through public and private information that was used by the presidents and ministers of interior. CISEN's structures and resources have been used by PRI and PAN [National Action

Party] governments to address their political agendas putting aside the national security interests.[38]

Alexia Barrios G., a journalist specializing in security issues, asserts that between 2000 and 2012, the presidential administrations of the PAN political party directly promoted and disqualified civil servants within CISEN.[39] Individuals with extensive career experience were relieved from their positions on claims that they failed to meet the new institutional requirements (for example, a degree from a private university).[40] Hence, CISEN preserved its pre-transition modus operandi, which involved personal influence/recommendation as the main recruitment criteria; lack of effective accountability/control mechanisms; devoid of insightful evaluation; incertitude; and the absence of a "culture of intelligence" in which the society becomes an interested stakeholder that monitors CISEN activity through the media. [41]

However, General Jorge Carrillo Olea, founder of CISEN, notes some positive developments during CISEN's existence. The organization provided benefits and the attractive possibility of career progression, which resulted in recruitment of very capable people.[42] CISEN also increased and expanded relationships and cooperation with international intelligence agencies, which helped bolster its effectiveness.[43]

Control and Oversight

Mexican intelligence doctrine defines strategic intelligence as "systemized and hierarchized knowledge that has the main objective of providing an evaluative and prospective reference framework to make decisions that address integral vulnerabilities, risks, and threats through the ponderation of the link between security, defense, and development in its three dimensions: human, politic-military, and economic-environmental."[44] Nevertheless, in the view of Jorge Enrique Tello Peón, former CISEN director (1994–1999), one of the fundamental weaknesses in Mexico is the confusion among decision makers between the strategic, operational, or tactical intelligence functions, which unnecessarily complicates making correct and time-sensitive decisions.[45]

Mexico does not formulate long-term strategic intelligence objectives. Russell G. Swenson and Susana C. Lemozy assert that a nation's democratic intelligence system must evolve in a sequential order. First, long-term national intelligence objectives must be defined, which allows for the elaboration of a framework for strategic intelligence, and finally legitimate intelligence organizations will be devised as a response to national necessity.[46] During the last year of President Peña Nieto's administration, he espoused strengthening the intelligence service's identity and strategic intelligence cooperation. For instance, the creation of the CENFI, in 2015, facilitated the exchange of strategic information and the planning of joint operations involving members of the Ministry of Interior, Ministry of Defense, Ministry of Navy, General Prosecutor, National Security Commission, CISEN, and Federal Police.[47]

However, politicians still generally lack expertise or knowledge in intelligence or national security and maintain parochial interests that can be counterproductive to national security objectives.[48] A clear example took place during the Calderón presidency, when the war against drugs became an obsession. Thus the personal vendetta of the president focused national strategic intelligence objectives and allocation of resources on targeting of the heads of the drug cartels, which only worsened national security because the ensuing power vacuum was occupied by more criminal organizations—at times led by even more ruthless and better organized leaders. According to President Calderón "organized crime seeks the territorial control, and it will be a war without quarter because there is no possibility of coexisting with the drugs dealers . . . there is no coming back, it is them or us."[49]

Current civil control of intelligence in Mexico must be understood through the lens of its executive-centric political system and utilization of the intelligence community to further presidential prerogatives. Mexico's political system designates the executive branch as legally responsible for defining national security intelligence policy. In addition, the executive coordinates policy implementation with the Mexican States.[50] Further, the Ministries of Defense and Navy manage Section 2 Intelligence (intelligence gathered by the Mexican Armed Forces mirrors the U.S. intelligence gathering construct, due to cooperation between both nations), and the resulting reports are provided to the executive to fulfill commander-in-chief duties.[51] The legal-programmatic dimension provides the legal hierarchal configuration for the different entities within the system and how intelligence activities are to be conducted. Additionally, the National Development Plans organization, comprised of the Risk National Agenda (classified) and the Program for National Security (public), provides essential information to assist executive decision making.

Nevertheless, the political control of intelligence—exercised by the executive, legislative, and judicial branches—presents challenges to achieving harmony between effectiveness and transparency in Mexico, attributed to the lack of trust in politicians responsible for devising intelligence or national security.[52]

It has been argued that during the intelligence reform process, the greatest challenge has been the relationship between intelligence producers and consumers (government, especially, the executive branch). For example, as Alejandro Alegre Rabiela, former director of CISEN (1999–2000) laments,

[I]f today I was asked, what could have been done better? I would ask our consumer or decision maker if our products were useful. Because as a producer, one believes that the goods fabricated are what the decision maker needs. However, there was never an adequate feedback loop with the Head of the Executive branch nor the rest of the bodies of the Cabinet of National Security, nor the local governments or other branches of the government. We did not know if what CISEN was producing was useful, exactly what they needed or if they were missing something else.[53]

Professionalism and Effectiveness

Mexico's lack of a strategic vision or a plan, vis-à-vis the role and status of intelligence in Mexican democracy, has negatively affected the efficacy of the intelligence agencies. On the one hand, as Manuel Balcázar Villareal expounds, a deficient legal framework for intelligence has fueled politicization; CISEN has frequently been co-opted as a political-party instrument instead of focusing on the supreme interest of the state and addressing national security risks and threats.[54] This inappropriate utilization has led to the misallocation of finite intelligence resources and consequently permitted unabated national security threats to gain power.

There are three primary explanations for Mexican intelligence failures: (1) decision makers underestimate, if not disdain, the utility of strategic intelligence; (2) national strategic decisions are formed without consulting intelligence products, and special-interests group and personal agendas are elevated above national priorities; and (3) intelligence producers have not been professionalized or empowered to advise the executive, rather they are relegated to fulfill the role of document handlers. This threefold dynamic obstructs current intelligence endeavors and Mexico's strategic intelligence aspirations have failed simply because they have never received adequate attention.[55] In addition, national intelligence production is not an integrated analysis from all services—but rather an array of analytical products sent separately by each agency, due to a lack of trust among agencies in the central government and also among the local and state agencies[56]—which hinders intelligence effectiveness.[57]

Another element that precludes the formation of a national intelligence strategic vision is the antagonistic relationship between the executive branch with the other two branches—particularly with the legislative branch. According to the National Security Law, through the Bicameral National Security Commission, the legislature is legally allowed to request and review intelligence products. However, no legal powers have been assigned to legislators to act as a counterweight to the executive and judicial with the design, implementation, and evaluation of national intelligence policies. Thus it is fairly safe to say that in Mexico, there are no checks and balances through which the legislative branch might intervene in the intelligence sector.

Training

CISEN personnel acquire their professional training and development at the Academy of Intelligence for National Security (ESISEN), created in 2009.[58] Primarily ESISEN was created to provide training to CISEN members; therefore, the ranks of various CISEN sectors share common training experiences. Secondarily, a series of courses and seminars were regularly offered to personnel that belong to other institutions in the Mexican National Security Cabinet and other state government security agencies. Courses included intelligence analysis, emerging threat exploration, and language training. Intelligence studies has gradually expanded to civilian education institutions; for example, Universidad Anahuac offers intelligence bachelor of arts programs. Additionally, the Mexican Secretariat of National Defense (SEDENA) has developed military intelligence courses for its military personnel at the Military School of Intelligence (EMI).[59]

Nonetheless, Mexico's increase in professional intelligence education offerings has not translated into a fully formed solution. Limited information sources and meager opportunities to receive training remains problematic, which in turn affects the capabilities of intelligence agencies to carry out their roles and missions effectively.

Budgeting

Mexico lacks a state policy related to intelligence; this power resides exclusively with the executive branch, which can allocate a budget based on any criteria. Table 2.1, below, illustrates the random annual budget allocations to CISEN.

The budget reflects that the organization enjoyed consistent increases from 2000 to 2015, with the exception of 2010. However, in 2016 there was a significant funding reduction, and the budget has precipitously declined since, without any logical explanation or justification.

Table 2.1. Budget of the CISEN (2000–2018) and CNI (2019) in millions of Mexican pesos

2000	2001	2002	2003	2004	2005	2006	2007	2008	2009
$900	$980	$1,034	$886	$996	$869	$1,153	$1,114	$1,269	$2,379

2010	2011	2012	2013	2014	2015	2016	2017	2018	2019
$2,140	$2,244	$2,766	$2,744	$7,537	$7,616	$3,273	$2,823	$2,888	$2,491

Sources[60]

CONCLUSION

Mexico's challenges to democratic consolidation have had a spillover effect into the country's intelligence culture. As such, several lacunae surrounding Mexico's attempt to democratize its intelligence agencies need decision makers' immediate attention:

- The absence of a coherent and comprehensive intelligence community—a system with a common approach—that responds to the logic of the state[61] and helps to provide rationality to the decision-making process. According to Yehezkel Dror, former adviser to government of Mexico, current decisions "can influence the direction that the society should follow in the future."[62] Specially, the endemic violence is a critical issue that jeopardizes the right to life, and actions must be taken to reduce the homicide rate.
- Decision makers failure in distinguishing and separating tactical, operational, and strategic intelligence, giving priority to the strategic realm.[63]
- The absence of a national model on strategic intelligence capable of consolidating the information produce by all national security, local, and municipal entities.[64]
- Lack of continuous feedback between producers and consumers (decision makers) to facilitate an efficient system.
- The political dimension affecting the intelligence sphere and making it a political "currency" to distribute political appointments opposed to meritorious means.
- Lack of a culture of intelligence that according to Jorge Enrique Tello Peón should be developed within the federal government structures with the CNI as the axis of a national intelligence system with the participation of the federal government. Furthermore, to convince the citizens of their equal stake in the success of the intelligence community.[65]
- Unbalance between the personnel of the different intelligence segments at the three levels of government—federal, local, and municipal—especially in terms of analysis of the intelligence service collected.[66]

To attain a higher level of democratic consolidation and functionality of the intelligence system, Mexico first must distill, communicate, and implement national objectives. Second, a system that respects the prerogatives of the three coequal government branches and citizens will allow for a more equitable, responsive, and efficient intelligence apparatus. This framework will allow for the construction and iterative improvement of the system to capture and agilely respond to changing realities to better safeguard Mexican national interests. A proposed path for advancement has been formulated; however, receptiveness and implementation may prove problematic in creating a more fully developed democratic intelligence structure.

NOTES

1. Partido Revolucionario Institucional (PRI) and Instituto de Capacitación Política (ICAP), "Capítulo I Fundación del Partido," in *Historia Documental del Partido de la Revolución* (Mexico: PRI, 1981), 24–141, https://www.pri.org.mx/ban cosecretarias/files/Archivos/Pdf/594-1-11_32_45.pdf (accessed February 21, 2021).

2. Vicente Fox won the elections with over 42 percent of the vote. Fox was the first president elected from an opposition party since Francisco I. Madero in 1910. D. Nohlen (2005), *Elections in the Americas: A Data Handbook*, volume I; Murilo Kuschik (September 2000), Las encuestas y la elección del año 2000, *Revista Mexicana de Ciencias Políticas y Sociales*.

3. Juan J. Linz and Alfred Stepan, *Problems of Democratic Transition and Consolidation: Southern Europe, South America, and Post-Communist Europe* (Baltimore: Johns Hopkins University Press, 1996); Pablo González Casanova, *La Democracia en México* (Mexico: Era, 1965); Daniel Cosío Villegas, *El Sistema Político Mexicano* (Mexico: Joaquín Mortiz, 1972), 30–31; and Jorge Carpizo, *El Presidencialismo Mexicano* (Mexico: Siglo XXI, 1978).

4. https://web.oas.org/mla/en/Countries_Intro/en_mex-int-text-const.pdf

5. DFS emerged from the First Section intelligence agency created in 1918 within the Office for Governance, and which underwent several name changes until 1947, when it took the name of DFS. Sergio Aguayo Quezada, "Los Usos, Abusos y Retos de la Seguridad Nacional Mexicana, 1946–1990," in *En Busca de la Seguridad Perdida. Aproximaciones a la Seguridad Nacional Mexicana*, ed. Sergio Aguayo Quezada and Bruce Michael Bagley (Mexico: Siglo XXI, 1990), 107–45. Also see Tanalís Padilla and Louise E. Walker, eds., "Dossier: Spy Reports: Content, Methodology, and Historiography in Mexico's Secret Police Archive," *Journal of Iberian and Latin American Research* (July 2013).

6. The predecessor of DSC was established in 1918 by the constitutionalist President Venustiano Carranza (1917–1920) as an "intelligence agents' service" in the Ministry of Interior. Since its origins, more importance was given to the loyalty and discretion of its personnel rather than its honesty and observance of legality. Hence, recruitment processes and selection were exclusively based on the recommendations of the personnel already in the institution (nepotism). Sergio Aguayo Quezada, *La Charola: Una Historia de los Servicios de Inteligencia en México* (Mexico: Grijalbo, 2001), 200ff.

7. Malcolm Beith, *The Last Narco* (New York: Grove Press, 2010), 41; Carlos Moncada, *Del México Violento: Periodistas Asesinados* (Mexico: Edamex, 1991).

8. Centro de Investigación y Seguridad Nacional (CISEN), in *Official Journal of the Federation* (Mexico, February 13, 1989).

9. CISEN, *20 años de Historia. Testimonios Febrero 2009* (México: CISEN, 2009), 111–13.

10. CISEN, 1989; Jorge Carrillo Olea, *México en Riesgo. Una Visión Personal sobre un Estado a la Defensiva* (Mexico: Grijalbo, 2011), 247–48.

11. Marco Estrada Saavedra, "El levantamiento zapatista de 1994," in *Arqueología Mexicana* (September/October 2011): 60–63, https://arqueologiamexicana.mx/mex ico-antiguo/el-levantamiento-zapatista-de-1994 (accessed February 21, 2021).

12. *Plan Nacional de Desarrollo 2001–2006* (Mexico: Executive Power of the Federation, 2001). Translation by the author.

13. Marcos Pablo Moloeznik, *Tratado sobre Pensamiento Estratégico-Militar: Enseñanzas para el Sistema de Defensa de México* (Mexico: Colectivo de Análisis de la Seguridad en Democracia, CASEDE, 2018), 478–79, http://www.casede .org/index.php/biblioteca-casede-2-0/defensa-y-fuerzas-armadas/fuerzas-armadas -mexicanas/410-tratado-sobre-pensamiento-estrategico-militar (accessed February 21, 2021).

14. "3.1. Independencia, Soberanía y Seguridad Nacional," in *Primer Informe de Gobierno* (Mexico: Executive Power of the Federation, September 1, 2001).

15. For instance, the plan acknowledged that Mexico needed accurate and reliable information to guarantee national security and combat threats to national peace and well-being. It defined CISEN's role in strategic intelligence—planning, collection, processing, dissemination, and exploitation of intelligence—aimed at combating threats related to organized crime, subversion, terrorism, public security; demographic dynamics; counterintelligence; border security and migration; ecological hazards; global economy risks; democratic governability and rule of law; corruption; and institution strengthening, using such modern techniques and technologies, including scientific methodology for the intelligence analysis. *Plan Nacional de Desarrollo 2001–2006* (Mexico: Executive Power of the Federation, 2001), 128. CISEN, "Doctrina de Inteligencia" (Mexico: CISEN, 2000), http://www.cisen.gob.mx/html/ doctrina.htm (accessed February 21, 2021). Law of National Security defines intelligence as knowledge obtained through the collection, processing, dissemination, and exploitation of information, to be used in the decision-making process on matters related to national security. "Ley de Seguridad Nacional," in *Official Journal of the Federation* (Mexico: House of Representatives, January 31, 2005; last modified December 26, 2005), article 29. Translation by the author.

16. The government would therefore direct intelligence agencies to carry out illegal surveillance activities against opponents or critics of the government, in the name of national security—mostly because the strong executive the political opposition was viewed as a threat to the interest of the group maintaining power. https://mvsnoticias .com/noticias/nacionales/calderon-y-fox-deben-ser-investigados-por-caso-espionaje -morena.

17. The government would therefore direct intelligence agencies to carry out illegal surveillance activities against opponents or critics of the government, in the name of national security—mostly because the strong executive the political opposition was viewed as a threat to the interest of the group maintaining power. https://mvsnoticias .com/noticias/nacionales/calderon-y-fox-deben-ser-investigados-por-caso-espionaje -morena.

18. *Plan Nacional de Desarrollo 2013–2018* (Mexico: Executive Power of the Federation, 2013), 9, http://pnd.gob.mx/ (accessed February 21, 2021).

19. *Plan Nacional de Desarrollo 2013–2018* (Mexico: Executive Power of the Federation, 2013), 9; CISEN, *Amenazas y Riesgos* (Mexico, 2014), and *Programa para la Seguridad Nacional 2009–2012* (Mexico: Executive Power of the Federation, 2009), sec. 1.2.2.1 and 1.2.2.2, http://www.dof.gob.mx/nota_detalle.php?codigo=510 6082&fecha=20/08/2009 (accessed February 21, 2021).

20. Manuel Ignacio Balcázar Villareal, "Modernización del Sistema de Inteligencia Estratégica para la Seguridad Nacional en México," *Revista de Estudios en Seguridad Internacional* (July 2019), 72, http://www .seguridadinternacional.es/revista/?q=content/modernizaci%C3%B3n-del-sistema -de-inteligencia-estrat%C3%A9gica-para-la-seguridad-nacional-en-m%C3%A9xico (accessed February 21, 2021).

21. Alexia Barrios G., "Las Graves Confesiones," https://www.periodicoacceso .com/2013/11/29/las-graves-confesiones-de-guillermo/ (accessed February 21, 2021).

22. Government of Mexico, Executive Power of the Federation, "México en Paz," in *Sexto Infrome de Gobierno (2017–2018),* President Enrique Peña Nieto (Mexico, 2014), 20, https://www.gob.mx/epn/articulos/sexto-informe-de-gobierno -173378?idiom=es.

23. Approximately 99 percent of the 3,600 of CISEN's personnel and five of seven in leadership continue to work for CNI. The legal basis for CNI is Law on National Security of 2005. Centro Nacional de Inteligencia, CNI (2019), https://www .gob.mx/cni; Miguel Badillo, "Centro de Inteligencia opera con 99% de personal del CISEN," *Revista Contralínea* (April 3, 2019), https://www.contralinea.com.mx/ archivo-revista/2019/04/03/centro-de-inteligencia-opera-con-99-de-personal-del-cisen/ (accessed February 21, 2021).

24. Agustín Maciel Padilla, *Understanding Mexico's National Security Conundrum* (UK: Routledge | Taylor & Francis Group, 2021).

25. Alejandro Hope, "CISEN: Los Limites de la Apertura," *El Universal* (Mexico, January 25, 2019), https://www.eluniversal.com.mx/columna/alejandro-hope/nacion/ cisen-los-limites-de-la-apertura (accessed February 21, 2021); David Ramírez de Garay, "La 4T y los Servicios de Inteligencia," *México Evalúa* (March 12, 2019), https://www.mexicoevalua.org/la-4t-los-servicios-inteligencia/ (accessed February 21, 2021).

26. *Plan Nacional de Desarrollo 2019–2024* (Mexico: Executive Power of the Federation, 2019), 22, https://lopezobrador.org.mx/temas/plan-nacional-de-desar rollo-2019-2024/ (accessed February 21, 2021).

27. *Plan Nacional de Paz y Seguridad 2018–2024* (Mexico: Executive Power of the Federation, 2018), 20, https://lopezobrador.org.mx/wp-content/uploads/2018/11/ PLAN-DE-PAZ-Y-SEGURIDAD_ANEXO.pdf (accessed February 21, 2021).

28. Manuel Ignacio Balcázar Villareal, "Retos y Perspectivas de la Inteligencia Estratégica en México—Estado de situación" (Author's Unpublished Paper: Tuxtla Gutiérrez, July 2019), 4.

29. "Ley de Seguridad Nacional," in *Official Journal of the Federation* (Mexico: House of Representatives, January 31, 2005. Last modified December 26, 2005).

30. Alejandro Alegre Rabiela, "Hacia una Ley de Inteligencia para la Seguridad Nacional," *Revista de Administración Pública, RAP* (2000): 1–4, http://www

.inap.mx/portal/images/REVISTA_A_P/rap_101_2000.pdf (accessed February 21, 2021); Marcos Pablo Moloeznik, "Apuntes sobre Inteligencia e Instrumentos Estratégicos en México: Tensión entre la Legalidad y la Realidad," in *Inteligencia Estratégica Latinoamericana. Perspectivas y Ejes Predominantes para la Toma de Decisiones Estratégicas ante un Mundo en Cambio–Antología*, eds. José Gabriel Paz and Roberto Román (Buenos Aires: Ministerio de Defensa, Dirección de Inteligencia Estratégica-Militar, 2015), 140, https://drive.google.com/file/d/0B5QwcH3cZi9EWnBpTHFaWEkyOUU/view (accessed February 21, 2021). Even the Constitution has some elements of contradiction with regard to the intelligence and wider security sector activity. For instance, in its article 1 there are many provisions on human rights, while at the same time it contains elements such as preventive prison (misuse and in clear contradiction to the presumption of innocence) or the right to declare a foreigner as persona non grata and expel them from the territory without due process.

31. "Ley de Seguridad Nacional," in *Official Journal of the Federation* (Mexico: House of Representatives, January 31, 2005. Last modified December 26, 2005), article 21.

32. "Estatuto Laboral del Centro de Investigación y Seguridad Nacional," in *Official Journal of the Federation* (Mexico: House of Representatives, November 29, 2006), article 1, http://www.cisen.gob.mx/pdfs/marco_normativo/Estatuto_laboral _cisen.pdf.

33. "Estatuto Laboral del Centro de Investigación y Seguridad Nacional," in *Official Journal of the Federation* (Mexico: House of Representatives November 29, 2006), article 1, http://www.cisen.gob.mx/pdfs/marco_normativo/Estatuto_laboral _cisen.pdf.

34. Anonymous interview 1, Former director of CISEN (June 25, 2015); Anonymous interview 2, Former intelligence agent of the Presidency of Mexico and the Intelligence Unit of the Ministry of the Navy (SEMAR) (June 26, 2015); Anonymous interview 3, Former executive of ESISEN (June 23, 2015).

35. Jorge Torres, *CISEN. Auge y Decadencia del Espionaje Mexicano* (Mexico: Debate, 2009), 21.

36. Torres, *CISEN. Auge y Decadencia*, 21.

37. Torres, *CISEN. Auge y Decadencia*, 21.

38. Torres, *CISEN. Auge y Decadencia*, 12 and 19.

39. Alexia Barrios G., "Las Graves Confesiones de Guillermo Valdés,"*Periódico Acceso*, November 2013. https://www.periodicoacceso.com/2013/11/29/las-graves -confesiones-de-guillermo/ (accessed February 21, 2021).

40. Alexia Barrios G., "Las Graves Confesiones de Guillermo Valdés,"*Periódico Acceso*, November 2013. https://www.periodicoacceso.com/2013/11/29/las-graves -confesiones-de-guillermo/ (accessed February 21, 2021).

41. Sergio Aguayo Quezada, *La Charola*.

42. Jorge Carrillo Olea, *México en Riesgo*, 145.

43. CISEN, *20 años de Historia*, 44 and 45.

44. *Programa para la Seguridad Nacional 2014–2018* (Mexico: Executive Power of the Federation, 2014), 44, http://cdn.presidencia.gob.mx/programa-para-la-seguri dad-nacional.pdf (accessed February 21, 2021).

45. CISEN, *20 años de Historia*, 42.

46. Russell G. Swenson and Susana C. Lemozy, eds., *Democratización de la Función de Inteligencia. El Nexo de la Cultura Nacional y la Inteligencia Estratégica.* (Washington, DC: National Defense Intelligence College, 2009), xv and xvii.

47. "México en Paz," in *Sexto Infrome de Gobierno (2017–2018)*, President Enrique Peña Nieto (Mexico: Executive Power of the Federation, 2014), 20, https://www.gob.mx/epn/articulos/sexto-informe-de-gobierno-173378?idiom=es (accessed February 21, 2021).

48. Moloeznik, "Apuntes sobre inteligencia," 135; Balcázar Villareal, "Modernización del Sistema," 77.

49. Felipe de Jesús Calderón Hinojosa, interview by Jorge Zepeda Patterson, "El Crimen Organizado es la Mayor Amenaza a los Derechos Humanos," *El Universal* (Mexico: February 27, 2009), quoted in Raúl Benítez Manaut, Abelardo Rodríguez Sumano, and Armando Rodríguez Luna, eds., "La Guerra al Crimen Organizado." *Atlas de la Seguridad y la Defensa de México 2009* (Mexico: CASEDE, 2009), http://www.casede.org/PublicacionesCasede/Atlas2009/analisis_de_seguridad_1.pdf (accessed February 21, 2021).

50. Balcázar Villareal, "Modernización del Sistema," 77–78.

51. Balcázar Villareal, "Modernización del Sistema," 78.

52. Balcázar Villareal, "Modernización del Sistema," 77; and Javier Borredá, "Entrevista al General Jorge Carrillo Olea, Fundador del Centro de Investigación y Seguridad Nacional (CISEN)," *Revista Segurilatam* (May 7, 2019), 2, http://www.segurilatam.com/entrevistas/entrevistas/el-exito-de-la-inteligencia-al-servicio-de-la-seguridad-nacional-depende-de-la-confianza-del-presidente-del-pais.

53. CISEN, *20 años de Historia*, 52. Translation by the author.

54. Manuel Ignacio Balcázar Villareal, "Retos y Perspectivas de la Inteligencia Estratégica en México-Estado de situación" (Author's Unpublished Paper: Tuxtla Gutierrez, July 2019), 1.

55. Strategic intelligence consists of collating information to be distributed to decision-making authorities regarding national security matters from a comprehensive prospective and long-term vision. For example, the nation lacks the expertise to produce nationally scoped and relevant intelligence products and the capacity to adapt to complex situations. This approach ensures that Mexico will address national issues in a reactive, opposed to proactive, manner until a semblance of long-term vision and execution complimented by a democratically governed intelligence hierarchy is established. Balcázar Villareal, "Retos y perspectivas," 4.

56. This prevents Mexico from having a real national intelligence system.

57. Borredá, "Entrevista al General Jorge Carrillo Olea," 2, http://www.segurilatam.com/entrevistas/entrevistas/el-exito-de-la-inteligencia-al-servicio-de-la-seguridad-nacional-depende-de-la-confianza-del-presidente-del-pais.

58. See CISEN, *ESISEN* (Mexico: CISEN, 2015), http://www.cisen.gob.mx/Esisen.html (accessed February 21, 2021); "Estatuto Laboral del Centro de Investig-

ación y Seguridad Nacional," in *Official Journal of the Federation* (Mexico: House of Representatives, November 29, 2006), article 1, http://www.cisen.gob.mx/pdfs/marco_normativo/Estatuto_laboral_cisen.pdf; and "Acuerdo por el que se crea la Escuela de Inteligencia para la Seguridad Nacional del Centro de Investigación y Seguridad Nacional (ESISEN)," in *Official Journal of the Federation* (Mexico: House of Representatives, April 16, 2009), http://www.cisen.gob.mx/pdfs/acuerdo_escuela_inteligencia.pdf (accessed February 21, 2021).

59. Military Intelligence School depends on the Army and Air Force Studies Center, http://www.diputados.gob.mx/documentos/Defensa/35.pdf (accessed February 21, 2021).

60. Armando Rodríguez Luna, Patricia Quintanar, and Keyla Vargas, "Presupuestos: Seguridad y Defensa 2000–2016," in *Atlas de la Seguridad y la Defensa de México,* eds. Raúl Benítez Manaut and Sergio Aguayo Quezada, 303–34 (Mexico: Colectivo de Análisis de la Seguridad con Democracia CASEDE, 2016), https://www.casede.org/PublicacionesCasede/Atlas2016/Presupuestos.pdf; Nación321, "¿Qué Hace y Cuánto nos Cuesta a los Ciudadanos el CISEN?" Last modified February 13, 2018. https://www.nacion321.com/gobierno/que-hace-y-cuanto-nos-cuesta-a-los-ciudadanos-el-cisen (accessed February 21, 2021); Badillo, Miguel. "Centro de Inteligencia opera con 99% de personal del CISEN," *Revista Contralínea* (April 3, 2019), https://www.contralinea.com.mx/archivo-revista/2019/04/03/centro-de-inteligencia-opera-con-99-de-personal-del-cisen/ (accessed February 21, 2021).

61. CISEN, *Comunidad de Inteligencia* (Mexico: CISEN, 2015), http://www.cisen.gob.mx/intComunidadInt.html (accessed February 21, 2021).

62. Yehezkel Dror, *La capacidad de gobernar: Informe al Club de Roma* (Mexico: Fondo de Cultura Económica, 1994), 31.

63. Balcázar Villareal, "Modernización del Sistema," 75.

64. Balcázar Villareal, "Modernización del Sistema," 75.

65. CISEN, *20 años de historia*, 47.

66. Eduardo E. Estévez, "La actividad de inteligencia en nuevos contextos normativos democráticos-adaptando la inteligencia realizada en el ámbito interior," paper presented at *Seminário internacional 'a atividade de inteligência e os desafios contemporâneos'* (Argentina-Brasil: Gabinete de Segurança Institucional da Presidência da República (GSIPR), Agência Brasileira de Inteligência (ABIN), December 1–2, 2005), pp. 7 and 24, http://fas.org/irp/world/argentina/actividad.pdf (accessed February 21, 2021).

Part II

NEW DEMOCRACIES

Chapter Three

Argentina

María Alejandra Otamendi, Germán E. Gallino, and Eduardo E. Estévez

With a significant history of military coups and human rights abuses, Argentina began the process of transitioning to democracy in 1983. It was not until 2001 that new intelligence legislation was enacted, formally stipulating civilian control and establishing oversight mechanisms. However, democratic civilian control of the intelligence sector has been precarious due to the executive branch's repeated attempts to politicize intelligence and virtually nonexistent legislative oversight. This chapter reviews Argentina's intelligence apparatus from its formation. The review begins with a historical origins overview through non-democratic periods, followed by analysis of the transition to democracy, and recently instituted reforms.[1] In order to assess Argentina's degree of democratization, the Democratic Governance of Intelligence Matrix (DGI) discussed in the introduction of this handbook is applied in the last section of the chapter.

HISTORICAL BACKGROUND: INTELLIGENCE FROM PERONISM TO STATE TERRORISM

Between 1930 and 1983, Argentina suffered successive ruthless military dictatorships, with short periods of democratic governance.[2] In 1946, democratically elected president Juan Domingo Perón instituted the first intelligence service, the Coordination of Information of the Presidency, which, in 1976, at the beginning of the last dictatorship, became the State Intelligence Secretariat (SIDE).[3] At that time, the agency was charged with the planning, direction, and supervision of actions against communism, both domestically and abroad.[4] Additional intelligence agencies had operated since the 1940s within the Armed Forces branches.[5] Likewise, several law enforcement intelligence services—most notably the Federal Coordination Directorate[6] created in 1944 under the Argentine Federal Police (PFA) and the Federal Coordination Information Corps[7]—carried out similar roles during the last dictatorship aimed at countering surreptitious action of foreign powers, subversive groups, or persons who constituted a threat to state security.

The National Intelligence Center (CNI), created by National Defense Law No. 16970 of 1966, was tasked with the coordination and centralization of intelligence related to national security policy and national strategy planning, providing intelligence to the National Security Council, and formulating intelligence doctrine. There was no civilian control of the intelligence apparatus during the dictatorship. Military officers exercised the management of civilian intelligence agencies, the police, and security forces.[8]

This period marked by the use of coercive state powers against opposition parties produced a secret state legacy.[9] In this sense, in the context of the Cold War, the military dictatorship known as National Reorganization Process (1976–1983) implemented a "dirty war" between 1976 and 1983 by using the intelligence services under the "national security doctrine."[10] This doctrine coalesced the notions of national defense with that of internal security—regarding political dispute as threats to national security.[11] As a consequence, the dirty war involved state terrorism against political, social, religious, labor organizations, student leaders, and many other citizens through measures that included the systematic kidnapping of opponents' babies; the illegal detention of people that resulted in the "disappeared," killings, tortures, and human rights abuses of thousands of people.[12]

INTELLIGENCE UNDER TRANSITION AND DEMOCRATIC ADMINISTRATIONS

The non-democratic regime ended in collapse in 1983, when the Argentine armed forces, which started a war with Great Britain to recapture the Malvinas Islands in 1982, were defeated; additionally, the political pressure of human rights organizations such as *Madres* and *Abuelas de Plaza de Mayo* and the Nobel Peace Prize winner Pérez Esquivel was considerable.[13] Argentina transitioned to democracy in December 1983 after general elections, which resulted in the election of President Raul Alfonsín (1983–1989).[14] The political process that began in 1983 attracted the attention of academics who laid the epistemic foundations to advance the democratization of the defense and security sector under the paradigm of civil-military relations.[15] The demilitarization of politics and the depoliticization of military affairs became synonymous with democratization for both civil society and political leaders.[16]

President Alfonsín undertook several intelligence systems reforms. For the first time in the country's history, he appointed civilian officials as heads of the SIDE and the CNI. The new civilian leadership of intelligence in turn fired most of the military officers in those agencies, an unprecedented depuration of these institutions.[17] Civilian intelligence chiefs during Alfonsín's tenure also tried, though without success, to empower the CNI to lead the coordination of the intelligence community. In this regard, the SIDE obstructed the operation of the CNI from the beginning. That was possible because the CNI was never afforded independent resources and staff to gather and obtain information. In addition, there was no organic policy governing the sector and political power was weak.

A NEW LEGAL ARCHITECTURE IN CONTEXT

Legislative debate during the democratic transition resulted in congress passing three laws with specific articles to govern the intelligence sector. The first two were the 1988 National Defense Law No. 23554 that established a prohibition of using military intelligence to perform domestic intelligence functions; and the 1992 Internal Security Law No. 24059, which set up the first parliamentary intelligence oversight committee created in Latin America, and administrative regulations for a domestic intelligence system.[18]

In the aftermath of two terrorist bombings in the country's capital city, Buenos Aires, in 1992 and 1994—which the intelligence agencies failed to prevent—the Carlos Menem administration (1989–1999) attempted to strengthen Argentina's counterterrorism capabilities, including developing intelligence cooperation at regional and subregional levels.[19] In May 1996 President Menem signed Argentina's participation in the Tri-border Tripartite Command to operate at the confluence of the cities of Puerto Iguazú (Argentina), Foz de Iguazú (Brazil), and Ciudad del Este (Paraguay), an area that is considered a terrorist and organized crime hub, which enabled intelligence cooperation and sharing on terrorism and organized crime.[20] Despite these attempts, the intelligence agencies during this administration were involved in a number of illegal surveillance scandals—military involvement in domestic intelligence operations and the ungoverned rise in secret expenditures.[21]

The administration of Fernando De la Rúa (2000–2001) made several positive changes to the SIDE: approximately one thousand personnel were dismissed; secret budget was cut by 60 percent; qualified and expert human resources were hired; and a new organizational structure was established.[22] Nevertheless, SIDE's reform remained stalled until December 2001, when President De la Rúa enacted the National Intelligence Law No. 25520, instituting the judicial and functional basis of the National Intelligence System.[23]

Under the 2001 Law, three intelligence agencies became the leading bodies: The Secretariat of Intelligence (SI), the National Directorate for Criminal Intelligence (DINICRI), and the National Directorate for Strategic Military Intelligence (DNIEM). The SI replaced both SIDE and CNI, while DINICRI was rooted in the intelligence body created by the Internal Security Law and DINIEM in the National Defense Law. SI, under the presidency, had the mission of managing the intelligence system and producing national intelligence; the DINICRI, under the Interior Security Secretariat of the Ministry of Interior,[24] was tasked with the production of criminal intelligence and responsible for the functional management and coordination arrangement of the Federal Police and other federal security forces (National Gendarmerie, Naval Coast Guard, and the Airport Security Police), in addition to the twenty-three provincial police forces, intelligence activities; and finally the DINIEM, under the Defense Ministry, had the mission to produce strategic military intelligence.

Intelligence Law No. 25520 was important, but incomplete in advancing the objective of democratizing the state intelligence sector. The proposed statutes placed within the bill by Congress were not adopted during the implementation phase by the executive, weakening the democratization process.

INTELLIGENCE SCANDALS AND FURTHER REFORM

Since the 2001 legal changes, Argentina has undergone several intelligence-related scandals and subsequent transformations of the intelligence sector. For example, after a 2006 scandal involving military intelligence elements performing illegal domestic surveillance operations against the relatives of "Trelew massacre" victims—the event transpired in 1972[25]—the administration of President Nestor Kirchner (2003–2007) attempted to strengthen civilian control over military intelligence through the Ministry of Defense, centralizing functions previously retained by each branch of the armed forces (Resolution No. 381/06 and Decrees No. 727 and 1076 of 2006). Additionally, to enhance criminal intelligence during 2006–2008, the *Policía de Seguridad Aeropuertuaria* (PSA), a special police for airport security, was created after a scandal involving drug smuggling. Furthermore, the declassification of archived repression records, the government policy on declassification of secret decrees, and the reopening of human rights abuse cases during the state terrorism era marked democratization improvements.

Nevertheless, illegal wiretapping continued to occur, generating public concern.[26] This apprehension increased in December 2003 when the National Congress passed Law No. 25873 on Data Retention known as the "spy law" due to the threats it posed to privacy. Then, Decree No. 1563 of 2004 amended and refined the Data Retention Law. However, because of this scandal, President Kirchner issued Decree No. 357 of 2005 suspending Law No. 25873 application.[27] Finally, in February 2009 the Supreme Court of Justice adjudicated the unconstitutionality of both the Data Retention Law and its regulatory decree.[28]

On December 16, 2014, an official announcement put the SI on the cover of Argentina's top newspapers.[29] President Cristina Fernández de Kirchner (2007–2015) appointed new officials to head the SI, displacing the secretary and the undersecretary of intelligence,[30] who held their respective positions for more than ten years.[31] SI Director General of Operations Horacio Antonio Stiuso, along with other agents of his team, was also removed from office, suspected of plotting against the government.[32] More substantial changes arrived after the death under unclear circumstances of the federal prosecutor, Alberto Nisman, who was in charge of the criminal investigation of the 1994 bombing of the Argentine Israelite Mutual Aid Association (AMIA).[33] Some days later, President Kirchner submitted a bill to the National Congress to amend Law No. 25520 of National Intelligence, with a central proposal of dissolving the SI and the creation of the Federal Intelligence Agency (AFI).[34] After public consultation, the bill became Law No. 27126 on February 25, 2015,[35] later complemented by Regulatory Decree No. 1311 in July 2015.[36]

The following changes introduced by the new legislation were significant: the transfer of the SI interception of communications division to the National Prosecutor Office; the protection of personal data in a supervised intelligence database, which archives must be destroyed after a period of time; the "New Doctrine of National Intelligence" established by Regulatory Decree No. 1311 that promoted a national intelligence activity oriented by "problems" and not by the doctrine of the Cold War and of the so-called new threats; and the establishment of a transparency criteria in the performance of intelligence activities by banning personnel from setting up relationships with judges, officials, and staff at the federal, provincial, or local level.[37] In fact, the only authorized contacts between judges and intelligence was vested within the director and the deputy director of AFI in order to prevent the politicization of intelligence. In a parallel effort to counter politicization of the intelligence system, the appointment of the director and deputy director of the new intelligence agency must be confirmed by the senate, not solely appointed by the executive. It also required intelligence personnel to file affidavits of property under Public Ethics Law No. 25168.[38] More recently, President Alberto Fernández signed the Executive Decree of Need and Urgency (DNU) No. 52 on December 20, 2019, thereby revoking Decree No. 656 of 2016 signed by President Macri, reinstating Regulatory Decree No. 1311 of 2015, and reallocating secret intelligence expenses for strategic nutritional and educational programs to address societal needs.[39] Additionally, Alberto Fernández intervened against the AFI due to the scandals of wiretaps during the previous administration. These reforms boosted the democratization of the management of human resources, budget, and archives by reducing the level of secrecy and increasing accountability.

DEMOCRATIC GOVERNANCE OF INTELLIGENCE IN ARGENTINA

This section will assess the level of democratic governance of the intelligence sector in Argentina by applying the democratic governance of intelligence (DGI) matrix. The DGI matrix will be used to outline academically accepted specific intelligence governance requirements. However, the requirements will not be scored for the Argentina case.

Regarding *legislative* reforms, Argentina has developed a rich legal basis—on paper—since the transition to democracy in 1983. As mentioned above, this legal framework includes three laws with specific articles governing the intelligence sector: The National Defense Law No. 23554 of 1988, the 1992 Internal Security Law No. 24059 of 1992, and the National Intelligence Law No. 25520 of 2001, instituting the legal, organic, and functional basis of the National Intelligence System; further amended in 2015 by Law No. 27126 and Regulatory Decree No. 1311. However, this legal framework has been less than optimal. For example, Law No. 25520 did not solve the dispute on whether to centralize or decentralize intelligence authority. As a consequence, the intelligence sector remained a hybrid model for many years, blending a concentration of power at the top, the powerful SI, with de-centralized power at the secondary leadership level, the heads of the Ministry of Security and Ministry of Defense, while dividing some executive control and accountability responsibilities with the SI.[40] These organizational arrangements make coordination and sharing of information difficult. However, this obstacle was reduced with the creation of the AFI by Law No. 27126 in 2015, as the central body of the national intelligence system.

With regard to *collection of information*, Law No. 25520 forbids the misuse of intelligence and provides for the protection of rights and guarantees regardless of race, religion, cultural orientation, and political affiliation or ideology. Additionally, two important measures were imposed in 2015 to mitigate this problem: the transfer of SI's interception of communications division to the National General Attorney's office, and the establishment of the "New Doctrine of National Intelligence." Nevertheless, illegal collection of information on private citizens persisted. This trend was accentuated during the tenure of President Mauricio Macri (2015–2019), who in May 2016 issued new AFI guidelines through Decree No. 656, which hindered intelligence democratization, by allowing intelligence agencies to operate with full secrecy.[41] Consequently, AFI was relegated to its historic role as an ancillary unit to the criminal justice system, especially for cases involving politicians, which implied political manipulation and utilization as an instrument to further political agendas. This dynamic was crystallized by a 2019 court case investigating an illegal espionage network extorting businessmen, linking AFI intelligence agents, journalists, judges, prosecutors, and foreign intelligence services.[42] As a corrective measure, President Alberto Fernández (2019–) signed a decree in March 2020 aimed at ending the incestuous relationship between the judiciary and intelligence agents, and therefore reducing the risk of illegal wiretapping and extortion by prohibiting intelligence agencies from carrying out repressive tasks, compulsive powers, or performing police or criminal investigation.[43]

Irrespective of the real motives of the advancement in the democratization process launched with the 2015 amendments to Law No. 25520, much of them were disassembled by the mentioned Decree No. 656 signed by President Macri in 2016. In addition, a systematic leak of wiretaps during the Macri administration aroused the interest of the United Nations Special Rapporteur on the right to privacy, Joseph Cannataci, who visited Argentina in May 2019 and observed

> a general lack of trust on Argentina's intelligence services. Possibly due to Argentina's [illiberal] past, a strong culture of opacity and some highly publicized cases of illegal surveillance, many persons in Argentina suspect that they are personally under surveillance and that intelligence agents act without oversight or supervision.[44]

In terms of *political control*, the democratically elected president exercises executive control and coordination of defining strategic intelligence and general national intelligence policy objectives. In addition, Law No. 25520 provides secret expenditure control mechanisms and requires judicial authorization for interceptions of communications. Furthermore, Law No. 27126 and Regulatory Decree No. 1311 established the selection process and appointment of AFI's director and deputy director; both positions are nominated by the president but require congressional approval. Finally, all interactions with AFI agents must be synchronized through these two designated AFI authorities, strengthening political control over the intelligence apparatus.

With the December 20, 2019, AFI intervention, the intelligence apparatus became more accountable. President Alberto Fernández instructed the appointed intervener, Cristina Caamaño, to conduct a comprehensive evaluation of the national intelligence system, in particular the AFI. On June 12, 2020, the intervention was extended for a further 180 days. So far, the intervener has formalized complaints regarding political espionage and for fraudulent AFI purchases and contracts.[45]

In regard to *recruitment and training*, Law No. 25520 forbade the recruitment of intelligence officers who had conducted war crimes, crimes against humanity, or for human rights violations. This law, in concert with Regulatory Decree No. 950 of 2002, includes doctrinal definitions, criminal provisions, and regulations managing personnel and training. As previously mentioned, Decree No. 1311 also established a professionalizing recruitment process for AFI,[46] and specific training syllabus according to three facets.[47] Nevertheless, professionalization of the intelligence agencies remains problematic; one challenge has been the lack of an intelligence background many political and technical experts possess. The appointment of senior officials with modest expertise in the field inculcated the latest reform efforts with a dilettantish air, which prevented the requisite coordination to address the lingering resistance to reform within the intelligence organization.[48]

Additionally, Law No. 25520 provided for *external oversight*, mandating the Congressional Joint Committee for the Oversight of Intelligence Activities and Agencies.[49] The committee's responsibilities include assessing the legality of intelligence activities, intelligence policy, management and administration of the intelligence agencies, their effectiveness, career progression and associated education plans, secret budget and expenditures, communication interception and data retainment, and administrative processes to receive public complaints about the agency or its personnel. In general, this committee lacks expert knowledge, possesses limited proficiency in practical application, and has little political capital to exert its prerogatives.[50] However, in more recent times, this committee has been more active and with more political power. In fact, it has conducted an investigation on illegal espionage during the Macri administration (2016–2019).[51] This report, promoted by the official legislators of the committee, was rejected by members of the opposition party, claiming bias and invalid evidence.[52]

In terms of *economic-financial oversight*, Law No. 25520 established annual intelligence budget procedures: expenditures are publicly accessible and subject to budgetary supervision processes; additionally, the joint committee is qualified to oversee and exert control over the intelligence secret budget. Furthermore, the committee may intervene in proposed national budget bill related legislative debates, further creating checks and balances against the executive. In terms of *financial oversight*, amendments to Law No. 25520 in 2015 improved public availability of intelligence budget expenses and limited the amount of reserved intelligence activities funds. This improvement was temporarily lost during the implementation of Decree No. 656 during the Macri administration but recovered recently after its derogation.

Finally, regarding *public oversight*, Argentina has a civil society, media, and academia sectors committed to public scrutiny and debate on intelligence issues, particularly in response to scandals, contributing to a transparent environment. Through the Regulatory Decree No. 1311 of 2015, and for the first time since the recovery of democracy, the detailed doctrinal, organizational, and functional basis of intelligence was made public,[53] a breakthrough in the democratization of the intelligence sphere. The impact of the decree was not so much felt by the intelligence branch—rather on the relationship between the intelligence community and society, which now exercises greater *public oversight*, and examines the role of the intelligence services in Argentina[54]—greater access to information remains integral in achieving substantive results. An impediment to this type of oversight persists due to scarce civil society actors or organizations with intricate knowledge on intelligence and with the social legitimacy to act as mediators and decoders of policies of this highly technical sector.[55] This myopic focus may lead to the positive purposes and successful achievements of the intelligence segment being ignored while scandals are highly debated and sensationalized, this overshadowing may erode intelligence community legitimacy. Due to its high level of politicization, inherent secretive nature of intelligence leading to a perceived dubious transparency, and secret budgets have created a narrative that the intelligence sector is always a threat to democracy, instead of its guardian.

CONCLUSION

In sum, challenges associated with institutionalizing an intelligence culture in Argentina have involved demilitarizing the intelligence sector, exerting civilian control, establishing congressional oversight, controlling the secret budget, limiting domestic intelligence, refocusing military intelligence, and approving new legislation—all facets of democratic governance.

Intelligence democratization in Argentina is still driven by scandal and politics.[56] Despite a rich legal foundation for reinstitution of democratic intelligence practices after the intelligence crisis of late 2014 and early 2015, the culture, practices, and uses of intelligence data collection remain opaque and distorted in Argentina since the transition to democracy in 1983. The challenge remains balancing what sometimes resemble competing principles between intelligence services and democracy—secrecy in order to effectively conduct intelligence operations while not empowering state actors to operate extrajudiciously—undermining the prerogatives of duly elected officials, the citizens, and democracy. On the contrary, intelligence services can not only be democratized, but even more, they can help to strengthen democratic governance and the rule of law, guaranteeing citizens' rights, freedom, and security.

NOTES

1. This account draws heavily on the lengthy unpublished work by Eduardo E. Estévez, "Argentina's Intelligence in the Twenty-First Century/After Twenty-Five Years of Democracy," paper presented at the 51st International Studies Association Annual Convention, New Orleans, Louisiana, February 17–20, 2010. Part of this historical analysis was published in Alejandra Otamendi and Eduardo E. Estévez, "El Gobierno Democrático de la Inteligencia en América Latina: Matriz de Análisis y los Casos Testigo de Argentina y Perú," in *Estado, Seguridad y Política Criminal*, eds. E. Mizrahi and A. Di Leo Razuk (Buenos Aires: SAAP & FONCYT, 2018), 15–41. And the matrix to assess democratic governance was published previously in English at Alejandra Otamendi and Eduardo Estévez, "Intelligence Challenges in Latin America: A Comparative Matrix on Democratic Governance," in *¿Nuevos Paradigmas de Vigilancia? Miradas desde América Latina. Memorias del IV Simposio Internacional Lavits, Buenos Aires*, ed. Camilo Ríos (Córdoba: Fundación Vía Libre, 2017), 277–94. Available at http://lavits.org/wp-content/uploads/2017/08/P5_Otamendi_etal-1.pdf.

2. Juan Linz and Alfred Stepan, *Problems of Democratic Transition and Consolidation: Southern Europe, South America, and Post-Communist Europe* (Baltimore, MD: The Johns Hopkins University Press, 1996): 296–306; Guillermo O'Donnell and Philippe C. Schmitter, *Transitions from Authoritarian Rule: Tentative Conclusions about Uncertain Democracies* (Baltimore, MD: The Johns Hopkins University Press, 1989).

3. Decree "S" No.15078/1951. Decree No. 416 of May 13, 1976.

4. Decree-Law No. 4500 of 1963, issued by de facto president José María Guido, expanded its mission to also producing intelligence in the interest of the nation safety, for the conduct of State affairs, and actions against communism; secret Law No. 20195 of 1973, published on September 21, 2006 under provisions of Law No. 26134.

5. See Jaime Cañás, *Espionaje en la Argentina* (Buenos Aires: Editorial Mundo Actual, 1969), 177–78. For an approach to the Peronism's conception about national defense, see Marcelo Saín, "Defensa Nacional y Fuerzas Armadas: El Modelo Peronista (1943–1955)," in *La Construcción de la Nación Argentina: El rol de las Fuerzas Armadas* (Buenos Aires: Ministerio de Defensa, 2010), 333–43.

6. For an early history of this police intelligence element engaged in political surveillance, see Martin Edwin Andersen, *La Policía: Pasado, Presente y Propuestas para el Futuro* (Buenos Aires: Editorial Sudamericana, 2002), 136–40.

7. See Decree-Law "S" No. 2075 of 1958, Decree-Law "S" No. 9021 of 1963, and secret Law No. 17488 of 1967, published in 2006 under provisions of Law No. 26134.

8. See E. Martínez Codó, *Reseña Histórica de la Inteligencia Militar del Ejército Argentino* (Buenos Aires: Editorial Puma, 1999), 254; Iván Poczynok, "La Evolución de la Política de Inteligencia Militar Argentina: Rupturas y Continuidades (1990–2015)," *URVIO, Revista Latinoamericana de Estudios de Seguridad*, no. 21 (2017): 39–55, available at https://revistas.flacsoandes.edu.ec/urvio/article/view/2855/2012.

9. Laura Kalmanowiecki, "Origins and Applications of Political Policing in Argentina," *Latin American Perspectives* 27, no. 2 (2000): 37–40.

10. For an approach to the National Security Doctrine in the Argentine case, see Ernesto López, "La Introducción de la Doctrina de Seguridad Nacional en el Ejército Argentino," in *La Construcción de la Nación Argentina: El Rol de las Fuerzas Armadas* (Buenos Aires, Ministerio de Defensa, 2010), 389–403; Germán Soprano, "El Ejército Argentino en Democracia: De la 'Doctrina de la Seguridad Nacional' a la Definición de las 'Nuevas Amenazas' (1983–2001)," *Revista Universitaria de Historia Militar* 7, vol. 4 (RUHM, 2015): 86–107, available at https://ri.conicet .gov.ar/bitstream/handle/11336/52165/CONICET_Digital_Nro.945f7cd6-6e91-4a26 -ba73-3ee906172740_A.pdf?sequence=2.

11. For an approach to the normative organization of the last Argentine military dictatorship (1976–1983), see Marcelo Saín, "Condiciones Institucionales del Control Parlamentario de las Actividades y Organismos de Inteligencia del Estado," in *Papeles de trabajo: Control Democrático de los Organismos de Seguridad Interior de la República Argentina* (Buenos Aires: CELS, 1997), 113–39.

12. Max G. Manwaring, "Shadows of Things Past and Images of the Future: Lessons for the Insurgencies in Our Midst," *Strategic Studies Institute (SSI) Monograph*, Carlisle, PA, 2004, 17. Available at http://www.strategicstudiesinstitute.army.mil/ pubs/display.cfm?pubID=587. For an official account of human rights abuses and the systematic organization of state-led repression during military rule from 1976 to 1983, see *Nunca Más, Informe de la Comisión Nacional sobre Desaparición de Personas (CONADEP)* (Buenos Aires: Eudeba, 1984). For a comparative perspective on the role of intelligence services in the Southern Cone dictatorships, see Alfred Stepan, *Repensando a los Militares en Política—Cono Sur: Un Análisis Comparado* (Buenos Aires: Planeta, 1988), 30–47, and Francisco Javier Morales, "Organismos de Inteligencia y Seguridad en el Marco de las Dictaduras Militares de Brasil, Argentina y Chile. Perspectivas de Análisis y Puntos de Comparación," *Papeles de Trabajo: La Revista Electrónica del IDAES* 10, no.17 (2016): 74–103.

13. See Linz, and Stepan, *Problems of Democratic Transition and Consolidation,* 190–91; and Guillermo O'Donnell, Philippe C. Schmitter, and Laurence Whitehead, *Transitions from Authoritarian Rule: Prospects for Democracy*, t 4 (Baltimore: Johns Hopkins University Press, 1986).

14. See Linz, and Stepan, *Problems of Democratic Transition and Consolidation,*" 190–91.

15. For a development of civil-military relations in Argentina, see Gustavo Druetta, Eduardo Estévez, Ernesto López, and José E. Míguens, *Defensa y Democracia: Un Debate entre Civiles y Militares* (Buenos Aires: PuntoSur, 1990); Marcelo Saín, *Alfonsín, Menem y las Relaciones Cívico-militares: La Construcción del Control Civil sobre las Fuerzas Armadas en la Argentina Democrática (1983–1995)*,

Phd. Thesis de doctorado, Universidad Estadual de Campinas, Brasil (1999); José Manuel Ugarte, "Una Visión desde Latinoamérica de la Organización de la Defensa y Relaciones Civiles-militares," in *Organización de la Defensa y Control Civil de las Fuerzas Armadas en América Latina*, eds. David Pion-Berlin and José Manuel Ugarte (Buenos Aires: Jorge Baudino Ediciones, 2013); Ruth Diamint, *Sin Gloria: La Política de Defensa en la Argentina Democrática* (Buenos Aires: EUDEBA, 2014); Germán Montenegro, Marcelo Fabián Saín, and Juan Gabriel Tokatlian, *De Militares a Policías: La "Guerra contra las Drogas" y la Militarización de Argentina* (Buenos Aires: Capital Intelectual, 2018).

16. For a systematic reading of the paradigm of civil-military relations in Argentina, see Sabina Frederic, *Los Usos de la Fuerza Pública: Debates sobre Militares y Policías en las Ciencias Sociales de la Democracia* (Buenos Aires: Biblioteca Nacional, 2008), 30–48.

17. Gerardo Young, *SIDE: La Argentina Secreta* (Buenos Aires: Planeta, 2006).

18. On the parliamentary process and the political agreements for the promulgation of laws that regulate the intelligence sector in Argentina, see Priscila Carlos Brandão Antunes, "Establishing Democratic Control of Intelligence in Argentina," in *Reforming Intelligence: Obstacles to Democratic Control and Effectiveness*, eds. Thomas C. Bruneau and Steven C. Boraz (Austin: University of Texas Press, 2007), 195–218.

19. The attacks targeted the Embassy of Israel in 1992, and the AMIA, a Jewish community center building, in 1994.

20. On this, see Thomaz G. Costa and Gastón H. Schulmeister, "The Puzzle of the Iguazu Tri-Border Area: Many Questions and Few Answers Regarding Organized Crime and Terrorism Links," *Global Crime* 8, no. 1 (2007): 26–39.

21. Actually, after President Carlos Menem ended his term, he was sentenced under criminal charges of illegal use of secret budget in 2015. For more on this, see J. Patrice McSherry, "National Security and Social Crisis in Argentina," *Journal of Third World Studies* 17, no. 1 (2000). And for the judicial case, see https://www.cij. gov.ar/nota-19200-Condenaron-a-Menem-y-Cavallo-en-un-juicio-oral-por-el-pago -de-sobresueldos.html.

22. Florencia Fontán Balestra, "Towards a Democratic Control of Argentina's Intelligence Community," 2000, 24–46. Available at http://www.law.harvard.edu/ programs/criminal-justice/argentina.pdf. See also *Clarín*, "El Servicio de Inteligencia Estatal," editorial, February 18, 2000. Available at http://www.clarin.com/ diario/2000/02/18/i-01601d.htm.

23. For a full text of the law approved in 2002, in English, see DCAF, "Intelligence Legislation Model–Argentina. The Argentinean National Intelligence Law, 2001 and the Regulation of the National Intelligence Act, 2002," Geneva Centre for the Democratic Control of Armed Forces (DCAF) (2011).

24. Currently, DINICRI is under the Ministry of Security, created in 2010.

25. For the "Trelew massacre" and the espionage that occurred in 2006, see Eva Muzzopappa, "Inteligencia militar en Argentina: Reflexiones desde un archivo naval," *URVIO, Revista Latinoamericana de Estudios de Seguridad* 21 (2017): 87–103.

26. See "Escuchas ilegales y cultura política," *Clarín*, Buenos Aires, December 22, 2007. Available at http://www.clarin.com/diario/2007/12/22/opinion/o-04201.htm

27. For example, see Gustavo Ybarra and Lucas Colonna, "Sigue en vigor la polémica ley espía, *La Nación*, Buenos Aires, May 2, 2005. Available at https://www.lanacion.com.ar/politica/sigue-en-vigor-la-polemica-ley-espia-nid700765/.

28. Halabi, Ernesto against Executive Power—Law No. 25873 Decree No. 1563/04, by Law No. 16986, National Supreme Court of Justice (H. 270. XLII), Sentence, Buenos Aires, February 24, 2009.

29. Clarín, "Cristina descabezó la ex SIDE y vuelve Anibal," December 17, 2014, available at https://tapas.clarin.com/tapa.html#20141217; Raúl Kollmann, "Escoba Nueva," *Página/12*, December 17, 2014, available at https://www.pagina12.com.ar/diario/elpais/1-262147-2014-12-17.html; Mariana Verón, "Cristina descabezó la ex SIDE por las internas y la ofensiva judicial," *La Nación*, December 17, 2014, available at http://edicionimpresa.lanacion.com.ar/la-nacion/20141217/textview.

30. Oscar Parrilli, the general secretary of the presidency, and Juan Martín Mena, chief of cabinet of the Ministry of Justice and Human Rights were appointed respectively as director and deputy director of AFI.

31. Hector Icazuriaga held the post of Secretary of Intelligence between 2013 and December 2015. See https://www.argentina.gob.ar/normativa/nacional/decreto-1225-2003-91014 and http://servicios.infoleg.gob.ar/infolegInternet/verNorma.do?id=239611.

32. In April 2015, the Executive filed a legal complaint against Stiuso and other intelligence agents on failure to comply with the duties of a public servant charges. See https://www.casarosada.gob.ar/informacion/archivo/28536-la-si-denuncia-penalmente-al-ex-agente-antonio-stiuso. For a journalistic account on agent Stiuso, see Gerardo Young, *SIDE: La Argentina Secreta* (Buenos Aires: Planeta, 2006); Gerardo Young, *Código Stiuso: La SIDE, La Política desde las Cloacas y la Muerte de Nisman* (Buenos Aires: Planeta, 2015).

33. In January 2015, Prosecutor Nisman was filing a complaint against President Cristina Kirchner on concealment charges related to a 2013 agreement with Iran on the AMIA bombing investigation, "Memorandum de Entendimiento entre el Gobierno de la República Argentina y el Gobierno de la República Islámica de Irán sobre temas vinculados al ataque terrorista a la sede de la AMIA en Buenos Aires el 18 de julio de 1994." See the complaint at https://www.pagina12.com.ar/fotos/20150121/notas/denuncia-nisman.pdf. See Cass R. Sunstein and Adrian Vermeule, "Symposium on Conspiracy Theories: Causes and Cures," *The Journal of Political Philosophy* 17, no. 2 (2009): 202–27. Regarding the Nisman *affair*, see Leopoldo Rodriguez, and Shawn Smallman, "Political Polarization and Nisman's Death: Competing Conspiracy Theories in Argentina," *Journal of International and Global Studies* 8, no. 1 (2016): 20–39. On different interpretations, see https://www.dw.com/es/qui%C3%A9n-mat%C3%B3-a-nisman-hay-inexistencia-absoluta-de-pruebas-sobre-un-homicidio/a-52031627 and https://www.lanacion.com.ar/politica/polemico-libro-de-la-prima-de-alberto-nisman-asegura-que-lo-asesinaron-y-que-el-poder-esta-involucrado-nid1798016.

34. Cristina Fernández, "Anuncio de la presidenta de la Nación de reforma del sistema de Inteligencia del Estado," Presidencia de la Nación, Buenos Aires, 26 de enero de 2015. See https://www.casarosada.gob.ar/informacion/archivo/28321-reforma-del-sistema-de-inteligencia-del-estado-anuncio-de-la-presidenta-de-la-nacion-por-cadena-nacional and http://www.senado.gov.ar/prensa/12753/noticias.

35. See https://www.boletinoficial.gob.ar/detalleAviso/primera/121060/20150305?busqueda=1.

36. See http://www.senado.gov.ar/prensa/12753/noticias. During this legislative process, some important changes proposed by security, defense, and intelligence experts were included in the bill. In addition, the Citizens' Initiative for the Control of the Intelligence System (ICCSI), a network of specialized NGOs, remained very active in the public debate. For more, see Cámara de Senadores de la Nación, *Reunión Plenaria de las Comisiones de Asuntos Constitucionales y Justicia y Asuntos Penales*, Honorable Senado de la Nación, Buenos Aires, 4 de febrero de 2015. Available at http://www.senado.gov.ar/prensa/12755/noticias.

37. The only authorized officials are the director and deputy director of AFI; article 15bis of Law No. 25520.

38. Article 15ter, Law No. 25520.

39. See article 8 of Decree of Need and Urgency No. 52. Available at https://www.boletinoficial.gob.ar/detalleAviso/primera/224049/20191221.

40. Eduardo E. Estévez, "Comparing Intelligence Democratization in Latin America: Argentina, Peru, and Ecuador Cases," *Intelligence and National Security* 29, no. 4 (2014). See also, Eduardo E. Estévez, "Executive and Legislative Oversight of Intelligence in Argentina," in *Who's Watching the Spies? Establishing Intelligence Service Accountability*, eds. Hans Born, Loch Johnson, and Ian Leigh (Washington, DC: Potomac Books, 2005), 171–72; José M. Ugarte, "Nueva Ley de Inteligencia," *La Nación*, December 14, 2001.

41. See ICCSI report. Available at http://www.iccsi.com.ar/agencia-federal-de-inteligencia-vuelta-al-oscurantismo/.

42. On this, see https://www.hcdn.gob.ar/prensa/noticias/2019/noticias_0924.html.

43. Executive Decree of Need and Urgency No. 214, of March 2020, introduced this change to the Intelligence Law 25520. Available at https://www.boletinoficial.gob.ar/detalleAviso/primera/226271/20200305.

44. UN Human Rights Council, "Statement to the media by the United Nations Special Rapporteur on the right to privacy, on the conclusion of his official visit to Argentina, May 6–17, 2019," by Special Rapporteur Joseph A. Cannataci, Buenos Aires, May 17, 2019. Available at https://www.ohchr.org/EN/NewsEvents/Pages/DisplayNews.aspx?NewsID=24639&LangID=E.

45. For results of current intervention of AFI, see https://www.telam.com.ar/notas/202006/472845-cristina-caamano-afi-inteligencia-denuncia-espionaje-ilegal-mauricio-macri.html and https://www.pagina12.com.ar/287703-afi-macrista-nueva-denuncia-por-compras-irregulares.

46. For details, see Decree 1311 of 2015, Annexes IV, V, and VI. Available at https://www.iccsi.com.ar/recursos/.

47. Decree No. 1311 organized three hierarchical areas within AFI: Intelligence, including collectors and analysts; Security, including counterintelligence and security personnel; and Support, including management, administrative, technology, and Juridical assistance personnel.

48. On the obstacles during the implementation process, see Marcelo Saín, *La Casa que No Cesa. Infortunios y Desafíos en el Proceso de Reforma de la Ex SIDE* (Buenos Aires: Editorial Octubre, 2016), 103–19.

49. For an analysis of the functioning the Congressional Joint Committee for the Oversight of Intelligence Activities and Agencies between 2001 and 2013, see Tomás Bieda, "El Control Parlamentario en la Argentina," *POSTData* 20, no. 1 (2015): 185–219. See also José Manuel Ugarte, "Un Gran Reto Democrático: Controlar la Inteligencia," in *Los Macro y Micro Desafíos de la Seguridad en Democracia. Contradicciones y Vulnerabilidades en América Latina*, eds. Bertha García Gallegos and José Manuel Ugarte (Quito: Pontificia Universidad Católica del Ecuador, 2018). Available at https://www.researchgate.net/publication/326071054_UN_GRAN_RETO_DEM OCRATICO_CONTROLAR_LA_INTELIGENCIA.

50. See Eduardo E. Estévez, "Gobierno de la Inteligencia en la Argentina y el Perú antes y después de la Crisis," *Ciencia Política* 15, no. 29 (2020): 249–85. For a discussion on the need of transparency and accountability of intelligence, see Florina Cristiana Matei and Thomas C. Bruneau, "Policymakers and Intelligence Reform in the New Democracies," *International Journal of Intelligence and CounterIntelligence* 24, no. 4 (2011): 656–91.

51. See https://www4.hcdn.gob.ar/comisiones/especiales/cbinteligencia/In forme%20Comision%20Bicameral%20Inteligencia%202021-04-20.pdf.

52. See https://www4.hcdn.gob.ar/comisiones/especiales/cbinteligencia/Dicta men%20MINORIA%20Comision%20Bicameral%20Inteligencia%202021-04-20. pdf.

53. See Saín, *La Casa que No Cesa*: 118.

54. See Saín, *La Casa que No Cesa*: 25–30. Also see Gerardo Young, "Diez Años de Espionaje Nacional y Popular," *La Nación*, July 28, 2013. Available at https://www .lanacion.com.ar/opinion/diez-anos-de-espionaje-nacional-y-popular-nid1604944.

55. An exception is the Citizens' Initiative for the Control of the Intelligence System (ICCSI), a network created in 2012 that includes a number of NGOs: Asociación por los Derechos Civiles (ADC), Fundación Vía Libre, Núcleo de Estudios sobre Gobierno y Seguridad de la Universidad Metropolitana para la Educación y el Trabajo (UMET), Instituto Latinoamericano de Seguridad y Democracia (ILSED), and Centro de Estudios Legales y Sociales (CELS). See https://www.iccsi.com.ar/.

56. According to Estévez, during democratic transition and until 2014, the democratization of intelligence did not suffer any critical juncture of such magnitude that would have induced profound changes; in fact, the process is best described as "incremental policy change" where restructuring rather than reform was the political choice. Estévez, "Comparing Intelligence Democratization in Latin America," 577.

Chapter Four

Bolivia

Eduardo E. Estévez

An Andean country with multiple cultures and ethnic groups, Bolivia[1] has a history of coups and military governments, expressed as weak democracies.[2] After the election of Evo Morales as president in the 2005 election, Bolivia became a socialist and populist democracy.[3] Currently, intelligence functions are performed by the police and the armed forces under the political supervision of their respective civilian ministers. Despite attempts to legislate on these matters, intelligence activities have yet to become transparent to the population that these agencies are meant to protect and serve. This chapter reviews Bolivia's intelligence sector. It finds that the Bolivian intelligence apparatus has not fully democratized. Rather, it has been plagued by the lack of a comprehensive legal framework, ineffective oversight, and poor interagency coordination.

BACKGROUND: HISTORY OF
MILITARISM AND THE ROLE OF INTELLIGENCE

Bolivia has a long history of military interventions in politics, undermining democracy and the rule of law and resulting in either civilian or military or civilian-military authoritarian regimes[4]—which lasted until 1982, when democracy was reestablished.[5] More often than not, the Bolivian police forces supported the traditionally dominant military. Created in 1826, the state police—known as National Police and since 2009 as the Bolivian Police—was the instrument of the elites' oppression and repression of the Bolivian population—rather than a crime prevention–focused law enforcement agency—operating outside of the law, committing human rights abuses, and plagued by cronyism, patronage, corruption, ineffectiveness in crime prevention, and a negative public image.[6]

Several other institutions were created by the Bolivian military dictatorships to repress dissent, initially housed in the Ministry of Government.[7] In January 1954, the government of Víctor Paz Estenssoro established the Department for Control and Political Security (Political Control), a civilian repressive body that enabled a centralized and almost autonomous management of emerging political opposition problems.[8] In February 1959, elected civilian president Hernán Siles Suazo (1956–1960) created, by Supreme Decree No. 5154, the Directorate-General for State Information and Security (DGISE) under the Ministry of Government, a civilian intelligence service focused on public order, and internal and external security; it was empowered to carry out proactive measures and use of armed force in cases of disruption of public order or serious danger to institutional stability and state security.[9] Later, in September 1960, through Supreme Decree No. 5564, elected civilian president Víctor Paz Estenssoro (1960–1964), abolished the DGISE, transferring its offices and staff to the police, a decision justified by the fact that the circumstances that motivated its creation had been overcome.[10] Moreover, in November 1964, General Barrientos Ortuño dissolved the intelligence department (Political Control) created in 1954, as stated in Decree Law 6947.[11]

The Cold War prompted, as in other Latin American countries influenced by the "national security doctrine,"[12] the Bolivian government to move the police under the auspices of the armed forces—a temporary loss of police autonomy, a policy later reversed by the dictatorial government of Colonel Banzer (1971–1978).[13] In 1971, during the brief administration of General Juan José Torres (1970–1971), as part of a police reform initiative, the repressive intelligence apparatus was split into two services contained within the police—the Department of Political Order and the Department of Social Order—which were primarily tasked with fighting drug trafficking.[14] During this period, the police managed to outpace the military in the fight against drugs, which reduced the decade-long dominance of the security sector by the armed forces.[15]

TRANSITION TO DEMOCRACY

With a legacy of social exclusion and pauperization of the population—a by-product of military governments during the 1960s and 1970s—the precarious democratic governance implemented during the 1980s and 1990s showed an increase in popular resistance with the emergence of such new political actors as the social movements in defense of indigenous rights, water, gas, and natural resources.[16] The 1980s economic crisis, characterized by inefficient trade and financial instability caused by hyperinflation and recession, was followed by fiscal adjustment and privatizations.[17] This context paved the way for democratic transition in 1982, via a "pacted democracy."[18] Nevertheless, after economic stabilization, a new period of trade-related hardship occurred in the late 1990s and early 2000s, which halted economic progress and led to dissatisfaction with the government's policies, mass protests, and popular uprisings against privatization during 2000,[19] and culminating in democratic backslide in 2005.[20] The multiclass and multiethnic coalition that won the December 2005 elections—led by Evo Morales, the Socialist Movement (MAS) party, and the coca growers (*cocaleros*) union coalition—promised a radical rebuilding of the state.[21] Far-reaching structural reforms were introduced, including a new constitution, the nationalization of energy resources, the implementation of a new economic model where the state became the dominant player controlling state-owned companies, the rejection of International Monetary Fund (IMF), the advent of strong social policies, and land reform.[22]

PUBLIC SECURITY AND COUNTER-DRUG EFFORTS

After the restoration of democracy in 1982, public order and social control became paramount to national defense policy. The armed forces quickly transitioned to the new national security policy, while the police veered between contempt and sedition actions amid ongoing decline and corruption. Since March 1985, the police are governed by the Organic Law of National Police No. 734, which stipulates that as a centralized body, the mission is to preserve public order, defend the society, and ensure compliance with laws. Unfortunately, the law fails to define the need for intelligence agencies to protect human rights while conducting essential operations.[23]

As for the fight against drugs, much of the operational decision making, control, and financing of intelligence activities was virtually in the hands of foreign agencies; this dynamic was made possible due to Bolivia receiving substantial support and cooperation from the United States.[24] An eight-month antidrug joint operation called "Blast Furnace" carried out in 1986 by U.S. troops in Bolivia (Beni, Chapare, and Santa Cruz regions) generated high-impact political controversies with opposition forming from the coca growers and the political class; ultimately, the operation was declared a violation of national sovereignty by Congress and ruled as unconstitutional.[25] Despite this challenge, U.S. influence on the Bolivian security and intelligence sector persisted.[26] For example, the 1987 creation of the Special Antinarcotics Force (FELCN)—a national police entity—with its own intelligence service obtained extensive support from the U.S. Drug Enforcement Administration (DEA) and the Narcotics Affairs Section (NAS) of the U.S. Embassy in Bolivia in the form of training, advanced equipment, intelligence information, special operations, and logistical support.[27] While such assistance was viewed through a counternarcotics lens as beneficial to Bolivian stability, these actions were deleterious to the Bolivian democratic consolidation effort.

Regarding public security policies for crime prevention, frequently a neglected issue for military regimes, in the mid-1990s some outlines were devised, although overshadowed by incessant international pressure to resolve the drug problem.[28] For example, in 1997, with the aim of expanding citizen participation, improving security, and crime prevention mechanisms, the "Citizen Security and Protection Plan" was proposed by the executive, which promoted several legal and institutional reforms aimed at transforming the police; lamentably this plan was not implemented.[29]

These situations and events contributed to the police crisis in the early 2000s: the lack of interest of the civilian political leadership to promote democratic security policies and police reform; the police force continuance as a repressive political instrument of the executive; police militarization and politicization; and pacts of reciprocity between political power and police to further parochial interest.[30] In April 2000 and February 2003, Bolivia faced police insubordination and even riots.[31]

SECURITY AGENDA UNDER EVO MORALES

Morales, who won the 2005 election supported by social movements and coca growers, was again reelected in 2009 and 2014, and as further explained by Steen Christensen,

> [i]ntroduced a state-led development strategy with nationalizations and a focus on greater social and political inclusion of all groups, including previously disenfranchised indigenous groups. On the foreign policy front, Bolivia, like Venezuela, pursued counter-hegemonic foreign policies aiming at strengthening Bolivia's autonomy and reducing U.S. influence.[32]

According to José Rocabado Sánchez, the hallmark of the new state power structure was founded by the trilogy state: social movements/unions, the military, and under strong presidential leadership.[33] Morales substantially changed the roles and missions of the military. The armed forces were empowered and integrated into the MAS project; a civil-military, people-military alliance became part of the official discourse.[34] Its role as a development factor included three axes: recovery and protection of natural resources (including petroleum nationalization); promotion of social policies; and combatting corruption, smuggling, and crimes against the state.[35]

There was also a shift in the strategic focus and a counter-hegemonic posture to reduce U.S. regional influence.[36] The Morales administration's national security vision incorporated a neo-development model based on a counter capitalistic global free-market economy model with corresponding projects to promote human security, sustainable development, improvement of institutional capacity and longevity, and distributive policies. As for regional security, the objective was to ensure the complex interdependencies of the globalized world, on the one hand, and the guarantee of self-determination of countries, on the other, would create a less precarious and safer region.[37]

Regarding the fight against drug trafficking, and as part of his confrontation with the United States,[38] Morales's administration declared the U.S. ambassador persona non grata and in November 2008 suspended DEA activities in the country, as well as USAID activities in the coca production areas. U.S. influence was replaced by other countries,[39] further expounded in this chapter.

While the country's constituent assembly convened in September 2008 to discuss new constitutional text, protests among inhabitants of the department of Pando seeking autonomy from central government escalated to violence. President Morales declared a state of emergency, justified on the grounds of a coup instigated by the department authorities.[40] As a result, a new constitution—defining Bolivia as a Unitary Social State of Plurinational Communitarian Law—was passed on January 25, 2009.[41] According to Article 298, "State Security, defense, the Armed Forces, and the Bolivian Police" are under the central authority of the state. Further, Article 244 established the mission of the armed forces as follows: "the defense and preservation of the independence, security and stability of the State, and the honor and sovereignty of the country; to assure the supremacy of the Constitution; to guarantee the stability of the legitimately constituted Government; and to participate in the development of the country"; and Article 251 set the Bolivian Police's mission as follows: "to defend the society and conserve public order, and to assure compliance with the law. . . . It shall carry out the police function in a comprehensive, indivisible manner and under a single command, pursuant to the Organic Law of the Bolivian Police and the other laws of the State."[42]

In April 2011 the government enacted Law No. 100 on comprehensive development and border security, aimed to establish institutional articulations to promote thorough development, strengthen the state's presence, and prevent, control, and combat smuggling and other illicit activities.[43] The new internal security agenda of the military included reappropriation of the border territories, protection of natural resources, and affirmation of territorial integrity in the face of internal threats from sectors that sought to divide.[44]

In 2012 crime rates soared because of the impact of drug trafficking, including gangland killing, human trafficking, robbery, and lynching.[45] In June of the same year, the Bolivian Police started a riot that lasted almost a week, with demands including a salary increase; retirement on the basis of 100 percent of salary; and the abrogation of the new police disciplinary regime law no. 101 of 2011.[46] Meanwhile, the police security system was still co-opted by corruption.[47] Drug trafficking persists where the state still does not possess an effective presence[48]—for example, in Ichilo province, known as the "drug trafficking capital city," although police officials claimed that the FELCN forces exercise authority throughout the national territory.[49] Cocaine seizures increased during the 2006–2011 period, but 2013 figures showed a decrease, which was explained by reduced intelligence capabilities of the country as a consequence of the departure of the DEA, as well as by the presence of international organized crime.[50]

In March 2016 the minister of the presidency expressed the necessity for a state intelligence agency to protect the Plurinational State. The idea did not prosper, because the government minister stated that he was unaware of the proposal, which demonstrated internal government disagreements on this issue.[51] As in the cases of Perú and Ecuador, for example, Morales's administration appointed scholars with expertise in security affairs in key areas; however, they were not successful in promoting achieving changes.

According to an International Security Sector Advisory Team (ISSAT) report, although the Morales administration security and police reform intents "have so far been fractious, reactive and often stymied by corruption . . . , Bolivia has demonstrated it is open to international engagement when it comes to the security forces' attempts to tackle drug production and trafficking, despite its ongoing dispute with the United States."[52] As previously illustrated, Bolivia has been active in international cooperation on the hemispheric drug problem which is recognized by the Inter-American Drug Abuse Control Commission (CICAD). CICAD takes note that in the fourth round (2005–2006), Bolivia exchanged information with other countries in the hemisphere regarding drug trafficking. In addition, CICAD observes with satisfaction that as of the seventh round (2014–2018), secure communication channels were established for sharing intelligence information on drug interdiction and control.[53]

Finally, it should be noted that in November 2019, Morales was displaced from office,[54] opening a stage of uncertainty. The interim government announced general elections were to occur in May 2020.

Concerning state violence during the massive anti- and pro-Morales protests in October and November 2019, UN High Commissioner for Human Rights, Michelle Bachelet, in August 2020, expressed serious concern "that, nine months on, not a single person has been held accountable for the deaths in Sacaba and Senkata nor for the majority of the killings that happened during the period covered by our report."[55]

From the reading, it appears that Morales attempted to transform the nation into a new Plurinational State. His thought is that this nation-building strategy would be a panacea that would be adopted, inculcate, and fix historical wrongs. However, parochial interests and differing opinions have not been adopted by all and fixed this endemic problem. In 2020 the MAS party won election, and Luis Arce is the new president of the country.

Bolivia developed new regional and international collaboration arrangements to confront the drug problem. Police and intelligence bilateral cooperation with Brazil broadened as both countries prioritized border security. Intelligence sharing includes information on illicit drug trafficking, transnational criminal networks, drug trafficking modalities, and even telephone call interception.[56] It is also worth mentioning Venezuela and Iran military assistance, and security and intelligence cooperation, described by Maria Velez de Berliner as follows:

> Iran's influence in the country is thus limited to intelligence gathering and security of the executive branch. A large part of Bolivia's security and intelligence is outsourced to Venezuela, and it is through the work Iran does in these areas in Venezuela that Iran becomes an actor in Bolivia's security of the executive branch and in Bolivia's intelligence corps.[57]

However, changes in Bolivian geostrategic posture produced unintended consequences. The Brazilian organized crime group First Capital Command (PCC), as observed by Douglas Farah and Kathryn Babineau, "has gained a significant foothold in Bolivia, primarily in the Santa Cruz and Beni regions that border Brazil. The most visible evidence of this incursion is a series of high-profile bank robberies and the proliferation of cocaine laboratories under PCC control."[58]

Nonetheless despite the aforementioned changes, it appears that there were no strategic intelligence requirements, and to this day, there exists no strategic intelligence agency to fulfill such requirements. The apparent lack of formulated intelligence policy suggests a coordination deficiency between agencies.[59]

A LIMITED DEMOCRATIC GOVERNANCE OF INTELLIGENCE

Because there is no specific intelligence *legislation*, this section will rely on several academic and legal sources to recognize as faithfully as possible the topic under study.

Currently, the Bolivian intelligence sector is comprised of the Directorate of State Intelligence (DIE) under the Ministry of Government; the National Intelligence Directorate under the Bolivian police; Departments II of Intelligence of each of the armed forces, under the Ministry of Defense; and the FELCN intelligence elements aimed at combating drug trafficking. At the highest echelons of intelligence power brokers is the National State Security Council, which coordinates the State Intelligence Service (SIE), and the DIE.[60]

Rear Admiral Raúl Mejía Ibáñez notes the lack of a national intelligence system and therefore the absence of a management body that integrates the efforts of all existing intelligence subsystems to guide collection efforts and determine the essential elements of information required by decision makers. In general, the subsystems already established have worked in isolation, each focused on their specific function.[61] Thus specific or sectoral regulations provide the clearest description of the intelligence sector.

The 1985 Organic Police Law stipulates that the National Intelligence Directorate is responsible for obtaining, evaluating, and processing information to carry out preventive police security actions.[62] This is currently framed in Article 251 of the 2009 Constitution, which states that the Bolivian Police mission is defending society and the preservation of public order, and enforcement of laws throughout the territory. As mentioned in a country profile report by ISSAT, "there is also a police intelligence unit, the Special Centre of Police Investigations (CEIP), which operates under the supervision of prosecutors."[63]

The FELCN was established in 1987 through Supreme Decree No. 21666 as a specialized unit against drug trafficking, under the Ministry of Government, which deployed the Intelligence and Special Operations Group (GIOE).[64]

Regarding military intelligence, as established in Article 40 of the Armed Forces Organic Law of 1992, the commander in chief of the armed forces— a military officer appointed by the president—is responsible for directing strategic intelligence and psychological operations. According to Article 47 of the same law, it is for the chief of staff general to coordinate and supervise the elaboration of the strategic intelligence plan and the psychological operations plan.[65]

As for *collection* of information, broadly speaking, Bolivian intelligence analyzes traditional threats such as terrorism, drug trafficking, money laundering, illegal migration, social conflict, neighborhood environment, environmental deterioration, and proliferation of weapons of mass destruction.[66] It is worth noting the creation of the Interinstitutional Intelligence Center in airports and border checkpoints within the framework of the National Citizen Security Plan 2012–2016.[67]

On *training*, it is particularly noteworthy that the army, as retired Rear Admiral Raúl Mejía Ibáñez recounts, has historically given a significant boost to academic training in military intelligence, which has led to contributions to national defense and political authorities' decision making.[68]

The issue of secret expenditures is especially relevant in the matter of *financial and economic oversight*. In 2004, interim constitutional President Carlos Mesa (2003–2005) issued Supreme Decree No. 23745, updating the procedure for the formulation, approval, implementation, and control of secret expenditures. Strikingly, Article 10 directed that after their accountability to the Office of General Comptroller of the Republic, supporting documentation should be destroyed or incinerated.[69] Then in April 2006, President Morales issued Supreme Decree No. 28686 repealing all supreme decrees that irregularly supported financial accounts referred to as secret expenditures.[70]

Public oversight appears to be weak. Fernando Torres Gorena highlights the existing gap in academic literature and journalistic research on the Bolivian intelligence sector.[71]

THE INTELLIGENCE BILL OF 2010

As explained above, Bolivia lacks a national unified intelligence system, with the army's intelligence structure being the most cogent but operating with great autonomy and without any control or oversight. In 2008, the minister of defense at the time made public the intention to create the Central State Agency (AECIE) consolidating the information of the armed forces and the police, aimed at protecting natural resources, fighting international organized crime, and planning the role of the state in a new scenario and under a new political constitution.[72]

In 2010 the government proposed a bill for the creation of a Plurinational State Intelligence Directorate (DIDEP).[73] Its function would be to produce strategic intelligence and analyze the geographical, economic, political, psychosocial, technological, scientific, transport, and telecommunications components. It would centralize and integrate intelligence produced by the ministries of Government, Defense, Foreign Affairs, Economics, Transparency, and Combating Corruption and Autonomy. It would embrace three areas: military strategic intelligence, strategic state intelligence, and tactical and operational intelligence. It would be composed of officials from the ministries of Defense, Government, and military and police officers. Regarding external control, it should be carried out by the Plurinational Assembly through a special committee, and by the Supreme Defense Council. The bill did not regulate judicial or legislative control of intelligence operations. Important to note is that the bill understands intelligence in terms of comprehensive security, covering the protection of the state and people against threats or risks, and the protection of the well-being of people, granting intelligence agencies virtually unlimited powers.[74] Submitted by the minister of defense along with a package of fifteen other defense bills, none of them were addressed by the national assembly.

CONCLUSION

In Bolivia, intelligence activities, as acknowledged by Fernando Torres Gorena, have been superficially studied by social sciences, except when issues that compromised national security or public safety were publicly disclosed.[75]

The similarities of the police force mission[76] and intelligence policies between neoliberal and left-wing governments are striking. Neither police reform nor intelligence democratization has been achieved since the recovery of democracy. It can be argued that Bolivia serves as a test case of how a new leftist regime lasting from 2005 to 2019 managed the security and the intelligence sectors.[77]

Ultimately, Bolivia's intelligence culture is weak. At present Bolivia has neither a national intelligence agency to fulfill strategic intelligence requirements, nor an intelligence law to govern the system; the bill introduced last decade was not passed. Full democratic governance of intelligence and review of this peculiar system is awaiting.

NOTES

1. For a recent history, see Herbert S. Klein, *Historia Mínima de Bolivia* (México D.F.: El Colegio de México, 2016).

2. Including weak state institutions, poor governance, inequality, presence of drug trafficking organizations. For further reading, see George Gray Molina, "The Crisis in Bolivia: Challenges of Democracy, Conflict and Human Security," in *Democracy, Conflict and Human Security: Further Reading* (Volume 2) (Stockholm: International Institute for Democracy and Electoral Assistance, 2006), 25–34, available at http://www.idea.int/publications/dchs/upload/dchs_vol2_sec1_2.pdf; and Allan Gillies, "Theorising State Narco Relations in Bolivia's Nascent Democracy (1982–1993): Governance, Order and Political Transition," *Third World Quarterly* 39, no. 4 (2018): 727–46.

3. See James Rochlin, "Latin America's Left Turn and the New Strategic Landscape: The Case of Bolivia," *Third World Quarterly* 28, no. 7 (2007): 1330–33. The diverse and polarized views (populist, revolutionary, reformist) of scholars debating on the Evo Morales administration and MAS party have been grouped by Webber "on

an order-to-insurrection continuum, beginning with what I would term *the guardians of order*, followed by *masista loyalists*, and finally *the critical left*." Jeffery R. Webber, "Bolivia in the Era of Evo Morales," *Latin American Research Review* 45, no. 3 (2010): 249. For an account on social and economic changes, also see Rosemary Thorp et al., "Group Inequalities and Political Violence: Policy Challenges and Priorities in Bolivia, Guatemala and Peru," CRISE Overview no. 2 (Oxford, UK: Centre for Research on Inequality, Human Security and Ethnicity, 2010).

    4. In the terms of Juan J. Linz and Alfred Stepan, *Problems of Democratic Transition and Consolidation: Southern Europe, South America, and Post-Communist Europe* (Baltimore: Johns Hopkins University Press, 1996).

    5. See the chronology by Klein, *Historia Mínima de Bolivia*, 348. These regimes initially assumed a populist character, but subsequently became conservative (undertaking conservative economic reforms). These authoritarian governments were corrupt—often collaborating or being co-opted by drug trafficking groups—and highly repressive. As Matthes underscores, these regimes suspended "all civil rights, [suppressing] the workers' movement, [banning] the peasant syndicates and [sending] the military to occupy the mines." Britta Katharina Matthes, *From National to Pluri-National: Rethinking the Transformation of the Bolivian State through Struggles for Autonomy*, PhD thesis, University of Bath, 2017, 104, 271–77, available at https://purehost.bath.ac.uk/ws/portalfiles/portal/187928612/MATTHES_Britta Katharina_PhD_Thesis_29_01_2018.pdf. Loreta Tellería Escobar, "Fuerzas Armadas, Seguridad Interna y Democracia en Bolivia: Entre la Indefinición Estratégica y la Criminalización Social," in *El Papel de las Fuerzas Armadas en América Latina Seguridad Interna y Democracia*, eds. David Álvarez Veloso et al. (Buenos Aires: CLACSO, 2012), 110.

    6. Loreta Tellería Escobar, "Política Policial en Bolivia: Entre la Continuidad y el Cambio," *Delito y Sociedad* 26, no. 44 (2017): 120, 150. Also, see H. C. Felipe Mansilla, "Estructuras, Funciones y Problemas de la Policía Boliviana: Un Esbozo Introductorio," in *Justicia en la Calle: Ensayos sobre la Policía en América Latina*, ed. Peter Waldmann (Bogotá: Konrad Adenauer Stiftung-CIEDLA, 1996), 160; Juan Ramón Quintana, coord., *Policía y Democracia en Bolivia: Una Política Institucional Pendiente—Resultados Preliminares* (La Paz: Programa de Investigación Estratégica en Bolivia, 2003), 16; and H. C. F. Mansilla, *La Policía Boliviana: Entre los Códigos Informales y los Intentos de Modernización* (La Paz: Plural Editores, 2003).

    7. Ministerio Público Fiscal, Argentina, "Contexto Histórico de Bolivia," in *Edición digital del alegato expuesto por el Ministerio Público Fiscal en las Causas 1504, 1951, 2054 y 1976 ("Plan Cóndor")*. Available at https://www.mpf.gob.ar/plan-condor/paises/bolivia/. This document cites the work by Gerardo Irusta Medrano, *Espionaje y Servicios Secretos en Bolivia (1930–1980), Operación Cóndor en Acción* (La Paz: author's edition, 1995). Several other institutions were created by the military dictatorships in Bolivia to repress dissent, initially housed in the Ministry of Government.

    8. Juan Ramón Quintana, coord., *Policía y Democracia en Bolivia: Una Política Institucional Pendiente* (La Paz: Fundación PIEB—Programa de Investigación Estratégica en Bolivia, 2005), 52.

9. Decreto Supremo No. 5154/1959. Decree available at https://www.derechoteca .com/gacetabolivia/decreto-supremo-5154-del-24-febrero-1959/. As Gómez de la Torre and Medrano Carmona explain, Bolivia was the forerunner country in South America in creating a national intelligence agency at the political-strategic level within a democratic regime; although in Argentina elected president General Juan Domingo Perón created the State Information Coordinator (CIDE) in 1946, it ascribed a military/authoritarian character. Andrés Gómez de la Torre and Arturo Medrano Carmona, "Orígenes en el Proceso de Inteligencia en el Perú," *URVIO, Revista Latinoamericana de Estudios de Seguridad* 21 (2017): 1010–1111.

10. Decreto Supremo No. 05564/1960. Decree available at http://www.gacetaofi cialdebolivia.gob.bo/edicions/view/1.

11. Decreto Ley No. 06947/1964. Decree available at http://www.gacetaoficialde bolivia.gob.bo/edicions/view/217

12. See introduction.

13. Eduardo Gamarra and Raúl Barrios M., "Seguridad Ciudadana y Seguridad Nacional: Relaciones entre Policías y Militares en Bolivia," in *Justicia en la Calle,* ed. Peter Waldmann, 109–114.

14. Quintana, *Policía y Democracia en Bolivia*, 2003, 73. Bolivia has been a drug trafficking hub, with small local "crime families," and a source and transit country for human trafficking. ISSAT, *Bolivia Country Profile*, International Security Sector Advisory Team, online, updated October 2, 2015. Available at https://issat.dcaf.ch/ Learn/Resource-Library2/Country-Profiles/Bolivia-Country-Profile. According to Dreyfus, "In Bolivia, the illicit drug traffic is not managed by coalitions of criminal organizations but by 20 to 30 organizations (often referred to as 'families' due to the fact that most of the businesses are managed by landowner families) with serious conflicts and grievances between them." Pablo G. Dreyfus, *Border Spillover: Drug Trafficking and National Security in South America*, Thèse présentée pour l'obtention du grade de Docteur en Relations Internationales, Institut Universitaire de Hautes Études Internationales, Université de Genève (2002): 104.

15. With the defeat in the Chaco War (1932–1935), the Bolivian military lost prominence and thus the police were tasked with public security. With the 1952 revolution, the police consolidated as first choice instrument in public security. Subsequently the police played various roles but always subordinate to the military. In the early 1980s, the police displaced the military once again. Decades later, the military would regain prominence in public security policies, which focus on crime prevention and which is the task of police, not the armed forces, whose job is to implement national defense policies (focused on territorial defense against external or military threats). This old dispute between the military and the police was also present within the intelligence sector (rivalries between military and police intelligence services). Peter Waldmann, "¿Protección o Extorsión? Aproximación al Perfil Real de la Policía en América Latina," in *El Estado Anómico. Derecho, Seguridad Pública y Vida Cotidiana en América Latina*, ed. Peter Waldmann (Caracas: Nueva Sociedad, 2003), 126. See also Gamarra and Barrios, "Seguridad Ciudadana y Seguridad Nacional," 114–25; Joaquín Chacin Barragán, "Institucionalidad y Gestión Local de la Seguridad Ciudadana y la Violencia en Bolivia," in *Por esos Lugares no Camino . . .*

Reflexiones Teórica-conceptuales para Comprender la Violencia y la Inseguridad en Ámbitos Urbanos, ed. Alejandra Ramírez Soruco (Cochabamba: CESU-UMSS, 2015), 168–69. Also see Quintana, *Policía y Democracia en Bolivia,* 2005; Carlos Maldonado, "Desafíos de los Servicios de Inteligencia en la Región Andina," in *SIN Arcana Inmperii, Inteligencia en Democracia,* ed. Andrés Gómez de la Torre Rotta (Lima: Foro Libertad & Seguridad, 2007), 275.

16. Martin Edwin Andersen, *Peoples of the Earth: Ethnonationalism, Democracy, and the Indigenous Challenge in "Latin" America* (Lanham: Lexington Books, 2010), 94; Loreto Correa Vera, "De la Violencia Social a la Imposición Estatal: El Caso Boliviano de los Hidrocarburos," in *El Prisma de las Seguridades en América Latina: Escenarios Regionales y Locales,* coord. Alejo Vargas Velásquez (Ciudad Autónoma de Buenos Aires: CLACSO, 2012), 296. For a review of the various interpretations on the development of political institutions, indigenism, and issues of identity, see chapter 7, "Bolivia: Unraveling a Present Past," in Andersen, *Peoples of the Earth;* Klein, *Historia Mínima de Bolivia,* 21, 58.

17. Steen Christensen, "The Impact of China on South America Political and Economic Development," in *Regionalism, Development and the Post-Commodities Boom in South America,* ed. Ernesto Vivares (Cham: Palgrave Macmillan, 2018), 86.

18. See Willem Assies, "Bolivia: A Gasified Democracy," *Revista Europea de Estudios Latinoamericanos y del Caribe/European Review of Latin American and Caribbean Studies,* no. 76 (2004): 25–43.

19. See Otto Birke and Steffen Böhm, "'The People' and Resistance against International Business: The Case of the Bolivian 'Water War,'" *Critical Perspectives on International Business* 2, no. 4 (2006): 299–320.

20. Christensen, "The Impact of China on South America Political and Economic Development," 86.

21. Andersen, *Peoples of the Earth,* 101. See also Juan Carlos Lopera Téllez, "La Multidimensionalidad del Concepto de Seguridad: Breve Acercamiento al Caso de Bolivia," *Estudios en Seguridad y Defensa* 5, no. 10 (2010): 51–60.

22. Juan Ramón Quintana Taborga, "Introducción: La Cultura de la Dependencia Imperial," in *BoliviaLeaks: La Injerencia Política de Estados Unidos contra el Proceso de Cambio 2006–2010,* ed. Juan Ramón Quintana Taborga (Buenos Aires/La Paz: CLACSO / Estado Plurinacional de Bolivia. Ministerio de la Presidencia, 2016), 371; Klein, *Historia Mínima de Bolivia,* 333; Rochlin, "Latin America's Left Turn and the New Strategic Landscape," 1330–33.

23. Mansilla, "Estructuras, Funciones y Problemas de la Policía Boliviana," 158–59.

24. Juan Ramón Quintana Taborga, "La Policialización de la Agenda de Seguridad de Bolivia," in *Agenda de Seguridad Andino-Brasileña: Primeras Aproximaciones,* eds. Marco Cepik and Socorro Ramírez (Bogotá: Fescol/Iepri/Universidade Federal Do Rio Grande Do Sul, 2004): 114.

25. Jaime Malamud-Goti, "Soldiers, Peasants, Politicians and the War on Drugs in Bolivia," *The American University Journal of International Law and Policy* 6, no. 1 (1990): 41–43; Dreyfus, *Border Spillover,* 121–22.

26. On this topic, see Fernando Germán Torres Gorena, *La Influencia Norteamericana en los Organismos Policiales El Caso Boliviano (1993–1997)* (Quito: FLACSO, Sede Ecuador, 2012).

27. Torres Gorena, *La Influencia Norteamericana en los Organismos Policiales El Caso Boliviano (1993–1997)*, 47–48.

28. Theo Roncken, "Bolivia: Seguridad Ciudadana y Vivir Bien. La Seguridad Ciudadana en el Horizonte del Vivir Bien," in *La Inseguridad y la Seguridad Ciudadana en América Latina*, coord. José Alfredo Zavaleta Betancourt (Ciudad Autónoma de Buenos Aires: CLACSO, 2012), 207.

29. Alfonso M. Dorado E., "La Policía en el Estado de Derecho Latinoamericano: El Caso de Bolivia," in *La Policía en los Estados de Derecho Latinoamericanos*, eds. K. Ambos, J. L. Gómez Colomer, and R. Vogler (Bogotá: Editorial Gustavo Ibañez in cooperation with Friedrich-Ebert-Stiftung and Max Planck Institut für ausländisches und internationales Strafrecht, 2003), 93.

30. Quintana, *Policía y Democracia en Bolivia,* 2003, 21. Based on an analysis of four historical cycles, 1900–1937, 1937–1952, 1952–1964, and 1964–1982. Also, see Quintana Taborga, "La Policialización de la Agenda," 114, 136. On armed forces involvement in citizen security see also José Rocabado Sánchez, "La Seguridad Ciudadana en Bolivia: ¿Hay Espacio para las Fuerzas Armadas?" *URVIO, Revista Latinoamericana de Estudios de Seguridad* 12 (2012): 25–40.

31. See Marcelo Varnoux Garay, "La Seguridad Ciudadana en Bolivia: Entre la Delincuencia y los Motines Policiales," *Diálogo Político* 20, no. 3 (2003); Alberto Arturo Gutiérrez Fernández, *Lineamientos Jurídicos e Institucionales para Reforma de la Normativa de la Policía Boliviana Destinada a Evitar Actos de Insubordinación*, PhD thesis, Universidad Mayor de San Andrés, 2009; Gregorio Careaga, *La Policía en el Escenario Institucional de la Democracia en Bolivia. Formación de Movimiento Corporativo en las Crisis Estatales de Abril del 2000 y Febrero del 2003*, PhD thesis, Universidad Mayor de San Andrés, 2008.

32. Christensen, "The Impact of China on South America," 86.

33. José Rocabado Sánchez, "Las Fuerzas Armadas de Bolivia en un Contexto Internacional en Transformación, 2006–2018, in *El Nuevo Rol de las Fuerzas Armadas en Bolivia, Brasil, Chile, Colombia, Ecuador y Perú: Red de Política de Seguridad* (Lima: Konrad Adenauer Stiftung, Pontificia Universidad Católica del Perú, Instituto de Estudios Internacionales, 2018), 140.

34. Sonia Alda Mejías, "Los Cambios en las Fuerzas Armadas y la Defensa en la 'Revolución Democrática' de Evo Morales," in *Anuario 2010 de Seguridad Regional en América Latina y el Caribe*, eds. Hans Mathieu and Catalina Niño Guarnizo (Bogotá: Friedrich Ebert Stiftung en Colombia, 2010), 222–23.

35. Fernando Mayorga, "Bolivia: Seguridad Regional, Crisis Política y Conflictos," in *Anuario 2009 de Seguridad Regional en América Latina y el Caribe*, eds. Hans Mathieu and Paula Rodríguez Arredondo (Bogotá: Friedrich Ebert Stiftung en Colombia, 2009), 28–29.

36. For an analysis of the political economy context, and the emergence of new security themes see Rochlin, "Latin America's Left Turn."

37. Manuel Mejido Costoya, "Neodesarrollismo y Seguridad en América Latina: El Caso de Bolivia," *Revista Política y Estrategia*, no. 114 (2009): 158.

38. On Evo Morales, measures related to security and intelligence in 2006, see Loreta Tellería Escobar, "Wiki Revelación: Las Relaciones entre las Fuerzas Armadas y la Embajada de Estados Unidos en Bolivia (2007–2008)," in *BoliviaLeaks*, ed. Juan Ramón Quintana Taborga, 176–77.

39. Mayorga, "Bolivia," 32–35.

40. Mayorga, "Bolivia," 30–32.

41. https://www.constituteproject.org/constitution/Bolivia_2009.pdf.

42. https://www.constituteproject.org/constitution/Bolivia_2009.pdf.

43. Gustavo Bonifaz Moreno, "Tensiones de la Agenda de Seguridad en la Transición a un Estado Plurinacional con Autonomías," in *Anuario 2011 de Seguridad Regional en América Latina y el Caribe*, eds. Hans Mathieu, and Catalina Niño Guarnizo (Bogotá: Friedrich Ebert Stiftung en Colombia, 2011), 31.

44. Bonifaz Moreno, "Tensiones de la Agenda de Seguridad," 32.

45. Campero, "La Seguridad en Bolivia, 2011–2012," 40–43. On lynching as a kind of neoliberal violence, see Daniel M. Goldstein, "Flexible Justice: Neoliberal Violence and 'Self-Help' Security in Bolivia," *Critique of Anthropology* 25, no.4 (2005): 393–95.

46. José Carlos Campero, *El Motín Policial en Bolivia en Junio de 2012*, Policy Paper 45, (Bogotá: Friedrich-Ebert-Stiftung, Programa de Cooperación en Seguridad Regional, 2012).

47. José Carlos Campero, "Balance de la Seguridad en Bolivia, 2012–2013," in *Anuario 2013 de Seguridad Regional en América Latina y el Caribe*, ed. Catalina Niño Guarnizo (Bogotá: Friedrich Ebert Stiftung en Colombia, 2013), 21–23.

48. Boris Miranda, "Etnografía de la Vulnerabilidad: Escenarios Críticos del Narcotráfico en Bolivia," in *Anuario 2015 de Seguridad Regional en América Latina y el Caribe*, ed. Catalina Niño Guarnizo (Bogotá: Friedrich Ebert Stiftung en Colombia, 2015), 46.

49. Miranda, "Etnografía de la Vulnerabilidad," 43–48.

50. See ISSAT, *Bolivia Country Profile*; Campero, "Balance de la Seguridad en Bolivia," 7.

51. See "Quintana Anuncia Creación de una Agencia de Inteligencia," *Los Tiempos*, March 1, 2016, available at http://www.lostiempos.com/actualidad/nacional/20160301/quintana-anuncia-creacion-agencia-inteligencia; "Equipo de Inteligencia de Quintana no prosperó," *Los Tiempos*, April 21, 2016, available at http://www.lostiempos.com/actualidad/nacional/20160421/equipo-inteligencia-quintana-no-prospero.

52. ISSAT, *Bolivia Country Profile*.

53. CICAD, "Bolivia. Evaluation Report on Drug Policies," Multilateral Evaluation Mechanism (MEM), Inter-American Drug Abuse Control Commission (CICAD), Organization of American States (OAS), July 2019, 31. Available at http://www.cicad.oas.org/mem/reports/7/Full_Eval/Bolivia-7thRd-ENG.pdf.

54. Fernando Molina, "El Ejército Obliga a Evo Morales a Renunciar como Presidente de Bolivia," *El País*, November 11, 2019. Available at https://elpais.com/internacional/2019/11/10/actualidad/1573386514_263233.html.

55. UN Office of the High Commissioner for Human Rights, "Bolivia: UN Human Rights Chief urges structural changes to prevent crises," Geneva, August 24, 2020. Available at https://www.ohchr.org/EN/NewsEvents/Pages/DisplayNews.aspx?NewsID=26184&LangID=E. Also see Carwil Bjork-James, "Mass Protest and State Repression in Bolivian Political Culture: Putting the Gas War and the 2019 Crisis in Perspective," *Human Rights Program, Harvard Law School* (2020). Available at http://hrp.law.harvard.edu/wp-content/uploads/2020/05/CBjork-James_20_003-1.pdf.

56. Campero, "La Seguridad en Bolivia, 2011–2012," 33. José Rocabado Sánchez, "Nuevos Retos para la Lucha contra el Narcotráfico: Una Aproximación a las Redes del Narcotráfico en Bolivia," in *La Reconfiguración del Fenómeno del Narcotráfico en Bolivia, Brasil, Chile, Colombia, Ecuador y Perú Red de Política de Seguridad*, Jaime Baeza Freer et al. (Lima: Pontificia Universidad Católica del Perú, Instituto de Estudios Internacionales (IDEI)—Konrad Adenauer Stiftung, 2017), 103.

57. Maria Velez de Berliner, "The Middle East and Latin America: Implications for Latin America's Security," in *Routledge Handbook of Latin American Security*, eds. David R. Mares and Arie M. Kacowicz (New York: Routledge, 2016), 318.

58. Douglas Farah and Kathryn Babineau, *A Strategic Overview of Latin America: Identifying New Convergence Centers, Forgotten Territories, and Vital Hubs for Transnational Organized Crime*, Institute for National Strategic Studies—*Strategic Perspectives*, No. 28. (Washington, DC: National Defense University Press, 2019), 20.

59. Policy makers cannot be the analysts of the pieces of information produced by each intelligence agency. A coordination body has to do such a job and provide policy makers consolidated assessments based on their intelligence policy and requirements.

60. See Raúl L. Mejía Ibáñez, "La Realidad de la Inteligencia Nacional y la Importancia que Tiene en la Vida del Estado Boliviano," in *Democratización de la Función de Inteligencia—El Nexo de la Cultura Nacional y la Inteligencia Estratégica*, eds. Russell G. Swenson and Susana C. Lemozy (Washington, DC: National Defense Intelligence College Press 2009), 291–306; Carolina Sancho Hirane, "Cooperación en Inteligencia y UNASUR: Posibilidades y Limitaciones," paper presented at the XXXI International Congress of the Latin American Studies Association (LASA) Washington, DC, May 29–June 1, 2013; FLACSO, *Reporte Sector Seguridad en América Latina y el Caribe 2006: Informe Nacional Bolivia* (Santiago de Chile: FLACSO-Chile, 2006), available at https://issuu.com/flacsochile5/docs/informe_nacional_bolivia.

61. Mejía Ibáñez, "La Realidad de la Inteligencia Nacional," 292–95.

62. Bolivia, Ley No. 734 de 8 de abril de 1985—Ley Orgánica de la Policía Nacional. Available at https://www.acnur.org/fileadmin/Documentos/BDL/2002/0861.pdf.

63. ISSAT, *Bolivia Country Profile*.

64. See FELCN webpage: http://www.felcn.gob.bo.

65. Bolivia, Ley Orgánica de las Fuerzas Armadas de la Nación, 30 de diciembre de 1992. Available at https://www.mindef.gob.bo/mindef/sites/default/files/LOFA .pdf.

66. Sancho Hirane, "Cooperación en Inteligencia y UNASUR," 10.

67. Ramiro Orias A., "Políticas de Seguridad Ciudadana y Justicia Penal en Bolivia," in *Anuario 2014 de Seguridad Regional en América Latina y el Caribe*, ed. Catalina Niño Guarnizo (Bogotá: Friedrich Ebert Stiftung en Colombia, 2014), 63.

68. Mejía Ibáñez, "La Realidad de la Inteligencia Nacional," 291–306. Also see the Army's Military Intelligence School webpage: https://ejercito.mil.bo/then3wpag/ files/emie.php.

69. Decreto Supremo No. 27345 de 31 de enero de 2004. Available at http://www .gacetaoficialdebolivia.gob.bo/edicions/view/2564.

70. Decreto Supremo No. 28686, 24 de abril de 2006. Available at http://www.gac etaoficiadebolivia.gob.bo/edicions/view/2879. For more on this, see Magaly Victoria Churruarrín Saavedra (Directora General de Programación y Gestión Presupuestaria, Ministerio de Economía y Finanzas Públicas, Bolivia), "La Administración de Personal y Política Salarial para el Cumplimiento de Objetivos y metas en la Gestión Pública," XLIV Seminario Internacional de Presupuesto Público, Asociación Internacional de Presupuesto Público, Quito, Ecuador, November 10, 2017. Available at http://asip.org.ar/wp-content/uploads/2017/08/Adm-Pers-en-Bolivia.pptx.

71. Fernando G. Torres Gorena, "Inteligencia Boliviana," *El País—Noticias Tarija Bolivia*, November 23, 2017. Available at https://www.elpaisonline.com/index.php/ sociales-2/item/274160-inteligencia-boliviana.

72. Alda Mejías, "Los Cambios en las Fuerzas Armadas," 225.

73. See Oscar Jiménez Gonzales, "Sistemas de Inteligencia en el Perú y otros países de Iberoamérica," Informe de Sistematización Temática No.15/2011–2012, Área de Servicios de Investigación del Departamento de Investigación y Documentación Parlamentaria, Lima, 24 de enero de 2012; Francisco Rogger Carruitero Lecca, "Cambios en la Legislación Iberoamericana sobre Inteligencia—2011–2013," Informe de Investigación No. 27/2014–2013, Área de Servicios de Investigación del Departamento de Investigación y Documentación Parlamentaria, Lima, 21 de noviembre de 2013. Also, Andrés Gómez de la Torre Rotta, and Arturo Medrano Carmona, "Intelligence Laws in Peru and Latin America—Historical, Legal, and Institutional Evolution," in *Intelligence Management in the Americas*, eds. Russell Swenson and Carolina Sancho (Washington, DC: National Intelligence University Press, 2015), 29–47.

74. José Manuel Ugarte, "¿En qué Cambia, en qué Persiste, y hacia Dónde Va la Actividad de Inteligencia Latinoamericana?" (paper presented at FLACSO Ecuador-ISA Joint International Conference, Quito, Ecuador, July 25–27, 2018), 17.

75. Torres Gorena, "Inteligencia Boliviana."

76. See Loreta Tellería Escobar, "Política Policial en Bolivia," 120, 150.

77. This finding is in line with what Sánchez-Sibony suggests: "Alongside other contemporary hybrid regimes, the Bolivian MAS government offers comparativists an important research agenda; namely, the relationship between electoral authoritarian

rule, radicalization-cum-polarization, and the role of militaries in adjudicating high-stakes political disputes." Omar Sánchez-Sibony, "Competitive Authoritarianism in Morales's Bolivia: Skewing Arenas of Competition," *Latin American Politics and Society* 63, no. 1 (2021): 118–44, DOI: https://doi.org/10.1017/lap.2020.35. Also see Brendan de Brun, "Bolivia: A Tale of Praetorianism," in *The Routledge Handbook of Civil-Military Relations*, eds. Florina Cristiana Matei, Carolyn Halladay, and Thomas C. Bruneau (London: Routledge, 2021).

Chapter Five

Brazil

Marco Cepik[1]

This chapter assesses Brazil's intelligence democratization since the end of the military regime in the 1980s. Structurally speaking, Brazil's state apparatus has been built in the context of persistent authoritarian political culture and a highly unequal society.[2] From an interactional perspective, rigid hierarchies historically reproduced in Brazil (figure 5.1) tend to afflict daily interactions between individuals and groups with low levels of mutual trust and the recurrent use of coercion to resolve conflicts.[3] Such uncooperative political dynamics acutely stress democratic institutions, making the Brazilian political system a litmus test for democratization.

Historically, Brazilian intelligence is oriented against "internal enemies," labeled communists or corrupt actors in different contexts, and persistently resisted meaningful democratic accountability.[4] As a result, weak democratic governance[5] of intelligence caused chronic legitimacy deficits, inefficiencies, and political crises.[6]

HISTORICAL BACKGROUND ON THE MILITARY REGIME AND THE ROLE OF INTELLIGENCE

Between 1964, when a military coup overthrew the government of elected President João Goulart (1961–1964), and 1985, when the National Congress elected the first civilian president, Brazil was a non-democratic regime. The military regime used the intelligence services—most notably the National Information Service (SNI)—to repress the population under the pretext of combatting internal threats posed by subversion and communism, as defined in the Brazilian national security doctrine formed in the context of the Cold War.[7]

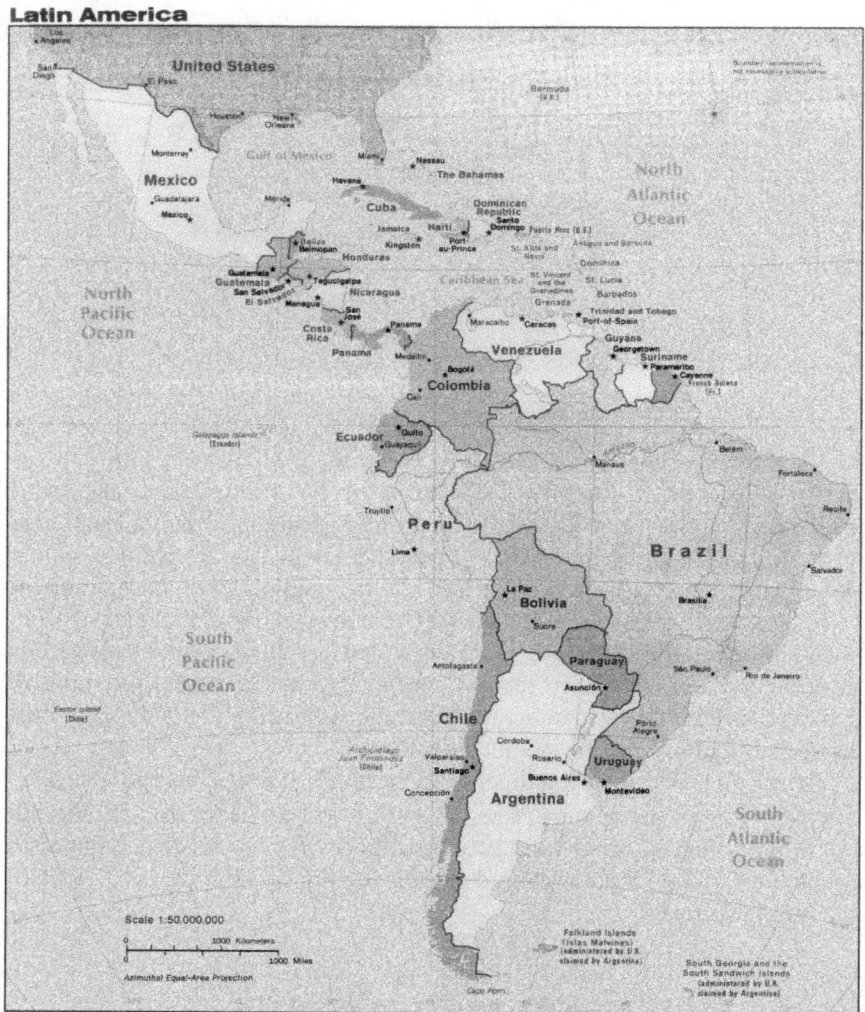

Figure 5.1. Map of Latin America
Courtesy of the Perry-Castañeda Library Map Collection at the University of Texas

As an entity under the president, the SNI was tasked with supervising and coordinating information and counterintelligence activities, establishing a national information apparatus encompassing every level of society.[8] Nevertheless, its primary focus was eliminating dissent toward the military government.

Although the SNI was conceived initially as a civilian agency subordinate to the executive branch, this agency became a military-dominated organization.[9] In 1968, the government created the National Internal Security System (SISSEGINT), an interagency arrangement comprised primarily of the SNI and the intelligence agencies of the three Brazilian military services (army, navy, and air force). Marco Cepik and Priscila Antunes revealed that this network engaged in "monitoring virtually every aspect of civilian life, especially those perceived as internal threats to national security. Its operations resulted in the violation of citizens' rights, since torture, violation of correspondence, telephone bugging, and arrests without a warrant were accepted practices during the military regime."[10] In 1971, the National School of Information (ESNI) was created to further solidify SNI's preeminence by monopolizing intelligence training of civilian and military personnel.[11] Between 1974 and 1985, the SNI lost legitimacy due to its politically repressive activities; however, it retained power in the slow transition to democracy.

In sum, the SNI became a "parallel power." As illustrated by Scott D. Tollefson, it "served as the backbone of the military regime's system of control and repression."[12] It had high penetration of society and was insulated from external accountability.[13] The SNI even survived the end of the military regime.

BACKGROUND ON DEMOCRATIC
TRANSITION AND INTELLIGENCE DEMOCRATIZATION

After twenty-one years of military rule, in 1985, the military regime initiated a transition to democracy, by transferring its governing power to a civilian president, José Sarney (1985–1990). In December 1989, Brazil's first democratic direct election led to the election of President Fernando Collor de Mello.[14] In 1990, President Collor disbanded the SNI. Since then, three distinct periods have marked the development of the post-dictatorial Brazilian intelligence system: 1990–1999, 2000–2014, and 2015–present.[15]

The first period (1990–1999) was a transitional one, involving some minor structural reforms.[16] The first step was changing the names of some intelligence agencies, to indicate a departure from past modus operandi. For instance, the secret services operating under the military included "intelligence" in their titles, to signal compatibility between their practices and those of their counterparts from democratic countries. In 1991, President Collor established the Secretariat for Strategic Affairs (SAE), a civilian body under the presidency that performed various functions, including intelligence activities.[17] An executive decree authorized the remaining SNI personnel, facilities, and technical means to operate within the newly formed SAE. The military and police intelligence branches continued to conduct surveillance against "subversive" social movements and political parties while simultaneously supporting "organic security" (internal affairs). The services established their priorities, responding to their threat perceptions.[18]

President Collor submitted a bill regulating intelligence activities to the National Congress in 1990, but the stigma of the secret services persisted.[19] Due to past experiences and the fact that legislation inherited from the military dictatorship was still in place, concerns about human rights violations and power abuses were prominent among journalists, parliamentarians, academics, and civil society. Throughout the decade, the government and opposition parliamentarians, especially from the Workers' Party (PT), debated new legislation to adapt Brazilian intelligence to what would become the democratic 1988 Federal Constitution. The main points of contention were determining the proper balance of power between the new civilian intelligence service and the legislative and judiciary's proper roles regarding authorization and oversight.

On December 7, 1999, Congress passed Law 9.883, enacted by President Fernando Henrique Cardoso (1995–2002) from the Brazilian Social Democracy Party, (PSDB). Article 1 of the law instituted a Brazilian Intelligence System (SISBIN), committed to defending the constitution and international treaties signed by Brazil.[20] The same article defined intelligence and counterintelligence activities. Under the law, intelligence should combine overt and secret efforts to acquire relevant domestic and international information. This information was aggregated, correlated, and identified immediate or potential threats and appropriate responses to decision makers. The law also defined counterintelligence as aiming to neutralize opposing countries, or organizations' intelligence capabilities.[21] Article 6 of the law has determined that the National Congress should exert external control and supervision of intelligence activities. Additionally, according to Article 11 of the law, the Senate brandishes the power to confirm or refuse the ABIN's director-general candidate proposed by the president.[22]

The Ministry of Defense and its subordinate entities—the intelligence centers of the navy (CIM), the army (CIE), and the air force (CIAER), the intelligence subsection of the Joint Chiefs of Staff (EMCFA), and the Center for the Amazon Security Protection System (CENSIPAM)—participate in the SISBIN. Ministry of Justice and Public Security also participate in the SISBIN, with the following entities: the intelligence departments of the Federal Police; the Federal Highway Police; the intelligence units of the departments in charge of the penitentiary system, ports, public security, special operations, asset recovery, and international legal cooperation. The Ministry of Infrastructure—eight associated agencies—also participate in SISBIN, including regulatory and implementation bodies in the transport and infrastructure sectors. Brazil's other sixteen ministries are part of the SISBIN council by at least one intelligence representative. Interestingly, of the forty-eight federal agencies, departments, and units participating in the SISBIN Council, less than a third directly support national security decisions.

The second period (2000–2014) involved SISBIN's consolidation and expansion. President Cardoso introduced additional and lasting institutional changes during his second term (1999–2002).[23] First, ABIN became subordinated to the newly created Institutional Security Office (GSI) of the presidency. Formerly known as the Presidency's Military Cabinet, the GSI is the ministry in charge of security affairs in the Brazilian federal government. Since then, the director of ABIN has been a civilian whose name has to be approved by the Senate. However, the person who heads ABIN is hierarchically subordinate to the chief minister of the GSI, since 1999 an army general appointed by the president of the republic.[24] Second, the president and the minister of justice created a Public Security Intelligence Subsystem (SISP) through an executive decree to better coordinate law enforcement intelligence at the federal and state levels.[25] Third, the minister of defense established an independent Defense Intelligence System (SINDE) through an administrative ordinance.[26] SINDE's goal was to integrate the intelligence services of the armed forces' three services, as well as the intelligence components of the joint chiefs of staff (EMCFA) and the Amazon Protection System Management and Operational Center (CENSIPAM). Fourth, an executive decree established which agencies would be part of the Brazilian intelligence system and belong to the interagency SISBIN Consultive Council. The SISBIN Council has no direct authority over the participating agencies but performs a potentially vital role to facilitate cooperation and intelligence policy implementation.[27]

Finally, as mandated by the 1999 intelligence law, the Brazilian legislative branch formally established the Joint Commission for the Control of Intelligence Activities (CCAI) in 2000. Nonetheless, the National Congress took another thirteen years to approve CCAI's powers, composition, and internal rules. According to the National Congress Resolution Number Two adopted on November 22, 2013, CCAI is a permanent commission of the National Congress, composed of six senators and six federal deputies, with powers to inspect all SISBIN's participating agencies and any other intelligence and counterintelligence components of the national public administration inside Brazil and abroad.[28] CCAI approves the nominee appointed by the president to direct ABIN and can conduct inspections at any intelligence-related facilities, initiate investigations, further investigate after receiving any complaints, and request documents, regardless of classification level.[29]

Additionally, the Joint Commission is responsible for evaluating the National Intelligence Policy (PNI) and the National Intelligence Strategy (ENINT), revising and amending budget proposals, conducting commission studies, preparing and requesting reports, proposing legislation, and holding public and secret hearings. Unjustified refusal to meet CCAI's demands constitutes a crime. Entrusted with such a range of formal powers, CCAI's poor performance over the years is frustrating.[30]

Lula da Silva (PT) retained the legal framework of SISBIN during his two presidential terms (2003–2006 and 2007–2010). However, he increased the number of intelligence branches and boosted resource allocation significantly. Two factors facilitated the rapid expansion of the intelligence community.[31] First, Lula's regional and global foreign and defense policy initiatives were diverse and ambitious—necessitating increased knowledge collection abilities and capacities—leading to employing a more significant number of personnel and facilities. Similarly, during Dilma Rousseff's (PT) first presidential term (2011–2014), Brazil hosted several important international events such as the United Nations Conference of Sustainable Development (2012) and the FIFA World Cup (2014). Additionally, Brazil's public security environment deteriorated alarmingly during Dilma's administration. In 2011, for example, there were 47,215 intentional violent deaths in Brazil, which rose to 53,646 in 2013 and 63,880 in 2017.[32] The combination of more ambitious international goals and a public security crisis resulted in the expansion of military and law enforcement intelligence spending and activities between 2000 and 2014.

During Cardoso, Lula, and Rousseff's presidencies, political crises linked to reports of abuse or intelligence failures were dealt with under the general framework established by the 1988 democratic constitution.[33] In 2013, for example, the National Congress established a Parliamentary Investigation Commission (CPI) to assess the validity of accusations against the U.S. government of allegedly conducting espionage against Brazil's presidency and Petrobras. The CPI concluded that security and counterintelligence failures transpired, necessitating legislative and organizational reforms.[34] Another positive development was the legislative process leading to the enactment of the Law of Access to Information (LAI), a federal law that governed citizen's access to information and official government secrets, sanctioned by President Rousseff in 2011 (Law 12,527).[35] Generally speaking, between 1988 and 2014, Brazil obtained significant simultaneous gains in democracy, security, and socioeconomic development.[36]

In striking contrast, the third period (2015–present) has been marked by the deterioration of previously achieved results. The economic situation worsened drastically following the international fall in commodity prices, the consequences of the COVID-19 pandemic, and the macroeconomic policy choices made by the federal government. The average annual growth of the Brazilian GDP was −1.06 percent within the above date range, with more pronounced declines in 2015 (−3.5 percent), in 2016 (−3.3 percent), and 2020 (-4.4 percent).[37] Social unrest and political polarization followed the deteriorating economic environment, punctuated by the impacts of the Car Wash operation, the deposition of Dilma Rousseff by the National Congress in 2016, the imposition of a harsh austerity plan combined with labor and pensions deregulations during Michel Temer's transitional government (2016–2018), and former President Lula's arrest followed by Jair Bolsonaro's controversial election in 2018.[38]

Between 2016 and 2018, as Temer's popular approval rates decreased to a mere 3 percent, the former vice president appealed to the armed forces to contain protests and intervene in Rio de Janeiro. Law enforcement and military intelligence agencies have benefited from the symbiotic relationship of government officials requiring assistance, and intelligence and security agencies providing it with associated resourcing and autonomous management with minor oversight. Commanded by an influential and prominent army general, the GSI established by executive decree a National Intelligence Policy (2016) and a National Intelligence Strategy (2017).

The PNI document (Executive Decree 8,793 of June 2016) identified eleven priority threats to guide SISBIN's intelligence work, albeit in a generic fashion and without prioritization: espionage, sabotage, external interference, actions contrary to national sovereignty, cyber-attacks, terrorism, illegal use of sensitive technologies, weapons of mass destruction, organized crime, corruption, and activities contrary to the Democratic Rule of Law.[39] In December 2017, another executive decree approved a National Intelligence Strategy (ENINT) to complement the new policy.[40] ENINT has four structuring axes: networking, technology and training, international projection, and security. ENINT's objectives include, inter alia: foster a culture of knowledge protection; improve cryptography capabilities; consolidate foreign intelligence activities; target corruption; combat organized crime, transnational crimes, and terrorism; create protocols for integrated SISBIN actions; and establish an early warning system. Although ABIN remains the sole federal agency with an exclusive intelligence mission, both PNI and ENINT are tasked with guiding the intelligence components of all SISBIN participating agencies in their respective policy realms.

In 2018, the Temer government authorized ABIN to hire three hundred new employees. By then, the agency had specialized directorates for intelligence operations, analysis, counterintelligence, counterterrorism, transnational crime, the Intelligence School (ESINT), and the Center for Research and

Development of Secure Communications (CEPESC). ABIN has superinten-
dencies in all Brazilian states and official attachés in twenty countries.[41]

Jair Bolsonaro's relationship with intelligence organizations has been
contradictory. On the one hand, Bolsonaro's policies have favored intelligence agencies. For instance, he appointed thousands of military officers—
active and retired—to relevant positions in the government. In parallel, the
Bolsonaro administration has endeavored to dilute oversight and accountability of intelligence.[42] On the other hand, he publicly declared his mistrust
in established intelligence organizations, amid concerns with potential misuse
of intelligence components obliged by hierarchy and loyalty in law enforcement and the armed forces, enabled by Bolsonaro's far-right stance against
human rights.[43] In August 2020, for example, the Brazilian Supreme Court
(STF) ordered the suspension of the compilation of a dossier against political
opponents produced by an Intelligence Directorate (DINT/SEOPI) under the
Ministry of Justice and Public Security (MJSP). In March 2021, Bolsonaro's
attorney general argued before the STF to utilize the National Security Law
(LSN) to investigate and prosecute people who criticize his government. LSN
was adopted by the Military Dictatorship in 1983 and was only revoked by
the National Congress in August 2021.[44] Conversely, Bolsonaro declared in a
televised cabinet meeting in 2020 that he trusted his "informal" intelligence
network, not the government's civilian intelligence agencies.[45] It has been difficult to reconcile a commitment to truth and respect for scientific evidence
underlying intelligence analytical work with the president's far-right ideology. In May 2020, for example, a secret ABIN report released by the press
indicated that Bolsonaro ignored and failed to act in response to the seriousness of the COVID-19 pandemic.[46]

In sum, Bolsonaro's contradictory claims and actions vis-à-vis intelligence
have obstructed intelligence democratization in Brazil. The expansion of
SISBIN in the last two decades also poses challenges for assessing the control
and accountability of intelligence activities.

ANALYSIS

The preceding discussion reveals that in contrast to the rapid expansion of
the SISBIN, the institutions for oversight and control are fewer and weaker.
The next section provides an evaluation of the gaps and unbalances between
the size of the Brazilian intelligence system and the ability of the selected
entities to exercise external democratic controls over the SISBIN agencies.[47]
Table 5.1 summarizes the preliminary findings and an overall performance
assessment of each selected institution.

Table 5.1. Oversight institutions, attributes, and performance

Institution	Mandate	Focus	Scope	Resources	Profile	Performance
CREDEN-CG	Decree	evaluate	cluster	insufficient	soft	weak
CISET-PR	Decree	audit	agency	sufficient	hard	strong
CGU	Law	investigate	system	sufficient	hard	strong
TCU	Constit	audit	system	outstanding	hard	strong
CCAI	Law	evaluate	system	insufficient	soft	weak
CPI	Constit	investigate	system	sufficient	hard	weak
CNJ	Constit	evaluate	cluster	outstanding	soft	weak
CNMP	Constit	investigate	cluster	outstanding	soft	weak
MPM	Law	investigate	cluster	sufficient	soft	weak
MEDIA	Constit	evaluate	system	sufficient	hard	medium

Source: Elaborated by the author.

In the executive branch, there is a significant gap between CREDEN's potential to improve the democratic governance of intelligence in Brazil and its current level of irrelevance in this realm.[48] CREDEN's legal mandate includes monitoring and evaluating the PNI and ENINT implementation programs.[49] However, the GSI minister chairs the CREDEN. In other words, the same minister (an army general) who has direct authority over ABIN and coordinates the SISBIN council is responsible for evaluating and monitoring how well the executive branch of the federal government implements the intelligence policy/strategy.[50] As of March 2021, no evidence exists of technical groups and reports assessing any such objectives. In this sense, CREDEN-CG fails to provide vital control and oversight (monitoring and evaluation), is insufficiently resourced, displays low assertiveness (soft), and achieves poor overall performance.

The CGU is the central organ of an Internal Control System for the Federal Executive Branch.[51] The comptroller general's mandate extends to all civilian bodies of SISBIN (the military has its own legal and disciplinary regime). The Internal Control Secretariat of the Presidency (CISET-PR) is also part of the Federal Internal Control System, so the GSI and the ABIN are under its purview. Under the terms of law 13,844 of 2019, CGU has auditing powers and executive functions of ombudsman, inspectorate, and internal affairs.[52] The power to sanction individuals contributes to making CGU and CISET effective oversight instruments regarding the legal conformity of officials' conduct. CGU is well funded and has been assertive in performing its mission in general.[53] There is one glaring problem, however. The CGU is also a member of the SISBIN Council, which precludes it from being considered an external and independent overseer. For example, in 2020, CGU and ABIN signed a Technical Cooperation Agreement for information sharing and anti-corruption training.[54]

In the legislative branch, there is a similar contrast between the Federal Court of Accounts (TCU) high performance within its narrow mission and the low performance of the CCAI. Based on the Federal Constitution (Article 71) and its organic law,[55] the TCU is empowered to inspect, audit, investigate, and judge the accounts of all the institutions and persons responsible for the money, assets, and currency of the Federative Republic. Transparency measures (online Budget Panel) allow citizens to critically monitor public spending on security, defense, intelligence, and even secret actions.[56] With outstanding resources and an assertive approach, the TCU has demonstrated a strong performance in auditing intelligence spending, at least in the case of ABIN.[57]

In contrast, despite its broad formal powers to evaluate, investigate, and audit, CCAI lacks minimal resources and displays low levels of expertise and interest (soft profile) as an overseer.[58] Its activities are intermittent and unfocused, setting a low standard for what Loch Johnson described as "sporadic patrolling and ad hoc responses to fire alarms."[59] Even further regulatory action from the Joint Commission, which could be expected in such situations, has failed.[60] For example, in 2015, the CCAI leadership introduced Bill 3,578 to regulate intelligence operations. The bill was shelved in 2019 without being voted upon.[61] Without a clear definition of what constitutes intelligence operations and analysis, something the original SISBIN law failed to provide, it is challenging to have effective oversight over such an elusive puzzle.

After twenty years, CCAI remains poorly institutionalized; therefore, the efficacy of its functioning depends on who presides over it, which alternates between the chairs of the Defense and Foreign Affairs Commissions of the Chamber of Deputies and the Senate. In 2019, for example, the son of the president, Federal Deputy Eduardo Bolsonaro, held the vice presidency of CCAI, creating an egregious conflict of interest. The Parliamentary Commissions of Inquiry (CPIs), designed to react with greater incisiveness and granted special investigative powers to rectify exceptional situations, cannot fulfill their roles in the absence of CCAI's cooperation. They tend to produce inconclusive and generic reports, as was the case with the CPI's investigation into allegations of espionage activities conducted by the U.S. government against Brazil in 2013–2014.[62]

In the judicial branch, the National Council of Justice (CNJ) is the body mandated by the constitution to guarantee the independence of justice and to inspect, audit, sanction, monitor, and evaluate the Brazilian judicial system. Experts contend CNJ is generally not very effective in performing oversight functions. Between 2007 and 2018, the average annual incident rate of sanctions was 0.14 percent of the total procedures initiated.[63] Concerning SISBIN, a potentially relevant area of activity for the CNJ would be monitoring and evaluating judicial authorizations for interception of communications, signals, and data. ABIN does not possess police powers and cannot request judicial approval to conduct wiretaps. However, law enforcement organizations conduct information interceptions in criminal investigations and intelligence operations with judicial authority. Data from the National Telephone Interception Control System (SNCI) indicates 19,213 court decisions regarding communication transmission intercepts between 2015 and 2020.[64] The CNJ should investigate the rationale behind such interception requests and possible abuses of power from law enforcement and intelligence agencies. However, no evidence of discussions about such matters by the council can be found.

Similarly, since the 1988 Constitution, the National Council of the Brazilian Public Prosecutor's Office (CNMP) has been the supervisory, audit, and evaluation body of the public ministry (MP), a Brazilian body of independent public prosecutors at the federal and state levels. Over the years, the MP has acquired increasing autonomy and enormous resources, with positive effects in several areas like environmental protection and human rights. However, more power was coupled with lackadaisical accountability and great latitude to individual agenda setting and engendering legal abuses and political biases that became evident in the aftermath of the Car Wash anticorruption operation.[65] Regarding intelligence oversight, there are two additional problems. First, the CNMP effectively renounced its constitutional duties to oversee and carry out external control of the police forces, including police intelligence.[66] Second, although the intelligence units of the various public prosecutor branches are not formally part of SISBIN, there are many informal collaboration channels, joint training, socialization mechanisms, and coordinated agendas limiting CNMP's independence as an external control institution.[67] An even softer profile characterizes the Military Public Ministry (MPM) relationship with military intelligence agencies.[68] As the delineation between intelligence and intelligence oversight entities becomes blurred, the net results are costly and potentially harmful to the citizens.

In the case of the media, the Brazilian Constitution guarantees freedom of expression and independence. Sufficient resources exist within Brazil for critical and independent coverage. Following the pattern identified by Loch Johnson,[69] the Brazilian media has been assertive in denouncing abuses, failures, and scandals ("fire alarms").[70] However, coverage was intense only during crises and primarily focused on ABIN.[71] The relative scarcity of complaints about abuses committed by the intelligence services against citizens, compared with those against police violence, may indicate that SISBIN does not perform direct repressive functions. Even so, little is known about the system's social penetration and surveillance capacity, topics essential in determining democratic consolidation.

Moreover, the Brazilian media is weakened by dependence on selective leaks and official sources. Brazil ranks 107th among 180 countries in the World Press Freedom Index of the organization Reporters Without Borders.[72] Three main factors hinder freedom of the press in Brazil: excessive concentration (TV, radio, printed, and online media cross-ownership), recurrent violence against journalists, and the exponential amount of disinformation circulating through social media and unchecked digital outlets.[73]

CONCLUSION

The institutional design of Brazil's intelligence oversight is comprehensive, especially considering Latin America's legacy of opacity.[74] However, three serious problems persist.

First, more than twenty years after the establishment of SISBIN, the most effective oversight mechanisms are neither evaluation nor investigation but auditing. Considering what Russell Swenson and Carolina Sancho called the forward-looking and preventive governance model, simultaneous evaluation policies and investigating agencies are the most crucial tasks for attaining intelligence democratization.[75] In the case of Brazil, the institutions that should evaluate intelligence policies of the federal executive (CREDEN-CG), legislative (CCAI), and judiciary (CNJ) branches are those with the weakest performance. According to Frans Leeuw and Jan-Eric Furubo,[76] the four conditions for evaluation systems to become institutionalized are an explanatory (not merely normative) epistemological perspective, clear organizational responsibilities, permanence, and a focus on the uses of evaluation reports to improve the policy cycle. In 2019, a Public Policy Monitoring and Evaluation Council was created in the federal government, creating no distinguishable impact thus far in intelligence oversight.[77]

The second problem arises from the vague definition of intelligence adopted in the law that devised SISBIN, which allowed excessive growth (forty-eight federal agencies so far) and the risk of undue securitization in various public policy realms. Additionally, military intelligence and law enforcement agencies are not subjected to any meaningful external oversight mechanisms by the executive, legislative, judiciary, and prosecutorial powers. They receive only a fraction of the media's attention in comparison with ABIN. Further research remains essential to assess intelligence oversight's challenges at the federal, state, and municipal levels, including private companies.

Third, since 2016 democracy has weakened in Brazil, a trend that has only worsened under Bolsonaro. Systematic attacks on social and civil rights are coupled with a weakening of accountability institutions. Building a legitimate and effective intelligence system depends on national and international political dynamics. Authoritarian temptations, either from government officials or sectors of military, police, and intelligence bureaucracies, can only be averted if society ascertains a minimal consensus around democratic rules of coexistence among a plurality of interests and opinions, as well as harmonizing sustainable and equitable development goals. To be part of the solution, all components of the SISBIN should adopt a strong ethical commitment to intelligence based on evidence, logical consistency, rule of democratic law, critical thinking, and self-reflection.

According to Peter Gill[78] and Patrick Obuobi,[79] effective oversight may be prevented by official secrecy and the power derived from technical expertise. According to Edward Shils,[80] secrets are compulsory retention of knowledge reinforced by the prospect of sanction in case of unauthorized disclosure. Therefore, official secrecy is a public form of regulating information flow, with limits and procedures that require public justification, legal and administrative procedures, and proper control and oversight. For David Luban,[81] first-order justifications for government secrecy are potentially valid and compatible with a democratic regime. However, when the very foundations of secrecy rules become secret, second-order reasons became increasingly incompatible with democracy. In Brazil, the federal information access law is very recent (2011) and has been under attack since the beginning of Bolsonaro's government. Intelligence oversight bodies could use LAI more frequently to address official secrecy from both perspectives, material (how many documents are being classified and by whom?) and ethical (which justifications, if any, are being offered by the authorities?).

The technical complexity of intelligence activities also hinders democratic accountability. Obtaining information, overtly and clandestinely, from human sources and the electromagnetic spectrum (cyberspace) is technically demanding.[82] The cryptology and cryptography legal framework and practical consequences are challenging topics to be addressed by the National Congress.[83] However, public policies in different areas require technological and scientific knowledge. To effectively conduct intelligence oversight, one possible remedy would be to increase staff and officials' expertise.[84] In contrast, the fact that CCAI has only one staff person in 2021 to support the Joint Commission in the National Congress to oversee forty-eight federal agencies tells a lot about Brazil's current state of democratic intelligence governance.

NOTES

1. Acknowledgments: This text is dedicated to Michael Herman (*in memoriam*). I would like to thank Peter Gill, Russell Swenson, Cristiana Matei, Eduardo Estévez,

Carolyn Halladay, Aline Hellmann, and Luciano Da Ros for their patience and valuable feedback. The author also expresses gratitude to Victoria Ellwanger Pires, Fernanda Boldrin, and Camila Souza for their research assistance. Disclosure statement: The author reported no potential conflict of interest. Funding: The author acknowledges financial support from the Brazilian National Council for Scientific and Technological Development (Conselho Nacional de Pesquisa Científica—CNPq), grant number 312939/2020-5.

2. Lilia Moritz Schwarcz, *Sobre o Autoritarismo Brasileiro* (São Paulo: Companhia das Letras, 2019).

3. Bruno Reis, *Modernização, Mercado e Democracia* (Porto Alegre: Editora UFRGS, 2020).

4. Marco Cepik, "Intelligence and Security Services in Brazil Reappraising Institutional Flaws and Political Dynamics," *The International Journal of Intelligence, Security, and Public Affairs* 23, no. 1 (2021): 81–102, doi: 10.1080/23800992.2020.1868784.

5. According to the distinction proposed by Peter Gill, the democratic governance of intelligence systems involves control, authorization, and oversight. Peter Gill, "Of Intelligence Oversight and the Challenge of Surveillance Corporatism," *Intelligence and National Security* 35, no. 7 (2020): 970–89, doi: 10.1080/02684527.2020.1783875. By control, the author understands the direction exercised by governors and leaders on intelligence agencies' priorities and actions. Authorization would mean the responsibility assumed by government officials and supervisory bodies regarding the authorized activities. Finally, oversight involves scrutinizing the intelligence actions carried out, both by internal and external agencies. In this sense, oversight is a precondition for the existence of accountability, which would be the obligation to explain, be accountable, and, if necessary, suffer consequences for errors and violations.

6. Marco Cepik and Christiano Ambros, "Intelligence, Crisis and Democracy: Institutional Punctuations in Brazil, Colombia, South Africa and India," *Intelligence and National Security* 29, no. 4 (2014): 523–51, doi: 10.1080/02684527.2014.915176.

7. The first civilian intelligence agency of the country was created in 1946 under the name of Federal Information and Counter-Information Service (SFICI), which was later incorporated to the National Security Council. Two decades later, the first comprehensive and integrated intelligence system in Brazil emerged during the military dictatorship (1964–1985). In June 1964, the military regime replaced SFICI with SNI. Priscila Antunes, *SNI & ABIN: Uma Leitura da Atuação dos Serviços Secretos Brasileiros ao Longo do Século XX* (Rio de Janeiro: FGV Editora, 2002).

8. Alfred Stepan, *Rethinking Military Politics: Brazil and Southern Cone* (Princeton, NJ: Princeton University Press, 1988), 16.

9. Scott D. Tollefson, "National Security," in *Brazil: A Country Study*, ed. Rex A. Hudson. (Washington, DC: Library of Congress, 1998), 358.

10. Marco Cepik and Priscila Antunes, "Brazil's New Intelligence System: An Institutional Assessment," *International Journal of Intelligence and CounterIntelligence* 16, no. 3 (2003): 353, doi: 10.1080/713830446.

11. Stepan, *Rethinking Military Politics*, 19.

12. Tollefson, "National Security," 359.

13. Peter Gill, *Intelligence Governance and Democratisation: A Comparative Analysis of the Limits of Reform* (New York: Routledge, 2016).

14. According to Linz and Stepan, "The Brazilian transition's origins in a hierarchically controlled military regime did, of course, have numerous deleterious consequences for the democratization process." Juan J. Linz and Alfred Stepan, *Problems of Democratic Transition and Consolidation: Southern Europe, South America, and Post-Communist Europe* (Baltimore: Johns Hopkins University Press, 1996), 166.

15. On this historical background and the role of intelligence, see Marco Cepik and Priscila Antunes, "Brazil's New Intelligence System"; Thomas C. Bruneau, "Intelligence Reforms in Brazil: Contemporary Challenges and the Legacy of the Past," *Strategic Insight* 6, no. 3 (May 2007); Marco Cepik, "Structural Change and Democratic Control of Intelligence in Brazil," in *Reforming Intelligence: Obstacles to Democratic Control and Effectiveness,* eds. Thomas C. Bruneau and Steven C. Boraz (Austin: University of Texas Press, 2007), 149–69; Marco Cepik, and Thomas Bruneau, "Brazilian National Approach towards Intelligence: Concept, Institutions and Contemporary Challenges," in *PSI Handbook of Global Security and Intelligence: National Approaches,* eds. Stuart Farson, Peter Gill, Mark Phythian, and Shlomo Shpiro (Westport, CT: Praeger, 2008), 112–29; Thomas C. Bruneau, "Intelligence Reform in Brazil: A Long, Drawn-Out Process," *International Journal of Intelligence and CounterIntelligence* 28, no. 3 (2015): 502–59.

16. Antunes, *SNI & ABIN.*

17. See Cepik and Antunes, "Brazil's New Intelligence System"; and Tollefson, "National Security."

18. It is worth mentioning that it is common for the security and intelligence services to conflate internal affair investigations as "counterintelligence" in Brazil. Thomas Bruneau and Florina C. Matei, "Intelligence in the Developing Democracies: The Quest for Transparency and Effectiveness," in *The Oxford Handbook of National Security,* ed. Loch Johnson (New York: Oxford University Press, 2010), 757–73.

19. Priscila C. Brandão, *Serviços Secretos e Democracia no Cone Sul: Premissas Para uma Convivência Eficiente, Legítima e Eficaz* (Niterói: Impetus, 2010).

20. Lei 9.883, 7 de dezembro de 1999. Available at https://www.planalto.gov.br/ccivil_03/leis/l9883.htm.

21. Lei 9.883, 7 de dezembro de 1999. Available at https://www.planalto.gov.br/ccivil_03/leis/l9883.htm.

22. Lei 9.883, 7 de dezembro de 1999. Available at https://www.planalto.gov.br/ccivil_03/leis/l9883.htm. Between 2002 and 2021, the number of federal agencies participating in SISBIN increased from twenty-two to forty-eight. Such bodies are subordinate to nineteen different ministries. Agência Brasileira de Inteligência, "Seis órgãos têm ingresso aprovado no SISBIN," https://www.gov.br/abin/pt-br/assuntos/noticias/seis-orgaos-tem-ingresso-aprovado-no-sisbin.

23. Cepik, "Structural Change and Democratic Control of Intelligence in Brazil."

24. Medida Provisória (MP) 1.911-10, 24 de setembro de 1999. Available at http://www.planalto.gov.br/ccivil_03/mpv/antigas/1911-10.htm.

25. Decreto 3.695, 21 de dezembro de 2000. Available at http://www.planalto.gov.br/ccivil_03/decreto/d3695.htm.

26. Portaria Normativa 295/MD, 3 de junho de 2002. Available at Portaria Normativa No 295/MD, de 3 de junho de 2002.

27. Decreto 4.376, 13 de dezembro de 2002. Available at http://www.planalto.gov .br/ccivil_03/decreto/2002/D4376compilado.htm.

28. Resolução 02, 2013—CN. Available at https://cutt.ly/fcEbUpD.

29. Resolução 02, 2013—CN. Available at https://cutt.ly/fcEbUpD.

30. Bruneau, "Intelligence Reform in Brazil."

31. Cepik, "Intelligence and Security Services in Brazil."

32. Fórum Brasileiro de Segurança Pública [FBSP], *Anuário Brasileiro de Segurança Pública* no. 9 (2014). Available at https://forumseguranca.org.br/storage/8_anuario_2014_20150309.pdf.

33. Cepik and Ambros, "Intelligence, Crisis, and Democracy," 534–38.

34. Senado Federal, *Relatório Final da CPI da Espionagem*, Brasília: Diário do Senado Federal, Ano LXIX, Sup. "C" n. 51, 17 de abril de 2014.

35. Karina Rodrigues, "The Politics of Brazil's Access to Information Policies: History and Coalitions," *Rev. Adm. Pública* 54, no. 1 (2020): 142–61, doi: 10.1590/0034-761220180369x.

36. Cepik, "Intelligence and Security Services in Brazil," 16.

37. Banco Central do Brasil. Available at https://www3.bcb.gov.br.

38. Ernesto Lodoño and Letícia Casado, "A Collapse Foretold: How Brazil's CO-VID-19 Outbreak Overwhelmed Hospitals," *New York Times*, March 27, 2021. Also, see https://cutt.ly/Nx9W3p4. https://calhoun.nps.edu/handle/10945/59691.

39. Decreto 8793, 26 de junho de 2016. Available at http://www.planalto.gov.br/ ccivil_03/_ato2015-2018/2016/decreto/D8793.htm.

40. Decreto de 15 de dezembro de 2017. Available at http://www.planalto.gov.br/ ccivil_03/_ato2015-2018/2017/dsn/Dsn14503.htm.

41. Gabinete de Segurança Institucional, *Relatório de Gestão 2018* (Brasília: Gabinete de Segurança Institucional, 2019). Available at https://bit.ly/3h8Vcql.

42. He repudiated transparency mechanisms established by Rousseff's government, like, for example, the National Truth Commission (CNV) and the Information Access Law (LAI). In 2019, his government attempted to extinguish federal collegiate councils and bodies with civil society representatives (Decree 9,759) and reduced the access to information made through LAI requests. Raul Durlo, *Relatório: Negativas de Acesso à informação pioram sob governo Bolsonaro* (São Paulo, Transparência Brasil, 2020). Available at https://www.transparencia.org.br/downloads/publicacoes/ Negativas_de_acesso_a_informacao_pioram_sob_governo_Bolsonaro.pdf.

43. Cepik, "Intelligence and Security Services in Brazil," 14.

44. Rayssa Motta and Pepita Ortega, "STF é pressionado para derrubar Lei de Segurança Nacional," *Terra*, March 25, 2021, https://bit.ly/2P6R6V4.

45. "Brazil court releases explosive Bolsonaro video as coronavirus cases soar," YouTube video, 5:25, posted by "DW News," May 23, 2020, https://www.youtube .com/watch?v=R45NG9tsNJk.

46. Mateus Vargas, "Informes da Abin destacam benefício da quarentena e citam subnotificação," *O Estado de São Paulo,* May 31, 2020. Available at https://cutt.ly/ VxSXQXq.

47. A relevant sample of national oversight institutions was selected for evaluation. The following ten oversight institutions were selected from the three coequal branches of government, the public prosecutor, and the media:

- From the Executive Branch, the National Defense and External Relations Chamber of the Government Council (CREDEN-CG), the Internal Control Secretariat of the Presidency (CISET-PR), and the Comptroller General of Brazil (CGU).
- From the Legislative Branch, the Federal Court of Accounts (TCU), the Intelligence Activities Control Commission (CCAI), and Parliamentary Investigation Committee (CPI).
- From the Judicial Branch, the National Council of Justice (CNJ).
- In the Public Prosecutor system, the National Council of the Brazilian Public Prosecutor's Office (CNMP) and the Military Public Ministry (MPM).
- The Media, in general, not particular business corporations or outlets, will be treated as an institution. Scores were assigned to each based on political science concepts, Brazilian documents, scientific articles, books, and the author's direct observation. Luciano Da Ros kindly shared thoughts on their insightful concept of accountability as the sum of transparency, oversight, and sanctioning, moderated by overseers' capacity, plus engagement minus political dominance of those under scrutiny: $A = (T + O + S) * (C + E - D)$. Luciano Da Ros and Matthew M. Taylor, "Accountability na Era Bolsonaro: continuidades e mudanças," in *Governo Bolsonaro: Retrocesso Democrático e Degradação Política*, ed. Leonardo Avritzer et al. (São Paulo, Editora Autêntica, 2021), 187–204. The preliminary assessment for each institution is based on five attributes. First, the institutions' oversight varies as the legal mandates come primarily from the Constitution, public laws, or executive decrees. The second attribute is the focus of the oversight, classified as evaluation, investigation, and auditing capacity. The third attribute was the scope of the oversight authority exercised by each institution, classified as encompassing one single agency, a cluster of agencies, or the entire SISBIN. Fourth, the oversight institutions were categorized according to the general level of resources they can marshal to conduct their respective missions. Finally, following the division proposed by Loch Johnson, the overseers' ability to compel responsiveness and accountability of the intelligence agencies and their leaders they were responsible for monitoring were classified as hard (positive) or soft (negative). Loch Johnson, "Governing in the Absence of Angels: On the Practice of Intelligence Accountability in the United States," in *Who's Watching the Spies? Establishing Intelligence Service Accountability*, ed. Hans Born, Loch Johnson, and Ian Leigh (Washington, DC: Potomac Books, 2005), 57–78.

48. Andreia Verdélio, "Bolsonaro preside hoje 39ª Reunião do Conselho de Governo," *Agência Brasil*, November 19, 2020, https://agenciabrasil.ebc.com.br/politica/noticia/2020-11/bolsonaro-preside-hoje-39a-reuniao-do-conselho-de-governo.

49. Decreto 9819, 03 de junho de 2019. Available at http://www.planalto.gov.br/ccivil_03/_ato2019-2022/2019/decreto/D9819.htm.

50. "Conselho de Governo," Brasília, March 30, 2021. Available at https://www.gov.br/planalto/pt-br/acao-governamental/conselho-de-governo/conselho-de-governo.

51. Decreto 3591, 06 de setembro de 2000. Available at http://www.planalto.gov.br/ccivil_03/decreto/d3591.htm.

52. Lei 13.844, 18 de junho de 2019. Available at http://www.planalto.gov.br/ccivil_03/_Ato2019-2022/2019/Lei/L13844compilado.htm.

53. Portal da Transparência, "Controladoria-Geral da União—Unidades com vínculo direto—CGU," https://portaldatransparencia.cgu.gov.br/orgaos/37000-minis terio-da-transparencia-e-cgu.

54. Controladoria Geral da União, "Acordo de Cooperação Técnica n. 11, de 10 de julho de 2020," https://repositorio.cgu.gov.br/handle/1/46082.

55. Lei 8.443, 16 de julho de 1992. Available at http://www.planalto.gov.br/ccivil_03/leis/l8443.htm.

56. SIOP—Sistema Integrado de Planejamento e Orçamento. Available at https://www.siop.planejamento.gov.br/.

57. Tribunal de Contas da União, "Relatório de Auditoria TC 023.480/2016-5 Gastos Sigilosos ABIN." Available at https://bit.ly/3jLwSga.

58. "Atividades Legislativas: Comissão Mista de Controle das Atividades de Inteligência," Senado Federal. Available at https://legis.senado.leg.br/comissoes/comissao?codcol=449.

59. Loch Johnson, "A Shock Theory of Congressional Accountability for Intelligence," in *Handbook of Intelligence Studies*, ed. Loch Johnson (New York: Routledge, 2009), 343–60.

60. Matthew D. McCubbins and Thomas Schwartz, "Congressional Oversight Overlooked: Police Patrols versus Fire Alarms," *American Journal of Political Science* 28, no. 1 (1984): 165–79, doi: 10.2307/2110792.

61. "Publicações," Agência Brasileira de Inteligência. ABIN. Available at https://www.gov.br/abin/pt-br/centrais-de-conteudo/publicacoes.

62. Senado Federal, *Relatório Final da CPI da Espionagem*.

63. Fábio Kerche, Vanessa Elias de Oliveira, and Cláudio Gonçalves Couto, "The Brazilian Councils of Justice and Public Prosecutor's Office as Instruments of Accountability," *Revista de Administração Pública* 54, no. 5 (2020): 1334–60, doi: 10.1590/0034-7612201900212.

64. "Painel do Sistema Nacional de Interceptações de Comunicações—SNIC," Conselho Nacional de Justiça. Available at https://bit.ly/31LnAad.

65. Rogério B. Arantes and Thiago M. Moreira, "Democracia, instituições de controle e justiça sob a ótica do pluralismo estatal," *Opinião Pública* 25, no. 1 (2019): 97–135, doi: 10.1590/1807-0191201925197.

66. Murilo Strätz, "O Sistema Brasileiro de Inteligência e a amplitude do controle externo da atividade policial federal exercido pelo Ministério Público da União," *Revista da SJRJ* 19, no. 34 (2012): 209–23, https://www.jfrj.jus.br/revista-sjrj/artigo/o-sistema-brasileiro-de-inteligencia-e-amplitude-do-controle-externo-da.

67. Carlos S. Arturi and Júlio C. Rodriguez, "Democratization and Intelligence and Internal Security Agencies: A Comparative Analysis of the Cases of Brazil and Portugal (1974–2014)," *Brazilian Political Science Review* 13, no. 02 (2019), doi: 10.1590/1981-3821201900020005.

68. Ministério Público Militar, "MPM em Visita ao Centro de Inteligência do Exército," January 27, 2021, https://www.mpm.mp.br/mpm-em-visita-ao-centro-de-inteligencia-do-exercito/.

69. Johnson, "A Shock Theory of Congressional Accountability for Intelligence," 345.

70. Bela Megale, "Chefe da Abin depõe por 3 horas em inquérito sobre ataques de Bolsonaro às urnas eletrônicas," *O Globo*, August 26, 2021, https://blogs.oglobo .globo.com/bela-megale/post/chefe-da-abin-depoe-por-3-horas-em-inquerito-sobre -ataques-de-bolsonaro-urnas-eletronicas.html.

71. Jaseff Raziel Yauri-Miranda, "Principles to Assess Accountability: A Study of Intelligence Agencies in Spain and Brazil," *International Journal of Intelligence and CounterIntelligence* (2020), doi: 10.1080/08850607.2020.1809954.

72. "Brazil," Reporters Without Borders, accessed March 15, 2021, https://rsf.org/ en/brazil.

73. Observatório da Imprensa, http://www.observatoriodaimprensa.com.br/.

74. Russel Swenson and Carolina Sancho, "The Governance Model of Intelligence Services in the Americas: A Comparative Assessment" (unpublished manuscript, 2021), 27.

75. Swenson and Sancho, "Governance Model of Intelligence," 1.

76. Frans L. Leeuw and Eric Furubo, "Evaluation Systems: What Are They and Why Study Them?" *Evaluation* 14, no. 2 (2008): 157–69, doi 10.1177/1356389007087537.

77. Decreto 9.834, 12 junho de 2019. Available at http://www.planalto.gov.br/ ccivil_03/_ato2019-2022/2019/decreto/D9834.htm.

78. Gill, "Intelligence Oversight and Challenge of Surveillance Corporatism," 13.

79. Patrick Obuobi, "Evaluating Ghana's Intelligence Oversight Regime," *International Journal of Intelligence and CounterIntelligence* 31, no. 2 (2018): 328, doi: 10.1080/08850607.2017.1375841.

80. Edward Shils, *The Torment of Secrecy* (Chicago: Ivan R. Dee Inc, 1996), 26.

81. David Luban, "The Publicity Principle," in *The Theory of Institutional Design*, ed. Robert Goodin (Cambridge: Cambridge University Press, 1996), 154–98.

82. Michelle Cayford, Wolter Pieters, and Constant Hijzen, "Plots, Murders, and Money: Oversight Bodies Evaluating the Effectiveness of Surveillance Technology," *Intelligence and National Security* 33, no. 7 (2018): 999–1021, doi: 10.1080/02684527.2018.1487159.

83. Diego Canabarro and Paulo Renã, "Veja dez razões para rejeitar artigo 10 do projeto sobre fake news, que rastreia mensagens," *Folha de São Paulo*, August 4, 2020, https://www1.folha.uol.com.br/poder/2020/08/veja-dez-razoes-para-rejeitar-artigo-10-do-projeto-sobre-fake-news-que-rastreia-mensagens.shtml.

84. Thorsten Wetzling, "Options for More Effective Intelligence Oversight," Stiftung Neue Verantwortung, 2017. Available at https://www.stiftung-nv.de/de/publika tion/options-more-effective-intelligence-oversight.

Chapter Six

Chile

John "Clay" Oeffinger, Shane Moran, and Florina Cristiana Matei

The story of Chilean intelligence since the Pinochet era has been mostly about decentralization following the authoritarian regime's toppling with an associated institutionalization of democratic civilian control, then a slow recentralization under incremental democratic safeguards. In this context, while progress has occurred in terms of political control over the intelligence agencies, reshaping their roles and missions, and developing interagency processes, such challenges as military resistance to change and sporadic interest in intelligence—the legacy of the Chilean non-democratic past—continue to hinder intelligence democratization.

BACKGROUND ON THE NON-DEMOCRATIC REGIME AND TRANSITION TO DEMOCRACY

Within the context of the global Cold War, Chile's 1973 military coup—that led to the installation of a military dictatorship under army general Augusto Pinochet (1973–1990)—bore the common traits of a U.S.-Soviet ideological proxy conflict, complete with an anti-communist right-wing military coup d'état that forcibly removed a socialist government from power.[1] Indeed, the 1970 Chilean presidential election of Marxist politician Salvador Allende (1970–1973) had precipitated internal unrest within Chile, as well as substantial concern in Washington, DC. President Richard Nixon, fearing another communist Cuba situation following Allende's election, described Chile as the latest slice of "red sandwich" that eventually could include all of Latin America.[2] For Pinochet, the reasons for the coup reached further back than Cold War politics, however; he and many others within the armed forces viewed Allende's election as an existential threat to the Chilean state.

Before the 1973 military coup, Chile had established itself as one of Latin America's longest standing democracies.[3] Chile's armed forces were constitutionally sworn to defend national sovereignty against external enemies—which they had done on several occasions, most notably, against Bolivia and Peru. The Chilean armed forces also had a domestic role. The army possessed a significant intelligence capability that it presently turned inward to thwart the perceived threat of communism. Indeed, since the late 1940s, the Chilean government combatted the incipient red threat by outlawing armed forces members from joining or associating with the Communist Party, and exiling Communist Party members to prison camps in the Atacama Desert.[4] Allende's early presidential policies, including the nationalization of the copper industry amid a faltering economy, stoked fears within the armed forces leadership of internal decline.

The Chilean constitution also granted the military a special role as "guardians of the institutional order."[5] The question then became just which order (and which institutions) the armed forces aimed to protect—and how. The first major fissure within the Allende government came in June 1973, when a small group of right-wing military personnel attempted to topple the government in what became known as the failed *Tanquetazo* coup.[6] The Chilean armed forces quelled the attempted coup, but the episode demonstrated a deterioration in the armed forces' trust in the Allende government.

Following the *Tanquetazo* coup attempt, General Pinochet—who at the time appeared to support the Allende government—was named the army commander in chief.[7] Within a month of taking command, however, Pinochet and three other generals led the September 11 coup, toppling the Allende government. Pinochet's power grab was under the pretense of national renewal through securing national sovereignty, which he perceived was increasingly vulnerable to attack. Pinochet viewed the dilemma, as external security relying upon addressing internal weakness and subversion, particularly from leftist political factions.[8]

In the months immediately following the coup, Pinochet ordered each of the Chilean armed forces to conduct unrestrained repression operations against any individual deemed a threat to the new military government, an effort described in a U.S. Department of State cable as a mission to "eradicat[e] Marxist cancer from Chilean life."[9] This campaign of repression came to include torture, state-sponsored violence, unwarranted arrests, and death squads.[10]

In this same vein, Pinochet legally[11] unified the Chilean intelligence community and granted it *carte blanche* authority to suppress opposition, restrict freedom of information and opinion, and monitor the activities of Chilean citizens of all ideological stances.[12] The new national intelligence system, known as the National Intelligence Directorate (DINA), was created by bringing several military[13] and civilian services (e.g., the five military intelligence organizations, the Intelligence Service of the Carabineros [SICAR], and Chile's national police intelligence apparatus) under one central authority.[14] DINA came under the command of army colonel Juan Manuel Contreras—an officer well known for his ruthlessness and ambition—hand-picked by Pinochet for the job.[15] Contreras was unwaveringly loyal to Pinochet and would personally brief the general every morning of the day's intelligence activities.[16] Additionally, several DINA officers joined the army officers responsible for the "Caravan of Death," a military unit that traversed the nation between September 30 and October 22, 1973, rounding up and executing individuals considered enemies of the state.[17]

In three years, DINA achieved complete control of its component military agencies, notably the most coercive intelligence organizations in Chile's Air Force and the Joint Staff.[18] The highest rates of human rights violations by DINA and its subordinate agencies occurred during the initial years of Pinochet's regime, when fifty persons a month were "disappearing."[19] DINA's additional tasks included neutralizing enemies of the regime abroad—the most notorious such operation being the assassination in 1976 of a former Allende minister, Orlando Leterlier, in the streets of Washington, DC, in broad daylight.[20] Ultimately, DINA's egregious human rights abuses led to vehement internal and external criticism.

In 1977, mounting criticism of DINA's modus operandi prompted Pinochet to replace DINA with the National Information Center (CNI). On paper, the new national intelligence organization came under civilian control, having to report directly to a civilian minister of the interior, rather than retaining a direct connection to the president.[21] Yet Contreras retained the director's role until 1979, thanks to his close relationship to Pinochet.[22] Furthermore, while less repressive, CNI continued its systematic repression of opponents to the Pinochet regime, broadly defined. Moreover, the CNI acquired considerable judicial powers, as it was in charge of military tribunals that prosecuted civilians.[23]

All in all, DINA and CNI abused and tortured over forty thousand people; of these, at least three thousand disappeared.[24] Most of the disappearances occurred under Contreras's close watch. Chile comes in second, after Argentina, in mass disappearances by the hand of the military dictatorships in the region.

DEMOCRATIC TRANSITION, CONSOLIDATION, AND INTELLIGENCE DEMOCRATIZATION EFFORTS

In 1989, Pinochet's departure from the presidency and the country's return to a democratically elected government ushered in a return to civilian-led national government and the restoration of many civil-military relations.[25]

Yet Chilean intelligence agencies would prove quite resistant to civilian-led reform. Most notably, the armed forces strongly held onto key prerogatives, such as the autonomy of their intelligence agencies from civilian oversight and control.[26] The national intelligence agency led by the military, disbanded CNI in 1990, though it was not replaced with a civilian-led equivalent organization for three years.

Each of the five intelligence agencies of the armed forces and national police remained, however. Furthermore, the few years immediately following Pinochet's departure witnessed a sharp rise in radical left-wing attacks that threatened the legitimacy of the new Chilean democratic government. They also seemed to pose a renewed existential threat that militates for a robust intelligence function and thus provided a certain retroactive legitimacy to the former military dictatorship's actions. [27] A special intelligence agency colloquially named *la oficina* was established in 1991 under the authority of the presidency and Ministry of Interior to counter and disarm radical left groups—including Manuel Rodríguez Patriotic Front, Lautaro Youth Movement, and the Revolutionary Left Movement.[28] This office became the Public Security Directorate (DISPI) on April 30, 1993, the first formalized civilian-led national intelligence agency of the post-Pinochet era.

DISPI, unlike its predecessors, lacked operational capabilities; instead, it was tasked with an analytical mission set. DISPI functioned under the Ministry of Interior, and it was predominantly staffed with analysts from the ruling *Concertación* coalition, determined to diminish the intelligence services' powers.[29] Still, DISPI was incapable of reducing military and national police intelligence agencies' prerogatives, and they continued to operate with scant oversight from the executive and ministerial levels. The new civilian-government lacked the requisite political capital to counter this pushback from the armed forces and associated intelligence agencies.[30] Only those reforms that did not directly relinquish military prerogatives to a powerful, civilian-led national intelligence agency were palatable to senior leaders within the armed forces. As these agencies harbored ex-DINA/CNI personnel, old Pinochet-era practices continued after the transition to democracy.[31] As such, military intelligence reform in Chile stagnated for over a decade following the Pinochet dictatorship.

Then the terrorist attacks of September 11, 2001, in the United States effected a shift in national security objectives throughout the world, including Chile.[32] In October of the same year, the Chilean congress began conducting comprehensive conversations and debates regarding the creation of a new national intelligence organization under, somehow, a more muscular civilian oversight. Importantly, the political initiative also had the backing of the armed forces, with the expectation that a new centralized intelligence agency could improve collection and coordination in combatting terrorist threats against Chilean interests.[33]

After three years of debate, the Chilean congress approved via Law No. 19074 the creation of a new and more robust unified intelligence agency, the National Intelligence Agency (ANI) on October 5, 2004.[34] The current public law governing Chile's intelligence system is encapsulated in the 2004 Law No. 19974.[35] This law established the state's intelligence system and organization structure of the ANI, the congressional document focused on codifying the rules, intelligence reform, objectives, and Chilean intelligence norms complicating democratic rule.

ANI's main functions comprise the following: provide relevant intelligence to the president and other governmental institutions, as determined by the president; safeguard critical information; request and obtain intelligence from the intelligence agencies within the armed forces, police, and other state institutions; produce intelligence related to terrorist groups and transnational crime; and counterintelligence.[36] Law No. 19974 does not attribute to ANI any operational capabilities, though; it only permits the agency to focus on analysis based on access to open sources information from the media, informants, and all the intelligence gathered by other security agencies.[37] If the agency cannot acquire national security–related information via open sources, ANI can engage in several kinds of intrusive activities, including the following: (1) the interception of telephone, computer, radio communications, and correspondence; (2) conducting systems and networks surveillance operations; (3) conducting wiretapping and video recording; and (4) using other technological systems for the transmission, storage, communication, or processing of information.[38]

Law No. 19974 stipulates that ANI personnel are entirely civilian, with educational and experience requirements falling upon a spectrum from highly educated and technical skills to basic high school education.[39] Law No. 19974 additionally mandates that the entire ANI is limited to ninety-eight employees.[40] The relative small size of the organization and no method to expand staffing levels is a concern, given that Chile's population has grown from 16 million in 2004 to over 18 million in 2019 according to the World Bank's population analysis.[41] To compound this problem, the intelligence services of the *Carabineros* and the Armed Forces' military intelligence institutions' manpower are not restricted by Law No. 19974—which creates a drastic staffing disparity between the small civilian intelligence service and the uniformed services, providing military intelligence disproportionate influence and undermines democratic intelligence reform.[42] Matei and de Castro explain that five hundred personnel are assigned to intelligence tasks between the *Carabineros* and civilian police intelligence units.[43] This figure is over five times the number of ANI personnel. Each branch of the armed forces possesses a separate intelligence agency—leading to what Gregory Weeks proposes, a potential competition with one another for resources.[44] This dichotomy between civilian and military intelligence carries through to how recruitment is handled for intelligence within Chile.[45]

Law No. 19974 stipulates that ANI must compete for public funds as any other governmental agency.[46] Appropriated ANI funds must be utilized in accordance with pre-established laws detailing the financial limitations placed upon the executive branch.[47] Chile's 2018 directorate of the budget released a detailed national budget that elucidated the use of public funds for ANI operations.[48] The budget also itemized specific personnel activities, goods and services, as well as asset acquisition expenditures totaling $6 billion Chilean pesos.[49] While the director of ANI is required to account for public funds, no data is publicly released to account for classified funds, other than a yearly report by the director to congress.[50] In addition, while the *Contraloría General de la República,* an official institution (autonomous from the executive branch and other public bodies)[51] that has the authority to verify the legality of the activities of state agencies, can check the legality of ANI's hiring process, and its spending, it cannot exercise any oversight over ANI's special funds, which the agency uses to pay informants and for classified operations.[52] According to Matei and de Castro, "Only the ANI Director, who knows the funding allocation, can assure the Contraloría of the lack of budgetary illegalities."[53] Such lack of fiscal transparency, arguably, permits corruption and misappropriation of funds.[54]

Law No. 19974 also details military intelligence as a role specific to the armed forces, thereby necessitating Chilean forces to not be funded solely through the public budgetary process—hence, military intelligence funding does not proceed through a public budgetary process.[55] The so-called "Copper Law," as noted by Matei and Robledo, has directly funded the Chilean armed forces without the need to petition the national legislature, and their constituents, for the right to utilize the funds.[56]

Consuelo Ferrer of *El Mercurio,* one of the largest newspapers in Chile, noted that two Chilean army chiefs of staff were charged with embezzlement for using public funds and funneling them to the retirement coffers of several generals within the Armed Forces.[57] In terms of actual intelligence scandals related to the use of secret funds, Matei and de Castro note a 2015 case, where Chile was accused of paying two Peruvian military informants.[58] While ANI lacks any operational capabilities, the agency can engage in several forms of intrusive intelligence gathering to acquire information when open source methods are unavailable.[59] Yet whether this can be considered an abuse of secret intelligence funds is debatable, especially given that Law No. 19974 gives the military authority to set its own security objectives. Lack of a uni-fied intelligence construct and ability to dictate funding and oversight of legal authorities has hindered intelligence reform advancement.

Additionally, Law No. 19974 delineates and codifies intelligence over-sight. Within the law, Article 37 states that the Chamber of Deputies, the lower house of Chile's bicameral Congress, has the right to request and be provided information from all organizations comprising Chile's national intelligence system.[60] Equally important, Article 39 states that the preceding articles do not prevent Chile's Senate, Chamber of Deputies, or other govern-mental bodies from requesting additional background information on intel-ligence activities, though it does require that requested information be routed through the minister of the interior, the minister of defense, or the director of the National Intelligence Agency, depending on what section of the intel-ligence system is being examined.[61]

Law No. 19974 established a committee within the Chilean Chamber of Deputies that has oversight over the various organizations that make up Chile's intelligence apparatus.[62] Additionally, the law requires the director of ANI to provide an annual report to the committee on the activities of the na-tional intelligence system.[63] This stipulation was further strengthened in 2015 in the only passed reform to Law No. 19974, which detailed the scope of the director's report more thoroughly.[64] Furthermore, the director's report was not limited to unclassified information. The revision to Law No. 19974 estab-lished the requisite structure for the intelligence committee to hold meetings in secure locations, allowing discussion of classified intelligence activities. This reform eliminated one of the easiest methods of intelligence agencies to shirk oversight, which has been the requirement of secrecy for many intel-ligence activities. Yet, a principal problem with Law No. 19974 is that the law does not go into detail regarding the establishment of specific timelines that the various intelligence agencies must answer congressional inquiries. The intelligence community has excessively delayed requested information to circumvent external oversight.

Law No. 19974 of 2004 also provides for judicial review of intelligence activities. In this connection, intelligence agencies must obtain authorization from judges for special collection activities.[65] ANI can only conduct wiretap-ping and video surveillance after receiving approval from a minister within the Court of Appeal. The military and police intelligence agencies can en-gage in such operations like running undercover agents and informants upon authorization granted only by their respective leadership, unfortunately not requiring prior judicial authorization.[66]

The comprehensive intelligence law discusses not only the control mecha-nisms and oversight of the intelligence system but also its use of public funds.

However, intelligence reform has been slow since 2004. In 2019, Chile's Congress initiated the much needed and monumental process of significantly revising the existing intelligence legislation, the first major intelligence reformation since the passing of the original Law No. 19974 in 2004.[67]

In this connection, Bill No. 12234-02, titled Fortify and Modernize the National Intelligence System, improves the organization and functioning of the intelligence system.[68] This bill, if passed, has the potential to improve the resourcing, integration, strategic vision, and culture of Chile's intelligence system.[69] In line with the bill, ANI will become the de facto lead agency, while other intelligence agencies will gradually lose power and be subordinate to the government.

One of the proposed law's critical goals appears to be integrating and unifying the disparate intelligence agencies within Chile's current stove-piped system. Additionally, the new bill seeks to add an intelligence advisory board to integrate and unify efforts of the various intelligence agencies that make up the Chilean intelligence system.[70] As noted earlier, a central problem within the Chilean intelligence system is the lack of cohesive efforts between its various entities, as well as independent funding sources and lack of concerted resource allocation. The proposed law seeks to change a majority of these issues. The new advisory board would be the primary linkage and impartial intermediate between Chile's president and the intelligence system.[71] Furthermore, reforms incorporating non-military-related intelligence services such as the *Carabineros* and Customs formally into Chile's national intelligence system and providing the directors of these organizations seats on the intelligence advisory board are on the agenda. However, refining the composition of national intelligence architecture is only part of the proposed law.

Simply incorporating formerly separate organizations into the intelligence system would be insufficient. Rather, developing a legal framework and culture of unifying all Chilean intelligence efforts with strategic resourcing is essential. The proposed law also seeks to change this current weakness by tasking the Chilean Financial Analysis Unit and the Internal Revenue Service with strategic intelligence analysis, and providing neutral examination to lawmakers and senior leaders to project for long-range strategic intelligence needs.[72] The proposed law would also create a Strategic National Intelligence document that would outline Chile's national intelligence strategic objectives quadrennially.[73] This document would be written by the director of ANI, with the assistance of the ministers of Public Security, Interior, and Defense.[74] These reforms demonstrate an earnest commitment to long-range strategic planning, signaled by this law requiring the various ministries to cooperate and with greater transparency achieve national security objectives. Yet strategic planning and increased integration, are not the only deficiencies that the proposed law tackles.

The seminal goal the law seeks to address is expanded power and influence of ANI over the separate military and civilian intelligence agencies.[75] The proposed law has several concrete measures to increase the effectiveness of ANI, such as institutional metrics to establish an ANI subdirector who would decrease the ANI director's administrative burden and also provide an additional person within the hierarchy to handle administrative functions.[76] Additionally, ANI would be charged with developing standardized plans and programs that would strengthen all branches' intelligence training and mature ANI's intelligence professionals to better integrate with Chile's other intelligence organizations. Equally important, ANI's ability to request and obtain information from other intelligence communities would be strengthened under the new law, legally compelling greater cooperation between the disparate Chilean intelligence agencies. Yet, increasing the effectiveness of intelligence is not the sole aim of these legal reforms; ANI will become the focal Chilean intelligence agency to which all other intelligence agencies will directly report and be held accountable.

The proposed law also seeks to increase the legislative oversight on the various components of Chile's intelligence system, particularly ANI given its new prominence. The new law would significantly increase the power of the Chamber of Deputies' oversight committee by requiring more frequent reports and justifications for expenditures from ANI's director, as well as establishing more closed-door classified briefings by ANI's director to the oversight committee.[77]

Overall, the new law appears to provide the most comprehensive reform of Chilean intelligence since 2004 by significantly increasing the cohesiveness and effectiveness of the rest of Chile's various intelligence systems and increasing democratic intelligence oversight—unfortunately the law does not heavily impinge on the prerogatives of military intelligence. Nevertheless, at the time of the writing of this chapter (August 2021), the Chilean Congress has not yet approved the bill.[78]

ANALYSIS

The preceding discussion reveals that Chile has made important progress in democratizing its intelligence agencies. Nevertheless, it has yet to achieve an acceptable tradeoff between transparency and the effectiveness of the post-Pinochet intelligence services, due to a host of interconnected challenges, many of them emerging from the legacy of the past. Indeed, according to Matei and de Castro, "Chile's military intelligence still bears the stigma derived from the long period of dictatorship . . . [d]elinking the actual need for intelligence from that dismal period of Chile's history has been difficult.

That factor has also affected and delayed the creation and development of an intelligence culture that allows training professionals in several areas of interest."[79] As a result, democratic civilian control remains underdeveloped, while the agencies' capabilities to combat threats are limited.

Control and Oversight

Control over the intelligence agencies has involved devising a legal framework for intelligence, creating civilian-led agencies, and developing such formal oversight mechanisms as the Intelligence Oversight Committee and judicial bodies. The limited involvement of the civilian intelligence agencies in direction and guidance vis-à-vis intelligence priorities coupled with the relatively limited power of oversight bodies over the armed forces have resulted in perfunctory oversight. In other words, as Matei and de Castro point out, "Chilean policymakers . . . tend to ignore the reality that creating security institutions . . . involves, among other actions, devising a strategic plan, then developing political capital, and authorizing human and financial resources."[80] As a result, oversight has rather been reactive, responding largely to media "fire alarms" about various scandals or intelligence failures.[81]

Informal oversight by the civil society and the media has also been lackadaisical. Chile's civil society, despite its robustness regarding social and economic issues, currently lacks a vigorous intelligence community accountability reform movement—a consequence of the transition to democracy. As Juan Linz and Alfred Stepan conclude, throughout Pinochet's reign, he retained the support of influential national power brokers, leading to the authoritarian government retaining a strong position as the regime transitioned away from power.[82] They further noted that the military's strong civil society support core was predicated on a reciprocal relationship; the military maintained social order in return for allowing the military's supporters a freer hand to control the economic progress of the country that benefited the majority of the citizens.[83] This viewpoint, preservation of social order being paramount, continues to this day. A 2016 study by *Latinobarometro* found that 51 percent of Chileans valued preserving social order at all costs, while 45 percent of Chileans viewed the preservation of individual rights to be more important.[84] Understanding Chile's military, elite class, and citizens' demand for a social order paradigm partially explains the lack of domestic pressures to reform intelligence collection and helps explain why until only recently, Chile has not witnessed a major intelligence reformation.

Professionalism and Effectiveness

Recruitment is based on Law No. 19974, which designates strict legal re-quirements and discriminators for each ANI level and rank. Requisites range from high school education to master's level degrees.[85] Additionally, Article 16 states that promotions will follow authorized guidelines detailed in other regulations related to intelligence.[86] Unfortunately, there are several prob-lems related to how Chilean intelligence recruitment is conducted. Primar-ily recruitment parameters are established through Law No. 19974, and as previously noted, no significant revision occurred until 2019. Thus, in the intervening decades there had been little adaptation and change within ANI to ensure that recruitment was meeting national intelligence objectives and requirements. Matei and de Castro note that the military's personnel organi-zation in fact had not seen revision until 2010.[87] The lack of coherency with regard to hiring practices within the military and civilian Chilean intelligence system creates an uneven structure that, when combined with the static nature of Chilean law, infuse a rigidity and opaqueness to Chilean intelligence that hinders meaningful intelligence reform and efficacy.

Unlike the codified rules detailed in Law No. 19974 pertaining to Chilean civilian intelligence recruitment, currently no law defines ANI personnel training requirements, particularly in respecting citizens' freedoms includ-ing but not limited to freedom of expression, movement, and association. This training deficiency may be due to the robust legal protections already guaranteed by Chile's 1980 constitution with regard to the aforementioned freedoms.[88] However, there is one potential conflict in Chile's constitutional freedom of association. Chile's constitution prohibits associations that are contrary to national security and moral public order.[89] This stipulation is especially concerning given that both DINA and CNI had targeted specific groups of individuals who were deemed subversive as discussed by Matei and de Castro.[90]

Enhanced rights-of-association training could serve to place stricter bound-aries on lawful interpretation of this difficult concept and create a balance of effective intelligence execution and protecting citizens' rights. Currently, publicly available information pertaining to Chile's intelligence agencies' methodology of freedom of association training is unavailable. Addition-ally, training problems are compounded by Chilean military and civilian intelligence services not receiving standardized training, nor do the separate agencies train collaboratively. Furthermore, as Matei and de Castro assert, military intelligence services continue to not perceive ANI personnel as being true intelligence professionals due to the latter not having trained at the same institutions as the former.[91] This organizational disconnect places significant barriers in the cross-institutional relationships between the various Chilean intelligence agencies. Avendaño Rojas discusses how the lack of joint training with the military intelligence services has negatively impacted ANI's ability to create an operational mission set.[92] The continued opaqueness of intelligence training, as well as the lack of a cross-institutional collaborative framework, will continue to negatively impact Chile's intelligence systems transparency and effectiveness.

As with civil liberties, the Chilean government relies on laws other than Law No. 19974 to delineate intelligence information declassification. Law No. 19974 exclusively mandates the need to guard classified information, as well as defining the potential penalties for violating protection of classified information.[93] In 2008 Law No. 20285 was ratified by the executive branch, which specifically handles the process of releasing information about government activities to the public. Typically, any agency has five years to declassify an information request commenced by citizens or legislature, though a five-year extension may be granted to evaluate the damage declassification could cause.[94] However, there are unique circumstances and areas that prevent specific information from ever being declassified, particularly regarding national security concerns: information that could compromise the territorial integrity of Chile, gravely damage Chile's international relationships, and threaten Chile's international rights.[95] Nevertheless, these declassification restrictions are still a positive departure from the previous military dictatorship regime. During the Pinochet era, the very concept of declassification was nearly unheard of and rarely occurred. The culture shift within the Chilean intelligence legislation regarding declassification rules can also be seen in the aforementioned Peruvian military intelligence scandal.[96] The Chilean intelligence collection activity was externally oriented and involved the bribing of Peruvian military members to provide information related to external threats to Chile's security, in sharp contrast to the hallmark tactics of the Pinochet regime's propensity to torture or blackmail in return for information on critics of the regime. Additionally, the Peru scandal demonstrated a departure from DINA/CNI's traditionally internally focused intelligence operations to a more external aligned focus.[97] The listed cultural shifts in information collection and declassification exhibit Chile's intelligence system commitment to greater accountability.

CONCLUSION

The story of Chilean intelligence culture in the democratic era has been one of slowly reforging a national intelligence system in the wake of the deleterious Pinochet era. For fourteen years from the fall of Pinochet to the passage of Law No. 19974, Chile's intelligence apparatus underwent a complete balkanization. The passage of 19974 and the current bill under congressional discussion has made significant strides to reintegrate the disparate parts of the Chilean intelligence apparatus. Yet while, progress has been made in creating an effective and democratically controlled intelligence system, Chile has yet to achieve a deeper integration of the nation's various military intelligence agencies under the civilian-led ANI and reshaping its use of intelligence for internal security in addition to its external focus. Matei and de Castro's conclusion in 2016 is, therefore, still valid.

> Chile is thus an intriguingly paradoxical case of 'intelligence and democracy,' whereby the country has achieved democratic consolidation, particularly in terms of free and fair elections, political pluralism, a free market economy, and even civil–military relations, yet without much progress in democratizing intelligence. The improvement of transparency, accountability, and civilian political control of intelligence is still a work in progress. Nevertheless, the intelligence agencies are now considerably distanced from the Pinochet-era's ruthlessly abusive services, and this accomplishment is worth noting.[98]

NOTES

1. Tanya Harmer, "Fractious Allies: Chile, the United States the Cold War, 1973–1976," *Diplomatic History* 37, no. 1 (January 2013): 109.

2. Graham Hovey, "Nixon Saw Cuba and Chile Enclosing Latin America," *New York Times*, May 26, 1977, https://www.nytimes.com/1977/05/26/archives/nixon-saw-cuba-and-chile-enclosing-latin-america.html.

3. Juan J. Linz and Alfred Stepan, *Problems of Democratic Transition and Consolidation: Southern Europe, South America, and Post-Communist Europe* (Baltimore: The Johns Hopkins University Press, 1996); Thomas C. Bruneau and Florina Cristiana Matei, *The Routledge Handbook of Civil-Military Relations* (New York: Routledge, 2013).

4. Pamela Constable and Arturo Valenzuela, *A Nation of Enemies: Chile under Pinochet* (New York: W. W. Norton Company, 1991), 46.

5. Pablo Policzer, *Rise and Fall of Repression in Chile* (Notre Dame, IN: University of Norte Dame Press, 2009), 42.

6. United States Central Intelligence Agency, *Consequences of a Military Coup in Chile* (1973), 2.

7. Tito Drago, *Chile: Un Doble Secuestro* (Spain: Universidad Complutense, 1993), 124.

8. Tanya Harmer, "Fractious Allies: Chile, the United States the Cold War, 1973–1976," 117.

9. Davis Airgram, *The Military Junta at One Month* (Washington, DC: Department of State, October 12, 1973).

10. Tanya Harmer, "Fractious Allies: Chile, the United States the Cold War, 1973–1976," 112 and 141.

11. Via a decree that created the National Prisoners Service (SENDET). "Manuel Contreras and the Birth of DINA," Latin American Studies.org. Available at http://www.latinamericanstudies.org/chile/DINA-birth.htm.

12. Florina Cristiana Matei and Andrés de Castro García, "Chilean Intelligence after Pinochet: Painstaking Reform of an Inauspicious Legacy," *International Journal of Intelligence and CounterIntelligence* 30, no. 2 (2017): 342.

13. Even if Chile had a long tradition of military-dominated intelligence apparatuses with limited civilian oversight since the establishment of the army's intelligence service in 1891, following Pinochet's seizure of the country, the intelligence community's role with civilian repression and detention leapt to unprecedented levels of brutality in order to quell any opposition or threats to the military junta's rule. Gregory Weeks, "A Preference for Deference: Reforming the Military's Intelligence Role in Argentina, Chile, and Peru," *Third World Quarterly* 29, no. 1 (2008): 50; Saul Landau and John Dinges, *Assassination in Embassy Row* (New York: Pantheon Books, 1980), 4.

14. Landau and Dinges, *Assassination in Embassy Row*, 3.

15. Policzer, *Rise and Fall of Repression in Chile*, 58.

16. Peter Kornbluh, *The Pinochet File: A Declassified Dossier on Atrocity and Accountability* (New York: The New Press, 2013), 174.

17. Carlos Huneeus, *El Régimen de Pinochet* (Santiago, Chile: Editorial Sudamericana, 2000), 101–3, 103–8, and 160–65.

18. Policzer, *Rise and Fall of Repression in Chile*, 112.

19. DINA's officers were in charge of more than one thousand clandestine detention centers, where real and imaginary enemies of the regime were tortured, via electric shocks, waterboarding, beatings, and sexual abuse. The prisoners that the regime considered as the most subversive were "disappeared" by the regime, meaning they were not going to be seen again. Matei and de Castro García, "Chilean Intelligence after Pinochet Government of Chile." "Rettig Report. Report of the Chilean National Commission on Truth and Reconciliation," available at http://www.gob.cl/infor merettig/. In this connection, journalists from the *Hindustan Times* note, "Contreras supervised the apprehension of thousands of suspected leftists after the coup as Santiago's national soccer stadium was transformed into a detention center where hundreds were held and tortured. About 150 bodies, many of them weighed down by sections of railroad track, were thrown from helicopters into the ocean and lakes, the military has acknowledged." "Chile's Feared Secret Police Chief Dies at Age 86," *Hindustan Times,* August 8, 2015. Available at https://www.hindustantimes.com/world/chile-s-feared-secret-police-chief-dies-at-age-86/story-8v89kXGfAbQnruNnCOrP8K.html.

20. J. Patrice McSherry, "Tracking the Origins of a State Terror Network: Operation Condor," *Latin American Perspectives*, 29, no. 1 (January 2002): 54.

21. Policzer, *Rise and Fall of Repression in Chile*, 13.

22. Ultimately, amid accusations of the regime's egregious human rights abuses toward the end of the military rule, the relationship between Contreras and Pinochet waned, as each started to blame the other for corruption and human rights abuses. In this connection, the *Hindustan Times* journalists explain, "While Contreras alleged his former boss amassed a fortune trafficking drugs to Europe, Pinochet accused the spy chief of acting without his consent and committing the era's worst abuses." "Chile's Feared Secret Police Chief Dies at Age 86."

23. Matei and de Castro García, "Chilean Intelligence after Pinochet."

24. Some of the bodies of the disappeared are yet to be found. Government of Chile, "Rettig Report" "Chile Recognises 9,800 More Victims of Pinochet's Rule," BBC News, August 18, 2011. Available at https://www.bbc.com/news/world-latin-america-14584095.

25. Chile began its transition to democracy in 1988 when a coalition of the main parties that opposed the Pinochet regime—the Christian Democrats, Socialists, Radicals, and the Party for Democracy, known as the *Concertación* de Partidos Por la Democracia, or simply Concertación—won a constitutionally authorized plebiscite on whether Pinochet should continue to be president for another eight years. Matei and de Castro García, "Chilean Intelligence after Pinochet." Marcos Robledo, "Democratic Consolidation in Chilean Civil-Military Relations: 1990–2005," in *Global Politics of Defense Reform*, eds. Thomas C. Bruneau and Harold A. Trinkunas (New York: Palgrave MacMillian, 2008); Bruneau and Matei, *The Routledge Handbook of Civil-Military Relations*.

26. Matei and de Castro García, "Chilean Intelligence after Pinochet."

27. Paul Hathazy, "Crafting Public Security: Demilitarization, Penal State Reform and Security Policy-Making in Postauthoritarian Chile," *Global Crime* 19, no. 3–4 (2018): 270.

28. Paul Hathazy, "Crafting Public Security," 270.

29. Rodrigo Vera Lama, *Sistema de Inteligencia del Estado a la luz del Derecho* (Santiago, Chile: Librotecnia, 2008), 201. Matei and de Castro, "Chilean Intelligence after Pinochet."

30. Vera Lama, *Sistema de Inteligencia del Estado a la luz del Derecho*, 201; and Matei and de Castro, "Chilean Intelligence after Pinochet."

31. For instance, in 1992, the military intelligence service spied on various center-right party members, and when a civilian judge designated to conduct the investigation into why the armed forces carried out such invasive acts, the armed forces closed the case. Kevin Ginter, "Latin American Intelligence Services and the Transition to Democracy," *Journal of Intelligence History* 8, no. 1 (2008): 69–93. The hard work of several human rights committees established after Chile's transition to democracy made possible the apprehension of many DINA/CNI officers responsible for the disappearances. These bodies were the National Commission on Truth and Reconciliation 1990–1991 (known as the Rettig Commission) and the National Commission on Political Imprisonment and Torture (known as the Valech Commission; Valech I, 2004–2005, and Valech II, 2011). Matei and de Castro, "Chilean Intelligence after Pinochet"; Robledo, "Democratic Consolidation in Chilean Civil-Military Relations";

Bruneau and Matei, *The Routledge Handbook of Civil–Military Relations*. Another example of abuse occurred in 1992, when a retired Navy officer, Humberto Palamara, attempted to publish a book, and the navy seized all the copies and put him on trial. When appealed to the InterAmerican Court of Human Rights, the court acted in his favor. Indeed, in 2006, the court ruled that Chile had violated Palamara's rights, because, as Russell Swenson and Carolina Sancho Hirane argue, the navy "applied prior restraint, having violated the guarantee of due process upon illegitimately subjecting Palamara to military jurisdiction, and having violated the right to private property by denying him the use and enjoyment of his intellectual creation. Beyond paying compensation and allowing the publication of the confiscated book, Chile had to bring its military justice up to international standards." Russell Swenson and Carolina Sancho. *Intelligence Management in the Americas* (Washington, DC: National Intelligence University, 2015), 98.

32. André Gómez de la Torre Rotta, "Servicios de Inteligencia y Democracia en América del Sur: Hacia una Segunda Generación de Reformas Normativas?," *Agenda International* 16, (2009): 119–30.

33. Weeks, "The Military and Intelligence Reform in Chile," 260. The rationale behind the armed forces' support for such an agency was the terrorist attacks in the United States on September 11, 2001. Matei and de Castro, "Chilean Intelligence after Pinochet."

34. ANI is the primary national intelligence organization, with congressionally mandated authority over the intelligence agencies of the armed forces and the national police, though civilian oversight continues to be a difficult challenge for the government to implement, as it would threaten existing prerogatives of the armed forces.

35. On the State Intelligence System and the Creation of the National Intelligence Agency, Law No. 19.974, 2004, trans. John Oeffinger, http://web.uchile.cl/archivos/derecho/CEDI/Normativa/Ley%2019.974%20Sobre%20el%20Sistema%20de%20Inteligencia%20del%20Estado%20y%20Crea%20la%20Agencia%20Nacional%20de%20Inteligencia.pdf.

36. On the State Intelligence System, Article 47.

37. On the State Intelligence System, Article 47; Matei and de Castro, "Chilean Intelligence after Pinochet."

38. On the State Intelligence System, Article 47.

39. On the State Intelligence System, Article 14.

40. On the State Intelligence System, Article 15.

41. "Population Total—Chile," *World Bank*, June 18, 2019, https://data.worldbank.org/indicator/SP.POP.TOTL?locations=CL&most_recent_year_desc=false.

42. On the State Intelligence System, Article 17.

43. Matei and de Castro, "Chilean Intelligence after Pinochet," 349.

44. Weeks, "A Preference for Deference," 50.

45. ANI viewed as a second-tier intelligence organization by the Military. Matei and de Castro, "Chilean Intelligence after Pinochet."

46. On the State Intelligence System, Article 20.

47. On the State Intelligence System, Article 19.

48. 2018 Public sector Annual Budget, Law No. 21.053, 2017, trans. John Oeffinger, http://www.dipres.gob.cl/597/articles-172496_doc_pdf.pdf, 79.

49. 2018 Public Sector Annual Budget, 79.

50. On the State Intelligence System, Article 37.

51. Similar to the Government Accountability Office (GAO) in the United States and the Courts of Audits in Europe; Matei and de Castro, "Chilean Intelligence after Pinochet."

52. Matei and de Castro, "Chilean Intelligence after Pinochet."

53. Matei and de Castro, "Chilean Intelligence after Pinochet."

54. However, there have been no reported cases of significant financial embezzlement or abuse of secret funds within ANI. Consuelo Ferrer, "Amounts, Use and Embezzlement: What Is the Debate about Expenses Used in the Rest of the World," *Emol Nacional*, July 6, 2019, trans. John Oeffinger, https://www.emol.com/noticias/Nacional/2019/07/06/953626/Montos-uso-y-presunta-malversacion-En-que-esta-el-debate-sobre-los-gastos-reservados-en-el-resto-del-mundo.html.

55. On the State Intelligence System, Article 20.

56. Florina Cristiana Matei and Marcos Robledo, "Democratic Civilian Control and Military Effectiveness: Chile," in *The Routledge Handbook of Civil-Military Relations*, ed. Thomas C. Bruneau and Florina Cristiana Matei (New York: Routledge, 2013), 288. However, in 2019 the Copper Law was abolished, which diminished the funds for modernization. "Chile Abolishes Law Requiring State-Run Copper Miner to Finance Military," *VOA*, July 24, 2019. Available at https://www.voanews.com/americas/chile-abolishes-law-requiring-state-run-copper-miner-finance-military.

57. Consuelo Ferrer, "Amounts, Use and Embezzlement."

58. Matei and de Castro, "Chilean Intelligence after Pinochet," 351.

59. Matei and de Castro, "Chilean Intelligence after Pinochet," 351.

60. On the State Intelligence System, Article 37.

61. On the State Intelligence System, Article 39.

62. On the State Intelligence System, Article 37.

63. On the State Intelligence System, Article 37.

64. In 2015 the first and only revision of law 19974 occurred; the director of intelligence is compelled to provide the Chamber of Deputies an annual report. Modification of Law No. 19.974, Bill 10029-02, trans. John Oeffinger, 363rd Congress, 19th sess, trans. John Oeffinger, 287, https://www.camara.cl/pley/pley_detalle.aspx?prmID=10451&prmBL=10029-02.

65. Matei and de Castro, "Chilean Intelligence after Pinochet."

66. Matei and de Castro, "Chilean Intelligence after Pinochet."

67. Fortify and Modernize the National Intelligence System, Section I, http://www.senado.cl/appsenado/templates/tramitacion/index.php?boletin_ini=12234-02.

68. Fortify and Modernize the National Intelligence System, Section II.

69. The bill was already approved unanimously by the Senate. Shirley Bernd, "Senado aprueba proyecto que moderniza el Sistema de Inteligencia del Estado," *EMOL*, January 23, 2020. Available at https://www.emol.com/noticias/Nacional/2020/01/23/974350/Senado-aprueba-proyecto-inteligencia-Estado.html.

70. Fortify and Modernize the National Intelligence System, Section III.

71. Fortify and Modernize the National Intelligence System, Section III.

72. Fortify and Modernize the National Intelligence System, Section III.

73. Fortify and Modernize the National Intelligence System, Section III.

74. Fortify and Modernize the National Intelligence System, Section III.

75. Fortify and Modernize the National Intelligence System, Section III.

76. Fortify and Modernize the National Intelligence System, Section III.

77. Fortify and Modernize the National Intelligence System, Article 1.

78. Boletín 12234-02, "Fortalece y moderniza el sistema de inteligencia del Estado," https://www.senado.cl/appsenado/templates/tramitacion/index.php?boletin _ini=12234-02.

79. Matei and de Castro, "Chilean Intelligence after Pinochet."

80. Matei and de Castro, "Chilean Intelligence after Pinochet."

81. Matei and de Castro, "Chilean Intelligence after Pinochet."

82. Juan J. Linz and Alfred Stepan, *Problems of Democratic Transition and Consolidation: Southern Europe, South America, and Post-Communist Europe* (Baltimore, MD: Johns Hopkins University Press, 1996), loc. 3777 of 1417, Kindle.

83. Linz and Stepan, *Problems of Democratic Transition and Consolidation.*

84. Latinobarómetro Corporation, *Informe 2016,* trans. John Oeffinger (Santiago, Chile: Latinobarómetro, 2016), http://www.latinobarometro.org/latContents.jsp.

85. On the State Intelligence System, Article 20.

86. On the State Intelligence System, Article 16.

87. Matei and de Castro, "Chilean Intelligence after Pinochet," 351.

88. Chilean Constitution, trans. John Oeffinger, Article 15, https://www.camara.cl/ camara/media/docs/constitucion_politica.pdf.

89. Chilean Constitution, trans. John Oeffinger, Article 15, https://www.camara.cl/ camara/media/docs/constitucion_politica.pdf.

90. Matei and de Castro, "Chilean Intelligence after Pinochet," 343.

91. Matei and de Castro, "Chilean Intelligence after Pinochet," 354.

92. Andrés Avendaño Rojas, "El Sistema de Inteligencia del Estado de Chile, La Producción de Inteligencia Estratégica y Otros Asuntos Relaciones," *Centro De Investigaciones y Estudios Estratégicos,* trans. John Oeffinger, no. 2 (March 2018): 10.

93. On the State Intelligence System, Article 44.

94. About the Public Access of Information, Law No. 20285, 2008, trans. John Oeffinger, Article 22, https://www.leychile.clN?27363&f=2016-01-05&p=.

95. About the Public Access of Information.

96. Matei and de Castro, "Chilean Intelligence after Pinochet," 351.

97. Matei and de Castro, "Chilean Intelligence after Pinochet," 352.

98. Matei and de Castro, "Chilean Intelligence after Pinochet."

Chapter Seven

Ecuador

Fredy Rivera Vélez and Renato Rivera Rhon

Political intelligence, a characterizing feature of Ecuadorean intelligence, was executed by military entities generally at the operational level by groups directly attached to the Ministry of Government or the National Police, whose mission was to infiltrate social movements, opposition political parties, labor unions, trade unions, or other perceived internal security threats. This institutionalized abuse against Ecuadorian citizens has fostered a stubborn legacy of abuse, corruption, and social scars that have been endemic for more than fifty years.[1]

Despite persistent attempts to modernize and reform the intelligence sector, including the 2009 legislation that established the National Intelligence Secretariat (SENAIN), Ecuador remains unable to implement democratic intelligence institutions subordinate and accountable to elected civilian authorities—founded on the balance among the executive, legislative, and judicial powers of the state—exerting an equilibrium of control while optimizing intelligence effectiveness.[2] Until 2020, intelligence service reforms were cosmetic political platitudes that did not foundationally consolidate the institution in terms of organic modernization, professionalism, and technological advancement.

This chapter provides an assessment of the legal, political, and doctrinal changes that have occurred within the Ecuadorian national intelligence system from 1960 to 2020. Specifically, the following reform-related issues are evaluated: the role of the military and the National Security Doctrine, the role of armed forces in the modernization and development of the country, the transformation of security and intelligence services during the democratic transition, and the new paradigm after 2009. The chapter concludes that Ecuadorean intelligence prerogatives have impeded the establishment of

structural reform and effective democratic modernization based on legislative controls, the thorough supervision of expenditures and allocated funds,
the integration of the media and civil society, and the existence of medium-
and long-term national plans with clear objectives that encompass national
and regional realities. Additionally, without doctrinal changes, military and
political intelligence has further resisted reform under the guise of national
security while cultivating the political influence that dominated the sector for
more than five decades.

BACKGROUND ON THE NON-DEMOCRATIC
REGIME AND THE ROLE OF INTELLIGENCE

Peru's invasion of Ecuadorean territory in 1941, the ensuing war, and the consequences of defeat stated in the terms of the Rio de Janeiro Protocol of 1942
in which Ecuador was forced to accept its military defeat and transfer 240,000
square kilometers of its territory to Peru, created the confluence of factors that
formed the identity of military intelligence and doctrine of national security
in Ecuador until the late 1990s. During this period, the notion of the "open
wound" was held as the permanent discursive principle in safeguarding territorial defense and national sovereignty and relegated all other social issues to
the periphery, providing the armed forces carte blanche authority. This power
continued throughout the next decades.

Between 1960 and 1979, the armed forces had a preponderant role in
developing national security doctrine and associated intelligence services.
Throughout two decades of operation, Ecuadorian intelligence agencies
and security institutions did not experience profound institutional and legal
changes, so they continued to exercise their prerogatives behind the scenes.[3]

The intelligence system incorporated the military notions of maintaining
external and internal defense.[4] First, the apparatus proceeded on the permanent hypothesis of a potential war with Peru. Second, at the internal defense
level, the concept of internal defense as a nationalist principle aimed at
combatting the threat of communism aligned with and complemented U.S.
national security doctrine, which extended across Latin America and the intelligence agencies in the region.

As a result of the increasing influence of communism in Latin America under the ideological tutelage of the 1959 Cuban Revolution, plus the security
risk represented by guerrilla insurgencies in several Latin American countries, the United States advanced a security policy incorporating diplomatic,
military, and economic levers to contain the regional spread of communism.
The economic and diplomatic strategy called "Alliance for Progress" aimed

to promote development, representative democracy, and the improvement of civil institutions through economic assistance programs worth over $20 billion in equivalent contemporary dollars.[5] In addition to isolating Cuba from this Hemispheric Plan, the strategy solidified the hegemony of U.S. regional objectives in the promotion of democracy, peace, capitalistic economic system, and institutional development.

The second strategic prong defined the characteristics of the National Security Doctrine (DSN): legitimization of military intervention, the adaptation of armed forces doctrine from an emphasis of large-scale conflict to anti-subversive activities, and a national intelligence apparatus aimed at reducing, neutralizing, or eliminating the capabilities of political dissidents of a socialist or communist inclination. This comprehensive blueprint was accompanied by the political support of the U.S. Embassy and the assistance of the U.S. Agency of International Development, charged with training and equipping police and military forces to counter the growth of the political left. In time this doctrine would become the impetus within Latin America to militarize the concept of security,[6] by harmonizing military functions intricately with the development of national institutions, social well-being, communications, and imbuement of popular support in the typical Ecuadorean nationalist.

The CIA's Ecuador operations in 1960 focused on "infiltrating the communist party, working with diplomatic officials, [and] supporting the propaganda efforts of the United States Information Agency," according to Becker.[7] This external dynamic altered the legal and organic structure; however, it did not fully inculcate and transform the basis of the intelligence organization's principles and doctrine.

The primary reason behind these developments was the armed forces' preponderant role in developing strategic intelligence policy, which excluded essential civilian government authorities from intelligence institutions, and security policies—further insulating from legislative accountability. The "National Security Doctrine" sponsored by the United States during the Cold War in Latin America constituted the protective umbrella of intelligence. In this sense, this section describes the military's role in shaping the discourse of Ecuadorian National Security Doctrine between 1960 and 1972, and it precipitated the implementation of modernization and development policies.

In 1960, President José María Velasco Ibarra (1960–1961) promulgated a law on national security that he dubbed the "Law of National Defense."[8] The law stipulated that the authority for national defense resides with the president of the Republic who had two advisory bodies: the Council for National Defense and the General Staff of the Armed Forces.[9] The Council for Defense housed the Directorate General for Information (DGI), a body that for a short time was responsible for national intelligence activity. The advisory bodies were controlled by military personnel responsible for centralizing security information and intelligence through the DGI, a subsection of the National Defense Council.

In 1963 the armed forces mounted a coup against President Carlos Julio Arosemena Monroy (1961–1963), a controversial president who established diplomatic relations with Cuba, abstained from voting for the expulsion of Cuba from the Organization of American States in 1961, and continued Velasco Ibarra's defense and oceanic preservation policy of seizing fishing boats—many of which were U.S. registered. These actions resulted in a military junta supported by the CIA that exercised power between 1963 and 1966.[10]

In 1964, the military junta, with legislative support, enacted the first Law of National Security, which links the concepts of the Doctrine of National Security and both external and internal defense under the same interpretive framework.[11] These reforms included the establishment of the Joint Armed Forces Command (COMACO), the National Security Council (COSENA), and the School of State Information. The intelligence activity carried out by the DGI was subordinate to the organic structure of the National Security Council, which was commanded by the armed forces.

In the following year (1965), Ecuador promoted agrarian reform, which combined the economic objectives of agricultural modernization with social objectives—colonization of vacant arable lands by the peasant population.[12] The junta also promoted new developmentalism[13] reforms—disillusioned with primary-exporter schemes—inspired by the Alliance for Progress to provide the country an overdue functioning national economic growth model.[14] Concurrently, the actions of military intelligence with the support of the junta and the CIA, prompted the formation of such anticommunist university groups as Ecuadorean Anti-Communist Action (AAE). This structural environment was conducive to the formation of several armed subversive groups with the goal of strengthening traditional parties like the Conservatives, who supported such offshoot organizations as the Social Christian Movement (MSC) and the Ecuador Nationalist Revolutionary Action (ARNE)—organizations that tacitly enforced the anticommunist government agenda but never received explicit directions or funding.[15] Moreover, the AAE and MSC worked closely with the CIA through operations that infiltrated communist groups and handled informants,[16] comprising the nucleus of the so-called *Pesquisas*, police officers linked to government structures who carried out intelligence operations.

Through establishing the preeminence of the armed forces with conducting national security activities and territorial protection—both an internal and external defense doctrine—over the following years the Ecuadorean State devised a strategy to combat exogenous and local communism. Combatting political forces of the left or any action or organization considered liable to alter or generate social instability were considered a priority in national security affairs. Destabilizing social and political actors included students, professional associations, trade unions, peasant farmers, and indigenous peoples. The expansive dissident list stifled democratic consolidation of the intelligence system, which did not undergo any principle and doctrine reform until the creation of the National Directorate for Intelligence (DNI) in the 1970s.

In 1972, General Guillermo Rodríguez Lara became de facto president (1972–1976). His nationalist and revolutionary government took advantage of the oil boom, internal industrial growth, and social advancements through the application of agrarian reform to achieve modernization. At the same time, the military administration announced a series of measures that restricted such individual and collective freedoms as the right to strike and community association without state authorization.[17] The military government maintained the Law of National Security of 1964 and reinforced the role of the DGI as the regime's political police.[18]

In 1976, following several months of friction within the armed forces, Rodriguez Lara was deposed from the presidency due to the dissatisfaction of the military and economic sector power brokers linked to intermediary capital, which led to the elimination of any semblance of political power retained by the militant left. This disagreement arose from the protectionist economic measures undertaken by Rodríguez Lara's finance minister to protect national manufacturing, to stimulate the development of trade union organizations, and to propose oil wealth reforms.[19] A military triumvirate surreptitiously gained control of the state through the establishment of the Supreme Governing Council. Initial tasks of the council included executing the Regulations and Law of National Security endorsed that same year, with the objective of exercising greater control over the population and neutralizing possible subversive communist actions. Intelligence functions, parameters, and institutional schemes codified within the Law of National Security of 1964 remained unaltered due to the prevalence of military doctrine permeating intelligence affairs.

However, in 1976 and again in 1979, the codification of the Law of National Security through the secretariat of the National Security Council created sectors called "Fronts": military, external, internal, and the new economic focuses as part of the National Security Operation.[20] Under the institutional and legal umbrella of the National Security Law, national planning, development policies, as well as programmatic security economic planning, were subsumed under the responsibility of the armed forces. This decision bolstered the nationalist vision and the idea of the military's sovereign use of natural resources, which arose from the inability of social communities and the political elites to generate leadership and promotion of development policies to benefit the whole of Ecuadorian society.[21] Simultaneously, the external Front maintained its attention on a potential conflict with Peru while the Internal Front sustained the mission of developing programs that counteracted divisive tendencies among Ecuadoreans and to maintain national unity at all costs as provided in the 1979 Law on National Security.

Under this framework, the DGI became a body under the general secretariat of the National Security Council. Concomitantly, a reserved (secret) regulation issued by the Supreme Governing Council tasked DGI with centralizing the information provided by the Fronts; additionally, coordinating the search for internal and external strategic information in the political, economic, social, and military fields. Furthermore, the council exercised the authority of coordinating DGI activities—conducting operations and collating information as it deemed appropriate—for the Council for National Security, the Joint Command of the Armed Forces, and the Directorates of the Fronts. Generally, operational planning was administered by military personnel.[22]

It is important to note that Ecuador played a role in the 1970s Condor Plan; declassified U.S. CIA archives indicate that in mid-January 1978, Ecuador joined the initiative with the code "Condor 7," which illustrated that "[t]he Army through the Directorate General of Intelligence (DGI) is responsible for intelligence reporting and the exchange of information among various members."[23]

Although the Ecuadorian Joint Command of the Armed Forces denied participating in the Condor Plan, the functions, and the operatives of the DGI between 1975 and 1979, demonstrated a correlation between the reform of the regulation to the law and greater access by that body to information emanating from the countries that endorsed the Condor Plan.[24] When the dictatorship came to an end in 1979, it appeared possible that the information originating from the Internal Front could have been used to carry out such polemical acts as the assassination of the opposition politician Abdón Calderón Muñoz in 1977, with the tacit involvement of state police and the interior minister of the triumvirate.[25]

Of further interest, although the democratic transition began in 1979, as explained in greater detail within following sections of this chapter, the military took over several democratic civilian governmental functions, installing a tutelary and cooperative institutional scheme that lasted until 2009—part of the problem of democratic consolidation in Ecuador.[26]

TRANSITION TO DEMOCRACY AND REFORM

In 1979 the country returned to a democratic path with Jaime Roldós Aguilera (1979–1981). However, as elected authorities rebalanced power to foster democratic ideals, the armed forces retained some non-democratic past prerogatives, including the new Law of National Security of 1979 that lasted until 2009,[27] which reconfigured the security and intelligence structure. This newly approved body of doctrine stayed relatively unchanged, replicating the Cold War logic—notably, the focus on "subversives"—and preserving its legacy of political police practices, but modified the system of security and intelligence—a rather negative development.[28] In an attempt to transition power slowly from the military to avoid shock, possibly leading to democratic backsliding, a protective legacy strategy was adopted—strategic intelligence was taken over by military interests with negligible participation from civil authorities—with the aspirations of slowly professionalizing the intelligence and military services with civilian oversight and control.

The 1980s in Ecuador marked the application of intelligence strategies associated with the traditional interpretation of internal threats interwoven with criteria relating to subversion and counterinsurgency. During the León Febres Cordero Presidency (1984–1988), the primary identified or prioritized threat for the Internal Front fixed on such urban guerrilla groups as *Alfaro Lives, Dammit!* (AVC) and *Free Nation Montoneras* (MPL), which promoted a nationalist discourse, emancipatory with regard to U.S. hegemony, and an ideology that claimed to extend democracy.[29] The presence of independent and diverse polities in concert with communist and socialist ideals constituted the recognized threat to the state and its military and police forces. As the government considered AVC and MPL subversive groups, they were monitored and dealt with by specialized policing units that egregiously violated human rights in the name of national security.[30]

In 1984 a covert counterterrorism unit called SIC-10 was created that was neither institutionalized nor located within the National Police or the DNI structure; it was intended to be secret and to combat terrorism and subversion through extrajudicial means. The SIC-10 was comprised of officers, troops, and police under the command of the General Commandant of Police, the Government Minister, and the President of the Republic. Its actions included infiltration and the use of torture to obtain information, as stated in the Report of the Truth Commission of 2010.[31] In addition to these groups, two other units were formed: the Antisubversive Intelligence Unit (UIAS) and the Special Investigations Unit (UIES). All these intelligence agencies had the technical and financial assistance of U.S. security agencies that encouraged local paramilitary forces to expand national security concepts, including the notion of the "War on Drugs"—a new U.S. strategy to cope with new types of threats.

These secretive activities and informal agreements were intentionally not monitored by the National Security Council.[32] Although the special units carried out specific intelligence operations, some of the funds were allocated for tactical intelligence of a political nature, conducted by the national security system and without any legislative control.

In general, the method of financing the operations of police or political intelligence was taken on as an autonomous discretional aspect of the fiscal expenditure of the government minister, without prior authorization from any higher authority or recorded reports of concluded activities. The minimal accountability was limited to a special examination by the comptroller general, who, having completed the analysis, proceeded to have the documentation burned.[33]

Later, in 1987, the government ministry passed a new law detailing the organizational structure of government intelligence[34] that maintained the same problematic relationship with national security and circumvented civilian control over the intelligence apparatus. The law allowed *Pesquisas* to be implemented through networks of civilian informants who did not belong to the National Police; thereby no actual reform occurred. The political intelligence work and the processing of information continued in the traditional four subfronts of internal security, which emerged from the U.S.-sponsored National Security Doctrine of the Cold War era: political, indigenous, workers, and student, indicating the persistence of the ingrained doctrinal approach that steered intelligence decisions.

The transition to the "War on Drugs" as part of the national security agenda acquired importance for Ecuador at the end of the 1980s, due to the seriousness of the border situation amid the escalating levels of violence precipitated by Colombia's devolvement into chaos.[35] It was a complex and difficult time for intelligence organizations—devising new tactics and structural methods to face new threats—while contemporaneously combatting endemic traditional threats. On the one hand, the regional situation of drug trafficking demanded much attention due to U.S. prioritization and conditionality for cooperation and interests. On the other hand, the traditional and conventional tensions with Peru necessitated inordinate intelligence resources, due to a prevalence of a warlike confrontational posture that took place in early 1995. With the ink still fresh on the peace agreement with Peru in 1998, Ecuador had maneuvering room to reallocate assets toward its participation in the "War on Drugs" through the instauration of the United States Forward Operating Location at the Manta military airport. This outpost assisted the collection of formal and informal intelligence that was aggregated and bolstered U.S.

intelligence and logistics military strategy against illegal drugs trafficking, designed to align with hemispheric objectives.

The 1995 war caused the military intelligence service to establish the Military Intelligence Arm in 1996 as an army function.[36] In 1998, a peace and boundaries agreement was brokered with Peru, and the intelligence service returned to its traditional duties; however, the DNI was excluded from the production of strategic intelligence. The DNI exemplifies the corrupt procedures of the military personnel within the intelligence apparatus due to its ranks replete with retired officers. The institution recruited military and police officers, hindering civil employees from curtailed military intelligence activities, slowed civilian appraisal of the system, and obscured expenses and operations to the legislative branch. In this way, the DNI acted as a kind of employment agency for military personnel and their client networks over which the civil powers had no means of intervention or control.

By the late 1990s, one challenge of note was the national security doctrine and no associated answer to the involvement and infiltration of organized crime in state institutions and the society. The semi-autonomous police units that rarely engaged with intelligence police agencies continued to develop parochial operations through the DGI. Unfortunately, the outmoded policies of corporatization and patronage devoid of necessary change and agreed-upon consolidated security missions were not debated. Military personnel traditionally did not consider the National Police to be an entity that could coordinate intelligence matters because their role consisted of solely providing classified strategic intelligence information that only the armed forces had the authority to process.[37] In short, although the scenario changed, the concept and doctrine of national security did not adapt to the challenge of organized crime, and both military intelligence and police intelligence continued business as usual, a mistaken and retrograde criterion at a time of intense national debate regarding the concept of public safety that was having a profound effect on the concerns of the Ecuadorean political class.

Although the military and the police shared the same national security doctrine, they failed to construct a comprehensive and complementary intelligence community. Both military personnel and police were unable to establish the requisite mechanisms for aggregating, processing, and disseminating strategic advice to political authorities. Hence, the DNI has remained isolated, retained its traditional character, and is subject to the bureaucratic pressure of the military sector—living in a mythical and glorified past—which was not practical for the needs of a democratic and modern state that requires an iterative strategic intelligence platform to agilely respond to changing domestic and international realities. This dynamic persisted and was illustrated through various Laws of National Security and the functions assigned to the DGI and DNI until 2009.[38]

The implementation of Plan Colombia in the late 1990s increased participation of the Ecuadorian State and deepened involvement of the police and armed forces in the Colombian conflict. This condition modified the risk calculus and threat analysis of the Ecuadorian intelligence community. This mind-set shift brought to the fore a broad discussion on the criticality of updating Ecuadorian intelligence doctrine, which included incorporating drug trafficking and Colombian guerrillas operating within the sovereign territory of Ecuador as threats.

One such reform posited the construction of an intelligence community outside the traditional influence of the military carried great weight in the political and democratic sphere.[39] This objective of exercising civil authority over the military became imperative in ensuing years because the armed forces again intervened in the country's democratic process by executing a coup in the 2000s through a military civic triumvirate that lasted a few hours. Nevertheless, the coup reasserted the military's role within the political sphere, which culminated in the election of Lucio Gutiérrez (2003–2005), a former armed forces colonel.[40]

As expected, the international political pressure from such multinational bodies as the Organization of American States and governments of the region, added to internal citizen mobilization, provoking compelling mechanisms to force a return to the rule of law within a few days. However, the need to revise the internal and external security doctrine remained at a legal and democratic loggerhead because it was difficult to balance the desire for civilian control over the military when the armed forces reserved the undisputed authority as "guarantors" of the Ecuadorean Democratic Constitution. This guarantee came to an end in 2008 with the new constitution's ratification that limited the powers and functions of the military.[41]

The Ecuadorian political and economic lens of the first years of the twenty-first century was marked by chronic governmental instability and lack of democratic governance. Different administrations were unable to amalgamate defense and intelligence matters, except for the President Alfredo Palacio period (2005–2007) who in 2005 issued a national defense white paper. There is no reference to intelligence in the document, although regional challenges represented by Colombia are cited as examples of ongoing internal conflict and the extraterritorial consequences of the violence caused by different armed insurgent groups in neighboring countries.[42]

NEW THREATS AND LEGISLATION

In 2007, Ecuador changed political direction with the crushing electoral victory of Rafael Correa (2007–2017). The new government implemented a series of institutional reforms and enacted a new constitution under the heading of Citizens Revolution. However, it was not until the 2008 Angostura crisis[43]—the Colombian incursion into Ecuadorian territory to kill rebel leaders—that the government decided to implement changes to Ecuador's intelligence service under the Law of Public Security and the State in 2009,[44] thereby replacing the 1979 Law of National Security.

The 2009 law establishes the System of Public Security for defense, public order, and the prevention and management of risk. In contrast to previous laws approved since the 1970s, the intelligence community was now regulated by the National Secretariat of Intelligence (SENAIN). Additionally, the law abolished the Fronts (internal, external, and economic), it prioritized citizens' protection, it abolished the COSENA that was wielded by the armed forces, and it created the Council for State and Public Security, which included the participation of the attorney general, the chancellor, and the judiciary. The law also determined the functions, expenditures, operations, classification of documents, and the limitations of intelligence practices. However, it did not create accountability structures for the use of reserved expenditure, and it did not include political consequences to executed questionable decisions. Furthermore, the 2009 law established a permanent fund for allocated expenses; the figure was published in the state general budget to increase transparency. The 2009 law attempted to remove the principal impediment that maintained an antagonistic relationship between military intelligence and citizens—"one of the main threats was between society and the diverse ways in which it is structured . . . by disregarding the idea of considering social, trade union, and political organizations as potentially threatening."[45]

The Angostura crisis was a violation of Ecuadorian sovereignty and revealed the low operational capacity of the Ecuadorean intelligence services to counter foreign incursions and to inform political leadership of serious events within a timely manner. President Correa initially assumed that the crisis was an infiltration by foreign national intelligence service operatives to conceal transgressions.[46] Moreover, this event illustrated the Colombian government's security and intelligence doctrine, characterized by preemptive strikes, the use of the euphemistic language of "collateral damage," unilateralism as a legitimate principle extending beyond Colombian borders, and the strategy of involving regional neighbors in an internal problem that is the sovereign responsibility of Colombia.

Despite the FARC camp being located on Ecuadorian territory, the Colombian government did not communicate the incursion in Angostura, which was interpreted by the Ecuadorian authorities as a violation of national sovereignty, a violation of territorial integrity, and a lack of mutual trust and cooperation between the countries.[47] Finally, these factors had to be considered when formulating national security legislation and the aspiration to promote the modernization of the intelligence service within a realistic context.

Following the Angostura crisis, President Rafael Correa signed Decree 1080 on May 15, 2008, the Commission for the Investigation of Ecuadorean Military and Police Intelligence Services, with the power to issue criteria regarding the civil, penal, and administrative responsibilities of those who managed information relating to the 2008 Colombian incursion into Ecuadorean territory. In this regard, the report issued by the Commission revealed the following:[48]

- Foreign interests managed to penetrate military and police intelligence organizations under the pretext of fighting drug trafficking. There was little control from civil authorities and a lamentable account of cooperation received.
- There was no intelligence law that provides mechanisms for monitoring, supervision, and coordination between different organizations.
- There was no network that enables information to be shared appropriately and securely between units of the military intelligence subsystem.
- The DGI of the police did not have a database, nor an encrypted communication system. The staff lacked technical and professional training.
- Both the military and the police intelligence organizations had carried out informal tasks that were distributed arbitrarily by those who held political power or to satisfy personal or institutional interests.
- Informal practices were treated as criminal offenses, as in the case of concealing witness, documentary, or material evidence.

Analysis of the commission's report led to the political decision to reform the intelligence services, to devise a new security law that vested greater control with civilian authorities and integrated the civil authorities who were responsible for oversight of the intelligence services to manage and assess the intelligence institutions. Additionally, this comprehensive review sought to carry out proceedings and sanctions against those responsible for the unsatisfactory management of the Ecuadorian intelligence system.

It is important to note that, until 2009, there were no procedures for investigation and enforcing accountability regarding the performance of intelligence services—except for two events that are worthy of mention, and which ended in the judiciary. The first incident related to the misuse of earmarked funds for internal security, which resulted in a former government minister and vice president in the 1990s fleeing the country.[49] The second was linked to an investigation of the Truth Commission that identified abuses and violations of human rights by elements of the police and military intelligence services in the 1980s. The findings of the commission boosted the participation of social organizations and opened debate and political intervention that prompted further intelligence reforms—the elimination of the 1979 Law of National Security and the approval of the Law of Public Security and the State of 2009—as mentioned above.[50]

Although the intelligence system was not completely dismantled, the 2009 law fundamentally changed some traditional standards. First, the National Directorate for Intelligence was seized from the military and transferred to SENAIN—civil management and accountability (see figure 7.1). As stated by the law, SENAIN is the governing body of the National System that plans, standardizes, and coordinates the collection, processing, and production of

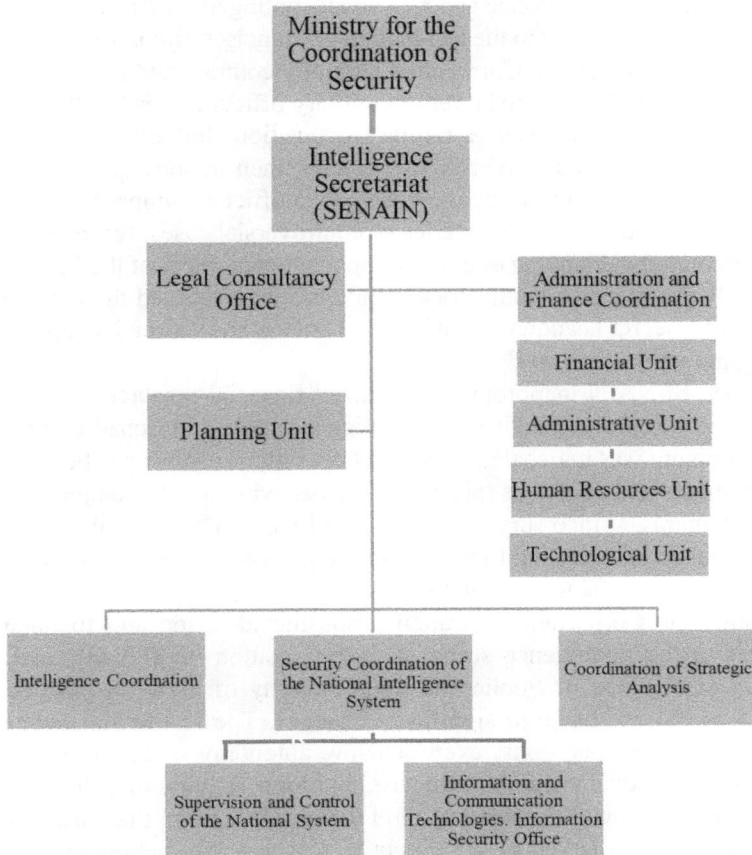

```
                    Ministry for the
                    Coordination of
                       Security
                          |
                     Intelligence
                      Secretariat
                       (SENAIN)

  Legal Consultancy              Administration and
       Office                    Finance Coordination
                                          |
                                     Financial Unit
                                          |
    Planning Unit                   Administrative Unit
                                          |
                                  Human Resources Unit
                                          |
                                   Technological Unit


  Intelligence        Security Coordination of    Coordination of Strategic
  Coordnation         the National Intelligence          Analysis
                             System

                  Supervision and Control    Information and
                  of the National System     Communication
                                             Technologies. Information
                                             Security Office
```

Figure 7.1.   Chart of the National Intelligence Secretariat (SENAIN)

intelligence for the purposes of public and state security, while executing oversight of the National Intelligence System.

SETBACK

Soon after Rafael Correa's administration established machinations for the modernization of public and state security, legal confusion concerning intelligence responsibilities and authorities arising from the new Law of Public and State Security became apparent. From 2010, SENAIN became involved in a vicious cycle of strategic failures, new clientelism, mission distortion, and acts of corruption that are still being actively investigated.[51]

The politically polarizing issue and the coup attempt led by a discontented section of the National Police and by a small contingent of air force personnel in September 2010,[52] led to the resignation of Francisco Jijón, the first civilian SENAIN chief. President Correa then promptly contradicted one of his civil-military tenets and appointed a retired military officer as head of the national intelligence agency to placate military opposition. Initially, a retired vice admiral was appointed as SENAIN secretary, then in subsequent years this function was transferred to active duty police officers—improperly loyal to the president and discharged a series of controversial cases, for example, the 2012 attempted kidnapping of a former opposition member of the Ecuadorean Assembly Fernando Balda in Bogotá—a critic who accused the government of having a secret headquarters where politicians and journalists opposed to the regime were spied on.[53]

Further, SENAIN inappropriately utilized financial resources allocated to modernize and professionalize the intelligence service in Ecuador; however, this equipment was marshaled to conduct operations against political opposition members. Examples of this egregious behavior was the employment of CCTV cameras—video surveillance system ECU 911[54]—for political spying on the public and reverting to the dictatorial persecution practices utilized by the political police since the 1970s.

Despite the Correa administration proposing idealistic and foundational changes to the intelligence sector with the creation of SENAIN and ratification of the Law of Public and State Security of 2009, in practice, the institution did not undergo significant changes. The institution maintained legacy *Pesquisa* operations, exercised low autonomy in its decisions free from unprofessional political influence, and most importantly, the secretary possessed little power to steer and audit the mission. Ergo, the third mandate (2013–2017) was marked by the executive resisting external policy changes, repelling accountability by the legislative branch, and a notable absence of civilian control over the intelligence sector's prerogatives.

OUTCOME

From the onset of President Lenín Moreno's tenure (2017–2021), a series of scandals emerged when SENAIN's political espionage activities were disclosed: monitoring of 335 press conferences, 943 assemblies, 328 demonstrations, 4 hunger strikes, and nearly 2,100 events during 2016.[55] SENAIN underwent serious questioning, and in an attempt to pacify public outrage in April 2018, the secretariat changed the organization's name to the Center for Strategic Intelligence (CIES); nevertheless, the institution preserved its practices of being a political espionage instrument.

This situation proved paradoxical because although the Law of Public and State Security of 2009 established structural reforms, refusal to subordinate to civilian leadership was retained plus the co-option of the institution responsible for national strategic intelligence to fulfill the parochial political concerns of the president. In essence, intelligence reform created unintended consequences manipulated by nefarious actors. The new system was exponentially more powerful and dedicated almost exclusively to opposition political espionage, imbued with a low accountability mechanism and personnel dedicated to discrediting opposition politicians through trolls or cyberattacks. The legislative branch retained certain intelligence oversight activities—for example, receiving annual accountability reports from SENAIN—but exercised anemic evaluation of secret operations expenditures. This ineffectual paradigm led to SENAIN accommodating the political interests of President Rafael Correa, who failed to connect national objectives with strategic intelligence—episodically outmaneuvering the other two governmental branches to accumulate greater power in the executive.

Superficial changes to the Ecuadorian community have obscured the sincere desire of reform with political banality. Ecuadorian intelligence remains a resilient government service subject to ongoing political pressures and has prioritized political intelligence collection, leaving strategic intelligence activities to the military sector, including internal state security activities. Finally, given its legal ambivalence and the unique nature of its objectives and operations, Ecuadorian intelligence has struggled with corruption and assisting political government authorities' parochial interests.[56] The kidnapping and subsequent murder of three *El Comercio* newspaper journalists in 2018 by members of the Armed Group "Oliver Sinisterra" that occurred on the border between Ecuador and Colombia revealed that the institution was incapable of anticipating, communicating, and proposing strategies to decision makers. The government and CIES were paralyzed by the inability to synchronize efforts and to articulate the subsystems of intelligence from a strategic intelligence perspective to resolve the crisis.

Between April 2018 and May 2021, the CIES has been led by four directors with little or no experience within the field, maintained a low organic institutionalism, experienced moderate professional participation, and conducted near autonomous operational discretion without being subject to annual and strategic accountability. Above all, the organization failed to devise an intelligence community capable of dissuading local and international security threats.

The intelligence system in Ecuador remains on a pendulum between corporate interests of the armed forces and the political interests of the executive using the institution as a platform for espionage and political intelligence, hence, the institutional and legal reforms of 2009 aimed at restructure and creation of a functional equilibrium for the national intelligence service. In practice, the system preserved its corporate structure, limited its activities to political intelligence, did not properly train its staff, and focused entirely on political threats to internal stability—failing to complete its foundational objectives of anticipation, action, and prediction of risks and threats to the Ecuadorian State.

CONCLUSION

Intelligence services in Ecuador have succeeded in being effective during different historical periods and subservient to the governments in office, regardless of their ideological stance; however, intelligence has failed to materially adopt a democratic model. Without having introduced greater doctrinal changes up to the present, military and political intelligence dominated the agenda for more than three decades, developing corporate and client structures within official institutions, and further codified by the laws of national security. This behavior, related to a specific classification of democracy, tends to vest power and decisions with the executive, has impeded the establishment of structural reform and effective democratic modernization based on legislative controls, obscured supervision of cost and allocated funds, and incorrectly monitors the media and civil society. It has also ignored the existence of medium- and long-term national plans with clear objectives that encompass national and regional realities; and more importantly, the institution has failed to anticipate and propose strategies to decision makers.

Between 1979 and 2009, strategic intelligence was a prerogative of the military with minimal civil authority participation. The past decade that witnessed the creation of SENAIN by the Law of Public and State Security of 2009 has been characterized by intelligence agencies demonstrating ambivalence and contradictory actions, as well as demonstrating signs of corruption and operating with impunity, thereby, squandering the historic opportunity to construct reliable, technical, and professional institutions in keeping with the international parameters of intelligence in democratic societies. The 2018 establishment of CIES did not result in any concrete results toward a democratic culture of intelligence based on the intelligence community aligning strategic and security interests of the state and the collective well-being and peace of its inhabitants.

Ecuador must progress toward an intelligence law that promotes meaningful structural reform and effective democratic modernization, which establishes independent legislative audits, enforced standards that guarantee professionalism, adequate technical personnel training, and strategic intelligence vision implementation.[57]

NOTES

1. Fredy Rivera Vélez and Katalina Barreiro, "Political Intelligence and National Security in Ecuador: A Retrospective Reading," *Journal of Power, Politics & Governance* 2, no. 3–4 (2014): 131.

2. See Eduardo Estévez, "Comparing Intelligence Democratization in Latin America: Argentina, Peru, and Ecuador Cases," *Intelligence and National Security* 29, no. 4 (2014): 553.

3. Rivera Vélez and Barreiro, "Political Intelligence."

4. Fredy Rivera Vélez, "Inteligencia Estratégica e Inteligencia Política: Los Claro-oscuros del Caso Ecuatoriano," in *Inteligencia Estratégica Contemporánea: Perspectivas desde la Región Suramericana*, edited by Mariano Bartolomé et al. (Quito: Universidad de las Fuerzas Armadas, ESPE, 2016), 133–48.

5. General Orlando F. Aguirre, "La Alianza para el Progreso ¿Promoción del Desarrollo o Disciplinamiento Estatal?," paper presented at II Jornadas de Economía Política, Universidad Nacional de General Sarmiento, Buenos Aires, 2008. Available at https://www.ungs.edu.ar/cm/uploaded_files/file/ecopol/2da_jornada/Aguirre.pdf.

6. Francisco Leal, "La Doctrina de Seguridad Nacional: Materialización de la Guerra Fría en América del Sur," *Revista de Estudios Sociales* 15 (2003): 75.

7. Marc Becker, *The CIA in Ecuador* (Durham and London: Duke University Press, 2020).

8. Ley de Seguridad Nacional de la República del Ecuador. Quito, Registro Oficial No. 892 de 9 de agosto de 1979.

9. Fredy Rivera Vélez, *La Seguridad Perversa. Política, Democracia y Derechos Humanos en el Ecuador: 1998–2006* (FLACSO Sede Ecuador-Universidad Nacional de Cuyo, 2012).

10. Rivera Vélez, "Inteligencia Estratégica e Inteligencia Política."

11. Fredy Rivera Vélez, "La Inteligencia Ecuatoriana: Tradiciones, Cambios y Perspectivas," in *Inteligencia Estratégica y Prospectiva*, edited by Fredy Rivera Vélez (Quito-Ecuador: FLACSO-SENAIN, 2011), 47–73.

12. Pierre Gondard and Hubert Mazurek, "30 años de Reforma Agraria y Colonización en el Ecuador (1964–1994): Dinámicas Espaciales," in *Dinámicas Territoriales: Ecuador, Bolivia, Perú, Venezuela*, edited by Pierre Gondard and León Juan Bernardo (Quito-Ecuador: Colegio de Geógrafos del Ecuador (CGE) / Corporación Editora Nacional (CEN) / Institut de Recherche pour le Développement (IRD) / Pontificia Universidad Católica del Ecuador, 2001): 15–40.

13. According to Bresser-Pereira, "Whereas the structuralist thinking was a Latin American version of development economics, national developmentalism was the respective national development strategy. As a state-led strategy, it understood that markets are effective in resource allocation provided that they are combined with economic planning and the constitution of state-owned enterprises. National-developmentalism was a strategy sponsored in one way or another by industrialists, the public bureaucracies, and urban workers. It faced intellectual opposition from neoclassical or monetarist economists and political opposition from the liberal middle classes and the old oligarchy whose interests were based on the export of primary goods." Luiz Carlos Bresser-Pereira, "From Old to New Developmentalism in Latin America," *The Oxford Handbook of Latin American Economics*, eds. José Antonio Ocampo and Jaime Ros (Oxford: Oxford University Press, 2011), 108–29.

14. See Augusto Varas and Fernando Bustamante, *Fuerzas Armadas y Política en Ecuador.* (Quito: FLACSO-Ecuador, 1977).

15. Milton Reyes, "La Inteligencia China, Un Acercamiento Histórico Cultural," in *Inteligencia Estratégica y Prospectiva*, edited by Fredy Rivera Vélez (Quito-Ecuador: FLACSO-SENAIN, 2011), 197–211.

16. Philip Agee, *Inside the Company. CIA Diary* (New York: Stonehill Publishing Company, 1975); Silva E. Quintero R, *Ecuador: Una Nación en Ciernes* (Quito: Abya-Yala, 1998).

17. Fredy Rivera Vélez, Katalina Barreiro Santana, and Gilda Alicia Guerrero Salgado, *¿Dónde está el Pesquisa? Una Historia de la Inteligencia Política en Ecuador* (Quito: Pontificia Universidad Católica del Ecuador, 2018).

18. For example, the existence, between 1972 and 1976, of special courts and the establishment of the "*Fumisa*" police unit, whose aim was to neutralize the leaders of the peasant farmers' cooperatives who were fighting for access to land, as well as the creation of paramilitary groups whose mission was to destabilize the student movement and its organizations in the principal cities. See Fredy Rivera Vélez, "Inteligencia Estratégica e Inteligencia Política," 138.

19. See Varas and Bustamante, *Fuerzas Armadas y Política en Ecuador.*

20. "These fronts were designed to prevent, alert, supervise and combat the following: external threats; war threats (international policies and the border problem with Peru); threats of foreign political interference (subversion); and natural disasters (earthquakes, volcanic eruptions, etc.)." Rivera Vélez and Barreiro, "Political Intelligence," 124.

21. See Varas and Bustamante, *Fuerzas Armadas y Política en Ecuador*.

22. In conformity with the Regulations to the National Security Law. Decreto No. 913-F, Reglamento General de la Ley de Seguridad Nacional. Quito, Registro Oficial No. 231, del 13 de diciembre de 1976.

23. Central Intelligence Agency, "Ecuador Participation in Operation Condor," FOIA (Freedom of Information Act) Collection, document no. 0000345205, January 2, 1978 (released June 11, 1999). Accessed on May 7, 2019. Available at https://www.cia.gov/library/readingroom/docs/DOC_0000345205.pdf.

24. Rivera Vélez, *La Seguridad Perversa.*

25. Víctor Granda Aguilar, *La Masacre de Aztra: El Crimen más Espantoso de la Dictadura del Triunvirato Militar* (Cuenca, Ecuador: Facultad de Ciencias Económicas de la Universidad de Cuenca, 1979).

26. See Thomas C. Bruneau, "Ecuador: The Continuing Challenge of Democratic Consolidation and Civil-Military Relations," *Strategic Insights* 5, no. 2 (February 2006).

27. Fredy Rivera Vélez, *Democracia Minimalista y "Fantasmas" Castrenses en el Ecuador Contemporáneo* (Quito: FLACSO Sede Ecuador, 2003). Available at http://www.flacso.org.ec/docs/ffaaydec.pdf.

28. Also being abetted by the ambiguous definition and porous concept between external and internal security contributed to the combination and superposition of tasks, roles, missions, and structures that were present in the intelligence tasks contained in the National Security Law of 1979. Rivera Vélez, "Inteligencia Estratégica e Inteligencia Política."

29. Rivera Vélez, "Inteligencia Estratégica e Inteligencia Política."

30. During the government of Febres Cordero two elite groups of the National Police appeared: the Intervention and Rescue Group (GIR) and the secret and informal Criminal Investigation Service (SIC-10). For the four years of his government persecution, harassment, arbitrary detention, torture, and disappearance were legitimized as valid methods. Comisión de la Verdad, *Informe de la Comisión de la Verdad, Ecuador 2010. Sin Verdad No Hay Justicia, Resumen Ejecutivo* (Quito: Edicuatorial, 2010): 164–194.

31. Comisión de la Verdad, *Informe de la Comisión de la Verdad,* 222–24.

32. See Fredy Rivera Vélez, "Perspectivas Analíticas para la Paz, Seguridad y Desarme." Documento de Trabajo. Secretaría Nacional de Planificación y Desarrollo. (Quito: SENPLADES, 2010); also Rivera Vélez, "Inteligencia Estratégica e Inteligencia Política."

33. See Rivera Vélez, *La Seguridad Perversa.*

34. Ministerio de Gobierno, Reglamento Orgánico Funcional de Ministerio de Gobierno, December 17, 1987.

35. See Fredy Rivera Vélez, "Ecuador: Untangling the Drug War," in *Drugs and Democracy in Latin America. The Impact of U.S. Policy,* edited by Colleta Youngers and Eiileen Rosin (Boulder, CO. Lynne Rienner Publishers, 2005).

36. Rivera Vélez, "La Inteligencia Ecuatoriana," 52.

37. Rivera Vélez, *La Seguridad Perversa.*

38. Rivera Vélez, "La Inteligencia Ecuatoriana," 47–73.

39. Rivera Vélez, "Inteligencia Estratégica e Inteligencia Política."

40. The Armed Forces, besides being highly popular among the citizens, maintain a doctrine of leadership and their corporate purpose lies in strengthening their institution hand in hand with the development of national institutions. This relationship

largely explains the military interest in Ecuador to establish its social and political function of strengthening the State as a whole. See Varas and Bustamante *Fuerzas Armadas y Política en Ecuador*, 123.

41. For an historical account on the military, see Katalina Barreiro Santana, Milton Reyes Herrera, and Diego Pérez Enríquez, "The Role of the Ecuadorian Armed Forces: Historical Structure and Changing Security Environments," *Revista de Estudos e Pesquisas Avançadas do Terceiro Setor* 2, no. 2 (2019): 50–72.

42. See Rivera Vélez, *La Seguridad Perversa*.

43. On March 1, 2008, on the Colombian-Ecuadorean border, specifically in the Province of Sucumbíos and the town called Angostura, an unauthorized armed incursion by the Colombian Armed Forces and National Police took place into an encampment of the Revolutionary Armed Forces of Colombia People's Army (FARC-EP), where among others they found Luis Edgar Devia Silva, alias Raúl Reyes, second in command of the insurgents and part of the leadership of the guerrilla organization. Further information in Rivera Vélez, "Inteligencia Estratégica e Inteligencia Política."

44. Ley de Seguridad Pública y del Estado. Quito, Registro Oficial Suplemento 35 del 28 de septiembre de 2009.

45. Francisco Jijón Calderón, "El Nuevo Ecuador y la Secretaría Nacional de Inteligencia," in *Inteligencia Estratégica y Prospectiva*, edited by Fredy Rivera Vélez (Quito-Ecuador: FLACSO-SENAIN, 2011), 18.

46. President Correa "said that Ecuador's intelligence systems were 'totally infiltrated and subjugated to the C.I.A.' He accused senior military officials of sharing intelligence with Colombia, the Bush administration's top ally in Latin America." Simon Romero, "Ecuador's Leader Purges Military and Moves to Expel American Base," *New York Times*, April 21, 2008, https://www.nytimes.com/2008/04/21/world/americas/21ecuador.html.

47. On this case, see "Angostura: Radiografía de la crisis de Ecuador y Colombia," *El Telégrafo*, May 20, 2017. Available at https://www.eltelegrafo.com.ec/noticias/politiko/1/angostura-radiografia-de-la-crisis-de-ecuador-y-colombia.

48. Comisión para la Investigación de los Servicios de Inteligencia Militares y Policiales. *Informe de penetración de la CIA en las Fuerzas Armadas y Policía Nacional*. Quito: Comisión para la Investigación de los Servicios de Inteligencia Militares y Policiales, 2008. Available at https://inredh.org/informe-de-penetracion-de-la-cia-en-fuerzas-armadas-y-policia-nacional/.

49. On this case, see "Dahik Huyó Ayer a Costa Rica," *El Tiempo*, October 13, 1995, https://www.eltiempo.com/archivo/documento/MAM-422975.

50. Rivera Vélez, "La Inteligencia Ecuatoriana," 65; Estévez, "Comparing Intelligence Democratization in Latin America," 568.

51. "SENAIN priorizó la Inteligencia Política, no la Seguridad Nacional," *El Telégrafo*, March 25, 2018, https://www.eltelegrafo.com.ec/noticias/politica/3/senain-priorizo-la-inteligencia-politica-no-la-seguridad-nacional. See *Plan V*, "¿Ecuador tiene una Estructura de Inteligencia debilitada?" February 26, 2018, http://www.planv.com.ec/historias/politica/ecuador-tiene-una-estructura-inteligencia-debilitada.

52. On September 30, 2010, a police revolt occurred when former President Rafael Correa was held by rebels in the police hospital. The conflict arose on account of the legal reform that was to be enacted for internal security that purportedly affected the police force. The revolt involved the intervention of the Armed Forces, with armed clashes resulting in 274 wounded and 5 dead. See Carlos De la Torre, "Corporatism, Charisma, and Chaos: Ecuador's Police Rebellion in Context," *NACLA Report on the Americas* 44, no. 1 (2011): 25–32. Also see Daniel Pontón and Fredy Rivera Vélez, "Postneoliberalismo y Policía: Caso de Ecuador 2007–2013," *Desafíos* 28, no. 2 (2016): 229–31.

53. "Secuestro de un Opositor Ecuatoriano en Cedritos: La Verdadera Historia," *Revista Semana*, June 6, 2018, https://www.semana.com/nacion/articulo/historia-del -secuestro-del-ecuatoriano-fernando-balda-flores-en-colombia/570148.

54. Paul Mozur, Jonah M. Kessel, and Melissa Chan, "Hecho en China y Exportado a Ecuador: El Aparato de Vigilancia Estatal," *The New York Times*, April 24, 2019, https://www.nytimes.com/es/2019/04/24/ecuador-vigilancia-seguridad-china/.

55. *Plan V*, "Las Perspectivas del Cambio en los Servicios de Inteligencia," October 1, 2018, https://www.planv.com.ec/historias/politica/perspectivas-del-cambio -servicios-inteligencia.

56. Executive Decree No. 526, Quito, Ecuador, September 21, 2018, https://www .cies.gob.ec/archivos/4574.

57. "Expertos Declaran la Necesidad de una Ley de Inteligencia," *La Hora*, March 26, 2018, https://lahora.com.ec/quito/noticia/1102145049/expertos-declaran-la-nece sidad-de-una-ley-de-inteligencia.

Chapter Eight

Peru

Victor Ray[1]

Intelligence scandals have been a recurrent feature of Peruvian politics since the fall of Alberto Fujimori's authoritarian regime in 2000. To assess the current state of Peruvian intelligence civilian governance, this chapter examines three cycles of intelligence scandals—2000–2001, 2001–2015, and 2015–present—in Peru since its transition to democracy in 1978 and subsequent efforts at legislative and institutional reform. The chapter analyzes Peru's attempts to reform the intelligence policy apparatus—specifically, the National Intelligence Directorate (DINI) and its institutional predecessors. Peru's reactive approach to intelligence reform has resulted in incrementally advancing positive legislation; however, insufficiently specific legislation and inadequate civil society national security engagement remain major obstacles to effective democratic intelligence governance reforms.[2]

BACKGROUND ON THE NON-DEMOCRATIC REGIME AND THE ROLE OF INTELLIGENCE

Between 1992 and 2000, Peru was an authoritarian regime under Alberto Fujimori.[3] President Fujimori was elected in 1990 as a political outsider during a brutal insurgency and an economic crisis. As a result of popular dissatisfaction with the ineffectual democratic administrations that had governed since 1980, Peruvian citizens largely approved when Fujimori, in cooperation with the armed forces, carried out a "self-coup" in April 1992 that shut down congress and the judiciary and permitted him unilaterally to reshape the state.[4]

After the coup, the National Intelligence Service (SIN)—which was originally formed in 1960—became Fujimori's personal political police, under the directorship of Vladimiro Montesinos,[5] who used it to assert control over the military, the press, and politicians through bribes and threats.[6] Abetted by Montesinos, Fujimori effectively dismantled independent legislative and judicial checks over national security services.[7] Still, Fujimori's measures and his government enjoyed wide approval at this time, fueled by Peru's economic recovery and a series of successes against the major insurgent movements.[8]

Ironically, in 2000, the Fujimori regime failed amid its own successes—in the midst of a corruption and bribery scandal, suspicion about the legality of his election, and a military revolt.[9] Irrefutable video evidence in 2000—of Montesinos bribing an opposition politician—diluted public support for the Fujimori regime and precipitated the regime's collapse and the transition back to democracy.[10] Shifting public sentiment prompted Fujimori to deactivate SIN, which in turn resulted in Montesinos fleeing the country.[11] Fujimori, unable to maintain his position, fled to Japan shortly thereafter, resigning his presidency from Japanese soil to avoid extradition.[12] The interim presidency fell to Valentin Paniagua (2000–2001), who marshaled a democratic transitional government until free elections were conducted in 2001.[13]

DEMOCRATIC REFORMS: THREE
CYCLES OF SCANDAL AND REFORM, 2000–PRESENT

Since 2000, Peru's intelligence community has undergone three major cycles of scandals, which in turn produced three corresponding reform cycles. In the first cycle (2000–2001), Fujimori began the formal dismantling of the SIN in an effort to separate himself from Montesinos's corrupt activities, as well as to obscure the nature of the organization's past activities under his regime and reduce his culpability.[14] In June 2001, the Peruvian Congress under President Paniagua's transitional government passed Law No. 27479. The law reorganized the National Intelligence System (SINA) established in 1970 and stipulated the hierarchal structure of top-level intelligence agencies and various ministries.[15] The SIN's functions were transferred to the National Intelligence Council (CNI) and the National Directorate of Strategic Intelligence (DINIE) within CNI.[16]

The law was flawed from its inception, because it provided for duplicate roles among agencies (e.g., between CNI and DINIE) and lacked provisions for democratic civilian control of intelligence organizations (e.g., no provisions for judicial oversight over the collection of information on citizens and no limit on intelligence agencies' ability to suspend citizens' rights to privacy were established).[17] Nevertheless, it was symbolically important as the first law governing intelligence to be passed through the normal legislative process rather than presidential decree.[18]

Furthermore, in 2001 President Paniagua created the Commission on Truth and Reconciliation to investigate crimes and human rights violations committed by terrorist organizations, state agents, and paramilitary groups during the internal armed conflict (1980–2000) and the Fujimori regime.[19] Its 2003 final report[20] made recommendations to improve intelligence democratization such as the implementation of democratic civilian control of the military intelligence agencies, restricting them to the production of defense intelligence, as well as the passage of a legal framework strengthening CNI's role.[21]

In 2004, by presidential decision, the CNI was subject to restructuring and concurrently a Special Commission monitoring CNI restructuring was created with the main purpose of promoting democratic controls, efficiency, protection of rights, and transparency. In December 2005, Peruvian Congress adopted by consensus Law 28664, revamping the structure of the intelligence system.[22]

The second cycle (2001–2006) emerged under the backdrop of an intelligence crisis during the presidency of Alejandro Toledo in the same years and the formation of DINI. Between the turbulent years of 2001 and 2004, seven different individuals led CNI, one of whom held the post twice; interpersonal politics and competition between CNI presidents, DINIE directors, and political rivals partially explain the high rate of turnover—a struggle to form the future intelligence organizations in the shape that disparate members viewed as correct.[23] The personal infighting and inconsistent leadership that plagued the senior ranks of CNI affected all levels of intelligence personnel, manifested by a massive exodus of ex-SIN members through firings, political purges, and resignations.[24]

Within this hyperpolitical environment, leaks to the press from former and current CNI employees to undermine political rivals abounded.[25] These actions culminated in 2004 with the revelation of a "laughable . . . war of intelligence inside of the government"—as Ocampo highlights—wherein the Interior Ministry's own intelligence agency, the Intelligence Directorate, detected and revealed attempts by the CNI and DINIE to smear the reputation of the interior minister himself, former CNI chairman Fernando Rospigliosi.[26] This scandal, which plainly revealed the degree of infighting in Toledo's government and the intelligence community's role therein, initiated a process of reform that resulted in a second major reorganization of the high-level intelligence apparatus.[27]

This period also saw the adoption of more robust intelligence legislation. Aided by a Harvard University Project on Justice in Times of Transition, the Peruvian Congress developed a new intelligence law codified in January 2006. Law No. 28664, for example, replaced CNI with the National Intelligence Council (COIN) and DINI (which simply removed "strategic" from the name of DINIE, its predecessor), and clearly delineated the roles of each body vis-à-vis each other.[28] At the highest levels of the intelligence community, DINI became the lead agency in the intelligence sector and the governing organization of the SINA.[29] COIN in turn shifted from an intelligence agency to a true interagency council, and the executive director of DINI became the chair of COIN, theoretically improving SINA's unity of effort, because for the first time, Peru had a strategic coordinator of the intelligence organizations and activities.[30]

The 2006 law also created a Congressional Intelligence Committee, "which has the authority to obtain classified and unclassified information from any of SINA's components, to investigate agencies ex officio, to supervise the annual plan of intelligence and its derived policies, and to request an annual secret report from the DINI";[31] judicial review, specifically necessitating the approval of two judges to conduct intrusive operations, like, for example, wiretapping;[32] and mandatory scheduled declassification and a formal process through which citizens could request early declassification.[33]

The newly formed Congressional Intelligence Committee and the intelligence community disputed the appropriate limitations of the type and level of classified information that should be provided to Congress.[34] The intelligence community clearly distrusted legislators, suspecting with some justification that they would leak classified information for political purposes; additionally, the new law did not specify punitive actions for unauthorized disclosures by intelligence committee members.[35] The intelligence community's distrust also extended to the judicial branch, making the episodic appointments of judges to approve special domestic operations that were intrusive upon Peruvian citizen's privacy problematic.[36] Moreover, impromptu assignments to handle intelligence cases reduced the judiciary's ability to formulate specialized expertise and the ability to develop an equilibrium—conducting effective intelligence operations, while respecting citizens' rights.[37]

In spite of these shortcomings, the 2006 reforms enacted at the end of the Toledo regime marked a significant improvement over previous legislation, and they facilitated the relative stability of the Peruvian intelligence system over the course of the administration of Toledo's successor, Alan Garcia (2006–2011).[38]

The third phase occurred during the presidency of former army officer Ollanta Humala (2011–2016). In 2012, Congress delegated to the Humala administration the authority to decide unilaterally on matters related to the "modernization" of a wide array of national security organizations, including SINA, for a period of ninety days.[39] This situation led to Legislative Decree (DL) No. 1141 of 2012, later amended by Law No. 30535 of 2016, which remains the primary statute governing intelligence in Peru. DL No. 1141 was similar to Law No. 28664 in structure and content; however, it restructured the DINI. The addition of authorities aimed at consolidating its role as the central agency of SINA provided foundational reform. DINI's leader, previously its executive director, became the "National Intelligence Director," thereby solidifying the agency's leadership of SINA and subordinating the intelligence agency to civilian control.[40] In 2013, a bipartisan coalition in the Congress submitted to Peru's Constitutional Court a case alleging that Articles 36 and 37 of DL 1141, which governed the composition and function of the Congressional Intelligence Committee, were deemed unconstitutional.[41] The lawmakers argued that the executive had no constitutional right to regulate a congressional committee by decree and that Congress could not legally delegate authority to regulate itself to the executive.[42] The case was largely symbolic; stalling within the judicial system until 2017, by which time Congress had already significantly modified Article 36 through Law No. 30535. Nonetheless, the elaboration of a formal argument by congressional members to claim their legislative right to oversee against executive encroachment represents a major step in the desire of the congress to interject in intelligence governance. The changes to Law No. 30535 enabled the committee to initiate investigations of SINA components and provided more specificity on DINI information requests by the committee, including its budget.[43]

Unfortunately, it is alleged that Humala's administration routinely used DINI to monitor domestic political actors who disagreed with his policies—notably the vice president and Congress members, as well as civil society, including journalists.[44] Ultimately, Congress censured the prime minister for allowing spying on politicians and civil society representatives.[45]

Responding to the public outcry, the Humala administration created a Reorganization Commission of civilian experts to report on the state of DINI and propose appropriate reforms. The report of the Reorganization Commission links undemocratic DINI practices and abuses with ineffectiveness.[46] This finding prompted a renewed effort at intelligence reform. For example, Law No. 30535 defines strategic intelligence as "useful knowledge . . . for the formulation and execution of the general policy of the government, with the object of guaranteeing respect for human rights, protecting the population from threats to their security, defending national sovereignty, and promoting the general well-being and integral development of the Nation."[47] Nevertheless, this definition, with vague references to "general well-being" and "development," did not capture the essence of strategic intelligence as defined in the report.[48] In a promising sign, in 2018, Congress approved a bill to define more precisely strategic intelligence, as well as tactical and operational intelligence, but as of this writing the laws have not promulgated the intelligence organizations responsible for legal enactment.[49]

On September 30, 2019, President Martin Vizcarra dissolved the Peruvian Congress following an extended period of deadlock between the executive and legislative branches over political reforms aimed at curbing corruption. The Congress, which had been controlled by an opposition coalition led by the Fujimorista Party, Fuerza Popular, denounced the dissolution as a coup, although the move comported with Article 134 of the Peruvian constitution.[50] The legislature's loss of legitimacy and public support seemed to bode ill for future congressional intelligence oversight.

Vizcarra enacted new elections in January 2020, yet his party did not gain a governing coalition in congress. In this context, the new congress impeached him twice in 2020. The second impeachment was successful and forced Vizcarra to leave office in November 2020. The head of the legislature, Manuel Merino, who opposed Vizcarra's reforms, succeeded Vizcarra on November 10, 2020, but only lasted five days in office. Francisco Sagasti, an academic involved with international organizations on development, replaced him.[51]

Peru held presidential elections on April 11, 2021. After a run-off between the two top candidates—Pedro Castillo, from left-wing Free Peru party, and Keiko Fujimori, Alberto Fujimori's daughter and the leader of the right-wing Popular Force—on June 6, 2021, Castillo won.[52] Peru's political environment continues to be plagued by defective decision making, which triggers unrest in the country.[53]

ANALYSIS

Peru has not achieved considerable progress in democratizing its intelligence agencies. The legacy of the past—including retention of many SIN agents, who continued their non-democratic modus operandi—fickle strategic leadership, and arbitrary decision making has obstructed reform. These obstacles have resulted in incomplete legal framework, weak formal and informal control and oversight mechanisms, and underdeveloped professional norms. Under these circumstances, intelligence agencies remain highly politicized and limited in their operational effectiveness.

Control and Oversight

Intelligence oversight has been cyclical and complementary to political crises. Formal intelligence oversight, for one, has mostly involved responding to crises or occasional fire alarms[54] sounded by the civil society and/or the media. In this connection, what Matei and Bruneau wrote in 2011 is still valid: "Although Peru's decisionmakers, including members of Congress, have shown interest in intelligence reform, including civilian democratic control, transparency, and effectiveness, their efforts have yet to be fully implemented."[55]

With some exceptions, civil society, the press, and academia in Peru have not sustained the kind of interest in intelligence matters necessary to produce a broad and reflective public debate.[56] Whereas intelligence scandals generate brief media attention, the press often fails to comment on the legality or illegality of the actions involved, let alone the possible shape of legal reforms that might prevent future abuses.[57] Meanwhile, for the average Peruvian, local issues of everyday security against petty crime maintained greater relevance than strategic issues of national security, and the decades-long parade of scandals from high-level intelligence agencies has inculcated a sentiment that spying on citizens is simply normal.[58] Ultimately, then, oversight has been ineffective, which has allowed politicization of intelligence.

Professionalism and Effectiveness

The massive exodus of former SIN personnel after the democratic transition was never followed by a concerted effort to systematize the recruitment and training of civilian personnel with specific qualifications for strategic intelligence. The stigma of the authoritarian past made the field especially unattractive to young potential recruits, and the general disinterest in intelligence matters within academia reduced the pool of qualified candidates.[59] The result was recruitment by "cronyism and clientelism" rather than meritocracy.[60] As an example, of the 374 individuals permanently employed by DINI in 2015, only 158 held at least a bachelor's degree, only 4 had studied political science, and none had studied international relations.[61] This issue, coupled with DINI's aging permanent workforce (62 percent over the age of forty) illustrates DINI's challenge to recruiting qualified, young candidates with educational backgrounds relevant to strategic-level national security affairs.[62] Moreover, DINI lacks a career progression structure to encourage long-term development and promotion for its employees.[63]

This lack of career mobility likely explains another odd statistic: despite the overwhelming predominance of employees over the age of forty, more than 46 percent of DINI employees had less than five years of services with the organization.[64] In such an environment, politicization flourishes; the Reorganization Committee describes a disturbing practice whereby Peruvian political parties secretly send loyalists to join ("infiltrate") DINI and leak information on their behalf.[65]

To be sure, the National Intelligence School (ENI) provides a number of courses to educate members on various SINA competencies, ranging from two to eight months. ENI's courses are generally well received by students, but they fail to provide robust instruction on issues related to the ethics and legality of certain orders and operations.[66] Moreover, the segmentation between civilian academia and the national security establishment appears to extend to higher-level intelligence courses as well. Gomez de la Torre lamented in 2009 that academic literature on intelligence in Latin America is not assigned in the ENI, and in 2015, Céspedes called on DINI and ENI to assume responsibility in connecting the intelligence community to civilian academia.[67] There is, unfortunately, little available information on the depth and frequency of the de facto intelligence-academia outreach. At the minimum, this lacuna is an indicator that Peru's intelligence outreach and transparency are still limited.

CONCLUSION

The trajectory of Peru's intelligence culture transformation follows some broader regional trends. Many Latin American nations have encountered institutional, political, and civilian resistance when attempting to transition to a Western intelligence civilian authority model that controls the nation's respective intelligence apparatuses. Additionally, the legacy of vesting disproportionate power in the executive, lack of legal enforcement between three-coequal branches of government, weak legacy of military subordination to civilian control, and detachment of the civilian population in reforming Peru's intelligence system have been problematic. On the one hand, the recurrent personalistic abuse of intelligence services is a product of the personalistic politics of Peru, which is a widely noted feature of Latin American politics.[68] On the other hand, the prolonged disinterest of Peruvian legislators, academics, and the press in meaningfully engaging with intelligence issues is consistent with the broader findings of the literature on Latin American democratic transition and security services.[69] As demonstrated in this chapter, only when an intelligence scandal transpires, of a proportion that cannot be ignored, rudimentary actions to rectify the transgression through legal means—at times constitutionally questionable and counterproductive—are implemented.

However, Peru's iterative transformation of civilian control of the intelligence community has shown promise of a more robust and durable democracy. The continued engagement of Peru's civilian population and elected officials in demanding accountability and meaningful intelligence reforms, shifting the intelligence community's focus toward achieving national strategic objectives opposed to furthering personal domestic political gains, and understanding that reform does not possess a defined timetable and patience is required will set the conditions for Peru's positive transition. Peru has begun the foundational steps of establishing and enforcing laws to form a governmental system of equal justice. Additional iterative steps and resistance to democratic backsliding may provide manners to tailor lasting intelligence reforms to better civil-military intelligence relations.

NOTES

1. The views expressed in this chapter are the author's own and do not reflect the official positions of the United States Marine Corps, the Department of Defense, or the United States government.

2. In this chapter, I implicitly treat the subordination of the security services to democratic civilian institutions as a normatively desirable goal. I accept, for the purposes of this chapter, the basic propositions of Terry Lynn Karl and Philippe Schmitter's 1991 definition of "modern political democracy" as "a system of governance in which rulers are held accountable for their actions in the public realm by citizens, acting indirectly through the competition and cooperation of their elected representatives." In the context of modern democracy, I accept Mark Lowenthal's description of the legitimate purpose of intelligence as supporting policy makers in the following ways: "to avoid strategic surprise; to provide long-term expertise; to support the policy process; and to maintain the secrecy of information." Other uses of intelligence are "either wasteful or illegal." I hold, along with Florina Cristiana Matei and Thomas Bruneau, that new democracies face special challenges in simultaneously gaining democratic control of intelligence services and achieving intelligence effectiveness, although I believe that these goals can be (though often are not) mutually reinforcing if they receive the dedicated attention of policy makers and civil society. See Terry Lynn Karl and Philippe C. Schmitter, "What Democracy Is . . . and Is Not," *Journal of Democracy* 2, no. 3 (Summer 1991): 75–80; Mark M. Lowenthal, *Intelligence: From Secrets to Policy*, 7th ed. (Los Angeles: CQ Press, 2017), 2; Thomas C. Bruneau and Florina Cristiana Matei, "Intelligence in the Developing Democracies: The Quest for Transparency and Effectiveness," in *The Oxford Handbook of National Security Intelligence*, ed. Loch K. Johnson (Oxford: Oxford University Press, 2010), 759–62; Florina Cristiana Matei and Thomas Bruneau, "Intelligence Reform in New Democracies: Factors Supporting or Arresting Progress," *Democratization* 18, no. 3 (June 2011): 607–15.

3. See Carlos Contreras and Marcos Cueto, *Historia del Perú Contemporaneo*, 6th ed. (Lima: Instituto de Estudios Peruanos, 2018). Between 1930 and 1980, military governments prevailed and there were failed efforts to establish a strong democratic regime. The country's chief trauma of the twentieth century was the brutal terrorism of Shining Path, a rural Maoist terrorist group whose rise and development the intelligence services failed to adequately appreciate in the early 1980s. The intelligence services' failure to appreciate and understand Shining Path in the 1980s is tied to the country's intense geographic and cultural divisions that have historically resulted in

the Lima-centrism of Peruvian politics. Alberto Bolivar Ocampo ably describes the effects of "Lima-centric glasses" on the institutional culture of the Peruvian security services, an immensely important issue that, due to space constraints, I will not be able to address meaningfully in this chapter. See Alberto Bolívar Ocampo, "Cultura, Periodos Culturales y Servicios de Inteligencia en el Perú, 1960–2008," in *Democratización de la Función de Inteligencia: El Nexo de la Cultura Nacional y la Inteligencia Estratégica*, ed. Russell G. Swenson and Susana C. Lemozy (Washington: National Defense Intelligence College Press, 2009), 261; Andrés Gómez de la Torre Rotta, "Hacia una Cultura de Inteligencia: Un Desafío para el Perú," in *Democratización de de la Función de Inteligencia: El Nexo de la Cultura Nacional y la Inteligencia Estratégica*, ed. Russell G. Swenson and Susana C. Lemozy (Washington: National Defense Intelligence College Press, 2009), 311–12; Michael L. Burgoyne, "The Allure of Quick Victory: Lessons from Peru's Fight against Sendero Luminoso," *Military Review* 90, no. 5 (2010): 70; Juan J. Linz and Alfred Stepan, *Problems of Democratic Transition and Consolidation. Southern Europe, South America, and Post-Communist Europe* (Baltimore: Johns Hopkins University Press, 1996).

4. Also known as a civilian-military coup, or coup from above, an *autogolpe* is initiated by "an elected president who allies with the military to exert dominance over the other branches of government." Daniel C. Hellinger, *Comparative Politics of Latin America: Democracy at Last?* (Routledge, 2020), 336. For additional definitions of a self-coup, see the following literature: Wendy Hunter, "Continuity or Change? Civil-Military Relations in Democratic Argentina, Chile, and Peru," *Political Science Quarterly* 112, no. 3 (1997): 453–75; David Pion-Berlin, *Civil-Military Relations in Latin America: New Analytical Perspectives* (Chapel Hill: University of North Carolina Press, 2003); Steven Levitsky, "Fujimori and Post-Party Politics in Peru," *Journal of Democracy* 10, no. 3 (1999): 78–92, https://doi.org/10.1353/jod.1999.0047. "Fujimori under Fire," *Economist*, July 26, 1997, https://www.economist.com/the-americas/1997/07/24/fujimori-under-fire; Philip Mauceri, "Return of the Caudillo: Autocratic Democracy in Peru," *Third World Quarterly* 18, no. 5 (1997): 901–2.

5. Some Peruvian military officers believed that Fujimori was "in the hip pocket" of Montesinos and the SIN. Montesinos may thus be better described as Fujimori's key collaborator rather than his puppet master. Army Intelligence and Threat Analysis Center, "Who Is Controlling Whom?," counterintelligence periodic summary, October 23, 1990, and "Peru: Does Fujimori's Unofficial Advisor Control the Peruvian Intelligence Community?" in *Fujimori's Rasputin: The Declassified Files on Peru's Former Intelligence Chief, Vladimiro Montesinos*, ed. Tamara Feinstein (Washington, DC: The National Security Archive and Chadwyck-Healy, 2001), Documents 1 and 2. Available at https://nsarchive2.gwu.edu/NSAEBB/NSAEBB37/. The extreme version of this argument would suggest that Fujimori's Peru matched Peter Gill's conception of an "independent security state," in which security agencies operate "autonomously of the government and the rest of the state machine." It is perhaps more plausible that, to borrow Gill's terminology, there was a strong alliance between the "secret state" and the "executive branch" and that the strongest layer of the "Gore-Tex state" thus began outside of those two circles. See Peter Gill, *Policing Politics: Security Intel-*

ligence and the Liberal Democratic State (London: Routledge, 1994), 80–82. Also see Levitsky, "Fujimori and Post-Party Politics," 80–81; Catherine M. Conaghan, *Fujimori's Peru: Deception in the Public Sphere* (Pittsburgh: University of Pittsburgh Press, 2005), 5–6, 13, 28–30; Andrés Gómez de la Torre, "Política y Legislación de Inteligencia en el Perú e Iberoamérica: Tendencias y Perspectivas, Documento 1 (Lima: Instituto de Estudios Internacionales, 2013), 12–13.

6. Ernesto Garcia Calderon, "Peru's Decade of Living Dangerously," *Journal of Democracy* 12, no. 2 (April 2001): 49–51; Fernando Rospigliosi, *Montesinos y las Fuerzas Armadas: Cómo Controló Durante una Década las Instituciones Militares* (Lima: Instituto de Estudios Peruanos, 2000), 201; John McMillan and Pablo Zoido, "How to Subvert Democracy: Montesinos in Peru," *The Journal of Economic Perspectives* 18, no. 4 (2004): 76–82; McMillan, "Montesinos in Peru," 74–89; Rospigliosi, *Montesinos y las Fuerzas Armadas*, 202. It should be noted that the SIN also employed violence in some cases to achieve its ends, evidenced by the massacres carried out by the SIN-connected Colina Group in the early 1990s. However, it appears that Montesinos largely preferred nonviolent tools such as bribery and threats to achieve political control, as McMillan documents (p. 75), and these appear to have been the most widespread implements of the SIN's corrupt power.

7. Rospigliosi, *Montesinos y las Fuerzas Armadas*, 214–25.

8. Established in the 1970s by Abimael Guzmán, the Shining Path, or *Sendero Luminoso*, is an insurgent group that started a campaign against the newly established Peruvian democratic government. The group emerged from the National University of San Cristóbal of Huamanga. Kenney, Fujimori's Coup. Tubbs notes that the Shining Path and the Túpac Amaru Revolutionary Movement (MRTA) "controlled approximately one-third of Peru and were responsible for thousands of civilian deaths in various terrorist activities including the destruction of infrastructure and public executions." Christian D. Tubbs, "Conditions of Democratic Erosion: Has US Democracy Reached a Tipping Point?" (master's thesis, Naval Postgraduate School, 2018), available at http://hdl.handle.net/10945/61290. Also see Rospigliosi, *Montesinos y las Fuerzas Armadas*, 198; Gómez de la Torre, *Política y Legislación de Intelligencia*, 13–14. Some scholars have sought to downplay the role of Montesinos's state security apparatus in delivering the main blow to Shining Path, the 1992 capture of its leader, Abimael Guzman. Rospigliosi and others have asserted that the SIN had "no participation" in the operation, which was planned and carried out by a special police task force. However, that the SIN played no role in Guzman's capture seems to contradict the consensus (which these same individuals support) that the SIN established control of virtually all state security organizations. Regardless of the SIN's role in the matter, it is clear that the capture bolstered the popularity of Fujimori's government.

9. Kurt Weyland, "The Rise and Decline of Fujimori's Neopopulist Leadership," in *The Fujimori Legacy: The Rise of Electoral Authoritarianism in Peru*, ed. Julio F. Carrión (University Park, PA: Penn State University Press, 2006), 20; Julio F. Carrión, "Conclusion: The Rise and Fall of Electoral Authoritarianism in Peru," in *The Fujimori Legacy*, 317; "Agony in the Andes," *Economist*, November 7, 2002, available at https://www.economist.com/unknown/2000/11/07/agony-in-the-andes; "Cleaning Up," *Economist*, November 30, 2000, available at https://www.economist

.com/the-americas/2000/11/30/cleaning-up; "Fujimori under Fire," *Economist*, July 26, 1997, available at https://www.economist.com/the-americas/1997/07/24/fujimori -under-fire; Samuel E. Finer, *The Man on Horseback: The Role of Military in Politics* (London: Pall Mall Press, 1962); Clay Oeffinger and Florina Cristiana Matei, "Peru: When Presidents Go *Praetorian*," in *The Routledge Handbook of Civil-Military Relations*, eds. Florina Cristiana Matei, Carolyn Halladay, and Thomas C. Bruneau (London: Routledge, 2021).

10. Sally Bowen and Jane Holligan, *El Espía Imperfecto: La Telaraña Siniestra de Vladimiro Montesinos* (Lima: PEISA, 2003), 422–29.

11. Carlos Basombrío and Fernando Rospigliosi, *La Seguridad y sus Instituciones en el Perú a Inicios del Siglo XXI: Reformas Democráticas o Neomilitarismo* (Lima: Instituto de Estudios Peruanos, 2006), 251; Bowen and Holligan, *El Espía Imperfecto*, 434–45.

12. Contreras, *Historia del Perú*, 429. It was possible for Fujimori to flee and stay in Japan indefinitely because he had dual citizenship: Peruvian and Japanese. "Fujimori a Japanese, Can Stay: Kono," *The Japanese Times*, December 12, 2000. Available at https://www.japantimes.co.jp/news/2000/12/13/national/fujimori-a-japanese-can-stay-kono/.

13. Contreras, *Historia del Perú*, 429–30.

14. Jaris Mujica, "La Desactivación del Servicio de Inteligencia Nacional: De la Salida del Personal de Inteligencia al Desarrollo de las Agencias Privadas de Inteligencia en el Perú," *Revista de Ciencia Política y Gobierno* 1, no. 2 (2014): 132, 136–37.

15. Law No. 27479, Article 11. Outside of the top-level intelligence agencies (such as the present-day DINI), the Ministry of the Interior and the Ministry of Defense each have several subordinate intelligence organizations.

16. In theory, the CNI would serve as the "governing body of highest level of the SINA" and would consist of the leaders of each of Peru's main intelligence organizations, as well as a chairman appointed by the president. The text of the law implied that the DINIE's function was to produce intelligence, whereas the CNI's role was to direct the overall SINA. Law No. 27479, Articles 15, 17, 20, and 28. Besides the CNI's chairman and DINIE's director, the CNI's members included the head of the intelligence division of the armed forces' joint staff, the director of intelligence for the Ministry of the Interior, a representative from the Ministry of Foreign Relations, and representatives from the Ministries of Finance and Education.

17. Law No. 27479, Articles 22, 32. Examples of overlap and ambiguity are rife within these articles, which establish the "functions" of the CNI and the DINIE. For instance, the CNI is tasked to "establish objectives and policies of the SINA that orient its activities," while the DINIE is to "orient the effort of the search for information." Andrés Gómez de la Torre Rotta, "Perú: Frustraciones en los Intentos por Reconstruir Su Sistema de Inteligencia," in *Profesionalismo de Inteligencia en Las Américas, Edición Revisada*, ed. Russell G. Swenson and Susana C. Lemozy (Washington: Joint Military Intelligence College, 2004), 168–69; Gómez de la Torre, *Política y Legislación de Inteligencia*, 16.

18. Gómez de la Torre, *Política y Legislación de Inteligencia*, 16.

19. Supreme Decree No. 065 of June 2, 2001.

20. See Comisión de la Verdad y Reconciliación, *Informe Final de la Comisión de la Verdad y Reconciliación del Perú*, Lima: CVR, 2003.

21. Eduardo Estévez, "Comparing Intelligence Democratization in Latin America: Argentina, Peru, and Ecuador Cases," *Intelligence and National Security* 29, no. 4 (2014): 552–80.

22. Law 28664.

23. Bolívar Ocampo, "Cultura y Servicios de Inteligencia," 270–71; Gómez de la Torre Rotta, "Perú: Frustaciones," 184; Mujica, "La Desactivación del SIN," 137. Juan Velit, the first civilian intelligence chief in Peru's history, had to contend with Toledo's selection of a retired general, Daniel Mora, as his nominally subordinate DINIE director. Mora, for his part, used the law's ambiguity to establish his own de facto independence from the CNI chairman; he apparently resented "having a civilian as a superior, especially in an entity as identified with the Armed Forces as intelligence was." Gómez de la Torre Rotta, "Perú: Frustaciones," 159–61 and 308–9; Basombrío and Rospigliosi, *La Seguridad y sus Instituciones*, 267–68, 72. Also, see Gregory Weeks, "A Preference for Deference: Reforming the Military's Intelligence Role in Argentina, Chile and Peru," *Third World Quarterly* 29, no. 1 (2008): 54–55.

24. Mujica, "La Desactivación del SIN," 137–41, 46–48; and Juan Velit, "Inteligencia Sin Espejismos," interview by Pablo O'Brien, *Caretas*, May 23, 2002, http://www2.caretas.pe/2002/1722/articulos/inteligencia.phtml. However, many of these former intelligence members found alternate employment within the growing industry of private security firms.

25. Mujica, "La Desactivación del SIN," 145; Gómez de la Torre Rotta, "Perú: Frustaciones," 184.

26. Bolívar Ocampo, "Cultura y Servicios de Inteligencia," 270–71; Gómez de la Torre Rotta, "Perú: Frustaciones," 184; Basombrío and Rospigliosi, *La Seguridad y sus Instituciones*, 274.

27. Bolívar Ocampo, "Cultura y Servicios de Inteligencia," 270–71; Gómez de la Torre Rotta, "Perú: Frustaciones," 184; Basombrío and Rospigliosi, *La Seguridad y sus Instituciones*, 274.

28. Basombrío and Rospigliosi, *La Seguridad y sus Instituciones*, 253–66; Gómez de la Torre Rotta, "Hacia una Cultura de Inteligencia," 314; Gómez de la Torre Rotta, "Perú: Frustaciones," 169–72,185, 256, and 81; Harvard University Project on Justice in Times of Transition, *Recomendaciones para la Reforma de Inteligencia en el Perú a la Luz de la Experiencia de Otros Países del Mundo*, 2002, 2.

29. Law No. 28664, Article 8.

30. Law No. 28664, Articles 7, 23–24.

31. Florina Cristiana Matei and Thomas C. Bruneau, "Policymakers and Intelligence Reform in the New Democracies," *International Journal of Intelligence and CounterIntelligence* 24, no. 4 (2011): 656–91. The law did not provide for budgetary control of intelligence budget, although the comptroller general of the Republic had the power to control special resources by the DINI director. The law did not stipulate any control over Peru's military intelligence, although it oversees SINA. Also, see Law No. 28664, Article 21.

32. Law No. 28664, Article 20, Glossary.

33. Law No. 28664, Article 17. These declassification periods ranged from ten to twenty years, depending on the classification level. This was later changed to remove the distinction in classification levels; currently, all classified material has a mandatory declassification period of twenty years. See DL No. 1141, Article 6.

34. Andrés Gómez de la Torre Rotta and Arturo Medrano Carmona, "La Reorganización de Inteligencia en el Perú: Aspectos Jurídicos, Políticos, y Comparativos en la región," in *Inteligencia Estratégica Latinoamericana: Perspectivas y Ejes Predominantes para la Toma de Decisiones Estratégicas ante un Mundo en Cambio*, ed. José Gabriel Paz (Buenos Aires: Ministerio de Defensa, 2015), 183.

35. This reasoning is outlined by Basombrio and Rospigliosi, who indicate that the lack of a framework for preventing unauthorized disclosure by politicians encouraged the intelligence community to subvert it and withhold information from Congress. A Peruvian subject matter expert echoed this argument to me in a personal conversation in 2019. See Basombrío and Rospigliosi, *La Seguridad y sus Instituciones*, 284.

36. Basombrio and Rospigliosi point out that the ad hoc appointment fell short of the recommendations of the 2004 reform commission, which proposed that judges be appointed to address such cases for a period of three years. See Basombrío and Rospigliosi, *La Seguridad y sus Instituciones*, 284.

37. See Gómez de la Torre Rotta, "Perú: Frustaciones," 173. Meanwhile, the stigma of intelligence matters, associated with Montesinos-era excesses and more recent scandals, discouraged judges further from getting involved in them; as a result, intelligence agencies might simply bypass an inexperienced and uninterested judiciary. Discussion, in 2019 with a Peruvian subject matter expert.

38. It should be noted that this legislative stability does not imply a lack of abuses. While no scandals emerged that might force another suspension of intelligence activities and require a new round of reforms, leaks and abuses within the SINA continued, several of which would be revealed during the administration of Garcia's successor. See Bolívar Ocampo, "Cultura y Servicios de Inteligencia," 271–72.

39. Law 29915, Articles 1–2. The bill (1380.2012/PE) proposing this delegation of authority cited increasing levels of "crime and insecurity" as its impetus. This decision questions the will and expertise of the Peruvian Congress to perform its oversight role effectively. This questionable temporary transfer of power from the legislative to executive branch occurred under Article 104.

40. DL 1141, Article 19. See Sentencia 0016-2013-PI/TC, 12–20. The case was largely decided in favor of the opposition congressmen on the grounds that DL 1141 imposed on Congress's ability to regulate itself.

41. Resoluciones del Tribunal Constitucional, 0016-2013-PI/TC, August 21, 2013, and October 30, 2013. Documents and decisions of the Constitutional Tribunal are available on the body's website at https://www.tc.gob.pe/.

42. Congresistas de la Republica c. Poder Ejecutivo, Sentencia 0016-2013-PI/TC, 2017, 4.

43. Law No. 30535, modification of DL No. 1141 Article 36. The law does not specify whether this includes the secret budget, which is typically referred to as "special resources."

44. "Parte policial confirmaría reglaje a la vicepresidenta Marisol Espinoza," *El Comercio*, January 19, 2015. Officials claimed that the agent was in the area of Espinoza's residence in response to the possibility of increased threats to the U.S. Embassy. The press largely rejected this version of events, citing the distance between the embassy and Espinoza's residence. "Aparecen nuevos nombres rastreados por Dirección Nacional de Inteligencia," *El Comercio*, March 26, 2015; "En los últimos seis meses del gobierno de García se rastreó a más de 700 personas," *El Comercio*, March 21, 2015; "La DINI rastreó bienes de empresarios, periodistas, y miembros de Estado," *El Comercio*, March 20, 2015; and Fernando Rospigliosi, "La Crisis de los Espías," *El Comercio*, May 22, 2015. Although President Humala and Vice President Espinoza were very close when Humala became president in July 2011, Espinoza ultimately disagreed with Humala's shift from leftist (as he campaigned for presidency) to right policies. For example, when Humala adopted a new youth labor law in 2015, Espinosa urged him to revise it, upon protests from students and union representatives who worried that it would limit labor rights in favor of the private sector. Humala refused. https://www.peruviantimes.com/22/police-intelligence-officials-reported-spying-on-vice-president/23658/.

45. "Perú: primera ministra Ana Jara, obligada a renunciar a su cargo," BBC News, March 31, 2015. Available at https://www.bbc.com/mundo/ultimas_noticias/2015/03/150331_ultnot_peru_ministra_jara_renuncia_lav.

46. Comisión Reorganizadora de la Dirección Nacional de Inteligencia, *Informe de la Comisión Reorganizadora de la Dirección Nacional de Inteligencia*, 2015, 19, 20. Also see Christian Schambaher Céspedes, *Claves para Entender la Crisis de Inteligencia en el Perú y Propuestas de Solución* (Lima: Escuela Conjunta de la Fuerzas Armadas, 2015). Fernando Rospigliosi, "La DINI: Una alternativa," *El Comercio*, April 12, 2015; and Comisión Reorganizadora, *Informe*, 19–20. For example, it is noteworthy that, at the height of the SIN's abuse of its power in 1995, Peru was strategically surprised by Ecuador. This example provides compelling evidence that intelligence democratization, which can serve to orient intelligence agencies toward their legally defined missions, can increase intelligence effectiveness in the big picture of national security.

47. Law No. 30535, modification of DL 1141, Article 2.

48. Law No. 30535, modification of DL 1141, Article 16.

49. See Bill 2468/2017-CR. It should be noted that this amendment to the Law No. 30535 was not passed. The delay in the bill's progress appears to have come as a result of the Intelligence Committee's recommendation, after the successful vote, to change elements of one article of the new text, as expressed in Oficio 077-2018-2019-MMA-CI-CR. The bill may also be a casualty of the legislative-executive deadlock that has characterized current Peruvian politics.

50. http://www.congreso.gob.pe/Docs/files/CONSTITUTION_27_11_2012_ENG.pdf. However, it quickly became clear that both public opinion and the armed forces were firmly behind Vizcarra; Congress was widely viewed as corrupt, obstructionist, and ineffective. Also in accordance with the law, Peru held new parliamentary elections in January 2020.

51. Merino was forced to leave office by ongoing protests in support of Vizcarra, which were handled by the police very brutally, causing several deaths and disappearances. Sonia Goldenberg, "Is Peru Ungovernable," *The New York Times*, January 5, 2021, available at https://www.nytimes.com/2021/01/05/opinion/is-peru-ungovernable.html; Adam Taylor, "Peru Had Three Presidents in One Week. Now It Has Four Months to Fix the System," *The Washington Post*, November 20, 2020, available at https://www.washingtonpost.com/world/2020/11/20/peru-third-president-francisco-sagasti/; "Martín Vizcarra Dismisses Peru's congress," *The Economist*, October 5, 2019, available at https://www.economist.com/the-americas/2019/10/03/martin-vizcarra-dismisses-perus-congress; Oeffinger and Matei, "Peru: When Presidents Go *Praetorian.*"

52. "Peru Election: Socialist Pedro Castillo Claims Victory Ahead of Official Result," *The Guardian*, June 16, 2021, available at https://www.theguardian.com/world/2021/jun/16/peru-election-socialist-pedro-castillo-claims-victory-ahead-of-official-result; "Peru election: Why has no winner been declared?," BBC News, June 17, 2021, available at https://www.bbc.com/news/world-latin-america-57511485; Mitra Taj and Julie Turkewitz, "Pedro Castillo, Leftist Political Outsider, Wins Peru Presidency," *New York Times*, July 19, 2021, available at https://www.nytimes.com/2021/07/19/world/americas/peru-election-pedro-castillo.html.

53. On July 29, 2021, Castillo named Guido Bellido—a member of his political party—as prime minister. The nomination signaled Castillo's shift from a moderate governance approach—which he campaigned on—to a more leftist one, which triggered massive protests in the country. "Designación de Guido Bellido en la PCM pondría en riesgo la lucha contra el terrorismo, según expertos," *El Comercio*, July 30, 2021, available at https://elcomercio.pe/lima/designacion-de-guido-bellido-en-la-pcm-pondria-en-riesgo-la-lucha-contra-el-terrorismo-pedro-castillo-noticia/; Marco Aquino and Marcelo Rochabrun, "Peru's Castillo Names Far-Left PM; No Finance Minister in Cabinet," Reuters, July 30, 2021, available at https://www.reuters.com/world/europe/peru-president-castillo-names-member-far-left-party-prime-minister-2021-07-29/; "Peru Protesters Rally against Pedro Castillo's New Government," *Aljazeera*, August 1, 2021, available at https://www.aljazeera.com/news/2021/8/1/peru-protesters-rally-against-pedro-castillos-new-government.

54. Matthew D. McCubbins and Thomas Schwartz, "Congressional Oversight Overlooked: Police Patrols versus Fire Alarms," *American Journal of Political Science* 28, no. 1 (1984): 165–79. doi: 10.2307/2110792.

55. Matei and Bruneau, "Policymakers."

56. Harvard University, *Recomendaciones para la Reforma de Inteligencia*, 3–4; Florina Cristiana Matei, "The Media's Role in Intelligence Democratization," *International Journal of Intelligence and CounterIntelligence* 27, no. 1 (2014): 73–108. Matei provides a detailed study of the importance of the media in the democratic reform of intelligence. Also see Gómez de la Torre Rotta, "Perú: Frustaciones," 156; Gómez de la Torre Rotta, "Hacia una Cultura de Inteligencia," 313; Basombrío and Rospigliosi, *La Seguridad y sus Instituciones*, 281; Mujica, "La Desactivación del SIN," 131; Céspedes, *Claves para Entender la Crisis de Inteligencia*, 5.

57. See Comisión Reorganizadora, *Informe*, 5, 36, 44. The Commission writes, "The press has accused DINI of carrying out actions that were legal in addition to accusing it of others that were not."

58. In 2006, Basombrío and Rospigliosi noted that "almost all civilian politicians" in Peru believe that in the "natural order of things . . . the intelligence services always spy on politicians and on all classes of people and institutions, no matter the government." In 2015, the Reorganization Committee noted widespread public suspicion of DINI espionage in its discussion of intelligence culture in Peru and attributed such distrust to the intelligence services' history since the Fujimori era. That Peruvians simply expect that intelligence services regularly spy on citizens was further confirmed to me in multiple conversations with Peruvian subject matter experts in 2019. See Comisión Reorganizadora, *Informe*, 43; Basombrío and Rospigliosi, *La Seguridad y sus Instituciones*, 248.

59. Basombrío and Rospigliosi, *La Seguridad y sus Instituciones*, 269.

60. Gómez de la Torre Rotta, "Perú: Frustaciones," 158.

61. Comisión Reorganizadora, *Informe*, 27–28. The report breaks down the DINI's pool of university degrees by discipline: forty-seven engineering (23 percent), thirty-eight law (19 percent), twenty-one administration (10 percent), nineteen accounting (9 percent), four political science (2 percent), ten sociology (5 percent), two anthropology (1 percent), and sixteen communication science (8 percent).

62. Comisión Reorganizadora, *Informe*, 27. The breakdown by age is as follows: 28 from ages 25 to 30 (7 percent), 52 from ages 31 to 35 (14 percent), 63 from ages 36 to 40 (17 percent), 111 from ages 41 to 50 (30 percent), 77 from ages 51 to 60 (21 percent) and 43 from ages 61 to 70 (11 percent). In addition, its 374 members, DINI also has 275 temporary attachments from the armed forces.

63. Comisión Reorganizadora, *Informe*, 30.

64. Comisión Reorganizadora, *Informe*, 27. The breakdown by years of service is as follows: 31 with less than 1 year (8 percent), 142 with 1–5 years (38 percent), 85 with 6–10 years (23 percent), 99 with 11–20 years (26 percent), 17 with more than 21 years (5 percent).

65. Comisión Reorganizadora, *Informe*, 29-30.

66. Comisión Reorganizadora, *Informe*, 35; and Santiago Llop Meseguer, Luis Martínez Enríquez, Fernando Valeriano-Ferrer González, *Apuntes de Inteligencia Básica* (Callao: Escuela Superior de Guerra Naval, 2013.

67. Gómez de la Torre Rotta, "Hacia una Cultura de Inteligencia," 313; Céspedes, *Claves para Entender la crisis de inteligencia*, 16–-17. The 2017 Law 30618 stipulates that the ENI should conduct outreach to universities. Law No. 30618, modification to DL 1141, Article 17.16.

68. Including vesting the preponderance of power within a strong executive; unequal power and enforcement mechanisms for the three coequal branches (executive, legislative, and judicial); and weak legacy of military subordination to civilian control. See Kurt Weyland, "Neopopulism and Neoliberalism in Latin America: How Much Affinity?," *Third World Quarterly* 24, no. 6 (2003): 1095–115; Paul Sondrol, "The Presidentialist Tradition in Latin America," *International Journal of Public*

Administration 28, no. 5–6 (2005): 518–22; Estévez, "Comparing Intelligence Democratization in Latin America"; Eduardo Estévez, "Intelligence in Peru: Between Democratic Reform and Regression," *Journal of Mediterranean and Balkan Intelligence* 7, no. 1 (June 2016): 107–24

69. See Matei, "Intelligence Reform in New Democracies," 611–13. Peru's case aligns well with many elements of Matei and Bruneau's findings. However, it is noteworthy that Matei and Bruneau identify the maintenance of personnel in the intelligence services from the non-democratic regime as a factor that is prone to cause abuses and scandals. Peru offers a counterpoint to this stance. In the Peruvian case, there was in fact a mass exodus of ex-SIN personnel following the democratic transition, but, as we have seen, scandals persisted anyways as a result of executive abuse and personnel instability in the intelligence services.

Chapter Nine

Uruguay

Nicolás Alvarez

After a five-year-long debate, at the end of 2018, the Uruguayan legislature approved the creation of a National System of State Intelligence through Law No. 19696—making Uruguay the last South American country to achieve legislation that guarantees regulation and democratic civilian control of intelligence. This chapter provides an assessment of the partial democratic reforms of the Uruguayan intelligence services since the democratic transition in 1984.[1]

HISTORICAL BACKGROUND OF URUGUAY AND THE ROLE OF INTELLIGENCE AGENCIES

In 1973 Uruguay became an authoritarian military regime, through a successful military coup d'état, which replaced political parties in control of the state apparatus.[2] The roots of the military dictatorship are twofold. First, a deep economic, social, and political crisis after World War II produced violent civilian armed groups, prompting an equally aggressive state response.[3] Second, as in the case of other Latin American countries studied in this volume—most notably, Argentina—the Cold War context compelled Uruguay to align with a superpower, like the United States.

These developments granted intelligence agencies a disproportionate amount of power in Uruguay, while both East and West jockeyed for influence. The USSR, on the one hand, managed to infiltrate its spies into the region and Uruguay was no exception.[4] On the other hand, when communist guerrillas emerged in Uruguay, the United States—which desired to maintain Latin America as a region free of Communism—intensified its training of the

Uruguayan security forces to fight these groups, including intelligence agencies, with virtually no attention to democratic oversight. In this connection, the United States conducted training for the intelligence agency, established in 1947, called the Intelligence and Liaison Service (SIE), whose main goal became fighting communism, and the Ministry of Defense's Defense Information Service (SID), created in 1965.[5] The training focused on counterinsurgency tactics—by any means and to great effect—but lacked a corresponding discussion about human rights.

Although guerrilla forces were defeated in 1972, the country next plunged into one of the darkest periods in its history—the civil-military dictatorship (1973–1985),[6] when the state control over the population became complete and repressive, with the help of the willing Uruguayan intelligence apparatus. Virtually all public agencies had a military officer posted for liaison purposes as well as maintaining surveillance, and a registry was created that classified every resident in the country according to their propensity to challenge or comply with the regime's directives.[7] Additionally, to prevent the creation of an autonomous intelligence service, all military officers were trained in intelligence tasks, with the ultimate goal of spying on one another.[8] In other words, Uruguay became a complete surveillance and police state, with the intelligence agencies—especially the National Directorate of Information and Intelligence (DNII)—being the regime's political police. The whole intelligence apparatus under the coordination of the Coordinating Agency for Anti-Subversive Activities (OCOA), created in 1973, collaborated with counterparts from other Latin American nations, with managerial oversight from the notorious Operation Condor organization.[9]

DEMOCRATIC TRANSITION AND CONSOLIDATION

The armed forces sought to legitimize the coup government through a constitutional plebiscite in 1980, but the vote came out negative. After this adverse result, the regime gradually lost strength. Democratic elections occurred in 1982, commenced Uruguay's transition to democracy. Finally, in 1984, representatives of the Colorado Party (PC), the Broad Front (FA), and the Civic Union (UC) negotiated the end of the regime with the military leadership in the well-known "Naval Club Pact."[10] In this context, the Uruguayan armed forces at least appeared to receive some new prerogatives—like, for example, immunity to military officers from prosecution of human rights abuses carried out during the dictatorship[11]—in exchange for seeming to surrender power to the new government and its civilianized order.

Nevertheless, the intelligence agencies, did not embrace the return to civilian rule. Rather Uruguay's military and intelligence services adopted peacekeeping operations without civilian consent to isolate the military artificially from civilian oversight. This opportunity was provided by the closing of the Cold War and the resulting global geopolitical shift; Uruguay's armed forces had to contemplate their roles and missions within a new ideological construct. During the 1980s–1990s, Uruguay began to reconcile the relationship among society, the armed forces, and the government and sought domestic democratic transition and consolidation. Conventional wisdom of developed nations prescribed adoption of peacekeeping operations as the silver bullet to achieve democratic reforms.[12] The reality of the situation is more nuanced and adoption of peacekeeping operations by the Uruguayan military (intelligence service) has stunted civil-military relationships, because the impetus was to maintain autonomy from civilian control, opposed to expediting democratic consolidation.

Uruguay's previous experience with democracy allowed the country—after negotiations between civilians and the military officers—to rebuild quickly such requisite democratic institutions as free and fair elections, political pluralism, freedom of speech and association, individual rights and liberties, democratic civil-military relations, and free market economy, to name a few.[13] However, Uruguay has no civilian or political institutions that oversee or control the military's UN peacekeeping role.[14] The few civilians embedded in the defense sector have abdicated decision-making authority over troop deployments and UN reimbursement to the armed forces.[15] Essentially, the military has dictated the military budget without civilian control from 1985 to 2010.[16] To further illustrate, utilizing specific data points, in 2006 the Uruguayan military, and by extension the intelligence agencies, was compensated US$56 million for troop compensation and equipment reimbursement. This figure accounted for 26 percent of the entire defense budget of Uruguay for that year.[17] Another data point is from 2002 in relation to the civil sector. The Uruguayan military complex received US$20 million in personnel compensation for peacekeeping in the Democratic Republic of Congo. In comparison Uruguay's major domestic export, beef, totaled US$16 million in the same year. Therefore, peacekeeping operations were the most profitable export of Uruguay.[18] The military and intelligence agencies are able to enhance military wages, replace aging equipment, perform training and mission readiness.[19] Uruguay's military perfected utilizing UN PKO (peacekeeping operations) to supplement military members' wages and update its equipment. Unfortunately, this policy provided the defense sector greater latitude to operate without civilian oversight and not place the military under the sphere of civil authority.[20]

The armed forces accepted the authority of the democratically elected authorities, while maintaining traditional management autonomy.[21] Consequently, the legacy of the past intelligence culture and *praxis,* developed in the particular context of the civil-military dictatorship, became one of the most endemic challenges faced by successive democratic governments that attempted to reform intelligence. It has become apparent that military leadership did not negotiate to relinquish autonomy to civilian oversight that has delayed democratic transition and consolidation.

CONSOLIDATION AND ATTEMPTS AT REFORM

In November 1984, Uruguay regained a semblance of a democratic civil society with independent executive and legislative authorities by means of free and fair elections. Dr. Julio María Sanguinetti, a member of the PC elected at that time (1985–1990), was able to quickly restore a general climate of representative democracy. Political prisoners were released, dismissed public officials were reinstated, and the parliamentary and judicial branches were reinstated.[22]

However, the new democratic government was ineffective in requiring the armed forces to appear before civilian courts for trials. Consequently, the Sanguinetti administration decided to promote the Law on the Expiry of the Punitive Claim of the State (Law No. 15848), which—*grosso modo*—granted amnesty to the military.[23] The National Party (PN), which had not participated in the previous negotiations between civilians and the military, decided to support Law No. 15848, on grounds that military amnesty was an "implicit fact" of the agreements, whereas the FA, which had participated together with the PC in the negotiations, rejected the initiative, arguing against amnesty.[24] Despite these differences, the law was passed in 1986 with the majority support of the PC and PN members as a manner to accelerate political closure and usher democratic governance. Subsequently, different social movements and the FA succeeded in having Law No. 15848 submitted to an annulment referendum in 1989.[25] The law was voted on by the public for revocation—57 percent voted for annulment—and became codified law.

With regard to intelligence agencies, in the aftermath of the 1984 elections, the military government approved Law No. 15663, by which the SID became known as the Armed Forces Information Service (SIFFA) and was directly dependent on the Board of Commanders in Chief of the Armed Forces. However, two years later, the Expiry Law determined that this service would be renamed the Directorate General of Defense Information (DGID) and would again report to the Ministry of National Defense. Finally, by Law No. 15848, the DGID was organized into a General Directorate with a single director and three subdirectorates in charge of senior officers distributed among the three forces (army, navy, and air force). The renaming of the intelligence organization and bureaucratic reshuffling did not change or diminish the substantive power of the intelligence apparatus. The new organization—heir of the dictatorship—continued to be led by the armed forces and maintained its prerogative in unilaterally conducting high profile intelligence missions both domestically and internationally to fulfill parochial interest, devoid of civilian oversight and benefit to the nation's citizens. Additional problems derived from the lack of democratic civilian control of intelligence agencies created further friction or nonaligned governmental agencies.

The kidnapping and subsequent murder in Uruguay, in 1992, of the Chilean biochemist Eugenio Berríos—agent of the Chilean dictator Augusto Pinochet and member of the National Intelligence Directorate (DINA)—confirmed the magnitude of the problem: armed forces not complying with civilian authorities and extrajudicial killings.[26] The body of the former Chilean intelligence operator was found on the Uruguayan coast in 1995, and a decade later, in 2006, three Uruguayan soldiers were extradited to Chile to account for the killing of Berríos and sentenced to prison by that country's justice system.[27] In an interview conducted in 2008, then Uruguayan President Luis Alberto Lacalle (1990–1995) acknowledged the situation "as a relationship between members of the intelligence services acting outside their specific functions and guided by personal relationships and commitments."[28]

The "Berríos case" revealed the power and autonomy that the intelligence services continued to maintain during democratic transition. This extrajudicial killing led to the second restructuring of the intelligence community by President Julio María Sanguinetti (1995–2000) and the transformation of the DGID into the National Directorate of State Intelligence (DINACIE) by Decree No. 405/99. According to Alejandro Bihar, Decree 405/999 charged DINACIE, with the implementation of "a State Intelligence System that—in favor of the capitalization of existing organizations and resources—plans, coordinates, and executes intelligence at the highest level of the state, with the purpose that it is timely and truthfully available to the Executive Branch."[29] However, to better exercise civil control, according to press sources at the time, the civilian elites had the intention of "diminishing the autonomy granted to the services and achieving an effective coordination";[30] the legality of a decree superseded the law and, together with limited parliamentary authority, produced a controversial tone to the discussion of the new body and harkened of authoritarianism.[31]

During 1995–2000, the executive and legislature discussed passing an intelligence law for the first time and creating an accountable "Intelligence

Community."[32] Contemporary press sources detailed the executive's desire to create a General Intelligence Secretariat to coordinate different state services and maintain appropriate oversight. This construct would designate a civilian director; however, the military and police surreptitiously scuttled this necessary program to minimize encroachment upon their power structure.[33]

According to the approved regulations, DINACIE would continue to be responsible for aggregating and disseminating intelligence at the highest level through the coordination and planning of all information and counter-information activities developed by the various existing specialized agencies. The organization maintained control over external and internal security. DINACIE was led by the National Director-General Officer. The position rotated every two years and alternated among the three military forces. A general coordinator—who must be an army colonel—and five divisions within the exterior and the interior of the organization must be consulted and ratify the National Director-General Officer selection. The existence of a state intelligence governing body controlled by the military and with the capacity to produce internal intelligence generated unease among the police forces that later claimed autonomy from the new body.[34]Additionally, external civilian control mechanisms were not established.

The friction between agencies and the controversies over the decree that gave form to DINACIE became inconsequential in 2001 during the presidency of Dr. Jorge Batlle, a member of the PC party. The events of September 11, 2001, drastically changed the global security dynamic, producing an era of nations desiring to avoid the appearance of supporting or harboring terrorists from U.S. and coalition nations. Accordingly, the Uruguayan government proactively granted DINACIE the responsibility of conducting counterterrorism intelligence within the nation's territory to conform with U.S. global counterterrorism objectives in order to signal support, gain access to resources, and curtail possible U.S. intervention.[35] During this rapid shift, two issues faded from prominence, even though they had proved insurmountable for previous democratic governments: the military monopoly on intelligence matters and the contribution of the armed forces to the internal security tasks of the state.[36]

In this context, FA entered into the national government in 2005. With this entry the balance of defense, security, and intelligence constituted a real challenge for a left-wing political party historically characterized by its critical stance toward the leadership model of the traditional parties (PN and PC). Still, the administration, as well as its predecessors, did not manage, in principle, to effect substantive changes in intelligence matters—intelligence agencies, thus, remained powerful. One year after the government took office, the Ministry of Defense initiated the "National Debate on Defense" with the aim of further subordinating military and intelligence agencies under civilian control and supporting citizens' interest. The debate, which did not include intelligence as it was considered to have "its own status,"[37] culminated in the adoption of the National Defense Framework Act (no. 18860). The act establishes an unprecedented set of provisions, granting civilian control over the military.[38] Although intelligence reform remains incomplete because of powerful, entrenched Uruguayan individuals and organizations, and the distortive effects of U.S.-led global counterterrorism efforts, the Defense Framework Law centralized matters related to military intelligence within the General Staff of Defense—a military ministerial advisory body that reported directly to civilian authorities. [39]

In parallel, President Tabaré Vázquez (2005–2010) created, by Law No. 17930 (National Budget 2005–2010), the position of Coordinator of the State Intelligence Services. Initially, the new body was declared autonomous by the president, escaping any kind of external control. In little more than a decade, the office suffered from a series of corruption that reflected the hierarchal weaknesses of the organization, particularly the lack of oversight. As a result of the controversies generated within the political system, the office was neither regulated nor staffed during the first administration of the FA. Since its creation, the position remained vacant for greater than half of the time.[40] Then, in approximately a five-year span, it had three incumbents, one civilian and two retired generals: Augusto Gregori (2010–2013), Ramón Bonilla (2013–2015), and Washington Martínez (2016–2018), respectively. This churn led to much turmoil as many military and intelligence agencies filled a position for a few years and switched people out to combat cronyism and complacency.

In this context, the political opposition legislator, José Amy (PC), presented to parliament two bills that sought to generate external controls of intelligence activities and for those carried out by the intelligence coordinator. Following this event, the General Assembly, with the support of all political parties, decided in 2011 to create an *ad hoc* independent state intelligence commission to better investigate the inner workings of the intelligence apparatus. The findings of the special commission suggested the creation of a National Intelligence System to restructure the foci of power toward civilian control and increase transparency.

After more than five years of debating the characteristics of Law No. 19696, the legislature ratified the law in 2018, thereby creating the National System of State Intelligence. Additionally, the position of Coordinator of the State Intelligence Services was dissolved. Moreover, Law No. 19355 of 2015 was amended, the DINACIE was renamed as the Strategic Intelligence Directorate (DIE) and placed under the General Staff of Defense to seize control of intelligence functions into the domain of civil servants. Furthermore, subsequent Law No. 19670 of 2018, also passed by the legislative branch, created the National Police Investigations Directorate (DIP), which currently directs and supervises the General Directorate of Information and Intelligence (DGII)—heir of the DNII.[41] These complementary laws and amendments are instruments with which the coequal branches of government can begin rebalancing the intelligence agencies, power hierarchy in favor of a democratically consolidated form of governance.

Almost two election cycles were exhausted between negotiations and polemics, advances and setbacks. Intelligence reform was interrupted by the confluence of an intense electoral campaign, which revealed the government's excessive powers, and the most important intelligence scandal in the country's history. As one Uruguayan columnist observed with suspicion, it is possible to argue that the Intelligence Law was "the most discussed initiative in Parliament since the return of democracy."[42]

The creation of the parliamentary intelligence commission in 2011 represented the first serious attempt to reform the sector since the restoration of democracy. The various party representatives came to the negotiating table with more agreements than differences. The projects initially presented by the PC were quickly complemented with two initiatives that the FA and the PN presented to the parliamentary commission. Subsequently, the executive branch submitted a bill that, in general terms, was closely related to the initiatives presented by the parliament. The commission finished its activity in 2014 and presented a bill that, in addition to being supported by all the parliamentary political parties, had the direct assistance of the prestigious Geneva Centre for Security Sector Governance (DCAF). However, with the arrival of the 2014 legislative and presidential elections, the bill did not get to be discussed in plenary and the issue was not part of the electoral campaign that shelved the commission's proposal. The reason for obfuscating the bill and further inquiries was to protect powerful political members that had participated in illegal activities.

Friday, September 2, 2016, was no ordinary day in Uruguay. The weekly newspaper *Brecha*, in a note titled *Continued Services*,[43] stated that Uruguayan intelligence services had been carrying out illegal espionage activities—against presidents, former presidents, senators, deputies, judges, prosecutors, political parties, unions, and social organizations—since the restoration of democracy. Samuel Blixen, the journalist in charge of disseminating this information, based his statements on two expert witnesses' reports that had been commissioned by Judge Beatriz Larrieu as a result of the material seized from the private home of the late Colonel Elmar Castiglioni at the end of 2015. The so-called *Castiglioni archive*, which had been confiscated by the Justice Department, was linked to an intelligence file seized in 2006 by the then head of the Ministry of Defense, Azucena Berruti—the *Berruti archive*.[44]

This intelligence maleficence was corroborated, not mere speculation. As a result, the civilian elites decided to create a parliamentary investigatory commission with the aim of studying the Berruti archive in depth. Barely a month after the creation of the commission, in November 2016, the executive decided to submit a bill to parliament with the purpose of creating a National State Intelligence System. This bill reflected the work of the intelligence commission that had worked from 2011 to 2014. Finally, after two years of parallel legislative work, in August 2018, the investigative commission confirmed the occurrence of illegal espionage, transferred its results to the justice system, and recommended to the parliament the approval of the bill that instituted the state intelligence system.

As of the following month, the Special Commission on Security and Cohabitation, which included—among its members—representatives of the investigative commission and the former intelligence commission, expedited the processing of the bill, which, in October 2018, was approved by both legislative chambers and promulgated by the executive (Law No. 19.696).

ANALYSIS

The Uruguayan Parliament unanimously ratified the proposal of the executive power to appoint General Washington Martínez as Secretary of Strategic Intelligence. Currently, while parliament is working on the creation of the bicameral parliamentary intelligence commission, the executive is attempting to restrict the administrative aspects that will allow the new secretary of state to function and maintain oversight.

Although it is too early to evaluate the impact of the new legal framework on the democratic governance of the intelligence sector, it is possible to unravel the benefits and eventual challenges of the Uruguayan reform. The following subsections briefly review the four categories developed by Otamendi and Estévez in the *matrix on intelligence governance*.[45] (1) resources: legislative and financial; (2) organization: political leadership, recruitment, and training; (3) procedures: special procedures, classification, and declassification of information; and (4) relations: external and public supervision.

Control and Oversight

One of the main new features of the legislation are the *checks-and-balances* mechanisms. Internally, the director or head of each intelligence agency is designated responsible and ultimately accountable to the president for his personnel's actions, as well as the respective authorities in the hierarchical chain of the administration. The priority areas of this control are the human and technical resources administered by each agency, including the SIEE.

In addition to the external control established through the authorizations granted by the Judiciary Power, the legal basis grants the General Assembly the power to create a bicameral parliamentary commission. Such a commission is composed of legislators from all political parties with parliamentary representation, and its main task will be to control and supervise the performance of the SNIE.

The relationship between parliament and the executive power utilizes the director of the SIEE and/or the ministers members of the SNIE to liaise between the two governmental branches. Additionally, the executive is obligated to provide detailed activity information on intelligence operations to the parliament, as well as allowing access to archives and files, and allow visits to audit facilities. The president can only refuse a request due to imperative reasons of protection of the sources or protection of the identity of third parties. Such a refusal should be substantiated before the bicameral parliamentary committee. On the other hand, legislators who take possession of classified information are obliged to comply with the security standards established to safeguard the disclosure thereof, even after their functions have ceased.[46]

The establishment of a legislative commission for external control of intelligence activities was one of the most eagerly awaited aspects of the new legislation. Nonetheless, in the last decade Uruguay has made significant progress in aspects related to public supervision of intelligence activities through the declassification of documents. The constant pressure of the various human rights movements and their associated political parties connected with media coverage has renewed the call for intelligence reform.

In terms of legislative resources, Uruguay is taking a historic step. Prior to the approval of the law, the country lacked reliable institutional mechanisms to control the activities carried out by the intelligence services, and in particular, with regard to the definition of competencies, limitations, and controls that the various agencies must uphold.

The new regulations establish a system requiring strict compliance with the Constitution of the Uruguayan Republic, a republic democratic regime of governance, and full respect to human rights. In this regard, prohibitions are established for the performance of repressive tasks (police functions or criminal investigation), intervention in the political, social, or economic activity of the country (foreign affairs, life of political parties, media, and other social organizations), and the disclosure of any type of information acquired in the exercise of their functions. In addition to providing the services with a new organizational structure, the legislation establishes limits on the special intelligence powers, rules for the processing, protection, and use of personal data, and control and supervision mechanisms to which the various intelligence agencies must obey.

Regarding financial resources, the new legislation grants the Strategic Intelligence Secretariat the power to design the programs and budgets established in the National Intelligence Plan. This plan must be reported to parliament in the Annual Report submitted by the secretariat. At the present time, the financial information of the country's main intelligence agencies is public, although it is difficult to disaggregate and ensure complete adherence due to the organization of the Uruguayan budget.

The organizations are underfunded but still getting funds from other illicit or alternative sources. This development is allowing them to maintain power and not listen to civilian authorities. By way of example, the DIE—ex-DINACIE—currently depends on the General Staff of Defense. Although it is possible to consult the budget of the latter, it is not possible to determine the amount that the DIE receives. The same situation applies at the police level, where the exact funding amount of the DGII—ex DNII—which depends on the recently created DIP, is unknown. The last annual budget of the DINACIE, and DNII, prior was roughly 0.4 percent. Currently, the General Staff of Defense, which includes the expenses of the DIE, represents only 0.5 percent of the annual defense budget. The crime prevention and repression program, which includes the expenses of the DGII, and multiple agencies and programs, represents 17.4 percent of the annual public security budget. Presumably, DGII, like its predecessor, continues to have a marginal budget.[47]

Professionalism and Effectiveness

The new National State Intelligence System (SNIE) aspires to bring together, under the coordination of the Secretariat of Strategic State Intelligence (SIEE), the main intelligence and counterintelligence agencies of Uruguay. Although the law does not enumerate all intelligence agencies, it mentions the most prominent, which fall under the Ministers of the Interior, National Defense, Foreign Affairs, and Economy and Finance.[48]

With respect to *political leadership*, the SIEE is created as a decentralized organization subject to the executive branch, with the president of the Republic creating consensus with the aforementioned ministers. At this point,

Uruguay has opted for an intermediate path that excludes the possibility that the SNIE reports exclusively to the Presidency of the Republic or a single ministry, as happens in other countries of the region. This design seeks to create greater transparency and accountability.

Given that Uruguayan law vests great power in the Presidency of the Republic with few mechanisms to check the executives' power, only the constitution can define such powers, and a simple law cannot alter the power structure.[49] This dynamic creates presidential autonomy, placing the president above reproach of any other governmental branch; therefore, any limits on the executive would be unconstitutional. On the other hand, the alternative of the SNIE being under the stewardship of a single ministry was not present at the negotiating table.

Laws mandate the head of the SNIE will be the director of the SIEE, who is appointed by the president of the Republic, acting in agreement with the aforementioned ministers, upon previous authorization by the Chamber of Senators. For a director of the SNIE to be dismissed, notice must be provided to the dismissal body. The position is of exclusive dedication and incompatible with any other activity, and the director's mandate may not be extended for more than six consecutive years.

In terms of organization and management of the various agencies, the SIEE is responsible for coordinating the operation of the SNIE. Although the management of each agency is reserved to the ministries on which they depend, the law establishes powers for the director of the SIEE to request the information deemed necessary for the fulfillment of their functions. At the same time, it obliges the various agencies to provide requested information. The cooperation and exchange of information to produce strategic intelligence may be organized through the creation by the director of SIEE of an intelligence coordinating board that aggregate information pertaining to the specific intelligence tasks.

With regard to the training and recruitment of intelligence agents, Uruguay lacks a unified specialized manner to recruit, evaluate, and train. At the military level, the National Army is the only force provided with a specialized intelligence training institution.[50] Although it is not possible to access specific information on the curricula, according to the latest legal amendment (Decree No. 427/018), the Army Intelligence School—subject to the Military Institute of Weapons and Specialties—under its main objectives, forms and trains chiefs, officers, subordinate personnel, and specialists in intelligence activities.[51] On the other hand, the Military Institute of Higher Studies also exists, the purpose of which is to prepare senior officers and chiefs for the functions of command, direction, and staff, offering strategic intelligence courses within its undergraduate and postgraduate study plans.[52]

At the police level, no specific intelligence training is offered. The National Police School, under the National Directorate of Police Education, provides police officers a bachelor's degree in police science and short courses dedicated to training in information and intelligence.[53] Finally, at the civilian level, there is no training or investigation center dedicated exclusively to intelligence activities. The only area of civilian training in strategic matters is the Center for Higher National Studies, which, although it is part of the Ministry of National Defense organization, does not constitute a military training institute. Within the Academic Extension Courses of the institute, a basic seminar in strategic planning and intelligence—intended for civilian, police, and military professionals—is offered.[54]

Additionally, the Uruguayan armed forces created their own Peacekeeping Operations School in which there are no manuals or debriefing—essentially no civilian oversight—further bringing many to question the true degree of intelligence reform within the nation, Uruguayan intelligence restructuring has stagnated in a nebulous location that will not be apparent for some time. While many laws have been signed to wrest control of the intelligence apparatus from those opposing reform to independent civilian control, the ability to enforce these laws remains problematic. This situation could possibly be explained by a lag from the time a law is authorized until it is truly institutionalized and produces results or wonton disregard for the law among current intelligence position holders that is stifling progress.

Regarding the procedures for collecting information and its subsequent classification and declassification, Uruguay is once again taking an important step forward. According to the approved regulations, any operation to be carried out by any SNIE body involving special communications interception procedures—telephonic, computer, radio, or other technological systems—must be authorized by the judiciary power. However, two figures have been created: the *informant* and the *undercover agent*, which guarantee intelligence actions within the framework of an investigation.[55]

With respect to information, the law establishes that all SNIE member bodies must adopt standardized procedures to classify, reclassify, or declassify information—something that does not currently happen. Classification duration limitations have been created: a maximum period of twenty-five years and the obligation to maintain secrecy—for officials and other people with a need to know and possessing a nondisclosure agreement. This limit was created to improve transparency and block intelligence personnel and bureaucrats from effectively hiding inappropriate operations by indefinitely prohibiting others from viewing the requested information, thus, reducing accountability and civilian control. In regard to safeguarding classified and sensitive information, one exemption exists for an individual to publicly disclose such information—violation of human rights or being relevant to preventing or investigating human rights violations.

CONCLUSION

In comparative terms, Uruguay's situation after the democratization of the 1980s has not been very different from its South American counterparts. Despite the nation's institutions being deemed healthy and functional, the country has not managed to escape the most frequent difficulties of balancing intelligence-democracy priorities: politicization and autonomy.

Having approved a robust legal framework, the Uruguayan political system faces the challenge of consolidating and practicing civilian control over the intelligence community. As much of the specialized literature has argued,[56] the democratization of intelligence is not based solely on normative processes. In other words, the law by itself will not guarantee a change in the culture and *praxis* of the sector.

In addition to consolidating a culture of intelligence, Uruguay will have to confront three pending issues in the short term: (1) the fight against the so-called "new threats" and in particular terrorism; (2) surveillance in the digital era; and (3) the regulation of intelligence activities unconnected to the state. Regarding the first issue, Uruguay lacks a legal framework that clearly defines the competencies, limits, and coordination between the different security forces that combat terrorism in the national territory, including the intelligence services. Although the pressure exerted by the Financial Action Task Force led to a fast revision of the rules on the financing of terrorism,[57] parliament was unable to agree on aspects relating to the definition of the phenomenon itself, the structure, and the national coordination for fighting it.

Another topic for consideration is directly linked to the burgeoning technology sector and unforeseen privacy rights concerns, and how such flaws within certain technology can be exploited by intelligence organizations and other nefarious entities. Currently, the country lacks the legal tools to guarantee the right to privacy with the proliferation of devices capable of eavesdropping, telephone interception, or electronic surveillance of persons. The importing, commercialization, and use of these devices must be the subject of state regulation to respond to this dynamic situation. The magnitude of these vulnerabilities cannot be comprehensively understood at this juncture, but it is necessary for the Uruguayan government to begin delving into how to manage this emerging circumstance.

Finally, the tasks performed by private investigators in Uruguay are pending regulation. Unlike the multiple security companies not connected to the state, which comply with precise regulations and are subject to state control, the centennial job of "private detective" dwells in a legal limbo. Ultimately, as O'Donnell suggested in this regard, "effective institutions and practices favorable to them cannot be built in a day."[58] This tacit allowance of private security companies operating beyond reproach of the government continues to be Uruguay's modus operandi.

Uruguay remains a nation with an incomplete transition to a consolidated democracy. The authoritarian government of the 1970s and 1980s allowed for the military and intelligence apparatus to exercise full control over civil affairs. As the Cold War waned, the military and intelligence services found that feigning regret for previous actions would allow for greater maneuvering room—to dictate terms and actively devise the new civil-military structure. The military and intelligence service adeptly shifted from internal operations, to international and PKOs. The reorientation of the intelligence community's mission tasks allowed these services to maintain their financial freedom of the Uruguayan civil government, gain public support, and access legitimate foreign financing to supplement Uruguayan military/intelligence members' salaries and equipment procurement. This rather unusual dynamic continues to stymie Uruguay's democratic consolidation, and true reform will be difficult until the military and intelligence services become subordinate to civil leadership and reduction of parochial prerogatives.

NOTES

1. This chapter focuses on three historical moments: the civil-military dictatorship (1973–1985); the democratic transition and consolidation, which included the first attempts of intelligence reform (1985–2010); and the creation of the National Intelligence System (2011–2018). The emphasis is placed on the evaluation of the changes introduced by Uruguay for the democratic management of intelligence, pointing out the problematical areas and future challenges.

2. Juan Rial, "Los Militares en tanto Partido Político Sustituto frente a la Redemocratización en Uruguay," in *La Autonomía Militar en América Latina*, coords. Augusto Varas and Felipe Agüero (Caracas: Nueva Sociedad, 1988).

3. Benjamín Nahum, *Manual de Historia del Uruguay, vol. 2, 1903–2000* (Montevideo: Ediciones Banda Oriental, 2002), 183–229, 272.

4. For example, the so-called Mesutti affair—which revealed that Oscar Mesutti, who worked in Uruguay's foreign office archive, gave classified information to the Soviet Embassy—shocked public opinion and led to the expulsion of the Soviet delegation in 1961. Fernando Aparicio, Roberto García, and Mercedes Terra, *Espionaje y Política*, 153–84. Likewise, Africa de las Heras, a Spanish citizen (who became a KGB spy), managed to settle in Uruguay in 1948 and direct, from there, the Soviet espionage network in Latin America. See Group of Interdisciplinary Studies on the

Recent Past, "Trías Collection," http://www.geipar.udelar.edu.uy/index. php/2018/10/03/coleccion-trias/ (accessed on March 6, 2019); and Mauro Abranches and Vladimír Petrilák, *La SBT: El Brazo de la KGB en Uruguay* (Montevideo: Planeta, 2018). On the same note, declassified documents of the communist-era Czechoslovak intelligence agency StB show the participation of the Soviet satellite in Uruguay, who managed to recruit a historic leader of the Socialist Party in Uruguay. See Group of Interdisciplinary Studies on the Recent Past, "Trías Collection"; and Abranches and Petrilák, *La SBT: El Brazo de la KGB en Uruguay*.

5. Before World War II, the Montevideo Police Department and the Armed Forces maintained "liaison relations" with United States intelligence. See Philip Age, *La CIA por Dentro: Diario de un Espía* (Buenos Aires, Editorial Sudamericana, 1987), 282; Benjamín Nahum, *Manual de Historia del Uruguay*, 241; Fernando Aparicio, Roberto García, and Mercedes Terra, *Espionaje y Política*, 17–25; and Benjamín Nahum, *Informes Diplomáticos de los Representantes de España en Uruguay, vol. 2, 1948–1958* (Montevideo: UDELAR, 2001), 12. Different historiographic researches on the Uruguayan case have shown that not only had the surveillance lines already been functioning in the police headquarters in Montevideo since the early 1940s but that the SIE as well had been assigned to monitor activities of the Uruguayan Communist Party (PCU). These roles continued after SIE became the Directorate of Information and Intelligence (DII) in 1967, and then the National Directorate of Information and Intelligence (DNII) in 1971. Fernando Aparicio, Roberto García, and Mercedes Terra, *Espionaje y Política*. Once the Joint Forces were constituted, the police and its intelligence service were subordinated to the Armed Forces and thus maintained until the democratic restoration. Álvaro Rico, *Investigación Histórica sobre la Dictadura y el Terrorismo de Estado en el Uruguay 1973–1985* (Montevideo: UdelaR, CSIC, FHCE, CEIU, 2008), 415–33.

6. A civil-military dictatorship involves a system of governance based on an alliance between civilians (politicians, technocrats, business representatives) and military leadership. See José Miguel Busquets and Andrea Delbono, "La Dictadura Cívico-Militar En Uruguay (1973–1985): Aproximación a su Periodización y Caracterización a la Luz de Algunas Teorizaciones sobre el Autoritarismo," *Revista de La Facultad de Derecho* (2° Época), no. 41 (December 2016): 61–102. Available at http://dx.doi.org/10.22187/rfd201624.

7. Julián González Guyer, "Relaciones Militares: El Impacto del 11 de Setiembre en el Cono Sur," Paper presented at the Seminar on Research and Education in Defense and Security Studies, Brasilia, August 2002, 14.

8. Alfred Stepan, *Repensando a los Militares en Política* (Buenos Aires: Planeta, 1988), 39.

9. Intelligence agencies had additional tasks, besides containment of subversion, such as fighting drugs, in the context of the U.S. "war on drugs" policy. See Álvaro Rico, *Investigación Histórica*, 422–25. See "Documents on Uruguay in the National Archives and Records Administration," http://www.geipar.udelar.edu.uy/index.php/ category/documentos_hist/eeuu/ (accessed on March 6, 2019); and Central Intelligence Agency, "Freedom of Information Act Electronic Reading Room—Uruguay," https://www.cia.gov/library/readingroom/search/site/Uruguay (accessed on March 6, 2019). Initiated in 1975 with support from the U.S. government, Operation Condor

was a regional collaborative effort among the various military regimes' intelligence agencies aimed at assassination of these regimes' political opponents. J. Patrice Mc-Sherry, "Operation Condor: Clandestine Inter-American System," *Social Justice 26*, no. 4 (78) (1999): 144–74.

10. Luis Eduardo González, "Transición y Restauración Democrática," in *Uruguay y la Democracia*, coord. Charles Gillespie (Montevideo: Ediciones Banda Oriental, 1985), 109–19.

11. Alejandro M. Bihar, "Civil Liberties in the Absence of Legislative Intelligence Oversight: Lessons Learned from Uruguay," thesis, Naval Postgraduate School, Monterey, CA, June 2018. Available at http://hdl.handle.net/10945/59689.

12. The rationale asserted that peacekeeping operations would transfer forces to international locations to allow domestic politics the ability to restructure with fewer constraints and pressures from military forces. Developing nations' militaries would professionalize through interaction with professional militaries and adopt international norms, and civil-military relations would improve with little effort. Chiyuki Aoi, Cedric De Coning, and Ramesh Chandra Thakur, *Unintended Consequences of Peacekeeping Operations* (Tokyo: United Nations University Press, 2007), 171.

13. Historically, Uruguayan democracy has enjoyed a privileged position on the regional stage. In comparative terms, Uruguay is one of the Latin American countries that has lived longer under democratic governments. Daniel Chasquetti and Adolfo Garcé, "Futuros Posibles de la Democracia Uruguaya," in *La Aventura Uruguaya ¿Naides más que Naides?*, coords. Gerardo Caetano and Rodrigo Arocena (Montevideo: Random House, 2011). About the transition in Uruguay, see Gerardo Caetano and José Rila, *Breve Historia de la Dictadura* (Montevideo: CLAEH/EBO, 1986). Gerardo Caetano coord., *20 años de Democracia. Uruguay: 1985–2005. Miradas Múltiples* (Montevideo: Taurus, 2005).

14. Chiyuki Aoi, De Coning, and Thakur, *Unintended Consequences of Peacekeeping Operations*, 182.

15. Kai Michael Kenkel, *South America and Peace Operations Coming of Age* (London: Routledge, 2013), 127.

16. Kenkel, *South America*, 126.

17. Kenkel, *South America*, 125.

18. Arturo C. Sotomayor Velázquez, "Peacekeeping Effects in South America: Common Experiences and Divergent Effects on Civil–Military Relations." *International Peacekeeping* 17, no. 5 (November 2010): 632–33, ProQuest.

19. Kenkel, *South America*, 124.

20. Velázquez, "Peacekeeping Effects in South America," 638–40.

21. Thomas C. Bruneau and Florina Cristiana Matei, eds., *The Routledge Handbook of Civil-Military Relations* (New York: Routledge, 2013).

22. Gerardo Caetano, *20 años de Democracia*, 305–7.

23. Francisco Gallinal, "La Ley de Caducidad," *El País*, February 28, 2009. Available at https://web.archive.org/web/20100812064807/http://www.elpais.com.uy/09/02/28/predit_401629.asp.

24. Gallinal, "La Ley de Caducidad."

25. To annul the entire law.

26. Sergio Israel, *Silencio de Estado: Eugenio Berríos y el Poder Político Uruguayo* (Montevideo: Aguilar, 2008).

27. "Tres Militares Uruguayos Extraditados a Chile por Caso Berríos," *Hoy*, April 18, 2006. Available at https://hoy.com.do/tres-militares-uruguayos-extraditados-a -chile-por-caso-berrios-2/.

28. Sergio Israel, *Silencio de Estado*, 258.

29. Bihar, "Civil Liberties in the Absence of Legislative Intelligence Oversight." Also see Alejandro M. Bihar, "Uruguay's Attempt at Intelligence Oversight," *International Journal of Intelligence and CounterIntelligence* 33, no. 2 (2020): 214–47, doi: 10.1080/08850607.2019.1663701.

30. *La República*, "Sanguinetti creó Dirección de Inteligencia Nacional por Decreto," January 6, 2000, political section, 4–5.

31. Julián González Guyer, "Relaciones Militares," 11.

32. Jorge Jouroff, "Inteligencia y Cultura: Una Oportunidad para Uruguay," in *Democratización de la Función de Inteligencia. El Nexo de la Cultura Nacional y la Inteligencia Estratégica*, coords. Russell G. Swenson and Susana C. Lemozy (Washington, DC: Colegio Nacional de Inteligencia y Defensa, 2009), 149.

33. *La República*, "Sanguinetti creó Dirección," 4.

34. *La República*, "Sanguinetti creó Dirección," 4.

35. Luis Casal Beck, "El Terrorismo Sigue en la Mira," *El Observador*, January 26, 2002, political section, 8–9.

36. Julián González Guyer, "Relaciones Militares," 10.

37. As revealed by Julián González (organizing member of the National Debate on Defense), interviewed for a previous work by the author.

38. As revealed by Julián González (organizing member of the National Debate on Defense), interviewed for a previous work by the author.

39. As revealed by Julián González (organizing member of the National Debate on Defense), interviewed for a previous work by the author.

40. The charge was regulated and occupied during the Mujica administration (2010–2015).

41. For a detailed analysis on this stage, see Nicolás Álvarez, "The Long Road towards Democratization: Reform of Intelligence in Uruguay (1985–2015)," *Journal of Mediterranean and Balkan Intelligence* 1, no. 7 (2016): 49–70.

42. Daniel Isgleas, "Inteligencia Estratégica: Los Ojos y Oídos del Estado Bajo Control," *El País*, September 30, 2018, https://www.elpais.com.uy/informacion/politica/inteligencia-estrategica-ojos-oidos-control.html#_=_ (accessed on May 6, 2019).

43. Samuel Blixen, "Servicios Continuados," *Brecha*, September 2, 2016, https://brecha.com.uy/servicios-continuados/.

44. For the multiple journalistic investigations on the case, see Samuel Blixen, "Infiltrados: Espionaje Militar en Democracia," special publication *Brecha*, February 2017, https://issuu.com/semanariobrecha/docs/infiltrados_brecha.

45. Alejandra Otamendi and Eduardo Estévez, "Intelligence Challenges in Latin America: A Comparative Matrix on Democratic Governance," in *¿Nuevos Paradigmas de Vigilancia? Miradas desde América Latina*, ed. Camilo Ríos (Córdoba: Fundación Vía Libre, 2017): 277–94.

46. See Parlamento del Uruguay, Comisión Especial de Control y Supervisión del Sistema Nacional de Inteligencia de Estado, https://parlamento.gub.uy/camara sycomisiones/asambleageneral/comisiones/1186; Álvarez, "The Long Road towards Democratization."

47. It is possible to consult the budget in the General Accounting Office of the Nation, "Budget Execution of All Items," https://www.cgn.gub.uy/innovaportal/v/83013/5/innova.front/consultas-de-ejecucion-presupuestal.html (accessed on June 1, 2019).

48. Namely, Strategic Intelligence Directorate, Department S2 (Army), N2 (Navy), A2 (Air), Ministry of Defense; National Directorate of Investigations of the Police and National Directorate of Information and Police Intelligence, of the Ministry of the Interior; Financial Analysis Unit, Ministry of Economy; and Political Affairs Directorate of the Ministry of Foreign Affairs.

49. Considerations made by experts in constitutional law who collaborated with the special intelligence commission (2011–2014).

50. Decrees no. 35/000 and no. 39/000, regulate the promotion and qualification systems of the Superior and Junior Personnel of DINACIE, currently D.I.E.

51. The information can be consulted in Military Institute of Weapons and Specialties, "School of Army Intelligence," http://www.imae.edu.uy/escuela-EIE.html (accessed on May 28, 2019).

52. The information can be consulted in Military Institute of Advanced Studies, "Careers and Courses 2019," http://www.imes.edu.uy/new/?page_id=684 (accessed on May 28, 2019).

53. The information can be consulted in National School of Police, "Plans of Study," https://www.enp.edu.uy/index.php/institutos/i-u-p/plan-de-estudio (accessed on May 28, 2019).

54. The information can be consulted in Center for Higher National Studies, "Course of Analysis of Strategic Information Applied to National Defense," http://calen.edu.uy/wp-content/uploads/calen-analisis-informacion-2019.pdf (accessed on May 28, 2019).

55. There is no additional available information on these assets. Arguably, Uruguayan intelligence organizations intentionally utilize such human assets or pose as such to skirt the law and conduct investigations under a technicality that does not follow the spirit of the law.

56. Eduardo E. Estévez, "Escenarios Actuales de Inteligencia: Desafíos en las Dimensiones Estratégica y Criminal. Legados, Cambio, Prioridades," paper prepared for the congress of the Association of Latin American Studies, Chicago, Illinois, May 21–24, 2014, p. 32.

57. "¿Qué Propone el Proyecto Antiterrorista que Aprobó el Senado y a Quiénes Afecta?" *El Observador*, May 7, 2019, https://www.elobservador.com.uy/nota/-que-propone-el-proyecto-antiterrorismo-que-aprobo-el-senado-y-a-quienes-afecta--201957174836 (accessed on June 1, 2019).

58. Guillermo O´ Donnell, "¿Democracia Delegativa?" in *La Democracia Hoy,* coord. Jaime Barba (San Salvador: Istmo, 1994), 21.

Chapter Ten

Costa Rica

Gerardo Hernández-Naranjo,
Marco Vinicio Méndez-Coto, and
Carlos Humberto Cascante-Segura

Like other consolidated democracies around the world,[1] Costa Rica has striven to balance its democratic and peaceful principles with its requirements to maintain security and intelligence services. Costa Rican national identity is associated with peace, disarmament, and human rights; however, its intelligence services are rooted in Costa Rica's past militaristic institutions and authoritarian rule. During the last two decades, Costa Rica's political leaders have discussed the closure of the Directorate of Intelligence and National Security (DISNA)—the current national intelligence agency—considered a remnant of the Cold War and a permanent menace to national democratic values and the protection of human rights; yet the organization remains.

In that context, this chapter discusses the development and transformation of Costa Rican intelligence services since 1948, the year of the last military conflict in the country. Specifically, it analyzes the challenges to intelligence reform amid democratic consolidation, and it further explores how the current intelligence culture engenders debates about its institutional permanence in the twenty-first century.[2] It finds that Costa Rica lacks a strategic vision of the role and responsibilities of the intelligence service in Costa Rica's democracy. As a result, democratic civilian control and oversight of the intelligence service in Costa Rica have been weak, marked by lack of understanding and indifference toward intelligence. As such, an uncertain future afflicts the intelligence services in Costa Rica.

HISTORICAL BACKGROUND (1821–1940)

Costa Rica declared its independence from the Spanish empire in 1821. This period is widely regarded as a pacific process because it did not entail a war

189

of independence against Spain. However, it is also accepted that the first decades of independent governance were characterized by the adversarial relations between the local elites and the commercial elites—intellectuals and rich oligarchic families (mostly merchants and coffee planters) in the capital of San José, which was the most important economic city during the period—who sought centralization of the public powers.[3]

Costa Rica suffered internal disputes between these antagonistic power brokers, who ultimately facilitated authoritarian rule motivated by the desire to impose a centralistic state in an effort to overcome the substantial resistance from local leadership, which wanted to preserve the colonial-era system of government and parochial prerogatives. In the 1850s, the centralization process created a set of new institutions that appropriated the powers exercised by local elites. In this same period, amid foreign disputes and border disagreements with neighbors, Costa Rica developed a national army, which rapidly become one the most important institutions of the state until the final decade of the nineteenth century.[4]

Upon the completion of the state centralizing project, disputes within the oligarchy became evident, thus allowing leaders of the national army to interject their power to resolving these disagreements. In 1870, the military corps decided to seize power from civilian authorities, staging a coup that overthrew the civilian government of Jesús Jiménez Zamora (1863–1866 and 1868–1870) and installing General Tomas Guardia Gutiérrez as president. His presidential tenure, which was expanded until 1882, saw the rise and proliferation of such nineteenth-century intelligence practices as espionage, enemy tracking, and intimidation of political adversaries. Guardia held control of all state institutions and tried to subdue any form of opposition, brutally persecuting his enemies. These acts of repression were conducted by police authorities, members of the national army, and provincial governors, but importantly, no single agency or organization was granted autonomous jurisdiction to execute such measures.[5]

Once Guardia died in 1882, two of his closest loyalists assumed the presidency and the level of authoritarian rule decreased. During this period, a group of liberal lawyers—nicknamed "*El Olimpo*,"[6] due to their "detached arrogance and self-assured elitism," as Palmer notes,[7] akin to the Greek gods—was called to serve in important government positions. This transition inaugurated a process of liberalizing state institutions: using education, judicial stability, and electoral process as established forms of social control. Even if espionage, intimidation, and violence remained a frequent part of the electoral process, after 1902 Costa Rica recovered a semblance of political stability, and the accusations of political repression diminished substantially.[8] During this period, no intelligence agency was created by the police or military organizational laws.

This political stability was short lived and gave way to crisis due to the economic consequences of World War I. In 1917, by means of a coup d'état, Federico Tinoco Granados assumed the presidency. The new government was plunged into diplomatic isolation after the United States refused to recognize it. The regime had no policies to contain the fiscal problems that had grown out of the wartime coffee-export restrictions, and the lingering economic troubles caused a general protest in the major cities of Costa Rica against Tinoco's rule. The administration relied so heavily on the national army that it was necessary to increase its budget; the force used repressive tactics against Tinoco's political opponents to further his control.[9]

One of the measures undertaken by the Tinoco administration was the creation of the Detectives National Corps or DNC. On the one hand, this new corps operated under strict limits; its formal objective was to prosecute crimes and not to take preventive measures. On the other hand, organically, it was part of the national army and reported directly to the minister of war and navy, who was President Ticono's brother—General Joaquín Tinoco. Perhaps unsurprisingly, DNC leaders immediately began spying and persecuting adversaries and critics of the Tinoco administration, who, according to Fernández Morales, came to deride the corps as a band of "flunkies that lurked everywhere."[10]

After Tinoco's ousting in August 1919, the DNC was disbanded, but a scant few years later, in 1923, a similar entity was formed, called the Corps of Investigative Agents (CIA). This new institution was subordinate to the national army. However, the previous repression against the citizenry and its affiliation with the Tinoco administration tarnished the army's.[11] The new corps was strictly prohibited from any kind of political intervention; its established purpose was solely to use scientific methods to study crime and criminals.[12]

The CIA was integrated into the Police Organization Law in 1940, which established a formal relation between all the police forces of the state under the rule of the secretary of public security—the new name adopted by the Minister of War and Navy in the 1920s to establish civilian rule over the National Army—and the commander in chief of the National Army.[13] In the end, the CIA was the closest attempt to institutionalize and centralize intelligence functions in Costa Rica in the twentieth century.

DEMOCRATIC CONSOLIDATION AND INTELLIGENCE SERVICE INSTITUTIONAL EVOLUTION (1940–2005)

The 1940s and 1950s were decades of intense political turmoil in Costa Rica. Internal frictions among political forces and economic problems caused a rupture not only within the elites themselves but also between national elites and the society, and produced problems in government transitions—which occurred in conjunction with World War II and then the Cold War.[14] This turmoil caused not only a civil war in March–April 1948 but also two attempts by members of the deposed government to return to power with the assistance of Nicaragua, Venezuela, and the Dominican Republic in December 1948 and January 1955.[15] Additionally, there were also external threats and the influence of United States intelligence objectives.

In the context of World War II, the Calderón administration (1940–1944) of the National Republican Party completely aligned with the U.S. policy in opposition toward Nazi Germany. To this end, the Calderón administration received American military, security, and intelligence cooperation, and local police corps took part in the espionage and capture of German, Italian, and Spanish citizens in Costa Rica.[16] Calderón, in addition, played to the American preferences and thwarted the national opposition, which he tarred with accusations of corruption and Communist sympathies. During the Picado administration (1944–1948), also linked with the National Republican Party, the United States reduced its cooperation with the government and maintained a degree of neutrality during the 1948 civil war; at the end of the conflict, Washington accepted the triumph of the forces led by José Figueres Ferrer, who pledged to carry out policies that favored the U.S. government objective of combatting communism.[17]

Figueres and his group organized a transitional government called "Founding Board of the Second Republic"—or "*La Junta*"—which governed until November 1949. "La Junta" used abusive espionage and intimidation methods against political enemies, especially Communist Party members who faced imprisonment with some party leaders murdered by security and intelligence forces.[18]

Figueres sought to instate major political reforms. In 1948, he convened with other political forces to call for elections to designate a National Constitutional Assembly;[19] the 1949 Constitution completed the process of proscribing it as a permanent institution. Military forces could only be organized in specific cases—for example, for national defense or by continental agreement—which would then be subordinated to civil authorities (Art. 12). According to the same provision, police forces oversee monitoring and preserving public order. Thus, internal and external security have been tasked to different civil police forces, commanded by the Ministry of Public Security (originally in charge of crime prevention and surveillance) and the Ministry of Government (originally in charge of immigration and border control).[20]

A large portion of Costa Rica's National Army was disbanded, and the process of building a new civil National Police Corps began with members loyal to Figueres and "La Junta." This process continued during the second

Figueres administration (1953–1958),[21] in which the Ministry of Public Security was founded.[22] However, the police modernization process was never fully completed. In fact, during the following decades, ruptures within the political elite class, and instability and fear, enabled the successive governments to remove police personnel hired by the previous government and replace them with officers loyal to the current government—which obstructed police professionalization.[23]

Internationally, the Figueres administration conducted intelligence activities in Central America and Caribbean countries, ultimately prompting presidents Anastasio Somoza García (Nicaragua) and Rafael Leonidas Trujillo (Dominican Republic) to accuse the Costa Rican leadership of conspiring with exiles and opposition forces to overthrow their governments.[24] Figueres in turn accused these dictators of plotting against his life and his government, but no detailed studies exist of these secret missions or the Costa Rican intelligence service's involvement.

There is no historical research on the activities conducted by the Corps of Investigative Agents during this period. The CIA was incorporated into the new Ministry of Security in 1953.[25]

Two new institutions were created in the 1960s: the "Agencia de Seguridad Nacional" (National Security Agency), created in 1963, and "Organismo de Investigación Judicial" (Judicial Investigation Corps) in 1974; the latter was responsible for the investigation of conventional criminality.[26] The National Security Agency (NSA) was a department in the Ministry of Public Security,[27] although no law or executive order authorized such an agency to exist. Perhaps, its foundation was a consequence of President John F. Kennedy's visit to Costa Rica, because before the visit, the Costa Rican government (by means of the Corps of Investigative Agents) and the U.S. Central Intelligence Agency (CIA) cooperated to control possible terrorist acts against Kennedy. Members of Costa Rica's Communist Party and some foreigners were arrested for revolutionary activities. After this experience, U.S. officials concluded Costa Rica struggled with containing subversive activities and needed to strengthen its security services.[28]

More broadly, NSA was a product of the Cold War Western Hemisphere doctrine and the National Security Doctrine, the Cuban Revolution (1959), and the expansion of revolutionary movements in Latin America. In 1965, the Central American Defense Treaty was signed with a particular emphasis on the threat of international communism, subversive movements, and irregular warfare. The treaty established mechanisms for coordination, cooperation, and information exchange among states. The United States continued to provide financial, technical, and equipment assistance, as well as education and training for police and intelligence forces.[29] Nevertheless, comprehensive research is required to understand properly the different manners in which this training and narratives were adapted by national authorities and agents.

In 1968, the NSA changed its name to the División Nacional de Seguridad (National Security Division or NSD). The 1972 CIA Handbook notes that

> investigation of subversive activities is the responsibility of the National Security Division (NSD) of the Civil Guard's Directorate of Criminal Investigations (DIC), which has a total of 110 member[s]. . . . It has powers of arrest, search and seizure [subversive activities] but it normally does not use them, the NSD generally collects evidence of subversive activities and then turns it over to other components of DIC or other government agencies for appropriate action.[30]

During the 1970s and 1980s, Cold War attitudes affected NSD practices. In fact, the agency acted as the government's political police, targeting left-wing parties, students, and labor leaders—all considered "comunistas."[31] These abuses persisted even after 1985, when NSD underwent a critical reform and became the Dirección de Inteligencia y Seguridad (Director of Intelligence and Security or DIS). The DIS reported to the Presidency Office and was regulated through Executive Order 16398, but its budget program was part of the Ministry of Public Security. This executive order also stipulated that the agency was legally authorized to conduct "investigations and surveillance related to national security [as directed by] the President of the Republic," as well as domestic and international intelligence interagency cooperation and collaboration.[32]

After the end of the Cold War, efforts to democratize security institutions in Central America prompted further reform. In 1994, the General Police Law[33] and the Bylaws of Organization and Operation of the Directorate of Intelligence and Security Executive Order were codified.[34] Among other changes, these laws renamed the agency the Directorate of Intelligence and National Security (DISNA), and defined its obligations and operational constraints. DISNA's main task became advising the president on national security matters. In practice, within legal parameters, the president yields DISNA's strategic coordination and decision-making process to the Ministry of the Presidency, which in the Costa Rican political system is the Executive Branch Cabinet coordinator.

In accordance with these regulations, DISNA also was tasked with strategic internal and external criminal intelligence, collecting and analyzing information on international threats. Furthermore, DISNA was approved to participate in international intelligence cooperation and information sharing. These regulations firmly forbid DISNA from conducting interrogations, issuing citations, or detaining suspects; also, DISNA requires judicial authorization to partake in coercive actions with competent police bodies. Moreover, its internal reports and documents are qualified as confidential, but to be declared a secret of state, presidential permission is required—a manner to improve transparency and preclude intelligence organizations from obfuscating information from civil authorities.[35]

From 1994 to 2005, DISNA was submitted to additional institutional reforms. Originally, DISNA oversaw the Special Intervention Unit (UEI), which is a police force specialized in high-risk operations against terrorism and drug trafficking activities,[36] but the agencies were separated, budgetarily and administratively, in 1998.[37] Finally, a more detailed and comprehensive regulation was defined by the Organization and Operation Bylaws Executive Order in 2005.[38] This order preserved the basic organization as defined in 1994, but it provided several revised regulations detailing staff members, selection, recruitment, and training; measures for information and document classification; administrative procedures and penalties for violating laws committed by the staff; characterizing procedures and restrictions for intrusive operations; and limitations upon secret funds used for collecting and confirming information.

DISNA's Current Organization Chart, Budget, and Human Resources

In accordance with legal basis and budgetary information, DISNA's organizational chart is rather simplistic, as shown in figure 10.1.

The most important subcomponent is the Operative Department, which is charged with proposing and executing data collection and analysis. During the last decades, this department has focused on drugs control and "international threats management" (it remains unclear what constitutes a threat and is placed within this category).[39] This situation relegates DISNA's primary role to domestic criminal/police intelligence, even if the legal framework grants DISNA a transnational strategic intelligence role.

According to senior officials of DISNA and data from the Ministry of Finance, it is estimated that DISNA possesses a staff of 170 employees, and an annual budget of approximately US$5.5 million in 2019, equivalent to 32.15 percent of the Ministry of the Presidency budget and 1.2 percent of the 2019 Ministry of the Public Security budget.[40] Of these allocated funds, 84.6 percent is dedicated to salaries, as shown in table 10.1.

It should be noted that these figures do not take into account several other intelligence activity units, which operate within the judiciary branch, the Minister of Public Security, the Drug Control Police, or various other institutions focused on commercial, financial, and tax affairs.

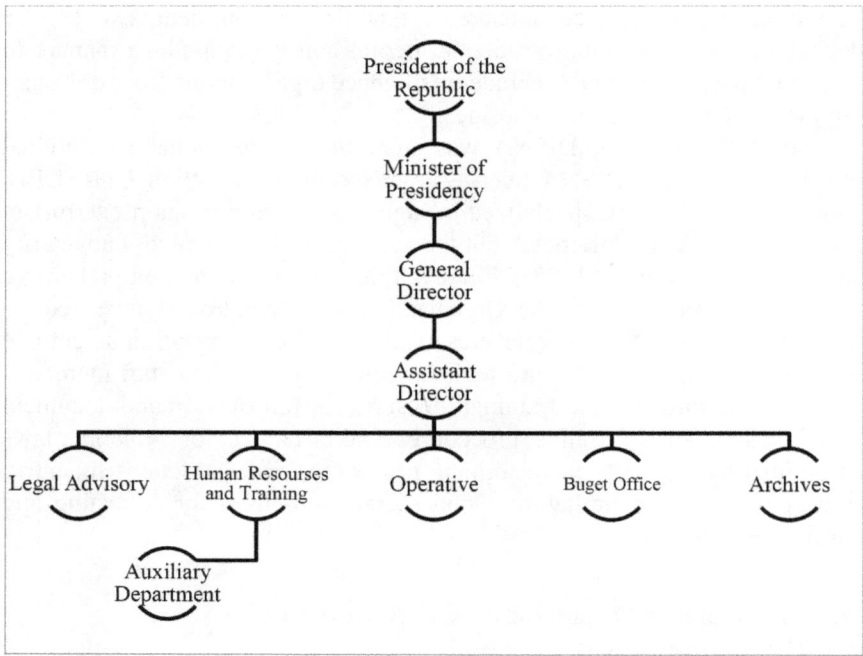

Figure 10.1.   DISNA Organization Chart

DISNA officials have raised the long-standing issue of their headquarters conditions, even indicating that their ability to work is affected by the over-crowded and under-equipped facility.[41] Officials have highlighted the shortage of technological resources and means of transportation. Even this scarce funding has been reappropriated from other agencies.[42]

Although one can postulate the characteristics of Costa Rica's intelligence services functions, it is not possible to determine with much clarity the current strategies for collecting information.[44] In general terms, it is inferred that

Table 10.1.   DISNA Ordinary Budget 2019, US dollars

Item	Amount	Percentage
Salaries	4,596,964.46	84.6%
Services	668,685.64	12.3%
Materials and supplies	97,054.32	1.8%
Transferences	62,166.86	1.1%
Durable goods	6,810.83	0.1%
Total	5,431,682.10	100.00%

Source: Ministry of Finance (2019).

the vast majority of the information is provided by collecting publicly available sources or open-source intelligence (OSINT) or from international intelligence and/or law enforcement cooperation networks such as, INTERPOL.[44] DISNA employs interpersonal contact or "human intelligence" (HUMINT) but for budgetary reasons this method is legally restrained. Additionally, only in certain situations does Costa Rica invest in advanced technological resources to augment intelligence activities. For example, during its last border conflict with Nicaragua, Costa Rica purchased satellite images to monitor the zone in dispute (Isla Calero-Portillos).[45] Such a dramatic shift owed to the urgency of the situation, rather than the emergence of a new pattern of Costa Rican intelligence actions.

Despite this fundamental reform activity, DISNA has been unable to assume a legitimate place within Costa Rican society, in part because of its antecedents.

DEMOCRATIC INTELLIGENCE GOVERNANCE AND ACCOUNTABILITY IN PRACTICE (2005–PRESENT)

Intelligence service governance and accountability has been one of the most pressing issues on Costa Rica's political agenda. DISNA still has legal problems, as well as challenges regarding the budget, human resources, and administrative organization; recruitment and training; political and civil control; and a functioning intelligence culture possessing a strategic perspective. The final segment of this chapter is dedicated to these dynamics.

Legal Framework

During the last decades, there has been an effort to subordinate the intelligence community to civilian control to finalize democratic consolidation. Both the General Police Law of 1994 and the executive decrees have striven to build a better delineated, more stable, and professional domestic intelligence service institutional framework in contrast to previous decades.[46] However, this legal framework lacks clear provisions and mechanisms to apportion control and oversight powers among the executive branch, the legislative branch, the judicial branch, and internal officials. Moreover, these regulations provide the president and Ministry of the Presidency an ample and discretional scope to define DISNA priorities. This fragile and fragmented legal structure has also failed to build a culture of intelligence that allows citizens and political officials the ability to understand the relevance of the intelligence services in supporting the democratic system.

The most recent legislative debate on institutional changes to the intelligence services has ranged from proposals to dissolve previous agencies and transfer their mission sets to other organizations, concentrate all intelligence activities and agencies within a modernization effort, expanding the sector, and nuanced proposals that reside in between the current proposals, as shown in table 10.2.

In 2019 the executive branch proposed a new bill before the Legislative Assembly, advocating for extensive DISNA reform, but different initiatives and controversies rapidly proliferated.[48] In this context, political actors have

Table 10.2.   Law Proposals Presented to Legislative Assembly to Closure or Reform DISNA

Legislative File	Presentation Date	Proposal
17266	January 21, 2009	Reform to the General Police Law to disband DISNA, transfer its assets to the Ministry of Security and files to the Ministry of the Presidency.
17345	April 28, 2009	Repeal DISNA, redefine the mandate of the President of the Republic and transfer files to the National Archive.
17993	February 8, 2011	Reform the General Police Law to repeal DISNA, transfer equipment and goods to the Ministry of Security, files to the Ministry of the Presidency, and transfer the organization's officials to other units.
19125	May 21, 2014	Repeal DISNA, transfer functions and budget to the Ministry of Security, its files to the Ministry of the Presidency which may transfer them to the Ministry of Security or the Judicial Investigation Agency.
19165	June 19, 2014	Creation of the National Security System Law. The Intelligence and Security Police is created, whose head would be the President, who may delegate such responsibility either to the Ministry of the Presidency or the Ministry of Security.
19330	September 30, 2014	Repeal DISNA, transfer personnel to the Ministry of Security and files to the Ministry of the Presidency, which may be submitted by the Judicial Investigation Agency or the Ministry of Security.
19346	October 1, 2014	Creation of a new law to transform DISNA into the Directorate of National Strategic Intelligence (DIEN).

Source: Cátedra Seguridad y Convivencia Democrática (2016).[47]

failed to build a consensus, so the country continues to lack a clear intelligence service definition in paradigmatic and operational terms. These deficiencies deter the intelligence service from reaching optimal performance and fortifying democratic consolidation.

Democratic Civilian Control and Oversight

Political and civil control over Costa Rican intelligence has faced numerous challenges. The most prominent one is difficulty establishing political, criminal, and administrative responsibilities; in this sense, when failures of intelligence have occurred, public perceptions and the practices themselves remain unchanged.[49]

A consolidated democracy requires that both criminal and administrative penalties must be unambiguously established by law and applied with the utilization of due process. Additionally, the Legislative Assembly is obliged to supervise intelligence authorities and review intelligence activities and operations, as well as passing laws to enumerate powers. The legislative branch is tasked with preserving its prerogative to define Costa Rican domestic and transnational threats. In a functioning checks-and-balances system, ideally, the judiciary and the Constitutional Court conduct legal reviews of specific intelligence service actions and ensure that coercive actions are properly performed in accordance with law requirements and mitigate human rights violations associated with specific actions.[50]

The Costa Rican legal framework confers the president and Minister of Presidency exclusive control and supervision over DISNA, while legislative control and oversight is absent from the current regulations. Furthermore, a mandate obliging DISNA to regularly inform the Legislative Assembly does not exist, which obstructs accountability and democratic consolidation. Although, the legislative branch retains a general power to subpoena the general director and any other staff members to the plenary or any legislative commission for legislative oversight, this is an incidental fact and not frequently exercised by the members of congress.

On the other hand, Costa Rica has striven to establish judicial review of intelligence services. DISNA's intrusive operations—including wiretapping—require prior authorization from the Minister of the Presidency, as established in Article 19 of Decree No. 32522 (Organization and Operation Regulation). Another oversight protocol compels DISNA to request judicial permission before conducting justified coercive activities with competent authorities, in accordance with Article 20 of the regulations. Specifically, the article states, "Petitions before the competent judicial authority must be submitted, without exception, by the General Director and in the absence of this by the Deputy

General Director of the institution, with prior authorization of the hierarchy, with the consequent responsibility within of the extremes of their participation."[51] This sort of judicial oversight has been relevant to avoid a resurgence of abuses committed during 1970s and 1980s.

Professionalization and Effectiveness

Costa Rica employs a General Directorate of the Civil Service, which is a "technical-legal entity for the management of human resources that provide their services to the institutions of the Central Government."[52] It allows any qualified citizens the ability to compete for available positions in the public administration. However, DISNA is not ruled by the Civil Service Statute; therefore the recruitment process is internal and subject to the provisions of the Organization and Functioning Regulation, which establishes in Article 12 that DISNA applicants must

> a) Be a Costa Rican Citizen; b) Be of legal age; c) Be of faultless conduct; d) Having completed the third cycle of basic general education, without prejudice to the additional requirements determined for each position; e) Pass medical and psychological exams, which are practiced in accordance with the law; f) Complete the training processes and eligibility requirements established by the Statute in accordance with their specific work area; g) Have a license to drive vehicles in cases where the position requires it; and of the type that traffic regulations demand.[53]

These basic requirements are analogous to police recruitment standards because DISNA officials perform functions outlined in the Police Statute, as established in the 1994 Police General Law.

DISNA does not publicize its available vacancies. However, senior officials have indicated that any interested citizen can apply to the positions and be included in the DISNA recruitment databases, eventually becoming part of the selection process that involves psychological exams and other professional requirements.[54]

Successful applicants are trained at the National Police Academy, which has a specialized intelligence program. In addition, Article 13 of the Internal Regulations establish that the DISNA staff are compelled to participate in all national or international training programs, related to their specialty and follow General Directorate instructions, or when appropriate Ministry of the Presidency directives.[55]

It is important to mention that there are no intelligence academic degrees or postgraduate degrees in Costa Rican universities; therefore, officials usually have majored in such specialties as criminology, law, political sciences, and international relations. Presumably, some intelligence-sector members have studied abroad to receive advanced degrees in strategic and emerging intelligence. DISNA officials acknowledge that international cooperation with such governments as the United States, Colombia, and Israel has been essential in improving organizational knowledge and skills,[56] but—as has been mentioned previously—this training dependence is an obstacle to the national intelligence culture.

Costa Rica's modern national identity has been built around such values as peace, freedom, and democracy, displayed by the armed forces' utilization and conduct. DISNA has not been able to modify its inherited reputation, previous to and including the Cold War era. Since 1995, scandals, controversies, and public debates have surrounded this institution—and called into question the appropriateness of the agency and its functions in modern Costa Rica. For example, in 1995, a scandal over wiretapping led to the opening of a Special Investigative Commission in the Legislative Assembly, prompting some legislators to demand the closure of DISNA. In 2007, during the referendum campaign on the U.S.–Central America Free Trade Agreement (CAFTA), DISNA was criticized for disclosing several photographs of a congressman opposed to the treaty alongside a Colombian FARC leader. In 2008, the attorney general of the republic himself defined DISNA as a political police agency; and in 2009, the University Council of the University of Costa Rica, the most prestigious university in the country, issued a statement calling for DISNA closure in view of previous human rights abuses and the legal absence of accountability parameters.[57] Finally, between 2014 and 2017, DISNA was accused of losing a large part of its confidential files[58] as well as paying bribes and intimidating journalists.[59] Therefore, Jorge Torres, assistant director of DISNA argues, "Costa Rica does not have a developed intelligence culture, which has implied a slow process to get out of the deep ostracism in which it had been since the mid-1980s."[60] Even if Costa Rica has an intelligence culture, DISNA certainly lacks legitimacy and social approval.

This less than favorable evaluation of the intelligence sector is partially symptom and partially cause of a larger strategic problem. Costa Rica has delayed debates on emerging threats and security priorities against which efforts with medium- and long-term objectives should be targeted.[61] In addition to the well-known drug trafficking problem, Costa Rica must face such perils as international money laundering and drug trafficking organizations' intervention in national politics. Currently resourceful international terror organizations are exploiting gaps in the intelligence system to execute operations from Costa Rica sovereign territory. Also, Costa Rica has been defined as a transit point to the United States for illicit goods, thus necessitating information collaboration with more robust international security organizations.[62] In addition, one of the most pressing challenges for the region, and Costa Rica in particular, is criminal cyberactivity (economic crimes, cyberterrorism, cyberespionage, destabilization, and ideologic radicalization promotion).[63] With these mounting issues, Costa Rica lacks a National Security Strategy to guide the necessary efforts.

The absence of a National Security Strategy affects efforts to consolidate a coherent group of priorities and assign appropriate resources.[64] In the Costa Rican context, DISNA perceives security risks differently from the rest of Latin American intelligence services. Specifically, security is understood "fundamentally as risk management of non-traditional threats such as the protection of natural resources . . . , energy sources, marine resources and diverse ecosystems to which . . . concepts such as the fight against terrorism, transnational organized narco-activity, cyber-crime and/or the need for critical infrastructure protection have been added"; additionally the country deems itself free from traditional threats "with the exception of the ancient border conflict with the Republic of Nicaragua."[65] No real political or public discussion has anchored DISNA's activities in any kind of policy to support this vision in a sensible—or democratic—fashion.

These controversies have increased under the current administration. To be sure, in 2019 the Alvarado administration (2018–2022) proposed a national security policy; however, the scope of the discussion has been limited to specific political/intelligence organizations and has not been openly debated by the electorate. Also, there have been contradictory governmental proposals as to DISNA's institutional future (one portion of the spectrum demands its closure, another suggests a possible return to Ministry of Public Security), a jumble that well reflects the Costa Rican security paradox.[66]

CONCLUSION: COSTA RICAN SECURITY PARADOX AND INTELLIGENCE SERVICES

Costa Rica's intelligence culture is paradoxical. On the one hand, Costa Rica stands out as a recognized stable democratic regime, albeit one threatened by certain security risks. On the other hand, use of non-democratic intelligence tactics during the Cold War has left an incomplete and unsuccessful institutional and legal framework for the democratic governance of the nation's intelligence services.

Costa Rica's inadequate institutional framework has led to not defining the meaning, purpose, and doctrine that should guide a state intelligence service according to its democratic regime. This imprecise structure favors external influencers and vests disproportionate power to the executive branch in determining DISNA's priorities and methods. Beyond the budgetary and administrative controls applicable to state entities, as well as the judicial authorizations required by DISNA for coercive actions, political controls are not well delineated, both within the executive and especially regarding the legislative branch. This incomplete legal framework promotes DISNA legal functions to be misunderstood—or, worse, ignored—by public opinion. Both the need and the opportunity for change, despite the inertia of more than a century of unhappy experience, are real and urgent.

NOTES

1. According to Democracy Matrix, 2020, Costa Rica ranks 10th in the world. See https://www.democracymatrix.com/ranking. Also, according to Freedom House, "People have the right to organize in different political parties without undue obstacles. The historical dominance of the PLN and the Social Christian Unity Party (PUSC) has waned in recent years, as newly formed parties have gained traction, leading to the collapse of the traditional two-party system." Also, "Power regularly alternates in Costa Rica and opposition parties compete fiercely in presidential and legislative elections. Luis Guillermo Solís won the 2014 presidential election as the candidate of PAC, an opposition party at the time. Parties along a wide spectrum of the political order freely competed in the 2018 elections, and the PRN made major gains, winning 14 seats in the legislature after capturing just 1 seat in the 2014 contest." Freedom House, *Freedom in the World (Democracy in Retreat)*, Freedom House, 2019. Available at https://freedomhouse.org/country/costa-rica/freedom-world/2019.

2. The chapter is segmented into three parts. The first section provides a historical overview of the Costa Rican governmental activities conventionally linked with intelligence service in the final decades of the ninetheenth century and first decades of the twentieth century, until 1948, when Costa Rica was an authoritarian regime. The second one studies the institutional evolution of the intelligence service in the context of Costa Rican democratic consolidation process during the second part of the twentieth century. Finally, the third section explores the current Costa Rican intelligence sector, focused on such dimensions as the legal framework; budgetary issues and administrative organization; recruitment and training; information collection; and political and civil control.

3. Iván Molina Jiménez, *Costa Rica (1800–1850), El Legado Colonial y la Génesis del Capitalismo* (San José: Editorial Universidad de Costa Rica, 1era edición, 2da reimpresión, 2002): 437–44. Also see Elizabeth Fonseca, *Centroamérica: Su Historia* (San José: FLACSO-EDUCA, 1998).

4. David Díaz Arias, *La Era de la Centralización: Estado, Sociedad e Institucionalidad en Costa Rica 1848–1870.* (San José: Editorial UCR, 2015), 33–34; Esteban Corella Ovares, "El Gasto Militar del Estado Costarricense, 1821–1870." Universidad de Costa Rica. *Diálogos, Revista Electrónica de Historia* 18, no. 1 (2017): 26; Esteban Corella Ovares, "El Ejército en Costa Rica: Organización de las Fuerzas

Armadas, Sistema de Reclutamiento y la Construcción del Estado, 1812–1870," master's thesis. on history, Universidad de Costa Rica, Costa Rica, 2013. Also see David Díaz Arias, *Construcción de un Estado Moderno. Política e Identidad Nacional en Costa Rica, 1821–1914* (San José, Editorial UCR, 2005).

5. Efraín Pérez Zumbado, *El Control y la Dominación Política en el Régimen de Tomás Guardia* (San José: EUNED, 2013): 115–17.

6. Meaning "the Olympus," a reference to Greek mythology. Mount Olympus was the mountain where the Greek gods lived.

7. Steven Palmer, "Confinement, Policing, and the Emergence of Social Policy in Costa Rica, 1880–1935," in *The Birth of the Penitentiary in Latin America: Essays on Criminology, Prison Reform, and Social Control, 1830–1940*, eds. Ricardo D. Salvatore and Carlos Aguirre (Austin: University of Texas Press, 1996, Kindle edition, no page).

8. Iván Molina Jiménez and Fabrice Lehoucq, *Urnas de lo Inesperado. Fraude Electoral y Lucha Política en Costa Rica (1901–1948)* (San José: Editorial Universidad de Costa Rica, 1999), 6.

9. Jesús Fernández Morales, *Las Presidencias del Castillo Azul* (San José: Litografía e Imprenta Lil, 2010), 176.

10. Fernández Morales, *Las Presidencias del Castillo Azul,* 178.

11. Mercedes Muñoz, "Costa Rica: La Abolición del Ejército y la Construcción de la Paz Regional," *Historia y Comunicación Social* 19 (2014): 386; Mercedes Muñoz, *El Estado y la Abolición del Ejército 1914–1949* (San José: Editorial Porvenir, 1990).

12. Law No. 93, April 17, 1923.

13. Law No. 114, July 6, 1940.

14. Monica Flores Chacon, "Debunking the Pura Vida: Costa Rican Exceptionalism Is Under Threat," master's thesis, Naval Postgraduate School, Monterey, California, 2021. Available at http://hdl.handle.net/10945/67710.

15. Jorge Sáenz Carbonell, *Historia Diplomática de Costa Rica (1948–1970)* (Heredia: Escuela de Relaciones Internacionales, 2013): 14–15, 102–3.

16. Laura Moreno-Rodríguez, "La Presencia de José Figueres en México: Del Unionismo a La Insurrección, 1942–194," *Temas De Nuestra América. Revista De Estudios Latinoamericanos* 33 (septiembre, 2017): 107. Available at https://doi.org/10.15359/tdna.33-e.4. Also see Jacobo Schifter, *Costa Rica 1948. Análisis de Documentos Confidenciales del Departamento de Estado* (San José: EDUCA, 1982).

17. Jacobo Schifter, *Las Alianzas Conflictivas: Las Relaciones de Estados Unidos y Costa Rica desde la Segunda Guerra Mundial a la Guerra Fría* (San José: Libro Libre, 1986), 307.

18. Silvia Molina-Vargas, "La Violencia Política contra los Comunistas tras la Guerra Civil en Costa Rica (1948–1949)," *Cuadernos Inter.c.a.mbio sobre Centroamérica y el Caribe* 15, no. 1 (Abril–setiembre, 2018): 138–39.

19. David Díaz Arias, *Crisis Social y Memorias en Lucha: Guerra Civil en Costa Rica (1940–1948)* (San José: Editorial UCR, 2015): 285–86.

20. During this period, except for a failed attempt to retake power by arms in 1955 through a military incursion from Nicaragua led by forces that had been defeated in the 1948 Civil War, the country has not experienced internal or external armed

conflicts. In cases of violations of sovereignty and even armed attacks such as those carried out by the National Guard of Nicaragua during the Somoza dictatorship in the late 1970s, Costa Rica has resorted to the legal and defense mechanisms of the OAS, as well as cooperation from friendly countries. In the most recent territorial conflict with Nicaragua over Portillos Island / Harbor Head Costa Rica attended the International Court of Justice in The Hague. Rafael Obregón Loría, *Hechos Militares y Políticos de Nuestra Historia Patria* (Alajuela: Museo Histórico Cultural Juan Santamaría, 1981); Kirk Bowman, "¿Fue el Compromiso y Consenso de las Élites lo que llevó a la Consolidación Democrática en Costa Rica? Evidencias de la década de 1950," *Revista de Historia*, no. 41 (enero 2000): 91–127, available at https://www.revistas.una.ac.cr/index.php/historia/article/view/1868; Marco Méndez-Coto, "The Social Construction of External Aggression in Latin America: A Comparison between Costa Rica and Ecuador," *AUSTRAL: Brazilian Journal of Strategy & International Relations* 7, no. 14 (2018).

21. Figueres was president three times: 1948–1949, 1953–1958, and 1970–1974.

22. Executive Order No. 3, November 19, 1953.

23. Indeed, once in government, political parties preferred to change the major part of police corps members designated by previous administrations.

24. Carlos Humberto Cascante Segura, *La Política Exterior de Costa Rica (1850–2010)* (San José: EUCR, 2015), 33.

25. Executive Order No. 3, November 8, 1953; Until 1960, the CIA was still part of the Ministry of Public Security. Executive Order No. 45, May 24, 1960.

26. Law No. 5524, May 7, 1974.

27. Paul Cháves, "Los Espías No Bastan: Definiendo las Políticas Públicas en Materia de Servicios de Inteligencia en Costa Rica," paper presented at the Panel on Intelligence, Center for Hemispheric Defense Studies, 2001. Available at http://www.fas.org/irp/world/costa_rica/chaves.html.

28. CIA, Security Conditions in Costa Rica, March 6, 1963: 7–8.

29. Daniel Matul Romero and Andrés Palacios Rodríguez, "De CONDECA al Tratado Marco de Seguridad Democrática: La Nueva Institucionalidad Regional en Materia de Seguridad," *Revista Centroamericana de Administración Pública,* no. 66–67 (2014): 43–78; Cháves, "Los Espías No Bastan."

30. CIA, Update 1970 Handbook, December 1972: III–5

31. Marielos Aguilar, "Las Restricciones de los Derechos Políticos de los Costarricenses en la Década de 1980," *Revista de Ciencias Sociales* 67 (March 1995): 49–51; Daniel Camacho, "Democracia y Democratización en Centroamérica," in *Democracia y Democratización en Centroamérica,* Regina Steichen (compilator) (San José: EUCR, 1993), 234.

32. Executive Order No. 16398, June 6, 1985.

33. Law No. 7410, May 30, 1994.

34. Executive Order No. 23758, November 18, 1994.

35. Executive Order No. 23758, November 18, 1994.

36. Executive Order No. 32523, July 27, 2005.

37. Executive Order No. 27474, December 3, 1998.

38. Executive Order No. 32522, July 27, 2005.

39. National Budget, 2019. Available at https://www.hacienda.go.cr/docs/5c095b1c2ad61_Ley202.pdf.

40. National Budget, 2019. Available at https://www.hacienda.go.cr/docs/5c095b1c2ad61_Ley202.pdf.

41. Legislative Assembly, Permanent Commission of Income and Public Expenditure, Act 26°, October 23, 2014: 17–18.

42. AR.com, La DIS es como entrar a un "ghetto" en un precario, afirma Subdirector de la entidad. *AR.com*, October 23, 2014. Available at https://www ameliarueda.com/nota/la-dis-es-como-entrar-a-un-ghetto-en-un-precario-afirma-sub director-de-la-e.

43. Jorge Torres, *Requerimiento* [Informe de inteligencia] (San José: Dirección de Inteligencia y Seguridad del Estado, 2016).

44. See INTERPOL's National Central Bureau (NCB) in San Jose, Costa Rica, website: https://www.interpol.int/en/Who-we-are/Member-countries/Americas/COSTA-RICA.

45. Esteban Oviedo, "País contrata fotografías satelitales para vigilar incursión de ejército nicaragüense." *La Nación,* November 2, 2010. Available at https://www .nacion.com/archivo/pais-contrata-fotografias-satelitales-para-vigilar-incursion-de -ejercito-nicaraguense/DTSWANAZLBEA7J4G4RUGHPDTSM/story/.

46. See chapter 1 (or intro…).

47. Cátedra Seguridad y Convivencia Democrática, *¿Reformar o Cerrar la DIS? Aportes para el Debate,* Documento de Trabajo (San José: Universidad de Costa Rica, 2016).

48. Natalia Díaz Zeledón, "Otro proyecto de ley aspira a cerrar la DIS y redistribuir sus 3.188 millones a Seguridad," *Semanario Universidad*, February 28, 2020. Available at https://semanariouniversidad.com/pais/otro-proyecto-de-ley-aspira-a -cerrar-la-dis-y-redistribuir-sus-%C2%A23-188-millones-a-seguridad/.

49. Enrique Sáiz, "Unas Primeras Aproximaciones a los Sesgos Cognitivos en el Análisis de Inteligencia," *Inteligencia y Seguridad: Revista de Análisis y Prospectiva* 7 (2010): 231–36.

50. Daniel Matul-Romero and Carlos Torres, *Nuevo Arreglo Institucional a la Inteligencia en Costa Rica. Hacia una Reforma por una Gobernanza Democrática y Transparente.* Serie Análisis no. 2. (San José: FES—América Central, 2015).

51. Executive Order No. 32522, July 27, 2005.

52. Dirección General de Servicio Civil (DGSC). "About." Available at http://www.dgsc.go.cr/dgsc_descripcion.html.

53. Executive Order No. 32522, July 27, 2005. Translation by the authors.

54. Torres, *Requerimiento.*

55. Executive Order No. 32522, July 27, 2005.

56. Torres, *Requerimiento.*

57. Gerardo Hernández, "Debates sobre la Dirección de Inteligencia y Seguridad (DIS) y Propuesta para Abrir un Espacio Académico de Análisis sobre Seguridad y Convivencia Democrática en Costa Rica," paper presented at the 2° Congress on Intelligence: Intelligence Culture as an Element for Reflection and Collaboration, Madrid, 2010.

58. Esteban Mata, "Mariano Figueres: Cada gobierno limpió los archivos de operaciones de la DIS," *La Nación*, October 20, 2014. Available at https://www .nacion.com/el-pais/politica/mariano-figueres-cada-gobierno-limpio-los-archivos-de -operaciones-de-la-dis/LRSMN5HQIBCYBFDK3OCQSZENXI/story/.

59. José Arce, "Figueres: 'DIS nunca ni sobornó ni intimidó a ningún periodista,'" *AMPrensa*, March 16, 2017. Available at https://amprensa.com/2017/03/figueres-dis -nunca-soborno-intimido-ningun-periodista/.

60. Torres, *Requerimiento*.

61. Marco Méndez-Coto and Fredy Rivera Vélez, "The Intelligence Service in Costa Rica: Between the New and the Old Paradigm," *The International Journal of Intelligence, Security, and Public Affairs* 20, no. 1 (2018): 6–19; Carlos Humberto Cascante Segura and Nery Mata Argüello, "Rasgos de una Política de Defensa de Costa Rica. Entre la Paz y la Inseguridad," *Revista de Estudios en Seguridad y Defensa*, 13 (25): 93.

62. OSAC, *Costa Rica 2020 Crime and Safety Report* (Washington DC: OSAC, 2020). Available at https://www.osac.gov/Content/Report/e21b7a07-15a4-4fda-93ca -18e81f6fbd8c.

63. Prosic, *Ciberseguridad en Costa Rica*. San José: Programa de Sociedad de la Información Conocimiento (UCR), 2010: 25–26. Costa Rica has proactively and successfully formed the Computer Security Incident Response Center (C-SIRT), which does have the budget or personnel to handle this twenty-first century challenge.

64. Daniel Matul Romero and Roger Juárez, *Reforma de la Dirección de Inteligencia y Seguridad (DIS). Lineamientos para la Construcción de una Hoja de Ruta*, Serie Perspectivas no. 6. (San José: ESF—América Central, 2014): 20.

65. Torres, *Requerimiento*.

66. Carlos Mora, "Ministro contradice a presidente sobre futuro de la Dis," *CRhoy*, September 10, 2020. Available at https://www.crhoy.com/nacionales/ministro-contra dice-propuesta-de-presidente-sobre-futuro-de-la-dis/.

Chapter Eleven

Guatemala

Eduardo E. Estévez

Between 1839, when the Republic of Guatemala gained its independence from Spain, and 1996—when a peace agreement put an end to a bloody internal conflict that had plagued the country since 1962—this Central American country was marked by political instability, social conflicts, and repression,[1] manifested in a revolving door between democratic governance and military authoritarianism.[2] The late 1990s found the country engaged in a peace process and transitioning to democracy. Since then, Guatemala has striven to achieve democratic consolidation.

This chapter reviews the efforts and new legislation adopted to accomplish intelligence governance and accountability as part of the democratic security paradigm that replaced the counterinsurgent state model. These legal reforms occurred in the context of weak democratic institutions, corruption, bad actors disregarding laws with impunity, and the presence of clandestine and illegal security apparatuses as revealed by the International Commission Against Impunity in Guatemala (CICIG), convened between 2007 and 2019. Guatemala's post-conflict transition to democracy has made minimal impact on the military's control of the intelligence community. It was not until the 2000s that the civil intelligence agency, outlined within the 1996 peace agreements, was created by law; a corresponding legal framework for the intelligence system was adopted by the 2008 law on the national security system. Changes adopted during this century have not yet led to effective and enduring civilian control of the intelligence sector, and more broadly in the demilitarization of security in the country. These are but a few challenges Guatemala's intelligence democratization faces.

HISTORICAL BACKGROUND
ON THE NON-DEMOCRATIC REGIME

The October 1944 popular revolution that overthrew a long-lasting dictator-ship[3] led to elected governments promoting social and economic reforms.[4] These reforms upset both the elites—landowners in Guatemala—and the U.S. government, which was worried about the spread of Communism in the coun-try. In 1946, the government created the army's first military intelligence unit, following a collaborative framework devised during the four-year agreement with the United States that additionally instituted a military mission within the country.

After several failed military coups attempted by the Guatemalan armed forces over the proceeding ten years against the Guatemalan socialist govern-ment, the United States decided to take matters into its own hands.[5] President Eisenhower directed the Central Intelligence Agency to carry out Operation PBSUCCESS—a covert operation that combined propaganda, coup, and paramilitary activities, with the objective of toppling the Guatemalan gov-ernment.[6] PBSUCCESS commenced on December 9, 1953, and led to the overthrow of President Jacobo Arbenz on June 27, 1954.[7] Carlos Castillo Armas—an exiled former military officer handpicked by the United States—replaced Arbenz.

Abetted by the military, Castillo Armas immediately halted the reforms implemented by the Arbenz administration, while devising new legislation that infringed upon citizens' rights—for example, rescinding the right to vote for illiterate citizens.[8] Seeking a greater role in Guatemala's governance, the military established an administrative capacity over all facets of the country, by creating partnerships with the elites, including political parties and the ec-onomically powerful civilian oligarchy.[9] As such, the 1954 coup established a fragile constitutional order.

Armas's harsh reforms prompted unhappy Guatemalan citizens to organize against the government—by carrying out protests, which were violently sup-pressed by the government. In the 1950s, during the Cold War, the Guate-malan National Security Council was created to coordinate new intelligence tasks, integrating the Department of Defense Against Communism and the Department of Security, the latter in charge of presidential security and intel-ligence functions.[10] At that time, repressive intelligence against dissent was mainly conducted by internal security forces, including the investigative unit of the National Police, the Treasury Police, the Mobile Military Police (PMA), and other actors.[11]

The government's policies and response to protests made Armas unpopular. In this context on July 26, 1957, Romeo Vásquez Sánchez, a leftist sympathizer presidential guard member assassinated Armas.[12] In 1958, General José Miguel Ramón Fuentes was elected president. In 1963 the military eliminated its political partners and assumed full control. The army became the country's primary vanguard of power, setting up a "counterinsurgent military regime."[13]

The state's counter-revolutionary focus since the mid-1950s[14] transitioned to internal armed conflict that lasted thirty-four years, between 1962 and 1996. The first guerrilla movement emerged in 1962 from a group of low-ranking military officers that failed in an earlier military uprising.[15]

On this background, counterinsurgency activities began in 1962 with the creation of the Special Group under the National Security Council, a ministerial-level body that coordinated the development of new doctrine and tactics. As guerrilla operations increased, the state reacted by expanding civilian repression and developing an environment of terror through its counterinsurgency strategy. Its choice was to implement "a 'mailed fist' strategy which also proved effective (albeit brutal)" as illustrated by Steven Metz and Raymond Millen.[16] U.S. assistance was critical to this effort;[17] intelligence and counterintelligence structures (like, for example, communications networks) were established through the formation of intelligence specialized units and communications networks synchronizing the entirety of the nation's intelligence organizations.[18] Ultimately, the government also categorized oppositional social and political actors unrelated to the armed insurgency as enemies of the state—thereby providing the pretense for collecting information and conducting illegal operations on such groups—performing covert paramilitary and psychological operations to further state hegemony.[19] All these developments paved the way for the politicization of the intelligence sector.[20] Between the late-1970s and 1980s, such elements as D-2 military intelligence and police counterintelligence acquired the following roles: technical and computer collection developments, human resources training, international cooperation, and the implementation of human intelligence networks that utilized the population as an information source during the conflict.[21] Guatemala's utilization of the intelligence system to repress domestic dissidents resulted in two situations antithetical to democracy: (1) the absence of an intelligence regulatory framework, and (2) the excessive concentration of intelligence without oversight in the EMDN's D-2 military intelligence body.[22]

In the early 1980s, eager to focus only on counterinsurgency, the military junta decided to give up its administrative task and restore democratic rule in Guatemala—a rather paradoxical move,[23] considering that at that moment it was carrying out a horrid genocide.[24] To this end, in 1983, the military junta appointed General Efraín Ríos Montt to initiate a democratic transition. As he drifted from military guidance, the junta replaced him with General Mejía Víctores, who convened a Constitutional Assembly in 1984, organized national elections in 1985, and handed over formal political authority to elected officials in 1986. [25]

In May 1985, a constitutional reform was ratified, distinguished by greater democratic openness. It defined, among other aspects, a special emphasis on the preservation and defense of human rights; the possibility of a second round of elections; the independence of the Supreme Electoral Court; the creation of the Human Rights Attorney General's Office; the establishment of the Constitutional Court; and banning presidential reelection and the election of persons who had participated in coups.[26] In December 1985, free and fair general elections were held with Vinicio Cerezo (1986–1991)[27] elected as president. Nevertheless, the military remained a powerful force,[28] especially in the context of intelligence.[29] Additionally, the D-2 military intelligence element under the Military Chiefs of Staff Office (EMDN), and the Presidential General Staff (EMP), an intelligence unit under presidential authority informally known as "Archivo,"[30] played a disproportionate role during the transition process, focused on working against political opponents and human rights activists.[31] Military intelligence sought to continue Guatemala's internal conflict during the transition process.[32] The EMP devised manners to constrain civilian authorities from diminishing the organization's unchecked power—persistently providing the executive intelligence information on hypothetical or real political opponents.[33]

On this background—and in parallel with the democratic transition—Guatemala also started a peace process, which started in 1987 when the government created a National Commission for Reconciliation, which facilitated national dialogue.[34] Participants in the peace process included the government, the military, the URNG, political parties, and social sectors.[35]

ATTEMPTS AT INTELLIGENCE
REFORMS SINCE THE DEMOCRATIC TRANSITION

The peace agreements did not considerably reduce the influence of the armed forces or intelligence agencies. The military continued to carry out domestic security roles and engage in domestic political spying.[36] Furthermore, during the first half of the 1990s, military intelligence was tasked, in addition to combating insurgency, with pursuing organized crime, drug trafficking, and common crime, which gave intelligence agencies carte blanche to engage in illicit activities under the name of security—which triggered criticism by human rights watchdogs.[37]

Under these circumstances, the impetus for fundamental intelligence reform attempts started in the 1990s. First, in 1993, the "Archivo" was renamed the Secretariat of Strategic Affairs in an effort to build a new agency. The organization's operational units were deactivated, and an analysis division was established, becoming the entity's sole function.[38] Then, in 1995, the Secretariat was formalized through a Gubernative Agreement—the equivalent of an executive order in the United States. This executive decision, which was later declared unconstitutional due to the executive branch exercising excessive legislative power, was the first step toward what would later be known as the Secretariat of Strategic Analysis (SAE), accountable to the president.[39] Specifically, Article 13 of the 1997 Law of the Executive Branch reestablished the SAE as a civilian body tasked to provide the president with information and advice to anticipate, prevent, and resolve situations of risk or threat of a different nature to the democratic state and its inhabitants.[40] This project, the country's first effort toward meaningful regulation of the intelligence sector, marked the beginning of the Guatemalan intelligence services' democratic transition as well.[41]

As part of the peace accords, in September 1996 the *Agreement on the Strengthening of Civilian Power and on the Role of the Armed Forces in a Democratic Society* was signed in Mexico City, the impetus for Guatemalan intelligence reform.[42] This agreement envisaged the following:

- A Civilian Intelligence and Information Analysis Department (DICAI), under the Ministry of the Interior, responsible for obtaining information on organized crime and ordinary crime.
- A Strategic Analysis Secretariat, a civilian body subordinate to the executive, tasked with informing and advising the president; additionally, to anticipate, prevent, and resolve situations posing a danger or threat to the democratic state.
- An Intelligence Department under the Chief of Staff for National Defense excluded from performing domestic intelligence and limited to external defense.

The agreement encouraged congress to adopt a law establishing an intelligence oversight committee and a law stipulating provisions on classification and declassification procedures and levels.[43] The 1996 Agreement also advanced the creation of a presidential Advisory Council on Security, to act as a strategic security coordinator. Moreover, the dissolution of the EMP and its replacement by a new body was emphatically prescribed. [44] Additionally, President Portillo appointed Edgar Gutiérrez, a human rights activist, as head of the SAE.[45] In September 2000 President Portillo issued, without consultations, a gubernative agreement creating the DICAI, but this decision was later declared unconstitutional and therefore suspended—the Constitutional Court considered that the president lacked the legislative powers to create the organization, stating congress was the only institution that retained the requisite legal authority.[46] Police intelligence reforms involved the abolishment of the PMA, the National Police, and the Treasury Police; all organizations were replaced by the new and demilitarized PNC.[47]

The legal framework and reform attempts resulted in the following intelligence sector components in Guatemala:

- The Secretary of Intelligence (SIE),[48] under the presidency, earlier known as SAE, which was established in 1997, is the civil intelligence agency charged with supporting the president, coordinating the National Intelligence System, and tasked with the production of strategic intelligence.
- The DIGICI, under the Ministry of Government, created by a 2005 law, is tasked to produce intelligence related to organized crime and ordinary crime.
- The Military Intelligence Directorate for National Defense Staff (DIEMDN) is tasked, as outlined by the LMSNS law (discussed later in this chapter), with the collection and production of information on external military threats.
- The police intelligence components of the PNC. According to a gubernative agreement of December 2005,[49] the Sub-Directorate for Police Investigations of the PNC is responsible for obtaining, analyzing, interpreting, and disseminating criminal information, also maintaining the Police Information Division.[50] Recently it was proposed to establish a Sub-Directorate for Police Intelligence.[51]

To institutionalize intelligence governance and accountability, the Guatemalan Congress passed two significant pieces of legislation: the DIGICI law of 2005[52] and the Framework Law for the National System of Security of 2008 (LMSNS).[53] The DIGICI law details the intelligence cycle phases designed to protect the country from organized crime and common crime by specifying the structural, organizational, and intelligence control mechanisms. It also established that the DIGICI is accountable to the Ministry of Government and that the minister in charge appoints the head of such bodies. The DIGICI law specified that to perform interception of communications, prior authorization from an appeals court is required. Furthermore, the DIGICI law specified that a congressional commission be responsible for ensuring compliance with the law.

DIGICI law unequivocally defined that the DIGICI will not intervene in investigations subject to judicial proceedings nor in police operations arising from intelligence the organization produced. The LMSNS law—which provides for the coordination of internal security, external security, and intelligence activities to anticipate and respond effectively to risks, threats, and vulnerabilities—deepened this precept, prohibiting the SIE, the DIGICI, and the DIEMDN from conducting operations derived from their own investigations. Article 26 of the LMSNS law further amplifies the coordinative objectives of the National Intelligence System. The LMSNS law established the National Security Council to coordinate the national security sector.[54]

A gubernative agreement issued in May 2011 by President Salvador Alvaro Colom (2008–2012) regulated the LMSNS law.[55] This gubernative agreement set guidelines for the coordination of the intelligence system, its meetings, production, dissemination of reports, legal enforcement, interinstitutional cooperation, and secrecy. A professionalized intelligence system career path for intelligence personnel is provided for in Article 30 of the LMSNS law. The legislation in force does not provide definitions and legitimate scope of reserved intelligence expenditure, declassification procedures, nor does it explicitly provide for criminal penalties.[56] Also, regarding congressional control, the LMSNS law created the Specific Legislative Commission on National Security and Intelligence Affairs with the power to analyze intelligence plans and programs, to monitor and maintain budgetary control of the intelligence sector, and to contribute an opinion on any draft legislation or matter that is relevant to or linked to intelligence activities. Lastly, Article 27 of the LMSNS law also provided for judicial control of the special procedures for collecting information by the agencies comprising the national intelligence system.

ANALYSIS

Ultimately, these reforms did not result in achieving democratic governance of the Guatemalan intelligence agencies. Indeed, as a report released by Amnesty International in 2003 indicates, "In recent decades, virtually the entire history of Guatemalan military and paramilitary intelligence structures and attempts at their reform suggests a systematic and deliberate pattern of institutional behavior whereby following public calls for reform, abusive structures were concealed rather than abolished."[57] MINUGUA reports noted the lack of political will and the relentless influence of clandestine groups hindering security and intelligence reform decisions, which impeded civilian control of intelligence and the demilitarization of the security and intelligence apparatuses.[58]

Control and Oversight

These reform attempts did not result in effective intelligence oversight. Regrettably, parliamentary control has not fully matured and therefore has not exerted its authority.[59] Likewise, the current constitution still designates public security as one of the functions of the armed forces, contrary to modern concepts of a consolidated and healthy democracy. These lacunae in turn permitted intelligence corruption and politicization.[60] For example, a case of corruption involving then president Otto Pérez Molina (2012–2015), a retired general and former head of D-2 military intelligence, led to civic protests that ended with his resignation and arrest on corruption charges in 2015.[61] Likewise, during the last two administrations, the National System of Security and SIE were headed by officials with military backgrounds, whose management has not always been aligned with the principles of democratic consolidation of security institutions.[62] A troubling recent occurrence has been President Alejandro Giammattei (2020–) appointing as head of the SIE an individual alleged by CICIG to be participating in a parallel intelligence network of lawyers, military members, and prosecutors known as *La Oficinita*, engaged in illegal espionage.[63] Thereby potentially relegating intelligence oversight to criminal entities and their ability to manipulate democratic progress to further parochial interests.

On the other hand, public oversight of intelligence has made positive effects. For example, the security environment in Guatemala—dominated by common crime, organized crime, and private security companies—has led to a favorable climate for civil society debates and proposals for a new intelligence and security legislative paradigm.[64] A noteworthy endeavor was the project "Toward a Security Policy for Democracy" (POLSEDE), a United Nations Development Program (UNDP) initiative launched in 1999 as a research-and-dialogue process implemented by Guatemalan academic and civil society institutions until 2002—focused on military, security, and intelligence challenges precipitated from peace agreements.[65] Additionally, concerning public oversight, especially transparency and truth-seeking, the release of the former National Police archives in 2005 is a significant step toward rectifying previous injustices.[66] Similarly, the DIGICI law and the LMSNS law were influenced by active civil society organizations working as congressional technical advisors.[67]

Professionalism

The Guatemalan intelligence system has been ineffective in combating the nefarious security threats that have plagued the country since the end of the civil war. On the one hand, military intelligence has neglected border security and associated threats. On the other hand, the DIGICI, newly began to strengthen and technologize its criminal intelligence structure in five regions.

CONCLUSION

Guatemalan intelligence culture has been challenged by weak democratic institutions, insecurity, corruption, impunity demonstrated toward the rule of law, and the CIACS[68] unveiled by the CICIG. [69] Legislative changes adopted this century to achieve intelligence democratization have not yet crystallized into effective and enduring civilian control.

This outcome falls within the broader field of civil-military relations, as well as in the process of demilitarization of security and intelligence apparatuses and their negative legacies. In this respect, Bernardo Arévalo and Ana Glenda Tager contend that "the implementation of the security reform process and the broader peace agreement has been limited by the weakness of the Guatemalan state and inadequate civilian capacity for coherent policy formulation and implementation."[70]

Meanwhile, intelligence challenges both in the strategic field and issues of violence and organized crime[71] remain top priorities. In addition to these challenges are myopic decisions by political elites that clash with the essence of democratic reforms and intelligence governance. Guatemala's complex case illustrates the relevance of enduring political will to foster the institutionalization of civilian democratic authority upon the intelligence sector.

NOTES

1. Kristin Marsh, "Republic of Guatemala," in *World Encyclopedia of Political Systems and Parties, Fourth Edition,* eds. Neil Schlager and Jayne Weisblatt (New York: Facts On File, 2006): 521.

2. Arévalo notes that Guatemala's authoritarianism was "organized following hierarchical and exclusionary patterns." Bernardo Arévalo de León, "Civil-Military Relations in Post-Conflict Guatemala," *Revista Fuerzas Armadas y Sociedad* 20, no. 1 (2005): 64. Also, see Nicholas Copeland, *The Democracy Development Machine: Neoliberalism, Radical Pessimism, and Authoritarian Populism in Mayan Guatemala* (Ithaca and London: Cornell University Press, 2019): 1; and Duilia Mora Turner, "Violent Crime in Post-Civil War Guatemala: Causes and Policy Implications," master's thesis, Naval Postgraduate School, Monterey, California, 2015, available at http://hdl .handle.net/10945/45266.

3. General Jorge Ubico (1931–1944) headed the regime. Piero Gleijeses, "La Aldea de Ubico: Guatemala, 1931–1944," *Mesoamérica* 10, no. 17 (1989): 25–60.

4. Gustavo Berganza, *Compendio de Historia de Guatemala, 1944–2000* (Guatemala: Asociación de Investigación y Estudios Sociales, 2004), 2–18.

5. Piero Gleijeses, *Shattered Hope: The Guatemalan Revolution and the United States, 1944–1954* (Princeton: Princeton University Press, 1991). Regarding implications of this fact for the region, see Max Paul Friedman, "Significados Transnacionales del Golpe de Estado de 1954 en Guatemala: Un Suceso de la Guerra Fría Internacional," in *Guatemala y la Guerra Fría en América Latina, 1947–1977*, ed. Roberto García Ferreira (Guatemala: CEUR-USAC, 2010), 19–28.

6. On the scale of covert operations, see Mark M. Lowenthal, *Intelligence: From Secrets to Policy*, 7th ed. (Los Angeles: CQ Press, 2017); also, see Ruben Arcos's chapter "Covert Operations" in *The Conduct of Intelligence in Democracies: Processes, Practices, Cultures*, eds. Florina Cristiana Matei and Carolyn Halladay (Boulder: Lynne Rienner Publishers, 2019): 97–106.

7. Mora Turner, "Violent Crime in Post-Civil War Guatemala."

8. Mora Turner, "Violent Crime in Post-Civil War Guatemala."

9. Marsh, "Republic of Guatemala," 521.

10. Bernardo Arévalo de León, "Del Estado Violento al Ejército Político: Violencia, Formación Estatal y Ejército en Guatemala, 1500–1963," PhD thesis, University of Utrecht, 2015, 205, 276–277. Available at http://dspace.library.uu.nl/handle/1874/330737.

11. At that time, the military did not engage in any repression activities. Manolo Vela, "De Peras y Olmos: La Reforma de los Servicios de Inteligencia en Guatemala," *Revista de la Secretaría de Análisis Estratégico de la Presidencia de la República* 1, no. 1 (2002): 70–72.

12. Gleijeses, *Shattered Hope*.

13. Comisión para el Esclarecimiento Histórico (CEH), *Guatemala, Memoria de Silencio*, vols. 1–12 (Guatemala City: CEH, 1999), paragraphs 396 and 397.

14. Arévalo de León, "Civil-Military Relations in Post-Conflict Guatemala," 64.

15. As summarized by Copeland, "Guatemala's armed conflict was one of the longest and bloodiest in modern Latin American history . . . [organized] by peasant, indigenous, student, religious, and workers' organizations, along with several armed revolutionary groups—motivated by anti-imperialism, land reform, equality, and social democracy—that were all violently opposed by a fascistic military dictatorship backed by national elites and the US government." Copeland, *The Democracy Development Machine*, 1. In February 1982, the Guatemalan National Revolutionary Unity (URNG) materialized as a leftist guerrilla alliance. According to Sabine Kurtenbach, the URNG never reached a military strength to effectively endanger the existing status quo. Sabine Kurtenbach, *Guatemala's Post-War Development: The Structural Failure of Low Intensity Peace*, Project working paper no. 3, Institute for Development and Peace (INEF) (Germany: University of Duisburg-Essen, 2008), 1.

16. Steven Metz and Raymond Millen, "Insurgency and Counterinsurgency in the 21st Century" (Strategic Studies Institute, United States Army War College, Carlisle, PA, 2004), 11–12.

17. US "military assistance was directed towards reinforcing the national intelligence apparatus and for training the officer corps in counterinsurgency techniques,

key factors which had significant bearing on human rights violations during the armed confrontation." CEH, *Guatemala: Memory of Silence. Report of the Commission for Historical Clarification. Conclusions and Recommendations* (Guatemala City: CEH, 1999), paragraph 13.

18. Arévalo de León, "Del Estado Violento al Ejército Político," 321–22, 335–36. In its initial phase, the process of preparing military intelligence resources included the assembly of the Regional Telecommunications Center; reorganizations operated in the military intelligence service; and the completion of the first courses in counterintelligence in 1965. Vela, "De Peras y Olmos," 73. Also see Álvaro Cremades Guisado, *Inteligencia y Secreto en Guatemala: La Trascendencia del Archivo Histórico de la Policía Nacional* (Guatemala: Escuela de Ciencia Política, Universidad de San Carlos de Guatemala, 2017), 37–47.

19. In the context of the internal armed conflict, the military determined the roles and missions of intelligence agencies. POLSEDE, "Aportes para el Estudio de la Inteligencia de Estado en Guatemala," Subgrupo de Trabajo No. 4 Inteligencia Civil, Proyecto Hacia una Política de Seguridad para la Democracia, FLACSO—WSP—IGEDEP, Guatemala, 2002, 9–10. Available at https://www.interpeace.org/resource/a-contribution-to-the-study-of-the-intelligence-apparatus-in-guatemala/.

20. As noted in a report published by a UN-backed truth commission on Guatemala's civil war, the intelligence apparatus dominated every dimension of the counterinsurgency effort: "the driving force of a state policy that took advantage of the situation resulting from the armed confrontation, to control the population, the society, the State and the Army itself. This total domination was based on a political-military strategy and was put into practice using mechanisms which violated human rights, the Constitution and the laws of the Republic." Comisión para el Esclarecimiento Histórico (CEH), *Guatemala, Memoria de Silencio*, vols. 1–12 (Guatemala City: CEH, 1999). This report detailed conclusions on the following items: human rights violations committed by the State; anti-communism and the National Security Doctrine; massacres and the devastation of the Mayan people; disappearances; arbitrary executions; rape of women; death squads; denial of justice; forced and discriminatory military recruitment; the legal order affected; institutional responsibility; acts of genocide; as well as items related to acts of violence committed by the guerrillas.

21. Vela, "De Peras y Olmos," 77–80.

22. Manolo Vela, "Dilemas de la Reforma del Sistema de Inteligencia en Guatemala," *Diálogo* 3 (1999): 6. See also Carmen Rosa De León-Escribano Schlotter, "Estructuras de Inteligencia en Guatemala," in *Inteligencia Policial—Compilación de Textos*, ed. Carmen Rosa De León-Escribano Schlotter, Cuadernos de IEPADES no. 1 (Guatemala: Instituto de Enseñanza para el Desarrollo Sostenible, 2000), 7–21.

23. As Bernardo Arévalo elaborates, this transition was not the result of political pressure from civil society or political parties over the army to relinquish power—as in many cases in other parts of the continent—but a strategic decision of the military to retreat from political administrative functions in order to concentrate in the internal armed confrontation: democratization as a tool for counterinsurgency. Arévalo de León, "Civil-Military Relations in Post-Conflict Guatemala," 68.

24. In the early 1980s the military regime reacted brutally to the growing social mobilization all over the country. Over six hundred Maya communities in the highlands were destroyed, a million men forced into "civilian self defence patrols" (PAC), and military-controlled settlements, so-called "development poles," established. The alliance included the Guerrilla Army of the Poor (EGP), the Revolutionary Organization of the People in Arms (ORPA), the Rebel Armed Forces (FAR), and the core of the Guatemalan Labour Party (PGT). Berganza, *Compendio de Historia de Guatemala*, 67; Kurtenbach, *Guatemala's Post-War Development*, 1. Retired General Efraín Ríos Montt, who was selected by the military junta to rule the country from March 1982 to August 1983, led this genocide. Kees Koonings, "Civil Society, Transitions and Post-War Reconstruction in Latin America: A Comparison of El Salvador, Guatemala, and Peru," *Iberoamericana (Stockholm)* 32, no. 2 (2002): 56; Arévalo de León, "Civil-Military Relations in Post-Conflict Guatemala," 68.

25. Kees Koonings, "Civil Society, Transitions and Post-War Reconstruction in Latin America," 56; and Arévalo de León, "Civil-Military Relations in Post-Conflict Guatemala," 68. According to Linz and Stepan, Guatemala is an example of electoralist nontransitions "where a previously ruling military [e.g., in Guatemala in the 1980s], though relinquishing direct control of government, retains such extensive prerogatives that the democratically elected government is not even *de jure* sovereign." Juan J. Linz and Alfred Stepan, *Problems of Democratic Transition and Consolidation: Southern Europe, South America, and Post-Communist Europe* (Baltimore, Johns Hopkins University Press, 1996): 4. On Guatemalan military role in politics, see Silvina María Romano, "Entre la Militarización y la Democracia: La Historia en el Presente de Guatemala," *Latinoamérica. Revista de Estudios Latinoamericano* 55 (2012): 215–44.

26. Berganza, *Compendio de Historia de Guatemala*, 68.

27. He was a democratic politician, Guatemalan Christian Democracy Party. He promoted the peace agreements in Central America known as Esquipulas I and Esquipulas II.

28. Linz and Stepan, *Problems of Democratic Transition and Consolidation*, 4. In this connection, the military retained several prerogatives, including, for example, a role in internal security. Kurtenbach, *Guatemala's Post-War Development*, 18. On prerogatives, see Alfred Stepan, *Rethinking Military Politics: Brazil and the Southern Cone* (Princeton, NJ: Princeton University Press, 1988). Three military coup attempts during his tenure (1987, 1988, and 1989), a rather odd development considering that the administration granted the armed forces amnesty for the recent human rights abuses. Mora Turner, "Violent Crime in Post-Civil War Guatemala."

29. Intelligence continued under military control under the logics of the counterinsurgency strategy.

30. "The EMP was officially created in the early 1980s to absorb the intelligence functions of its predecessor, the . . . Special Communications Services for the Presidency, (commonly known as La Regional, the Regional). . . . Its official name in 1982 was . . . General Information and Support Services for the President of the Presidential High Command, at which time it was assigned explicit counterinsurgency functions." Amnesty International, *Guatemala Accountable Intelligence or Recycled Repres-*

sion? Abolition of the EMP and Effective Intelligence Reform, Index number: AMR 34/031/2003 [online] (London: Amnesty International, June 9, 2003): 2. Available at https://www.amnesty.org/en/documents/AMR34/031/2003/en.

31. See Edgar Gutiérrez, *Hacia Un Paradigma Democrático del Sistema de Inteligencia en Guatemala*. (Ciudad de Guatemala, Guatemala: Fundación Myrna Mack, 1999); Vela, "De Peras y Olmos," 76; Amnesty International, *Guatemala Accountable Intelligence or Recycled Repression?*

32. Gutiérrez, *Hacia Un Paradigma Democrático*, 17. Also see, Jennifer Schirmer, "The Guatemalan Politico-Military Project: ¿Legacies for a Violent Peace?," *Latin American Perspectives* 26, no. 2 (1999): 92–107.

33. Vela, "De Peras y Olmos," 82.

34. Koonings, "Civil Society, Transitions and Post-War Reconstruction in Latin America," 50. On these three postwar transformations—pacification, democratization, and market liberalization—also see Welmoed Barendsen, "The Political Economy of Peacebuilding: A Study into Power Relations and the Triple Transition in Guatemala," master's thesis, Utrecht University, 2015, available at https://dspace.library.uu.nl/bitstream/handle/1874/320417/FINAL%20THESIS%203494713.pdf%3Bseque; https://peacemaker.un.org/centralamerica-esquipulasI86 and https://peacemaker.un.org/centralamerica-esquipulasII87; United Nations, General Assembly Security Council. *Agreement on the Procedure for the Search for Peace by Political Means*. A/45/1007 S/22563 (May 2, 1991), available at https://peacemaker.un.org/sites/peacemaker.un.org/files/GT_910426_MexicoAgreement.pdf.

35. The UN performed an observatory role through its Mission for the Verification of Human Rights and of Compliance with the Comprehensive Agreement on Human Rights in Guatemala (MINUGUA), deployed between 1994 and 2004. Civil society organizations "played an important role in triggering the peace process, offering platforms and being a partner in the process. Neither the military nor the ruling party nor the URNG were in a position to subordinate or control civil society. As a result, [civil society organizations] have developed into major stakeholders in the implementation of the peace agreements and the deepening of democratic governance through expanding voice and strengthening peaceful consensus." Koonings, "Civil Society, Transitions and Post-War Reconstruction in Latin America," 63. Subsequently, negotiations progressed with the Oslo Agreements, and the adoption of the *Agreement on a Firm and Lasting Peace* of December 1996 officially ceased civil war hostilities and legally recognized all the agreements previously signed. See William Stanley, *Enabling Peace in Guatemala: The Story of MINUGUA* (Boulder: Lynne Rienner Publishers, 2013); United Nations, General Assembly Security Council, *Agreement on a Firm and Lasting Peace*, A/51/796 S/1997/114 (February 7, 1997), available at https://peacemaker.un.org/guatemala-firmlastingpeace96. For an account on the negotiation process see Jeremy Armon, Rachel Sieder, and Richard Wilson, eds., *Negotiating Rights: The Guatemalan Peace Process* (London: Conciliation Resources, 1997); William Stanley and David Holiday, "Broad Participation, Diffuse Responsibility: Peace Implementation in Guatemala," in *Ending Civil Wars: The Implementation of Peace Agreements*, eds. Stephen John Stedman, Donald Rothchild, and

Elisabeth Consuens (Boulder, CO: Lynne Rienner Press, 2002): 421–62; Berganza, *Compendio de Historia de Guatemala*, 73–89.

36. Stanley, and Holiday, "Broad Participation, Diffuse Responsibility," 448–49.

37. Gutiérrez, *Hacia Un Paradigma Democrático*, 52–54.

38. The various secretariats created during transition, which can be confusing, responded to the need to comply with the agreements while retaining some functions and staff of the deactivated agencies. These cosmetic actions indicate little political interest in their final dismantling. A recommended reading is Alexander H. Joffe, "Dismantling Intelligence Agencies," *Crime, Law and Social Change* 32, (1999): 325–46.

39. Vela, "De Peras y Olmos," 89.

40. Guatemala Congress, Legislative Decree No. 114 of 1997, Law of the Executive Branch. Available at https://www.mem.gob.gt/wp-content/uploads/2015/06/12 ._Ley_del_Organismo_Ejecutivo_Decreto_114_97.pdf.

41. Vela, "De Peras y Olmos," 90.

42. United Nations, General Assembly Security Council, *Agreement on the Strengthening of Civilian Power and on the Role of the Armed Forces in a Democratic Society*, A/51/410 S/1996/853 (October 16, 1996). Available at https://peacemaker .un.org/sites/peacemaker.un.org/files/GT_960919_AgreementStrengtheningCivilian Power.pdf.

43. United Nations, *Agreement on the Strengthening of Civilian Power.*

44. United Nations, *Agreement on the Strengthening of Civilian Power.* Despite specific language in the agreement, the EMP remained in operation; in fact, between 1999 and 2002 its budget was tripled. Finally, however, President Alfonso Portillo (2000–2004) took initiative to abolish the agency. In September 2003, the Secretariat of Administrative Affairs and Security of the Presidency (SAAS) was established by law as a civilian body to ensure the security of the president, vice president, and their families, with no intelligence functions. Article 20 of the same law dissolved the EMP. Susan C. Peacock and Adriana Beltrán, *Hidden Powers in Post-Conflict Guatemala: Illegal Armed Groups and the Forces behind Them* (Washington, DC: Washington Office on Latin America, 2003): 22; Guatemala Congress, Legislative Decree No. 50, of 2003; Law for the Secretariat of Administrative Affairs and Security of the Presidency (SAAS), https://www.saas.gob.gt/historico/informacion-publica/ley-de -saas/category/4-ley-de-saas?download=2:ley-de-saas.

45. Amnesty International, *Guatemala Accountable Intelligence or Recycled Repression?*, 11.

46. See Ana Glenda Tager Rosado, "Inteligencia y Democracia en las Américas: Guatemala en Perspectiva Comparada," paper presented at the Center for Hemispheric Defense Studies' 4th Annual Conference on Research and Education in Defense and Security Studies, Washington, DC, May 22–25, 2001. Only in October 2005 did the Congress pass a law that created the body provided for in the agreements, under the name General Directorate for Civilian Intelligence (DIGICI). Guatemala Congress, Legislative Decree No. 71, of 2005, Law for the General Directorate for Civilian Intelligence (DIGICI), http://ww2.oj.gob.gt/es/QueEsOJ/EstructuraOJ/UnidadesAd-

ministrativas/CentroAnalisisDocumentacionJudicial/cds/CDs%20leyes/2005/pdfs/decretos/D071-2005.pdf.

47. Created by a law passed in February 1997 that was criticized because it lacked human rights protection standards, the botched PNC implementation process by President Álvaro Arzú's administration (1996–2000) showed many deficiencies. Guatemala Congress, Legislative Decree No. 11, of 1997, Law for the National Civil Police, https://www.acnur.org/fileadmin/Documentos/BDL/2016/10660.pdf. The 1997 law provides among the missions assigned to the PNC, to acquire, receive, and analyze any data of interest to public security. William Stanley, "Building New Police Forces in El Salvador and Guatemala: Learning and Counter-Learning," in *Peacebuilding and Police Reform*, eds. Tor Tanke Holm and Espen Barth Eide (London: Frank Cass, 2000), 125. Also see Marie-Louise Glebbeek, *In the Crossfire of Democracy: Police Reform and Police Practice in Post-Civil War Guatemala* (Amsterdam: Rozenberg, 2003); and Marie-Louise Glebbeek, "Post-War Violence and Police Reform in Guatemala," in *Policing Insecurity: Police Reform, Security, and Human Rights in Latin America*, ed. Niels Uildriks (Lanham: Lexington Books, 2009), 79–94.

48. SIE webpage: https://www.sie.gob.gt/portal/.

49. Presidency of Guatemala, Gubernative Agreement No. 662 of December 2005, Regulation of the National Civil Police, https://pnc.edu.gt/wp-content/uploads/2013/07/Acuerdo-Gubernativo-662-2005.pdf.

50. Presidency of Guatemala, Gubernative Agreement No. 172 of June 2014, Modifying the Regulation of the National Civil Police, https://pnc.edu.gt/wp-content/uploads/2015/11/Acuerdo-Gubernativo-172-2014.pdf.

51. "Nuevos subdirectores y supresión de divisiones anuncia PNC," *Diario 1*, February 10, 2016. Available at http://diario1.com/nacionales/2016/02/nuevos-subdirectores-y-supresion-de-divisiones-anuncia-pnc/. See PCN chart, as of March 2021, at http://www.pnc.gob.sv/portal/page/portal/informativo/institucion/estructura_organizativa/organigrama%20pnc.jpg.

52. Guatemala Congress, Legislative Decree No. 71, of 2005.

53. Guatemala Congress, Legislative Decree No. 18, of 2008, Framework Law for the National System of Security, https://stcns.gob.gt/wp-content/uploads/2018/09/06_Ley_Marco_SNS_.pdf.

54. This council is headed by the president and includes a seat for the SIE, among other top officials.

55. Presidency of Guatemala, Gubernative Agreement No. 166 of May 2011, Regulation of the Framework Law for the National System of Security, https://stcns.gob.gt/wp-content/uploads/2018/09/06_Ley_Marco_SNS_.pdf.

56. Reserved expenses are expenditures that are not included in the annual budget that is unclassified—the equivalent of the secret budget in the United States.

57. Amnesty International, *Guatemala Accountable Intelligence or Recycled Repression?*, 12.

58. Kana Akizuki, "La Direccionalidad Política del Estado Guatemalteco en el Marco de la Inteligencia, Situación y Perspectivas," master's thesis, Guatemala, FLACSO, Sede Guatemala, 2003. Available at http://hdl.handle.net/10469/2053; Stanley, *Enabling Peace in Guatemala*, 4.

59. Jahir Dabroy (coord.), "Desclasifiquemos el Modelo de Inteligencia en Guatemala," *Revista Política y Sociedad*, no. 53 (2016): 43–71.

60. Francisco Jiménez Irungaray, "La Seguridad de la Nación: Un Balance Estratégico-Político en la Guatemala de Hoy," in *La Construcción de la Paz en Guatemala: Reconciliación, Seguridad y Violencia en una Democracia Precaria*, ed. Bernardo Arévalo de León (Guatemala: FLACSO, Sede Guatemala, 2019), 89. Available at https://www.flacso.edu.gt/publicaciones/wp-content/uploads/2019/11/Libro-la-construccion-de-la-paz-1-1.pdf.

61. "La Línea" was a fraud case relating to imports investigated by CICIG. See Charles Call and Jeffrey Hallock, "Too Much Success? The Legacy and Lessons of the International Commission Against Impunity in Guatemala," *The Legacy and Lessons of the International Commission Against Impunity in Guatemala (January 1, 2020)*. *CLALS Working Paper Series* 24 (2020), 25–31.

62. Guatemala, Procurador de los Derechos Humanos, *Informe Anual Circunstanciado de Actividades y Situación de los Derechos Humanos. 2019* (Guatemala: PDH, 2020), 76.

63. Ferdy Montepeque, "Un integrante de 'La Oficinita' será el secretario de Inteligencia de Giammattei," *El Periódico*, January 16, 2020. Available at https://elperiodico.com.gt/nacion/2020/01/16/un-integrante-de-la-oficinita-sera-el-secretario-de-inteligencia-de-giammattei/. The SIE secretary was replaced in January 2021. See https://lahora.gt/van-cuatro-cambios-en-secretarias-del-ejecutivo-hasta-ahora/.

64. Pedro Trujillo Álvarez, "La Falta de Institucionalización de la Inteligencia y su Impacto en la Seguridad: El Caso de Guatemala," *Inteligencia y Seguridad, Revista de Análisis y Prospectiva* 5 (2008–2009): 149.

65. POLSEDE project was implemented by FLACSO—Guatemala, the Guatemalan Institute for Development and Peace (IGEDEP) and War-Torn Societies Project International (WSP). Documents on intelligence produced include *Guidelines for the Study of State Intelligence in Guatemala*; *General Criteria for Intelligence System Reform in Guatemala*; *Guatemala: Fundamentals of the Intelligence System*; *Democratic Intelligence System Controls in Guatemala*; *Organic Structure and the Intelligence System Profession in Guatemala*; and *Conceptual Framework and Areas of Competence, Intelligence Subsystem for Internal Security*. Project GUA/99/022, *WSP in Guatemala. Toward A Security Policy for Democracy*. Consultation Report: Systematization of the development of the project, and lessons learned, (Project: Toward a Security Policy for Democracy, FLACSO–WSP–IGEDEP, Guatemala, 2002), available at https://www.interpeace.org/wp-content/uploads/2002/02/2002_Guat_Interpeace_Toward_A_Greater_Security_Policy_For_Democracy_ENG.pdf. Also see Bernardo Arévalo de León and Ana Glenda Tager, "POLSEDE, Civil Society, and Security Sector Reform in Guatemala," in *Civil Society, Peace, and Power*, eds. David Cortright, Melanie Greenberg, and Laurel Stone (Lanham: Rowman & Littlefield, 2016), 207–30; and DCAF Case Study "Guatemala: Toward a Democratic Security Policy," available at https://issat.dcaf.ch/Learn/Resource-Library2/Case-Studies/Guatemala-Toward-a-Democratic-Security-Policy.

66. See Kirsten Weld, *Paper Cadavers: The Archives of Dictatorship in Guatemala* (Durham, NC: Duke University Press, 2014); and Cremades Guisado, *Inteligencia y Secreto en Guatemala*.

67. Arévalo de León and Glenda Tager, "POLSEDE," 220.

68. Known as Clandestine and Illegal Security apparatuses (CIACS). Edgar Gutiérrez, former head of SAE, explained that these organizations are comprised of elements "which had military discipline and organization, as well as knowledge of local terrain and networks within state security structures [and] took on operations for drug cartels and private security firms." Edgar Gutierrez, "Guatemala Elites and Organized Crime," InsightCrime and IDRC, 2016: 16. Available at https://idl-bnc-idrc .dspacedirect.org/bitstream/handle/10625/55847/IDL-55847.pdf.

69. WOLA, *La Comisión Internacional contra la Impunidad en Guatemala (CICIG): Un instrumento innovador contra redes criminales y para el fortalecimiento del Estado de derecho* (Washington, DC: Oficina en Washington para Asuntos Latinoamericanos, 2015), 27. For a sound analysis of CICIG, see Call and Hallock, "Too Much Success?."

70. Arévalo de León and Tager, "POLSEDE," 225.

71. Since early 1990s, rising crime and violence—homicides, drug trafficking and organized crime, violent gang activity, and so on—became a public security challenge. Stanley, "Building New Police Forces in El Salvador and Guatemala," 129; A. Douglas Kincaid, "Demilitarization and Security in El Salvador and Guatemala: Convergences of Success and Crisis," *Journal of Interamerican Studies and World Affairs* 42, no. 4 (2000): 51–56; Duilia Mora Turner, "Root Causes of Violence in Post-Civil War Guatemala: A Literature Review," *E-International Relations* (E-IR) (2015), available at https://www.e-ir.info/2015/04/08/root-causes-of-violence-in -post-civil-war-guatemala-a-literature-review/.

Chapter Twelve

The Bahamas, Jamaica, and Trinidad and Tobago

Kevin Peters

The Bahamas, Jamaica, and Trinidad and Tobago are some of the longest-established democracies in the Caribbean. Each respective nation has endured difficult threats to internal security as they have transitioned from former colonial-ruled regimes to functional, constitutional democracies. In this connection, each nation has striven to institutionalize intelligence agencies that are capable of effectively addressing threats, while remaining under democratic civilian control and oversight.

This chapter examines the role of intelligence reform in building legal frameworks for intelligence activities, accountability and oversight of federal spending on intelligence programs, and the need for transparency and rules-based parameters in collection of information.

HISTORICAL BACKGROUND—THREAT ENVIRONMENT IN THE COLONIAL ERA

From their discoveries, settlements, and colonization by European powers, the Bahamas, Jamaica, and Trinidad and Tobago have confronted a diverse range of security threats that have evolved to present-day transnational criminal and radicalization challenges. The three former British colonial possessions initially confronted threats ranging from illicit maritime smuggling; piracy and privateering; the slave trade and the long-term implications of post-slavery reform; to an increase in immigration of former slaves and other groups seeking opportunities in the new world. In the centuries that succeeded the so-called golden era of piracy in the Caribbean from 1691 to 1724,[1] new maritime smuggling threats of illicit maritime drug trafficking emerged, and the Caribbean remains today an important crossroads for cocaine and heroin smuggling between South America, Mexico, the United States, Europe, and Asia.[2]

Race relations, the legacy of slavery, and income inequality all led to twentieth-century social unrest and societal challenges that shaped the roles of future security and intelligence services in the three island nations. Trinidad and Tobago, in particular, experienced more immigration than the Bahamas and Jamaica during the Colonial Era. Trinidad and Tobago were separate nations until 1888 and in the years following the end of slavery, more than 150,000 immigrants and indentured laborers from India, China, and Portugal would arrive in the dual island nation, resulting in a diverse mix of cultures and customs.[3] The seeds of today's small Muslim community in Trinidad and Tobago—a societal aspect that differentiates Trinidad and Tobago from present day Bahamas and Jamaica—also were planted during the Colonial Era, and continuous migration from African slaves, free African immigrants, Indian indentured immigrants, and eastern Mediterranean immigrants permanently resettled in the Caribbean nation.[4] In the modern era and in contrast to the Bahamas and Jamaica, Trinidad and Tobago would confront a significant domestic extremist threat from members of the Islamic group Jamaat-al-Muslimeem, who on July 27, 1990, attacked parliament and took the prime minister hostage.[5] Additionally, in recent years Trinidad and Tobago had one of the highest number of citizens in the Western Hemisphere who traveled to fight with the Islamic State.[6]

The intelligence services that existed in the three countries before their independence were influenced by English-provincial control and mostly served as outposts of the United Kingdom's intelligence services and overseas presence.[7] The Bahamian colonial authorities created the principal domestic security agency, the Royal Bahamas Police Force (RBPF), on March 1, 1840, under the command of Inspector General John Pinder.[8] RBPF was comprised of sixteen members, and all, with the exception of Pinder, were likely former slaves.[9] The police force originally only patrolled the largest island of New Providence, and in subsequent years it would grow in force structure and expand its presence to all seven hundred islands. The RBPF, like many British colonial security forces, was primarily a land-based police force until 1958 when it began conducting maritime patrolling of Bahamian territorial waters.[10] It is difficult to ascertain when the Bahamas intelligence services were first created, but it appears that a special branch in the Bahamas was an active intelligence partner, possibly in the decades prior to Bahamian independence. According to a declassified U.S. Federal Bureau of Investigations (FBI) report from 1968, American investigators were collaborating with Britain's MI-5 and the Bahamas Special Branch on anti-Fidel Castro investigations that related to the assassination of President John F. Kennedy.[11]

It is unclear if Jamaica and Trinidad and Tobago possessed formal intelligence services prior to their respective independence and formation of military services of both nations developed in the late eighteenth century. The West India Regiment—a British colonial regiment created in the late eighteenth century (1795)—was the predecessor to the current Jamaican Defense Force (JDF). The West India Regiment was disbanded in 1926 due to economic reasons, and was reconstituted from 1958 to 1962 as part of the West Indies Federation's military force.[12] Likewise, Trinidad and Tobago created the Volunteers in 1879, which was later renamed the Trinidad Regiment until the organization's termination in 1948, when Trinidad and Tobago joined the West Indies Federation.[13] After the Trinidad Regiment was dissolved, Trinidad and Tobago lacked an independent military force until the Defence Act of 1962 established the Trinidad and Tobago Defence Force (TTDF).[14] At the time of independence, all three Caribbean nations had established military organizations by which to develop intelligence capabilities to support national defense and public security missions.

POST-COLONIAL ERA: TRANSITION TO DEMOCRACY / ROLE OF INTELLIGENCE IN DEMOCRATIZATION

The three island nations transitioned peacefully from British colonial rule and began to develop and expand their intelligence services and capabilities with heavy emphasis on supporting domestic security and law enforcement operations. The Bahamas was the last of the three nations to gain its independence and in 1973, under a new constitution, an agreement with London created the new nation of the archipelago of seven hundred islands.[15] Jamaica and Trinidad and Tobago gained their independence over a decade earlier in 1962 with such foreign dignitaries as British Princess Margaret and U.S. Vice President Lyndon Johnson attending the Jamaican Independence ceremonies.[16] Trinidad and Tobago gained independence under the leadership of Oxford University–educated Eric Williams, whose ground breaking book *Capitalism and Slavery* challenged the widely held perception that the English abolitionist movement of the prior century was based on the noble sentiment of the English people.[17] Willams, instead argued that market economics, the Industrial Revolution in Britain, and unprofitability had lead to the slave emancipation as opposed to the previously accepted belief that enlightened humanitarianism had ended slavery in British colonial possessions.[18] Williams represented a foundational figure in Trinidad and Tobago, becoming the first prime minister of the free dual nation and remaining in office until his death in 1981.

Soon after obtaining independence, the three Caribbean countries began to develop military and intelligence services, which all had similar missions aimed at safeguarding domestic security and combating transnational and regional security threats. As such, in 1980, the Bahamas created the Royal Bahamas Defence Force (RBDF), under the Ministry of National Security and assumed RBPF's responsibilities as the primary naval force for the Bahamas.[19] Although the RBDF relied on British military customs and culture, it differed from other former British colonial possessions in not having any land-based units.[20] In contrast to the RBDF, which was established almost two decades after independence, the Jamaica Defence Force (JDF) was constituted a few days prior to Jamaica becoming a soverign state, with veteran elements of the West Indies Federation's military force providing the nucleus.[21] The JDF was established in 1962 and had similar maritime policing and national defense responsibilities to the security forces of the Bahamas and Trinidad and Tobago; however, the JDF also was tasked with aiding civil authorities with civil defense and conducting humanitarian assistance and disaster relief operations.[22] The Jamaica Defence Force Military Intelligence Unit (JDFMIU) was established in 1976 with the initial focus—likely with pressure from the United States—of examining Cold War–related geopolitical threats as they related to Jamaican security, and in the 1980s the agency transitioned to a counterdrug focus.[23]

Likewise, Trinidad and Tobago's formal military organization, the Trinidad and Tobago Defence Force (TTDF) was established in 1962 and, similar to the JDF, was tasked with defending the sovereignty of the nation, supporting civil authorities in maintaining law and order, and in supporting humanitarian and disaster relief operations.[24] Although the TTDF was established following the creation as a sovereign state, the Trinidad and Tobago Police Service (TTPS) had existed for several centuries and possibily had an organic intelligence capacity based off of the British Special Branch that was in existence prior to gaining independence. The TTPS was the oldest public institution in the twin-island republic, founded in 1592,[25] and was heavily influenced by a postcolonial policing strategy derived from the Irish Constabulary, which utilized large police presences within local communities to suppress protests against the government.[26] The Special Branch existed as an arm of the Police Service, and it was criticized following the 1990 failed coup attempt for being overly insular and for not sharing intelligence with the TTDF or other partner agencies.[27]

Since their inception to the present, the intelligence services of each country have developed and undergone several reforms—mostly dictated by the evolution of the security environment in the region. Although the three island nations have made progress since gaining independence in developing intelligence capabilities to support national security priorities, the countries have struggled to establish intelligence services confined within legislative authorities, and mechanisms for ensuring civilian oversight and accountability. The Bahamas intelligence services grew from the colonial British elements and struggled in recent years to create a national intelligence service with legal standing and oversight mechanisms. Jamaica's intelligence elements derived from the British colonial security units to support policing services and law enforcement activities but also lacked transparency into their operations, likely due to high levels of gang-related corruption. Trinidad and Tobago's intelligence capabilities, like the other two nations, matured from British colonial structures and also lacked accountability processes and public visibility into the government's collection activities.

The Bahamas intelligence services have evolved based in large part amid influence from British models for supporting military and security service organizational structures. In the years following independence, the Bahamas established a Financial Intelligence Unit (FIU) to combat financial crimes and money laundering, and the RBDF created military intelligence units to support maritime enforcement missions.[28] In recent years the Bahamas also attempted to create a national-level intelligence organization to support the country's national security decision-making processes. The first iteration of the National Intelligence Agency (NIA) was short lived and highly controversial due to its lack of legislative authorization, failure to gain broad political support, and lack of transparency on its intelligence collection activities that potentially monitored Bahamain citizens. The initial process for the creation of the National Intelligence Agency was suspended, and the Bahamas is presently in the process of reforming this agency, which will, among other functions, provide security assessments to the National Security Council, and assist the Ministry of Foreign Affairs in collecting intelligence related to foreign powers or groups of nation-state actors.[29] The creation of the NIA and the 2019 legislative debate over the establishment of the new NIA highlight the importance of oversight and transparency being inculcated into an intelligence agency's foundational legislation and how public support is critical to the functions of legitimate intelligence services.

Jamaica's intelligence services followed a similar evolutionary trajectory as their Bahamian counterparts, and most Jamaican intelligence units reside within the JDF and the island's police force, the Jamaican Constabulary Force (JCF). The Criminal Investigation Bureau (CIB) is responsible for all major criminal investigations, is organized into several law enforcement sections, and it initially contained an intelligence unit. The CIB's Criminal Intelligence Unit became part of the Consolidated Intelligence Department based on a merger of Criminal Intelligence and the Special Branch.[30] Despite having distinct missions, the JDF has had occasion to reinforce the JCF in internal security operations, perhaps most notably in the 2010 joint operation to arrest "Shower Posse" drug gang leader Christopher "Dudus" Coke.[31] The attempted arrest and subsequent surrender of Coke in 2010 highlighted the power of gangs within the garrison communities, and Jamaican security forces allegedly had to seek permission from gang leaders prior to entering the community where the subsequent battle resulted in seventy-four people being killed.[32] This event drew the world's attention to Jamaican security challenges, and two years later the government published a comprehensive national strategy titled *National Security Policy for Jamaica, Towards a Secure and Prosperous Nation.*[33]

While the JDF and the JCF may have some overlapping responsibilities especially in terms of confronting drug trafficking-related threats to the island, the Jamaican Defence Force Military Intelligence Unit (JDFMIU) is the island's primary organization for producing counterdrug intelligence to support interdiction operations.[34] The JCF has several internal intelligence organizations to include the Special Branch, which conducts intelligence collection and dissemination to support domestic law enforcement operations, the Organized Criminal Investigative Division (OCID), and the National Firearm and Drug Intelligence Centre (NFDIC), along with smaller operational support units.[35] Other elements of the Jamaican government include organizations that conduct some level of tactical and operational intelligence support such as the Jamaica Customs, the Ministry of Finance and Public Service, the Immigration Citizenship and Passport Division, and the Ministry of Foreign Affairs and Foreign Trade.[36] All of Jamaica's various intelligence elements would be administratively aligned under a single national-level agency in the mid-2000s in an effort to increase information sharing and increase the operational effectiveness of Jamaica's intelligence services.[37]

On the same note, the number of intelligence services in Trinidad and Tobago grew in the aftermath of the 1990 failed coup d'état[38] and the public release of Sir David Simmon's Commission of Enquiry into the 1990 Coup created the justification for the creation of the Security Intelligence Agency (SIA) and the Strategic Services Agency (SSA).[39] The years following the attempted coup d'état dramatically changed Trinidad and Tobago's intelligence services as the island nation contended with growing threats of Islamic radicalization, its citizens traveling to fight with the Islamic State in Syria and Iraq, and the continual threat of drug trafficking and transnational organized crime. Trinidad and Tobago's security and intelligence services were criticized for failing to coordinate and share information related to Jamaat-al-Muslimeem's activities and intentions.[40] The failed 1990 coup galvanized significant changes and increased focus, at the national level, on the role of coordinated intelligence operations as a necessity to supporting public security. The Security Intelligence Agency, the Strategic Services Agency, and the Special Anti-Crime Unit of Trinidad and Tobago were all born in the aftermath of the coup.[41] The establishment of these agencies and the efficacy of intelligence-sharing processes became a public debate, highlighting the need for legislative authorities to establish a legal framework for intelligence services to operate effectively.[42]

The Bahamas', Jamaica's, and Trinidad and Tobago's transition to democracy enabled the creation of intelligence services that supported domestic security priorities; however, each nation struggled to establish appropriate mechanisms for accountability, oversight, and transparency necessary within a democratic society. As a result of a lack of legislative authorities, oversight of intelligence collection activities, and accountability of government spending on intelligence programs, each nation would contend with significant public backlash for the activities of their respective intelligence agencies.

DEMOCRATIC INTELLIGENCE GOVERNANCE AND ACCOUNTABILITY

In the past few decades, the Bahamas, Jamaica, and Trinidad and Tobago have labored to establish intelligence capabilities that are transparent and effectively support the security activities of the respective nations. However, these countries have struggled to build legal frameworks for politically neutral, transparent, and accountable intelligence services.[43] This section examines and analyzes the shortcomings of the three island nations, in terms of the legal basis for intelligence activities, the establishment of democratic control and oversight mechanisms, and the fostering of transparency between government institutions and the public with regards to intelligence activities.[44]

Legislation

Bruneau and Boraz note that legislatures in established and newer democracies often ensure that executive control is appropriate in terms of national security and in accordance with the rule of law, although it is common for many newer democracies to lack effective legislative oversight of intelligence activities.[45] The nearly decade-long saga of the Bahamian attempts to establish the National Intelligence Agency (NIA) demonstrates the importance of legislative authority, legal definitions of national security threats, and respect for human rights and civil liberties.[46] In comparison to the Bahamas' failure to explain the purpose for a national-level intelligence service, Jamaica's 2007 national strategy laid out a comprehensive, if not overly broad, rationale for the creation of a national intelligence agency and for an overarching framework for oversight and policy coordination.[47] Trinidad and Tobago, in contrast to the other two nations, has multiple national-level intelligence services, although they lack legislative authority and accountability mechanisms.[48]

Matei and Halladay highlight the importance of democratic institution building in balancing the roles of democracy and intelligence and the need for public education and transparency from intelligence elements of a government.[49] In the Bahamas, the lack of public awareness and transparency of the creation of the NIA ultimately doomed the initial launch of the agency. The Progressive Liberal Party's (PLP) efforts to establish a new national level intelligence service in 2012 set off a series of political and public debates and highlight the need for rigorous discussion on the roles and functions of intelligence within a democracy.[50] The initial efforts by the PLP to create the NIA ultimately failed due to the PLP not seeking congressional approval for the new agency, a lack of approved threat and national security definitions with legal standings, and clear limits on the role of intelligence collection within Bahamian society.[51] The PLP's failure to build public awareness and a political mandate for the NIA ultimately led to the disbandment of the NIA and restructuring of the agency in 2018 through 2020.[52]

An examination of Jamaican intelligence services, their respective governance structure, and accountability processes is complicated by systematic corruption within government institutions and by a lack of public transparency on the part of government officials.[53] Two years after the violent arrest of Jamaican drug trafficker Christopher "Dudus" Coke,[54] the Jamaican government published a comprehensive national strategy titled *National Security Policy for Jamaica, Towards a Secure and Prosperous Nation.*[55] The strategy recommended the creation of a National Intelligence Agency to provide intelligence to inform state decision-making on strategic or policy issues, coordinate intelligence with international partners, and deconflict intelligence operations among domestic intelligence units throughout Jamaica's security services.[56] The strategy also called for the establishment of a National Intelligence Consulting Group (NICG) to develop recognized definitions, functional responsibilities for various agencies, cooperative mechanisms for sharing information, coordinating functions between domestic and overseas units, reporting responsibilities, and oversight processes for Jamaica's intelligence services.[57] Although the strategy lacked specifics on how and when it would be implemented, it provided a macrolevel overview for public awareness of the direction of Jamaica's intelligence services and how they would be aligned within the existing security architecture.

Despite the 2007 national strategy and regular national security policy updates on Jamaican government websites, it is unclear how the strategy was implemented and if it had a role in reforming Jamaica's intelligence services. Furthermore, the national strategy lacked a legislative basis and was not enacted via democratic debate. In 2014, National Security Minister Peter Bunting confirmed that Jamaica was developing a new FBI-style agency to investigate issues that impact national security; however, it was unclear from Bunting's statements under what legal authorities the new agency would operate, if it would contain an intelligence capability, or if any collection activities on Jamaican citizens would be monitored or reviewed by Parliament.[58] In an opinion article following Bunting's announcement, Andrew King argued instead for merging two existing intelligence units within the JCF with the JDFMIU to form a new State Intelligence Agency governed by new intelligence legislation.[59] King's article, at a minimum, highlights a lack of public awareness of any improvements that may have developed after the 2007 national strategy, and it also demonstrates that Jamaica was bolstered by its security services to address endemic problems discussed in their national strategy seven years prior.

In comparison to the Bahamas and Jamaica, Trinidad and Tobago, especially in recent years, has become a hot spot for Islamic State radicalization; some have advocated that combatting violent extremism needs to be a higher national priority for the dual-island nation.[60] Others have argued that Trinidad and Tobago must focus on reforming its security agencies to combat terrorism and organized crime and that security issues have taken a lower priority due to the government's focus on improving health care, education, and the economy.[61] Multiple agencies were established, or at a minimum publicly acknowledged, by executive mandate in Sir David Simmon's Commission of Enquiry into the 1990 Coup. The government acknowledged that the Security Intelligence Agency, the Strategic Services Agency, and the Special Anti-Crime Unit of Trinidad and Tobago were established, although there was no mention of the missions or functions of the Security Intelligence Agency or the Special Anti-Crime Unit of Trinidad and Tobago.[62] Despite having multiple national level intelligence services, it is unclear if they have legislative mandates or if there are oversight hierarchies to review potential intelligence collection activities on Trinidadian citizens. The initial creation of a national intelligence agency without a legal framework is consistent with emerging democracies in Latin America and the Caribbean region, where policy makers have left strategic and operational planning of intelligence institutions to military and civilian intelligence leaders.[63]

Of the three island nations, the Bahamas appears to be making the most progress toward establishing a legislative framework for national-level intelligence activities. By May 2017, the original NIA was disbanded when the Freedom National Movement (FNM) took office and the legislative process began for what would become the National Crime Intelligence Agency Bill, which would eventually be passed in 2019.[64] The new NIA would be authorized in 2019 with legislative standing, oversight and budgetary transparency processes, and with a clearly defined civilian command structure.[65]

Oversight of Financial Resources

Caparini describes an aspect of intelligence oversight as seeking to determine the efficacy of an intelligence service and whether a service is making efficient use of public funds.[66] It is unclear how the Bahamas, Jamaica, and Trinidad and Tobago allocate resources to intelligence activities, and only sporadic information is publicly disclosed on how the three nations fund their intelligence programs. The lack of transparency in how public funds are used for intelligence operations may highlight the challenge of managing security services in an environment with significant and enduring drug trafficking and transnational criminal activity. The lack of fiscal awareness of intelligence activities undermines public trust, and critics of the three nations' respective intelligence services regularly highlight the need for more oversight of federal funding dedicated to intelligence activities.

In 2012, Bahamian critics of the National Intelligence Agency noted the lack of oversight on numerous fronts; they were quick to point out the need for fiscal transparency.[67] In August 2012, Minister of National Security Dr. Bernard Nottage acknowledged that the government had been working internally for months to build the NIA in order to protect Bahamas's borders, maintain public safety, and reduce crime.[68] Opposition political parties and privacy advocate groups soon questioned the legal authority of the NIA, and in 2014 FNM leaders declared the NIA and Prime Minister Christie's administration a threat to democracy and civil liberties.[69] A year later, Democratic National Alliance (DNA) leader Branville McCartney highlighted the ongoing lack of transparency in the NIA's operations, and in an opinion article, McCartney claimed that Bahamian citizens lacked a full understanding of the types of personal information that was being collected by the NIA, what operational actions were being taken, and how public funds were being allocated for intelligence purposes.[70]

In regard to Jamaica's intelligence services, it is difficult to examine the role of oversight given a lack of information on the structure and relationship of the various agencies. Issues of corruption and the need to protect sources and methods likely contribute to the lack of publicly available information, but it is unclear how civil society is able to participate in discussions of the role of their intelligence services.[71] In a 2011 article on policing and security in Jamaica, McDavid, Clayton, and Cowell argue that the level of corruption and criminal activity in Jamaica undermines the state's ability to provide security, education, and public health to its citizens.[72] In an environment where criminal gangs have demonstrated the ability to prevent law enforcement officials access to high crime areas, as previously highlighted during the operation to arrest Christopher "Dudus" Coke, it is unlikely that transparency on security spending, especially intelligence activities, can be made available for public review.

Trinidad and Tobago continues to confront high levels of crime and homicides[73] and the Minister of Finance's 2021 budget statement to congress highlights the challenges in understanding how federal funds are allocated toward intelligence activities.[74] Although Trinidad and Tobago provides annual state priorities updates to congress, limited information on the National Security infrastructure is disclosed. In the 2020 Budget Statement, the Minister of Finance laments that $5 billion (Trinidad/Tobago dollars) have been spent on national security over the last five years and that this amount could have been spent on other domestic priorities such as health care, education, road infrastructure, housing, rural development, and public utilities.[75] While this statement is insightful on the government's view of the security sector, it also shows the lack of transparency on how Trinidad and Tobago allocates federal funds to intelligence activities. In the same report, intelligence is only given a passing reference with a preponderance of national security focus allocated toward improvements to intelligence-led policing strategies and programs.[76] In the 2021 budget report, there is a reference to the creation of a National Intelligence Fusion Center, with the mission of sharing intelligence and resources to support operations; however, no further information on how much funds are being allocated for this new initiative is provided.[77]

Information Collection

Gill argues that oversight of intelligence activities exists in almost all forms of authoritarian intelligence systems; however, in democracies, control of collection activities is performed by agency leaders, legislative oversight committees, legal review experts, and governed by rules for intelligence sharing.[78] Of the three Caribbean nations, the Bahamas has made the most progress toward developing oversight of collection activities. In contrast, Jamaica and Trinidad and Tobago require more emphasis on oversight and transparency in their respective intelligence collection operations to advance the democratic governance of their institutions.

The debate over the role of the NIA in Bahamian society highlights the importance in a democracy of legislation authorizing intelligence activities and for clear definitions on what intelligence collection can be accomplished in the domestic and foreign arenas. The PLP's failure to work through the legislative process with the original creation of the NIA was inconsistent with established democratic practices of ensuring legislative branches create the key intelligence organizations, align personnel, develop legal oversight mechanisms, and provide balance to executive branch policies.[79] The lack of authorized legislation also resulted in public distrust in the NIA's intelligence activities, and the lack of a legal mandate raised questions as to how the government defined threats and what activities were authorized for domestic intelligence collection. Multiple definitions or ambiguity as to how intelligence activities are defined can lead to a diversity of interpretations and regulatory actions by those engaged in policy.[80] Although these shortcomings initially derailed the NIA, in the agency's second iteration, rigorous legislative debate resulted in legal definitions for approved intelligence activities and articulated how the NIA would operate within the broader government apparatus.[81]

Although it is very difficult to determine what oversight mechanisms exist in Jamaica that pertain to intelligence collection and retention of personal information, recent legislation in Trinidad and Tobago has expanded intelligence collection authorities without adding apparent, commensurate oversight protocols or processes. In recent years, the Strategic Services Agency was given expanded authorities and missions beyond drug interdiction and now include broader law enforcement coordination responsibilities and intelligence functions.[82] In 2020, Strategic Services Agency Regulations gave the agency sweeping authorities to collect and retain information without including requirements for public oversight or accountability.[83] Unfortunately, as the security and intelligences services have expanded their authorities and the scope of their operations, intelligence reform processes have not been addressed. Some have called for wide-scale reform of Trinidad and Tobago's intelligence services, and it is unclear if political will exists to match expanded intelligence authorities with protections necessary for democratic oversight of intelligence operations.[84]

CONCLUSION

An examination of the respective intelligence culture within the island nations of the Bahamas, Jamaica, and Trinidad and Tobago highlights the need for transparency, respect for the rule of law, and robust debate on the role of intelligence services within a society. The attempt to create a national intelligence agency, especially in the Bahamas and Trinidad and Tobago, demonstrates the importance of a legislative mandate and inclusion of all branches of government in the role of intelligence operations. Rule of law with intelligence services and building accountability into the legal framework is critical to transparency and a functional democracy. Public debate on the role of intelligence in domestic security operations is also a critical factor in determining what information of a nation's citizens can be collected and retained and under what circumstances. In a final analysis of the intelligence services of the Bahamas, Jamaica, and Trinidad and Tobago, we may be reminded that relatively new democracies need support from elder democratic nations on the methods for building accountability, governance, and intelligence operations oversight.

NOTES

1. Nigel Cawthorne, *A History of Pirates: Blood and Thunder on the High Seas* (Edison, NJ: Chartwell Books, Inc., 2006), 11.

2. Mark P. Sullivan et al., "Latin America and the Caribbean: U.S. Policy and Issues in the 116th Congress," CRS Report No. R46258 (Washington, DC: Congressional Research Service, 2021).

3. Carrie Gibson, *Empire's Crossroads: The Caribbean from Columbus to the Present Day*, (London: Atlantic Montly Press, 2001), 214–16.

4. Daniel P. Aldrich and Raghunath Mahabir, "Countering Violent Extremism in Trinidad and Tobago: An Evaluation," *SSRN Electronic Journal* (October 3, 2019), 2–7, https://doi.org/10.2139/ssrn.3450026.

5. Kathleen M. Collihan and Constantine P. Danopoulos, "Coup d'etat Attempt in Trinidad: Its Causes and Failure," *Armed Forces and Society*; Chicago 19, no. 3 (Spring 1993): 435.

6. Rhonda Krystal Rambally, "T&T Leading in Foreign Fighters per Capita" *Trinidad* Guardian, August 6, 2016, https://www.guardian.co.tt/article-6.2.356744. cb62081cbf.

7. Gregor William Davey, "Intelligence and British Decolonisation: The Development of an Imperial Intelligence System in the Late Colonial Period 1944–1966." (PhD diss., Kings College of London, 2014), 60.

8. "About the Royal Bahamas Police Force," Royal Bahamas Police Force, Accessed July 7, 2020, http://www.royalbahamaspolice.org/aboutus/?aboutus_id=1.

9. "About the Royal Bahamas Police Force."

10. "History of the RBDF," Royal Bahamian Defence Force, Accessed July 7, 2020, http://rbdf.gov.bs/history/.

11. Federal Bureau of Investigations, "Report on Bahamas Special Branch Collaboration with UK MI-5 Related to JKF Assassination Investigation," October 7, 1968, https://www.archives.gov/files/research/jfk/releases/docid-32329043.pdf.

12. Sanjay Badri-Maharaj, "Jamaica Defence Force: Balancing Priorities with Resources—Analysis," *Eurasia Review News and Analysis*, December 11, 2016, http://eurasiareview.com/11122016-jamaica-defence-force-balancing-priorities -with-resources-analysis/.

13. Elisabeth Wallace, "The West Indies Federation: Decline and Fall," *International Journal*; Toronto 17, no. 3 (Summer 1962): 269–88.

14. Dion Phillips, "The Trinidad and Tobago Defence Force: Origin, Structure, Training, Security and Other Roles," *Caribbean Quarterly*, February 3, 2016, 14–15, https://www.tandfonline.com/doi/pdf/10.1080/00086495.1997.11672099?needAcce ss=true.

15. Gibson, *Empire's Crossroads*, 270.

16. Gibson, *Empire's Crossroads*, 268.

17. Gibson, *Empire's Crossroads*, 266.

18. Gibson, *Empire's Crossroads*, 270.

19. Ivelaw L. Griffith, *The Quest for Security in the Caribbean: Problems and Promises in Subordinate States* (M.E. Sharpe, 1993), 86.

20. Griffith, *The Quest for Security in the Caribbean*, 88.

21. Jamaican Defence Force, "JDF History Jamaica Defence Force—Recruiting Website | Fit to Fight," History of the Jamaican Defence Force, accessed September 26, 2020, https://www.jdfweb.com/join/wp/jdf-history/.

22. Dameon Creary, "Jamaican Maritime Security: What Are the Capability Gaps That Limit the Jamaican Defence Force in the Execution of Its Roles in Maritime Security?" (master's thesis, US Army Command and General Staff College, 2014), 4–5, https://apps.dtic.mil/dtic/tr/fulltext/u2/1038597.pdf.

23. Trevor Leckie, "Enhancing the Jamaica Defence Force Military Intelligence Unit's Effectiveness to Conduct Counterdrug Missions" (master's thesis, US Army Command and General Staff College, 2006), 2–4, https://apps.dtic.mil/dtic/tr/fulltext/ u2/a452032.pdf.

24. Phillips, "The Trinidad and Tobago Defence Force," 15.

25. Gerard Besson, "The Caribbean History Archives: The Trinidad and Tobago Police Service," *The Caribbean History Archives* (blog), December 3, 2017, http:// caribbeanhistoryarchives.blogspot.com/2017/12/the-trinidad-and-tobago-police-ser vice.html.

26. David B. Wilson, Roger B. Parks, and Stephen D. Mastrofski, "The Impact of Police Reform on Communities of Trinidad and Tobago," *Journal of Experimental Criminology*; Dordrecht 7, no. 4 (December 2011): 375–405, http://dx.doi .org/10.1007/s11292-011-9131-y.

27. "Police Unable to Cope," *Trinidad and Tobago Newsday Archives*, March 25, 2014, https://archives.newsday.co.tt/2014/03/25/police-unable-to-cope-3/.

28. Khrisna Russell, "PLP's NIA Operated for 'Personal Gain,'" *The Tribune*, May 23, 2019, http://www.tribune242.com/news/2019/may/23/plps-nia-operated -personal-gain/.

29. "National Crime Intelligence Agency Bill Passed in HOA," *EyeWitness News*, May 23, 2019, https://ewnews.com/national-crime-intelligence-agency-bill-passed -in-hoa.

30. Anthony Harriot, *Police and Crime Control in Jamaica: Problems of Reforming Ex-colonial Constabularies* (Barbados: University of the West Indies, 2000), 430.

31. Badri-Maharaj, "Jamaica Defence Force."

32. Mattathias Schwartz, "A Massacre in Jamaica," *The New Yorker,* December 5, 2011, https://www.newyorker.com/magazine/2011/12/12/a-massacre-in-jamaica.

33. International Security Sector Advisory Team (ISSAT), *Jamaica Country Profile*, International Security Sector Advisory Team (ISSAT), February 2, 2015, http://issat.dcaf.ch/Learn/Resource-Library/Country-Profiles/Jamaica-Country-Profile.

34. Leckie, "Enhancing the Jamaica Defence," 2–4.

35. Jaimie S. A. Ogilvie, "Enhancing National Security in Jamaica through the Development and Employment of Special Operations Forces" (master's thesis, Naval Postgraduate School, 2005), 25–27, http://hdl.handle.net/10945/1889.

36. National Security Strategy Development Working Group for the Ministry and of National Security, *Jamaica: National Security Strategy* (Government of Jamaica, May 2006), https://www.files.ethz.ch/isn/156818/JamaicaSecurityStrategy.pdf.

37. Jamaica Information Service, "Govt. Seeks to Set Up Civilian Intelligence Agency," Jamaica Information Service, January 25, 2006, https://jis.gov.jm/govt-seeks-to-set-up-civilian-intelligence-agency/.

38. On July 27, 1990, members of the Jamaat-al-Muslimeen, under the command of Imam Yasin Bakr, attacked the Trinidad and Tobago Parliament building and took members of Parliament and the prime minister hostage. Muslimeem also took control of the state television station, demanded the prime minister's resignation and called for new elections. On August 1, 1990, the rebels surrendered following their release of Prime Minister Robinson, who had suffered a gunshot wound. Prime Minister Robinson agreed to resign and to give amnesty to the rebels. Despite the amnesty agreement, the government arrested Bakr and his followers and ended the attempted coup.Collihan and Danopoulos, "Coup d'etat Attempt in Trinidad"; John S. Jeremie, "Caribbean Terror," *Journal of Financial Crime*; London 18, no. 4 (2011): 296–318, http://dx.doi.org/10.1108/13590791111173669.

39. Derron Mc Clean, "Intelligence Reform—Considerations for Trinidad and Tobago" (master's thesis, Naval Postgraduate School, 2018), 2–3, https://calhoun.nps.edu/handle/10945/61223.

40. Aaron Barcant, "The Republic of Trinidad and Tobago: From Crown Colony to National Security State" (master's thesis, Concordia University, 2018), 12–14, https://spectrum.library.concordia.ca/984158/.

41. "Police Unable to Cope," *Trinidad and Tobago NewsDay*, March 25, 2014, https://archives.newsday.co.tt/2014/03/25/police-unable-to-cope-3/.

42. "Politicians Court Confusion over SSA, SIA," *Trinidad and Tobago NewsDay*, December 12, 2010, https://archives.newsday.co.tt/2010/12/12/politicians-court-confusion-over-ssa-sia/.

43. Florina Cristiana Matei and Carolyn Halladay, "The Role and Purpose of Intelligence in a Democracy," in *The Conduct of Intelligence in Democracies: Processes, Practices, Cultures*, eds. Florina Cristiana Matei, and Carolyn Halladay (Boulder: Lynne Rienner Publishers, 2019), 1–23.

Kevin Peters

44. Marina Caparini, "Controlling and Overseeing Intelligence Services in Democratic States," in *Democratic Control of Intelligence Services: Containing Rogue Elephants*, eds. Hans Born, and Marina Caparini (New York: Routledge, 2016).

45. Thomas C. Bruneau and Steven C. Boraz, *Reforming Intelligence: Obstacles to Democratic Control and Effectiveness* (Austin: University of Texas Press, 2009), 15.

46. Peter Gill, *Intelligence Governance and Democratisation: A Comparative Analysis of the Limits of Reform* (London: Routledge, 2016); also based on Hans Born and Fairlie Jensen, "Intelligence Services: Strengthening Democratic Accountability," in *Democratic Control of Intelligence Services: Containing Rogue Elephants*, eds. Hans Born and Marina Caparini (Aldershot: Ashgate, 2007), 257–69; Marina Caparini, "Controlling and Overseeing Intelligence Services in Democratic States," in Democratic Control of Intelligence Services: Containing Rogue Elephants, eds. Hans Born, and Marina Caparini (Aldershot: Ashgate, 2007), 3–24; Andrés Gómez de la Torre, *Política y Legislación de Inteligencia en el Perú e Iberoamérica: Tendencias y Perspectivas*, Documento 1, (Lima: Instituto de Estudios Internacionales, 2013); Juan Carlos Morales Peña, "Hacia una Revisión Estratégica del Sector de Inteligencia en El Salvador," *Revista Policía y Seguridad Pública* 5, No. 2, (2016): 209–84; Fred Schreier, "The Need for Efficient and Legitimate Intelligence," in *Democratic Control of Intelligence Services: Containing Rogue Elephants*, eds. Hans Born, and Marina Caparini (Aldershot: Ashgate, 2007), 25–44, among others.

47. Jamaica Information Service, "Govt. Seeks to Set Up Civilian Intelligence Agency."

48. Derron Mc Clean, "Intelligence Reform—Considerations for Trinidad and Tobago," 2–4.

49. Florina Cristiana Matei and Carolyn Halladay, eds., *The Conduct of Intelligence in Democracies. Processes, Practices, Cultures*, vol. 21, 2019, https://www.tandfonline.com/doi/full/10.1080/23800992.2019.1695719, 17.

50. Celeste Nixon, "Government Presses Ahead with Creation of National Intelligence Agency," *The Tribune*, August 10, 2012, http://www.tribune242.com/news/2012/aug/10/government-presses-ahead-with-creation-of/; Sharon Turner, "National Intelligence Agency to Be Progressed This Year," *The Nassau Guardian*, February 17, 2020, https://thenassauguardian.com/2020/02/17/national-intelligence-agency-to-be-progressed-this-year/.

51. Branville McCartney, "NIA = No Information Available," *The Bahamas Weekly*, February 21, 2015, http://www.thebahamasweekly.com/publish/bahamian-politics/McCartney_NIA_No_Information_Available40170.shtml.

52. Turner, "National Intelligence Agency to Be Progressed This Year."

53. International Security Sector Advisory Team (ISSAT), "Jamaica Country Profile."

54. Jamaica's garrison communities and the criminal gangs have their roots in the violent political conflict of the 1960s and 1970s between the Jamaica Labour Party (JLP) and the People's National Party (PNP). The poor neighborhoods endured terrible gun violence throughout this era, and Jamaican criminal groups developed deep ties with transnational criminal syndicates and international drug trafficking organizations. The attempted arrest of and subsequent surrender of Christopher (Dudus)

Coke in 2010 highlighted the power of gangs within the garrison communities, and Jamaican security forces allegedly had to ask permission of the gangs before entering the community and prior to the battle that resulted in seventy-four people being killed.

55. International Security Sector Advisory Team (ISSAT), "Jamaica Country Profile."

56. Government of Jamaica, "National Security Policy for Jamaica: Towards a Secure and Prosperous Nation," 2007, http://www.oas.org/csh/spanish/documentos/National%20Security%20Policy%20-%20Jamaica%20-%202007.pdf.

57. Government of Jamaica, "National Security Policy for Jamaica."

58. Andrew King, "Jamaica's FBI," *The Gleaner*, October 7, 2014, http://jamaica-gleaner.com/article/commentary/20141009/jamaicas-fbi.

59. Andrew King, "Jamaica's FBI."

60. Aldrich and Mahabir, "Countering Violent Extremism in Trinidad and To-bago," 2–7.

61. Ronald N Jeffrey, "A National Security Strategy Framework for the Republic of Trinidad and Tobago" (master's thesis, U.S. Army Command and General Staff College, 2012), 79–86.

62. Derron Mc Clean, "Intelligence Reform—Considerations for Trinidad and Tobago," 23.

63. Florina Cristiana Matei, Andres de Castro Garcia, and Darren Henfield, "Balancing Civilian Control with Intelligence Effectiveness in Latin America and the Caribbean: Current Trends and Lessons Learned," *Journal of Mediterranean and Balkan Intelligence,* 7 (2016): 15.

64. Khrisna Russell, "PLP's NIA Operated for 'Personal Gain.'"

65. "National Crime Intelligence Agency Bill Passed in HOA."

66. Caparini, *Democratic Control of Intelligence Services*, 9.

67. McCartney, "NIA = No Information Available."

68. Celeste Nixon, "Government Presses Ahead with Creation of National Intelligence Agency."

69. "FNM Deputy Says Govt May Be Spying," *The Nassau Guardian*, May 7, 2014, https://thenassauguardian.com/2014/05/07/fnm-deputy-says-govt-may-be-spying/.

70. McCartney, "NIA = No Information Available."

71. Gill, *Intelligence Governance and Democratisation*, 6–8.

72. Hilton McDavid, Anthony Clayton, and Noel Cowell, "The Difference between the Constabulary Force and the Military: An Analysis of the Differing Roles and Functions in the Context of the Current Security Environment in the Caribbean (The Case of Jamaica)," *Journal of Eastern Caribbean Studies*; Cave Hill 36, no. 3 (September 2011): 40–71, 78.

73. United Nations Office on Drugs and Crime, *Global Study on Homicide; Homicide Trends, Patterns, and Criminal Justice Responses 2019* (Vienna: 2019), 44, http://www.unodc.org/documents/data-and-analysis/gsh/Booklet2.pdf.

74. Government of Trinidad and Tobago, "National Budget 2021—Ministry of Finance," October 5, 2020, https://www.finance.gov.tt/2020/10/05/national-budget-2021/.

75. Government of Trinidad and Tobago, "The Government of the Republic of Trinidad and Tobago Budget Statement 2020," October 7, 2019, https://www.finance .gov.tt/wp-content/uploads/2019/10/BUDGET-STATEMENT-2020.pdf, 113.

76. Government of Trinidad and Tobago, "The Government of the Republic of Trinidad and Tobago Budget Statement 2020."

77. Government of Trinidad and Tobago, "National Budget 2021—Ministry of Finance."

78. Peter Gill, "Of Intelligence Oversight and the Challenge of Surveillance Corporatism," *Intelligence and National Security*, June 26, 2020, 1–20, https://doi.org/10 .1080/02684527.2020.1783875, 1–3.

79. Bruneau and Boraz, *Reforming Intelligence: Obstacles to Democratic Control and Effectiveness*, 15–16.

80. Jan Goldman and Susan Maret, *Intelligence and Information Policy for National Security: Key Terms and Concepts* (Lanham: Rowman & Littlefield, 2016), 9–11.

81. "National Crime Intelligence Agency Bill Passed in HOA."

82. Trinidad and Tobago Parliament, "Bill Essentials—The Strategic Services Agency (Amendment) Bill, 2016" (2016), http://www .ttparliament.org/documents/2338.pdf.

83. Trinidad and Tobago Parliament, "The Strategic Services Agency Regulations, 2020" (n.d.).

84. Derron Mc Clean, "Intelligence Reform—Considerations for Trinidad and Tobago," 110–23.

Chapter Thirteen

Paraguay

Eduardo E. Estévez and Florina Cristiana Matei

Paraguay's democratic transformation began in 1989, and has been rather slow, due to strong legacies of past military rule.[1] Continued military influence in politics, coupled with limited civilian expertise in intelligence and security, as well as endemic corruption have hindered the development of accountable and transparent intelligence agencies since the democratic transition. On the other hand, despite a challenging security environment involving a panoply of threats stemming from migration, corruption, and (transnational) organized crime, enabled by such ungoverned spaces as the Tri-Border Area (TBA) with Argentina and Brazil,[2] Paraguay has not invested in modernizing and creating effective intelligence agencies.[3] This chapter provides an overview of the attempts to develop democratic intelligence reform since Paraguay's democratic transition.[4]

BACKGROUND ON THE NON-DEMOCRATIC REGIME

Paraguayan independence dates to 1811. During the twentieth century, the country experienced an authoritarian period, 1940–1989, which began with a number of civilian provisional governments followed by military coups, and culminating in the military regime led by General Alfredo Stroessner, which lasted thirty-five years.[5]

Stroessner governed the country from 1954 to 1989. Unlike such dictatorships as those of Argentina or Chile, characterized as bureaucratic authoritarian regimes, Stroessner's rule—known in the literature as stronism[6]—had distinctive features.[7] Stronism relied on a hierarchical triangle of the Colorado Party, the state, and the armed forces—a phenomenon described by López as the "partidization" of the armed forces-military partisanship,[8] and the "militarization of the party."[9] Corruption was the means by which the regime exerted control over the military, with generals becoming landowners or entrepreneurs.[10] With the help of the United States, stronism successfully implemented a coercion machine aimed at repressing any political opposition[11] and influencing the subjugation of the population.[12] The repressive apparatus of stronism included the "*pyrahué*," civilians organized to control and inform on others—a central mechanism for the operation of controlling the movements of persons considered suspicious and affiliated with subversive social or political organizations—and exercised violence against urban and rural inhabitants as one of the ways to apply social control.[13]

Although there is scant information on the Paraguayan intelligence structure during this period, the existing literature notes that it was a mix of military and civilian institutions, which acted as the political police of the regime.[14] The intelligence apparatus comprised a domestic civilian intelligence agency known as the National Intelligence Secretariat charged with foreign intelligence, counter espionage, counter subversion, terrorism, and tri-border surveillance. Defense and military intelligence services performed basic collection capabilities, while the national police conducted domestic intelligence.[15] Paraguay was a leading participant in Operation Condor,[16] which in 1975 targeted government opponents under the veneer of fighting communism.[17] In this context, Paraguay's intelligence agencies carried out egregious human rights abuses, including kidnappings, brutal interrogation and torture, forced disappearances, and extrajudicial killings.[18] Ultimately, no oversight of intelligence existed other than Stroessner's personal control of the agencies.[19]

TRANSITION TO DEMOCRACY AND INTELLIGENCE DEMOCRATIC REFORM ATTEMPTS

A legitimacy crisis of the Stroessner regime, in parallel with the 1989 economic calamity, resulted in a military coup led by General Andrés Rodríguez in February 1989, marking the beginning of a democratic transition.[20] After the tenure of President Rodríguez (1989–1993), the next four presidents belonged to the Colorado Party, marked by its history as a main partner of stronism—which reveals that Paraguay's commitment to democracy was superficial. Transition to democracy was plagued by the preeminence of the Colorado Party, the absence of differing polity in power, and the remnants of an authoritarian political culture, to name a few impediments.[21]

The election of Fernando Lugo (2008–2012), who was not a member of the Colorado party, finally pronounced change for Paraguay. This seminal event was viewed as a historical triumph of democracy and signified an actual transformation.[22]

Reform of intelligence agencies has been rather slow, mimicking the transitional arc of democracy in Paraguay. Nevertheless, it is worth mentioning Paraguay's early success in transitional justice.[23] For example, in December 1992 secret archives were found in several stations and elements of the national police and in the National Directorate of Technical Affairs.[24] Known as *Archivos del Terror*, such files were relocated to the Asunción Supreme Court, at the Center of Documentation and Archives for the Defense of Human Rights. This centralized repository contains three hundred thousand documents, listing fifty thousand murdered; thirty thousand disappeared; and four hundred thousand imprisoned. The archives include interrogation transcripts and recordings, photos, and records of regional extrajudicial transfers (Operation Condor).[25] This material was analyzed by the Truth and Justice Commission (CVJ) created in 2003, which covered not only the years of the Stroessner regime but also the subsequent period until 2003, because of the incumbents' closeness to Stroessner.[26] The commission report, issued in 2008, noted that most repressive actions were precoordinated by a united intelligence and counterintelligence system, and an extensive network of special agents or undercover informants.[27] The report recommended the sanction of a law regulating the intelligence services, ensuring the unrestricted respect for human rights, the defense of national sovereignty, and establishing sanctions on officials who transgress them.[28]

An outcome of the discovery of the police archives was the criminal prosecution and conviction on human rights violations charges of a few repressors of the Stroessner regime, such as Pastor Milciades Coronel, among others.[29] The path opened by the CVJ on the construction of citizenship and collective memory was followed by the Directorate-General for Truth, Justice and Reparation established in 2009 in the Ombudsman's Office, charged with the implementation of symbolic and material reparation measures to the victims of the dictatorship, including Paraguayan exiles residing abroad.[30]

In the first year of his tenure, President Horacio Cartés (2013–2018), member of the Colorado Party, sent the legislative body a bill to amend Law 1337 of 1999 in regard to national defense and domestic security, which was passed in August 2013. The new Law 5036 widened the concept of national defense in order to confront both external and internal aggressions and authorized that during a state of exception, and other grave situations, the armed forces were to be active in performing public order and internal security tasks.[31] This amendment and the new roles of the armed forces, which have been considered unconstitutional, entailed the militarization of public security and in fact the empowerment of military intelligence to gather domestic intelligence, posing risks to society and democracy.[32]

In 2013, a Paraguayan defense white paper was published—the first of its kind.[33] Among the defense strategic pillars outlined in the paper, one referred to intelligence, listing the national imperative of forming an intelligence system directed toward economic, political, social, and military sectors.[34] Furthermore, the paper outlined national security threats such as the Paraguayan People's Army (EPP), a small insurgent group operating in the country's northern region since 2008;[35] and the Triple Border Area (TBA—Ciudad del Este, Paraguay; Foz do Iguazu, Brazil; and Iguazu, Argentina), notorious for organized crime, terrorist groups, and drug trafficking activities.[36]

DEMOCRATIC GOVERNANCE AND ACCOUNTABILITY IN PRACTICE

In 2014, Law 5241 was passed,[37] establishing the following institutions: the National Intelligence System (SINAI), comprised of the National Intelligence Council (CNI), the Ministry of Interior, the Ministry of Defense and the Armed Forces, the Permanent Secretary of the National Defense Council, and the National Antidrug Secretariat. SINAI's main focus is "detecting, neutralizing and counterbalancing the actions of domestic and international terrorist groups, and of transnational criminal organizations."[38] The CNI executes two strategic functions—coordination of SINAI agencies' intelligence activities and reviewing the annual intelligence plan. The National Intelligence Secretariat (SNI), a new intelligence agency, is tasked with the collection and processing of national and international intelligence information to provide global and sectoral assessments upon presidential and the Criminal Intelligence Directorate request.[39] Generally, these intelligence summonses encompass illegal activities affecting the constitution and legal norms.[40]

The president oversees the activities of SINAI, the SNI, the Secretariate for Money and Goods Laundering (SEPRELAD), and the National Antidrug Secretariat (SENAD). The president also oversees the Ministries of Interior and Defense and the Military Forces Command (CCFFAA), while the CCFFAA is in charge of the intelligence agencies that operate within the military services.[41] The SNI oversees the Criminal Intelligence Directorate created by the law.[42] In addition, the Ministry of Interior oversees the intelligence agencies operating under the Police Directorate.[43]

Currently, according to Law 5241 and its regulatory decree,[44] in addition to the SNI, the SINAI is composed of the following intelligence bodies:

- Strategic Intelligence Directorate of the Ministry of Defense
- Intelligence Directorate of the Ministry of Interior[45]
- Intelligence Directorate of the National Police
- Intelligence Directorate of the SENAD
- General Directorate for Financial Analysis of the SEPRELAD
- such other bodies as authorized by de CNI

Also, regarding intelligence activities and *collection of information*, Law 5241 provides for the protection of human rights and constitutional freedoms by stipulating that the intelligence agencies of SINAI must not perform repressive activities, have compulsive or detention powers, fulfill police functions or conduct criminal investigations; nor are they to obtain information, or keep data on individuals based on their race, religion, nationality, or due to their membership of any social group, private actions, political opinion, adherence or membership in party, social, trade union, community, cooperative, assistance, cultural or labor organizations, or because of legal activities performed within any field.

ANALYSIS

Paraguay has not made significant progress in democratizing its intelligence agencies. The legal framework is limited and deficient; political control and oversight is weak, while professional norms are precarious. These lacunae provide fertile ground for intelligence politicization, which in turn impedes intelligence effectiveness. The next sections analyze Paraguay's progress vis-à-vis political control and oversight and its professionalism and effectiveness.

Political Control and Oversight

Political control of intelligence is very low. Although the new intelligence agency, SNI,[46] was formally created in 2014, it was not until February 2018 that its first director was designated by President Mario Abdo Benítez (2018–present).[47] Further, only in 2019 was progress made in its official formation to execute state responsibilities through international training assistance.[48] Moreover, the first CNI meeting was held in November 2019, chaired by President Benítez, who proposed a national intelligence plan. An important contribution to transparency and *public oversight* was the publication on the SNI website of the CNI's 2019 National Intelligence Plan.[49] Following a situation analysis, this unclassified document explains the main threats—actions against sovereignty; foreign interference; cyberattacks; organized crime; terrorism; illegal armed groups; sabotage; espionage; corruption; weapons of mass destruction; and actions contrary to the democratic rule of law. The *collection of information* priorities that result from each of these threats are to be addressed by the agencies comprising the intelligence system in accordance with their legal authorities.

Congressional oversight, too, is virtually nonexistent. The law does not specifically mention any kind of congressional oversight nor explicitly provides for civilian external control of military intelligence, seriously constraining the powers of elected civilian officials and delaying democratic consolidation. Nevertheless, members of the Paraguayan Congress have occasionally conducted de facto oversight. As Wishart notes, "Legislators are not afraid to raise the debate in congress, and most importantly, . . . scandals have made intelligence oversight a policy issue of importance among lawmakers."[50] Despite these occasional fire-alarm-driven congressional actions, Paraguay's legislative oversight remains essentially absent.

Informal oversight by civil society and the media is also less than perfect. While the media allocates some space and time to intelligence-related coverage,[51] it does not foster a debate on the role and place of intelligence in Paraguay. Nor does it provide substantive exposure of wrongdoing or abuses to effect responsive government and (more) democratic reforms of intelligence.

Interestingly, the SNI adopted Resolution 56/2020, an internal control mechanism—its first citizen accountability plan—that sets out details on two main activities, one on the allocation and implementations of the SNI budget, and the other mandating the agency to produce reports for the presidency.[52] The 2020 year reports, for example, that between October and December 2020 SNI received 63 percent of the established goals in the budget implementation, due to pandemic policy restrictions, and 100 percent compliance in the issuing of intelligence reports.[53] This lack of robust oversight over the intelligence agencies in Paraguay increases the threat of intelligence politicization, as the agencies remain vulnerable to becoming the personal tools of the government *du jour* against political opponents.[54]

Professionalism and Effectiveness

Paraguay's current security landscape comprises a mix of quasi-insurgent groups and organized criminal bands, great power competition, and corruption (including corruption of government institutions).[55] This multifarious security context requires effective security institutions, including capable and professional intelligence agencies. To this end, Paraguay has endeavored to professionalize its intelligence agencies. In fact, Paraguay has encountered some progress, between 2016 and 2019, toward professionalization and effectiveness.

During 2019, SNI personnel were trained in such countries as Argentina, Austria, Brazil, Chile, Colombia, El Salvador, Germany, Nicaragua, Spain, Taiwan, and the United States. SNI also convened its first public competitive process for hiring new officials, with publicly disclosed tenets such as transparency, integrity, and the exclusive recognition of meritocracy.[56] At the international level, in 2020, the head of SNI highlighted the increasing intelligence cooperation with such countries as the United States, Qatar, Russia, and Israel.[57]

In terms of effectiveness, SNI has expanded its mission to the conduct of business intelligence, in collaboration with the Superintendence of Banks, and political and social intelligence. The organization employs big data resources through database connections with the Central Bank, the Civil Service Secretariat, the Automotive Registry, Identifications, Judiciary, and the Civil Registry. They rely on two systems: the Bravo System, a platform for the processing of information in real time from databases and delivering analytical products; and the System of Information and Analysis of Intelligence (SAI2), which involves intelligence analysis and information for various police decision processes.[58]

Nevertheless, since the SNI only has analytical rather than operational capabilities, its effectiveness in ensuring national security is limited, as it depends on other agencies to penetrate and collect information on organized criminal groups and other nefarious organizations that threaten Parguay's security, which in turn delays progress in combating these types of threats.[59] In addition, intelligence cooperation and sharing among Paraguay's intelligence agencies does not seem to function well.

Police intelligence also has attempted to professionalize by defining core competencies, formalizing standards, and expanding mission sets. Since October 2016, the National Police obtained the ISO 9001 international certification for quality collection management, processing, and analysis of information and dissemination of intelligence. The main emphasis is now on criminal intelligence, which works on the basis of a nationally distributed intelligence handbook issued in 2016.[60]

As Paraguay joined the GAFILAT, previously known as GAFISUD, its Financial Intelligence Unit (FIU), is a member of the Egmont Group, "a platform for the secure exchange of expertise and financial intelligence to combat money laundering and terrorist financing (ML/TF)."[61] Additional attempts to professionalize through interagency cooperation and joint training and education involve the membership in the Regional Intelligence Liaison Office—a global intelligence-sharing network comprised of customs authorities, under the umbrella of the Worldwide Customs Organization. It is also supported by the Customs Enforcement Network, which is an information system that provides specifics about the seizure of merchandise and controlled items from customs offices around the world.[62] The Ministry of Defense created an intelligence-focused curriculum—including combating terrorism and organized crime, for example—for the military, aimed at preparing the armed forces' personnel in effectively fighting the array of nonaligned threats that challenge the country's security.[63] The MOI's Intelligence Office (DI) and the MOD's DIE have been educating and training their officers within the education institutions of the armed forces, including the Institute of Advanced Strategic Studies (IAEE), which offers a strategic intelligence course.[64] The United States has also provided some education and training to Paraguay's intelligence officers in combating terrorism and organized crime.[65]

Internationally, too, the effectiveness of Paraguay's intelligence services has been less than perfect. In 1994, Argentina, Brazil, and Paraguay created a Tripartite Command to improve the Triple Border Area's security, notably through law enforcement and intelligence cooperation. Since 2006, it has operated more like a formal Regional Intelligence Center, which relied heavily on information and intelligence sharing. Indeed, as Trevisi notes, the three countries created "a common database for the identification of people and vehicles, and agreed to unprecedented operational collaboration and information sharing. Brazil and Paraguay, for example, have cooperated closely in anti-narcotics operations. In 2011, they agreed to ameliorate methods of sharing information and to coordinate research regarding drug trafficking. In May 2013, Paraguayan and Brazilian forces destroyed 26 tons of marijuana, in part of an extended operation that aims to eradicate the cultivation of cannabis in the border area between the two countries."[66]

While there have been several negative reports on the effectiveness of intelligence sharing among the three countries—which fault Paraguay's politicization and corruption for the lack of intelligence cooperation progress[67]—more recent assessments indicate that intelligence sharing has been improved.[68] Nevertheless, while overall Paraguay's participation in these endeavors deserves accolades, there is little available information to prove causation or even correlation with increased intelligence professionalization in Paraguay.

CONCLUSION

Paraguay's intelligence culture has yet to develop a robust intelligence culture, which supports both democracy and intelligence agencies. Despite some progress, the Paraguayan intelligence system is limited to analytical rather than operational capabilities, due to the political concerns of using intelligence organizations against opponents, and it is still vulnerable to politicization even after reform attempts.[69] Following a long autocratic period characterized by violating democratic ideals with impunity and human rights violations, and a path to democracy not without delays and difficulties, the intelligence sector is unfolding, although it is yet in its infancy in terms of democratic governance.

NOTES

1. José María Amarilla, "La Cara Oculta de la Seguridad Pública en el Paraguay," in *Seguridad Pública-Ciudadana en Paraguay; Enfoques, saberes, debates y prácticas*, eds. Carlos Peris and José Amarilla (Asunción: Universidad Nacional de Asunción, 2017), 87.

2. For other hubs for organized crime, such as the northern city of Pedro Juan Caballero near Brazil, see Marcelo Moriconi and Carlos Aníbal Peris, "Merging Legality with Illegality in Paraguay: The Cluster of Order in Pedro Juan Caballero," *Third World Quarterly* 40, no. 12 (2019): 2210–27. Available at https://doi.org/10.10 80/01436597.2019.1636225.

3. Bureau of Counterterrorism, *Country Reports on Terrorism 2019: Paraguay*, US Department of State. Available at https://www.state.gov/reports/country-reports -on-terrorism-2019/paraguay/.

4. The literature on Paraguay's intelligence agencies is rather scarce—way less developed as the literature on other Latin American countries' intelligence. Nevertheless, a few academic works are worth mentioning: Russell Swenson and Carolina Sancho, *Intelligence Management in the Americas* (Washington, DC: National Intelligence University, 2015); Eric Wishart, *Intelligence Networks and the Tri-Border Area of South America: The Dilemma of Efficiency versus Oversight* (master's thesis, Naval Postgraduate School, 2002), 43, available at http://www.dtic.mil/cgi-bin/Ge tTRDoc?AD=ADA411244&Location=U2&doc=GetTRDoc.pdf;_Florencia Prego, "Poststronismo, Reforma Constitucional y Transición Democrática: La Construcción de una Nueva Legalidad en Paraguay," *Sociohistórica* 43 (2019); Luis Roniger, Leonardo Senkman, and María Antonia Sánchez, "El Legado del Autoritarismo y la Construcción de Memoria Histórica en el Paraguay Poststronista," in *Las Luchas por la Memoria en América Latina: Historia Reciente y Violencia Política,* coords. Eugenia Allier Montaño and Emilio Crenzel (México: Bonilla Artigas Editores: UNAM, Instituto de Investigaciones Sociales, 2015); Marco Cepik, "Bosses and Gatekeepers: A Network Analysis of South America's Intelligence Systems," *International Journal of Intelligence and CounterIntelligence* 30, no. 4 (2017), 701–22, doi: 10.1080/08850607.2017.1297117.

5. Paraguay underwent a civil war in 1947, which occurred because the Colorado Party sought to depose and wrest control from the dictatorship of General Higinio

Morinigo. The Colorado Party then confronted and defeated the opposition consisting of Liberals, Febreristas, Communist parties, and various military rebels; the armed forces made a conservative turn that invited growing military partisanship and a weakened military profession; and the Colorado Party became hegemonic. As Magdalena López stated, between 1948 and 2008 twelve presidents were of the same political color, the Colorado Party, interchanging between authoritarian and democratic periods, but always including coup threats, electoral frauds, political patronage, and a personality-centered use of the state resources. See Magdalena López, *Transición y Democracia en Paraguay (1989–2017): "El cambio no es una cuestión electoral"* (Buenos Aires: Editorial Sb, 2018), 24, 60; and Sonia Winer, *Doctrina de inSeguridad Mundial: Paraguay como Laboratorio de Estados Unidos en la Región* (Buenos Aires: Prometeo Libros, 2015), 35.

6. According to Powers, "Stronism was not a class-based exclusionary regime like the bureaucratic authoritarian regimes of the 1970s, but rather was exclusionary on the basis of party affiliation." Nancy R. Powers, *The Transition to Democracy in Paraguay: Problems and Prospects. A Rapporteur's Report*, Working Paper no. 171, Helen Kellogg Institute for International Studies, University of Notre Dame, 1992. Available at https://kellogg.nd.edu/sites/default/files/old_files/documents/171_0.pdf. For more details on stronism see, Félix Pablo Friggeri, "Primitive Accumulation, Mafia Capitalism, and the Campesino Population in Paraguay," *Latin American Perspectives* 48, no. 1 (2021): 126–44. Available at https://journals.sagepub.com/doi/pdf/10.1177/0094582X20975002.

7. López, *Transición y Democracia en Paraguay,* 40.

8. Those armed forces that do not remain outside the realms of partisan politics. See, for example, Michael McNemey, "Military Partisanship," *Journal of Political and Military Sociology* 34, no. 2, (2006). Available at https://www.jstor.org/stable/45294228?seq=1.

9. López, *Transición y Democracia en Paraguay,* 35.

10. Winer, *Doctrina de inSeguridad Mundial,* 40.

11. Those political parties and actors outside the regime, those not belonging the Colorado Party, as mentioned above.

12. Winer, *Doctrina de inSeguridad Mundial,* 34, 43–45. Also see Fátima Myriam Yore, *La Dominación Stronista: Orígenes y Consolidación. "Seguridad Nacional" y Represión* (Asunción: BASE-IS, 1992).

13. López, *Transición y Democracia en Paraguay,* 35 and 44; and Winer, *Doctrina de inSeguridad Mundial,* 63; Numeral 174, Paraguay, *Informe Final (Conclusiones y Recomendaciones) de la Comisión Verdad y Justicia de Paraguay*, 2008, available at http://www.derechoshumanos.net/lesahumanidad/informes/paraguay/Informe_Comision_Verdad_y_Justicia_Paraguay_Conclusiones_y_Recomendaciones.htm. An important legacy was those related to the state terrorism and impunity effects that impacted in policing practices of the 1990s. Winer, *Doctrina de inSeguridad Mundial,* 86.

14. Wishart notes that "Paraguay's intelligence community remains a bit of a mystery." Wishart, *Intelligence Networks*, 43.

15. Carlos Anibal Peris Castiglioni, "Herederos del Fantasma Stronista Perspectiva Continuista del Pensador José Manuel Silvero aplicada a la Situación Actual de la Policía Nacional," in *Pensamiento Paraguayo: Reflexiones en torno a las Ideas de José Manuel Silvero Arévalos*, eds. Mariza Amaral Maciel and Sandra Escutia Díaz (Asunción: Ateneo de Lengua y Cultura Guaraní / Suindá Ediciones, 2019): 332. Neither the police nor the ministry of interior had criminal intelligence analysis capabilities. Amarilla, "La Cara Oculta de la Seguridad Pública en el Paraguay," 50, 53, 54, 87, 95.

16. See introduction.

17. See Greg Grandin, *The Last Colonial Massacre: Latin America in the Cold War* (Chicago: University of Chicago Press, 2011), 75; Walter L. Hixson, *The Myth of American Diplomacy: National Identity and U.S. Foreign Policy* (New Haven: Yale University Press, 2009), 223; Patrice McSherry, "'Industrial Repression' and Operation Condor in Latin America," in *State Violence and Genocide in Latin America: The Cold War Years*, edited by M. Esparza, Henry R. Huttenbach, and Daniel Feierstein (Abingdon/New York: Routledge, 2010), 107.

18. Diana Jean Schemo, "Files in Paraguay Detail Atrocities of US, Allies," *The New York Times*, August 11, 1999, available at https://www.nytimes.com/1999/08/11/world/files-in-paraguay-detail-atrocities-of-us-allies.html; Alex Henderson, "7 Fascist Regimes Enthusiastically Supported by America," Alternet, February 4, 2015, available at https://www.alternet.org/2015/02/7-fascist-regimes-enthusiastically-supported-america/; W. John Green, *A History of Political Murder in Latin America: Killing the Messengers of Change* (Albany: State University of New York Press, 2015): 266.

19. Wishart, *Intelligence Networks*, 43.

20. López, *Transición y Democracia en Paraguay,* 45–51.

21. Prego, "Poststronismo, Reforma Constitucional y Transición Democrática," *Sociohistórica* 43 (2019): 6 and 12. For Prego, who wonders whether Paraguayan political culture is one of the main obstacles to democratization, authoritarianism cannot be thought of as a practice confined to government or a partisan political arena but permeating the entire social fabric.

22. López, *Transición y Democracia en Paraguay,* 60.

23. Florina Cristiana Matei and Andrés de Castro García, "Transitional Justice and Intelligence Democratization," *International Journal of Intelligence and CounterIntelligence* 32, no. 4 (2019): 717–36.

24. See Palmira Vélez Jiménez, "Dictaduras, Derechos Humanos, Memoria y Archivos en Latinoamérica: El Caso Paraguayo," in *América: Poder, Conflicto y Política*, coords. Gabriela Dalla Corte Caballero, Ricardo Piqueras Céspedes, and Meritxell Tous Mata (Universidad de Murcia—Asociación Española de Americanistas, 2013). Available at https://dialnet.unirioja.es/descarga/libro/569094.pdf.

25. Open Society Justice Initiative, "Archives of State Security Service Records," Briefing Paper, January 2013. Also see Rosa M. Palau, "Paraguay: Archivo del Terror. Los Archivos de la Policía de la Dictadura," in *Trabajadores, Archivos, Memoria, Verdad, Justicia y Reparación: Reflexiones del 4° Seminario Internacional El Mundo de*

los Trabajadores y sus Archivos, orgs. Antonio José Marques, Inez Terezinha Stampa, and Sonia Troitiño (Rio de Janeiro: Arquivo Nacional; São Paulo: Central Única dos Trabalhadores, 2018): 39–57.

26. Roniger, Senkman, and Sánchez, "El Legado del Autoritarismo y la Construcción de Memoria Histórica en el Paraguay Poststronista," 157.

27. Numeral 30, Paraguay. *Informe Final (Conclusiones y Recomendaciones) de la Comisión Verdad y Justicia de Paraguay.*

28. Numeral 167. Paraguay. *Informe Final (Conclusiones y Recomendaciones) de la Comisión Verdad y Justicia de Paraguay.*

29. Coronel was in charge of the investigative branch of the National Police (1968–1989). Iván Nikolás Kronawetter Pino, "El Enjuiciamiento de Individuos por Crímenes de Derecho Internacional en el Orden Jurídico Paraguayo," master's thesis, Facultat de Dret, Universitat de Barcelona, 2017, 37–38. Available at http://hdl .handle.net/2445/120747.

30. Roniger, Senkman, and Sánchez, "El Legado del Autoritarismo y la Construcción de Memoria Histórica en el Paraguay Poststronista," 157.

31. Paraguay, Poder Legislativo, Ley N° 1337 de Defensa Nacional y Seguridad Interna, 14 de Abril de 1999, Paraguay, Poder Legislativo, Ley N° 5036 que modifica y amplía los artículos 2°, 3° y 56 de la Ley N° 1.337/99 "de Defensa Nacional y de Seguridad Interna," 22 de Abril de 2013. See Tamara Lajtman Bereicoa, "Dinámicas Securitarias y Guerra Preventiva en Paraguay," Aproximaciones a la Ley de Defensa Nacional y Seguridad Interna," *Crítica y Resistencias. Revista de Conflictos Sociales Latinoamericanos* 5 (2017): 139–58.

32. See Natalia Rodríguez, "Modificaciones en Materia de Defensa Nacional: Las Atribuciones Extraordinarias de las FF.AA. que Introdujeron la Ley 5036/13 y el Decreto del Poder Ejecutivo," *Boletín SERPAJ Paraguay 7*, no. 26 (2018): 3–5; Abel Enrique Irala, "Modificación de la Ley de Seguridad y Defensa del Año 2013," *Estudios Paraguayos* 34, no.1 (2016): 59–77; Juan A. Martens, "Entre el Miedo y la Militarización: La Política de (In) Seguridad de Paraguay," *Revista de la Facultad de Derecho de México* 67, no. 269 (2017): 229–47.

33. Paraguay, *Primer Libro Banco de la Defensa Nacional de la República del Paraguay* (Asunción: Presidencia de la República. Ministerio de Defensa Nacional— Consejo Permanente de Defensa Nacional, 2013).

34. Paraguay, *Primer Libro Banco,* 133.

35. EPP actions served as a justification for amending the defense legislation in 2013. Tamara Lajtman Bereicoa, "Dinámicas Securitarias y Guerra Preventiva en Paraguay, 144–45.

36. The presence of Brazilian organized crime group First Capital Command (PCC) in Paraguay is also worth mentioning. See R. Evan Ellis, "The Paraguayan Military and the Struggle against Organized Crime and Insecurity," *Military Review* (online exclusive) (January 2019), available at https://www.armyupress.army.mil/ Portals/7/Army-Press-Online-Journal/documents/2019/Ellis.pdf; Douglas Farah and Kathryn Babineau, *A Strategic Overview of Latin America: Identifying New Convergence Centers, Forgotten Territories, and Vital Hubs for Transnational Organized Crime*, Institute for National Strategic Studies—Strategic Perspectives, No. 28

(Washington, DC: National Defense University Press, 2019); Rex Hudson, "Terrorist and Organized Crime Groups in the Tri-Border Area (TBA) of South America," Federal Research Division, Library of Congress, Washington, DC, 2003; Sonia Alda Mejías, *Observatorio de Redes Criminales y Tráficos Ilícitos del Real Instituto Elcano*, Documento de Trabajo No. 4, Real Instituto Elcano, 2018; International Security Sector Advisory Team-ISSAT, Paraguay Country Profile, online, updated February 10, 2015, available at https://issat.dcaf.ch/Learn/Resource-Library2/Country-Profiles/Paraguay-Country-Profile.

37. Kyra Gurney, "Paraguay Congress Approves Intelligence Agency Following EPP Attacks," Brief, *InSight Crime*, July 14, 2014. Available at https://www.insight crime.org/news/brief/paraguay-congress-approves-intelligence-agency-following-epp -attacks/.

38. "Country Reports on Terrorism 2019: Paraguay," https://www.state.gov/reports/country-reports-on-terrorism-2019/paraguay/.

39. As Paraguay's principal intelligence coordinating organization, the SNI presides over the National Intelligence Council. Cepik, "Bosses and Gatekeepers."

40. The law stipulates the respect for the rule of law, citizens' rights and liberties. By Decree 2812 of December 18, 2014, the Executive Branch regulated such law. Paraguay, Poder Legislativo, Ley N° 5241 Que crea el Sistema Nacional de Inteligencia, Gaceta Oficial N° 160, 22 Agosto 2014.

41. Cepik, "Bosses and Gatekeepers."

42. The regulatory decree placed this directorate within the organizational structure of the SNI, which means that it is not under the Ministry of Interior.

43. The Department of Intelligence (DIPN), and the Secretariate for Terrorism Prevention and Investigation (SEPRINTE). Cepik, "Bosses and Gatekeepers."

44. Paraguay, Presidencia de la República, Decreto N° 2812, por el cual se reglamenta la Ley N° 5241, Que crea el Sistema Nacional de Inteligencia, 18 de Diciembre 2014.

45. Not the Criminal Intelligence Directorate, as previously explained.

46. SNI webpage: https://www.sni.gov.py/.

47. See "Martínez asume en Interior y Lezcano pasa a ser el Ministro de Inteligencia," *ABC Color,* February 3, 2018. Available at https://www.abc.com.py/edicion -impresa/judiciales-y-policiales/martinez-asume-en-interior-y-lezcano-pasa-a-ser-el -ministro-de-inteligencia-1671837.html.

48. See "Recién ahora implementan Secretaría de Inteligencia," *ABC Color*, April 24, 2019. Available at https://www.abc.com.py/edicion-impresa/politica/recien-ahora-implementan-secretaria-de-inteligencia-1683066.html.

49. See https://www.sni.gov.py/institucion/amenazas-detectadas/plan-nacional de-inteligencia.

50. Like, for example, the kidnapping of two left-wing activists by supposed vigilantes with alleged connections with the intelligence agencies. See Wishart, *Intelligence Networks*.

51. A recent example is the interview of SIN head Esteban Aquino Bernal by *La Nación* daily, where he explains the role of SIN domestically and internationally. "Trabajamos las 24 horas, los 7 días, para producir información oportuna," *La*

Nación, January 2, 2021, available at https://www.lanacion.com.py/politica_edicion
_impresa/2021/01/02/trabajamos-las-24-horas-los-7-dias-para-producir-informacion
-oportuna/. Another example is a critique of the role of CNI during pandemics by *El Independiente*, which stresses that the CNI lacks an adequate budget to combat the pandemic effectively. "Inteligencia, otro fracaso del Gobierno," *El Independiente*, March 23, 2021. Available at https://independiente.com.py/inteligencia-otro-fracaso -del-gobierno/.

52. Paraguay, Poder Ejecutivo, Secretaría Nacional de Inteligencia, Resolución N° 056 del 09 de Marzo de 2020, Aprueba Plan de Rendición de Cuentas al Ciudadano de la Secretaría Nacional de Inteligencia.

53. See https://www.sni.gov.py/transparencia/rendicion-de-cuentas.

54. Ellis, "The Paraguayan Military"; "Paraguay's First Intelligence Service Created," *MercoPress*, December 26, 2014, available at https://en.mercopress .com/2014/12/26/paraguay-s-first-intelligence-service-created. See also Wishart, *Intelligence Networks*.

55. Ellis, "The Paraguayan Military." Also see "Paraguay's First Intelligence Service Created," *MercoPress*.

56. See "Realizan primera reunión del Consejo Nacional de Inteligencia," *La Nación*, November 26, 2019. Available at https://www.lanacion.com.py/ ahora/2019/11/26/realizan-primera-reunion-del-consejo-nacional-de-inteligencia/.

57. "Secretaría de Inteligencia se fortalece con la cooperación internacional, asegura ministro," *La Nación*, August 20, 2020. Available at https://www.lanacion.com .py/politica/2020/08/20/secretaria-de-inteligencia-se-fortalece-con-la-cooperacion -internacional-asegura-ministro/.

58. Hernán Mayor and Oscar Pereira, "Formulación y Aplicación de Políticas Públicas en Seguridad Pública-Ciudadana," in *Seguridad Pública-Ciudadana en Paraguay: Enfoques, saberes, debates y prácticas*, eds. Carlos Peris and José Amarilla (Asunción: Universidad Nacional de Asunción, 2017): 114–18.

59. Ellis, "The Paraguayan Military." Also see "Paraguay's First Intelligence Service Created," *MercoPress*.

60. Mayor and Pereira, "Formulación y Aplicación de Políticas Públicas," 114–18. Freedom House categorizes Paraguay as "partly free" in 2016. Freedom House, *Freedom in the World 2016—Anxious Dictators; Wavering Democracies: Global Freedom under Pressure*, Freedom House, 2016, available at https://freedomhouse.org/sites/ default/files/FH_FITW_Report_2016.pdf. State Department's Report in 2016 notes Paraguay's democratic progress. Bureau of Democracy, *Paraguay 2016 Human Rights Report*, Human Rights and Labor, Country Reports on Human Rights Practices for 2016, United States Department of State, 2016, available at https://www.state .gov/wp-content/uploads/2019/01/Paraguay-1.pdf.

61. Egmont Group, "About," https://egmontgroup.org/en/content/about. GAFISUD/GAFILAT seeks to strengthen the professionalism of intelligence and law enforcement professionals who are working in the field of combating money laundering. Swenson and Sancho, *Intelligence Management in the Americas*. Also see Bureau of Counterterrorism, *Country Reports on Terrorism 2019: Paraguay*.

62. Swenson and Sancho, *Intelligence Management in the Americas*. Also see Bureau of Counterterrorism, *Country Reports on Terrorism 2019: Paraguay*.

63. Swenson and Sancho, *Intelligence Management in the Americas*.

64. Swenson and Sancho, *Intelligence Management in the Americas*.

65. For example, between 1994 when it was created and 2019 when it was restructured (and became the Institute for Security Governance) the Center for Civil Military Relations at the Naval Postgraduate School, would educate Paraguayan military officers who worked in the field of combating terrorism on the democratic toolkit of countering terrorist groups, in programs conducted both in residence and in Paraguay, under the Mobile Education Team. These programs contained intelligence-related lectures, focused both on effectiveness and accountability.

66. A. F. Trevisi, "Assessing the Terrorist Threat in the Tri-Border Area of Brazil, Paraguay and Argentina," *International Institute for Counter-Terrorism*, 48. Available at https://www.ict.org.il/UserFiles/Trevisi%202013.pdf.

67. Indeed, as Eric Wishart highlights, in Paraguay "the domestic security intelligence system is most likely very highly politicized. This politicization has produced a lack of trust by other intelligence agencies within the region and hinders the sharing of information. . . . [T]he Paraguayan intelligence Service . . . [is] most problematic, due to . . . corruption among agents and a hurry to produce results." Wishart, *Intelligence Networks*, 45. Similarly, Keshavarz notes that "[g]overnment corruption, the lack of proper law enforcement training and resources, and an inadequate justice system have proven the task force to be rather ineffective." This was even after the United States joined the force (known as the "3+1 group"). Alma Keshavarz, "Irán and Hezbollah in the Tri-Border Areas of Latin America: A Look at the 'Old TBA' and the 'New TBA,'" *Small Wars Journal* (2015). Available at https://smallwarsjournal.com/jrnl/art/iran-and-hezbollah-in-the-tri-border-areas-of-latin-america-a-look-at-the-%E2%80%9Cold-tba%E2%80%9D-and-the.

68. As Swenson and Sancho note, "Team leaders of intelligence units from these countries worked together in the center to share sensitive information and coordinate covert operations." However, these reports do not provide information whether Paraguay's intelligence agencies are still the weakest link of this intelligence cooperation endeavor. Swenson and Sancho, *Intelligence Management in the Americas*.

69. Ellis, "The Paraguayan Military."

Chapter Fourteen

El Salvador

Eduardo E. Estévez

From 1931 until 1992, El Salvador[1] was ruled by successive military governments (and their allies, the economic elite).[2] Several insurgency and counterinsurgency groups threatened the various military governments in the 1960s, which resulted in a civil war (1980–1992). This turmoil ended with a cease-fire and peace process mediated by the United Nations (UN), followed by transition to democratic rule in 1992 and several democratic reform attempts. These reform endeavors have also included transforming intelligence agencies—a tall order, given El Salvador's post-transition unstable political and security environment, amid social unrest, political conflict, violence and murder, poverty, corruption, and mass migration. This chapter aims to provide some insights into the Salvadoran attempt to transform its intelligence agencies and security sector since the 1992 democratic transition, which process coincides with the militarization of public security. Ultimately, it finds that intelligence reform remains incomplete in El Salvador—both a cause and symptom of an imperfect legal framework, lack of oversight, and ineffective intelligence agencies.

THE NON-DEMOCRATIC REGIME, CIVIL WAR, AND THE ROLE OF INTELLIGENCE

For decades since the 1930s, Salvadoran society has lived with violence—of either political or criminal origin. The political system—historically dominated by warlords, landowners, traders, and coffee growers—was taken over by the military in 1931 until the 1980s.[3] Public security became the central mission of the military.[4] As the UN Truth Commission on El Salvador explained, "Violence has formed part of the exercise of official authority, directly guided by State officials . . . reflected, throughout the country's history, in a pattern of conduct within the Government and power elites of using violence as a means to control civilian society."[5] This culture of violence strengthened during the civil war between the polarizing military government and the Farabundo Martí National Liberation Front (FMLN), a coalition of left-wing groups, from 1979 to 1992, which militarized the society and led to societal infighting.[6]

Since the beginning of the counterinsurgency campaign and during the civil war, El Salvador's security sector maintained three repressive and brutal components: police forces (National Police, National Guard, and Treasury Police), army, and paramilitary groups[7]—all trained under U.S. police assistance programs.[8] Isolation from the population allowed these militarized institutions to commit human rights violations with relative impunity.[9] These security forces organized their own intelligence units, which provided intelligence on insurgent movements to assist police and military operations.[10] Intelligence units, created in 1963 and 1966, respectively, included the Salvadoran Security Agency (ANSESAL), the nervous system of the counterinsurgency apparatus,[11] and the Nationalist Democratic Organization (ORDEN),[12] a body under the National Guard that ran a network of informants in rural areas—locations associated with insurgency recruitment, training, equipping, regrouping, and a citizenry generally sympathetic to the insurgents' cause.[13] The Territorial Service, an agency comprised by military reservists, was another paramilitary body; the organization's competencies included maintaining social control, gathering information, and providing operational support for counterinsurgency.[14] In early 1982, a Salvadoran military intelligence service was formed with the support of the United States, with the objective of subverting Communist movements.[15] Finally, in 1985, the National Intelligence Department (DNI)—established under the Armed Forces General Staff and reporting to the minister of defense—became the final counterinsurgency agency until it was abolished in 1992 under the Peace Agreements.[16]

These agencies used death squads,[17] interrogations, torture, and killings (a repertoire known as "dirty work") of trade unionists, university members, partisan militants, and peasants—as directed by the military, and with the military doing a significant share of the dirty work.[18] All these militarized security institutions were the regime's political police, which effectively suppressed "dissent while defending elite interests against labor and peasant organizers and other 'subversive' influences," as Stanley and Loosle note.[19] Stanley and Loosle further elaborate, "The brutality of the security forces was a crucial contributing factor in the expansion of support for guerrilla organizations and the eventual outbreak of civil war."[20]

TRANSITION TO DEMOCRACY, PEACE, AND REFORM

The gradual rebuilding of this war-torn country and its transition to democracy materialized through a negotiated peace agreement between the Salvadoran government ruled by the ARENA party, and the FMLN, under the auspices of the United Nations. Several agreements urged for the dismantling of the repressive apparatus and corresponding tactics and objectives:[21] the Mexico Agreement of April 27, 1991; The New York Agreement of September 25, 1991; and Final Peace Agreements of January 16, 1992, in Mexico City.[22]

Both the Salvadoran Constitution (Article 159) and peace agreements separated the roles of defense and public security, with the armed forces in charge of the former and a police force that was to be created in charge of the latter. These stipulations provided for the demilitarization of domestic security. In addition, the agreements stipulated the need for intelligence reform.

The agreements also proposed the creation of a truth commission to investigate egregious acts of violence that had occurred since 1980. The UN Truth Commission on El Salvador operated from July 1992 to March 1993. Its report "included specific findings on thirty-two particularly notorious or representative cases, and implicated virtually the entire High Command of the Salvadoran Armed Forces in the November 1989 murder of six Jesuit priests, their cook, and her daughter . . . [by] agents of the Salvadoran state."[23] Among its sundry recommendations, the report called for the exclusion of the armed forces from public security and intelligence functions.[24] Accordingly, the commission recommended that "Salvadorian institutions must make serious efforts to investigate the structural connection that has been found to exist between the death squads and State bodies."[25] As a result of these findings, the Salvadoran government and the UN agreed to establish the Joint Group for the Investigation of Illegal Armed Groups with Political Motivation in El Salvador, which investigated these linkages between December 1993 and July 1994. The Joint Group revealed that after the end of the civil war, the death squads—including the army—were seeking employment with their skill sets honed during the civil war with common and organized crime entities.[26]

El Salvador had to establish a new National Civil Police (PNC)—made up of members of the National Police, FMNL, and new personnel. The new government coalition also agreed to the creation of the National Academy of Public Security.[27] Interestingly, the government at first did not want to establish the PNC; initially, not allocating funds for the PNC's creation—hoping and claiming that such funds were to be provided by international donors.[28] Eventually, the PNC was established by law in June 1992, and it continues to operate at the time that this chapter was written, although its professionalization has been lackluster.[29] A low degree of professionalization has obstructed the country's efforts to address public security threats, and thus the ability of criminal intelligence to produce substantive results at the expense of the state.

In an effort to fulfill the peace agreements, subsequent administrations attempted to reform the inherited militarized public security regime—characterized by lack of political control, human rights violations, and corruption, with varying levels of success.[30] Constitutional reforms of 1992 were a political means to legally codify peace agreements, thereby subordinating the armed forces to the president and separation of national defense and public security functions.[31] However, public security has not ceased to be militarized since 1992, due to the rapid deterioration of the public safety environment and police forces' limited ability to combat security threats effectively, which in turn resulted in the military (which was viewed as a capable instrument to fight these security threats) undertaking domestic security roles. The current situation is marked by violent crimes, high homicide rates, the street gangs or *maras*, extortion and payment to gangs, kidnapping for ransom by criminal organizations, and illicit smuggling networks.[32] This dynamic has led to regression—extrajudicial killings and death squads aimed at Salvadoran citizens have reemerged[33]—in which military intelligence has been involved.[34] Additionally, a sense of validation has been conferred to previous human rights abuses conducted by the military, which further hinders democratic consolidation of the military and intelligence agencies.

The Path to Reforming Intelligence

The 1992 Peace Agreements also outlined an *intelligence reform*: "The National Intelligence Department [DNI] shall be abolished and State intelligence services [OIE] shall be entrusted to a new entity to be called the State Intelligence Agency, which shall be subordinated to civilian authority and come under the direct authority of the President of the Republic." The agreement called for a new legal and doctrinal basis to enhance democratic and human rights principles, independent external oversight of intelligence activities, and staff recruitment to be carried out with international assistance. Finally, for former DNI staff to maintain their position in the organization, they were submitted to rigorous evaluation of their past performance, abilities, adherence to human rights principles, and capacity to adapt to the new doctrine.[35]

Article 168/18 of the 1992 constitution stipulated that it was the president's responsibility to organize, lead, and maintain a new intelligence agency—the State Intelligence Agency (OIE). The intention was to replace the DNI, the intelligence body of previous authoritarian regimes, with a new body that was envisaged in the peace agreements. OIE was thus created by executive Decree No. 34 on April 28, 1992, issued by then President Alfredo Cristiani. Its main role was to advise the president on intelligence, especially in the political, economic, social, and security fields for the achievement of national security objectives. However, as OIE was under de facto military (and not civilian) control, it allegedly engaged in political surveillance, which triggered a series of inquiries in 2000 by the attorney general and the Assembly.[36] In September 2001, the Salvadorian Supreme Court decided on the unconstitutionality of the OIE executive decree of 1992.[37] In the same month, to overcome this institutional situation, the Assembly passed new legislation, the OIE Law.[38] According to this law, the OIE is mandated to inform and advise the president on intelligence, which is necessary to meet national security objectives linked to the development of the country, the security of the state, and the validity of the democratic regime. Thus, the law changed the agency's mission; however, it did not provide for legislative and judicial controls. The OIE Law complies with the intent of the peace agreements; however, the law does not regulate the entirety of the Salvadoran intelligence agencies, which illustrates a weakness in the legal framework.

Regarding *legislation* in force, the 2001 OIE Law[39] formalized in Article 5 the OIE's main roles: informing and advising the president on intelligence matters and coordinating and consolidating intelligence and counterintelligence information from the various executive institutions. OIE is specified in Article 3 of the law, as a civil, professional, and apolitical agency serving society and the state. It is important to emphasize that the law does not define other state agencies that produce intelligence and counterintelligence. According to Article 2 of the OIE Law, intelligence is a permanent and integral activity that is essential for state security, which penetrates all facets and levels of national activity. Compliance of OIE actions within constitutional bounds and laws is detailed in articles 6 and 7. In August 2016, President Salvador Sánchez Cerén (2014–2019) issued Decree No. 47 regulating the OIE Law.[40] The eleven articles of the OIE Law, complemented by its regulatory decree delineate the powers, principles, and legal bases of OIE. With regard to collection of information, according to Article 6 of Decree No. 47, the OIE is responsible for developing strategic and operative intelligence activities within the confines of established regulations and laws.

Regrettably, the OIE Law does not forbid clandestine operations and, as stated above, fails to regulate the functioning, competences, and activities of all state agencies that perform intelligence functions, placing security and state stability at risk.[41] In addition, the 2001 OIE Law grants extensive powers to the organization and only provides for the exercise of control by the executive under a veil of secrecy and devoid of accountability. As for the OIE, the 2001 law stipulates that all matters, activities, and documentation related to this agency are classified. In practice, relegating activities to opacity and far from scrutiny opposed transparency associated with democratic consolidation. As Amaya Cóbar notes, until 2007 the OIE had never been under democratic civilian control and its activities remain opaque to the public,[42] a situation that continues to the present, with the sole exception of the OIE intelligence budget.

Concerning police intelligence, the CIP, operating since 2001 under the bylaws of the PNC organic law, was tasked with producing intelligence analysis through the compilation, elaboration, processing, control, and dissemination of information to decision makers at all levels of the PNC.[43] Since 2005, CIP's territorial deployment has burgeoned—included a second organizational level composed of five regional intelligence centers—and since 2009, a third organizational level with police intelligence units in the twenty-two police delegations throughout the country.[44] This territorial deployment arose according to the need for field agents to collect information on criminal networks that operated in these ungoverned regions. And since a police reorganization in 2016, CIP became Sub-Directorate for Police Intelligence (SIPOL) and is now organized into four divisions.[45] In fact, CIP had—at least until 2016—problems with centralization and sharing of intelligence due to poor organization and the creation of various intelligence divisions within specialized police units, among other issues. Since its reorganization, the SIPOL began to take the necessary steps to reverse this situation, implementing a new information collection program, an information processing system, and a novel form of dissemination that encompasses the capabilities and expertise of the different intelligence and analysis offices of the PCN that until then had worked autonomously.[46] The PCN also envisaged in its planning the enactment of intelligence-led policing, needed to combat organized crime and gang-related violence.[47]

The Military Intelligence System comprises the Intelligence Directorate of the Armed Forces General Staff, and it is assigned with gathering information and producing intelligence at the strategic, operational, and tactical levels. It is subordinated to the Ministry of Defense and the Joint Chiefs of Staff, and under the structure of the Military Doctrine and Education Command.[48] Since 1994, it has been housing the School for Military intelligence, which was created in 1988.[49] Unfortunately, little is known about military intelligence regulations; there is no reference to them in the 1998 organic law, which is currently in force, nor in the antecedent law, which dates from 1994.[50] More appalling, although the 1992 agreements specified that the OIE was the only authorized state intelligence agency of the country, the armed forces have continued to maintain their own military intelligence system and apparatus, which remains free of both any legal framework and civilian control.[51] More recently, an attempted integration of military intelligence into the intelligence community to unify all state intelligence subsystems to prevent security threats—an effort made during the administration of President Mauricio Funes (2009–2014) of the FMLN party—failed due to the military maintaining its security-related prerogatives and ability to resist reforms.[52]

In terms of political control, the OIE, as stated in Article 4 of the 2001 law, is under the authority of the president, who defines its policies and lines of efforts. Moreover, according to Article 9 of the same law, all operational, administrative, staff, organizational, and functioning matters of the OIE should be regulated by the executive branch. Articles 4 and 5 of Decree No. 47 regulating the OIE Law prescribe that the president appoints the OIE director and deputy director. In addition, Decree No. 47 defines the director's powers and responsibilities. Importantly, Article 162 of the Constitution stipulates that the president appoints, removes, or accepts the resignations of the chief of Public Security and of the State Intelligence.

The legal framework for fiscal oversight is incomplete. According to a 2017 study on secret government expenditures conducted by Fundación Nacional para el Desarrollo—FUNDE, the national chapter of Transparency International—legislation on such matters did not delimit responsibilities, prohibitions, sanctions, or control mechanisms. The report also acknowledged that information on reserved expenses allocated to the Presidency of the Republic/OIE, the Ministry of National Defense, and the PNC was insufficient.[53] Moreover, in December 2019, under an agreement between the Legislative Assembly budget committee and the Bukele administration, the Budget Act of 2020 was amended and for the first time the secret budget figures for OIE were publicly released.[54] Furthermore, for the 2021 budget, the Legislative Assembly cut the OIE's funds by 50 percent from what was requested by the executive.[55]

As for training, since 2011, the National Public Security Academy (ANSP)—established in 1992 under the peace agreements[56]—proposes basic courses in police intelligence.[57] Together with CIP/SIPOL and the PNC training center, ANSP coordinated the organization and implementation of a complementary education system that would allow the use of personnel already specialized in intelligence and their physical and didactic resources. For example, between 2004 and 2006, 132 specialists in police intelligence graduated from the ANSP, compared to 722, between 2014 and 2016.[58] In addition, intelligence professionals from El Salvador have benefited from specific intelligence- and democracy-related education from U.S. International Military Education and Training (IMET) assistance programs. For example, in 2017, the Center for Civil-Military Relations (CCMR) conducted a one-week mobile education team (MET) seminar in San Salvador, which focused on the relationship between intelligence organizations, political elites, and society—putting a premium on ethics, oversight, and political neutrality, while also maintaining operational effectiveness.[59] Likewise, military officers from El Salvador have participated in U.S. Naval Postgraduate School's MA programs in civil–military relations and countering terrorism, where they have been exposed to intelligence and democracy courses.

As for external oversight, the OIE Law does not provide for any kind of oversight by the legislative and judicial branches. In 2019, a special parliamentary committee recommended that the assembly set up a standing oversight committee on public security and state intelligence.[60] To date, however, no such standing committee has been created.

Finally, regarding public oversight, although the truth commission produced tangible promissory successes during the transition, the contemporaneous 1993 Amnesty Law[61] became a significant stumbling block for transitional justice and criminal prosecution of human rights crimes.[62] In this context, the military repeatedly refused access to its secret archives.[63] In July 2016, the Supreme Court ruled on the unconstitutionality of the Amnesty Law. Strikingly, in 2019, on the last day of his term of office, Sánchez Cerén decreed the creation of a military archives review committee.[64] Additionally, the media has dealt with intelligence issues, such as those linked to illegal spying and the use of secret intelligence expenses—making them versed in intelligence overreach and charged with holding violators accountable. The media remains an integral organization to continue oversight activities.[65]

ANALYSIS

Despite these legislative changes, there has been little progress in the democratization of El Salvador intelligence. The legal basis does not provide for legislative oversight, judicial control, procedures for special operations, definition and scope of reserved expenditure, accountability, declassification procedures, nor does it explicitly provide for the control of military intelligence. In addition, poor coordination of information gathering by police intelligence, as well as lack of strategic analysis capabilities and trained analysts persist.[66] Efforts to reinforce police intelligence activities during the Sánchez Cerén administration as part of the national violence prevention strategy, and the reorganization of the PNC as outlined above, are encouraging.[67] As for the financial oversight dimension, it is evolving from opacity to greater attention and visibility, which is promising in terms of accountability.[68]

CONCLUSION

Ultimately, developing an intelligence culture in El Salvador remains a wicked problem.[69] The intelligence overlapping functions between the armed forces and the police, the lack of coordination between the diverse intelligence agencies, and the tendency toward militarization can be attributed to the lack of specific legislation covering the intelligence community that would condition policy makers to implement what is provided for in the peace agreements.[70] Additionally, excessive power vested within the executive branch and limited oversight mechanisms and manners of accountability for the legislative and judicial branches to contest such actions create the conditions to stall intelligence reform. Surprisingly, fragile democratic institutions and weak political culture do not hinder reform.[71] A profound transformation remains outstanding,[72] based on a new legislative framework for the entire Salvadoran intelligence community, including oversight and transparency provisions as well as measures guaranteeing a democratic governance of intelligence, and respect for human rights.

NOTES

1. For a brief on El Salvador, see Kristin Marsh, "Republic of El Salvador," in *World Encyclopedia of Political Systems and Parties, Fourth Edition,* eds. Neil Schlager and Jayne Weisblatt (New York: Facts On File, 2006): 404–11. Also see International Security Sector Advisory Team—ISSAT, *El Salvador Country Profile,* online, updated February 2, 2015. Available at https://issat.dcaf.ch/Learn/Resource -Library2/Country-Profiles/El-Salvador-Country-Profile.

2. The Salvadoran military state has been portrayed as a protection racket state. William Stanley, *The Protection Racket State: Elite Politics, Military Extortion, and Civil War in El Salvador* (Philadelphia: Temple University Press, 1996).

3. Carlos Gregorio López Bernal, "Las Claves de la Historia de El Salvador," in *El Salvador. Historia Contemporánea, 1808–2010,* ed. Carlos Gregorio López Bernal (San Salvador: Fundación Mapfre/Editorial Universitaria, Universidad de El Salvador, 2015), 38.

4. Gino Costa, *La Policía Nacional Civil de El Salvador (1990–1997)* (San Salvador: UCA Editores, 1999): 77, 195.

5. United Nations, General Assembly Security Council, *Report of the UN Truth Commission on El Salvador. From Madness to Hope, The 12 Year War in El Salvador.* S 25500 (April 1, 1993): 133–34. Available at https://undocs.org/ pdf?symbol=en/S/25500.

6. See José Miguel Cruz, Luis Armando González, Luis Ernesto Romano, and Elvio Sisti, *La Violencia en El Salvador en los Años Noventa: Magnitud, Costos y Factores Posibilitadores,* Documento de Trabajo R-338, Banco Interamericano de

Desarrollo (San Salvador: Instituto Universitario de Opinión Pública. Universidad Centroamericana José Simeón Cañas, 1998); Costa, *La Policía Nacional Civil*, 30–37; López Bernal, "Las Claves de la Historia de El Salvador," 34–43, 45; Carlos M. Vilas, "El Camino hacia la Revolución y la Guerra," in *Observatorio Latinoamericano 9. Dossier El Salvador* (Buenos Aires: Instituto de Estudios de América Latina y el Caribe, 2012), 47; Kevin A. Young, "El Salvador's FMLN and the Constraints on Leftist Government," in *Oxford Research Encyclopedia of Latin American Politics*, eds. Harry Vanden and Gary Prevost (New York: Oxford University Press, 2019), 2; Francisco Eliseo Ortiz Ruiz, "El Salvador 1991–1992: Acuerdo de Paz y Reforma Constitucional," *Perspectivas* no. 4 (San Salvador: Friedrich-Ebert-Stiftung, 2017), 6.

7. Costa, *La Policía Nacional Civil*, 27–28.

8. See Costa, *La Policía Nacional Civil*, 44–60.

9. Jaime Martínez Ventura, "La Policía en el Estado de Derecho Latinoamericano: El Caso de El Salvador," in *La Policía en los Estados de Derecho Latinoamericanos*, eds. K. Ambos, J. L. Gómez Colomer, and R. Vogler (Bogotá: Editorial Gustavo Ibañez in cooperation with Friedrich-Ebert-Stiftung and Max Planck Institut für ausländisches und internationales Strafrecht, 2003), 305.

10. Herard Von Santos, "Estudio Historiográfico sobre los Sistemas de Inteligencia de los Antiguos Cuerpos de Seguridad Pública Salvadoreños," *Revista Policía y Seguridad Pública* 5, no. 2 (2015): 298–321. Like the security institutions that they belonged to, these agencies were also involved in human rights abuses, as noted in the next paragraph.

11. Costa, *La Policía Nacional Civil*, 39.

12. According to Peñalva Torres, "The first paramilitary platform, ORDEN, was part of the Intelligence structure, however it was never officially included in the federal budget, and there were no laws, hearing, or any official regulation for it." Ana Paula Peñalva Torres, "Transitional Accountability Only for Some? Accountability Measures against Paramilitary Groups," master's thesis, Uppsala University, 2017, 35. Available at http://urn.kb.se/resolve?urn=urn:nbn:se:uu:diva-325009.

13. In 1979 ANSESAL and ORDEN were disbanded although these agencies remained active under different names and structures; ANSESAL was integrated to the Armed Forces Chief of Staff, and ORDEN was reallocated in a new civil defense unit and in the Territorial Service. In this context, Major Roberto D'Aubuisson, a top officer of ANSESAL—who, on March 24, 1980, orchestrated the murder of Archbishop Monsignor Oscar Arnulfo Romero (a vocal critic of genocide against civilian social movements prior to the civil war)—kept part of ANSESAL's archives, which he used to achieve his political goals and ambitions. Indeed, he used these files to blackmail security forces and the military. He created a new agency known as National Intelligence Agency (ANI) under the army headquarters and, in 1981, the conservative National Republican Alliance (ARENA) party. Costa, *La Policía Nacional Civil*, 40. United Nations, *Report of the UN Truth Commission on El Salvador*; Destiny Alvarez, "Roberto D'Aubuisson: A Right-Wing Leader's Rise to Power," PhD diss., The University of Texas at Austin, 2020, 19, available at https://hdl.handle.net/2152/84128; Cate Buchanan, and Joaquín Chávez, *Guns and Violence in the El Salvador Peace Negotiations*, HD Centre for Humanitarian Dialogue, 2008, 12, available at https://

www.files.ethz.ch/isn/95077/HD%20Centre%20NegDis%20El%20Salvador%20
Country%20Study%20PDF.pdf; Young, "El Salvador's FMLN," 2; López Bernal,
"El Salvador 1960–1992," 237–89; and Ralph Sprenkels, "La Memoria Militante:
Historia y Política en la Posguerra Salvadoreña," in *Observatorio Latinoamericano
9 Dossier El Salvador,* ed. Lucrecia Molinari (Buenos Aires: Instituto de Estudios de
América Latina y el Caribe (IEALC), Facultad de Ciencias Sociales, Universidad de
Buenos Aires, 2011), 186–200, available at http://iealc.sociales.uba.ar/publicaciones/
observatorio-latinoamericano-9/.

14. See HerardVon Santos, "El Servicio Territorial como parte del Sistema de
Control Social y Territorial del Estado Salvadoreño durante el Conflicto Armado
(1972–1992)," *Revista Policía y Seguridad Pública* (2016) 227–94. Since 1960, the
Territorial Service has added a second mission concerning assisting the State in social
and territorial control, joining forces in this task with ORDEN and ANSESAL, and
providing reports on the political, economic, and social situation of the populations
in which they lived.

15. Tactical intelligence courses prepared officers and senior enlisted personnel to
take intelligence staff positions throughout the military. CIA, "Draft [REDACTED]
paper on Salvadoran Military," UWCHR El Salvador Freedom of Information Act
(FOIA) Documents, June 13, 1984. Available at http://hdl.handle.net/1773/38759.

16. Costa, *La Policía Nacional Civil,* 100. According to Rex Hudson, the DNI's
mission was to provide strategic, political, and national intelligence, [but] the demands
of the war and a lack of training compelled it to develop mainly military operational
intelligence at the strategic and tactical levels, duplicating the C-2's [Intelligence of the
Armed Forces General Staff] principal mission." Rex A. Hudson, "National Security,"
in *El Salvador: A Country Study,* ed. Richard A. Haggerty (Washington, DC: Library
of Congress, 1990), 208–9; also see Ana Margarita Chavez Escobar, *From Authoritarian to Democratic Regimes,* The New Role of Security Intelligence," (master's thesis,
Naval Postgraduate School, Monterey, California, 2001), available at http://hdl.handle
.net/10945/2740. 71.

17. Especially, the intelligence section (S-II) in the armed forces units.

18. United Nations, *Report of the UN Truth Commission on El Salvador.* On
ANSESAL and ORDEN see María Eugenia Bonilla Ovallos, "Desempeño Policial
Democrático: El Caso de la Policía Nacional Civil de El Salvador" tesis doctoral,
Universidad de Salamanca, 2018, 87, available at https://gredos.usal.es/jspui/
bitstream/10366/139483/1/DDPG_BonillaOvallosME_Desempe%C3%B1oPolicial
.pdf; Carlos Reynaldo López Nuila, "La Seguridad Pública de El Salvador hasta
1994." *Entorno* 33 (2004–2005): 33; Herard Von Santos, "El Servicio Territorial: 231;
Lucrecia Molinari, "O Nascimento da Inteligência Contrainsurgente em El Salvador,"
O Istmo, online, March 29, 2016, available at https://oistmo.com/2016/03/29/analise-
o-nascimento-da-inteligencia-contrainsurgente-em-el-salvador/; Costa, *La Policía
Nacional Civil,* 39; Von Santos, "Estudio Historiográfico"; Brian D'Haeseleer, "The
Salvadoran Crucible: American Counterinsurgency in El Salvador, 1979–1992," PhD
thesis, American University, Washington, DC, 2015, 127–28, available at http://hdl.
handle.net/1961/auislandora:12413; Lucrecia Molinari, "Counterinsurgency and
Union Movement in El Salvador (1967–1968)," *Genocide Studies and Preven-*

tion: An International Journal 8, no. 1 (2013): 35. Also see Von Santos, "Estudio Historiográfico," 307; Carlos Gregorio López Bernal, "El Salvador 1960–1992: Reformas, Utopía Revolucionaria y Guerra Civil," in *As Revoluções na América Latina Contemporânea: Entre o Ciclo Revolucionário e as Democracias Restringidas*, eds. Marcela Cristina Quinteros, and Luiz Felipe Viel Moreira (Maringá: Ed. UEM-PGH-História; Medellín: Pulso & Letra: Universidad de Antioquia, 2017), 237–89; and Sprenkels, "La Memoria Militante."

19. William Stanley and Robert Loosle, "El Salvador: The Civilian Police Component of Peace Operations," in *Policing the New World Disorder*, eds. Robert B. Oakley, Eliot M. Goldberg, and Michale J. Dziedzic (Washington, DC: National Defense University Press, 1997); and Ana Margarita Chavez Escobar, "From Authoritarian to Democratic Regimes." As Rex Hudson recalled, "By the mid-1960s, ORDEN was a well-established, nationwide network of peasant informants and paramilitary forces, with a unit in most villages." Hudson, "National Security," 228.

20. Stanley and Loosle, "El Salvador." See also T. David Mason and Dale A. Krane, "The Political Economy of Death Squads: Toward a Theory of the Impact of State-Sanctioned Terror," *International Studies Quarterly* 33, no. 2 (1989), 175–98.

21. In the words of Chuck Call, "Future-oriented institutional reforms were rooted in the past, concerned especially with curbing the power of the armed forces in internal security and intelligence." Charles T. Call, "Democratization, War, and State-Building: Constructing the Rule of Law in El Salvador," *Journal of Latin American Studies* 35, no. 4 (2003): 847.

22. United Nations, General Assembly Security Council. *Peace Agreement*. A/46/664 S/23501 (January 30, 1992). Available at https://peacemaker.un.org/sites/peacemaker.un.org/files/SV_920116_ChapultepecAgreement.pdf.

23. Margaret Popkin, "Building the Rule of Law in Post-War El Salvador," in *El Salvador Implementation of the Peace Accords*, ed. Margarita S. Studemeister (Washington, DC: United States Institute of Peace, Peaceworks No. 38, 2001), 11.

24. Elena Martínez-Barahona, Sonia Rubio-Padilla, Héctor Centeno Martín, and Martha Gutiérrez-Salazar, "La Comisión de la Verdad para El Salvador: Manteniendo la paz a cambio de justicia," *CMI Report*, 2018, 16.

25. United Nations, *Report of the UN Truth Commission on El Salvador*, 137.

26. Grupo Conjunto para la Investigación de Grupos Armados Ilegales con Motivación Política en El Salvador, *Informe Grupo Conjunto para la Investigación de Grupos Armados Ilegales con Motivación Política* (San Salvador: Naciones Unidas, Julio de 1994), 56–57, available at https://www.transparencia.gob.sv/institutions/capres/documents/255838/download; WOLA, *El Estado Cautivo, Crimen Organizado y Derechos Humanos en América Latina* (Washington, DC: Washington Office of Latin America, 2007), 3–12, available at https://www.wola.org/sites/default/files/downloadable/Citizen%20Security/past/el_estado_cautivo%20FINAL.pdf.

27. PNC doctrine was to be founded on principles developed in consensus with the UN. Costa, *La Policía Nacional Civil*, 65–87.

28. William Stanley, "Building New Police Forces in El Salvador and Guatemala: Learning and Counter-Learning," in *Peacebuilding and Police Reform*, eds. Tor Tanke Holm and Espen Barth Eide (London: Frank Cass, 2000), 114, 116–17.

29. Decreto Legislativo No. 269, 25 de junio de 1992, Ley Orgánica de la Policía Nacional Civil. The law included provisions on guiding principles and UN instruments relating to the respect of human rights and incorporated a Code of Conduct for Law Enforcement Officers. One lesson learned was that "new personnel are likely to produce better results than 'recycled' personnel, especially in critical and politically sensitive areas; thereby threatening job security and power of entrenched bureaucrats and tenured police officials." Stanley, "Building New Police Forces," 119. The PNC is still under construction due to problems such as militarization, criminal infiltration, internal power disputes, professionalization, and internal control deficits. Edgar Baltazar Landeros, "La PNC de El Salvador durante los Gobiernos del FMLN," *Tensões Mundiais* 15, no. 28 (2019): 246–47.

30. Gino Costa, "Demilitarizing Public Security: Lessons from El Salvador," in *El Salvador Implementation of the Peace Accords*, ed. Margarita S. Studemeister (Washington, DC: United States Institute of Peace, Peaceworks No. 38, 2001), 20–26. Also see Stanley and Loosle, "El Salvador."

31. See Ortiz Ruiz, "El Salvador 1991–1992."

32. ISSAT, *El Salvador Country Profile.* The involvement of the military in public security to confront those threats, which contradicts the peace agreements and El Salvador constitution, remains the policy choice. HRW, "El Salvador, Events of 2020," *Human Rights Watch World Report 2021.* Available at https://www.hrw.org/world-report/2021/country-chapters/el-salvador. Also see Daira Arana Aguilar and Miguel Adrián Ramírez González, "La Remilitarización de la Seguridad Pública en el Triángulo Norte de Centroamérica y los Esfuerzos Internacionales para Garantizar la Protección de los Derechos Humanos en la Región," in *Contextualizaciones Latinoamericanas: Proceso de Militarización de la Seguridad Pública en América Latina*, eds. Marcos Pablo Moloeznik and Ignacio Medina Núñez (Guadalajara: CUCSH, Universidad de Guadalajara, 2019), 108–12. As such, to confront the *maras*, almost every administration since 1992 opted for Mano Dura policies. On the origins of *maras*, its relationship with organized crime, and mano dura policies, see Sonja Wolf, "El Nexo entre las Maras y el Crimen Organizado," in *Anuario 2012 de Seguridad Regional en América Latina y el Caribe*, eds. Hans Mathieu and Catalina Niño Guarnizo (Bogotá: Friedrich Ebert Stiftung en Colombia, 2012), 252–74. Also see María Eugenia Bonilla Ovallos, "Las Políticas de Seguridad y la Policía Nacional Civil en El Salvador," *Revista Mexicana de Análisis Político y Administración Pública* 4, no. 1 (2015): 63–84. For an account on public security policies in El Salvador between 1994 and 2019, see Viviana García Pinzón and Erika J. Rojas Ospina, "La Política de Seguridad en El Salvador: La Construcción del Enemigo y sus Efectos en la Violencia y el Orden Social," *Revista de Estudios Sociales,* no. 73 (2020): 96–108. Available at https://doi.org/10.7440/res73.2020.08. As such, the Salvadoran armed forces are making up lost ground after the Peace Agreements, increasing their prerogatives, and by 2019 they recorded the largest increase in the defense budget for the entire postcivil war period. Francisco J. Verdes-Montenegro Escánez and Érika M. Rodríguez-Pinzón, "Bukele y las Fuerzas Armadas: Un Tándem que Erosiona los Contrapesos de la Democracia Salvadoreña," in *Pensamiento Propio, Militarización y Seguridad Pública en las Américas*, eds. Thiago Rodrigues, Érika M. Rodríguez-Pinzón,

and Ole Wæver (CRIES, January–June 2020): 223–24. Available at http://www. cries.org/wp-content/uploads/2020/08/012-Montenegro.pdf. President Bukele issued in 2020 a decree establishing special provisions for the participation of the armed forces, in domestic operations, which was reissued for 2021. See República de El Salvador, Presidencia de la República, Decreto N° 36—Disposiciones Especiales Transitorias para la Participación de la Fuerza Armada, en Operaciones de Manten-imiento de la Paz Interna—9 de Marzo de 2020, available at https://www.transpar encia.gob.sv/institutions/capres/documents/352272/download; and República de El Salvador, Presidencia de la República, Decreto N° 46—Reforma a las Disposiciones Especiales Transitorias para la Participación de la Fuerza Armada en Operaciones de Mantenimiento de la Paz Interna—11 de Diciembre de 2020, available at https:// www.transparencia.gob.sv/institutions/mdn/documents/408343/download.

33. Ximena Mercedes Galvez Lima, "El Salvador: High Level of Armed Gang Violence," in *The War Report: Armed Conflicts in 2017*, ed. Annyssa Bellal (Geneva: The Geneva Academy of International Humanitarian Law and Human Rights, 2018), 70. One recent example includes the "Golden Grain Plan" for the protection of the coffee harvest, when the military was assigned patrolling duties—which marked a re-turn to remilitarization. Arana Aguilar, and Ramírez González, "La Remilitarización de la Seguridad Pública en el Triángulo Norte," 108–12. Also see Jeannette Aguilar, "El Rol del Ejército en la Seguridad Interna en el Salvador: Lo Excepcional Conver-tido en Permanente," in *Antología del Pensamiento Crítico Salvadoreño Contem-poráneo*, eds. Loida Mariela Castro, and Roberto Oswaldo López Salazar (Buenos Aires, CLACSO, 2018), 519–51; Edgardo Amaya Cóbar, "Militarización de la Se-guridad Pública en El Salvador, 1992–2012," *URVIO, Revista Latinoamericana de Estudios de Seguridad* 12 (2014): 80.

34. See Lester Cabrera Toledo, "Entre el Cambio y la Inercia Histórica: El Contexto Actual de la Inteligencia Militar en Suramérica," *URVIO, Revista Latino-americana de Estudios de Seguridad* 21 (2017): 8–21; Daniel Sansó-Rubert Pascual, "Inteligencia Militar y Criminalidad Organizada: Retos a Debatir en América Latina," *URVIO, Revista Latinoamericana de Estudios de Seguridad* 21 (2017): 22–38.

35. Chapter I-7 included the following points: "B. The legal regime, staff training, organisational lines, operational guidelines and in general, the doctrine of the State Intelligence Agency shall accord with democratic principles; the concept of State intelligence as a State function for the common good, free from all considerations of politics, ideology or social position or any other discrimination; and strict respect for human rights. C. The activities of the State Intelligence Agency shall be restricted to those required for compiling and analysing information in the general interest, by the means and within the limits authorised by the legal order and, in particular, on the ba-sis of strict respect for human rights. D. The activities of the State Intelligence Agency shall be supervised by the Legislative Assembly, using the oversight mechanisms established by the Constitution. E. Alternative employment and compensation shall be offered to staff currently attached to the National Intelligence Department who are not incorporated into the new State Intelligence Agency. International support shall be sought for that purpose. F. The incorporation into the State Intelligence Agency of staff of the National Intelligence Department who so request shall be permitted only

after rigorous evaluation of their past performance, abilities and capacity to adapt to the new doctrine. Such evaluation shall be made by the Director of the Agency, under the authority of the President of the Republic, with the support of international advisory services and United Nations verification. G. The State Intelligence Agency shall be organised by its Director, under the authority of the President of the Republic." United Nations, General Assembly Security Council. *Peace Agreement*.

36. On alleged wrongdoings, see IRB–Immigration and Refugee Board of Canada, "Activities and Mandate of the State Intelligence Organization (Organismo de Inteligencia del Estado, OIE); whether it continues to operate (1992–March 2002) [SLV38413.E]," March 25, 2002. Available at https://www.refworld.org/docid/3df4beac4.html.

37. https://www.jurisprudencia.gob.sv/DocumentosBoveda/D/1/2000-2009/2001/09/142F.PDF.

38. See IRB, "Activities and Mandate of the State Intelligence Organization."

39. Asamblea Legislativa de la República de El Salvador, Decreto Legislativo N° 554—Ley del Organismo de Inteligencia del Estado–, 21 de Septiembre de 2001. Available at https://www.asamblea.gob.sv/decretos/details/473.

40. República de El Salvador, Presidencia de la República, Decreto N° 47—Reglamento de la Ley del Organismo de Inteligencia del Estado–, 17 de Agosto de 2016. Available at https://www.diariooficial.gob.sv/diarios/do-2016/08-agosto/17-08-2016.pdf.

41. Aguilar, "El Rol del Ejército," 525–26.

42. Edgardo Amaya Cóbar, "Quince Años de Reforma Policial en El Salvador: Avances y Desafíos," *URVIO, Revista Latinoamericana de Estudios de Seguridad* 2 (2007): 134.

43. República de El Salvador, Presidencia de la República. Decreto N° 82–Reglamento de la Ley Orgánica de la Policía Nacional Civil–, 9 de Octubre de 2002. Available at https://www.lamjol.info/index.php/RPSP/article/view/3037/2786. Also see, José Osmín Bogran Acosta, Walter Reymundo Lazo Merino, and Douglas Elenilson Zometa, "El Impacto de la Inteligencia Policial en la Toma de Decisiones Estratégicas, Operativas y Tácticas en la Policía Nacional Civil de El Salvador," *Revista Policía y Seguridad Pública* 5, no. 2 (2015); Carmen Rosa de Leon-Escribano, "Capabilities of Police and Military Forces in Central America: A Comparative Analysis of Guatemala, El Salvador, Honduras and Nicaragua," *Western Hemisphere Security Analysis Center*, Paper 10 (2011), available at https://digitalcommons.fiu.edu/cgi/viewcontent.cgi?article=1009&context=whemsac.

44. Bogran Acosta et al., "El Impacto de la Inteligencia Policial," 369–71.

45. "Nuevos subdirectores y supresión de divisiones anuncia PNC." *Diario 1*, February 10, 2016. Available at http://diario1.com/nacionales/2016/02/nuevos-subdirectores-y-supresion-de-divisiones-anuncia-pnc/. See PNC chart, as of March 2021, at http://www.pnc.gob.sv/portal/page/portal/informativo/institucion/estructura_organizativa/organigrama%20pnc.jpg.

46. Herard Von Santos, "La Formación en Inteligencia Policial: Análisis de la Oferta Educativa de la ANSP," *Revista Policía y Seguridad Pública* 7, no. 2 (2017): 85, 126.

47. Von Santos, "La Formación en Inteligencia Policial," 112.

48. Aguilar, "El Rol del Ejército en la Seguridad Interna en el Salvador," 525.

49. CODEM, "Reseña Histórica de la Escuela Nacional de Inteligencia Militar (ESNACIN)," *Boletín Informativo* no. 95 (San Salvador: Comando de Doctrina y Educación Militar, June 2003). Available at http://codem.mil.sv/index.php/publicaciones/boletin-informativo/boletin-informativos-de-2003/boletin-junio-2003/detail.

50. Markus Schultze-Kraft, *Pacificación y Poder Civil en Centroamérica: Las Relaciones Cívico-Militares en El Salvador, Guatemala y Nicaragua en el Posconflicto* (Bogotá: Editorial Norma, 2005).

51. Bogran Acosta et al., "El Impacto de la Inteligencia Policial," 368–68.

52. Aguilar, "El Rol del Ejército," 526.

53. Jaime López, "Análisis sobre el Manejo de los Gastos Reservados en el Órgano Ejecutivo" (San Salvador: Fundación Nacional para el Desarrollo–FUNDE, Capítulo Nacional de Transparencia Internacional, February 16, 2017), available at http://www.repo.funde.org/1262/; and Jaime Alberto López, Rommel Reynaldo Rodríguez Trejo, and Jessica Estrada. "Manejo de los Gastos Reservados de la Presidencia: Hallazgos y Propuestas" (San Salvador: Fundación Nacional para el Desarrollo -FUNDE, Capítulo Nacional de Transparencia Internacional, 2018), 6–7, available at http://www.repo.funde.org/1472/2/InformeGR.pdf.

54. Gabriela Villarroel, "Reforma al presupuesto 2020 quitó reserva al gasto de OIE," *El Mundo*, December 27, 2019. Available at https://diario.elmundo.sv/reforma-al -presupuesto-2020-quito-reserva-al-gasto-de-oie/.

55. Jimmy Alvarado, "Asamblea recorta $450 millones en gastos opacos del presupuesto 2021," *El Faro.net*, December 29, 2020. Available at https://elfaro.net/es/202012/el_salvador/25113/Asamblea-recorta-$450-millones-en-gastos-opacos -del-presupuesto-2021.htm?st-full_text=all&tpl=11.

56. On ANSP, see Costa, *La Policía Nacional Civil*, 335–54.

57. For a detailed study, see Herard Von Santos, "La Formación en Inteligencia Policial," 81–141. Also see "37 policías de la Subdirección de Inteligencia Policial capacitados." *Academia Nacional de Seguridad Pública*. May 19, 2017. Available at https://www.ansp.gob.sv/37-policias-de-la-subdireccion-de-inteligencia-policial -capacitados/.

58. Von Santos, "La Formación en Inteligencia Policial," 98, 116. The basic course of intelligence describes the general concepts of police intelligence, focused on citizen security, addressing the doctrine that includes principles, values, technical and legal regulations; the organizational structure of police intelligence, as well as the stages of the intelligence cycle framed in the collection, evaluation, collation, analysis, and dissemination. Von Santos, "La Formación en Inteligencia Policial," 111.

59. In 2019, CCMR became Institute for Security Governance.

60. Griselda López, "Informe de comisión especial concluye que no existen vínculos de actores políticos en el alza de los homicidios," Asamblea Legislativa, República de El Salvador, November 28, 2019. Available at https://www.asamblea .gob.sv/index.php/node/9750.

61. Asamblea Legislativa de la República de El Salvador. Decreto Legislativo N° 486—Ley de Amnistía General para la Consolidación de la Paz, 22 de Marzo de 1993.

62. See Jo-Marie Burt, "Transitional Justice in the Aftermath of Civil Conflict: Lessons from Peru, Guatemala and El Salvador." (Washington, DC: Due Process of Law Foundation, 2018); Sabine Kurtenbach, "Judicial Reform—A Neglected Dimension of SSR in el Salvador," *Journal of Intervention and Statebuilding* 13, no. 1 (2019): 57–74; and Florina Cristiana Matei and Andrés de Castro García, "Transitional Justice and Intelligence Democratization," *International Journal of Intelligence and CounterIntelligence* 32, no. 4 (2019): 717–36.

63. Aguilar, "El Rol del Ejército en la Seguridad Interna en el Salvador," 534.

64. Valeria Guzmán and Nelson Rauda, "Casa Presidencial responde al juez que el Ejército no tiene archivos de El Mozote," *El Faro.net*, November 24, 2019, available at https://elfaro.net/es/201911/el_salvador/23810/Casa-Presidencial-responde-al -juez-que-el-Ej%C3%A9rcito-no-tiene-archivos-de-El-Mozote.htm; República de El Salvador, Presidencia de la República; Decreto N° 36—Creación de la Comisión Revisora de Archivos Militares relacionados al Conflicto Armado Interno de El Salvador–, 3 de Octubre de 2019, available at https://www.transparencia.gob.sv/institutions/ capres/documents/319882/download.

65. For example, see "Nueve casos de espionaje en El Salvador," *El Salvador. com*, January 27, 2017, available at https://historico.elsalvador.com/historico/310196/ nueve-casos-de-espionaje-en-el-salvador.html; Wiliam A. Hernández, "Acoso y espionaje aumentaron en los gobiernos del FMLN," *El Salvador.com*, May 11, 2019, available at https://historico.elsalvador.com/historico/592389/acoso-y-espionaje-au mentaron-en-los-gobiernos-del-fmln.html; Laura Jordán, "Desvío de fondos desde penales sirvió para financiar OIE," *La Prensa Gráfica*, July 10, 2021, available at https://www.laprensagrafica.com/elsalvador/Desvio-de-fondos-desde-penales-sirvio -para-financiar-OIE-20210709-0091.html.

66. Bogran Acosta, Lazo Merino, and Elenilson Zometa, "El Impacto de la Inteligencia Policial," 409–10.

67. See Óscar A. Fernández O., "Las Nuevas Políticas de Justicia, Seguridad Pública y Convivencia en El Salvador, 2014–2019," in *Anuario 2014 de Seguridad Regional en América Latina y el Caribe*, ed. Catalina Niño Guarnizo (Bogotá: Friedrich Ebert Stiftung en Colombia, 2014), 192–95.

68. In this connection, a 2021 FUNDE report noted that in terms of legitimacy and transparency, it remains to be expected that the government publishes more disaggregated OIE budget information. Fundación Nacional para el Desarrollo, "De los Gastos Reservados de la Partida 54315 de la Presidencia a los Gastos Reservados del OIE," Documento de Opinión (San Salvador: Fundación Nacional para el Desarrollo/FUNDE— Capítulo Nacional de Transparencia Internacional, 2021), available at http://www.repo .funde.org/id/eprint/1776/. Also see "Opacidad, corrupción, hipocresía," Editorial UCA, Universidad Centroamericana José Simeón Caña, El Salvador, July 26, 2021. Available at https://noticias.uca.edu.sv/editoriales/opacidad-corrupcion-hipocresia#.

69. Chavez Escobar, "From Authoritarian to Democratic Regimes," 75.

70. See María Eugenia Bonilla Ovallos and Jerónimo Ríos Sierra, "Luces y Sombras en la Profesionalización de la Policía Nacional Civil de El Salvador tras los Acuerdos de Paz de Chapultepec (1992–2017)," *Revista UNISCI/UNISCI Journal* 55 (2021): 131–57. In addition, with regard to the exercise of civil control over the armed

forces, as John Berg puts it, "Democratic oversight in El Salvador requires a reform of its Ministry of Defense to place more civilian leaders in the chain-of-command between the president and military generals." John R. Berg, "Insurgents to Presidents: Contemporary Civil-Military Relations in Brazil, El Salvador, and Uruguay," master's thesis, Naval Postgraduate School, Monterey, California, 2015. Available at http://hdl.handle.net/10945/48552.

70. A Human Rights Watch report stated, "Since taking office, President Nayib Bukele has undermined basic democratic checks and balances. In February 2020, he entered the Legislative Assembly with armed soldiers in an apparent effort to intimidate legislators into approving a loan for security forces. He has publicly defied three rulings by the Constitutional Chamber of the Supreme Court prohibiting arrests for violations of a Covid-19-related lockdown Bukele had decreed." HRW, "El Salvador, Events of 2020."

71. Alexander H. Joffe, "Dismantling Intelligence Agencies," *Crime, Law and Social Change* 32, (1999): 325–26.

Part III

NON-DEMOCRATIC REGIMES

Chapter Fifteen

Venezuela

Jacques (Jake) Suyderhoud
and Florina Cristiana Matei

Over a politically turbulent century that saw Venezuela expel military dictatorships, struggle during democratic openings, labor toward democratic consolidation, and then conclude with a populist surge that initiated the country's
retreat to authoritarianism, the predominant role of the nation's intelligence
services waivered only slightly. The common priority of Venezuelan intelligence institutions throughout this era, under whichever title conferred upon
them by the leadership of the day, has been to target the political opposition.
Beginning in the first decades of the 1900s, Venezuela's military leadership
used security forces to identify and eliminate resistant political organizations. Counterintuitively, despite the fall of military rule and the advance of
participatory politics in the century's second half, such democrats as Rómulo
Betancourt frequently turned to a lightly regulated intelligence apparatus to
secure their regimes against political foes. However, despite the consistency
of the mission, the capability and reliability of intelligence services to neutralize political opponents was transformed under the leadership of Hugo Chávez
and Nicolas Maduro. Following a failed military coup in 2002, Chávez
purged the government of disloyal agents and increased his direct control of
the intelligence services, looking to constrain not just opponents to his rule
but also independent and dissenting voices within his own government.

This chapter outlines the evolution of Venezuela's intelligence services
over the last century and describes the efforts to use intelligence institutions
to limit the maneuvering capacity of opposition movements. The chapter
first describes how, during the era of military rule, Venezuelan intelligence
was built from a tradition of using state security forces to target political
opponents. It then details reforms during the democratic era that did little to
increase oversight and accountability, often only providing new justifications
of old efforts to fortify political power. However, it was the reforms during

the Chávez and Maduro eras that made Venezuelan intelligence services a more effective instrument in the attempt to guarantee the survival of the governing regime. Through the consolidation of the intelligence services under the president's control and amid the establishment of parallel intelligence structures (including the empowering of foreign intelligence personnel), the reforms during these eras successfully reined in a praetorian military, neutralizing the traditional enablers of regime change in Venezuela. Instead of the coups and political volatility that checkered Venezuela's twentieth century, modern intelligence-sector reforms have provided stability to a regime that has lost both democratic legitimacy and the capacity to provide basic services to its citizens.

THE EVOLUTION OF INTELLIGENCE UNDER MILITARY RULE

The use of state security forces to eliminate political opposition began early in the first decades of the twentieth century. General Juan Vincente Gómez came to power in 1908 and used state security forces to help him consolidate political control. His forces quickly purged the leading political organizations of Venezuelan society, resulting in the dismantling of each of Venezuela's traditional political parties established in the nineteenth century.[1] Political debate survived only in academic hallways and underground movements. Stripped of the ability to assemble openly, the political parties that weathered this period were forced to develop in secrecy, relying on their own internal intelligence networks to avoid state persecution.[2]

A by-product of state-led repression was an increased resilience of the political movements that survived the political prohibition era. The Democratic Action (AD) political party, which would turn into a leading party during Venezuela's democratic era, grew from its underground roots to garner broad popular support throughout the country. The organization retained a hierarchical structure, and maintaining the strict party discipline that was required to protect its leadership from state persecution—for fear of recurring political discrimination—AD developed methods to organize despite being forced into the shadows. In 1945, mid-level military officers, disgruntled with the stagnation of the country under its latest military leader, General Isaías Medina Angarita, looked to collaborate with AD to lend legitimacy to their efforts to overthrow the ruling regime.[3] AD successfully mobilized support for the coup and, in 1947, again capitalized on its popularity to dominate Venezuela's first national election. However, the ability to organize underground did not translate to an ability to secure consensus while in power. Ambitious and unpopular reforms pushed forward by AD leaders fractured support for the government, and in 1948 the democracy was again overthrown by a military that was developing an increasingly praetorian instinct.[4]

Following this second coup in 1948, the new political leadership returned to the traditional practice of using the state's security apparatus to attack political threats to regime authority. Colonel Marco Pérez Jiménez, who also was instrumental in the uprising that overthrew Medina in 1945, emerged from the 1948 coup effort to become president. As president, he empowered the newly formed National Security Service (SN) to be his tool to constrain the political opposition.[5] Although de jure SN was tasked to be apolitical, de facto it was the regime's political police, focused on ensuring internal security and monitoring dissent from both citizens and members of the armed forces.[6] Political parties returned as central targets of the military regime. AD, as well as the Venezuelan Communist Party (PCV), were outlawed immediately. Ironically, even political parties such as COPEI (the Christian Socialist Party) and URD (the Democratic Republican Union), which had initially supported the coup, found themselves under strict surveillance and soon were banned by Pérez Jiménez.[7] Venezuela's political parties once again found their leaders exiled and their members persecuted by the state.[8]

Under the leadership of Pedro Estrada (SN Member), a well-resourced SN became a prominent institution in the Pérez Jiménez government. SN grew to a force of five thosand, responsible for intelligence collection and processing as well as running intelligence-based operations. Through these operations, the organization quickly gained notoriety as a violent check against political opponents.[9] However, SN was not just an effective tool against political dissidents. Its size, operational capacity, and prominent position in the Pérez Jiménez government made it an establishment institution that rivaled even the military. As Deborah Norden describes, "SN became synonymous with repression in Venezuela, as it routinely utilized torture and was empowered to arrest political opponents, both civilian and military . . . [it] served not only as a rival to the armed forces, but as a potential enemy."[10] However, though SN grew strong enough to compete with the military, it was not granted the authority and access required to infiltrate it. When Pérez Jiménez became ineffective and lost popularity, SN was not positioned to stop the military from acting against the regime.

In 1958, a military-led coup removed Pérez Jiménez and again installed a democratic regime. This time, however, the leading democratic parties concluded that their long-term survival, and the survival of the entire democratic system, would depend on their commitment to cooperate with one another. To ensure mutual support, AD, COPEI, and URD joined in an agreement to proportionally share power regardless of individual electoral outcomes.[11] The *Pact of Punto Fijo*, as the arrangement was called, stabilized the government through the country's democratic transition. Yet, those on the periphery of the compact were viewed as threats to the democratic movement. In response, the government of Rómulo Betancourt turned to its own intelligence networks to guarantee both the president's protection and the protection of Venezuela's inchoate democratic regime.

INTELLIGENCE REFORMS DURING THE DEMOCRATIC ERA

The persecution of each *Pact* signatory at the hands of SN did not dissuade the new coalition government from turning to intelligence institutions themselves once in power. Rómulo Betancourt came to office in 1959 facing a guerrilla campaign led by Venezuela's communist party (which had been excluded from the *Pact of Punto Fijo*), terrorist attacks at the hands of extreme leftist groups, and assassination attempts against him from the far right.[12] Although now in power, Betancourt viewed these attacks as a continuation of the battle for democratic survival. Just as the leading democrats had trusted their own internal intelligence systems in the struggle against Pérez Jiménez, the new government again looked to intelligence institutions to provide protection against a determined political opposition.[13]

Regrettably, the intelligence services during the democratic transition were often no better at respecting human rights than their predecessors had been. Though Betancourt replaced the notorious SN when he became president in 1959, it did not take long for the new service, known as the General Directorate of the Police (Digepol), to likewise become known for its abusive tactics. Digepol maintained SN's modus operandi and an anticommunist mission and was soon accused of politically motivated arrests, mistreatment of prisoners, and other actions antithetical to democratic governance.[14] Nevertheless, President Betancourt dismissed criticism of the intelligence service and instead asserted that a democratically elected president had the right to designate undemocratic enemies and use all available avenues to counter such threats.[15]

Despite the rule-by-consensus arrangement delineated under the *Pact of Punto Fijo*, there were few institutional checks to limit how Betancourt's used the country's intelligence assets. The legislature granted Betancourt significant leeway as the administration attempted to consolidate the new government, including the authority to suspend guarantees of personal and civil liberties, and neglected to take any formal oversight role over the regime's new intelligence agency.[16] Without fundamental institutional reform and oversight, the intelligence services continued the political repression that had been common during the authoritarian era.[17]

Nevertheless, during the democratic era, public outcry became a tool that could modify the practices of the intelligence services. Digepol's egregious human rights abuses made the agency extremely unpopular, especially as Venezuela's internal communist threat dissipated at the end of the 1960s.[18] As democracy in Venezuela consolidated and the presidency peacefully passed to the COPEI-led opposition and Rafael Caldera in 1968, public demands for intelligence reform grew.[19] Caldera again reorganized the intelligence services when he came to office, replacing Digepol with the Directorate for Intelligence and Prevention Services (DISIP). DISIP was instructed to divest from political operations, with a charge to focus on criminals rather than political opponents.[20] Despite this new mission, Caldera's top-down reforms did not change the nature of the intelligence services, and abuse remained common. Police operations launched during the Caldera administration, such as the anti-crime offensive *Operación Vanguardia*, again resulted in excesses that provoked popular anger, while reports of extrajudicial killings of leftist leaders by intelligence agents continued into the Carlos Pérez administration that followed. However, public outcry during the democratic era could be sufficient to prompt congressional investigations into intelligence overreach and cause operations such as *Vanguardia* to be abandoned or complicit intelligence leadership to be held to account for their actions.[21]

Abuses conducted by the intelligence services during the democratic era were also constrained by a fractured organizational structure. To avoid granting an exorbitant amount of unchecked power to a single individual or institution, as had been the case with SN under Pedro Estrada, the intelligence apparatus during the *Punto Fijo* era (1958–1998) was intentionally decentralized.[22] The Military Intelligence Directorate (DIM) fell under the Defense Ministry, while the Technical Judicial Police (PTJ) fell under the Minister of Justice.[23] In addition, the National Security Council, under the presidency, had its own intelligence capacity.[24] With the DISIP in the Ministry of the Interior, state intelligence assets during the democratic era were divided into four competing directorates, answerable to separate ministerial leadership. Tasked with unique responsibilities, all four agencies would present their opinions of the most pressing intelligence concerns facing the country.[25] The various intelligence services became rivals, competing for influence in the government and stressing their vision in the daily competition for resources.[26] Unfortunately, despite the structural limitations, the formal oversight of the intelligence services outside of the executive branch remained limited, allowing the president wide latitude in how to utilize the government's competing intelligence institutions.[27]

DISARMING THE PRAETORIAN
GUARD: INTELLIGENCE UNDER CHÁVEZ

Hugo Chávez rose to power in 1999 as an outsider, suspicious of Venezuela's political establishment and opposed to the country's traditional policy positions. To an extent not seen since Rómulo Betancourt, Chávez worked to remove potential political opponents[28] from Venezuela's intelligence institutions.[29] Chávez instructed DISIP's head to rid the agency of foreign influence, including Cuban exiles and Israelis whom the DISIP had long employed.[30] By 2001, the CIA cut its ties with DISIP, ending a relationship that spanned over thirty years.[31]

Following a failed uprising in 2002, Chávez redoubled his efforts to purge hostile political forces from government institutions. Aware of Venezuela's history of military-led coups (having organized a failed attempt himself as a colonel in 1992), Chávez was determined to eliminate the threat for good. Using voter registration data to determine allegiance, Chávez purged from his intelligence agencies any officers considered to be insufficiently loyal to his regime.[32] He then turned to these filtered intelligence services to enforce loyalty across the other institutions of government, in particular the military. The mission of the DIM was reoriented; it no longer prioritized Colombian military assessments, but rather was tasked to root out disloyalty in Venezuela's own armed services.[33] While nominally still under the Ministry of Defense, Chávez, a former military officer himself, tasked the DIM directly, taking personal responsibility for loyalty within the ranks.[34] Additionally, the Ministry of Justice was folded into the Ministry of the Interior, and the PTJ was rebranded the Center for Political Investigation and Criminal Containment (CPCC), directed to act in a supporting role to the DISIP.[35] Through these reforms, the horizontal separations of the intelligence services softened, allowing Chávez both more direct access to intelligence information and more direct control over the functions of his intelligence services.

As Chávez fought to eliminate disloyalty, Venezuela began to adopt practices associated with the intelligence services of Fidel Castro's Cuba. Though DISIP leadership had initially rebuffed assistance from Cuban intelligence offered shortly after Chávez's inauguration, Chávez's policy decisions soon directed reforms that mimicked Cuban methods.[36] In 2001, Chávez created the *Círculos Bolivarianos*, an organization with the stated purpose to "organize civil society, raise political consciousness to safeguard and widen the process of change, encourage the participation of all communities in government, and mobilize the community to confront opposition and to facilitate the meeting of social needs."[37] Opponents of the *Círculos*, however, argued that it was a tool that copied Cuba's "Committees for the Defense of the Revolution," serving as a means to encourage citizens to spy on each other on behalf of the Chávez regime.[38]

Eventually Chávez would formally import Cuban assistance to augment surveillance of Venezuelan dissidents. By 2003, Cuban intelligence advisors filtered into Venezuela, gaining a trusted position in Chávez's inner circle.[39] Rather than solely training Venezuelan intelligence forces, the Cuban advisors in the country developed a direct link to the Venezuelan president, offering intelligence assessments autonomous of, and often excluding, Venezuela's own agencies. By 2006, U.S. analysis indicated that Cuban intelligence officials maintained direct access to Chávez, providing their own information that was for the president's eyes only.[40]

In 2008, months after a constitutional referendum to remove presidential term limits failed at the polls, Chávez turned to his revolutionary mentor, Fidel Castro, for advice on how to better secure his position in power.[41] This cooperation launched Venezuelan intelligence down two major paths of intelligence reform. Using his decree power, Chávez instituted reforms that sought to replace the DISIP and the DIM with two new agencies, the General Intelligence Office and the General Counterintelligence Office, both of which would fall under his personal control.[42] The decree, drafted behind closed doors without input from the assembly or general public, also mandated that citizens and judges comply with requests to assist the new agencies and other loyalist groups—failure to do so would be punishable with up to six years in prison.[43] Opponents again vociferously noted the similarities of these policies to the internal intelligence practices of Cuba, assessing the motive to be an attempt to force the citizen-on-citizen intelligence gathering that they feared first began with the *Círculos*. Popular backlash was severe, with former Chávez allies also declaring the new laws to be "purely Cuban-style policy."[44]

Once again, as earlier in the democratic era, public backlash redirected intelligence policy and rolled back what popular majorities felt was a significant intelligence overreach. The harsh press and critical public sentiment forced Chávez to rescind the decrees. As Romero then described in the *New York Times*, "In some ways, the changes would merely refine the control Mr. Chávez already exerts over intelligence operations."[45] Community activist organizations had already become popular intelligence collectors, and previous reorganization had already consolidated Chávez's control over the intelligence services. Moreover, the superficial formal name changes would come in short order too. In 2010, the DISIP was rebranded the Bolivarian Intelligence Service (SEBIN), and in 2011 Chávez restructured the DIM, creating two military intelligence services: the General Military Intelligence Directorate (DGIM) and the General Military Counterintelligence Directorate (DGCIM), explicitly reinforcing the military's domestic counterintelligence priority.[46]

However, the deference to popular will that caused Chávez to back off his public decrees did not stop him from pursuing intelligence reforms surreptitiously. Concurrent with the failed May 2008 effort, Chávez was busy formalizing ties with Cuban intelligence that would increase his ability to guarantee loyalty within the ranks of the Venezuelan military. The first of two agreements between Venezuelan and Cuban defense ministers restructured the DIM in May 2008, promoting the creation of new units within the service and initiating training of DIM officers in Havana.[47] The second agreement created a committee of Cuban military experts called the GRUCE (the Coordination and Liaison Group of the Republic of Cuba) that would send Cuban advisors to Venezuela to train and inspect military units.[48]

While there was significant backlash to the public decrees on intelligence, the secret arrangements between Venezuela and Cuba continued unobserved and unchecked. In Cuba, a country with its own interest in safeguarding the Chávez regime to preserve the flow of oil assistance, DIM officers were indoctrinated with the mission to "infiltrate and control the military."[49] Cuban-trained military counterintelligence forces were instructed to train and live with their military counterparts, using internal surveillance and the threat of arrest and torture to dissuade military officers from rebelling against the regime.[50] The result gave the intelligence services, as described by a former DGCIM officer, an "iron grip" over the military.[51]

INTELLIGENCE AFTER CHÁVEZ

President Nicolas Maduro continued with reforms that pushed the intelligence services even further under the president's direct control. In April 2013, a month after assuming the presidency following Chávez's death in March, Maduro transferred authority over SEBIN from the Ministry of the Interior, Justice, and Peace to the vice president.[52] Maduro then created the Strategic Center for Homeland Security and Protection (CESSPA) at the beginning of 2014 to serve as a mandated collection point for all sensitive information accumulated by the various intelligence agencies.[53] In 2015, DGCIM was again reformed through presidential decree, emphasizing its primary roles to protect the president and secure the armed forces from subversive elements, whether internally or externally sourced.[54] These reforms brought the institutions primarily responsible for surveilling political dissent into even closer orbit to the presidency and ensured that any information warning of destabilizing movements would be presented to the president unfiltered.

Still, even these reforms have been augmented with back-channel connections that have provided Maduro more direct personal control over various aspects of the intelligence apparatus. Maduro has maintained direct lines of communication with SEBIN leadership that facilitate personal tasking of the agency's director general.[55] Likewise, a Special Affairs Unit has been created outside the DGCIM's formal structure, allowing the president to circumvent formal lines of authority to provide individual instructions to unit-level leadership.[56] The president reportedly has also established a separate intelligence processing center in the executive that has allowed intelligence to flow directly to the him rather than through CESSPA, which, as an institution under the Ministry of the Interior, is subject to a filter that Maduro appears eager to avoid.[57]

The result of these changes has been the creation of an intelligence system that possesses few institutional checks on its practices. Curti describes in her 2015 comparative analysis of South American intelligence systems that Venezuela's intelligence services are unique in that they have no legally defined control mechanisms.[58] Instead, as Ramos Pismataro elaborates, lacking an institutional control structure, SEBIN has "acquired a role of particular relevance in the political control of the regime, participating actively in controversial activities like the search for political opponents, even denying orders for the release of the accused for political reasons."[59] SEBIN was chartered with the responsibility "to carry out intelligence and civil counterintelligence activities to neutralize real or potential threats to the Venezuelan State, regardless of whether they are internal or external."[60] However, with this range of tasks, SEBIN, as Ramos notes, "participates in police actions for citizen security, in operations led by the DGIM, and in operations of the DGCIM, demonstrating the absence of a clear distinction in the roles and responsibilities of civil and military intelligence and counterintelligence organizations."[61] Devoid of civilian oversight and clear delineation of the roles of the intelligence services, Ramos continues, institutions such as SEBIN "initially built as a civil [intelligence body], ends up under military command and is converted into another instrument of the Government, partisan and focused on political and social control to preserve the revolution from its supposed internal and external enemies."[62]

Maduro also has diversified the alternate intelligence-collection sources that both supplement and check the official intelligence institutions of the state. One such institution is the "Special Brigade against the Actions of Groups Generating Violence." This group, formed in 2014, falls under the Ministry of the Interior but answers directly to the president; it has the role of "coordinating, analyzing, evaluating, organizing, directing, executing and collecting the information . . . to neutralize and control the activities of groups that generate violence."[63] Also in 2014, Maduro created the "System of Protection for Peace," designed as popular intelligence networks to report on criminal groups in social and cultural, economic, and political spheres.[64] This institution continues the popular intelligence tradition grown from the *Círculos Bolivarianos* and also extended to the Bolivarian Militia, which has become its own counterweight to the traditional military institutions. The militia, according to a UN report, "is made up of citizen volunteers, who assist the FANB [National Bolivarian Armed Forces] in the 'integral defense' of the nation and contribute to the system of intelligence and counter-intelligence."[65] Former intelligence officers also claim that Maduro has outsourced some surveillance and detention activities to partisan *colectivos* to enable intelligence work that can be accomplished extrajudicially.[66] Such reforms have caused a proliferation of intelligence agencies with a primary allegiance to the Maduro regime.

The politicization of the intelligence services and the lack of institutional oversight has again encouraged a politically repressive environment in Venezuela. An investigation by the UN has concluded that SEBIN and DGCIM have, in particular, played leading roles in the targeted repression of dissidents, including "political leaders at the forefront of protests, opposition politicians and military dissidents accused of rebellion, plotting coups or other conspiracies."[67] SEBIN has not only targeted political activists, such as Leopoldo López, for arrest without a warrant, but the intelligence service has also used its power to detain currently sitting and democratically elected officials, such as the mayor of Caracas, Antonio Ledezma.[68] According to a 2021 Organization of American States (OAS) report on Venezuela, "40% of the 80 opposition mayors in the country had been victims of targeted persecution as part of a systematic state practice of repression."[69] Unchecked and unsupervised operations directed by the president have targeted high-level officials, extinguishing an alleged surge in coup attempts against the government (according to the Maduro administration, growing in number from three between 2014 and 2016 to at least sixteen between 2017 and 2020).[70]

The transformation of Venezuelan intelligence into a political tool has resulted in the abuse of the Venezuelan population. Without judicial oversight or authorization, arbitrary detentions of political dissidents have become common and systematic.[71] Amnesty International details the "arbitrary measures being used by the Venezuelan state security forces . . . aimed at obstructing freedom of expression, association, and political participation."[72] The report specifically calls out SEBIN's practice of arresting political dissidents without a legal justification and detaining them even when ordered by the judiciary to release them.[73] Independent reports also have noted state-sanctioned torture, providing evidence that Maduro is not only aware of this abuse but that he explicitly orders such transgressions.[74]

CONCLUSION

Venezuela's intelligence culture is a culture of extreme politicization. The political opposition has constantly found itself centered in the sights of Venezuela's intelligence services. From the military regimes that opened the twentieth century, to the democrats that stabilized Venezuela while elsewhere Latin America revolutionaries were battling autocrats, Venezuela's intelligence services have been used as a tool to strike down political opponents and to fortify the governing regime. However, none of Venezuela's leaders has utilized intelligence for parochial interests as effectively as Hugo Chávez and Nicolas Maduro.

Venezuela's twenty-first century leaders have created an intelligence apparatus firmly built around their own personalistic leadership. By centralizing control of the intelligence services and proliferating the sources of intelligence outside traditional institutions, modern intelligence in Venezuela has become highly politicized, marked by its loyalty to the current governing class rather than to the civic or military institutions to which they belong. Indeed, the charters of the leading intelligence services force a tension between state security and the threat of destabilizing forces brought by the country's own internal civil and military enemies. The enlistment of partisan forces loyal to the administration and Cuban intelligence professionals dedicated to preserving Cuba's oil lifeline from Venezuela have fortified the ties from intelligence sources to the executive.[75] Such institutions, loyal above all to the current regime, serve as a check on the competing forces from within the traditional chambers of Venezuelan power brokers.

As such, one of the most significant results of the politicization of the intelligence institutions has been the effective dismantling of the armed forces as a praetorian institution. Venezuelan counterintelligence agents and their Cuban counterparts have infiltrated the ranks of the armed services to an unprecedented extent, creating an environment of fear and intimidation that has paralyzed the traditional praetorian tendencies of the Venezuelan military. Venezuela historically has relied on the support of its military to overturn unpopular and undemocratic regimes. However, under the watchful eye of the intelligence services, dissidents within the military have been arrested, tortured, and purged. After decades of attempts, the common ambition of Venezuela's presidents to coup-proof their regimes finally may have been realized. By this measure, at least, Maduro has been exceptional.

NOTES

1. José Molina and Carmen Pérez, "Evolution of the Party System in Venezuela, 1946–1993," *Journal of Interamerican Studies and World Affairs* 40, no. 2 (Summer 1998): 5, http://search.proquest.com/docview/59879034/.

2. Michael Coppedge, "Venezuela: Democratic despite Presidentialism," in *The Failure of Presidential Democracy*, ed. Juan J. Linz and Arturo Valenzuela (Baltimore: The Johns Hopkins University Press, 1994), 401; David Myers, "The Institutions of Intelligence in Venezuela: Lessons from 45 Years of Democracy," *Ibero-Americana* 33, no. 1 (2003): 90, https://www.readcube.com/articles/10.16993%2Fibero.164.

3. General Eleazar López Contreas took over the presidency following Gómez's death in 1935. In 1941, General Isaías Medina Angarita succeeded López. Increased investment in the military during these administrations led to a more educated and ambitious junior-officer corps that was dissatisfied with its uneducated senior leadership. This rift contributed to the *Acción Democractica*-supported coup in 1945.

4. Jacques Suyderhoud, "Designed to Fail: Proportional Representation and Presidentialism in Latin America" (master's thesis, Naval Postgraduate School, 2020), 68, https://calhoun.nps.edu/handle/10945/65450.

5. Myers, "The Institutions of Intelligence in Venezuela: Lessons from 45 Years of Democracy," 85; SN was a product of the 1938 "Ley Del Servicio Nacional de Seguridad," and reorganized into the form that Pérez Jiménez inherited it by the Revolutionary Junta, following the 1945 coup d'état.

6. Deborah L. Norden, "Venezuela: Coup-Proofing from Pérez Jiménez to Maduro," *Oxford Research Encyclopedia of Politics* (January 22, 2021): 5, https://doi.org/10.1093/acrefore/9780190228637.013.1955.

7. Molina and Perez, "Evolution of the Party System in Venezuela, 1946–1993," 7; Norden, "Venezuela: Coup-Proofing from Pérez Jiménez to Maduro," 5.

8. Molina and Perez, "Evolution of the Party System in Venezuela, 1946–1993," 7; Norden, "Venezuela," 3.

9. Myers, "The Institutions of Intelligence in Venezuela," 85.

10. Norden, "Venezuela," 5.

11. Suyderhoud, "Designed to Fail: Proportional Representation and Presidentialism in Latin America," 69. As Suyderhoud notes, "The Pact arranged that cabinet posts, congressional leadership positions, and governorships (which the president had the right to appoint) would be divided proportionally among the three parties regardless of which party won the upcoming elections. A common political program was also adopted to secure against extreme partisanship, and pledges for inclusionary commissions and decentralized public administration were made to ensure that the interests of civil society were reflected in the government." Although the major parties unified under the 1958 *Pact of Punto Fijo*, democratic transition was still vulnerable.

12. Coppedge, "Venezuela: Democratic despite Presidentialism," 412; Kevin Ginter, "Truth and Mirage: The Cuba-Venezuela Security and Intelligence Alliance," *International Journal of Intelligence and CounterIntelligence* 26, no. 2 (2013): 220, https://doi.org/10.1080/08850607.2013.758003; Stephen G. Rabe, "The Caribbean Triangle: Betancourt, Castro, and Trujillo and U.S. Foreign Policy, 1958–1963,"

Diplomatic History 20, no. 1 (Winter 1996): 60–64. Although elected just as Fidel Castro's revolutionaries were claiming victory, Betancourt was less concerned over Cuban calls for hemispheric revolution than the immediate threat from Rafael Trujillo in the Dominican Republic, whose anti-Betancourt policies included ordering a nearly successful assassination attempt by car bomb in June 1960. Trujillo, who had supported his dictatorial counterpart in Venezuela, Pérez Jiménez, feuded with Betancourt since Venezuela's short-lived democratic period from 1945–1948. For Trujillo, Betancourt was a product of the leftist revolutionary movement spreading throughout the region. Betancourt viewed Trujillo unfavorably as a symbol of the authoritarianism that the anti-communist movement had made acceptable. However, Betancourt, despite some communist sympathies in his youth, was also determined to prevent Cuban influence from undermining his program of moderate reform. After Trujillo's own assassination in 1961, Betancourt's view on the Castro regime hardened. He saw the Cuban influence in the street demonstrations of leftist movements in the country and broke relations with Cuba in November of that year.

13. Myers, "The Institutions of Intelligence in Venezuela," 90.

14. Judith Ewell, *Venezuela: A Century of Change* (Stanford: Stanford University Press, 1984), 129.

15. Ewell, *Venezuela: A Century of Change*, 129.

16. Ewell, *Venezuela: A Century of Change*, 129; Mark Ungar, *Elusive Reform: Democracy and Rule of Law in Latin America* (Boulder: Lynne Rienner Publishers, 2002), 100; Myers, "The Institutions of Intelligence in Venezuela," 88–89.

17. Mark Ungar, *Elusive Reform: Democracy and Rule of Law in Latin America*, 107.

18. By 1968, the guerrilla war led by the Venezuelan communist party (PCV) had mostly ended. PCV was legalized in 1969, MIR by 1973. Ewell, *Venezuela: A Century of Change*, 170; Coppedge, 400.

19. Ewell, *Venezuela: A Century of Change*, 170.

20. Ginter, "Truth and Mirage," 223; Ungar, *Elusive Reform*, 97.

21. Ewell, *Venezuela: A Century of Change*, 170, 205.

22. Myers, "The Institutions of Intelligence in Venezuela," 86.

23. Myers, "The Institutions of Intelligence in Venezuela," 88; Ungar, *Elusive Reform*, 97; DIM replaced the Armed Services Information Service in 1971 and the PTJ was established in 1958.

24. Myers, "The Institutions of Intelligence in Venezuela," 87.

25. DIM was tasked with collecting intelligence on military threats to the country and its borders, while PTJ focused on national-level criminal activity and drug activity and the National Security Council assessed internal and external threats.

26. Myers, "The Institutions of Intelligence in Venezuela," 88.

27. Myers, "The Institutions of Intelligence in Venezuela," 89.

28. Agents, both domestic and foreign, not attached to his leftist movement.

29. Myers, "The Institutions of Intelligence in Venezuela," 91.

30. Ginter, "Truth and Mirage," 228; Myers, "The Institutions of Intelligence in Venezuela," 91.

31. Myers, "The Institutions of Intelligence in Venezuela," 87; Ginter, "Truth and Mirage," 223.

32. Simon Romero, "Chávez Decree Tightens Hold on Intelligence," *New York Times*, June 3, 2008, A1, ProQuest.

33. Romero, "Chávez Decree Tightens Hold on Intelligence," A1; Myers, "The Institutions of Intelligence in Venezuela," 92.

34. Myers, "The Institutions of Intelligence in Venezuela," 93.

35. Myers, "The Institutions of Intelligence in Venezuela," 92.

36. Maye Primera, "¡Patria o muerte! Pero ¿mi patria o la tuya?" *El País*, May 24, 2010, https://elpais.com/diario/2010/05/24/internacional/1274652005_850215.html.

37. Cristóbal Valencia Ramírez, "Venezuela's Bolivarian Revolution: Who Are the Chavistas?" *Latin American Perspectives* 32, no. 3 (2005): 86, http://www.jstor.org/stable/30040243.

38. United States Bureau of Citizenship and Immigration Services, "Venezuela: Information on Círculos Bolivarianos," April 30, 2002, https://www.refworld.org/country,,USCIS,,VEN,,3dec9b4b4,0.html; Ginter, "Truth and Mirage," 229; Myers, "The Institutions of Intelligence in Venezuela," 92.

39. Primera, "¡Patria o muerte! Pero ¿mi patria o la tuya?"; Angus Berwick, "Imported Repression: How Cuba Taught Venezuela to Quash Military Dissent," Reuters, August 22, 2019, https://www.reuters.com/investigates/special-report/venezuela-cuba-military/.

40. Berwick, "Imported Repression."

41. Berwick, "Imported Repression"

42. Romero, "Chavez Decree Tightens Hold on Intelligence," A1.

43. Romero, "Chavez Decree Tightens Hold on Intelligence," A1.

44. Romero, "Chavez Decree Tightens Hold on Intelligence," A1.

45. Romero, "Chavez Decree Tightens Hold on Intelligence," A1.

46. Samanta Curti, *Reformas de Los Sistemas De Inteligencia En America del Sur*, (Konrad Adenauer Stiftung, 2015), 10, http://www.kas.de/wf/doc/17940-1442-1-30.pdf; Berwick, "Imported Repression."

47. Berwick, "Imported Repression." These three-month trainings supported as many as forty DIM officers at a time.

48. Berwick, "Imported Repression."

49. Berwick, "Imported Repression."

50. Harold Trinkunas, "The Transformation of the Venezuelan Bolivarian Armed Force under Chávez and Maduro," in *The Routledge Handbook of Civil-Military Relations*, ed. Florina Cristiana Matei, Carolyn Halladay, and Thomas C. Bruneau (New York: Routledge, 2021), 256, 260.

51. Berwick, "Imported Repression."

52. United Nations Humans Rights Council, *Detailed Findings of the Independent International Factfinding Mission on the Bolivarian Republic of Venezuela*, A/HRC/45/CRP.11 (September 15, 2020), 58. Under its organic law, the structure below the vice president includes a director general (appointed by the president), the subdirector general, the secretary general, and the unit-level directors for the major directorates.

53. United Nations Humans Rights Council, *Detailed Findings*, 58.

54. Presidential Decree No. 1605, *Official Gazette No. 40,599*, February 10, 2015, art. 2, http://www.franciscosantana.net/2016/02/reglamento-organico-de-la-direccion.html.

55. United Nations Humans Rights Council, *Detailed Findings*, 383.

56. United Nations Humans Rights Council, *Detailed Findings*, 386.

57. United Nations Humans Rights Council, *Detailed Findings*, 383.

58. *Curti, Reformas de Los Sistemas De Inteligencia En America del Sur*, 33.

59. Francesca Ramos Pismataro, "Los militares y el deterioro democrático en Venezuela" [The military and the deterioration of democracy in Venezuela], *Estudios Políticos* 53 (May 2018): 268, https://doi.org/10.17533/udea.espo.n53a12.

60. Presidential Decree No. 9,446, *Official Gazette No. 40,153*, April 1, 2013, art. 3, https://www.franciscosantana.net/2013/04/reglamento-organico-del-servicio.html.

61. Ramos Pismataro, "Los militares," 268.

62. Ramos Pismataro, "Los militares," 269.

63. "Nicolás Maduro crea brigada especial en Venezuela," June 27, 2014, América TeVé, video, 2:14, https://www.youtube.com/watch?v=IQlf0zeY7a4.

64. United Nations Humans Rights Council, *Detailed Findings*, 64.

65. United Nations Humans Rights Council, *Detailed Findings*, 51.

66. United Nations Humans Rights Council, *Detailed Findings*, 383; Chávez (and Maduro) gave the Bolivarian militia (which was made up by civilian volunteers who operated under the umbrella of the ministry of defense) together with the *colectivos* (community-based armed groups that aimed at safeguarding the Bolivarian "revolution") the military counterbalancing role and tasked DISIP with keeping tabs on political opponents.

67. United Nations Humans Rights Council, *Detailed Findings*, 66.

68. "Venezuela's Regime, Tyranny Looms" *The Economist*, vol. 414, issue 8927 (February 28, 2015): 29.

69. "Report of the General Secretariat of the Organization of American States and the Panel of Independent International Experts on the Possible Commission of Crimes against Humanity in Venezuela" (Washington, DC: Organization of American States, 2021), 30, http://www.oas.org/documents/eng/press/Informe-Panel-Independiente-Venezuela-EN.pdf.

70. United Nations Humans Rights Council, *Detailed Findings*, 70.

71. Amnesty International, *Silenced by Force: Politically-Motivated Arbitrary Detentions in Venezuela*, AMR 53/6014/2017 (Amnesty International, 2017), 4, https://www.amnesty.org/en/documents/amr53/6014/2017/en/.

72. Amnesty International, *Silenced by Force*, 3.

73. Amnesty International, *Silenced by Force*, 4.

74. Amnesty International, *Silenced by Force*, 4; "Report of the General Secretariat of the Organization of American States and the Panel of Independent International Experts on the Possible Commission of Crimes against Humanity in Venezuela," 40; United Nations Humans Rights Council, *Detailed Findings*, 79, 86. The UN report documented torture through heavy beatings with bats and sharp objects; leaving visible marks, broken bones and damaged organs; excessively tight handcuffs resulting in cuts to the wrists; asphyxiation with toxic substances and water; stress positions

known as "the octopus" and "crucifixions"; conditions including constant lighting, isolation in a dark room for days, no access to toilets, blindfolding; sexual and gender-based violence including forced nudity, threats of rape and rape; cuts and mutilations including in the bottom of the feet and the nails; electric shocks in sensitive parts of the body (including to the genitals); food and water deprivation, eating from the floor, forceful feeding of feces; psychological torture, including death threats to victim and family members.

75. Sarah Marsh and Marianna Parrga, "Oil-rich Venezuela and Russia Come to Aid of Ally Cuba, But Its Energy Woes Persist," Reuters, October 4, 2019, https://www.reuters.com/article/us-cuba-economy-analysis-idUSKBN1WJ2GS.

Chapter Sixteen

Cuba

Brendan J. de Brun

Cuba's intelligence community surfaced and then formalized throughout the twentieth century, quickly growing to be one of the most successful and infamous intelligence networks in history. Molded by postrevolutionary ideals and shaped under Soviet tutelage, Cuban intelligence bloomed in an effort to defend the small island nation from its myriad enemies while simultaneously exporting the nation's ideology across the hemisphere. However, unlike many of its formalized counterparts across the world, Cuba's intelligence networks never became truly accountable to a state-based bureaucratic structure. In fact, accountability of these agencies almost exclusively resided with the Castros—and to a lesser degree within the Revolutionary Armed Forces (FAR) or the Ministry of the Interior (MININT) leadership—rather than the public or government assemblies. This centralization not only caused a degree of institutional infighting throughout the years, but it also kept parallel intelligence components peripherally unaware of their counterparts' operations. Though the effort and funding dedicated to the evolution of Cuba's intelligence community undoubtedly generated one of the most prolific—and notorious—clandestine institutions in the world, the centralization of both power and information inhibited any potential growth of institutional accountability (whether truly communist or, even less so, democratic). As noted by Hal Klepak in his security analysis of Cuba, "[T]here is no tradition of democratic intelligence agencies in Cuba."[1]

HISTORICAL BACKGROUND

Under Spanish rule, structured intelligence gathering in Cuba was nonexistent, and in its place the colonial government relied heavily on loyalists to provide information on impending revolts, foreign attacks, and internal sabotage.[2] When the Americans arrived to the island after the 1898 revolution, these loyalists established one of the most powerful armed organizations in Cuba (numbering in the thousands), known as the Rural Guard.[3] As Klepak notes, the Guard itself did not have any formal intelligence training per se, but its close ties with American forces and the local police, coupled with its internal security role, "ensured that local informants were numerous."[4]

Despite lack of formalized training and institutional foundation building, Cuban intelligence nonetheless surfaced in a fashion predominant in Latin America during this era, as it largely focused on gathering information on political rivals through various means, as well as the general defense of the incumbent government. In 1933, Fulgencio Batista led the Sergeant's Revolt, a coup which effectively removed the elected government of Cuba and initiated a period of protracted political turmoil. In the aftermath of the revolt, Batista retained the military's loyalty and, by proxy, the burgeoning Cuban intelligence machine. This position of power eventually led Batista to take the presidency of Cuba in 1940. The early Batista years saw the first true development of the Cuban intelligence structure by forming the Military Intelligence Service (SIM).[5] SIM was largely an internal organization focused on routing out public and political opponents and neutralizing their efforts before they could become problematic to the reigning regime (though these operations invariably occurred abroad as well).[6] In this context, up until the end of World War II, Cuba's close ties with the United States led the island nation to be almost completely dependent on U.S. foreign intelligence for external matters.[7] By 1944, Batista stepped down as president, and his chosen successor was defeated in the following elections. The SIM remained, however, and its reputation became notorious in its conduct of both domestic and international operations, often illegal, and always in support of the current regime. In 1952, Batista returned to Cuba, again running for president. However, as his lead lagged in the time proceeding to the elections, he instead opted to lead a coup and took direct control of the country. The United States, though cautious after these events, nonetheless came to diplomatically recognize Batista's new regime due to his anticommunist rhetoric.

Batista's second presidential regime saw an invigoration and consolidation of the Cuban intelligence apparatus. Between 1952 and 1953, the Cuban military intelligence formalized into the Directorate of Intelligence (G-2). As was expected by the American government, in the years leading up to the Cuban revolution, Batista's regime became increasingly more repressive of its former Communist allies. By 1958, the regime had even created the Office of Suppression of Communist Activities (BRAC) to dismantle unions and crush communist opposition within the country.[8] The United States, in turn, began to provide additional training to the G-2 in the form of psychological warfare and direct intelligence training to crush the Communist uprising.[9] However, Cuba's increasing and thinly veiled criminal activity (backed by the Batista regime) fueled a spiral of corruption within the country. Coupled with the increasingly repressive tactics of the intelligence organizations, this confluence of factors ultimately proved to inspire, rather than suppress, revolutionary sentiment.

FIDEL CASTRO'S RULE

In January 1959, Fidel Castro led a successful revolution against Batista and put Cuba firmly under his control. One of his first acts was the culling of the previous regime's intelligence service in a swift and extensive fashion, often resorting to sham trials (or summary decisions) that resulted in the execution of many of the former intelligence and military officers of the previous regime.[10] With the new revolutionary ideology instated (combined with sweeping land reforms established by the new government), Castro rapidly alienated the previous elite, making it apparent that both external and internal threats to the revolutionary government were being scrutinized. Internally, the new revolutionary model stripped power and opportunity from the middle class as well, fracturing the population and forcing many to leave the country. Externally, the United States' tentative relationship with Cuba dissolved, leading to extreme American measures of communist suppression to include a failed invasion attempt against the Castro regime.[11] In the aftermath of the Bay of Pigs in April 1961, Cuba's public declaration of a Marxist-Leninist regime caused a cascade effect of worsening relations with the rest of the Americas. With most of the hemisphere turning against the Cuban regime, the looming threat of a world replete with enemies led to a burgeoning relationship with the USSR. This new affiliation served a symbiotic purpose: the Soviets would provide economic (trade and construction), military, and diplomatic assistance, and Cuba would provide the Russians with an ally at the doorstep of their primary enemy—the United States.

In this increasingly dangerous environment, Castro sought to energize the Cuban intelligence structure in 1961 and formed the General Intelligence Directorate (DGI), an organization soon to be controlled primarily by Manuel Piñeiro.[12] The DGI became Cuba's main intelligence service, charged with domestic and international intelligence collection and analysis—a role that, according to Klepak, continues to exist.[13] Brian Latell, a former director of the CIA Center for the Study of Intelligence, notes that "the Cuban Intelligence service, beginning in the 1960s, very quickly became one of the four or five best in the world, rivalling the CIA, the KGB, and the Israeli intelligence service."[14] Under Castro's control, the Cuban intelligence apparatus began to form into an incredibly powerful organization that rivaled many of its counterparts around the planet. However, unlike in the American case (or for that matter, even the Soviets'), Cuba's intelligence apparatus became steadily subordinate to an individual man (Fidel Castro) rather than either the government structure he presided over or the people.

It is feasible that Castro's Cuban intelligence culture emerged even before the institution was formalized under the revolutionary regime. Fidel Castro's views were prevalent far before the Cuban revolution was successful, first landing him in prison for twenty-two months after a failed attack on the Mocadada and Cespedes barracks in July 1953. After being released, he was effectively exiled to Mexico where he met an Argentinian doctor, Ernesto "Che" Guevara, and began training guerrilla insurgents to reattempt a revolutionary movement in Cuba, one that was ultimately successful in the following years. This fervor, amplified by his infamous partner, Che, and his brother Raul Castro, would go on to form the revolutionary bedrock from which the Cuban state would emerge. Unsurprisingly, after the solidification of Castro's rule in the early 1960s and the development of the DGI, the foundational culture from which the Cuban intelligence apparatus would materialize and invariably replicate (or at the very least emulate) the ideology espoused in Castro's leadership. It is important to note that Cuba bloomed as a country ideologically surrounded by enemies, both a literal and figurative island unto its own. As Klepak notes, "The Cuban government has developed a 'siege mentality' that is the base point for the development of a security services network,"[15] a staunch viewpoint that would shape the growth and transformation of the Cuban intelligence structure.

The extent of Cuban involvement in Latin American affairs since Castro's revolution in the 1950s is no secret, as the export of Cuban Marxism-Leninism was one of the key tenets of the Cuban intelligence community for much of the twentieth century, and to a degree, remains so to this day. Cuba's revolution in and of itself opened the floodgates across Latin America toward revolutionary ideology, and Cuba, as an exporter of this sentiment, rapidly became involved. Timothy Wickham-Crowley, in an analysis of guerrilla movements in Latin America throughout the latter half of the twentieth century, notes that many nations in the hemisphere viewed the Cuban revolutionary success as a path to emulate, providing a degree of hope, and provided the blueprint for achieving the same degree of success in their own nations.[16] Moreover, he writes that Cuba's success may have been the catalyst that kickstarted the first wave of guerrilla insurgencies that erupted across the hemisphere throughout the 1960s and 1970s. [17] This revolution model was further solidified through Che Guevara's published writings, which were often found by varying armed forces after overrunning guerrilla encampments.[18]

First and foremost, the FAR emerged as the formalized military institution of the state, built directly from the revolutionary army that deposed the Batista regime.[19] In fact, much of the civil-military context of the Cuban experience in the twentiethh century and beyond evolves from the fact that the modern Cuban military effectively won the Cuban Revolution and to a degree has remained in power since. William LeoGrande, who analyzed Cuba's civil-military relations in the context of communist systems, notes that the creation of the regime was formed by the military itself.[20] In the early stages of state formation in the post-revolutionary period, Castro directly commanded the armed forces in the initial development of the Communist Party system. In fact, LeoGrande notes that the revolutionary forces "performed all the tasks of a Leninist Party in the initial phases of a socialist revolution: [they] took administrative control of the old state bureaucracy; . . . seized means of production; . . . mobilized popular support; . . . and [they] constituted the organizational core around which the foundations of a new political system were laid."[21] Of note, due to the long-standing political weakness of the party proper, the FAR largely remained in control of various state functions and preserving the role of "civic soldiers"[22] all throughout the 1960s, remaining in control of many of the state's institutions to include its economy and production. Beginning in 1970, the Cuban Communist Party (PCC) began the strengthening of its role in the system, turning many of the previously military-controlled institutions over to civilian authorities. In fact, as LeoGrande observes, "there was no clear differentiation of civil and military roles before 1970."[23]

Because of this development, during the early years of the postrevolution regime, Cuba's intelligence structure began to form under the command of the FAR and Raul Castro himself. In 1959, members of the underground communist party and the FAR initially assembled into a counterintelligence unit known as the Department of Investigations of the Rebel Army (DIER). By 1960, however, the increasing perception of threats led to a split in intelligence responsibilities. Focused internally on counterintelligence (as an evolution of DIER) the Department of State Security (DSE) emerged, which would become popularly known as G-2. At the same time, the DGI was formed as the lead external intelligence agency that would come to bloom heavily under the tutelage of the USSR in the decades that followed. This organization was codenamed "M" and was led by the infamous Comandante Manuel Piñeiro Losada, or *Barbarroja* (codename "M-1"). These organizations remained under the direct control of Raul Castro and the FAR until 1961, and they functioned as the primary intelligence tools of state security. However, reorganization of the Cuban Intelligence structure occurred in 1961, placing both of these organizations under the MININT. Though MININT remained subordinate (at least in name) to the FAR, the differentiation between a state-based intelligence apparatus and that of the armed forces began to form. As such, the FAR created a similar intelligence structure to that of MININT, creating the Military Intelligence Directorate (DIM) and the Military Coun-terintelligence Directorate (CIM). Personal politics were heavily at play dur-ing this period, as the newly appointed leader of the MININT, Comandante Ramiro Valdes, and Raul Castro had been rivals throughout the revolutionary years.

In his article detailing the roles of Cuban intelligence agencies, Frank Mora notes that "the decision to separate DSE-MININT from MINFAR was made largely for practical reasons."[24] The FAR, as the armed force of Cuba, was to be primarily used to fend off invaders and minimize the impact of foreign aggression. MININT, on the other hand, would instead focus on both "domestic order (Counter-Intelligence, Fire Department, Police, Immigration and the Prison system) and Intelligence (foreign threats and special opera-tions abroad)."[25] As time later revealed, the nature of MININT's intelligence apparatus would soon outweigh the FAR's role in the protection of Cuba, and rapidly developed its own identity separate from its military oversight. Though it remained legally subordinate to the FAR, by 1962 the strategic environment—Fidel Castro's insistence on remaining intricately involved in intelligence affairs—allowed MININT to achieve its own individual reputa-tion while building autonomy and power.

Throughout the early 1960s and 1970s, increased access to Soviet support led to significant increases in training, equipment, and funding through close bilateral ties with the USSR.[26] Soviet support included the construction and operation of the Lourdes intelligence facility outside of Havana, where liai-son officers conducted intelligence, language, and structural instruction for the burgeoning Cuban Intelligence community. Due to their strategic position next to the United States, Cuba's communist affiliations gave its intelligence operators access to some of the most sophisticated counterintelligence and security apparatus on the planet, including East German state security intel-ligence training. The Cuban-Soviet relationship grew to include exchanges of agents, training, and capital, shaping the evolution of the Cuban intelligence apparatus. As the Cold War progressed, however, USSR–Cuba relations ebbed and waned due to a misalignment of political priorities and the Soviets' decreased emphasis on the region. Eventual collapse of the Soviet Union largely severed this intelligence relationship.

Throughout the 1960s, MININT's role in the Cuban intelligence realm grew significantly and began to diverge from the direct control and objectives of the FAR. MININT's prioritization as the lead intelligence agency was largely due to Fidel Castro's increased interest and involvement in the operations of both the DSE and DGI, providing MININT a higher degree of autonomy and power than its position under the FAR would imply. Mora attributes this growing wedge to a conflict of personal interest between the leadership of these institutions, and Fidel Castro's intentional manipulation of intelligence leadership to prevent the solidification of any power base that could oppose him.[27] As the commander of the FAR, and by proxy all intelligence agencies in Cuba, Raul Castro butted heads with the director of MININT, Ramiro Valdes. Raul and Valdes were bitter rivals during the revolutionary years, and the MININT's growing position of repute (growing in power and autonomy) from under the FAR's control further exacerbated the divide. Additionally, Fidel Castro's direct involvement in MININT activities further complicated the matter. His style was impulsive and often at the expense of governmental procedure, which chafed against some of the more methodical planning preferred by its ministers. As Mora notes, "[I]t was not uncommon for Fidel to issue directives to ministry personnel without the knowledge of the minister, or to hold secret meetings,"[28] habitually without the presence of the directors themselves. Furthermore, he continues that "Fidel created a climate of distrust, tension and competition within Minint [*sic*] and between FAR and the Ministry of Interior that lasted until 1989."[29] Overall, the higher echelons of Cuban intelligence culture were warped by the personalistic whims of the leadership at hand, and the organizations that emerged from this competition were invariably affected by this dynamic. Some of this animosity was relieved in 1970 when a confidant and friend of Raul was put in place as the MININT commander, Sergio del Valle. However, Fidel Castro's dislike of the man often led to him being skipped in the chain of command.

Regardless, much of this conflict had permeated down the ranks by this point, and both the FAR and the intelligence aspects of the MININT had begun a rivalry that would last for two more decades. For one, MININT officers often came from higher sociocultural strata than their counterparts in the FAR. Members of the former often came from the urban areas of Cuba, representative of previous upper-middle-class families and positions. FAR personnel, on the other hand, primarily came from the rural areas of the country and generally emerged from lower socioeconomic strata. Among other aspects, this caused a rift between the two branches of government, where the FAR looked at MININT operatives as bourgeoisie, and the others, in turn, called the soldiers "gorillas."[30] Additionally, other cultural aspects of the intelligence agencies began to broaden the rift. MININT operatives were often seen as people who played fast and loose with government regulation, whereas the FAR was exceptionally proud of its bureaucratic professionalism. Due to their connections abroad, MININT operatives generally had access to higher-quality goods that improved their quality of life, while those in the FAR did not (though in the 1970s *Comercio Militar*, a military-specific commissary, was instituted to give some privileges to the armed forces, but it was not equivalent). Conversely, education opportunities were more abundant for members of the FAR; much of the benefit of education and professional indoctrination was ultimately absent from the ministry and its intelligence organizations.

EXPORTING THE REVOLUTION

Throughout most of the 1960s and 1970s, the Cuban intelligence community also had an outsized regional role (external to the island), propagating its own breed of communism across the hemisphere. Far from being bystanders to this process, Cuban intelligence agencies (namely the DGI) became deeply involved in trying to help burgeoning communist paramilitary groups across the Americas gain a foothold to establish lasting change within their countries. Manuel "Barbarroja" Piñeiro (the initial commander of the DGI) firmly believed in Guevara's efforts to inspire revolution abroad, and actively sent personnel to enact this very mission.[31] In an article analyzing the Cuban and Soviet intelligence involvement in Allende's Chile, Kristian Gustafson and Christopher Andrew note that "in Latin America, Cuba would attempt to foment revolution with Che Guevara's *'foco'* theory."[32] They also assess that Cuban intelligence agencies, namely the DGI, would sometimes "develop a domestic base through some spark of revolutionary violence," or in Chile's case (which was already fairly energized under Allende) instead focused "their efforts towards radicalizing local parties."[33] In the rest of Latin America, Cuban intelligence often made the initial approach by enticing rebel groups with subversion tactics and guerrilla warfighting training.[34] Once recruited, these revolutionaries were handed over to the FAR for the majority of that instruction. These groups, like the Colombian National Liberation Army (ELN) and Chile's Leftist Revolutionary Movement (MIR), often visited Cuba for training before returning to their home country to initiate operations.[35] The numbers of leaders and trainees visiting Cuba during the 1960s is estimated to be in the range of two thousand to three thousand, which allowed for a sufficient ratio of guerrilla forces to combat their respective national opponents.

That said, Wickham-Crowley observes that "even where and when the Cubans were still involved with various national insurgencies, their presence and contacts with the locals were not always convivial."[36] He notes that in Bolivia and Venezuela, Cuba's support rapidly dwindled in the 1960s until eventually most of their involvement in those countries fizzled out.[37]

Che Guevara's death in October 1967 in Bolivia at the hands of counter-insurgent forces dealt a significant morale blow to insurgent forces across Latin America. By the end of the decade, Cuba's deepening relationship with the USSR gently removed it from the revolutionary sphere of influence of Latin America, and by 1968, Cuba's heavy-handed role in the first wave of insurgencies (including the funding they provided) had significantly decreased. Wickham-Crowley observes that "by 1969–1970, Cuba had withdrawn almost all of its rhetoric and support for guerrillas in neighboring countries," and some of the most supportive insurgent forces had "publicly turned against Fidel."[38] Furthermore, Cuba's regional objectives within Latin America often conflicted with the Soviets' view of how local situations should develop, often leading to friction between the KGB and DGI while operating in the same local areas.

Even more so in the case of Chile, Cuba's intelligence objectives often came in conflict with its own national goals, as the advanced training given to the MIR in many ways hampered Allende's ability to make socialism a more palatable option for Chile. In fact, Cuba's radicalization of the left across Latin America may have contributed to a psychological backlash from the right due to loss aversion (or a disproportionate popular rejection of the left), triggering much of the authoritarian turn prevalent throughout Latin America in the 1970s.[39] Cuban involvement in the second wave of guerrilla insurgencies resurfaced again in the 1970s and 1980s, again accepting revolutionaries from Nicaragua and El Salvador for training, and a large portion of Cuban funding was directed at the nascent Farabundo Martí Liberation Front in El Salvador, a Marxist revolutionary group aimed at deposing the nation's government.[40] Though less Cuban funding was directed at either Guatemala or Nicaragua, Wickham-Crowley nonetheless argues that "the Cuban authorities were apparently crucial in finally getting the three disputatious wings of the Sandinistas [to] truly cooperate in the movement to oust Somoza."[41]

Overall, Cuba's attempt to export revolution had mixed results. Invariably, the direct involvement in clandestine operations across the hemisphere and globally provided invaluable training, experience, and reach for the Cuban intelligence sector. Actions abroad provided valuable intel, aided the Cubans in destabilizing potential opponents, and at the very least, distracted their largest regional antagonist (the United States) away from directly targeting the Cuban homeland. Conversely, however, Cuban involvement in the affairs of other countries (especially on a clandestine level) caused a significant amount of regional resentment. Those countries that were not able to replicate the Cuban experiment (a permanent communist revolution in Latin America) invariably took a tougher position against Castro's regime. In fact, the disruptive actions of the Cuban intelligence service throughout the hemisphere even made the USSR wary of the ally it had cultivated in the region. The Soviet philosophy on the expansion of communism was fundamentally different from Cuba's vision, and this rift in a common objective would slowly come to create distance in the relationship between the two.

FROM THE END OF THE COLD WAR TO TODAY

In 1989, the Cold War was ending and Cuba's greatest ally in its stance against the hemisphere had seemingly dissolved overnight. The symbolic fight of capitalism versus socialism had ended, and Cuba's motivation to export its communist ideology across the hemisphere confronted the harsh reality that, from this point forward, it would be alone in this endeavor. As such, the Cuban intelligence community was forced to restructure. Changes began to bring the entire Cuban intelligence apparatus more securely under the control of the FAR, adjustments required to be relevant in the modern geopolitical paradigm; however, the process was violent, rapid, and temporarily crippling. Corruption and smuggling charges were levied against high-level officials in both the FAR and MININT, which led to the execution of various leaders, imprisonment of others, and the reorganization of the Cuban intelligence structure. During the purge, five hundred intelligence officers and leaders of the MININT were removed and replaced by members of the FAR.[42] In fact, the purge was so rapid and destructive that many of those purged had to be recalled to duty to regain some level of intelligence control. Mora states that "by December 1989, all the heads of MININT's departments and over 70 percent of the ministry's officer corps and staff were dismissed and replaced by young officers and cadres from MINFAR's Intelligence and Counter-Intelligence directorates."[43] In an interview with the *Miami Herald*, Juan Reinaldo Sanchez, a former member of Fidel Castro's security detail, noted that "ten years of work in intelligence and counterintelligence was lost"[44] during the purge, bringing the entire Cuban intelligence apparatus under the Intelligence Directorate (DI). In the years that followed the purge, the roles of the FAR and MININT reversed from where they were in the 1960s and 1970s. With the MININT firmly staffed by FAR personnel, many of the socioeconomic advantages that the MININT had were rapidly shut down. In fact, a degree of marked discrimination against MININT permeated the structure following the purge, and many of the privileges available to the FAR were never opened to MININT personnel. Still, after the initial restructuring, the MININT and its intelligence structure have been able to operate on a more mutually beneficial level with the rest of the FAR's intelligence community, building a more effective and mutually supportive intelligence community.

In 1989, the DGI was restructured in the Intelligence Directorate, and it remains the intelligence service dedicated to external matters, currently under the charge of MININT. It is led by a vice minister and is composed by various departments that focus on regional areas; for example, M-1 is directed primarily at the United States.[45] This M-1 department is further divided into sections, which focus on everything from political bodies (such as the U.S. Congress), intelligence and law enforcement agencies (CIA, FBI), all the way to industrial espionage. The DI focuses on three main areas, to include political and economic intelligence (partitioned into global regions), external counterintelligence, and military intelligence; smaller focus areas are dedicated to technical support. Internally, the MININT also controls the Counter-intelligence Directorate (DCI), which focuses primarily on internal counterespionage, insurgencies, and anticorruption efforts. Within the FAR, both the DIM and CIM remain active, but with modern objectives. Much like in the MININT organizations, DIM is focused on exogenous threats and manages a significant signal intelligence (SIGINT) unit. CIM focuses internally on military counterespionage, commands the FAR's political police, and focuses on countering U.S. SIGINT and electronic warfare.

CURRENT OPERATIONS

Though modern Cuban intelligence operations are clandestine in nature and typically difficult to identify, it is unequivocal that their influence and reach remains active throughout the world. In a report by the Congressional Research Service, Mark Sullivan writes that "various sources estimate that the number of Cuban military and intelligence advisers in Venezuela [in 2014] ranged from hundreds to thousands, coordinated by Cuba's military attaché in Venezuela."[46] In this report U.S. Secretary of State, Mike Pompeo noted that "Cuban military and intelligence services are deeply entrenched in the Venezuelan state"; Sullivan further claimed that Cuban intelligence operatives "provide physical protection and other support to President Maduro and those around him."[47]

Additionally, over the course of the last two decades Bolivia has been an area of focus for the Cuban intelligence community due to the political alignment of the two nations. Evo Morales, former president of Bolivia, ran the country under the socialist ideals of his party and retained close ties with the Cuban government throughout most of his tenure as president. However, in 2019 the Bolivian elections were fraught with societal upheaval and amplified by the pandemic, and eventually Morales was ousted by coup. Reporter Yuvinka Avilés noted that many of the presumed Cuban health workers allowed in the country during the chaotic period of elections were not actual medical technicians. She details that, according to the Bolivian communications minister, "about 700 presumed Cuban doctors, who were working in Bolivia as part of a health agreement signed by former President Evo Morales, weren't qualified to practice, because they lacked the necessary degrees or had fraudulent ones, and that their true mission in the South American nation was intelligence work."[48] Though the period following Morales's departure from the Bolivian presidency is marred with partisan finger-pointing, Avilés writes, "Bolivia's interim government said it had asked Venezuelan and Cuban officials to leave the country, including scores of Cuban doctors, accusing them of instigating unrest in the wake of the resignation of former president Evo Morales."[49]

Unsurprisingly, funding of the Cuban intelligence community is mostly masked and controlled behind the scenes by the party and state. Only personnel directly tied to the intelligence agencies or direct financing have full understanding of where the funds are allocated. Moreover, control is mainly held at the very top of the Cuban hierarchical structure, originally overseen by Fidel Castro, and in the last eight years, led by Raul. Although Raul Castro has officially stepped down from power as of April 18, 2021, analysts believe that the Castros' control over Cuba remains firm, held tightly in the hands of loyalists, confidents, and even family members. Marcell Felipe wrote in a *Wall Street Journal* article that much of the power in Cuba remains with Raul Castro's son-in-law, General Luis Lopez Callejas (head of the Armed Forces Business Enterprise Group—GAESA)[50] as well as his son, Colonel Alejandro Castro Espín who Felipe notes is a "powerful member of the intelligence apparatus."[51] With General Lopez Calleja's control over the majority of Cuba's economic functions and Colonel Castro Espín's considerable influence within the still influential intelligence community, Felipe evaluates that "the island still marches to the beat of the Castro family's drum."[52]

CONCLUSION

Due to its ideological and physical vulnerability throughout the twentieth century and beyond, it comes as no surprise that after sixty years of existence little is known about the Cuban intelligence structure or the state mechanisms that uphold it.[53] However, it is apparent throughout Cuba's history that the intelligence network built under Fidel Castro's rule was a tool that was beholden primarily to him, maintaining personal control of the activities both internal and external to the country. Very little accountability, both in financing and in action, goes beyond the direct line of control of their respective intelligence agencies, the FAR, and the top brass. Unlike the democratization of intelligence agencies across other countries in Latin America, Cuban leadership (namely the Castro family) has retained a firm grasp on all collection, counterintelligence, and espionage that emanates from this small island state. This situation owes, in large part, to the outsized personalities of the leaders that built it, the long-standing power of the FAR in almost all government affairs, and the mentality of isolated survival that permeates the culture of the Cuban intelligence structure to this day.

The Cuban intelligence apparatus, despite Soviet influence and the Cuban Communist Party that molded its evolution, fails to mimic other intelligence structures prevalent under other communist regimes. LeoGrande notes that "the significance of the Cuban case lies in the fact that neither of the traditional roles of Communist civil-military relations is able to provide an adequate account of the Cuban experience."[54] Whether judging by the Cuban intelligence community's highly centralized control, clandestine funding sources, or its external focus on exporting revolution, LeoGrande continues that "it is the character of this revolution and its success in resisting years of efforts by the United States to regain control of the island that have made Cuba far more prominent in world affairs than its small size would indicate."[55] As such, Cuba's intelligence culture is unlike any other intelligence community on the planet, and despite overt changes of Cuban leadership in 2021, it will likely remain both prolific within its realm and decidedly undemocratic in nature.

NOTES

1. Anthony Stuart Farson, Peter Gill, et al., eds., *PSI Handbook of Global Security and Intelligence: National Approaches, Intelligence and the Quest for Security* (Westport, CT: Praeger Security International, 2008), 147.

2. Farson, Gill et al., *PSI Handbook of Global Security and Intelligence*, 147, 148.

3. Farson, Gill et al., *PSI Handbook of Global Security and Intelligence*, 148.

4. Farson, Gill et al., *PSI Handbook of Global Security and Intelligence*, 148.

5. Farson, Gill et al., *PSI Handbook of Global Security and Intelligence*, 149.

6. Farson, Gill et al., *PSI Handbook of Global Security and Intelligence*, 149.

7. Farson, Gill et al., *PSI Handbook of Global Security and Intelligence*, 148.

8. Farson, Gill et al., *PSI Handbook of Global Security and Intelligence*, 149.

9. Farson, Gill et al., *PSI Handbook of Global Security and Intelligence*, 149.

10. Farson, Gill et al., *PSI Handbook of Global Security and Intelligence*, 150.

11. On April 17, 1961, the United States authorized and backed an attempted counterrevolution against the Castro regime. This consisted of over 1,400 exiled Cubans who opposed the communist regime. This force landed in the Bay of Pigs, but due to overwhelming resistance and lack of American air support, the invasion

attempt ended violently and quickly. This infamous failed attempt was dubbed nothing short of a fiasco, emboldening Cuban leadership and tarnishing the United States' reputation in the aftermath of the operation. David M. Barrett, "The Bay of Pigs Fiasco and the Kennedy Administration's Off-the-Record Briefings for Journalists," *Journal of Cold War Studies* 21 (2019): 3, 4.

12. Farson, Gill et al., *PSI Handbook of Global Security and Intelligence*, 150.

13. Farson, Gill et al., *PSI Handbook of Global Security and Intelligence*, 150.

14. "Castro's Secrets: The CIA and Cuba's Intelligence Machine | C-SPAN.Org," pt. 2:20, accessed April 11, 2021, https://www.c-span.org/video/?309426-4/castros -secrets-cia-cubas-intelligence-machine.

15. Farson, Gill et al., *PSI Handbook of Global Security and Intelligence*, 147.

16. Timothy Wickham-Crowley, "Two 'Waves' of Guerrilla-Movement Organizing in Latin America, 1956–1990," *Comparative Studies in Society and History* 56, no. 1 (January 2014): 218, https://doi.org/10.1017/S0010417513000674.

17. Wickham-Crowley, "Two 'Waves' of Guerrilla-Movement Organizing," 221.

18. Wickham-Crowley, "Two 'Waves' of Guerrilla-Movement Organizing," 221.

19. Dale R. Herspring, ed., *Civil-Military Relations in Communist Systems*, Westview's Special Studies on the Soviet Union and Eastern Europe (Boulder, CO: Westview Press [u.a.], 1978), 204.

20. William LeoGrande, "A Bureaucratic Approach to Civil-Military Relations in Communist Systems: The Case of Cuba," in *Comparative Communist Civil-Military Relations*, eds. Dale Herspring and Ivan Volgyes (Boulder: Westview Press, 1978).

21. William LeoGrande, "A Bureaucratic Approach to Civil-Military Relations in Communist Systems: The Case of Cuba," in *Comparative Communist Civil-Military Relations*, eds. Dale Herspring and Ivan Volgyes (Boulder: Westview Press, 1978).

22. Herspring, *Civil-Military Relations in Communist Systems*, 205.

23. William LeoGrande, "A Bureaucratic Approach to Civil-Military Relations in Communist Systems: The Case of Cuba," in *Comparative Communist Civil-Military Relations*, eds. Dale Herspring and Ivan Volgyes (Boulder: Westview Press, 1978).

24. Frank O. Mora, "Cuba's Ministry of Interior: The FAR's Fifth Army," *Bulletin of Latin American Research* 26, no. 2 (2007): 224.

25. Mora, "Cuba's Ministry of Interior," 224.

26. Farson, Gill et al., *PSI Handbook of Global Security and Intelligence*, 152.

27. Mora, "Cuba's Ministry of Interior," 226.

28. Mora, "Cuba's Ministry of Interior," 225.

29. Mora, "Cuba's Ministry of Interior," 226.

30. Mora, "Cuba's Ministry of Interior," 227.

31. Kristian Gustafson and Christopher Andrew, "The Other Hidden Hand: Soviet and Cuban Intelligence in Allende's Chile," *Intelligence and National Security* 33, no. 3 (April 16, 2018): 410, https://doi.org/10.1080/02684527.2017.1407549.

32. Gustafson and Andrew, "The Other Hidden Hand," 410.

33. Gustafson and Andrew, "The Other Hidden Hand," 410.

34. Gustafson and Andrew, "The Other Hidden Hand," 410.

35. Wickham-Crowley, "Two 'Waves' of Guerrilla-Movement Organizing," 222.

36. Wickham-Crowley, "Two 'Waves' of Guerrilla-Movement Organizing," 225.

37. Wickham-Crowley, "Two 'Waves' of Guerrilla-Movement Organizing," 225.

38. Wickham-Crowley, "Two 'Waves' of Guerrilla-Movement Organizing," 225.

39. Kurt Weyland, "Revolution and Reaction," Rocking Our Priors, pt. 10:00, accessed January 19, 2021, https://soundcloud.com/user-845572280/revolution-reac tion-professor-kurt-weyland. Weyland proposes that people are more likely to fight against loss than they are to fight for gains. This is due to loss aversion, a phenomenon proposed by Prospect Theory. In his application of the theory to politics in Latin America, he notes that radicalization of the left (even in small groups, like guerrillas) may have triggered a disproportionate popular counterreaction from the right that ultimately ushered in Latin America's wave of authoritarianism throughout the 1970s.

40. Wickham-Crowley, "Two 'Waves' of Guerrilla-Movement Organizing," 228.

41. Wickham-Crowley, "Two 'Waves' of Guerrilla-Movement Organizing," 228.

42. Juan O. Tamayo, "Arnaldo Ochoa—a Problem for Castro Brothers 25 Years Ago," *Miami Herald*, accessed June 27, 2021, https://www.miamiherald.com/news/ nation-world/world/americas/article1967653.html.

43. Mora, "Cuba's Ministry of Interior," 230.

44. Tamayo, "Arnaldo Ochoa—a Problem for Castro Brothers 25 Years Ago."

45. "Cuba I Inteligencia, Espionaje y Servicios Secretos," accessed April 11, 2021, https://www.intelpage.info/cuba.html.

46. Mark P. Sullivan, "Cuba: U.S. Policy in the 116th Congress and through the Trump Administration," n.d., 19.

47. Sullivan, "Cuba," 26.

48. Yuvinka Gozalvez Avilés / Voice of America, "Cuban Health Workers Were Not Doctors, Bolivia's Government Reports | Diálogo Americas," accessed June 28, 2021, https://dialogo-americas.com/articles/cuban-health-workers-were-not-doctors -bolivias-government-reports/.

49. "Bolivia Kicks Out Cubans, Venezuelans for Allegedly Fuelling Unrest," euronews, November 15, 2019, https://www.euronews.com/2019/11/15/bolivias -ousted-morales-can-return-but-would-face-inquiry-interim-president.

50. Grupo de Administracion Empresarial (GAESA). Felipe summarizes its function as a "military-run conglomerate that controls about 75% of the Cuban economy, including hotels, construction companies, shipping companies, hard-currency transmitters and currency exchanges." Marcell Felipe, "Opinion: The Castros Still Run Cuba," *Wall Street Journal*, April 18, 2021, sec. Opinion, https://www.wsj.com/ articles/the-castros-still-run-cuba-11618783289. According to Reuters writer Marc Frank, "GAESA's books, like those of other state-run companies, are not public." See "Cuban Military's Tentacles Reach Deep into Economy," Reuters, June 15, 2017, sec. Emerging Markets, https://www.reuters.com/article/us-usa-cuba-military -idUSKBN1962VK.

51. Felipe, "Opinion."

52. Felipe, "Opinion."

53. Farson, Gill, et al., *PSI Handbook of Global Security and Intelligence*, 147.

54. Herspring, *Civil-Military Relations in Communist Systems*, 214–15.

55. Gary Prevost, "Cuba in an Age of Economic Reform," *Oxford Research Encyclopedia of Politics*, 23 May 2019. https://doi.org/10.1093/acrefore/9780190228637 .013.1518. Also in Gary Prevost, "Cuba," in *Politics of Latin America: The Power Game*, eds. Harry E. Vanden and Gary Prevost (New York: Oxford University Press, 2002), 325.

Conclusion

Thomas C. Bruneau

I have two goals in this conclusion. The first is to discuss the background and some of the main elements of intelligence in new democracies. The second is to help make the reader aware that while democratic civilian control of intelligence is apparently not a problem in the United States, there is very serious concern whether the intelligence community (IC) is effective in providing decision makers—civilian and military—with the intelligence they need in the current global situation, which includes competition with China and Russia and the far-ranging impact of the COVID-19 pandemic. Alarmingly, arrogance, even hubris, abounds among intelligence professionals in the United States who generally disregard the pathologies facing intelligence agencies that form the focus of this book, while ignoring problems of the IC in the United States. The arrogance, while unacceptable, is comprehensible as the U.S. IC is huge, consisting of seventeen separate organizations of which nine are within the Department of Defense (DoD); in FY 2020, its appropriated budget was $85.5 billion.[1]

First, with regard to the *The Handbook of Latin America and Caribbean Intelligence Cultures*, it is a very great pleasure for me to write this conclusion. The volume is unique in that it provides case studies for the majority of countries in the region, including those where not only Spanish but also Portuguese and English are the official languages, and it further includes three different types of political regimes—consolidated democracies, consolidating democracies, and non-democratic regimes. It is useful as the case studies go beyond the legal framework for intelligence, which may or may not serve as a guide to anything, and it describes and analyzes the reality of intelligence as organization and process. Writing this conclusion is for me tremendously gratifying as well because five of the authors, which include two of the coeditors, have worked closely with me as we jointly created the scholarly subfield of intelligence in new democracies. We have cooperated in research in half of the countries analyzed here, in our publications, in helping to reorient the *International Journal of Intelligence and CounterIntelligence* to go beyond the study of intelligence in the United States and a few other democracies, and in expanding and enriching the Intelligence Studies Section of the International Studies Association. But our collaboration goes far beyond the scholarly study of intelligence in new democracies, not-so-new democracies, and non-democracies as together we have reformulated the analytical approach to not only intelligence but also the more general field of civil-military relations.

Traditionally the study of civil-military relations focused exclusively on democratic civilian control of the armed forces. To the extent that such scholarship was applied to intelligence, this control was conceptualized as oversight, mainly legislative oversight, as intelligence agencies are part of the executive branch of government. In civil-military relations, it is possible to envision means for democratically elected civilians to control the military, and there are several conceptual approaches vying for acceptance. In contrast, in intelligence, because the defining characteristic of intelligence is secrecy, control can neither be proven nor disproven. At most, in newer democracies, legislatures are empowered to conduct oversight of intelligence agencies, but as demonstrated in the case studies in this book—most notably Mexico—they are not provided with the means (funding and personnel) to in fact conduct oversight.

The biggest challenge by far with regard to both civil-military relations and intelligence is to prove effectiveness. In the former, maybe a total of ten countries have militaries that are equipped and trained to engage in armed conflict with other countries, and in the vast majority of countries the armed forces fulfill up to ten different roles and missions; from peacekeeping to military support to civilian authorities to diplomacy. In none of these other and more likely roles and missions, can success be proven or disproven. In the latter case, intelligence, it is totally impossible to prove effectiveness. Something could happen—or not—for a myriad of different reasons; and in any case, a decision maker, civilian, military, democratic or not, may have—or may not have—followed what the intelligence professionals might have discovered or recommended. In short, in both civil-military relations and intelligence effectiveness cannot be proven or disproven in terms of results that can be observed and measured. In our analysis, therefore, we have come to focus on what we have defined as requirements, without which effectiveness would be impossible.

Analysis of whether a country fulfills the posited requirements is simpler than one might imagine since in the vast majority of cases there is much rhetoric and very little fulfillment of requirements that involve primarily institutions and resources. In this book the chapter editors posit, and the chapter authors utilize, a Matrix on Intelligence Governance that, while heavy on control, includes recruitment and training and thus gets to personnel issues, which are crucial everywhere for effective intelligence.

In most countries analyzed in this book, as is the case globally, intelligence in prior, non-democratic regimes meant state security—that is, security of the regime, which in most instances was some form of dictatorship that could be military, civilian, or civilian under a Marxist-Leninist regime. Therefore, the biggest challenge everywhere was and is to overcome the experiences of the past that poses challenges to both control and effectiveness. One of the co-editors and authors in this book, Florina Cristiana Matei, and I published an article in the journal *Democratization* in 2011 in which we describe and discuss factors that impede or promote the democratization and effectiveness of intelligence.[2] I believe a review of the factors impeding reform and effectiveness of intelligence is relevant to the cases in this book as I know from personal experience one or more of these factors applies to virtually all of the countries included here.

A first factor that hinders progress is the complexity of intelligence reform itself. Democratization of intelligence is a complex process, involving a comprehensive overhauling of a host of security and intelligence concepts, policies, and procedures, to seek to achieve a balance in effectiveness and transparency. These changes must be integrated in a more comprehensive democratic transformation of the entire security and defense sectors (e.g., reform of the military, police, border control institutions, etc.), and, ultimately, of an overall economic, political, and societal reform. It is extremely challenging for new governments, without experience in running a democratic state, to handle such multiple and complex institutional and policy changes. Regimes in transition lack mature institutions in all domains of security, including intelligence, impeding their ability to achieve a balance between security and democracy. In most cases new democracies must develop from scratch structures and processes that would establish legal and organizational provisions that set the roles and missions, direction, and prioritizing tasks for the agencies; tools of interagency coordination and cooperation between intelligence and other security organizations; avenues for developing a working relationship with the executive, legislatures, civil society, and international groups; and effective mechanisms of democratic control and oversight.

The new institutions must establish sufficient legitimacy to be able to undertake a rigorous democratic reform of the intelligence services and/or execute a robust democratic control and oversight, which affect both the effectiveness and control (implemented via oversight) of the newly developed intelligence agencies. This balance becomes even more difficult when the legitimacy of the governments is in jeopardy, as they are repeatedly contested and questioned. Governments generally focus on maintaining their authority and not on security and intelligence reform; what is more, sometimes, instead of focusing on "democratizing intelligence," governments use intelligence in a non-democratic way (in line with "the bad old days") to maintain control. Additionally, even if the legitimacy issue is resolved, more pressing issues such as economic development, health care, and education, get higher priority on the governments' agendas, which receive more resources and time to the detriment of security, including intelligence.

A second impediment to intelligence democratization is the detrimental impact that the non-democratic past has on the general perception of intelligence. In virtually all new democracies, the intelligence agencies bear a stigma of their non-democratic past and misconduct. With a few exceptions, after a regime change, the new agencies tend to preserve the personnel, premises, and other assets of the non-democratic institutions. The residual personnel may perpetuate abuses and violations of human rights for personal or political reasons.

A third factor is the opposition by intelligence agencies to democratic reform for a variety of ideological, political, and bureaucratic reasons. Under the non-democratic regimes, intelligence agencies served an elite and highly privileged political class and enjoyed special benefits; thus they are more likely to be suspicious of any political change than other government organization due to their previous support for a very exclusive clique of society. Democratic reform means intelligence agencies would have to refrain from abusive practices and illegalities; undergo downsizing, vetting, and retrospective investigation of their past practices and actions; and lose prerogatives—which they, not surprisingly, try to resist. They may even use their special skills and access to files/records to stall or influence the reform by blackmailing or coercing decision makers. In addition, intelligence agencies challenge democratic reform (specifically, democratic control) as they generally lack confidence in the political decision makers' expertise on intelligence, doubt that national security is a high priority on the politicians' agenda, and consider that too much transparency or democratic scrutiny will undermine their effectiveness. Then, too, intelligence agencies are bureaucracies, and bureaucracies are hard to reform even in a democratic country—harder in a transition regime.

Not only intelligence agencies but also elected officials avoid or initially oppose reforming intelligence. To begin with, to avoid suspicion of having been involved in past political police transgressions, politicians may circumvent any involvement with the intelligence apparatus that carries the stigma of having been a tool of repression under the old regime; or they may avoid taking on radical reforms of intelligence and thorough democratic control from fear that intelligence agencies may have compromising and embarrassing information to utilize as leverage. Decision makers may also wish to be able to deny knowledge of illegal operations in order to avoid any possible suspicion that they tolerate illegal activities and practices. Lastly, politicians may refuse to undertake significant intelligence reforms for fear of resistance (fearing that intelligence personnel have accumulated, and maybe are still collecting, information that could be used against them). In fact, politicians frequently use intelligence agencies to collect "dirt" to blackmail or otherwise intimidate potential political enemies and journalists. An additional issue is that many new democracies tend to suffer from a so-called transition fatigue—a post-transition stagnation in political and social changes—which curbs interest in and keenness for reform.

A fourth factor is the lack of civilian expertise in what intelligence (let alone "democratic intelligence") involves, since their previous exposure (if any) to security and/or intelligence matters had been in an authoritarian environment, where fear and total secrecy prevailed. This lack of expertise in intelligence makes it extremely difficult for decision makers to have an informed opinion on the topic or to choose the best reform avenues, policies, and practices. With no prior knowledge, legislators are less likely to establish a vigorous legal framework for operating an intelligence system in a democracy; provide appropriate direction and tasking; conduct reviews of budgets, expenditures, and activities; carry out inquiries and interpellations; and/or provide feedback to the intelligence agencies, upon receipt of intelligence briefs and summaries. Similarly judicial bodies may be incapable of discerning when it is appropriate to grant a surveillance warrant. All these challenges, coupled with weak institutions, increase the potential for abuses (e.g., illegal wiretaps, surveillance, and informants), on the one hand, or lead to mutual tensions between decision makers and intelligence agencies that delay or oppose the democratic transformation, on the other hand.

Intelligence agencies of transition regimes often lack professionalism. A professional intelligence service in a democracy involves a series of formal and structured personnel commitments, such as strict entrance requirements, ongoing training and education programs, specific code of ethics (to include respect for human rights and liberties), and mechanisms enabling cumulative learning and improvement. Considering these many prerequisites, the natural tendency of the new democracies to rely on the intelligence "experts" from the former regime undermines the professionalization of the new intelligence agencies. The recycled personnel may continue to operate as in the past for their own personal or political parties' benefit (disregarding democratic principles of rule of law and respect for citizens' rights, freedoms, and private life), limit employment possibilities for a new generation of intelligence personnel, and/or convey their "best practices" to the new agents. Moreover, since the legal framework and democratic control mechanisms are not robust enough to effectively question and reprimand intelligence officers, they can, essentially, do whatever they want. Speedy retirement or firing of the old intelligence personnel, as well as hiring new personnel, are also problematic. For example, retired or fired personnel may create or join competing agencies in the private sector, often better supplied and equipped, or support or join organized crime networks.

A fifth factor is the lack of public support for intelligence and inexistent intelligence culture. As previously stated, for the general public, the legacy agencies continue to be viewed very negatively for a long time after the transition to democracy. Amid mistrust and even hatred, there can be almost no support for the intelligence functions at the beginning of transition. Citizens (including political elites) in new democracies more or less oppose creating new intelligence systems for fear of a return to a non-democratic regime. Lack of support for intelligence goes hand in hand with lack of intelligence culture and knowledge among the intelligence outsiders. In transition regimes, the population, civil society, as well as the elected and appointed officials lack understanding of why effective intelligence is needed, even in a democracy. Alternately, they may not know what effective intelligence involves (e.g., the need for some level of secrecy), or they may be unfamiliar with democratic control mechanisms (which would balance security with transparency).

Intelligence agencies in regimes undergoing transitions often lack (at least initially) both the organization and the expertise to develop robust public relations and outreach, to enable them to cleanse their image and gain popular support. Due to the excessive secrecy surrounding their past work (most of the time illegal and abusive) during the non-democratic regime, it is less likely intelligence agencies had public affairs offices or other means to conduct dialogues with the media or citizens. In addition, in many transition states, the media, which might theoretically have the means to promote intelligence agencies' images, fail to do so (they rather seek the opposite— discrediting intelligence agencies). Regrettably, public debate on intelligence issues is generally dominated by the sensationalist media, and intelligence agencies tend to remain hermetic. Even if formal oversight mechanisms exist and politicians have security clearances, it is difficult for intelligence outsiders to attain an intelligence culture/knowledge.

A sixth factor is corruption and organized crime. Following the transition to democracy, the fragile and contested legitimacy of the newly formed political elites and weakness of new institutions, open borders and free movement policies, rising poverty and inequality, potential conflicts in the neighboring areas and increased insecurity, as well as increased opportunities for enrichment through illegal avenues, may lead to mounting corruption and organized crime activities. Criminal groups are wealthy enough to corrupt the state institutions, or worse, to directly penetrate into the state institutions (including intelligence agencies); therefore democratic reform, in general, and of the intelligence in particular are seriously challenged.

A seventh factor is overall democratic regression. If transition states are incapable of providing basic human rights, freedoms, and liberties for its citizens, fall short in attaining political freedom and pluralism, lack free market economies, do not possess vigorous civil societies, and are incapable of bringing their security services (including intelligence) under civilian democratic control and oversight, they, by definition, fail to democratize. As these countries remain moderately or strongly authoritarian, more likely intelligence agencies remain unreformed and non-democratic. In Venezuela, for example, not only has the government failed in strengthening the democratic values and norms, but the military and intelligence agencies continue to be the chief prop of the regime to conduct clandestine activities against the population.

Awareness of these very negative factors arising from the background to intelligence in non-democratic regimes is fundamental to understanding the tremendous challenge of reforming intelligence in terms of both democratic civilian control and effectiveness. The chapters in this book provide ample evidence of this assertion.

Lest one, and particularly an American reader of this book, feel self-confident that all is well with the intelligence community in this country, it must be initially stated that currently in the United States, the system is facing the most serious challenge since its founding after World War II. This challenge, which is less about democratic civilian control—which seems to function—is mainly about effectiveness in terms of supporting the U.S. defense strategy. Therefore, in contrast to the primary focus on control, or lack thereof, in the chapters in this book, the IC in the United States is confronted with how effective it can be in the so-called great power competition (GPC) arena. After all, if the IC with its associated $80 billion annual budget is not up to the demands of the GPC, Americans have no justification to tout the U.S. IC over those of the countries included in this book. While official government documents globally include the term "strategy" somewhere in their titles, there is a great degree of formalism, and not all things that are termed "strategy" are in fact strategy. For example, an annual U.S. *National Security Strategy* is required by Article 603 as codified in Title 50, U.S. Code, Article 3043 of the Goldwater-Nichols Defense Reorganization Act of 1986 that directs the U.S. executive to publish such a document annually. Since the end of the Cold

War, U.S. administrations have ignored this requirement. Neither the George W. Bush administration nor the Barak Obama administration met the annual requirement; they each published only two during their eight-year administrations—even then, none was very useful.[3]

As a lead-in to the discussion on the U.S. National Defense Strategy later in this chapter, it seems appropriate to quote the first two lines of the chapter "Restoring Our National Security" by James O. Ellis Jr., James N. Mattis, and Kori Schake: "For the past twenty years, across administrations of both political parties, the United States has been operating largely unguided by strategy. We have been much too reactive to events and crises, and have allowed others to define the perception and outcomes of our engagement around the world."[4] This situation is now changing, and beginning from at least November 2014 during the administration of President Barak Obama in the *Third Offset Strategy*, the focus of DoD and the U.S. Armed Forces increasingly became "ensuring the ability of the United States to project military power in the face of an emergent suite of advanced military capabilities developed, deployed, and potentially sold by China, Russia, and others."[5] Beginning with the *Third Offset Strategy*, the U.S. government now defines the contemporary era as one of GPC thereby signaling a transition away from the Global Wars on Terror; more specifically, the United States is primarily focused on China, and to a lesser extent, Russia. Indeed, the most authoritative document of the U.S. government regarding national defense is the *National Defense Strategy* of 2018, which defines the "Strategic Environment" in the following terms: "The central challenge to U.S. prosperity and security is the *reemergence of long-term, strategic competition* by what the National Security Strategy classifies as revisionist powers. It is increasingly clear that China and Russia want to shape a world consistent with their authoritarian model—gaining veto authority over other nations' economic, diplomatic, and security decisions. . . . [L]ong-term strategic competitions with China and Russia are the principal priorities for the Department and require both increased and sustained investment, because of the magnitude of the threats they pose to U.S. security and prosperity today, and the potential for those threats to increase in the future."[6]

There is ample and ever-increasing evidence that the *National Defense Strategy* of 2018, in contrast to all so-called strategies since the end of the Cold War, is in fact a strategy and is being implemented. First of all, the policy-defining and funding body, which is the U.S. Congress, in the 2017 NDAA mandated the secretary of defense to produce a National Defense Strategy to articulate U.S. national security and defense strategy. The strategy also replaces the quadrennial defense review as a basis for resourcing decisions. The Congress also created a National Defense Strategy Commission, the members of which were appointed by Congress, to assess and evaluate the National Defense Strategy. The Commission produced *Providing for the Common Defense: The Assessment and Recommendations of the National Defense Strategy Commission*.[7] The Congressional Research Service utilized the report of the National Defense Strategy Commission, as only the Introduction of the Strategy is unclassified, to publish a report on the 2018 Strategy.[8] In short, Congress mandated the creation and was heavily engaged in the assessment of the strategy by the Commission. The 2020 NDAA, Section 1708 directs the secretary of defense to report on the implementation of the National Defense Strategy and further mandates two studies of its implementation, one of which is to be a non–U.S. government organization.[9] A summary of the FY 2021 NDAA, approved by the Congress on December 3, 2020, states the following: "Eyeing China's rise as a global military and economic power, lawmakers unveiled a compromise defense policy bill Thursday that targets China on multiple fronts, with $6.9 billion prescribed for a new Pacific Deterrence Initiative over two years."[10] The Congressional Research Service publishes, approximately twice a year, a long (approximately fifty pages) analysis of the status of GPC in the *Renewed Great Power Competition: Implications for Defense-Issues for Congress*.[11]

Second, the armed forces of the United States are in fact reorienting themselves from operations in line with the global war on terror (GWOT) to operations in line with GPC. For example, the U.S. Navy's Daily News Service includes a large section titled "Great Power Competition," (most recently renamed "Strategic Competition"). In addition, courses and certificate degree programs are being offered on the topic of GPC. The stimulus for these academic programs came from U.S. Navy staff, with fulfillment through various military institutions of higher education to include the Naval War College and the Naval Postgraduate School.[12] On March 17, 2020, the U.S. Navy, Marine Corps, and Coast Guard issued a new maritime strategy identifying China as the biggest long-term threat to the United States.[13] The U. S. Air Force has created a think tank, the Office of Commercial and Economic Analysis, to analyze "great power competition."[14] Further, the theme of great power competition has been picked up by think tanks of all political stripes.

Third, President Biden, in his report to Congress on April 28, 2021, highlighted GPC activities to counter both China and Russia. As stated in the lead paragraph by David E. Sanger, "President Biden has justified his broad vision to remake the American economy as the necessary step to survive long-run competition with China, a foot race in which the United States must prove not only that democracies can deliver, but that it can continue to out-innovate and outproduce the world's most successful authoritarian state."[15]

Fourth, the competition at the strategic military level with China, and to a lesser extent, Russia is real. For confirmation on China, one only needs to read *Un-Restricted Warfare* of 1999 or *Made in China 2025*. The former demonstrates how China can militarily defeat the United States. The latter is a national strategic plan to further develop the manufacturing sector of the People's Republic of China that seeks to make China dominant in global high-tech manufacturing technologies. The goal is to catch up with, and surpass, Western technological prowess in advanced industries, executed through a whole of government approach to include state-sponsored theft of intellectual property.[16] China is infamous for civil-military fusion that means the government has access to all information, including from the private sector, that could prove useful for military purposes. In short, the NDS seeks to reorient the U.S. strategy to global threats.[17] The IC cannot help but be completely involved in providing intelligence to the civilian and military decision makers in the context of the current great power competition.

It should be noted that the IC, as early as September 1999, was beginning to gear up for this competition by engaging with start-ups and others in Silicon Valley for new technologies, primarily in the cyber realm. I draw on here the more or less official description by Rick E. Yannussi of the founding and operation of the organization.[18] It was established as an independent nonprofit corporation with offices at the CIA in Langley, Virginia, and in Menlo Park, California. Its mission is to foster the development of new and emerging information technologies and to pursue research and development that produce solutions to the most difficult IT problems facing the IC. To accomplish this goal, it networks with those in industry, the venture capital community, academia, and any others who are at the forefront of IT innovation. "Through the business relationships that it establishes, In-Q-Tel creates environments for collaboration, product demonstration, prototyping, and evaluations. From these activities flow the IT solutions that the Agency seeks and most importantly, the commercial opportunities for product development by its partners."[19] According to Yannuzzi and other sources we have consulted, the model has been relatively successful at bringing in new technology.[20] However, despite these decades of preparation, the IC still lacks the capacity to identify and avert new security challenges—like, for example, recognizing the magnitude of the threat posed by the COVID-19 pandemic in 2020.[21]

In defining the challenge to effectiveness facing the IC in the context of the strategy of great power competition, I will now draw upon the 2021 CSIS Report *Maintaining the Intelligence Edge: Reimagining and Reinventing Intelligence Through Innovation.*[22] I am doing this for four reasons: First, the document is completely current—having been released in early 2021. Second, the report focuses on the whole IC, and in all imaginable aspects of intelligence explicitly in the context of great power competition. Third, while the report is unclassified, eleven of the twelve commissioners have all held extremely important positions in the IC, and the twelfth, Amy Zegart, who in fact was on the NSC, is maybe the most prolific and highly respected academic specializing in intelligence issues. The commission consulted widely, including both the executive branch and the two select intelligence committees in the legislative branch. Fourth, one of the co-chairs, Avril Haines, is now the director of National Intelligence; and one of two CSIS experts, Kathleen Hicks, is deputy secretary of defense. If there was ever a report by a think tank that is likely to be implemented, this is it. If the commission has its way, the CSIS report continues, "the dawning era of intelligence innovation must compel the IC to *reimagine* its tradecraft and missions to harness technology potential and *reinvent* its processes, partnerships, workforce, incentives, and yes-culture to embrace technological transformation."[23]

I believe it is worth quoting in full the first paragraph of the Executive Summary to convey the seriousness of the challenge facing the IC to maintain its effectiveness:

> The U.S. Intelligence Community (IC) stands at the dawn of a new era of technological innovation and transformation unprecedented in its history. Driven by artificial intelligence (AI) and associated emerging technologies, including cloud computing and advanced sensors, and big data analytics, the approaching "AI era" will transform both the nature of the global threats the IC is responsible for assessing and the IC's ability to accurately detect and assess them. Through all of this, the core mission of the IC will remain unchanged: to understand what is happening in the world, to deliver timely, accurate, and insightful analysis of those threats and developments to U.S. policymakers, and to provide U.S. leaders decision-making advantages over competitors. What will change is the IC's ability to fulfill this mission if it does not adapt to the new AI era.

In short, this book describes and analyzes the tremendous challenges to control and effectiveness in most countries in Latin America and the Caribbean. While the challenges are very different between those facing the intelligence agencies analyzed in this book and those facing the IC in the United States, they are all central to the future of democracy in the Western Hemisphere. At the minimum, thus, intelligence agencies in Latin America and the Caribbean Basin—as much as the politicians in the regions—must recognize that the troubles that loom for the United States are an omen for the intelligence services in their region.

NOTES

1. DeVine, Michael E., December 30, 2020, "Defense Primer: Under Secretary of Defense for Intelligence and Security," Congressional Research Service, IF10523.

2. Florina Cristiana Matei and Thomas Bruneau, "Intelligence Reform in New Democracies: Factors Supporting or Arresting Progress," *Democratization* 18 (2011): 3, 602–30. This article provides the empirical evidence and sources to support the short summary of main points provided here.

3. Catherine Dale,. "National Security Strategy: Mandates, Execution to Date, and Issues for Congress," *CRS Report for Congress,* August 6, 2013 (Washington, DC: CRS), Summary.

4. James O. Ellis Jr., James N. Mattis, and Kori Schake, "Restoring Our National Security," in George P. Schultz, ed., *Blueprint for America* (Stanford: Hoover Institution Press, 2016), 137.

5. Kathleen H. Hicks and Andrew Hunter, *Assessing the Third Offset Strategy* (Washington, DC: Center for Strategic International Studies, March 2017), 1. Available at https://www.csis.org/analysis/assessing-third-offset-strategy.

6. U.S. Department of Defense, *Summary of the 2018 National Defense Strategy of the United States of America: Sharpening the American Military's Competitive Edge.* Available at https://dod.defense.gov/Portals/1/Documents/pubs/2018-National-Defense-Strategy-Summary.pdf.

7. "Providing for the Common Defense: The Assessment and Recommendations of the National Defense Strategy Commission 2019." Available at https://www.hsdl.org/c/sign-in/?dest=abstract%26did%3D818823.

8. "Evaluating DOD Strategy: Key Findings of the National Defense Strategy Commission," March 19, 2019. *In Focus*, Congressional Research Service. Available at https://fas.org/sgp/crs/natsec/IF11139.pdf.

9. National Defense Authorization Act for 2020, which became Public Law No. 116-92 on December 20, 2019, It is available at https://www.congress.gov/bill/116th-congress/senate-bill/1790, p. 133.

10. Joe Gould, "Compromise Defense Bill Confronts a Rising China," *DefenseNews*, December 3, 2020. Available at https://www.defensenews.com/congress/2020/12/03/compromise-defense-bill-confronts-a-rising-china/?utm_source=Sailthru&utm_medium=email&utm_campaign=EBB%2012.04.20&utm_term=Editorial%20-%20Early%20Bird%20Brief.

11. The most recent in the hands of the authors is Ronald O'Rourke, January 27, 2021, *Renewed Great Power Competition: Implications for Defense—Issues for Congress*, Congressional Research Service R43838. The Federation of American Scientist website hosting these reports lists twenty-six leading up the January 27, 2021 version. Available at https://crsreports.congress.gov/product/details?prodcode=R43838.

12. See, for example, "NPS Launches Distance Learning Graduate Certificate in Great Power Competition," September 17, 2020. Available at https://www.navy.mil/Press-Office/News-Stories/Article/2351609/nps-launches-distance-learning-graduate-certificate-in-great-power-competition/.

13. Gina Harkins, "New Naval Strategy Zeroes in on China as Biggest Long-Term Threat to the US," Military.com, December 17, 2020. Available at https://www.military.com/daily-news/2020/12/17/new-naval-strategy-zeroes-china-biggest-long-term-threat-us.html.

14. United States Air Force, Office of Commercial and Economic Analysis. Available at https://www.afocea.com.

15. David E. Sanger, "Biden Calls for U.S. to Enter a New Superpower Struggle," *New York Times*, updated May 5, 2021. Available at https://www.nytimes.com/2021/04/29/us/politics/biden-china-russia-cold-war.html.

16. See Col. Quao Liang and Col. Wang Xiangsui, *Un-Restricted Warfare* (Brattleboro, VT: Echo Point Books & Media, 1999), and James McBride and Andrew Chatzky, "Is 'Made in China 2025' a Threat to Global Trade?" Council on Foreign Relations, *Backgrounder*, May 13, 2019, available at https://www.cfr.org/backgrounder/made-china-2025-threat-global-trade.

17. NA (February 5, 2018), "The 2018 National Defense Strategy: Fact Sheet," *CRS Report for Congress* (Washington, DC: CRS).

18. Rick E. Yannuzzi, "In-Q-Tel: A New Partnership between the CIA and the Private Sector," CIA, Center for the Study of Intelligence, 2000. Available at https://www.cia.gov/library/publications/intelligence-history/in-q-tel.

19. Yannuzzi, "In-Q-Tel," 2 of 9.

20. In addition to Yannuzzi, I have drawn upon the In-Q-Tel website and the following sources: Wendy Molzahn, "The CIA's In-Q-Tel Model: Its Applicability," *Acquisition Review Quarterly* (Winter 2003): 47–61, available at https://www.dau.edu/library/arj/ARJ/arq2003/MolzahnWT3.pdf; Damien Van Puyvelde, *Outsourcing US Intelligence: Contractors and Government Accountability* (Glasgow: Edinburgh University Press, 2019); John T. Reinert, "In-Q-Tel: The Central Intelligence Agency as Venture Capitalist," *Northwestern Journal of International Law & Business* 33, no. 3 (Spring 2013): 677–709, and Jon D. Michaels, "The (Willingly) Fettered Executive: Presidential Spinoffs in National Security Domains and Beyond," *Virginia Law Review* 97, no. 4 (May 2011): 801–98. Available at https://www.virginialawreview.org/articles/willingly-fettered-executive-presidential-spinoffs-national-security-domains-and/.

21. Erik Dahl, "Warnings Unheeded, Again: What the Intelligence Lessons of 9/11 Tell Us about the Coronavirus Today," *Homeland Security Affairs* 16, Article 7 (December 2020). Available at http://www.hsaj.org/articles/16304.

22. CSIS, *Maintaining the Intelligence Edge: Reimagining and Reinventing Intelligence through Innovation*, Center for Strategic and International Studies, January 13, 2021, p. ix. Available at https://www.csis.org/analysis/maintaining-intelligence-edge-reimagining-and-reinventing-intelligence-through-innovation.

23. CSIS, *Maintaining the Intelligence Edge*, p. x (emphasis in the original).

Bibliography

BOOK/ARTICLE TITLES

2018 Public Sector Annual Budget, Law No. 21.053, 2017. Trans. John Oeffinger. Available at http://www.dipres.gob.cl/597/articles-172496_doc_pdf.pdf.

"37 policías de la Subdirección de Inteligencia Policial capacitados." *Academia Nacional de Seguridad Pública.* May 19, 2017. Available at https://www.ansp.gob.sv/37-policias-de-la-subdireccion-de-inteligencia-policial-capacitados/.

About the Public Access of Information, Law no. 20285, 2008. Trans. John Oeffinger. Article 22. Available at https://www.leychile.clN?27363&f=2016-01-05&p=.

"Agony in the Andes." *Economist*, November 7, 2002. Available at https://www.economist.com/unknown/2000/11/07/agony-in-the-andes.

"Angostura: Radiografía de la crisis de Ecuador y Colombia." *El Telégrafo*, May 20, 2017, Available at https://www.eltelegrafo.com.ec/noticias/politiko/1/angostura-radiografia-de-la-crisis-de-ecuador-y-colombia.

"Aparecen nuevos nombres rastreados por Dirección Nacional de Inteligencia." *El Comercio*, March 26, 2015.

"Brazil Court Releases Explosive Bolsonaro Video as Coronavirus Cases Soar." YouTube video, 5:25. Posted by "DW News," May 23, 2020. https://www.eltelegrafo.com.ec/noticias/politiko/1/angostura-radiografia-de-la-crisis-de-ecuador-y-colombia.

"Castro's Secrets: The CIA and Cuba's Intelligence Machine | C-SPAN.Org." Accessed April 11, 2021. https://www.c-span.org/video/?309426-4/castros-secrets-cia-cubas-intelligence-machine.

"Chile Abolishes Law Requiring State-Run Copper Miner to Finance Military," *VOA*, July 24, 2019. Available at https://www.eltelegrafo.com.ec/noticias/politiko/1/angostura-radiografia-de-la-crisis-de-ecuador-y-colombia.

"Chile Recognises 9,800 More Victims of Pinochet's Rule." BBC News, August 18, 2011. Available at https://www.bbc.com/news/world-latin-america-14584095.

"Chile's Feared Secret Police Chief Dies at Age 86." *Hindustan Times*, August 8, 2015. Available at https://www.hindustantimes.com/world/chile-s-feared-secret-police-chief-dies-at-age-86/story-8v89kXGfAbQnruNnCOrP8K.html.

"Cleaning Up," *Economist*, November 30, 2000. Available at https://www.economist.com/the-americas/2000/11/30/cleaning-up.

"Colombia: Intelligence Reform Would be Incomplete." *Oxford Research Daily Brief Service*, November 3, 2009.

"Colombia: Military Announce Closure of 20th Intelligence Brigade." Associated Press, May 20, 1998.

"Cuba I Inteligencia, Espionaje y Servicios Secretos." Accessed April 11, 2021. https://www.intelpage.info/cuba.html.

"Cuban Military's Tentacles Reach Deep into Economy." Reuters, June 15, 2017, sec. Emerging Markets. https://www.reuters.com/article/us-usa-cuba-military-idUSKBN1962VK.

"Dahik Huyó Ayer a Costa Rica." *El Tiempo*, October 13, 1995. Available at https://www.eltiempo.com/archivo/documento/MAM-422975.

"Designación de Guido Bellido en la PCM pondría en riesgo la lucha contra el terrorismo, según expertos." *El Comercio*, July 30, 2021. Available at https://elcomercio.pe/lima/designacion-de-guido-bellido-en-la-pcm-pondria-en-riesgo-la-lucha-contra-el-terrorismo-pedro-castillo-noticia/.

"El fin de la era Jara." *El Comercio*, March 31, 2015.

"En los últimos seis meses del gobierno de García se rastreó a más de 700 personas." *El Comercio*, March 21, 2015.

"Equipo de Inteligencia de Quintana no prosperó." *Los Tiempos*, April 21, 2016. Available at http://www.lostiempos.com/actualidad/nacional/20160421/equipo-inteligencia-quintana-no-prospero.

"Evaluating DOD Strategy: Key Findings of the National Defense Strategy Commission," March 19, 2019. *In Focus*, Congressional Research Service. Available at https://fas.org/sgp/crs/natsec/IF11139.pdf.

"Expertos Declaran la Necesidad de una Ley de Inteligencia." *La Hora*, March 26, 2018. Available at https://lahora.com.ec/quito/noticia/1102145049/expertos-declaran-la-necesidad-de-una-ley-de-inteligencia.

"Freedom in the World: Latin America Report Card," March 10, 2020. https://theglobalamericans.org/2020/03/freedom-in-the-world-latin-america-report-card/#:~:text=In%20its%20recently%20released%20Freedom,world%2C37%20countries%20reported%20improvements.

"Fuerte respaldo de EEUU a la gestión de ministro de Inteligencia." *La Nación*, August 18, 2020. Available at https://www.lanacion.com.py/politica/2020/08/18/fuerte-respaldo-de-eeuu-a-la-gestion-de-ministro-de-inteligencia/.

"Fujimori a Japanese, Can Stay: Kono." *The Japanese Times*, December 12, 2000. Available at https://www.japantimes.co.jp/news/2000/12/13/national/fujimori-a-japanese-can-stay-kono/.

"Fujimori under Fire." *Economist*, July 26, 1997. Available at https://www.economist.com/the-americas/1997/07/24/fujimori-under-fire.

"Gobierno anuncia el cierre de la DINI para 'revisar' mechanismos de control." *El Comercio*, February 10, 2015.

"History | RBDF." Accessed June 28, 2020. https://rbdf.gov.bs/history/.

"Inteligencia, otro fracaso del Gobierno." *El Independiente*, March 23, 2021. Available at https://independiente.com.py/inteligencia-otro-fracaso-del-gobierno/.

"Jorge Noguera Pidió la Libertad con 11 de 25 Años de Pena Cumplida." *El Tiempo*, February 7, 2019. Available at https://www.eltiempo.com/justicia/investigacion/exdirector-del-das-jorge-noguera-pide-su-libertad-por-pena-cumplida-179996.

"Jorge Noguera, de Próspero Abogado a Condenado." *El País*, September 18, 2011. Available at https://www.elpais.com.co/colombia/jorge-noguera-de-prospero-abogado-a-condenado.html.

"La DINI rastreó bienes de empresarios, periodistas, y miembros de Estado." *El Comercio*, March 20, 2015.

"Manuel Contreras and the Birth of DINA." Latin American Studies.org. Available at http://www.latinamericanstudies.org/chile/DINA-birth.htm.

"Martín Vizcarra Dismisses Peru's congress." *Economist*, October 5, 2019. Available at https://www.economist.com/the-americas/2019/10/03/martin-vizcarra-dismisses-perus-congress.

"Martínez asume en Interior y Lezcano pasa a ser el Ministro de Inteligencia." *ABC Color*, February 3, 2018. Available at https://www.abc.com.py/edicion-impresa/judiciales-y-policiales/martinez-asume-en-interior-y-lezcano-pasa-a-ser-el-ministro-de-inteligencia-1671837.html.

"National Crime Intelligence Agency Bill Passed in HOA." *EyeWitness News*, May 23, 2019. https://ewnews.com/national-crime-intelligence-agency-bill-passed-in-hoa.

"Nueve casos de espionaje en El Salvador." *El Salvador.com*. January 27, 2017. Available at https://historico.elsalvador.com/historico/310196/nueve-casos-de-espionaje-en-el-salvador.html.

"Nuevos subdirectores y supresión de divisiones anuncia PNC." *Diario 1*, February 10, 2016. Available at http://diario1.com/nacionales/2016/02/nuevos-subdirectores-y-supresion-de-divisiones-anuncia-pnc/.

"Opacidad, corrupción, hipocresía." Editorial UCA, Universidad Centroamericana José Simeón Caña, El Salvador, July 26, 2021. https://noticias.uca.edu.sv/editoriales/opacidad-corrupcion-hipocresia#.

"Paraguay's First Intelligence Service Created." *MercoPress*, December 26, 2014. Available at https://en.mercopress.com/2014/12/26/paraguay-s-first-intelligence-service-created.

"Parte policial confirmaría reglaje a la vicepresidenta Marisol Espinoza." *El Comercio*, January 19, 2015.

"Peru Election: Socialist Pedro Castillo Claims Victory Ahead of Official Result." *The Guardian*, June 16, 2021. Available at https://www.theguardian.com/world/2021/jun/16/peru-election-socialist-pedro-castillo-claims-victory-ahead-of-official-result.

"Peru Election: Why Has No Winner Been Declared?" BBC News, June 17, 2021. Available at https://www.bbc.com/news/world-latin-america-57511485.

"Peru Protesters Rally against Pedro Castillo's New Government." Aljazeera, August 1, 2021. Available at https://www.aljazeera.com/news/2021/8/1/peru-protesters -rally-against-pedro-castillos-new-government.

"Perú: Primera ministra Ana Jara, obligada a renunciar a su cargo." BBC News, March 31, 2015. Available at https://www.bbc.com/mundo/ultimas_noticias/ 2015/03/150331_ultnot_peru_ministra_jara_renuncia_lav.

"Politicians Court Confusion over SSA, SIA." *Trinidad and Tobago Newsday Archives*, December 12, 2010. https://archives.newsday.co.tt/2010/12/12/politicians -court-confusion-over-ssa-sia/.

"Population Total—Chile." *World Bank*, June 18, 2019. Available at https:// data.worldbank.org/indicator/SP.POP.TOTL?locations=CL&most_recent_year _desc=false.

"Quintana Anuncia Creación de una Agencia de Inteligencia." *Los Tiempos*, March 1, 2016. Available at http://www.lostiempos.com/actualidad/nacional/20160301/ quintana-anuncia-creacion-agencia-inteligencia.

"Realizan primera reunión del Consejo Nacional de Inteligencia." *La Nación*, November 26, 2019. Available at https://www.lanacion.com.py/ahora/2019/11/26/ realizan-primera-reunion-del-consejo-nacional-de-inteligencia/.

"Recién ahora implementan Secretaría de Inteligencia." *ABC Color*, April 24, 2019. Available at Https://www.abc.com.py/edicion-impresa/politica/recien-ahora-im plementan-secretaria-de-inteligencia-1683066.html.

"Secretaría de Inteligencia se fortalece con la cooperación internacional, asegura ministro." *La Nación*, August 20, 2020. Available at https://www.lanacion.com .py/politica/2020/08/20/secretaria-de-inteligencia-se-fortalece-con-la-cooperacion -internacional-asegura-ministro/.

"Secuestro de un Opositor Ecuatoriano en Cedritos: La Verdadera Historia." *Revista Semana*, June 6, 2018. Available at https://www.semana.com/nacion/articulo/ historia-del-secuestro-del-ecuatoriano-fernando-balda-flores-en-colombia/570148.

"SENAIN priorizó la Inteligencia Política, no la Seguridad Nacional." *El Telégrafo*, March 25, 2018. Available at https://www.eltelegrafo.com.ec/noticias/politica/3/ senain-priorizo-la-inteligencia-politica-no-la-seguridad-nacional.

"The Government of the Republic of Trinidad and Tobago Budget Statement 2020." G, October 7, 2019. https://www.finance.gov.tt/wp-content/uploads/2019/10/BUD-GET-STATEMENT-2020.pdf.

"Tres Militares Uruguayos Extraditados a Chile por Caso Berríos." *Hoy*, April 18, 2006. Available at https://hoy.com.do/tres-militares-uruguayos-extraditados-a -chile-por-caso-berrios-2/.

"Venezuela's Regime, Tyranny Looms." *Economist*, Vol. 414, Issue 8927, February 28, 2015.

AUTHOR'S NAME

Abranches, Mauro, and Vladimír Petrilák. *La SBT: el Brazo de la KGB en Uruguay*. Montevideo: Planeta, 2018.

AFP. "ELN Say Will Keep Fighting in Colombia's Out-of-sight War." June 22, 2019.

Agee, Philip. *Inside the Company. CIA Diary.* New York: Stonehill Publishing Company, 1975. Available at https://ia802301.us.archive.org/16/items/pdfy-DAzR701t P2dL_DNu/inside-the-company-cia-diary-philip-agee.pdf.

Agência Brasileira de Inteligência. "Publicações." Available at https://www.gov.br/abin/pt-br/centrais-de-conteudo/publicacoes.

Agência Brasileira de Inteligência. "Seis órgãos têm ingresso aprovado no SIS-BIN." https://www.gov.br/abin/pt-br/assuntos/noticias/seis-orgaos-tem-ingresso-aprovado-no-sisbin.

Age, Philip. *La CIA por Dentro: Diario de un Espía.* Buenos Aires: Editorial Sudamericana, 1987.

Aguayo Quezada, Sergio. "Los Usos, Abusos y Retos de la Seguridad Nacional Mexicana, 1946-1990." In *En Busca de la Seguridad Perdida. Aproximaciones a la Seguridad Nacional Mexicana,* eds. Sergio Aguayo Quezada and Bruce Michael Bagley, 107–45. Mexico: Siglo XXI, 1990.

Aguayo Quezada, Sergio. *La Charola: Una Historia de los Servicios de Inteligencia en México.* Mexico: Grijalbo, 2001.

Aguilar, Jeannette. "El Rol del Ejército en la Seguridad Interna en el Salvador: Lo Excepcional Convertido en Permanente." In *Antología del Pensamiento Crítico Salvadoreño Contemporáneo,* eds. Loida Mariela Castro and Roberto Oswaldo López Salazar, 519–51. Buenos Aires: CLACSO, 2018.

Aguilar, Marielos. "Las Restricciones de los Derechos Políticos de los Costarricenses en la Década de 1980." *Revista de Ciencias Sociales* 67 (March, 1995): 45–54.

Aguirre, Orlando F. (General). "La Alianza para el Progreso ¿Promoción del Desarrollo o Disciplinamiento Estatal?" Paper presented at II Jornadas de Economía Política, Universidad Nacional de General Sarmiento, Buenos Aires, 2008. Available at https://www.ungs.edu.ar/cm/uploaded_files/file/ecopol/2da_jornada/Aguirre.pdf.

Akizuki, Kana. "La Direccionalidad Política del Estado Guatemalteco en el Marco de la Inteligencia, Situación y Perspectivas." Master's thesis. Guatemala, FLACSO, Sede Guatemala, 2003. Available at http://hdl.handle.net/10469/2053.

Alda Mejías, Sonia. "Los Cambios en las Fuerzas Armadas y la Defensa en la 'Revolución Democrática' de Evo Morales." In *Anuario 2010 de Seguridad Regional en América Latina y el Caribe,* eds. Hans Mathieu, and Catalina Niño Guarnizo, 221–41. Bogotá: Friedrich Ebert Stiftung en Colombia, 2010.

Alda Mejías, Sonia. *Observatorio de Redes Criminales y Tráficos Ilícitos del Real Instituto Elcano.* Documento de Trabajo No. 4, Real Instituto Elcano, 2018. Available at https://www.realinstitutoelcano.org.

Aldrich, Daniel P., and Raghunath Mahabir. "Countering Violent Extremism in Trinidad and Tobago: An Evaluation." *SSRN Electronic Journal*, October 3, 2019. https://doi.org/10.2139/ssrn.3450026.

Alegre Rabiela, Alejandro. "Hacia una Ley de Inteligencia para la Seguridad Nacional," *Revista de Administración Pública* 101,(2000): 1–4. http://www.inap.mx/portal/images/REVISTA_A_P/rap_101_2000.pdf.

Alsema, Adriaan. "Colombia's Cocaine Production Reaches All-Time High: US." *Colombia Reports*, March 7, 2020. Accessed on July 31, 2020. Available at https://colombiareports.com/colombias-cocaine-production-reaches-all-time-high-us/.

Alvarado, Jimmy. "Asamblea recorta $450 millones en gastos opacos del presupuesto 2021." *El Faro.net*, December 29, 2020. Available at https://elfaro.net/es/202012/el_salvador/25113/Asamblea-recorta-$450-millones-en-gastos-opacos-del-presu puesto-2021.htm?st-full_text=all&tpl=11.

Alvarez, Destiny. "Roberto D'Aubuisson: A Right-Wing Leader's Rise to Power." PhD dissertation, The University of Texas at Austin, 2020. Available at https://hdl.handle.net/2152/84128.

Álvarez, Nicolás. "The Long Road towards Democratization: Reform of Intelligence in Uruguay (1985–2015)." *Journal of Mediterranean and Balkan Intelligence* 7, no. 1 (2016): 49–70.

Álvarez, Nicolás. "Una Ventana de Oportunidad para Reformar la Inteligencia en Uruguay." *Revista Latinoamericana de Estudios de Seguridad*, no. 21 (2017): 121–39.

Amarilla, José María. "La Cara Oculta de la Seguridad Pública en el Paraguay," In *Seguridad Pública-Ciudadana en Paraguay: Enfoques, saberes, debates y prácticas*, eds. Carlos Peris and José Amarilla, 47–98. Asunción: Universidad Nacional de Asunción, 2017.

Amaya Cóbar, Edgardo. "Militarización de la Seguridad Pública en El Salvador, 1992–2012." *URVIO, Revista Latinoamericana de Estudios de Seguridad* 12 (2014): 71–82.

Amaya Cóbar, Edgardo. "Quince Años de Reforma Policial en El Salvador: Avances y Desafíos." *URVIO, Revista Latinoamericana de Estudios de Seguridad* 2 (2007): 127–44.

América TeVé. "Nicolás Maduro crea brigada especial en Venezuela." June 27, 2014. Video, 2:14. https://www.youtube.com/watch?v=IQlf0zeY7a4.

Amnesty International. *Annual Report: Colombia 2010*. Available at https://www.amnestyusa.org/reports/annual-report-colombia-2010/.

Amnesty International. *Annual Report: Colombia 2017/2018*. Available at https://www.amnesty.org/en/countries/americas/colombia/report-colombia/.

Amnesty International. *Guatemala Accountable Intelligence or Recycled Repression? Abolition of the EMP and Effective Intelligence Reform*. Index number: AMR 34/031/2003 [online]. London: Amnesty International, June 9, 2003. https://www.amnesty.org/en/documents/AMR34/031/2003/en.

Amnesty International. *Silenced by Force: Politically-Motivated Arbitrary Detentions in Venezuela*, AMR 53/6014/2017. Amnesty International, 2017. https://www.amnesty.org/en/documents/amr53/6014/2017/en/.

Andersen, Martin Edwin. *La Policía; Pasado, Presente y Propuestas para el Futuro*. Buenos Aires: Editorial Sudamericana, 2002.

Andersen, Martin Edwin. *Peoples of the Earth: Ethnonationalism, Democracy, and the Indigenous Challenge in "Latin" America*. Lanham: Lexington Books, 2010.

Anonymous interview 1. Former director of CISEN. June 25, 2015.

Anonymous interview 2. Former intelligence agent of the Presidency of Mexico and the Intelligence Unit of the Ministry of the Navy (SEMAR). June 26, 2015.

Anonymous interview 3. Former executive of ESISEN. June 23, 2015.

Anonymous interview 4. Former director of ESISEN and member of CASEDE. July 3, 2015.

Ansaldi, Waldo, and Mariana Alberto, "Muchos Hablan de Ella, Pocos Piensan en Ella: Una Agenda Posible para Explicar la Apelación a la Violencia Política en América Latina." In *América Latina: Tiempos de Violencias*, eds. Waldo Ansaldi and Verónica Giordano. Buenos Aires: Ariel, 2014.

Antunes, Priscila C. B. *SNI & ABIN: Uma Leitura da Atuação dos Serviços Secretos Brasileiros ao Longo do Século XX*. Rio de Janeiro: FGV Editora, 2002.

Aparicio, Fernando, Roberto García, and Mercedes Terra. *Espionaje y Política: Guerra Fría, Inteligencia Policial y Anticomunismo en el Sur de América Latina, 1947–1961*. Montevideo: Ediciones B Uruguay, 2013.

Aquino, Marco, and Marcelo Rochabrun. "Peru's Castillo Names Far-Left PM; No Finance Minister in Cabinet." Reuters, July 30, 2021. Available at https://www.reuters.com/world/europe/peru-president-castillo-names-member-far-left-party-prime-minister-2021-07-29/.

AR.com. La DIS es como entrar a un "ghetto" en un precario, afirma Subdirector de la entidad. *AR.com*, October 23, 2014. Available at https://www.ameliarueda.com/nota/la-dis-es-como-entrar-a-un-ghetto-en-un-precario-afirma-subdirector-de-la-e.

Arana Aguilar, Daira, and Miguel Adrián Ramírez González. "La Remilitarización de la Seguridad Pública en el Triángulo Norte de Centroamérica y los Esfuerzos Internacionales para Garantizar la Protección de los Derechos Humanos en la Región." In *Contextualizaciones Latinoamericanas. Proceso de Militarización de la Seguridad Pública en América Latina*, eds. Marcos Pablo Moloeznik and Ignacio Medina Núñez, 101–29. Guadalajara: CUCSH, Universidad de Guadalajara, 2019.

Arantes, Rogério, and T. M. Moreira. "Democracia, instituições de controle e justiça sob a ótica do pluralismo estatal." *Opinião Pública* 25, no. 1 (2019): 97–135. DOI: 10.1590/1807-0191201925197.

Arce, José. "Figueres: 'DIS nunca ni sobornó ni intimidó a ningún periodista.'" *AMPrensa*, March 16, 2017. Available at https://amprensa.com/2017/03/figueres-dis-nunca-soborno-intimido-ningun-periodista/.

Arcos, Ruben. "Covert Operations." In *The Conduct of Intelligence in Democracies: Processes, Practices, Cultures*, eds. Florina Cristiana Matei and Carolyn Halladay, 97–106. Boulder: Lynne Rienner Publishers, 2019.

Arévalo de León, Bernardo. "Civil-Military Relations in Post-Conflict Guatemala." *Revista Fuerzas Armadas y Sociedad* 20, no. 1 (2005): 63–108.

Arévalo de León, Bernardo. "Del Estado Violento al Ejército Político: Violencia, Formación Estatal y Ejército en Guatemala, 1500–1963." PhD thesis, University of Utrecht, 2015. Available at http://dspace.library.uu.nl/handle/1874/330737.

Arévalo de León, Bernardo, and Ana Glenda Tager. "POLSEDE, Civil Society, and Security Sector Reform in Guatemala." In *Civil Society, Peace, and Power*, eds. David Cortright, Melanie Greenberg, and Laurel Stone, 207–30. Lanham: Rowman & Littlefield, 2016.

Armon, Jeremy, Rachel Sieder, and Richard Wilson, eds. *Negotiating Rights: The Guatemalan Peace Process*. London: Conciliation Resources, 1997.

Army Intelligence and Threat Analysis Center. "Peru: Does Fujimori's Unofficial Advisor Control the Peruvian Intelligence Community?" In *Fujimori's Rasputin: The Declassified Files on Peru's Former Intelligence Chief, Vladimiro Montesinos*. ed. Tamara Feinstein. Washington, DC: The National Security Archive and Chadwyck-Healy, 2001. Available at https://nsarchive2.gwu.edu/NSAEBB/NSAEBB37/.

Army Intelligence and Threat Analysis Center. "Who Is Controlling Whom?" Counterintelligence Periodic Summary. October 23, 1990. In *Fujimori's Rasputin: The Declassified Files on Peru's Former Intelligence Chief, Vladimiro Montesinos*, ed. Tamara Feinstein. Washington, DC: The National Security Archive and Chadwyck-Healy, 2001. Available at https://nsarchive2.gwu.edu/NSAEBB/NSAEBB37/.

Arturi, Carlos S., and Júlio C. Rodriguez. "Democratization and Intelligence and Internal Security Agencies: A Comparative Analysis of the Cases of Brazil and Portugal (1974–2014)." *Brazilian Political Science Review* 13, no. 2 (2019). DOI: 10.1590/1981-3821201900020005.

Asamblea Legislativa de la República de El Salvador. Decreto Legislativo N° 353—Ley Orgánica de la Fuerza Armada. 30 de Julio de 1998. Available at https://www.asamblea.gob.sv/decretos/details/356.

Asamblea Legislativa de la República de El Salvador. Decreto Legislativo N° 486—Ley de Amnistía General para la Consolidación de la Paz. 22 de Marzo de 1993.

Asamblea Legislativa de la República de El Salvador. Decreto Legislativo N° 554—Ley del Organismo de Inteligencia del Estado–, 21 de Septiembre de 2001. Available at https://www.asamblea.gob.sv/decretos/details/473.

Asamblea Legislativa de la República de El Salvador. Decreto Legislativo N° 653—Ley Orgánica de la Policía Nacional Civil de El Salvador. 19 de Diciembre de 2001. Available at https://www.asamblea.gob.sv/decretos/details/3320.

Asociación por los Derechos Civiles. *El (Des)control Democrático de los Organismos de Inteligencia en Argentina*. Buenos Aires: ADC, 2015.

Assies, Willem. "Bolivia: A Gasified Democracy." *Revista Europea de Estudios Latinoamericanos y del Caribe/European Review of Latin American and Caribbean Studies*, no. 76 (2004): 25–43.

Avendaño Rojas, Andrés. "El Sistema de Inteligencia del Estado de Chile, La Producción de Inteligencia Estratégica y Otros Asuntos Relaciones." *Centro De Investigaciones y Estudios Estratégicos*, no. 2 (March 2018).

Badillo, Miguel. "Centro de Inteligencia opera con 99% de personal del CISEN." *Revista Contralínea*, April 3, 2019. https://www.contralinea.com.mx/archivo-revista/2019/04/03/centro-de-inteligencia-opera-con-99-de-personal-del-cisen/.

Badri-Maharaj, Sanjay. "Jamaica Defence Force: Balancing Priorities with Resources—Analysis." *Eurasia Review*, December 11, 2016. https://www.eurasiareview.com/11122016-jamaica-defence-force-balancing-priorities-with-resources-analysis/.

Balcázar Villareal, Manuel Ignacio. "Modernización del Sistema de Inteligencia Estratégica para la Seguridad Nacional en México." *Revista de Estudios en Seguridad Internacional* 5, no. 1 (2019): 71–81. http://www.seguridadinterna

cional.es/revista/?q=content/modernizaci%C3%B3n-del-sistema-de-inteligencia-estrat%C3%A9gica-para-la-seguridad-nacional-en-m%C3%A9xico.

Balcázar Villareal, Manuel Ignacio. "Retos y Perspectivas de la Inteligencia Estratégica en México—Estado de situación." *Chiapas*, July 2019.

Baltazar Landeros, Edgar. "La PNC de El Salvador durante los Gobiernos del FMLN." *Tensões Mundiais* 15, no. 28 (2019): 243–72.

Banco Central do Brasil. Available at https://www3.bcb.gov.br.

Barcant, Aaron. "The Republic of Trinidad and Tobago: From Crown Colony to National Security State." Master's thesis, Concordia University, 2018. https://spectrum.library.concordia.ca/984158/.

Barendsen, Welmoed. "The Political Economy of Peacebuilding: A Study into Power Relations and the Triple Transition in Guatemala." Master's thesis, Utrecht University, 2015. Available at https://dspace.library.uu.nl/bitstream/handle/1874/320417/FINAL%20THESIS%203494713.pdf%3Bseque.

Barreiro Santana, Katalina, Milton Reyes Herrera, and Diego Pérez Enríquez. "The Role of the Ecuadorian Armed Forces: Historical Structure and Changing Security Environments." *Revista de Estudos e Pesquisas Avançadas do Terceiro Setor* 2, no. 2 (2019): 50–72.

Barrios G., Alexia. "Las graves confesiones de Guillermo Valdés." *SDPnoticias*. Mexico: July 2015. http://www.sdpnoticias.com/columnas/2013/11/27/las-graves-confesiones-de-guillermo-valdes.

Basombrío, Carlos, and Fernando Rospigliosi. *La Seguridad y sus Instituciones en el Perú a Inicios del Siglo XXI: Reformas Democráticas o Neomilitarismo*. Lima: Instituto de Estudios Peruanos, 2006.

Becerra, Rafael Pérez. "Juez Pregunta por María del Pilar Hurtado y su Lugar de Reclusión." LAFM.COM. August 12, 2019. Available at https://www.lafm.com.co/judicial/juez-pregunta-por-maria-del-pilar-hurtado-y-su-lugar-de-reclusion.

Becerra, Rafael Pérez. "Niegan Libertad Condicional al Exdirector del DAS, Jorge Noguera." RCN Radio. February 28, 2019. Available at https://www.rcnradio.com/judicial/niegan-libertad-condicional-al-exdirector-del-das-jorge-noguera.

Becker, Marc. *The CIA in Ecuador.* Durham and London: Duke University Press, 2020.

Beith, Malcolm. *The Last Narco*. New York: Grove Press, 2010.

Berg, John R. "Insurgents to Presidents: Contemporary Civil-Military Relations in Brazil, El Salvador, and Uruguay." Master's thesis, Naval Postgraduate School, Monterey, CA, 2015. Available at http://hdl.handle.net/10945/48552.

Berganza, Gustavo. *Compendio de Historia de Guatemala, 1944–2000*. Guatemala: Asociación de Investigación y Estudios Sociales, 2004.

Bernd, Shirley. "Senado aprueba proyecto que moderniza el Sistema de Inteligencia del Estado." *EMOL*. January 23, 2020. Available at https://www.emol.com/noticias/Nacional/2020/01/23/974350/Senado-aprueba-proyecto-inteligencia-Estado.html.

Berwick, Angus. "Imported Repression: How Cuba Taught Venezuela to Quash Military Dissent." Reuters, August 22, 2019. https://www.reuters.com/investigates/special-report/venezuela-cuba-military/.

Besson, Gerard. "The Caribbean History Archives: The Trinidad and Tobago Police Service." *The Caribbean History Archives* (blog), December 3, 2017. http://caribbeanhistoryarchives.blogspot.com/2017/12/the-trinidad-and-tobago-police -service.html.

Bieda, Tomás. "El Control Parlamentario en la Argentina." *POSTData* 20, no. 1 (2015): 185–219. Available at http://www.revistapostdata.com.ar/2015/06/el-control-parlamentario-en-argentina-tomas-bieda/.

Bihar, Alejandro M. "Civil Liberties in the Absence of Legislative Intelligence Oversight: Lessons Learned from Uruguay." Thesis, Naval Postgraduate School, Monterey, CA, June 2018. Available at http://hdl.handle.net/10945/59689.

Bihar, Alejandro M. "Uruguay's Attempt at Intelligence Oversight." *International Journal of Intelligence and CounterIntelligence* 33, no. 2 (2020): 214–47. DOI: 10.1080/08850607.2019.1663701.

Birke, Otto, and Steffen Böhm. "'The People' and Resistance against International Business: The Case of the Bolivian 'Water War.'" *Critical Perspectives on International Business* 2, no. 4 (2006): 299–320.

Bjork-James, Carwil. "Mass Protest and State Repression in Bolivian Political Culture: Putting the Gas War and the 2019 Crisis in Perspective." *Human Rights Program, Harvard Law School* (2020). Available at http://hrp.law.harvard.edu/wp -content/uploads/2020/05/CBjork-James_20_003-1.pdf.

Blixen, Samuel. "Infiltrados: Espionaje Militar en Democracia." Special publication *Brecha*, February 2017. https://issuu.com/semanariobrecha/docs/infiltrados_brecha.

Blixen, Samuel. "Servicios Continuados." *Brecha*, September 2, 2016. https://brecha .com.uy/servicios-continuados/.

Bogran Acosta, José Osmín, Walter Reymundo Lazo Merino, and Douglas Elenilson Zometa. "El Impacto de la Inteligencia Policial en la Toma de Decisiones Estratégicas, Operativas y Tácticas en la Policía Nacional Civil de El Salvador." *Revista Policía y Seguridad Pública* 5, no. 2 (2015): 351–414.

Bolívar Ocampo, Alberto. "Cultura, Periodos Culturales y Servicios de Inteligencia en el Perú, 1960–2008." In *Democratización de la Función de Inteligencia: El Nexo de la Cultura Nacional y la Inteligencia Estratégica*, eds. Russell G. Swenson and Susana C. Lemozy, 257–74. Washington: National Defense Intelligence College Press, 2009.

Bolivia. Ley No. 734 de 8 de abril de 1985—Ley Orgánica de la Policía Nacional. Available at https://www.acnur.org/fileadmin/Documentos/BDL/2002/0861.pdf.

Bolivia. Ley Orgánica de las Fuerzas Armadas de la Nación. 30 de Diciembre de 1992. Available at https://www.mindef.gob.bo/mindef/sites/default/files/LOFA.pdf.

Bonifaz Moreno, Gustavo. "Tensiones de la Agenda de Seguridad en la Transición a un Estado Plurinacional con Autonomías." In *Anuario 2011 de Seguridad Regional en América Latina y el Caribe*, eds. Hans Mathieu, and Catalina Niño Guarnizo, 26–45. Bogotá: Friedrich Ebert Stiftung en Colombia, 2011.

Bonilla Ovallos, María Eugenia. *Desempeño Policial Democrático: El Caso de la Policía Nacional Civil de El Salvador*. Tesis doctoral, Universidad de Salamanca, 2018. Available at https://gredos.usal.es/jspui/bitstream/10366/139483/1/DDPG _BonillaOvallosME_Desempe%C3%B1oPolicial.pdf.

Bonilla Ovallos, María Eugenia. "Las Políticas de Seguridad y la Policía Nacional Civil en El Salvador." *Revista Mexicana de Análisis Político y Administración Pública* 4, no. 1 (2015): 63–84.

Bonilla Ovallos, María Eugenia, and Jerónimo Ríos Sierra. "Luces y Sombras en la Profesionalización de la Policía Nacional Civil de El Salvador tras los Acuerdos de Paz de Chapultepec (1992–2017)." *Revista UNISCI/UNISCI Journal* 55 (2021): 131–57.

Boraz, Steven C. "Establishing Democratic Control of Intelligence in Colombia." *International Journal of Intelligence and Counterintelligence* 19, no 1 (2006): 84–109.

Born, Hans, and Marina Caparini, eds. *Democratic Control of Intelligence Services: Containing Rogue Elephants* (Aldershot: Ashgate, 2007).

Born, Hans, Loch Johnson, and Ian Leigh, eds., *Who's Watching the Spies? Establishing Intelligence Service Accountability*. Washington, DC: Potomac Books, 2005.

Borredá, Javier. "Entrevista al General Jorge Carrillo Olea, Fundador del Centro de Investigación y Seguridad Nacional (CISEN)." *Revista Segurilatam*. Mexico, May 7, 2019. http://www.segurilatam.com/entrevistas/entrevistas/el-exito-de-la -inteligencia-al-servicio-de-la-seguridad-nacional-depende-de-la-confianza-del -presidente-del-pais.

Bowen, Sally, and Jane Holligan. *El Espía Imperfecto: La Telaraña Siniestra de Vladimiro Montesinos*. Lima: PEISA, 2003.

Bowman, Kirk. "¿Fue el Compromiso y Consenso de las Élites lo que llevó a la Consolidación Democrática en Costa Rica? Evidencias de la década de 1950." *Revista de Historia*, no. 41 (enero 2000): 91–127. Available at https://www.revistas.una .ac.cr/index.php/historia/article/view/1868.

Brandão Antunes, and Priscila Carlos. "Establishing Democratic Control of Intelligence in Argentina." In *Reforming Intelligence: Obstacles to Democratic Control and Effectiveness*, eds. Thomas C. Bruneau and Steven C. Boraz, 195–218. Austin: University of Texas Press, 2007.

Brandão, Priscila C. *Serviços Secretos e Democracias no Cone Sul: Premissas Para uma Convivência Eficiente, Legítima e Eficaz*. Niterói: Impetus, 2010.

Brandão, Priscila Carlos. *Serviços Secretos e Democracia no Cone Sul: Premissas para uma Convivência Legítima, Eficiente e Profissional*. Niterói: Editora Impetus, 2010.

Bresser-Pereira, Luiz Carlos. "From Old to New Developmentalism in Latin America." *The Oxford Handbook of Latin American Economics*, eds. José Antonio Ocampo and Jaime Ros, 108–29. Oxford: Oxford University Press, 2011.

Bruneau, Thomas C. "Democratic Politics in Brazil: Advances in Accountability Mechanisms and Regression in Civil-Military Relations." Unpublished manuscript, 2019.

Bruneau, Thomas C. "Ecuador: The Continuing Challenge of Democratic Consolidation and Civil-Military Relations." *Strategic Insights* 5, no. 2 (February 2006).

Bruneau, Thomas C. "Intelligence Reform in Brazil: A Long, Drawn-Out Process." *International Journal of Intelligence and CounterIntelligence* 28, no. 3 (2015): 502–19. DOI: 10.1080/08850607.2015.1022469.

Bruneau, Thomas C. "Intelligence Reforms in Brazil: Contemporary Challenges and the Legacy of the Past." *Strategic Insight* 6, no. 3 (May 2007).

Bruneau, Thomas C., and Kenneth R. Dombroski. "Reforming Intelligence: The Challenge of Control in New Democracies".

Bruneau, Thomas C., and Florina Cristiana Matei, eds. *The Routledge Handbook of Civil-Military Relations*. New York: Routledge, 2013.

Bruneau, Thomas C., and Florina Cristiana Matei. "Intelligence in the Developing Democracies: The Quest for Transparency and Effectiveness." In *The Oxford Handbook of National Security Intelligence*, ed. Loch K. Johnson, 757–73. Oxford: Oxford University Press, 2010.

Bruneau, Thomas C., and Scott D. Tollefson, eds. *In Who Guards the Guardians and How: Democratic Civil-Military Relations*, Austin: University of Texas Press, 2006.

Bruneau, Thomas C., and Steven C. Boraz. *Reforming Intelligence: Obstacles to Democratic Control and Effectiveness*. University of Texas Press, 2009.

Bureau of Counterterrorism. *Country Reports on Terrorism 2019: Paraguay*. US Department of State. Available at https://www.state.gov/reports/country-reports-on-terrorism-2019/paraguay/.

Bureau of Democracy. *Paraguay 2016 Human Rights Report*. Human Rights and Labor. Country Reports on Human Rights Practices for 2016, United States Department of State. 2016. Available at https://www.state.gov/wp-content/up loads/2019/01/Paraguay-1.pdf.

Burgoyne, Michael L. "The Allure of Quick Victory: Lessons from Peru's Fight against Sendero Luminoso." *Military Review* 90, no. 5 (2010): 68–73.

Burt, Jo-Marie. "Transitional Justice in the Aftermath of Civil Conflict: Lessons from Peru, Guatemala and El Salvador." Washington, DC: Due Process of Law Foundation, 2018.

Busquets, José Miguel, and Andrea Delbono. "La Dictadura Cívico-Militar En Uruguay (1973–1985): Aproximación a su Periodización y Caracterización a la Luz de Algunas Teorizaciones sobre el Autoritarismo." *Revista de La Facultad de Derecho* (2° Época), no. 41 (December 2016): 61–102. Available at http://dx.doi .org/10.22187/rfd201624.

Cabrera Toledo, Lester. "Entre el Cambio y la Inercia Histórica: El Contexto Actual de la Inteligencia Militar en Suramérica." *URVIO, Revista Latinoamericana de Estudios de Seguridad* 21 (2017): 8–21.

Caetano, Gerardo, coord. *20 años de Democracia. Uruguay: 1985–2005. Miradas Múltiples*. Montevideo: Taurus, 2005.

Caetano, Gerardo, and José Rila. *Breve Historia de la Dictadura*. Montevideo: CLAEH/EBO, 1986.

Calderon, Ernesto Garcia. "Peru's Decade of Living Dangerously." *Journal of Democracy* 12, no. 2 (April 2001): 46–58.

Calderón Hinojosa, Felipe de Jesús. Interview by Jorge Zepeda Patterson, "El Crimen Organizado es la Mayor Amenaza a los Derechos Humanos." *El Universal.* Mexico: February 27, 2009. Quoted in Raúl Benítez Manaut, Abelardo Rodríguez Sumano, and Armando Rodríguez Luna, eds., "La Guerra al Crimen Organizado."

Atlas de la Seguridad y la Defensa de México 2009. Mexico: CASEDE, 2009. http://www.casede.org/PublicacionesCasede/Atlas2009/analisis_de_seguridad_1 .pdf.

Call, Charles T. "Democratization, War, and State-Building: Constructing the Rule of Law in El Salvador." *Journal of Latin American Studies* 35, no. 4 (2003): 827–62.

Call, Charles, and Jeffrey Hallock. "Too Much Success? The Legacy and Lessons of the International Commission Against Impunity in Guatemala." *CLALS Working Paper Series* 24 (2020).

Camacho, Daniel. "Democracia y Democratización en Centroamérica." In *Democracia y Democratización en Centroamérica,* Regina Steichen, (compilator), 207–36. San José: EUCR, 1993.

Campero, José Carlos. "Balance de la Seguridad en Bolivia, 2012–2013." In *Anuario 2013 de Seguridad Regional en América Latina y el Caribe,* ed. Catalina Niño Guarnizo, 3–31o. Bogotá: Friedrich Ebert Stiftung en Colombia, 2013.

Campero, José Carlos. *El Motín Policial en Bolivia en Junio de 2012.* Policy Paper 45. Bogotá: Friedrich-Ebert-Stiftung, Programa de Cooperación en Seguridad Regional, 2012.

Campero, José Carlos. "La Seguridad en Bolivia, 2011–2012." In *Anuario 2012 de Seguridad Regional en América Latina y el Caribe,* eds. Hans Mathieu, and Catalina Niño Guarnizo, 28–55. Bogotá: Friedrich Ebert Stiftung en Colombia, 2012.

Canabarro, Diego, and Paulo Rená. "Veja dez razões para rejeitar artigo 10 do projeto sobre fake news, que rastreia mensagens." *Folha de São Paulo,* August 4th, 2020. https://www1.folha.uol.com.br/poder/2020/08/veja-dez-razoes-para-rejeitar -artigo-10-do-projeto-sobre-fake-news-que-rastreia-mensagens.shtml.

Cañás, Jaime. *Espionaje en la Argentina.* Buenos Aires: Editorial Mundo Actual, 1969.

Caparini, Marina. "Controlling and Overseeing Intelligence Services in Democratic States," in *Democratic Control of Intelligence Services: Containing Rogue Elephants,* eds. Hans Born, and Marina Caparini. New York: Routledge, 2016.

Careaga, Gregorio. *La Policía en el Escenario Institucional de la Democracia en Bolivia. Formación de Movimiento Corporativo en las Crisis Estatales de Abril del 2000 y Febrero del 2003.* Tesis de grado, Carrera de Ciencias Políticas, Facultad de Derecho y Ciencias Políticas, Universidad Mayor de San Andrés, 2008. https:// repositorio.umsa.bo/handle/123456789/8665.

Carpizo, Jorge. *El Presidencialismo Mexicano.* Mexico: Siglo XXI, 1978.

Carrillo Olea, Jorge. *México en Riesgo: Una Visión Personal sobre un Estado a la Defensiva.* México: Grijalbo, 2011.

Carrión, Julio F. "Conclusion. The Rise and Fall of Electoral Authoritarianism in Peru." In *The Fujimori Legacy: The Rise of Electoral Authoritarianism in Peru,* ed. Julio F. Carrión, 294–318. University Park: Penn State University Press, 2006.

Carruitero Lecca, Francisco Rogger. "Cambios en la Legislación Iberoamericana sobre Inteligencia, 2011–2013." Informe de Investigación No. 27/2014-2013. Área de Servicios de Investigación del Departamento de Investigación y Documentación Parlamentaria, Lima. 21 de noviembre de 2013.

Casal Beck, Luis. "El Terrorismo Sigue en la Mira." *El Observador,* January 26, 2002, political section, 8–9.

Cascante Segura, Carlos Humberto. *La Política Exterior de Costa Rica (1850–2010)*. San José: Editorial UCR, 2015.

Cascante Segura, Carlos Humberto, and Nery Mata Argüello. "Rasgos de una Política de Defensa de Costa Rica. Entre la Paz y la Inseguridad." *Revista de Estudios en Seguridad y Defensa*, 13 (25): 91–114. Available at https://doi.org/10.25062/1900 -8325.262.

Casey, Nicholas, and Federico Rios Escobar. "Colombia Struck a Peace Deal with Guerrillas, but Many Return to Arms." *New York Times*, September 18, 2018.

Casey, Nicholas, and Lara Jakes. "Colombia's Former FARC Guerilla Leader Calls for Return to War." *New York Times*, August 29, 2019.

Cátedra Seguridad y Convivencia Democrática. *¿Reformar o Cerrar la DIS? Aportes para el Debate*. Documento de Trabajo. San José: Universidad de Costa Rica, 2016.

Cawthorne, Nigel. *A History of Pirates: Blood and Thunder on the High Seas*. Edison, NJ: Chartwell Books, Inc., 2006.

Cayford, Michelle, Wolter Pieters, and Constant Hijzen. "Plots, Murders, and Money: Oversight Bodies Evaluating the Effectiveness of Surveillance Technology." *Intelligence and National Security* 33, no. 7 (2018): 999–1021. DOI: 10.1080/02684527.2018.1487159.

CEH. *Guatemala: Memory of Silence. Report of the Commission for Historical Clarification. Conclusions and Recommendations.* Guatemala City: Comisión para el Esclarecimiento Histórico, CEH / Historical Clarification Commission, 1999.

Center for Higher National Studies. "Course of Analysis of Strategic Information Applied to National Defense." http://calen.edu.uy/wp-content/uploads/calen-analisis -informacion-2019.pdf (accessed on May 28, 2019).

Central Intelligence Agency. "Ecuador Participation in Operation Condor." FOIA (Freedom of Information Act) Collection, document no. 0000345205, January 2, 1978 (released June 11, 1999). Accessed on May 7, 2019. Available at https://www .cia.gov/library/readingroom/docs/DOC_0000345205.pdf.

Central Intelligence Agency. "Freedom of Information Act Electronic Reading Room—Uruguay." https://www.cia.gov/library/readingroom/search/site/Uruguay (accessed on March 6, 2019).

Centro de Investigación y Seguridad Nacional (CISEN). *Official Journal of the Federation* (Mexico, February 13, 1989).

Centro Nacional de Inteligencia (CNI). 2019. https://www.gob.mx/cni.

Cepik, Marco, and Christiano Ambros. "Intelligence, Crisis, and Democracy: Institutional Punctuations in Brazil, Colombia, South Africa, and India." *Intelligence and National Security* 29, no. 4 (2014): 523–51. DOI: 10.1080/02684527.2014.915176.

Cepik, M., and Priscila Antunes. "Brazil's New Intelligence System: An Institutional Assessment." *International Journal of Intelligence and CounterIntelligence* 16, no. 3 (2003): 349–73. DOI: 10.1080/713830446.

Cepik, Marco, and Thomas Bruneau. "Brazilian National Approach towards Intelligence: Concept, Institutions and Contemporary Challenges." In *PSI Handbook of Global Security and Intelligence: National Approaches*, eds. Stuart Farson, Peter Gill, Mark Phythian, and Shlomo Shpiro, 112–129. Westport, CT: Praeger, 2008.

Cepik, Marco. "Bosses and Gatekeepers: A Network Analysis of South America's Intelligence Systems." *International Journal of Intelligence and CounterIntelligence* 30, no. 4 (2017): 701–22.

Cepik, Marco. "Intelligence and Security Services in Brazil Reappraising Institutional Flaws and Political Dynamics." *International Journal of Intelligence, Security, and Public Affairs* 23, no. 1 (2021): 81–102. DOI: 10.1080/23800992.2020.1868784.

Cepik, Marco. "Structural Change and Democratic Control of Intelligence in Brazil." In *Reforming Intelligence: Obstacles to Democratic Control and Effectiveness*, eds. T. C. Bruneau and S. C. Boraz, 149–69. Austin: University of Texas Press, 2007.

Céspedes, Christian Schambaher. *Claves para Entender la Crisis de Inteligencia en el Perú y propuestas de solución*. Lima: Escuela Conjunta de la Fuerzas Armadas, 2015.

Chacin Barragán, Joaquín. "Institucionalidad y Gestión Local de la Seguridad Ciudadana y la Violencia en Bolivia." In *Por esos Lugares no Camino. . . . Reflexiones Teórica-conceptuales para Comprender la Violencia y la Inseguridad en Ámbitos Urbanos*, ed., Alejandra Ramírez Soruco, 167–89. Cochabamba: CESU-UMSS, 2015.

Chasquetti, Daniel, and Adolfo Garcé. "Futuros Posibles de la Democracia Uruguaya." In *La Aventura Uruguaya ¿Naides más que Naides?*, coords. Gerardo Caetano and Rodrigo Arocena. Montevideo: Random House, 2011.

Cháves, Paul. "Los Espías No Bastan: Definiendo las Políticas Públicas en Materia de Servicios de Inteligencia en Costa Rica." Paper presented at the Panel on Intelligence, Center for Hemispheric Defense Studies, 2001. Available at http://www.fas.org/irp/world/costa_rica/chaves.html.

Chavez Escobar, Ana Margarita. "From Authoritarian to Democratic Regimes: The New Role of Security Intelligence." Master's thesis, Naval Postgraduate School, Monterey, CA, 2001. Available at http://hdl.handle.net/10945/2740.

Chilean Constitution. Trans. John Oeffinger. Article 15. https://www.camara.cl/camara/media/docs/constitucion_politica.pdf.

Chiyuki Aoi, Cedric De Coning, and Ramesh Chandra Thaku. *Unintended Consequences of Peacekeeping Operations*. Tokyo: United Nations University Press, 2007.

Christensen, Steen. "The Impact of China on South America Political and Economic Development." In *Regionalism, Development and the Post-Commodities Boom in South America*, ed. Ernesto Vivares, 77–100. Cham: Palgrave Macmillan, 2018.

Churruarrín Saavedra, Magaly Victoria (Directora General de Programación y Gestión Presupuestaria, Ministerio de Economía y Finanzas Públicas, Bolivia). "La Administración de Personal y Política Salarial para el Cumplimiento de Objetivos y metas en la Gestión Pública." XLIV Seminario Internacional de Presupuesto Público, Asociación Internacional de Presupuesto Público. Quito, Ecuador, November 10, 2017. Available at http://asip.org.ar/wp-content/uploads/2017/08/Adm-Pers-en-Bolivia.pptx.

CIA. Security Conditions in Costa Rica, March 6, 1963.

CIA. Update 1970 Handbook, December, 1972.

CIA. "Draft [REDACTED] Paper on Salvadoran Military." UWCHR El Salvador Freedom of Information Act (FOIA) Documents, June 13, 1984. Available at http://hdl.handle.net/1773/38759.

CICAD. "Bolivia. Evaluation Report on Drug Policies." Multilateral Evaluation Mechanism (MEM), Inter-American Drug Abuse Control Commission (CICAD), Organization of American States (OAS). July 2019. Available at http://www.cicad.oas.org/mem/reports/7/Full_Eval/Bolivia-7thRd-ENG.pdf.

CISEN (Centro de Investigación y Seguridad Nacional). *20 años de Historia: Testimonios Febrero 2009.* México, 2009.

CISEN (Centro de Investigación y Seguridad Nacional). Acuerdo por el que se crea la Escuela de Inteligencia para la Seguridad Nacional del Centro de Investigación y Seguridad Nacional (ESISEN). Mexico: House of Representatives, 2009. http://www.cisen.gob.mx/pdfs/acuerdo_escuela_inteligencia.pdf.

CISEN (Centro de Investigación y Seguridad Nacional). *Amenazas y Riesgos.* Mexico, 2014. http://www.cisen.gob.mx/snAmenazasRiesgos.html.

CISEN (Centro de Investigación y Seguridad Nacional). *Antecedentes.* Mexico, 2015. http://www.cisen.gob.mx/cisenAntecedentes.html.

CISEN (Centro de Investigación y Seguridad Nacional). *ESISEN.* Mexico, 2015. http://www.cisen.gob.mx/Esisen.html.

CISEN (Centro de Investigación y Seguridad Nacional). *Comunidad de Inteligencia.* Mexico, 2015. http://www.cisen.gob.mx/intComunidadInt.html.

CISEN (Centro de Investigación y Seguridad Nacional). *Doctrina de Inteligencia.* Mexico, 2000. http://www.cisen.gob.mx/html/doctrina.htm.

CISEN (Centro de Investigación y Seguridad Nacional). "Eduardo Medina-Mora, Director of the CISEN speech." Presented at *A los medios de los resultados del proceso de evaluación del CISEN.* Mexico, 2001. http://www.cisen.gob.mx/html/discurso.

Clarín. "Cristina descabezó la ex SIDE y vuelve Aníbal." December 17, 2014. Available at https://tapas.clarin.com/tapa.html#20141217.

Clarín. "El Servicio de Inteligencia Estatal." Editorial, February 18, 2000. Available at http://www.clarin.com/diario/2000/02/18/i-01601d.htm.

Clarín. "Escuchas ilegales y cultura política." December 22, 2007. Available at http://www.clarin.com/diario/2007/12/22/opinion/o-04201.htm.

CODEM. "Reseña Histórica de la Escuela Nacional de Inteligencia Militar (ESNACIN)." *Boletín Informativo* no. 95. San Salvador: Comando de Doctrina y Educación Militar, June 2003. Available at http://codem.mil.sv/index.php/publicaciones/boletin-informativo/boletin-informativos-de-2003/boletin-junio-2003/detail.

Collihan, Kathleen M., and Constantine P. Danopoulos. "Coup d'etat Attempt in Trinidad: Its Causes and Failure." *Armed Forces and Society;* Chicago 19, no. 3 (Spring 1993): 435.

Collins, Cath, ed. "The Uses of Truth—Truth Commission Archives, Justice and the Search for the Disappeared in El Salvador." Panel event, April 23, 2018. Available at http://www.dplf.org/sites/default/files/the_uses_of_truth_rapporteur_notes_final.pdf.

Comisión de la Verdad. *Informe de la Comisión de la Verdad, Ecuador 2010. Sin Verdad No Hay Justicia, Resumen Ejecutivo.* Quito: Edicuatorial, 2010.

Comisión Interamericana para el Control del Abuso de Drogas (CICAD) / Secretaría de Seguridad Multidimensional (SSM). *BOLIVIA Informe de Evaluación sobre Políticas de Drogas 2019*, Mecanismo de Evaluación Multilateral (MEM), Organización de los Estados Americanos (OEA). Available at http://www.cicad.oas.org.

Comisión para el Esclarecimiento Histórico (CEH). *Guatemala, Memoria de Silencio*, vols. 1–12. Guatemala City: CEH, 1999.

Comisión para la Investigación de los Servicios de Inteligencia Militares y Policiales. *Informe de penetración de la CIA en las Fuerzas Armadas y Policía Nacional.* Quito: Comisión para la Investigación de los Servicios de Inteligencia Militares y Policiales, 2008. Available at https://www.inredh.org/informe-de-penetracion-de -la-cia-en-fuerzas-armadas-y-policia-nacional.

Comisión Reorganizadora de la Dirección Nacional de Inteligencia. *Informe de la Comisión Reorganizadora de la Dirección Nacional de Inteligencia*, 2015.

CONADEP. *Nunca Más, Informe de la Comisión Nacional sobre Desaparición de Personas (CONADEP).* Buenos Aires: Eudeba, 1984.

Conaghan, Catherine M. *Fujimori's Peru: Deception in the Public Sphere.* Pittsburgh: University of Pittsburgh Press, 2005.

Conselho Nacional de Justiça. "Painel do Sistema Nacional de Interceptações de Comunicações—SNIC." Accessed March 13, 2021. https://bit.ly/31LnAad.

Constable, Pamela, and Arturo Valenzuela. *A Nation of Enemies: Chile under Pinochet.* New York: W. W. Norton Company, 1991.

Contreras, Carlos, and Marcos Cueto. *Historia del Perú Contemporaneo.* 6th ed. Lima: Instituto de Estudios Peruanos, 2018.

Controladoria Geral da União. "Acordo de Cooperação Técnica n. 11, de 10 de julho de 2020." https://repositorio.cgu.gov.br/handle/1/46082.

Copeland, Nicholas. *The Democracy Development Machine: Neoliberalism, Radical Pessimism, and Authoritarian Populism in Mayan Guatemala.* Ithaca & London: Cornell University Press, 2019.

Coppedge, Michael. "Venezuela: Democratic despite Presidentialism." In *The Failure of Presidential Democracy*, ed. Juan J. Linz and Arturo Valenzuela, 396–421. Baltimore: The Johns Hopkins University Press, 1994.

Corella Ovares, Esteban. "El Ejército en Costa Rica: Organización de las Fuerzas Armadas, Sistema de Reclutamiento y la Construcción del Estado, 1812–1870." Master's thesis on history, Costa Rica: Universidad de Costa Rica, 2013.

Corella Ovares, Esteban. "El Gasto Militar del Estado Costarricense, 1821–1870." Universidad de Costa Rica. *Diálogos, Revista Electrónica de Historia* 18, no. 1 (2017): 3–28.

Correa Vera, Loreto. "De la Violencia Social a la Imposición Estatal: El Caso Boliviano de los Hidrocarburos." In *El Prisma de las Seguridades en América Latina: Escenarios Regionales y Locales*, coord. Alejo Vargas Velásquez, 295–317. Ciudad Autónoma de Buenos Aires: CLACSO, 2012.

Cosío Villegas, Daniel. *El Sistema Político Mexicano.* Mexico: Joaquín Mortiz, 1972.

Costa, Gino. "Demilitarizing Public Security: Lessons from El Salvador." In *El Salvador Implementation of the Peace Accords*, ed. Margarita S. Studemeister. Washington, DC: United States Institute of Peace, Peaceworks No. 38, 2001, 20–26.

Costa, Gino. *La Policía Nacional Civil de El Salvador (1990–1997)*. San Salvador: UCA Editores, 1999.

Costa, Thomaz G., and Gastón H. Schulmeister. "The Puzzle of the Iguazu Tri-Border Area: Many Questions and Few Answers Regarding Organised Crime and Terrorism Links." *Global Crime* 8, no. 1 (2007): 26–39.

Creary, Dameon Ignatious. "Jamaican Maritime Security. What Are the Capability Gaps That Limit the Jamaica Defence Force in the Execution of Its Roles in Maritime Security?" Master's thesis, U.S. Army Command and General Staff College, 2017. https://apps.dtic.mil/dtic/tr/fulltext/u2/1038597.pdf.

Cremades Guisado, Álvaro. *Inteligencia y Secreto en Guatemala: La Trascendencia del Archivo Histórico de la Policía Nacional*. Guatemala: Escuela de Ciencia Política, Universidad de San Carlos de Guatemala, 2017.

Cruz, José Miguel, Luis Armando González, Luis Ernesto Romano, and Elvio Sisti. *La Violencia en El Salvador en los Años Noventa: Magnitud, Costos y Factores Posibilitadores*. Documento de Trabajo R-338, Banco Interamericano de Desarrollo. San Salvador: Instituto Universitario de Opinión Pública. Universidad Centroamericana José Simeón Cañas, 1998.

CSIS. *Maintaining the Intelligence Edge: Reimagining and Reinventing Intelligence through Innovation*. Center for Strategic and International Studies, p. ix. January 2012. Available at https://www.csis.org/analysis/maintaining-intelligence-edge-reimagining-and-reinventing-intelligence-through-innovation.

Curti, Samanta. *Reformas de Los Sistemas De Inteligencia En America del Sur*. Konrad Adenauer Stiftung, 2015. http://www.kas.de/wf/doc/17940-1442-1-30.pdf.

Da Ros, Luciano, and Matthew M. Taylor. "Accountability na Era Bolsonaro: Continuidades e mudanças." In *Governo Bolsonaro: Retrocesso Democrático e Degradação Política*, eds. Leonardo Avritzer et al., 187–204. São Paulo: Autêntica, 2021.

Dabroy, Jahir. Coord. "Desclasifiquemos el Modelo de Inteligencia en Guatemala." *Revista Política y Sociedad*, no. 53 (2016): 43–71.

Dahl, Erik. "Warnings Unheeded, Again: What the Intelligence Lessons of 9/11 Tell Us about the Coronavirus Today." *Homeland Security Affairs* 16, Article 7 (2020). http://www.hsaj.org/articles/16304.

Dale, Catherine. "National Security Strategy: Mandates, Execution to Date, and Issues for Congress." *CRS Report for Congress*. Washington, DC: CRS. Summary. 2016.

Davey, Gregor William. "Intelligence and British Decolonisation: The Development of an Imperial Intelligence System in the Late Colonial Period 1944–1966." PhD dissertation, Kings College of London, 2014.

Davies, Philip, and Kristian Gustafson, eds., *Intelligence Elsewhere: Spies and Espionage outside the Anglosphere*. Washington, DC: Georgetown University Press, 2013.

Davis Airgram. *The Military Junta at One Month.* Washington, DC: Department of State, October 12, 1973.

Davis, Dickie, David Kilkullen, Greg Mills, and David Spencer. *A Great Perhaps? Colombia: Conflict and Convergence.* London, UK: Hurst Publishers, 2016.

DCAF. "Intelligence Legislation Model—Argentina. The Argentinean National Intelligence Law, 2001 and the Regulation of the National Intelligence Act, 2002." Geneva Centre for the Democratic Control of Armed Forces (DCAF), 2011.

de Brun, Brendan. "Bolivia: A Tale of Praetorianism." In *The Routledge Handbook of Civil-Military Relations*, eds. Florina Cristiana Matei, Carolyn Halladay, and Thomas C. Bruneau. London: Routledge, 2021.

Decreto Legislativo N° 269, 25 de junio de 1992. Ley Orgánica de la Policía Nacional Civil.

De la Torre, Carlos. "Corporatism, Charisma, and Chaos: Ecuador's Police Rebellion in Context." *NACLA Report on the Americas* 44, no. 1 (2011): 25–32.

De León-Escribano Schlotter, Carmen Rosa. "Estructuras de Inteligencia en Guatemala." In *Inteligencia Policial—Compilación de Textos*, ed. Carmen Rosa De León-Escribano Schlotter, 7–21. Cuadernos de IEPADES no. 1. Guatemala: Instituto de Enseñanza para el Desarrollo Sostenible, 2000.

De Leon-Escribano, Carmen Rosa. "Capabilities of Police and Military Forces in Central America: A Comparative Analysis of Guatemala, El Salvador, Honduras and Nicaragua." *Western Hemisphere Security Analysis Center*, Paper no. 10 (2011), p. 54. Available at https://digitalcommons.fiu.edu/cgi/viewcontent.cgi?art icle=1009&context=whemsac.

DeVine, Michael E. "Defense Primer: Under Secretary of Defense for Intelligence and Security." Congressional Research Service. IF10523.

D'Haeseleer, Brian. "The Salvadoran Crucible: American Counterinsurgency in El Salvador, 1979–1992." PhD thesis, American University, Washington, DC, 2015. Available at http://hdl.handle.net/1961/auislandora:12413.

Diamint, Ruth. *Sin Gloria: La Política de Defensa en la Argentina Democrática.* Buenos Aires: EUDEBA, 2014.

Diamond, Larry. *Developing Democracy: Towards Consolidation.* Baltimore, MD: Johns Hopkins University Press, 1999).

Díaz Arias, David. *Construcción de un Estado Moderno: Política e Identidad Nacional en Costa Rica, 1821–1914.* San José: Editorial UCR, 2005.

Díaz Arias, David. *Crisis Social y Memorias en Lucha: Guerra Civil en Costa Rica (1940–1948).* San José: Editorial UCR, 2015.

Díaz Arias, David. *La Era de la Centralización: Estado, Sociedad e Institucionalidad en Costa Rica 1848–1870.* San José: Editorial UCR, 2015.

Díaz Zeledón, Natalia. "Otro proyecto de ley aspira a cerrar la DIS y redistribuir sus 3.188 millones a Seguridad." *Semanario Universidad*, February 28, 2020. Available at https://semanariouniversidad.com/pais/otro-proyecto-de-ley-aspira-a -cerrar-la-dis-y-redistribuir-sus-%C2%A3-188-millones-a-seguridad/.

Dirección General de Servicio Civil (DGSC). "About." Available at http://www.dgsc .go.cr/dgsc_descripcion.html.

Dorado E. and M. Alfonso. "La Policía en el Estado de Derecho Latinoamericano: El Caso de Bolivia." In *La Policía en los Estados de Derecho Latinoamericanos*, eds. K. Ambos, J. L. Gómez Colomer, and R. Vogler, 77–114. Bogotá: Editorial Gustavo Ibañez in cooperation with Friedrich-Ebert-Stiftung and Max Planck Institut für ausländisches und internationales Strafrecht, 2003.

Drago, Tito. *Chile: Un Doble Secuestro.* Spain: Universidad Complutense, 1993.

Dreyfus, Pablo G. *Border Spillover: Drug Trafficking and National Security in South America.* Thèse présentée pour l´obtention du grade de Docteur en Relations Internationales, Institut Universitaire de Hautes Études Internationales, Université de Genève (2002). Available at http://www.unige.ch/cyberdocuments/theses2002/DreyfusP/these.pdf.

Dror, Yehezkel. *La capacidad de gobernar. Informe al Club de Roma.* Mexico: Fondo de Cultura Económica, 1994.

Druetta, Gustavo, Eduardo Estévez, Ernesto López, and José E. Míguens, *Defensa y Democracia: Un Debate entre Civiles y Militares.* Buenos Aires: PuntoSur, 1990.

Durlo, Raul. *Relatório: Negativas de Acesso à informação pioram sob governo Bolsonaro.* São Paulo: Transparência Brasil, 2020. Available at https://www.transparencia.org.br/downloads/publicacoes/Negativas_de_acesso_a_informacao_pioram_sob_governo_Bolsonaro.pdf.

El Observador. "¿Qué Propone el Proyecto Antiterrorista que Aprobó el Senado y a Quiénes Afecta?" May 7, 2019. https://www.elobservador.com.uy/nota/-que-propone-el-proyecto-antiterrorismo-que-aprobo-el-senado-y-a-quienes-afecta--201957174836 (accessed on June 1, 2019).

Ellis, James O., Jr., James N. Mattis, and Kori Schake. "Restoring Our National Security." In *Blueprint for America,* George P. Schultz, ed. Stanford: Hoover Institution Press, 2016.

Estévez, Eduardo E. "Argentina's Intelligence in the Twenty-First Century/After Twenty-Five Years of Democracy." Paper presented at the 51st International Studies Association Annual Convention, New Orleans, Louisiana, February 17–20, 2010.

Estévez, Eduardo E. "Comparing Intelligence Democratization in Latin America: Argentina, Peru, and Ecuador Cases." *Intelligence and National Security* 29, no. 4 (2014): 552–80.

Estévez, Eduardo E. "Criminal Intelligence and the Challenge of Transnational Organized Crime in Latin America." *Journal of Mediterranean and Balkan Intelligence,* n.d., p. 18.

Estévez, Eduardo E. "Escenarios Actuales de Inteligencia: Desafíos en las Dimensiones Estratégica y Criminal. Legados, Cambio, Prioridades." Paper prepared for the congress of the Association of Latin American Studies, Chicago, Illinois, May 21–24, 2014, p. 32.

Estévez, Eduardo E. "Executive and Legislative Oversight of Intelligence in Argentina." In *Who's Watching the Spies? Establishing Intelligence Service Accountability,* eds. Hans Born, Loch Johnson, and Ian Leigh, 160–79. Washington, DC: Potomac Books, 2005.

Estévez, Eduardo E. "Gobierno de la Inteligencia en la Argentina y el Perú antes y después de la Crisis." *Ciencia Política* 15, no. 29 (2020): 249–85.

Estévez, Eduardo E. "Intelligence Community Reforms: The Case of Argentina." In *Intelligence Elsewhere: Spies and Espionage outside the Anglosphere*, eds. Philip Davies and Kristian Gustafson. Washington, DC: Georgetown University Press, 2013.

Estévez, Eduardo E. "La actividad de inteligencia en nuevos contextos normativos democráticos - adaptando la inteligencia realizada en el ámbito interior." Paper presented at Seminário internacional 'a atividade de inteligência e os desafioscontemporâneos.' Argentina-Brasil: Gabinete de Segurança Institucional da Presidência da República (GSIPR), Agência Brasileira de Inteligência (ABIN). December 1–2, 2005, pp. 7 and 24. http://fas.org/irp/world/argentina/actividad.pdf.

Estévez, Eduardo. "Intelligence in Peru: Between Democratic Reform and Regression." *Journal of Mediterranean and Balkan Intelligence* 7, no. 1 (June 2016): 107–24.

euronews. "Bolivia Kicks Out Cubans, Venezuelans for Allegedly Fuelling Unrest." November 15, 2019. https://www.euronews.com/2019/11/15/bolivias-ousted-morales-can-return-but-would-face-inquiry-interim-president.

Evan Ellis, R. "The Paraguayan Military and the Struggle against Organized Crime and Insecurity." *Military Review* (online exclusive) (January 2019). Available at https://www.armyupress.army.mil/Portals/7/Army-Press-Online-Journal/documents/2019/Ellis.pdf.

Ewell, Judith. *Venezuela: A Century of Change.* Stanford: Stanford University Press, 1984.

Executive Decree no. 526. Quito, Ecuador, September 21, 2018. Available at https://www.cies.gob.ec/archivos/4574.

Farah, Douglas, and Kathryn Babineau. *A Strategic Overview of Latin America: Identifying New Convergence Centers, Forgotten Territories, and Vital Hubs for Transnational Organized Crime*, Institute for National Strategic Studies–Strategic Perspectives, No. 28. Washington, DC: National Defense University Press, 2019.

Farson, Anthony Stuart, and Praeger Security International, eds. *PSI Handbook of Global Security and Intelligence: National Approaches. Intelligence and the Quest for Security.* Westport, CT: Praeger Security International, 2008.

Federal Bureau of Investigations. "Report on Bahamas Special Branch Collaboration with UK MI-5 Related to JKF Assassination Investigation." October 7, 1968. https://www.archives.gov/files/research/jfk/releases/docid-32329043.pdf.

Felipe, Marcell. "Opinion: The Castros Still Run Cuba." *Wall Street Journal*, April 18, 2021, sec. Opinion. https://www.wsj.com/articles/the-castros-still-run-cuba-11618783289.

Fernández Morales, Jesús, *Las Presidencias del Castillo Azul.* San José: Litografía e Imprenta Lil, 2010.

Fernández O., Óscar A. "Las Nuevas Políticas de Justicia, Seguridad Pública y Convivencia en El Salvador, 2014–2019." In *Anuario 2014 de Seguridad Regional en América Latina y el Caribe*, ed. Catalina Niño Guarnizo, 163–200. Bogotá: Friedrich Ebert Stiftung en Colombia, 2014.

Ferrer, Consuelo. "Amounts, Use and Embezzlement: What Is the Debate about Expenses Used in the Rest of the World." *Emol Nacional*, July 6, 2019. Trans. John Oeffinger. Available at https://www.emol.com/noticias/Nacional/2019/07/06/953626/Montos-uso-y-presunta-malversacion-En-que-esta-el-debate-sobre -los-gastos-reservados-en-el-resto-del-mundo.html.

Finer, Samuel E. *The Man on Horseback: The Role of Military in Politics.* London: Pall Mall Press, 1962.

Fiscal Year 2018 National Defense Authorization Act. "The 2018 National Defense Strategy: Fact Sheet." *CRS Report for Congress.* Washington, DC: CRS, 2018.

Fiscal Year 2021 National Defense Authorization Act. https://www.defensenews.com/congress/2020/12/03/compromise-defense-bill-confronts-a-rising-china/?utm_source=Sailthru&utm_medium=email&utm_campaign=EBB%2012.04.20&utm_term=Editorial%20-%20Early%20Bird%20Brief.

Flores Chacon, Monica. "Debunking the Pura Vida: Costa Rican Exceptionalism Is Under Threat." Master's thesis, Monterey, CA: Naval Postgraduate School, 2021. Available at http://hdl.handle.net/10945/67710.

Fonseca, Elizabeth. *Centroamérica: Su Historia.* San José: FLACSO-EDUCA, 1998.

Fontán Balestra, Florencia. "Towards a Democratic Control of Argentina's Intelligence Community." 2000. Available at http://www.law.harvard.edu/programs/criminal-justice/argentina.pdf.

Fortify and Modernize the National Intelligence System. Bill 12.234-02, 366th Congress, 66th sess. Trans. John Oefinger, Section I. Available at http://www.senado.cl/appsenado/templates/tramitacion/index.php?boletin_ini=12234-02.

Fórum Brasileiro de Segurança Pública [FBSP]. *Anuário Brasileiro de Segurança Pública*, no. 9 (2014). Available at https://forumseguranca.org.br/storage/8_anuario_2014_20150309.pdf.

Fox, Donald T., and Anne Stetson. "The 1991 Constitutional Reform: Prospects for Democracy and the Rule of Law in Colombia." *Case Western Reserve Journal of International Law* 24, no. 2 (1992): 139–63.

Frederic, Sabina. *Los Usos de la Fuerza Pública: Debates sobre Militares y Policías en las Ciencias Sociales de la Democracia.* Buenos Aires: Biblioteca Nacional, 2008.

Freedom House. *Freedom in the World (Democracy in Retreat).* Freedom House, 2019. Available at https://freedomhouse.org/sites/default/files/Feb2019_FH_FITW_2019_Report_ForWeb-compressed.pdf.

Freedom House. *Freedom in the World 2016—Anxious Dictators; Wavering Democracies: Global Freedom under Pressure.* Freedom House, 2016. Available at https://freedomhouse.org/sites/default/files/FH_FITW_Report_2016.pdf.

Friedman, Max Paul. "Significados Transnacionales del Golpe de Estado de 1954 en Guatemala: Un Suceso de la Guerra Fría Internacional." In *Guatemala y la Guerra Fría en América Latina, 1947–1977*, ed. Roberto García Ferreira, 19–28. Guatemala: CEUR-USAC, 2010.

Friggeri, Félix Pablo. "Primitive Accumulation, Mafia Capitalism, and the Campesino Population in Paraguay." *Latin American Perspectives* 48, no. 1 (2021): 126–44. Available at https://journals.sagepub.com/doi/pdf/10.1177/0094582X20975002.

Fundación Nacional para el Desarrollo. "De los Gastos Reservados de la Partida 54315 de la Presidencia a los Gastos Reservados del OIE." Documento de Opinión. San Salvador: Fundación Nacional para el Desarrollo -FUNDE, Capítulo Nacional de Transparencia Internacional, 2021. http://www.repo.funde.org/id/eprint/1776/.

Gabinete de Segurança Institucional. *Relatório de Gestão 2018*. Brasília: Gabinete de Segurança Institucional, 2019. Available at https://www.gov.br/gsi/pt-br/acesso-a -informacao/auditorias/relatorio_gestao_gsi_2018.pdf.

Gallinal, Francisco "La Ley de Caducidad." *El País*, February 28, 2009. Available at https://web.archive.org/web/20100812064807/http://www.elpais.com .uy/09/02/28/predit_401629.asp.

Galvez Lima, Ximena Mercedes. "El Salvador: High Level of Armed Gang Violence." In *The War Report: Armed Conflicts in 2017*, ed. Annyssa Bellal, 64–70. Geneva: The Geneva Academy of International Humanitarian Law and Human Rights, 2018.

Gamarra, Eduardo, and Raúl Barrios M. "Seguridad Ciudadana y Seguridad Nacional: Relaciones entre Policías y Militares en Bolivia." In *Justicia en la Calle: Ensayos sobre la Policía en América Latina*, ed., Peter Waldmann, 99–125. Bogotá: Konrad Adenauer Stiftung-CIEDLA, 1996.

Garcia, Richard Rocha. "Drug Trafficking and Its Impact on Colombia: An Economic Overview." *Canadian Journal of Latin American and Caribbean Studies* 28, no. 55/56 (2003): 277–304.

General Accounting Office of the Nation. "Budget Execution of All Items." https://www.cgn.gub.uy/innovaportal/v/83013/5/innova.front/consultas-de-ejecucion-pre supuestal.html (accessed on June 1, 2019).

Gentry, John A., and David E. Spencer. "Colombia's FARC: A Portrait of Insurgent Intelligence." *Intelligence and National Security* 25, no. 4 (2010): 453–78.

Gibson, Carrie. *Empire's Crossroads: The Caribbean from Columbus to the Present Day*. First edition. London: Atlantic Monthly Press, 2001.

Gill, Peter. *Intelligence Governance and Democratisation. A Comparative Analysis of the Limits of Reform*, London: Routledge, 2016.

Gill, Peter. "Of Intelligence Oversight and the Challenge of Surveillance Corporatism." *Intelligence and National Security* 35, no. 7 (2020): 970–89. DOI: 10.1080/02684527.2020.1783875.

Gill, Peter. *Policing Politics: Security Intelligence and the Liberal Democratic State*. London: Routledge, 1994.

Gill, Peter, and Michael Andregg, eds., *Democratization of Intelligence*. Oxford/New York: Routledge, 2015.

Gillies, Allan. "Theorising State–Narco Relations in Bolivia's Nascent Democracy (1982–1993): Governance, Order and Political Transition." *Third World Quarterly* 39, no. 4 (2018): 727–46.

Ginter, Kevin. "Latin American Intelligence Services and the Transition to Democracy." *Journal of Intelligence History* 8, no. 1 (2008): 69–93.

Ginter, Kevin. "Truth and Mirage: The Cuba–Venezuela Security and Intelligence Alliance." *International Journal of Intelligence and CounterIntelligence* 26, no. 2 (2013): 215–40. https://doi.org/10.1080/08850607.2013.758003.

Glebbeek, Marie-Louise. *In the Crossfire of Democracy: Police Reform and Police Practice in Post-Civil War Guatemala.* Amsterdam: Rozenberg, 2003.

Glebbeek, Marie-Louise. "Post-War Violence and Police Reform in Guatemala." In *Policing Insecurity: Police Reform, Security, and Human Rights in Latin America*, ed. Niels Uildriks, 79–94. Lanham: Lexington Books, 2009.

Gleijeses, Piero. "La Aldea de Ubico: Guatemala, 1931–1944." *Mesoamérica* 10, no. 17 (1989): 25–60.

Gleijeses, Piero. *Shattered Hope: The Guatemalan Revolution and the United States, 1944–1954.* Princeton: Princeton University Press, 1991.

Goldenberg, Sonia. "Is Peru Ungovernable." *New York Times*, January 5, 2021. Available at https://www.nytimes.com/2021/01/05/opinion/is-peru-ungovernable.html.

Goldman, Jan, and Susan Maret. *Intelligence and Information Policy for National Security: Key Terms and Concepts.* Lanham, MD: Rowman & Littlefield, 2016.

Goldstein, Daniel M. "Flexible Justice: Neoliberal Violence and 'Self-Help' Security in Bolivia." *Critique of Anthropology* 25, no. 4 (2005): 389–411.

Gómez de la Torre Rotta, Andrés. "¿Bolivarianización Jurídica de la Inteligencia en Bolivia?" Instituto Democrático para la Seguridad—IDS Perú, October 22, 2010. Available at https://idsperu.blogspot.com/2010/10/bolivarianizacion-juridica-de-la.html.

Gómez de la Torre, Andrés "Institucionalización y Crisis de Inteligencia: Perú en el Contexto Andino." In *Los Macro y Micro Desafíos de la Seguridad en Democracia*, pp. 243–44.

Gómez de la Torre Rotta, Andrés. "Hacia una Cultura de Inteligencia: Un Desafío para el Perú." In *Democratización de de la Función de Inteligencia: El Nexo de la Cultura Nacional y la Inteligencia Estratégica*, eds. Russell G. Swenson and Susana C. Lemozy, 307–28. Washington, DC: National Defense Intelligence College Press, 2009.

Gómez de la Torre Rotta, Andrés. "Perú: Frustraciones en los Intentos por Reconstruir Su Sistema de Inteligencia." In *Profesionalismo de Inteligencia en Las Américas, Edición Revisada*, eds. Russell G. Swenson and Susana C. Lemozy, 155–86. Washington, DC: Joint Military Intelligence College, 2004.

Gómez de la Torre, Andrés. "Política y Legislación de Inteligencia en el Perú e Iberoamérica: Tendencias y Perspectivas." Document 1. Lima: Instituto de Estudios Internacionales, 2013.

Gómez de la Torre Rotta, Andrés. "Servicios de Inteligencia y Democrácia en América del Sur: Hacia una Segunda Generación de Reformas Normativas?" *Agenda International* 16 (2009): 119–30.

Gómez de la Torre Rotta, Andrés, and Arturo Medrano Carmona. "Intelligence Laws in Peru and Latin America—Historical, Legal, and Institutional Evolution." In *Intelligence Management in the Americas*, eds. Russell Swenson and Carolina Sancho, 29–47. Washington, DC: National Intelligence University Press, 2015.

Gómez de la Torre Rotta, Andrés, and Arturo Medrano Carmona. "La Reorganización de Inteligencia en el Perú: Aspectos Jurídicos, Políticos, y Comparativos en la Región." In *Inteligencia Estratégica Latinoamericana: Perspectivas y Ejes Predominantes para la Toma de Decisiones Estratégicas ante un Mundo en Cambio*, ed. José Gabriel Paz, 177–89. Buenos Aires: Ministerio de Defensa, 2015.

Gómez de la Torre, Andrés, and Arturo Medrano Carmona. "Orígenes en el Proceso de Inteligencia en el Perú." *URVIO, Revista Latinoamericana de Estudios de Seguridad* 21 (2017): 104–20.

Gondard Pierre, and Hubert Mazurek. "30 Años de Reforma Agraria y Colonización en el Ecuador (1964–1994): Dinámicas Espaciales." In *Dinámicas Territoriales: Ecuador, Bolivia, Perú, Venezuela*, eds. Gondard Pierre and León Juan Bernardo. Quito-Ecuador: Colegio de Geógrafos del Ecuador (CGE)/Corporación Editora Nacional (CEN)/Institut de Recherche pour le Développement (IRD)/Pontificia Universidad Católica del Ecuador, 2001.

Gonsalves, Mark, Keith Stansell, and Tom Howes. *Out of Captivity*. New York: Harper, 2009, 413–29.

González Casanova, Pablo. *La Democracia en México*. Mexico: Era, 1965.

González Cussac, José Luis. "La Ley de Inteligencia Colombiana en Perspectiva Internacional." *Cuadernos de Derecho Penal* 15 (2016): 11–32.

González Guyer, Julián. "Relaciones Militares: El Impacto del 11 de Setiembre en el Cono Sur." Paper presented at the Seminar on Research and Education in Defense and Security Studies, Brasilia, August 2002.

González, Luis Eduardo. "Transición y Restauración Democrática." In *Uruguay y la Democracia*, coord. Charles Gillespie, 109–19. Montevideo: Ediciones Banda Oriental, 1985.

Government of Chile, "Rettig Report. Report of the Chilean National Commission on Truth and Reconciliation." Available at http://www.gob.cl/informerettig/.

Government of Jamaica. "A New Approach: National Security Policy for Jamaica. Towards a Secure and Prosperous Nation," 2014. https://cabinet.gov.jm/wp-con tent/uploads/2017/05/NATSEC-March-25-2014-1-1.pdf.

Government of Mexico. Executive Power of the Federation. "México en Paz." In *Sexto Informe de Gobierno (2017–2018)*. President Enrique Peña Nieto. Mexico, 2014. https://www.gob.mx/epn/articulos/sexto-informe-de-gobierno-173378?idiom=es.

Government of Mexico. Executive Power of the Federation. Official Journal of the Federation. "Acuerdo por el que se crea el Gabinete de Seguridad Nacional." Mexico, April 9, 2003. http://dof.gob.mx/nota_to_doc.php?codnota=2045345.

Government of Mexico. Executive Power of the Federation. *Plan Nacional de Desarrollo 2001–2006*. Mexico, 2001.

Government of Mexico. Executive Power of the Federation. *Plan Nacional de Desarrollo 2013–2018*. Mexico, 2013. http://pnd.gob.mx/

Government of Mexico. Executive Power of the Federation. *Plan Nacional de Desarrollo 2019–2024*. Mexico, 2019. https://lopezobrador.org.mx/temas/plan-nacional -de-desarrollo-2019-2024/.

Government of Mexico. Executive Power of the Federation. *Plan Nacional de Paz y Seguridad 2018–2024*. Mexico, 2018. https://lopezobrador.org.mx/wp-content/ uploads/2018/11/PLAN-DE-PAZ-Y-SEGURIDAD_ANEXO.pdf.

Government of Mexico. Executive Power of the Federation. *Programa para la Seguridad Nacional 2009–2012*. Mexico, 2009. http://www.dof.gob.mx/nota_detalle .php?codigo=5106082&fecha=20/08/2009.

Government of Mexico. Executive Power of the Federation. *Programa para la Seguridad Nacional 2014–2018*. Mexico, 2014. http://cdn.presidencia.gob.mx/ programa-para-la-seguridad-nacional.pdf.

Government of Mexico. Executive Power of the Federation. 3.1. Independencia, Soberanía y Seguridad Nacional." In *Primer Informe de Gobierno*. Mexico, September 1, 2001.

Government of Mexico. House of Representatives. "Acuerdo por el que se crea la Escuela de Inteligencia para la Seguridad Nacional del Centro de Investigación y Seguridad Nacional (ESISEN)." In *Official Journal of the Federation*. Mexico: April 16, 2009. http://www.cisen.gob.mx/pdfs/acuerdo_escuela_inteligencia.pdf.

Government of Mexico. House of Representatives. "Estatuto Laboral del Centro de Investigación y Seguridad Nacional." In *Official Journal of the Federation*. Mexico: November 29, 2006. http://www.cisen.gob.mx/pdfs/marco_normativo/ Estatuto_laboral_cisen.pdf.

Government of Mexico. House of Representatives. "Ley de Seguridad Nacional." In *Official Journal of the Federation*. Mexico: January 31, 2005. Last modified December 26, 2005.

Government of Mexico. Supreme Court of Justice, "Thesis XXV/96, XXVII/96, XXVIII/96, XXIX/96 y XXX/96." In *Semanario Judicial de la Federación,* ninth session, vol. 3 (México, March 1996).

Government of Trinidad and Tobago. "National Budget 2021—Ministry of Finance," October 5, 2020. https://www.finance.gov.tt/2020/10/05/national-budget-2021/.

Gozalvez Avilés, Yuvinka / Voice ofAmerica. "Cuban Health Workers Were Not Doctors, Bolivia's Government Reports | Diálogo Americas." Accessed June 28, 2021. https://dialogo-americas.com/articles/cuban-health-workers-were-not-doctors-bo livias-government-reports/.

Granda Aguilar, Víctor. *La Masacre de Aztra: El Crimen más Espantoso de la Dictadura del Triunvirato Militar*. Cuenca, Ecuador: Facultad de Ciencias Económicas de la Universidad de Cuenca, 1979.

Grandin, Greg. *The Last Colonial Massacre: Latin America in the Cold War*. Chicago: University of Chicago Press, 2011.

Gray Molina, George. "The Crisis in Bolivia: Challenges of Democracy, Conflict and Human Security." In *Democracy, Conflict and Human Security: Further Reading* (Volume 2), 25–34. Stockholm: International Institute for Democracy and Electoral Assistance, 2006. Available at http://www.idea.int/publications/dchs/upload/ dchs_vol2_sec1_2.pdf.

Green, W. John. *A History of Political Murder in Latin America: Killing the Messengers of Change*. Albany: State University of New York Press, 2015.

Grenoble, Alexander, and William Rose. "David Galula's Counterinsurgency: Occam Razor and Colombia." *Civil Wars* 13, no. 3 (2011): 280–311.

Griffith, Ivelaw L. *Caribbean Security in the Age of Terror: Challenge and Change*. Ian Randle Publishers, 2004.

Griffith, Ivelaw. *The Quest for Security in the Caribbean: Problems and Promises in Subordinate States*. M.E. Sharpe, 1993.

Griffith, Ivelaw L. *Strategy and Security in the Caribbean*. Greenwood Publishing Group, 1991.

Group of Interdisciplinary Studies on the Recent Past. "Documents on Uruguay in the National Archives and Records Administration." http://www.geipar.udelar.edu.uy/ index.php/category/documentos_hist/eeuu/ (accessed on March 6, 2019).

Group of Interdisciplinary Studies on the Recent Past. "Trías Collection." http://www .geipar.udelar.edu.uy/index.php/2018/10/03/coleccion-trias/ (accessed on March 6, 2019).

Grupo Conjunto para la Investigación de Grupos Armados Ilegales con Motivación Política en El Salvador. *Informe Grupo Conjunto para la Investigación de Grupos Armados Ilegales con Motivación Política*. San Salvador: Naciones Unidas, Julio de 1994. Available at https://www.transparencia.gob.sv/institutions/capres/docu ments/255838/download.

Guatemala Congress. Legislative Decree No. 11, of 1997. Law for the National Civil Police. https://www.acnur.org/fileadmin/Documentos/BDL/2016/10660.pdf.

Guatemala Congress. Legislative Decree No. 18, of 2008. Framework Law for the National System of Security. https://stcns.gob.gt/wp-content/uploads/2018/09/06 _Ley_Marco_SNS_.pdf.

Guatemala Congress. Legislative Decree No. 50, of 2003. Law for the Secretariat of Administrative Affairs and Security of the Presidency (SAAS). https:// www.saas.gob.gt/historico/informacion-publica/ley-de-saas/category/4-ley-de -saas?download=2:ley-de-saas.

Guatemala Congress. Legislative Decree No. 71, of 2005. Law for the General Directorate for Civilian Intelligence (DIGICI). http://ww2.oj.gob.gt/es/QueEsOJ/Es tructuraOJ/UnidadesAdministrativas/CentroAnalisisDocumentacionJudicial/cds/ CDs%20leyes/2005/pdfs/decretos/D071-2005.pdf.

Guatemala Congress. Legislative Decree No. 114 of 1997, Law of the Executive Branch. https://www.mem.gob.gt/wp-content/uploads/2015/06/12._Ley_del_Or ganismo_Ejecutivo_Decreto_114_97.pdf.

Guatemala. Procurador de los Derechos Humanos. *Informe Anual Circunstanciado de Actividades y Situación de los Derechos Humanos. 2019*. Guatemala: PDH, 2020.

Gurney, Kyra. "Paraguay Congress Approves Intelligence Agency Following EPP Attacks." Brief, *InSight Crime*, July 14, 2014. Available at https://www.insight crime.org/news/brief/paraguay-congress-approves-intelligence-agency-following -epp-attacks/.

Gustafson, Kristian, and Christopher Andrew. "The Other Hidden Hand: Soviet and Cuban Intelligence in Allende's Chile." *Intelligence and National Security* 33, no. 3 (April 16, 2018): 407–21. https://doi.org/10.1080/02684527.2017.1407549.

Gutiérrez, Edgar. "Guatemala Elites and Organized Crime." InsightCrime and IDRC, 2016. Available at https://idl-bnc-idrc.dspacedirect.org/bitstream/handle/ 10625/55847/IDL-55847.pdf.

Gutiérrez, Edgar. *Hacia Un Paradigma Democrático del Sistema de Inteligencia en Guatemala*. Ciudad de Guatemala, Guatemala: Fundación Myrna Mack, 1999.

Gutiérrez Fernández, Alberto Arturo. *Lineamientos Jurídicos e Institucionales para Reforma de la Normativa de la Policía Boliviana Destinada a Evitar Actos de Insubordinación.* Tesis de grado, Carrera de Derecho, Facultad de Derecho y Ciencias Políticas, Universidad Mayor de San Andrés, 2009. Available at https://repositorio.umsa.bo/handle/123456789/20066.

Guzmán, Valeria, and Nelson Rauda. "Casa Presidencial responde al juez que el Ejército no tiene archivos de El Mozote." *El Faro.net.* November 24, 2019. Available at https://elfaro.net/es/201911/el_salvador/23810/Casa-Presidencial-responde-al-juez-que-el-Ej%C3%A9rcito-no-tiene-archivos-de-El-Mozote.htm.

Harkins, Gina. "New Naval Strategy Zeroes in on China as Biggest Long-Term Threat to US." *Military Daily News,* December 17, 2020. https://www.military.com/daily-news/2020/12/17/new-naval-strategy-zeroes-china-biggest-long-term-threat-us.html.

Harmer, Tanya. "Fractious Allies: Chile, the United States the Cold War, 1973–1976." *Diplomatic History* 37, no. 1 (January 2013): 109–43.

Harriott, Anthony. *Police and Crime Control in Jamaica: Problems of Reforming Ex-Colonial Constabularies.* Barbados: University of the West Indies Press, 2000.

Harvard University Project on Justice in Times of Transition. *Recomendaciones para la Reforma de Inteligencia en el Perú a la Luz de la Experiencia de Otros Países del Mundo,* 2002.

Hathazy, Paul. "Crafting Public Security: Demilitarisation, Penal State Reform and Security Policy-Making in Postauthoritarian Chile." *Global Crime* 19, no. 3–4 (2018): 271–95.

Hellinger, Daniel C. *Comparative Politics of Latin America: Democracy at Last?* New York: Routledge, 2020.

Henderson, Alex. "7 Fascist Regimes Enthusiastically Supported by America." Alternet, February 4, 2015. Available at https://www.alternet.org/2015/02/7-fascist-regimes-enthusiastically-supported-america/.

Hernández, Gerardo. "Debates sobre la Dirección de Inteligencia y Seguridad (DIS) y Propuesta para Abrir un Espacio Académico de Análisis sobre Seguridad y Convivencia Democrática en Costa Rica." Paper presented at the 2° Congress on Intelligence: Intelligence Culture as an Element for Reflection and Collaboration, Madrid, 2010.

Hernández, Wiliam A. "Acoso y espionaje aumentaron en los gobiernos del FMLN." *El Salvador.com.* May 11, 2019. Available at https://historico.elsalvador.com/historico/592389/acoso-y-espionaje-aumentaron-en-los-gobiernos-del-fmln.html.

Herspring, Dale R., ed. *Civil-Military Relations in Communist Systems.* Westview's Special Studies on the Soviet Union and Eastern Europe. Boulder, CO: Westview Press [u.a.], 1978.

Hicks, Kathleen H., and Andrew Hunter. *Assessing the Third Offset Strategy.* March 16, 2017. Washington, DC: Center for Strategic International Studies, p. 1. Available at https://www.csis.org/analysis/assessing-third-offset-strategy.

Hixson, Walter L. *The Myth of American Diplomacy: National Identity and U.S. Foreign Policy.* New Haven: Yale University Press, 2009.

Hope, Alejandro. "CISEN: Los Limites de la Apertura." *El Universal*. Mexico, January 25, 2019. https://www.eluniversal.com.mx/columna/alejandro-hope/nacion/cisen-los-limites-de-la-apertura.

Hovey, Graham. "Nixon Saw Cuba and Chile Enclosing Latin America." *New York Times*, May 26, 1977. Available at https://www.nytimes.com/1977/05/26/archives/nixon-saw-cuba-and-chile-enclosing-latin-america.html.

HRW. "El Salvador, Events of 2020." *Human Rights Watch World Report 2021*. Available at https://www.hrw.org/world-report/2021/country-chapters/el-salvador.

Hudson, Rex A., ed. *Colombia: A Country Study*. Library of Congress Federal Research Division, 2010.

Hudson, Rex A. "National Security." In *El Salvador: A Country Study*, ed., Richard A. Haggerty, 195–260. Washington, DC: Library of Congress, 1990.

Hudson, Rex. "Terrorist and Organized Crime Groups in the Tri-Border Area (TBA) of South America." Federal Research Division, Library of Congress, Washington, DC, 2003.

Huneeus, Carlos. *El Régimen de Pinochet*. Santiago, Chile: Editorial Sudamericana, 2000.

Hunter, Wendy. "Continuity or Change? Civil-Military Relations in Democratic Argentina, Chile, and Peru." *Political Science Quarterly* 112, no. 3 (1997): 453–75.

Huntington, Samuel P. *The Third Wave: Democratization in the Late Twentieth Century*. Norman: University of Oklahoma Press, 1991.

International Security Sector Advisory Team (ISSAT). *Jamaica Country Profile*. International Security Sector Advisory Team (ISSAT), February 2, 2015. http://issat.dcaf.ch/Learn/Resource-Library/Country-Profiles/Jamaica-Country-Profile.

International Security Sector Advisory Team-ISSAT, *Paraguay Country Profile*, updated February 10, 2015. Available at https://issat.dcaf.ch/Learn/Resource-Library2/Country-Profiles/Paraguay-Country-Profile.

International Security Sector Advisory Team—ISSAT. *Bolivia Country Profile*, updated February 10, 2015. Available at https://issat.dcaf.ch/Learn/Resource-Library2/Country-Profiles/Bolivia-Country-Profile.

International Security Sector Advisory Team—ISSAT. *El Salvador Country Profile*, online, updated January 13, 2015. Available at https://issat.dcaf.ch/Learn/Resource-Library2/Country-Profiles/El-Salvador-Country-Profile.

Irala, Abel Enrique. "Modificación de la Ley de Seguridad y Defensa del Año 2013." *Estudios Paraguayos* 34, no. 1 (2016): 59–77.

IRB—Immigration and Refugee Board of Canada. "Activities and Mandate of the State Intelligence Organization (Organismo de Inteligencia del Estado, OIE); whether it continues to operate (1992–March 2002) [SLV38413.E]." March 25, 2002. Available at https://www.refworld.org/docid/3df4beac4.html.

Isgleas, Daniel. "Inteligencia Estratégica: Los Ojos y Oídos del Estado Bajo Control." *El País*, September 30, 2018, https://www.elpais.com.uy/informacion/politica/inteligencia-estrategica-ojos-oidos-control.html#_=_ (accessed on May 6, 2019).

Israel, Sergio. *Silencio de Estado: Eugenio Berríos y el Poder Político Uruguayo*. Montevideo: Aguilar, 2008.

Jamaica Information Service. "Govt. Seeks to Set Up Civilian Intelligence Agency." Jamaica Information Service, January 25, 2006. https://jis.gov.jm/govt-seeks-to -set-up-civilian-intelligence-agency/.

Jamaican Defence Force. "Jdf History Jamaica Defence Force—Recruiting Website | Fit to Fight." *History of the Jamaican Defence Force*. Accessed September 26, 2020. https://www.jdfweb.com/join/wp/jdf-history/.

Janetsky, Megan, and Anthony Faiola. "Colombian Guerrillas Are Using Coronavirus Curfews to Expand Their Control. Violators Have Been Killed." *The Washington Post*, July 26, 2020. Accessed on July 26, 2020. Available at https://www.washing tonpost.com/world/the_americas/colombia-coronavirus-farc-eln-guerrillas/2020/0 7/25/927d3c06-cb64-11ea-bc6a-6841b28d9093_story.html.

Jeffrey, Ronald N. "A National Security Strategy Framework for the Republic of Trinidad and Tobago." Master's thesis, U.S. Army Command and General Staff College, 2012.

Jeremie, John S. "Caribbean Terror; A Legal Analysis of the Allocation of Property Losses in Insurance Contracts in the Context of Terrorist Activity." *Journal of Financial Crime*; London 18, no. 4 (2011): 296–318. http://dx.doi .org/10.1108/13590791111173669.

Jijón Calderón, Francisco. "El Nuevo Ecuador y la Secretaría Nacional de Inteligencia." In *Inteligencia Estratégica y Prospectiva*, ed. Fredy Rivera Vélez. Quito-Ecuador: FLACSO-SENAIN, 2011.

Jiménez Gonzales, Oscar. "Sistemas de Inteligencia en el Perú y otros Países de Iberoamérica." Informe de Sistematización Temática No.15/2011–2012, Área de Servicios de Investigación del Departamento de Investigación y Documentación Parlamentaria, Lima, 24 de enero de 2012.

Jiménez Irungaray, Francisco. "La Seguridad de la Nación: Un Balance Estratégico-Político en la Guatemala de Hoy." In *La Construcción de la Paz en Guatemala: Reconciliación, Seguridad y Violencia en una Democracia Precaria*, ed. Bernardo Arévalo de León. Guatemala: FLACSO, Sede Guatemala, 2019, 61–90. Available at https://www.flacso.edu.gt/publicaciones/wp-content/uploads/2019/11/Libro-la -construccion-de-la-paz-1-1.pdf

Joffe, Alexander H. "Dismantling Intelligence Agencies." *Crime, Law and Social Change* 32 (1999): 325–46.

Johnson, Loch. "Governing in the Absence of Angels: On the Practice of Intelligence Accountability in the United States." In *Who's Watching the Spies? Establishing Intelligence Service Accountability*, eds. Hans Born, Loch Johnson, and Ian Leigh, 57–78. Washington, DC: Potomac Books, 2005.

Johnson, Loch. "A Shock Theory of Congressional Accountability for Intelligence." In *Handbook of Intelligence Studies*, ed. Loch Johnson, 343–60. New York: Routledge, 2009.

Jordán, Laura. "Desvío de fondos desde penales sirvió para financiar OIE." *La Prensa Gráfica*. July 10, 2021. Available at https://www.laprensagrafica.com/elsalvador/ Desvio-de-fondos-desde-penales-sirvio-para-financiar-OIE-20210709-0091.html.

Jouroff, Jorge. "Inteligencia y Cultura: Una Oportunidad para Uruguay." In *Democratización de la Función de Inteligencia: El Nexo de la Cultura Nacional y la Inteligencia Estratégica*, coords. Russell G. Swenson and Susana C. Lemozy. Washington, DC: Colegio Nacional de Inteligencia y Defensa, 2009.

Jurney, Corrine. "Netflix's Narcos Kingpin Pablo Escobar: A Look Back at His 7 Years on Forbes' Billionaires List." *Forbes*, September 18, 2015.

Kalmanowiecki, Laura. "Origins and Applications of Political Policing in Argentina." *Latin American Perspectives* 27, no. 2 (2000): 37–40.

Karl, Terry Lynn, and Philippe C. Schmitter. "What Democracy Is . . . and Is Not." *Journal of Democracy* 2, no. 3 (Summer 1991): 75–88.

Kenkel, Kai Michael. *South America and Peace Operations Coming of Age*. London: Routledge, 2013.

Kerche, Fábio, Vanessa Elias de Oliveira, and Cláudio Gonçalves Couto. "The Brazilian Councils of Justice and Public Prosecutor's Office as Instruments of Accountability." *Revista de Administração Pública* 54, no. 5 (2020): 1334–60. DOI: 10.1590/0034-7612201900212.

Keshavarz, Alma. "Irán and Hezbollah in the Tri-Border Areas of Latin America: A Look at the 'Old TBA' and the 'New TBA.'" *Small Wars Journal* (2015). Available at https://smallwarsjournal.com/jrnl/art/iran-and-hezbollah-in-the-tri-border-areas-of-latin-america-a-look-at-the-%E2%80%9Cold-tba%E2%80%9D-and-the.

Kincaid, A. Douglas. "Demilitarization and Security in El Salvador and Guatemala: Convergences of Success and Crisis." *Journal of Interamerican Studies and World Affairs* 42, no. 4 (2000): 39–58.

King, Ryan Thomas. "Sovereignty under Siege: Drug Trafficking and State Capacity in the Caribbean and Central America." Thesis. Monterey, CA: Naval Postgraduate School, 2016. https://calhoun.nps.edu/handle/10945/49507.

Kline, Harvey F. *Historical Dictionary of Colombia*. Plymouth, UK: Scarecrow Press, Inc., 2012.

Kollmann, Raúl. "Escoba Nueva." *Página/12*. December 17, 2014. Available at https://www.pagina12.com.ar/diario/elpais/1-262147-2014-12-17.html.

Koonings, Kees. "Civil Society, Transitions and Post-War Reconstruction in Latin America: A Comparison of El Salvador, Guatemala, and Peru." *Iberoamericana (Stockholm)* 32, no. 2 (2002).

Kornbluh, Peter. *The Pinochet File: A Declassified Dossier on Atrocity and Accountability*. New York: The New Press, 2013.

Kronawetter Pino, Iván Nikolás. "El Enjuiciamiento de Individuos por Crímenes de Derecho Internacional en el Orden Jurídico Paraguayo." Master's thesis, Facultat de Dret, Universitat de Barcelona, 2017. Available at http://hdl.handle.net/2445/120747.

Kurtenbach, Sabine. *Guatemala's Post-War Development: The Structural Failure of Low Intensity Peace*. Project working paper no. 3. Institute for Development and Peace (INEF). Germany: University of Duisburg-Essen, 2008.

Kurtenbach, Sabine. "Judicial Reform–A Neglected Dimension of SSR in el Salvador." *Journal of Intervention and Statebuilding* 13, no. 1 (2019): 57–74.

Kyle, Brett J., and Andrew G. Reiter. "A New Dawn for Latin American Militaries." *NACLA Report on the Americas* 51, Vol. 1 (2019).

La República. "Sanguinetti creó Dirección de Inteligencia Nacional por Decreto." January 6, 2000, political section, 4–5.

Lajtman Bereicoa, Tamara. "Dinámicas Securitarias y Guerra Preventiva en Paraguay. Aproximaciones a la Ley de Defensa Nacional y Seguridad Interna." *Crítica y Resistencias. Revista de Conflictos Sociales Latinoamericanos* 5 (2017): 139–58.

Landau, Saul, and John Dinges. *Assassination in Embassy Row.* New York: Pantheon Books, 1980.

Latinobarómetro Corporation, *Informe 2016.* Santiago, Chile: Latinobarómetro, 2016. Available at http://www.latinobarometro.org/latContents.jsp.

Leal, Francisco. "La Doctrina de Seguridad Nacional: Materialización de la Guerra Fría en América del Sur." *Revista de Estudios Sociales* 15 (2003): 74–87.

Leckie, Trevor Ray Anthony. "Enhancing the Jamaica Defence Force Military Intelligence Unit's Effectiveness to Conduct Counterdrug Missions." Master's thesis, US Army Command and General Staff College, 2006. https://apps.dtic.mil/dtic/tr/fulltext/u2/a452032.pdf.

Leeuw, Frans L., and Eric Furubo. "Evaluation Systems: What Are They and Why Study Them?" *Evaluation* 14, no. 2 (2008): 157–69. DOI: 10.1177/1356389007087537.

Legislative Assembly. Permanent Commission of Income and Public Expenditure. Act 26°. October 23, 2014.

Levitsky, Steven. "Fujimori and Post-Party Politics in Peru." *Journal of Democracy* 10, no. 3 (1999): 78–92.

Ley de Seguridad Pública y del Estado. Quito, Registro Oficial Suplemento 35 del 28 de septiembre de 2009.

Liang, Col. Quao, and Col. Wang Xiangsui, *Un-Restricted Warfare.* Brattleboro, VT: Echo Point Books & Media, 1999.

Linz, Juan J., and Alfred Stepan. *Problems of Democratic Transition and Consolidation: Southern Europe, South America, and Post-Communist Europe.* Baltimore: Johns Hopkins University Press, 1996.

Llop Meseguer, Santiago, Luis Martínez Enríquez, and Fernando Valeriano-Ferrer González. *Apuntes de Inteligencia Básica.* Callao: Escuela Superior de Guerra Naval, 2013.

Lodoño, Ernesto, and Letícia Casado. "A Collapse Foretold: How Brazil's COVID-19 Outbreak Overwhelmed Hospitals." *New York Times*, March 27, 2021. https://cutt.ly/Nx9W3p4.

Lopera Téllez, Juan Carlos. "La Multidimensionalidad del Concepto de Seguridad: Breve Acercamiento al Caso de Bolivia." *Estudios en Seguridad y Defensa* 5, no. 10 (2010): 51–60.

López, Ernesto. "La Introducción de la Doctrina de Seguridad Nacional en el Ejército Argentino." In *La Construcción de la Nación Argentina: El Rol de las Fuerzas Armadas*, 389–403. Buenos Aires: Ministerio de Defensa, 2010.

López, Griselda. "Informe de comisión especial concluye que no existen vínculos de actores políticos en el alza de los homicidios." Asamblea Legislativa, República de El Salvador, November 28, 2019. Available at https://www.asamblea.gob.sv/index.php/node/9750.

López, Jaime. "Análisis sobre el Manejo de los Gastos Reservados en el Órgano Ejecutivo." San Salvador: Fundación Nacional para el Desarrollo—FUNDE, Capítulo Nacional de Transparencia Internacional, February 16, 2017. Available at http://www.repo.funde.org/1262/.

López, Jaime Alberto, Rommel Reynaldo Rodríguez Trejo, and Jessica Estrada. "Manejo de los Gastos Reservados de la Presidencia: Hallazgos y Propuestas." San Salvador: Fundación Nacional para el Desarrollo—FUNDE, Capítulo Nacional de Transparencia Internacional, 2018. Available at http://www.repo.funde.org/1472/2/InformeGR.pdf.

López, Magdalena. *Transición y Democracia en Paraguay (1989–2017). "El cambio no es una cuestión electoral."* Buenos Aires: Editorial Sb, 2018.

López Bernal, Carlos Gregorio. "El Salvador 1960–1992: Reformas, Utopía Revolucionaria y Guerra Civil." In *As Revoluções na América Latina Contemporânea: Entre o Ciclo Revolucionário e as Democracias Restringidas*, eds. Marcela Cristina Quinteros, and Luiz Felipe Viel Moreira. Maringá: Ed. UEM-PGH-História; Medellín: Pulso & Letra: Universidad de Antioquia, 2017.

López Bernal, Carlos Gregorio. "Las Claves de la Historia de El Salvador." In *El Salvador. Historia Contemporánea, 1808–2010*, ed. Carlos Gregorio López Bernal, 27–52. San Salvador: Fundación Mapfre/Editorial Universitaria, Universidad de El Salvador, 2015.

López Nuila, Carlos Reynaldo. "La Seguridad Pública de El Salvador hasta 1994." *Entorno* 33 (2004–2005): 25–42. Available at http://hdl.handle.net/11298/824.

Lowenthal, Mark M. *Intelligence: From Secrets to Policy*, 7th ed. Los Angeles: CQ Press, 2017.

Luban, David. "The Publicity Principle." In *The Theory of Institutional Design*, ed. Robert Goodin, 154–198. Cambridge: Cambridge University Press, 1996.

Maciel Padilla, Agustín. *Understanding Mexico's National Security Conundrum*. UK: Routledge | Taylor & Francis Group, 2021.

Malamud-Goti, Jaime. "Soldiers, Peasants, Politicians and the War on Drugs in Bolivia." *The American University Journal of International Law and Policy* 6, no. 1 (1990): 35–55.

Maldonado, Carlos. "Desafíos de los Servicios de Inteligencia en la Región Andina." In *SIN Arcana Inmperii, Inteligencia en Democracia*, ed., Andrés Gómez de la Torre Rotta, 267–91. Lima: Foro Libertad & Seguridad, 2007.

Maldonado, Carlos. "Dilemas Antiguos y Modernos en la Inteligencia Estratégica en Sudamérica." *Interdisciplinary Journal of the Center for Hemispheric Defense Studies* 9, no. 1 (2009): 49–66.

Mansilla, H. C. Felipe. "Estructuras, Funciones y Problemas de la Policía boliviana. Un Esbozo Introductorio." In *Justicia en la Calle: Ensayos sobre la Policía en América Latina*, ed., Peter Waldmann, 141–60. Bogotá: Konrad Adenauer Stiftung-CIEDLA, 1996.

Mansilla, H. C. F. *La Policía Boliviana: Entre los Códigos Informales y los Intentos de Modernización*. La Paz: Plural Editores, 2003.

Manwaring, Max G. "Shadows of Things Past and Images of the Future: Lessons for the Insurgencies in Our Midst." *Strategic Studies Institute (SSI) Monograph.*

Carlisle, PA, 2004. Available at http://www.strategicstudiesinstitute.army.mil/pubs/display.cfm?pubID=587.

Mapping Militant Organizations. "National Liberation Army." Stanford University. Last modified July 2019. Accessed on July 25, 2020. Available at https://cisac.fsi.stanford.edu/mappingmilitants/profiles/national-liberation-army-eln.

Marsh, Kristin. "Republic of El Salvador." In *World Encyclopedia of Political Systems and Parties, Fourth Edition,* eds. Neil Schlager and Jayne Weisblatt, 404–11. New York: Facts On File, 2006.

Marsh, Kristin. "Republic of Guatemala." In *World Encyclopedia of Political Systems and Parties, Fourth Edition,* eds. Neil Schlager and Jayne Weisblatt, 521–29. New York: Facts On File, 2006.

Marsh, Sarah, and Marianna Parrga. "Oil-Rich Venezuela and Russia Come to Aid of Ally Cuba, But Its Energy Woes Persist." Reuters, October 4, 2019. https://www.reuters.com/article/us-cuba-economy-analysis-idUSKBN1WJ2GS.

Martens, Juan A. "Entre el Miedo y la Militarización: La Política de (In) Seguridad de Paraguay." *Revista de la Facultad de Derecho de México* 67, no. 269 (2017): 229–47.

Martin Merchan, Javiar. "Unmasking the Colombian Peace Accord." April 1, 2018. E-International Relations. Accessed on August 5, 2020. Available at https://www.e-ir.info/2018/04/01/unmasking-the-colombian-peace-accord-farc-strategy-in-a-never-ending-conflict/.

Martínez-Barahona, Elena, Sonia Rubio-Padilla, Héctor Centeno Martín, and Martha Gutiérrez-Salazar. "La Comisión de la Verdad para El Salvador: Manteniendo la paz a cambio de justicia." *CMI Report,* 2018.

Martínez Codó, E. *Reseña Histórica de la Inteligencia Militar del Ejército Argentino.* Buenos Aires: Editorial Puma, 1999.

Martínez Ventura, Jaime. "La Policía en el Estado de Derecho Latinoamericano: El Caso de El Salvador." In *La Policía en los Estados de Derecho Latinoamericanos,* eds. K. Ambos, J. L. Gómez Colomer, and R. Vogler, 305–52. Bogotá: Editorial Gustavo Ibañez in cooperation with Friedrich-Ebert-Stiftung and Max Planck Institut für ausländisches und internationales Strafrecht, 2003.

Mason, T. David, and Dale A. Krane. "The Political Economy of Death Squads: Toward a Theory of the Impact of State-Sanctioned Terror." *International Studies Quarterly* 33, no. 2 (1989): 175–98.

Mata, Esteban. "Mariano Figueres: Cada gobierno limpió los archivos de operaciones de la DIS." *La Nación,* October 20, 2014. Available at https://www.nacion.com/el-pais/politica/mariano-figueres-cada-gobierno-limpio-los-archivos-de-operacio nes-de-la-dis/LRSMN5HQIBCYBFDK3OCQSZENXI/story/.

Matei, Florina Cristiana. "The Media's Role in Intelligence Democratization." *International Journal of Intelligence and CounterIntelligence* 27, no. 1 (2014): 73–108.

Matei, Florina Cristiana, and Thomas Bruneau. "Intelligence Reform in New Democracies: Factors Supporting or Arresting Progress." *Democratization* 18, no. 3 (June 2011): 602–30.

Matei, Florina Cristiana, and Thomas C. Bruneau. "Policymakers and Intelligence Reform in the New Democracies." *International Journal of Intelligence and CounterIntelligence* 24, no. 4 (2011): 656–91.

Matei, Florina Cristiana, and Andrés de Castro García. "Chilean Intelligence After Pinochet: Painstaking Reform of an Inauspicious Legacy." *International Journal of Intelligence and Counterintelligence* 30, no. 2 (2017): 340–67.

Matei, Florina Cristiana, and Andres De Castro Garcia, eds. *Journal of Mediterranean and Balkan Intelligence* 7, no. 1 (2016).

Matei, Florina Cristiana, and Andrés de Castro García. "Transitional Justice and Intelligence Democratization." *International Journal of Intelligence and CounterIntelligence* 32, no. 4 (2019): 717–36.

Matei, Florina Cristiana, Andres de Castro Garcia, and Darren Henfield. "Balancing Civilian Control with Intelligence Effectiveness in Latin America and the Caribbean: Current Trends and Lessons Learned." *Journal of Mediterranean and Balkan Intelligence* 7 (2016): 15.

Matei, Florina Cristiana, and Carolyn Halladay, eds. *The Conduct of Intelligence in Democracies. Processes, Practices, Cultures*, vol. 21. 2019. https://www.tandfon line.com/doi/full/10.1080/23800992.2019.1695719.

Matei, Florina Cristiana, and Carolyn Halladay. "The Role and Purpose of Intelligence in a Democracy." In *The Conduct of Intelligence in Democracies: Processes, Practices, Cultures*, eds. Florina Cristiana Matei and Carolyn Halladay, 1–23. Boulder: Lynne Rienner Publishers, 2019.

Matei, Florina Cristiana, and Marcos Robledo. "Democratic Civilian Control and Military Effectiveness: Chile." In *The Routledge Handbook of Civil-Military Relations*, ed. Thomas C. Bruneau and Florina Cristiana Matei, 283–95. New York: Routledge, 2013.

Matthes, Britta Katharina. *From National to Pluri-National: Rethinking the Transformation of the Bolivian State through Struggles for Autonomy*. PhD thesis, University of Bath, 2017. Available at https://purehost.bath.ac.uk/ws/portalfiles/ portal/187928612/MATTHES_BrittaKatharina_PhD_Thesis_29_01_2018.pdf.

Matul Romero, Daniel, and Roger Juárez. *Reforma de la Dirección de Inteligencia y Seguridad (DIS). Lineamientos para la Construcción de una Hoja de Ruta.* Serie Perspectivas no. 6. San José: ESF—América Central, 2014.

Matul Romero, Daniel, and Andrés Palacios Rodríguez. "De CONDECA al Tratado Marco de Seguridad Democrática: La Nueva Institucionalidad Regional en Materia de Seguridad." *Revista Centroamericana de Administración Pública*, no. 66–67 (2014): 43–78.

Matul Romero, Daniel, and Carlos Torres. *Nuevo Arreglo Institucional a la Inteligencia en Costa Rica. Hacia una Reforma por una Gobernanza Democrática y Transparente.* Serie Análisis no. 2. San José: FES—América Central, 2015.

Mauceri, Philip. "Return of the Caudillo: Autocratic Democracy in Peru." *Third World Quarterly* 18, no. 5 (1997): 899–912.

Mayor, Hernán, and Oscar Pereira. "Formulación y Aplicación de Políticas Públicas en Seguridad Pública-Ciudadana." In *Seguridad Pública-Ciudadana en Paraguay.*

Enfoques, saberes, debates y prácticas, eds. Carlos Peris, and José Amarilla, 99–120. Asunción: Universidad Nacional de Asunción, 2017.

Mayorga, Fernando. "Bolivia: Seguridad Regional, Crisis Política y Conflictos." In *Anuario 2009 de Seguridad Regional en América Latina y el Caribe*, eds. Hans Mathieu and Paula Rodríguez Arredondo, 27–36. Bogotá: Friedrich Ebert Stiftung en Colombia, 2009.

McBride, James, and Andrew Chatzky. "Is 'Made in China 2025' a Threat to Global Trade?" May 13, 2019. CSIS, *Backgrounder*. Available at https://www.cfr.org/backgrounder/made-china-2025-threat-global-trade.

McCartney, Branville. "NIA = No Information Available," February 21, 2015. http://www.thebahamasweekly.com/publish/bahamian-politics/McCartney_NIA_No_Information_Available40170.shtml.

Mc Clean, Derron. "Intelligence Reform—Considerations for Trinidad and Tobago." Master's thesis. Monterey, CA: Naval Postgraduate School, 2018. https://calhoun.nps.edu/handle/10945/61223.

McCubbins, Matthew D., and Thomas Schwartz. "Congressional Oversight Overlooked: Police Patrols versus Fire Alarms." *American Journal of Political Science* 28, no. 1 (1984): 165–79. DOI: 10.2307/2110792.

McDavid Hilton, Anthony Clayton, and Noel Cowell. "The Difference between the Constabulary Force and the Military: An Analysis of the Differing Roles and Functions in the Context of the Current Security Environment in the Caribbean (The Case of Jamaica)." *Journal of Eastern Caribbean Studies*; Cave Hill 36, no. 3 (September 2011): 40–71,78.

Mc Lean, MAJ Jozette. "The Ability of the Trinidad and Tobago Defence Force (Ttdf) Logistics Infrastructure to Support Requirements in Response to Humanitarian and Disaster Relief (Hadr)." U.S. Army Command and General Staff College, 2017.

McMillan, John, and Pablo Zoido. "How to Subvert Democracy: Montesinos in Peru." *The Journal of Economic Perspectives* 18, no. 4 (2004): 69–92.

McNemey, Michael. "Military Partisanship." *Journal of Political and Military Sociology* 34, no. 2 (2006). Available at https://www.jstor.org/stable/45294228?seq=1.

McPhee, Glenn E. "Barriers to Collecting 'Secret Intelligence' in the Bahamas." *The International Journal of Intelligence, Security, and Public Affairs* 18, no. 2 (May 3, 2016): 93–109. https://doi.org/10.1080/23800992.2016.1196937.

McSherry, J. Patrice. "National Security and Social Crisis in Argentina." *Journal of Third World Studies* 17, no. 1 (2000).

McSherry, J. Patrice. "Operation Condor: Clandestine Inter-American System." *Social Justice* 26, no. 4 (78) (1999): 144–74.

McSherry, J. Patrice. "Tracking the Origins of a State Terror Network: Operation Condor." *Latin American Perspectives* 29, no. 1 (January 2002): 38–60.

McSherry, Patrice. "'Industrial Repression' and Operation Condor in Latin America." In *State Violence and Genocide in Latin America: The Cold War Years*, eds. M. Esparza, Henry R. Huttenbach, and Daniel Feierstein, 107–23. Abingdon/New York: Routledge, 2010.

Megale, Bela. "Chefe da Abin depõe por 3 horas em inquérito sobre ataques de Bolsonaro às urnas eletrônicas." *O Globo*, August 26, 2021. https://blogs.oglobo

.globo.com/bela-megale/post/chefe-da-abin-depoe-por-3-horas-em-inquerito-so
bre-ataques-de-bolsonaro-urnas-eletronicas.html.

Mejía Ibáñez, Raúl L. "La Realidad de la Inteligencia Nacional y la Importancia
que Tiene en la Vida del Estado Boliviano." In *Democratización de la Función de
Inteligencia—El Nexo de la Cultura Nacional y la Inteligencia Estratégica,* eds.,
Russell G. Swenson and Susana C. Lemozy, 291–306. Washington DC: National
Defense Intelligence College Press 2009.

Mejido Costoya, Manuel. "Neodesarrollismo y Seguridad en América Latina: El Caso
de Bolivia." *Revista Política y Estrategia,* no.114 (2009): 149–88.

Méndez-Coto, Marco. "The Social Construction of External Aggression in Latin
America: A Comparison between Costa Rica and Ecuador." *AUSTRAL: Brazilian
Journal of Strategy & International Relations* 7, no. 14 (2018). DOI: https://doi
.org/10.22456/2238-6912.84923.

Méndez-Coto, Marco, and Fredy Rivera Vélez. "The Intelligence Service in
Costa Rica: Between the New and the Old Paradigm." *The International Journal of Intelligence, Security, and Public Affairs* 20, no.1, (2018): 6–19 DOI:
10.1080/23800992.2018.1436387.

Metz, Steven, and Raymond Millen. "Insurgency and Counterinsurgency in the 21st
Century." Strategic Studies Institute, United States Army War College, Carlisle,
PA, 2004.

Michaels, Jon D. "The (Willingly) Fettered Executive: Presidential Spinoffs in
National Security Domains and Beyond." *Virginia Law Review* 97, no. 4 (2011):
801–98. Available at https://www.virginialawreview.org/articles/willingly-fettered
-executive-presidential-spinoffs-national-security-domains-and/.

Military Institute of Advanced Studies. "Careers and Courses 2019." http://www
.imes.edu.uy/new/?page_id=684 (accessed on May 28, 2019).

Military Institute of Weapons and Specialties. "School of Army Intelligence." http://
www.imae.edu.uy/escuela-EIE.html (accessed on May 28, 2019).

Ministerio de Gobierno, Reglamento Orgánico Funcional de Ministerio de Gobierno,
December 17, 1987.

Ministerio Público Fiscal, Argentina. "Contexto Histórico de Bolivia." In *edición
digital del alegato expuesto por el Ministerio Público Fiscal en las Causas 1504,
1951, 2054 y 1976 ("Plan Cóndor").* Available at https://www.mpf.gob.ar/plan
-condor/paises/bolivia/.

Ministério Público Militar. "MPM em Visita ao Centro de Inteligência do Exército." January 27, 2021. https://www.mpm.mp.br/mpm-em-visita-ao-centro-de-inteligencia
-do-exercito/.

Miranda, Boris. "Etnografía de la Vulnerabilidad: Escenarios Críticos del Narcotrá-
fico en Bolivia." In *Anuario 2015 de Seguridad Regional en América Latina y el
Caribe,* ed. Catalina Niño Guarnizo, 38–47. Bogotá: Friedrich Ebert Stiftung en
Colombia, 2015.

Modification of Law no. 19.974, Bill 10029-02. 363rd Congress, 19th sess. Trans.
John Oeffinger. Available at https://www.camara.cl/pley/pley_detalle.aspx?prmID
=10451&prmBL=10029-02.

Molina, Fernando. "El Ejército Obliga a Evo Morales a Renunciar como Presidente de Bolivia." *El País*, November 11, 2019. Available at https://elpais.com/interna cional/2019/11/10/actualidad/1573386514_263233.html.

Molina Jiménez, Iván. *Costa Rica (1800–1850), El Legado Colonial y la Génesis del Capitalismo.* San José: Editorial Universidad de Costa Rica, 1era edición, 2da reimpresión, 2002.

Molina Jiménez, Iván, and Fabrice Lehoucq. *Urnas de lo Inesperado. Fraude Electoral y Lucha Política en Costa Rica (1901–1948).* San José: Editorial Universidad de Costa Rica, 1999.

Molina, José, and Carmen Pérez. "Evolution of the Party System in Venezuela, 1946–1993." *Journal of Interamerican Studies and World Affairs* 40, no. 2 (Summer 1998): 1–26. ProQuest.

Molinari, Lucrecia. "Counterinsurgency and Union Movement in El Salvador (1967–1968)." *Genocide Studies and Prevention: An International Journal* 8, no. 1 (2013): 33–43.

Molinari, Lucrecia. "O Nascimento da Inteligência Contrainsurgente em El Salvador." *O Istmo*, online, March 29, 2016. Available at https://oistmo.com/2016/03/29/analise-o-nascimento-da-inteligencia-contrainsurgente-em-el-salvador/.

Molina-Vargas, Silvia. "La Violencia Política contra los Comunistas tras la Guerra Civil en Costa Rica (1948–1949)." *Cuadernos Inter.c.a.mbio sobre Centroamérica y el Caribe* 15, no. 1 (Abril-setiembre, 2018).

Moloeznik, Marcos Pablo. "Apuntes sobre Inteligencia e Instrumentos Estratégicos en México: Tensión entre la Legalidad y la Realidad." In *Inteligencia Estratégica Latinoamericana. Perspectivas y Ejes Predominantes para la Toma de Decisiones Estratégicas ante un Mundo en Cambio—Antología,* eds. José Gabriel Paz and Roberto Román, 133–60. Buenos Aires: Ministerio de Defensa, Dirección de Inteligencia Estratégica-Militar, 2015. https://drive.google.com/file/d/0B5QwcH3cZi9EWnBpTHFaWEkyOUU/view.

Moloeznik, Marcos Pablo. "Hacia una Interpretación del Proceso de Militarización de la Seguridad Pública en América Latina" In *Contextualizaciones Latinoamericanas. Proceso de Militarización de la Seguridad Pública en América Latina,* eds. Marcos Pablo Moloeznik and Ignacio Medina Núñez, 16–17. Guadalajara: CUCSH, Universidad de Guadalajara, 2019.

Moloeznik, Marcos Pablo. *Tratado sobre Pensamiento Estratégico-Militar. Enseñanzas para el Sistema de Defensa de México.* Mexico: Colectivo de Análisis de la Seguridad en Democracia (CASEDE), 2018. http://www.casede.org/index.php/bib lioteca-casede-2-0/defensa-y-fuerzas-armadas/fuerzas-armadas-mexicanas/410 -tratado-sobre-pensamiento-estrategico-militar.

Molzahn, Wendy Winter 2003. "The CIA's In-Q-Tel Model: Its Applicability." *Acquisition Review Quarterly.* 47–61 (Winter 2003): Available at https://www.dau.edu/library/arj/ARJ/arq2003/MolzahnWT3.pdf.

Moncada, Carlos. *Del México Violento: Periodistas Asesinados.* Mexico: Edamex, 1991.

Montenegro, Germán, Marcelo Fabián Saín, and Juan Gabriel Tokatlian. *De Militares a Policías. La "Guerra contra las Drogas" y la Militarización de Argentina.* Buenos Aires: Capital Intelectual, 2018.

Montepeque, Ferdy. "Un integrante de 'La Oficinita' será el secretario de Inteligencia de Giammattei." *El Periódico*, January 16, 2020. Available at https://elperiodico .com.gt/nacion/2020/01/16/un-integrante-de-la-oficinita-sera-el-secretario-de-in teligencia-de-giammattei/.

Mora, Carlos. "Ministro contradice a presidente sobre futuro de la Dis." *CRhoy*, September 10, 2020. Available at https://www.crhoy.com/nacionales/ministro -contradice-propuesta-de-presidente-sobre-futuro-de-la-dis/.

Mora, Frank O. "Cuba's Ministry of Interior: The FAR's Fifth Army." *Bulletin of Latin American Research* 26, no. 2 (2007): 222–37.

Mora Turner, Duilia. "Root Causes of Violence in Post-Civil War Guatemala: A Literature Review." *E-International Relations* (E-IR), (2015). Available at https:// www.e-ir.info/2015/04/08/root-causes-of-violence-in-post-civil-war-guatemala-a -literature-review/.

Mora Turner, Duilia. "Violent Crime in Post-Civil War Guatemala: Causes and Policy Implications." Master's thesis, Naval Postgraduate School, Monterey, CA, 2015. Available at http://hdl.handle.net/10945/45266.

Morales, Francisco Javier. "Organismos de Inteligencia y Seguridad en el Marco de las Dictaduras Militares de Brasil, Argentina y Chile. Perspectivas de Análisis y Puntos de Comparación." *Papeles de Trabajo: La Revista Electrónica del IDAES* 10, no.17 (2016): 74–103.

Moreno-Rodríguez, Laura. "La Presencia de José Figueres en México: Del Union-ismo a La Insurrección, 1942–1947." *Temas De Nuestra América. Revista De Estudios Latinoamericanos* 33 (septiembre 2017): 105–14. Available at https://doi .org/10.15359/tdna.33-e.4.

Moriconi, Marcelo, and Carlos Aníbal Peris. "Merging Legality with Illegality in Paraguay: The Cluster of Order in Pedro Juan Caballero." *Third World Quarterly* 40, no. 12 (2019): 2210–27. Available at https://doi.org/10.1080/01436597.2019 .1636225.

Motta, Rayssa, and Pepita Ortega. "STF é pressionado para derrubar Lei de Segu-rança Nacional." *Terra*, March 25, 2021. https://bit.ly/2P6R6V4.

Mozur, Paul, Jonah M. Kessel, and Melissa Chan. "Hecho en China y Exportado a Ecuador: El Aparato de Vigilancia Estatal." *The New York Times*, April 24, 2019. Accessed on May 23, 2019. Available at https://www.nytimes.com/es/2019/04/24/ ecuador-vigilancia-seguridad-china/.

Mujica, Jaris. "La Desactivación del Servicio de Inteligencia Nacional: De la Salida del Personal de Inteligencia al Desarrollo de las Agencias Privadas de Inteligencia en el Perú." *Revista de Ciencia Política y Gobierno* 1, no. 2 (2014): 129–55.

Müller, Jan-Werner. *What Is Populism?* Philadelphia: University of Pennsylvania Press, 2016.

Muñoz, Mercedes. "Costa Rica: La Abolición del Ejército y la Construcción de la Paz Regional." *Historia y Comunicación Social* 19 (2014): 375–88.

Muñoz, Mercedes. *El Estado y la Abolición del Ejército 1914–1949*. San José: Edito-rial Porvenir, 1990.

Muzzopappa, Eva. "Inteligencia Militar en Argentina. Reflexiones desde un Archivo Naval." *URVIO, Revista Latinoamericana de Estudios de Seguridad* 21 (2017): 87–103.

Myers, David. "The Institutions of Intelligence in Venezuela: Lessons from 45 Years of Democracy." *Ibero-Americana* 33, no. 1 (2003): 85–95. https://doi.org/10.16993/ibero.

Nación321. "¿Qué Hace y Cuánto nos Cuesta a los Ciudadanos el CISEN?." Last modified February 13, 2018. https://www.nacion321.com/gobierno/que-hace-y -cuanto-nos-cuesta-a-los-ciudadanos-el-cisen.

Nahum, Benjamín. *Informes Diplomáticos de los Representantes de España en Uruguay, vol. 2, 1948–1958.* Montevideo: UDELAR, 2001.

Nahum, Benjamín. *Manual de Historia del Uruguay, vol. 2, 1903–2000.* Montevideo: Ediciones Banda Oriental, 2002.

Nassau Guardian, The. "FNM Deputy Says Govt May Be Spying." *The Nassau Guardian,* May 7, 2014. https://thenassauguardian.com/2014/05/07/fnm-deputy -says-govt-may-be-spying/.

National Defense Authorization Act for 2020, which became public law no. 116-92 on December 20, 2019. It is available at https://www.congress.gov/bill/116th -congress/senate-bill/1790.

National School of Police. "Plans of Study." https://www.enp.edu.uy/index.php/ institutos/i-u-p/plan-de-estudio (accessed on May 28, 2019).

National Security Strategy Development Working Group for the Ministry and of National Security. *Jamaica: National Security Strategy.* Government of Jamaica, May 2006. https://www.files.ethz.ch/isn/156818/JamaicaSecurityStrategy.pdf.

Nixon, Celeste. "Government Presses Ahead with Creation of National Intelligence Agency," *The Tribune,* August 10, 2012. http://www.tribune242.com/news/2012/ aug/10/government-presses-ahead-with-creation-of/.

Norden, Deborah L. "Venezuela: Coup-Proofing from Pérez Jiménez to Maduro." *Oxford Research Encyclopedia of Politics* (January 22, 2021): 1–21. https://doi.org/10.1093/acrefore/9780190228637.013.1955.

O'Donnell, Guillermo. "¿Democracia Delegativa?" In *La democracia hoy,* coord. Jaime Barba. San Salvador: Istmo, 1994.

O'Rourke, Ronald. *Renewed Great Power Competition: Implications for Defense— Issues for Congress.* Congressional Research Service R43838, 2021. The Federation of American Scientist website hosting these reports lists twenty-six leading up to the January 27, 2021 version. Available at https://crsreports.congress.gov/ product/details?prodcode=R43838.

Obregón Loría, Rafael. *Hechos Militares y Políticos de Nuestra Historia Patria.* Alajuela: Museo Histórico Cultural Juan Santamaría, 1981.

Observatório da Imprensa. Accessed March 15, 2021. http://www.observatoriodaim prensa.com.br/.

Obuobi, Patrick P. "Evaluating Ghana's Intelligence Oversight Regime." *International Journal of Intelligence and CounterIntelligence* 31, no. 2 (2018): 312–41. DOI: 10.1080/08850607.2017.1375841.

O'Donnell, Guillermo, and Philippe C. Schmitter. *Transitions from Authoritarian Rule: Tentative Conclusions about Uncertain Democracies.* Baltimore, MD: The Johns Hopkins University Press, 1989.

O'Donnell, Guillermo, Philippe C. Schmitter, and Laurence Whitehead. *Transitions from Authoritarian Rule: Prospects for Democracy*, t 4. Baltimore: Johns Hopkins University Press, 1986.

Oeffinger, Clay, and Florina Cristiana Matei. "Peru: When Presidents Go Praetorian." In *The Routledge Handbook of Civil-Military Relations*, eds. Florina Cristiana Matei, Carolyn Halladay, and Thomas C. Bruneau. London: Routledge, 2021.

Official Diary of Colombia. Number 28343. November 10, 1953. Available at http://www.suin-juriscol.gov.co/viewDocument.asp?id=1778201.

Official Diary of Colombia. Number 30307. August 18, 1960. Available at http://www.suin-juriscol.gov.co/clp/contenidos.dll/Decretos/1801084?fn=document frame.htm$f=templates$3.0.

Ogilvie, Jaimie S. A. "Enhancing National Security in Jamaica through the Development and Employment of Special Operations Forces." Master's thesis, Naval Postgraduate School, 2005.

On the State Intelligence System and the Creation of the National Intelligence Agency, Law no. 19.974, 2004. Trans. John Oeffinger. Available at http://web.uchile.cl/archivos/derecho/CEDI/Normativa/Ley%2019.974%20Sobre%20el%20Sistema%20de%20Inteligencia%20del%20Estado%20y%20Crea%20la%20Agencia%20Nacional%20de%20Inteligencia.pdf.

Open Society Justice Initiative. "Archives of State Security Service Records." Briefing Paper, January 2013.

Organization of American States. "Report of the General Secretariat of the Organization of American States and the Panel of Independent International Experts on the Possible Commission of Crimes against Humanity in Venezuela." Washington, DC: Organization of American States, 2021. http://www.oas.org/documents/eng/press/Informe-Panel-Independiente-Venezuela-EN.pdf.

Orias A., Ramiro. "Políticas de Seguridad Ciudadana y Justicia Penal en Bolivia." In *Anuario 2014 de Seguridad Regional en América Latina y el Caribe*, ed. Catalina Niño Guarnizo, 51–74. Bogotá: Friedrich Ebert Stiftung en Colombia, 2014.

Ortiz Ruiz, Francisco Eliseo. "El Salvador 1991–1992: Acuerdo de Paz y Reforma Constitucional." *Perspectivas*, no. 4. San Salvador: Friedrich-Ebert-Stiftung, 2017.

OSAC. *Costa Rica Report*. Washington, DC: OSAC, 2020. Available at https://www.osac.gov/Content/Report/e21b7a07-15a4-4fda-93ca-18e81f6fbd8c.

Otamendi, Alejandra, and Eduardo Estévez. "El Gobierno Democrático de la Inteligencia en América Latina: Matriz de Análisis y los Casos Testigo de Argentina y Perú." In *Estado, Seguridad y Política Criminal*, eds. E. Mizrahi and A. Di Leo Razuk, 15–41. Buenos Aires: SAAP & FONCYT, 2018. Available at http://bit.ly/EsadoSeguridadyPolíticaCriminal.

Otamendi, Alejandra, and Eduardo Estévez. "Intelligence Challenges in Latin America: A Comparative Matrix on Democratic Governance." In *¿Nuevos Paradigmas de Vigilancia? Miradas desde América Latina*, ed. Camilo Ríos, 277–94. Córdoba: Fundación Vía Libre, 2017.

Oviedo, Esteban. "País contrata fotografías satelitales para vigilar incursión de ejército nicaragüense." *La Nación,* November 2, 2010. Available at https://www

.nacion.com/archivo/pais-contrata-fotografias-satelitales-para-vigilar-incursion-de
-ejercito-nicaraguense/DTSWANAZLBEA7J4G4RUGHPDTSM/story/.

Padilla, Tanalís, and Louise E. Walker, eds. "Dossier: Spy Reports: Content, Methodology, and Historiography in Mexico's Secret Police Archive." *Journal of Iberian and Latin American Research* 19, no. 1 (2013).

Palacios, Óscar. "Calderón y Fox deben ser investigados por caso espionaje: Morena." *MVS Noticias,* July 22, 2021. https://mvsnoticias.com/noticias/nacionales/calderon-y-fox-deben-ser-investigados-por-caso-espionaje-morena.

Palau, Rosa M. "Paraguay: Archivo del Terror. Los Archivos de la Policía de la Dictadura." In *Trabajadores, Archivos, Memoria, Verdad, Justicia y Reparación: Reflexiones del 4° Seminario Internacional El Mundo de los Trabajadores y sus Archivos,* orgs. Antonio José Marques, Inez Terezinha Stampa, and Sonia Troitiño, 39–57. Rio de Janeiro: Arquivo Nacional; São Paulo: Central Única dos Trabalhadores, 2018.

Palmer, Steven. "Confinement, Policing, and the Emergence of Social Policy in Costa Rica, 1880–1935." In *The Birth of the Penitentiary in Latin America: Essays on Criminology, Prison Reform, and Social Control, 1830–1940,* eds. Ricardo D. Salvatore and Carlos Aguirre, Kindle edition, n.p. Austin: University of Texas Press, 1996.

Paraguay, Consejo Nacional de Inteligencia. *Plan Nacional de Inteligencia.* Asunción—Paraguay, 2019. Available at https://www.sni.gov.py/institucion/amenazas-detectadas/plan-nacional-de-inteligencia.

Paraguay. *Informe Final (Conclusiones y Recomendaciones) de la Comisión Verdad y Justicia de Paraguay.* 2008. Available at http://www.derechoshumanos.net/lesahumanidad/informes/paraguay/Informe_Comision_Verdad_y_Justicia_Paraguay_Conclusiones_y_Recomendaciones.htm.

Paraguay. Poder Legislativo. Ley N° 1337 de Defensa Nacional y Seguridad Interna, 14 de Abril de 1999.

Paraguay. Poder Legislativo. Ley N° 5036 que modifica y amplía los artículos 2°, 3° y 56 de la Ley N° 1.337/99 "de Defensa Nacional y de Seguridad Interna." 22 de Abril de 2013.

Paraguay. Poder Legislativo. Ley N° 5241 Que crea el Sistema Nacional de Inteligencia. Gaceta Oficial N° 160, 22 de Agosto 2014.

Paraguay. Presidencia de la República. Decreto N° 2812, por el cual se reglamenta la Ley N° 5241, Que crea el Sistema Nacional de Inteligencia. 18 de Diciembre 2014.

Paraguay. *Primer Libro Banco de la Defensa Nacional de la República del Paraguay.* Asunción: Presidencia de la República. Ministerio de Defensa Nacional–Consejo Permanente de Defensa Nacional, 2013.

Parlamento del Uruguay. Comisión Especial de Control y Supervisión del Sistema Nacional de Inteligencia de Estado. https://parlamento.gub.uy/camarasycomisiones/asambleageneral/comisiones/1186.

Partido Revolucionario Institucional (PRI) and Instituto de Capacitación Política (ICAP). 1981. Capítulo I Fundación del Partido. In *Historia Documental del Partido de la Revolución,* 24–141. Mexico: PRI. https://www.pri.org.mx/bancosecretarias/files/Archivos/Pdf/594-1-11_32_45.pdf.

Peacock, Susan C., and Adriana Beltrán. *Hidden Powers in Post-Conflict Guatemala: Illegal Armed Groups and the Forces behind Them.* Washington, DC: Washington Office on Latin America, 2003.

Peñalva Torres, Ana Paula. "Transitional Accountability Only for Some? Accountability Measures against Paramilitary Groups." Master's thesis, Uppsala University, 2017. Available at http://urn.kb.se/resolve?urn=urn:nbn:se:uu:diva-325009.

Pérez Zumbado, Efraín. *El Control y la Dominación Política en el Régimen de Tomás Guardia.* San José: EUNED, 2013.

Peris Castiglioni, Carlos Anibal. "Herederos del Fantasma Stronista Perspectiva Continuista del Pensador José Manuel Silvero aplicada a la Situación Actual de la Policía Nacional." In *Pensamiento Paraguayo: Reflexiones en torno a las Ideas de José Manuel Silvero Arévalos,* eds. Mariza Amaral Maciel and Sandra Escutia Díaz, 319–35. Asunción: Ateneo de Lengua y Cultura Guaraní / Suindá Ediciones, 2019.

Phillips, Dion. "The Trinidad and Tobago Defence Force: Origin, Structure, Training, Security and Other Roles." *Caribbean Quarterly,* February 3, 2016. https://www.tandfonline.com/doi/pdf/10.1080/00086495.1997.11672099?needAccess=true.

Pion-Berlin, David. *Civil-Military Relations in Latin America: New Analytical Perspectives.* Chapel Hill, NC: University of North Carolina Press, 2003.

Pion-Berlin, David. *Military Missions in Democratic Latin America (Politics, Economics, and Inclusive Development).* New York: Palgrave Macmillan, 2016.

Plan V. "¿Ecuador tiene una Estructura de Inteligencia debilitada?" February 26, 2018. Available at http://www.planv.com.ec/historias/politica/ecuador-tiene-una-estructura-inteligencia-debilitada.

Plan V. "Las Perspectivas del Cambio en los Servicios de Inteligencia." October 1, 2018. Available at https://www.planv.com.ec/historias/politica/perspectivas-del-cambio-servicios-inteligencia.

Poczynok, Iván. "La Evolución de la Política de Inteligencia Militar Argentina: Rupturas y Continuidades (1990–2015)." *URVIO, Revista Latinoamericana de Estudios de Seguridad,* no. 21 (2017): 39–55. Available at https://revistas.flacsoandes.edu.ec/urvio/article/view/2855/2012.

Policzer, Pablo. *Rise and Fall of Repression in Chile.* Notre Dame, IN: University of Notre Dame Press, 2009: 42.

POLSEDE. "Aportes para el Estudio de la Inteligencia de Estado en Guatemala." Subgrupo de Trabajo No. 4 Inteligencia Civil, Proyecto Hacia una Política de Seguridad para la Democracia, FLACSO—WSP—IGEDEP. Guatemala, 2002, 9–10. Available at https://www.interpeace.org/resource/a-contribution-to-the-study-of-the-intelligence-apparatus-in-guatemala/.

Pontón, Daniel, and Fredy Rivera Vélez. "Postneoliberalismo y Policía: Caso de Ecuador 2007–2013." *Desafíos* 28, no. 2 (2016): 213–53.

Popkin, Margaret. "Building the Rule of Law in Post-War El Salvador." In *El Salvador Implementation of the Peace Accords,* ed. Margarita S. Studemeister, 10–19. Washington, DC: United States Institute of Peace, Peaceworks No. 38, 2001.

Porch, Douglas, and Jorge Delgado. "Masters of Today: Military Intelligence and Counterinsurgency in Colombia, 1990–2009." *Small Wars and Insurgencies* 21, no. 2 (2010): 277–302.

Portal da Transparência. "Controladoria-Geral da União—Unidades com vínculo direto—CGU." https://portaldatransparencia.cgu.gov.br/orgaos/37000-ministerio-da-transparencia-e-cgu.

Power, Timothy J., and Wendy Hunter. "Bolsonaro and Brazil's Illiberal Backlash." *Journal of Democracy* 30, no. 1 (2019): 68–82.

Powers, Nancy R. *The Transition to Democracy in Paraguay: Problems and Prospects. A Rapporteur's Report.* Working Paper No. 171, Helen Kellogg Institute for International Studies, University of Notre Dame, 1992. Available at https://kellogg.nd.edu/sites/default/files/old_files/documents/171_0.pdf.

Prego, Florencia. "Poststronismo, Reforma Constitucional y Transición Democrática. La Construcción de una Nueva Legalidad en Paraguay." *Sociohistórica* 43 (2019): e072–e072.

Presidency of Guatemala. Gubernative Agreement No. 166 of May 2011. Regulation of the Framework Law for the National System of Security. https://stcns.gob.gt/wp-content/uploads/2018/09/06_Ley_Marco_SNS_.pdf.

Presidency of Guatemala. Gubernative Agreement No. 172 of June 2014. Modifying the Regulation of the National Civil Police. https://pnc.edu.gt/wp-content/uploads/2015/11/Acuerdo-Gubernativo-172-2014.pdf.

Presidency of Guatemala. Gubernative Agreement No. 662 of December 2005. Regulation of the National Civil Police. https://pnc.edu.gt/wp-content/uploads/2013/07/Acuerdo-Gubernativo-662-2005.pdf.

Primera, Maye. "¡Patria o muerte! Pero ¿mi patria o la tuya?" *El País*, May 24, 2010. https://elpais.com/diario/2010/05/24/internacional/1274652005_850215.html.

Project GUA/99/022. *WSP in Guatemala. Toward a Security Policy for Democracy.* Consultation Report: Systematization of the Development of the Project, and Lessons Learned. Project: Toward a Security Policy for Democracy, FLACSO—WSP—IGEDEP, Guatemala, 2002. Available at https://www.interpeace.org/wp-content/uploads/2002/02/2002_Guat_Interpeace_Toward_A_Greater_Security_Policy_For_Democracy_ENG.pdf.

Prosic. *Ciberseguridad en Costa Rica.* San José: Programa de Sociedad de la Información Conocimiento (UCR), 2010.

"Providing for the Common Defense: The Assessment and Recommendations of the National Defense Strategy Commission 2019." Available at https://www.hsdl.org/c/sign-in/?dest=abstract%26did%3D818823.

Quintana Taborga, Juan Ramón. "Introducción: La Cultura de la Dependencia Imperial." In *BoliviaLeaks: La Injerencia Política de Estados Unidos contra el Proceso de Cambio 2006–2010*, ed. Juan Ramón Quintana Taborga. Ciudad Autónoma de Buenos Aires / La Paz: CLACSO / Estado Plurinacional de Bolivia. Ministerio de la Presidencia, 2016.

Quintana Taborga, Juan Ramón. "La Policialización de la Agenda de Seguridad de Bolivia." In *Agenda de Seguridad Andino-Brasileña: Primeras Aproximaciones*, eds. Marco Cepik and Socorro Ramírez, 97–143. Bogotá: Fescol/Iepri/Universidade Federal Do Rio Grande Do Sul, 2004.

Quintana, Juan Ramón, coord. *Policía y Democracia en Bolivia: Una Política Institucional Pendiente—Resultados Preliminares*. La Paz: Programa de Investigación Estratégica en Bolivia, 2003.

Quintana, Juan Ramón, coord., *Policía y Democracia en Bolivia: Una Política Institucional Pendiente*. La Paz: Fundación PIEB—Programa de Investigación Estratégica en Bolivia, 2005.

Quintero R, Silva E. *Ecuador: Una Nación en Ciernes*. Quito: Abya-Yala, 1998.

Rabe, Stephen G. "The Caribbean Triangle: Betancourt, Castro, and Trujillo and U.S. Foreign Policy, 1958–1963." *Diplomatic History* 20, no. 1 (Winter 1996): 55–78. https://www.jstor.org/stable/24913445.

Rambally, Rhonda Krystal. "T&T Leading in Foreign Fighters per Capita" *Trinidad Guardian*, August 6, 2016. https://www.guardian.co.tt/article-6.2.356744.cb 62081cbf.

Ramirez, Antonio. "An Introduction to Colombian Governmental Institutions and Primary Legal Sources." Hauser Global Law School Program—New York University. May 2007. Available at https://www.nyulawglobal.org/globalex/Colombia.html.

Ramírez de Garay, David. "La 4T y los Servicios de Inteligencia." *México Evalúa*. March 12, 2019. https://www.mexicoevalua.org/la-4t-los-servicios-inteligencia/.

Ramos Pismataro, Francesca. "Los militares y el deterioro democrático en Venezuela" [The military and the deterioration of democracy in Venezuela]. *Estudios Políticos* 53 (May 2018): 260–81. https://doi.org/10.17533/udea.espo.n53a12.

Regulations to the National Security Law. Decreto No. 913-F, Reglamento General de la Ley de Seguridad Nacional. Quito, Registro Oficial No. 231, del 13 de diciembre de 1976.

Reinert, John T. "In-Q-Tel: The Central Intelligence Agency as Venture Capitalist," *Northwestern Journal of International Law & Business* 33, no. 3 (Spring 2013): 677–709.

Reis, Bruno. *Modernização, Mercado e Democracia: Política e Economia em Sociedades Complexas*. Porto Alegre: Editora UFRGS, 2020.

Rempe, Dennis M., "The Origin of Internal Security in Colombia: Part I—A CIA Special Team Surveys La Violencia, 1959–1960." *Small Wars and Insurgencies.* vol. 10, no. 3 (1999): 24–61.

Reporters Without Borders. "Brazil." https://rsf.org/en/brazil.

República de Colombia. *Política de Defensa y Seguridad Democrática.* 2003.

República de El Salvador, Presidencia de la República, Decreto N° 36—Disposiciones Especiales Transitorias para la Participación de la Fuerza Armada, en Operaciones de Mantenimiento de la Paz Interna—, 9 de Marzo de 2020. Available at https://www.transparencia.gob.sv/institutions/capres/documents/352272/download.

República de El Salvador, Presidencia de la República, Decreto N° 46—Reforma a las Disposiciones Especiales Transitorias para la Participación de la Fuerza Armada en Operaciones de Mantenimiento de la Paz Interna—, 11 de Diciembre de 2020. Available at https://www.transparencia.gob.sv/institutions/mdn/documents/408343/download.

República de El Salvador, Presidencia de la República. Decreto N° 47—Reglamento de la Ley del Organismo de Inteligencia del Estado—, 17 de Agosto de 2016. Avail-

able at https://www.diariooficial.gob.sv/diarios/do-2016/08-agosto/17-08-2016
.pdf.

República de El Salvador, Presidencia de la República. Decreto N° 82—Reglamento
de la Ley Orgánica de la Policía Nacional Civil—, 9 de Octubre de 2002. Available
at https://www.lamjol.info/index.php/RPSP/article/view/3037/2786.

República de El Salvador, Presidencia de la República. Decreto N° 36—Creación
de la Comisión Revisora de Archivos Militares relacionados al Conflicto Armado
Interno de El Salvador—, 3 de Octubre de 2019. Available at https://www.transpar
encia.gob.sv/institutions/capres/documents/319882/download.

Reyes, Milton. "La Inteligencia China, Un Acercamiento Histórico Cultural." In
Inteligencia Estratégica y Prospectiva, ed. Fredy Rivera Vélez. Quito-Ecuador:
FLACSO-SENAIN, 2011.

Rial, Juan. "Los Militares en tanto Partido Político Sustituto frente a la Redemocratización en Uruguay." In *La Autonomía Militar en América Latina*, coords. Augusto Varas and Felipe Agüero. Caracas: Nueva Sociedad, 1988.

Rico, Álvaro. *Investigación Histórica sobre la Dictadura y el Terrorismo de Estado
en el Uruguay 1973– 1985*. Montevideo: UdelaR, CSIC, FHCE, CEIU, 2008.

Rivera Vélez, Fredy. *Democracia Minimalista y "Fantasmas" Castrenses en el Ecuador Contemporáneo*. Quito: FLACSO Sede Ecuador, 2003. Available at http://
www.flacso.org.ec/docs/ffaaydec.pdf.

Rivera Vélez, Fredy. "Ecuador: Untangling the Drug War." In *Drugs and Democracy
in Latin America: The Impact of U.S. Policy*, eds. Coletta Youngers and Eileen
Rosin. Boulder, CO. Lynne Rienner Publishers, 2005.

Rivera Vélez, Fredy. "Inteligencia Estratégica e Inteligencia Política: los Claro-
oscuros del Caso Ecuatoriano." In *Inteligencia Estratégica Contemporánea: Perspectivas desde la Región Suramericana*, eds. Mariano Bartolomé et al., 133–48.
Quito: Universidad de las Fuerzas Armadas, ESPE, 2016.

Rivera Vélez, Fredy. "La Inteligencia Ecuatoriana: Tradiciones, Cambios y Perspectivas." In *Inteligencia Estratégica y Prospectiva*, ed. Fredy Rivera Vélez, 47–73.
Quito-Ecuador: FLACSO-SENAIN, 2011.

Rivera Vélez, Fredy. *La Seguridad Perversa. Política, Democracia y Derechos Humanos en el Ecuador: 1998–2016*. FLACSO Sede Ecuador-Universidad Nacional
de Cuyo, 2012.

Rivera Vélez, Fredy. "Perspectivas Analíticas para la Paz, Seguridad y Desarme."
Documento de Trabajo. Secretaría Nacional de Planificación y Desarrollo. Quito:
SENPLADES, 2010.

Rivera Vélez, Fredy, and: Katalina Barreiro. "Political Intelligence and National
Security in Ecuador: A Retrospective Reading." *Journal of Power, Politics & Governance* 2, no. 3–4 (2014): 115–33.

Rivera Vélez, Fredy, Katalina Barreiro Santana, and Gilda Alicia Guerrero Salgado.
¿Dónde está el Pesquisa? Una Historia de la Inteligencia Política en Ecuador.
Quito: Pontificia Universidad Católica del Ecuador, 2018.

Robledo, Marcos."Democratic Consolidation in Chilean Civil-Military Relations:
1990–2005." In *Global Politics of Defense Reform*, eds. Thomas C. Bruneau and
Harold A. Trinkunas. New York: Palgrave MacMillian, 2008.

Rocabado Sánchez, José. "La Seguridad Ciudadana en Bolivia: ¿Hay Espacio para las Fuerzas Armadas?," *URVIO, Revista Latinoamericana de Estudios de Seguridad* 12 (2012): 25–40.

Rocabado Sánchez, José. "Las Fuerzas Armadas de Bolivia en un Contexto Internacional en Transformación, 2006–2018." In *El Nuevo Rol de las Fuerzas Armadas en Bolivia, Brasil, Chile, Colombia, Ecuador y Perú: Red de Política de Seguridad*, 139–70. Lima: Konrad Adenauer Stiftung, Pontificia Universidad Católica del Perú, Instituto de Estudios Internacionales, 2018.

Rocabado Sánchez, José. "Nuevos Retos para la Lucha contra el Narcotráfico. Una Aproximación a las Redes del Narcotráfico en Bolivia." In *La Reconfiguración del Fenómeno del Narcotráfico en Bolivia, Brasil, Chile, Colombia, Ecuador y Perú Red de Política de Seguridad*, eds. Jaime Baeza Freer et al., 83–114. Lima: Pontificia Universidad Católica del Perú, Instituto de Estudios Internacionales (IDEI)—Konrad Adenauer Stiftung, 2017.

Rochlin, James. "Latin America's Left Turn and the New Strategic Landscape: The Case of Bolivia." Third World Quarterly 28, no. 7 (2007): 1327–42.

Rodrigues, Karina F. "The Politics of Brazil's Access to Information Policies: History and Coalitions." *Revista de Administração Pública* 54, no. 1 (2020): 142–61. DOI: 10.1590/0034-761220180369x.

Rodríguez Luna, Armando, Patricia Quintanar, and Keyla Vargas "Presupuestos: Seguridad y Defensa 2000–2016." In *Atlas de la Seguridad y la Defensa de México* eds. Raúl Benítez Manaut and Sergio Aguayo Quezada, 303–34. Mexico: Colectivo de Análisis de la Seguridad con Democracia (CASEDE), 2016. https://www.casede.org/PublicacionesCasede/Atlas2016/Presupuestos.pdf.

Rodríguez, Johana. "Permiso de 72 Horas Sin Vigilancia a Exdirectora del DAS, María del Pilar Hurtado." RCN Radio. November 21, 2018. Available at https://www.rcnradio.com/judicial/permiso-de-72-horas-sin-vigilancia-exdirectora-del-das-maria-del-pilar-hurtado.

Rodriguez, Leopoldo, and Shawn Smallman. "Political Polarization and Nisman's Death: Competing Conspiracy Theories in Argentina." *Journal of International and Global Studies* 8, no. 1 (2016): 20–39.

Rodríguez, Natalia. "Modificaciones en Materia de Defensa Nacional: Las Atribuciones Extraordinarias de las FF.AA. que Introdujeron la Ley 5036/13 y el Decreto del Poder Ejecutivo." *Boletín SERPAJ Paraguay 7*, no. 26 (2018): 3–5.

Romano, Silvina María. "Entre la Militarización y la Democracia: La Historia en el Presente de Guatemala." *Latinoamérica. Revista de Estudios Latinoamericano* 55 (2012): 215–44.

Romero, Luis A. *A History of Argentina in the Twentieth Century*. Buenos Aires: Fondo de Cultura Económica, 2006.

Romero, Simon. "Chávez Decree Tightens Hold on Intelligence." *New York Times*, June 3, 2008. ProQuest.

Romero, Simon. "Ecuador's Leader Purges Military and Moves to Expel American Base." *New York Times*, April 21, 2008. Available at https://www.nytimes.com/2008/04/21/world/americas/21ecuador.html.

Roncken, Theo. "Bolivia: Seguridad Ciudadana y Vivir Bien. La Seguridad Ciudadana en el Horizonte del Vivir Bien." In *La Inseguridad y la Seguridad Ciudadana en América Latina*, coord. José Alfredo Zavaleta Betancourt, 205–32. Ciudad Autónoma de Buenos Aires: CLACSO, 2012.

Roniger, Luis, Leonardo Senkman, and María Antonia Sánchez. "El Legado del Autoritarismo y la Construcción de Memoria Histórica en el Paraguay Poststronista." In *Las Luchas por la Memoria en América Latina: Historia Reciente y Violencia Política*, coords. Eugenia Allier Montaño and Emilio Crenzel, 149–84. México: Bonilla Artigas Editores: UNAM, Instituto de Investigaciones Sociales, 2015.

Rospigliosi, Fernando. "La Crisis de los Espías." *El Comercio*, May 22, 2015.

Rospigliosi, Fernando. "La DINI: una alternativa." *El Comercio*, April 12, 2015.

Rospigliosi, Fernando. *Montesinos y las Fuerzas Armadas: Cómo Controló Durante una Década las Instituciones Militares*. Lima: Instituto de Estudios Peruanos, 2000.

Russell, Khrisna. "PLP's NIA Operated for 'Personal Gain,'" May 23, 2019. http://www.tribune242.com/news/2019/may/23/plps-nia-operated-personal-gain/.

Sáenz Carbonell, Jorge. *Historia Diplomática de Costa Rica (1948–1970)*. Heredia: Escuela de Relaciones Internacionales, 2013.

Saín, Marcelo. *Alfonsín, Menem y las Relaciones Cívico-militares: La Construcción del Control Civil sobre las Fuerzas Armadas en la Argentina Democrática (1983–1995)*. PhD thesis, Universidad Estadual de Campinas, Brasil, 1999.

Saín, Marcelo. *La Casa que No Cesa: Infortunios y Desafíos en el Proceso de Reforma de la Ex SIDE*. Buenos Aires: Editorial Octubre, 2016.

Saín, Marcelo. "Condiciones Institucionales del Control Parlamentario de las Actividades y Organismos de Inteligencia del Estado." In *Papeles de trabajo: Control Democrático de los Organismos de Seguridad Interior de la República Argentina*, 113–39. Buenos Aires: CELS, 1997.

Saín, Marcelo. "Defensa Nacional y Fuerzas Armadas. El Modelo Peronista (1943–1955)." In *La Construcción de la Nación Argentina: El rol de las Fuerzas Armadas*, 333–43. Buenos Aires: Ministerio de Defensa, 2010.

Sáiz, Enrique. "Unas Primeras Aproximaciones a los Sesgos Cognitivos en el Análisis de Inteligencia." *Inteligencia y Seguridad: Revista de Análisis y Prospectiva* 7 (2010): 231–36.

Sanahuja, José Antonio. "América Latina: Malestar democrático y retos de la crisis de la globalización." In *Panorama Estratégico 2019*, Instituto Español de Estudios Estratégicos, 241. España: Ministerio de Defensa, 2019.

Sánchez-Sibony, Omar. "Competitive Authoritarianism in Morales's Bolivia: Skewing Arenas of Competition." *Latin American Politics and Society* 63, no. 1 (2021): 118–44. DOI: https://doi.org/10.1017/lap.2020.35.

Sancho Hirane, Carolina. "Cooperación en Inteligencia y UNASUR: Posibilidades y Limitaciones." Paper presented at the XXXI International Congress of the Latin American Studies Association (LASA). Washington, DC, May 29–June 1, 2013.

Sanger, David E. "Biden Calls for US to Enter a New Superpower Struggle." *New York Times*, May 5, 2021. https://www.nytimes.com/2021/04/29/us/politics/biden-china-russia-cold-war.html.

Sansó-Rubert Pascual, Daniel. "Inteligencia Militar y Criminalidad Organizada: Retos a Debatir en América Latina." *URVIO, Revista Latinoamericana de Estudios de Seguridad* 21 (2017): 22–38.

Schemo, Diana Jean. "Files in Paraguay Detail Atrocities of US, Allies." *The New York Times*, August 11, 1999. Available at https://www.nytimes.com/1999/08/11/world/files-in-paraguay-detail-atrocities-of-us-allies.html.

Schifter, Jacobo. *Costa Rica 1948. Análisis de Documentos Confidenciales del Departamento de Estado.* San José: EDUCA, 1982.

Schifter, Jacobo. *Las Alianzas Conflictivas: Las Relaciones de Estados Unidos y Costa Rica desde la Segunda Guerra Mundial a la Guerra Fría.* San José: Libro Libre, 1986.

Schirmer, Jennifer. "The Guatemalan Politico-Military Project: Legacies for a Violent Peace?" *Latin American Perspectives* 26, no. 2 (1999): 92–107.

Schultze-Kraft, Markus. *Pacificación y Poder Civil en Centroamérica: Las Relaciones Cívico-Militares en El Salvador, Guatemala y Nicaragua en el Posconflicto.* Bogotá: Editorial Norma, 2005.

Schwarcz, L. *Sobre o Autoritarismo Brasileiro.* São Paulo: Companhia das Letras, 2019.

Schwartz, Mattathias. "A Massacre in Jamaica." *The New Yorker*, December 5, 2011. https://www.newyorker.com/magazine/2011/12/12/a-massacre-in-jamaica.

Senado Federal. "Atividades Legislativas: Comissão Mista de Controle das Atividades de Inteligência." Accessed March 17, 2021. Available at https://legis.senado.leg.br/comissoes/comissao?codcol=449.

Senado Federal. *Relatório Final da CPI da Espionagem.* Brasília: Diário do Senado Federal, Ano LXIX, Sup. "C" n. 51, 17 de abril de 2014.

Shils, Edward. *The Torment of Secrecy.* Chicago: Ivan R. Dee, 1996.

Shiraz, Zakia. "Intelligence Governance in Colombia: Lessons Learnt and Challenges for the Future." Paper presented at the 57th ISA (International Studies Association) Annual Convention, Atlanta, Georgia, USA, March 16–19, 2016.

Shiraz, Zakia, and John Kasuku. "Intelligence Culture and the Global South: China, Africa and Latin America." In *Secret Intelligence*, eds. Christopher Andrew, Richard J. Aldrich, and Wesley K. Wark. London: Routledge, 2019.

Sistema Costarricense de Información Jurídica (SCIJ). Online: Constitución Política de la República de Costa Rica, 1949; Ley General de Policía, N° 7.410; Decretos Ejecutivos: N°16.398, N°23.758, N°. 27,818, N° 29,459, N° 30.192, N° 32.522, N° 35.793, N°39.672, N° 41.096. http://www.pgrweb.go.cr/scij/.

Sistema Integrado de Planejamento e Orçamento—SIOP. Accessed March 17, 2021. https://www.siop.planejamento.gov.br/.

Smith, Sloan. "NCIA Bill Passes Senate." *The Nassau Guardian*, June 4, 2019. https://thenassauguardian.com/2019/06/04/ncia-bill-passes-senate/.

Sondrol, Paul. "The Presidentialist Tradition in Latin America." *International Journal of Public Administration* 28, no. 5–6 (2005): 517–30.

Soprano, Germán. "El Ejército Argentino en Democracia: De la 'Doctrina de la Seguridad Nacional' a la Definición de las 'Nuevas Amenazas' (1983–2001)." *Revista Universitaria de Historia Militar* 7, Vol. 4 (RUHM, 2015): 86–107. Available at https://ri.conicet.gov.ar/bitstream/handle/11336/52165/CONICET_Digital _Nro.945f7cd6-6e91-4a26-ba73-3ee906172740_A.pdf?sequence=2.

Sprenkels, Ralph. "La Memoria Militante: Historia y Política en la Posguerra Salvadoreña." In *Observatorio Latinoamericano 9 Dossier El Salvador,* ed. Lucrecia Molinari, 186–200. Buenos Aires: Instituto de Estudios de América Latina y el Caribe (IEALC), Facultad de Ciencias Sociales, Universidad de Buenos Aires, 2011. Available at http://iealc.sociales.uba.ar/publicaciones/observatorio-latino americano-9/.

Stanley, William. "Building New Police Forces in El Salvador and Guatemala: Learning and Counter-Learning." In *Peacebuilding and Police Reform*, eds. Tor Tanke Holm and Espen Barth Eide, 113–34. London: Frank Cass, 2000.

Stanley, William. *Enabling Peace in Guatemala: The Story of MINUGUA.* Boulder: Lynne Rienner Publishers, 2013.

Stanley, William. *The Protection Racket State: Elite Politics, Military Extortion, and Civil War in El Salvador*. Philadelphia: Temple University Press, 1996.

Stanley, William, and David Holiday. "Broad Participation, Diffuse Responsibility: Peace Implementation in Guatemala." In *Ending Civil Wars: The Implementation of Peace Agreements,* eds. Stephen John Stedman, Donald Rothchild, and Elisabeth Consuens, 421–462. Boulder, CO: Lynne Rienner Press, 2002.

Stanley, William, and Robert Loosle. "El Salvador: The Civilian Police Component of Peace Operations." In *Policing the New World Disorder*, eds. Robert B. Oakley, Eliot M. Goldberg, and Michale J. Dziedzic. Washington, DC: National Defense University Press, 1997.

Stepan, Alfred. *Repensando a los Militares en Política—Cono Sur: Un Análisis Comparado.* Buenos Aires: Planeta, 1988.

Stepan, Alfred. *Repensando a los Militares en Política.* Buenos Aires: Planeta, 1988.

Stepan, Alfred. *Rethinking Military Politics: Brazil and the Southern Cone*. Princeton, NJ: Princeton University Press, 1988.

Strätz, Murilo. "O Sistema Brasileiro de Inteligência e a amplitude do controle externo da atividade policial federal exercido pelo Ministério Público da União." *Revista da SJRJ* 19, no. 34 (2012): 209–23. https://www.jfrj.jus.br/revista-sjrj/ artigo/o-sistema-brasileiro-de-inteligencia-e-amplitude-do-controle-externo-da.

Sullivan, Mark P. "Cuba: U.S. Policy in the 116th Congress and through the Trump Administration," n.d., 82.

Sullivan, Mark P., June S. Beittel, Peter J. Meyer, Clare Ribando Seelke, Maureen Taft-Morales, and M. Angeles Villarreal. "Latin America and the Caribbean: U.S. Policy and Issues in the 116th Congress." Congressional Research Service Report. Congressional Research Service, January 8, 2021. https://crsreports.congress.gov/ product/pdf/R/R46258.

Sunstein Cass R., and Adrian Vermuele. "Symposium on Conspiracy Theories: Causes and Cures." *The Journal of Political Philosophy* 17, no. 2 (2009): 202–17.

Suyderhoud, Jacques. "Designed to Fail: Proportional Representation and Presidentialism in Latin America." Master's thesis, Naval Postgraduate School, 2020. https://calhoun.nps.edu/handle/10945/65450.

Swenson, Russell G., and Susana C. Lemozy, eds. *Democratización de la Función de Inteligencia: El Nexo de la Cultura Nacional y la Inteligencia Estratégica.* Washington, DC: National Defense Intelligence College, 2009.

Swenson, Russell G., and Susana C. Lemozy, eds., *Democratization of Intelligence* (English excerpts). Washington, DC: National Defense Intelligence College, 2009.

Swenson, Russell G., and Susana C. Lemozy, eds. *Intelligence Professionalism in the Americas.* Washington, DC: Joint Military Intelligence College, 2004.

Swenson, Russell, and Carolina Sancho. "The Governance Model of Intelligence Services in the Americas: A Comparative Assessment." Unpublished manuscript, 2021.

Swenson, Russell, and Carolina Sancho. *Intelligence Management in the Americas.* Washington, DC: National Intelligence University, 2015.

Tager Rosado, Ana Glenda. "Inteligencia y Democracia en las Américas: Guatemala en Perspectiva Comparada." Paper presented at the Center for Hemispheric Defense Studies' 4th Annual Conference on Research and Education in Defense and Security Studies, Washington, DC., May 22–25, 2001.

Taj, Mitra, and Julie Turkewitz. "Pedro Castillo, Leftist Political Outsider, Wins Peru Presidency." *New York Times*, July 19, 2021. Available at https://www.nytimes.com/2021/07/19/world/americas/peru-election-pedro-castillo.html.

Tamayo, Juan O. "Arnaldo Ochoa—a Problem for Castro Brothers 25 Years Ago." *Miami Herald.* Accessed June 27, 2021. https://www.miamiherald.com/news/nation-world/world/americas/article1967653.html.

Tavares, Rodrigo. *Security in South America: The Role of States and Regional Organizations.* Boulder, CO: Lynne Rienner Publishers, 2014.

Taylor, Adam. "Peru Had Three Presidents in One Week: Now It Has Four Months to Fix the System." *The Washington Post*, November 20, 2020. Available at https://www.washingtonpost.com/world/2020/11/20/peru-third-president-francisco-sagasti/.

Tellería Escobar, Loreta. "Fuerzas Armadas, Seguridad Interna y Democracia en Bolivia: Entre la Indefinición Estratégica y la Criminalización Social." In *El Papel de las Fuerzas Armadas en América Latina Seguridad Interna y Democracia*, eds. David Álvarez Veloso et al., 105–42. Buenos Aires: CLACSO, 2012.

Tellería Escobar, Loreta. "Política Policial en Bolivia: Entre la Continuidad y el Cambio." *Delito y Sociedad* 26, no. 44 (2017): 119–59.

Tellería Escobar, Loreta. "Wiki Revelación: Las Relaciones entre las Fuerzas Armadas y la Embajada de Estados Unidos en Bolivia (2007–2008)." In *BoliviaLeaks: La Injerencia Política de Estados Unidos contra el Proceso de Cambio 2006–2010*, ed. Juan Ramón Quintana Taborga, 145–84. Ciudad Autónoma de Buenos Aires / La Paz: CLACSO / Estado Plurinacional de Bolivia. Ministerio de la Presidencia, 2016.

Terkewitz, Julie. "Colombia Supreme Court Orders Ex-President Álvaro Uribe Detained." *The New York Times*, August 4, 2020. Available at https://www.nytimes.com/2020/08/04/world/americas/colombia-president-uribe-charged.html.

Thorp, Rosemary, Corinne Caumartin, George Gray, Maritza Paredes Molina, and Diego Zavaleta. "Group Inequalities and Political Violence: Policy Challenges and

Priorities in Bolivia, Guatemala and Peru." *CRISE Overview* No. 2. Oxford, UK: Centre for Research on Inequality, Human Security and Ethnicity (CRISE), 2010.

Tollefson, Scott D. "National Security." In *Brazil: A Country Study*, ed. by Rex A. Hudson, 33–412. Washington, DC: Library of Congress, 1998.

Torres Gorena, Fernando G. "Inteligencia Boliviana." *El País—Noticias Tarija Bolivia*, November 23, 2017. Available at https://www.elpaisonline.com/index.php/sociales-2/item/274160-inteligencia-boliviana.

Torres Gorena, Fernando Germán. *La Influencia Norteamericana en los Organismos Policiales El Caso Boliviano (1993–1997)*. Quito: FLACSO, Sede Ecuador, 2012.

Torres, Jorge. *CISEN. Auge y Decadencia del Espionaje Mexicano*. Mexico: Debate, 2009.

Torres, Jorge. *Requerimiento* [Informe de inteligencia]. San José: Dirección de Inteligencia y Seguridad del Estado, 2016.

Trevisi, A. F. "Assessing the Terrorist Threat in the Tri-Border Area of Brazil, Paraguay and Argentina." *International Institute for Counter-Terrorism*. Available at https://www.ict.org.il/UserFiles/Trevisi%202013.pdf.

Tribunal de Contas da União. "Relatório de Auditoria TC 023.480/2016-5 Gastos Sigilosos ABIN." https://pesquisa.apps.tcu.gov.br/#/documento/acórdão-completo/ABIN/%2520/DTRELEVANCIA%2520desc%252C%2520NUMACORDAOINT%2520de sc/8/%2520.

Trinidad and Tobago Newsday Archives. "Police Unable to Cope," March 25, 2014. https://archives.newsday.co.tt/2014/03/25/police-unable-to-cope-3/.

Trinidad and Tobago Parliament. "Bill Essentials—The Strategic Services Agency (Amendment) Bill, 2016 (2016)." http://www.ttparliament.org/documents/2338.pdf.

Trinidad and Tobago Parliament. "The Strategic Services Agency Regulations, 2020." n.d.

Trinkunas, Harold. "The Transformation of the Venezuelan Bolivarian Armed Force under Chávez and Maduro." In *The Routledge Handbook of Civil-Military Relations*, eds. Florina Cristiana Matei, Carolyn Halladay, and Thomas C. Bruneau, 239–65. New York: Routledge, 2021.

Trujillo Álvarez, Pedro. "La Falta de Institucionalización de la Inteligencia y su Impacto en la Seguridad: El Caso de Guatemala." *Inteligencia y Seguridad, Revista de Análisis y Prospectiva* 5 (2008–2009): 123–54.

Tubbs, Christian D. "Conditions of Democratic Erosion: Has US Democracy Reached a Tipping Point?" Master's thesis, Naval Postgraduate School, 2018. Available at http://hdl.handle.net/10945/61290.

Turner, Sharon. "National Intelligence Agency to Be Progressed This Year." *The Nassau Guardian*, February 17, 2020. https://thenassauguardian.com/national-intelligence-agency-to-be-progressed-this-year/.

Ugarte, José M. "Nueva Ley de Inteligencia." *La Nación*, December 14, 2001.

Ugarte, José Manuel. "¿En qué Cambia, en qué Persiste, y hacia Dónde Va la Actividad de Inteligencia Latinoamericana?" Paper presented at FLACSO Ecuador-ISA Joint International Conference, Quito, Ecuador, July 25–27, 2018.

Ugarte, José Manuel. "Una Visión desde Latinoamérica de la Organización de la Defensa y Relaciones Civiles-militares." In *Organización de la Defensa y control Civil de las Fuerzas Armadas en América Latina*, eds. David Pion-Berlin and José Manuel Ugarte. Buenos Aires: Jorge Baudino Ediciones, 2013.

Ugarte, José Manuel. "Un Gran Reto Democrático: Controlar la Inteligencia." In *Los Macro y Micro Desafíos de la Seguridad en Democracia: Contradicciones y Vulnerabilidades en América Latina*, eds., Bertha García Gallegos and José Manuel Ugarte. Quito: Pontificia Universidad Católica del Ecuador, 2018. Available at https://www.researchgate.net/publication/326071054_UN_GRAN_RETO_DEM OCRATICO_CONTROLAR_LA_INTELIGENCIA.

UN Human Rights Council. "Statement to the Media by the United Nations Special Rapporteur on the Right to Privacy, on the Conclusion of His Official Visit to Argentina, 6–17 May 2019," by Special Rapporteur Joseph A. Cannataci, Buenos Aires, May 17, 2019. Available at https://www.ohchr.org/EN/NewsEvents/Pages/ DisplayNews.aspx?NewsID=24639&LangID=E.

UN Office of the High Commissioner for Human Rights. "Bolivia: UN Human Rights Chief Urges Structural Changes to Prevent Crises." Geneva, August 24, 2020. Available at https://www.ohchr.org/EN/NewsEvents/Pages/DisplayNews .aspx?NewsID=26184&LangID=E.

Ungar, Mark. *Elusive Reform: Democracy and Rule of Law in Latin America*. Boulder: Lynne Rienner Publishers, 2002.

United Nations, General Assembly Security Council. *Agreement on the Procedure for the Search for Peace by Political Means*. A/45/1007 S/22563 (May 2, 1991). Available at https://peacemaker.un.org/sites/peacemaker.un.org/files/GT_910426_Mexico Agreement.pdf.

United Nations, General Assembly Security Council. *Agreement on the Strengthening of Civilian Power and on the Role of the Armed Forces in a Democratic Society*. A/51/410 S/1996/853 (October 16, 1996). Available at https://peacemaker .un.org/sites/peacemaker.un.org/files/GT_960919_AgreementStrengthening CivilianPower.pdf.

United Nations, General Assembly Security Council. *Peace Agreement*. A/46/664 S/23501 (January 30, 1992). Available at https://peacemaker.un.org/sites/peace-maker.un.org/files/SV_920116_ChapultepecAgreement.pdf.

United Nations, General Assembly Security Council. *Report of the UN Truth Commission on El Salvador. From Madness to Hope, The 12 Year War in El Salvador.* S 25500 (1 Abril 1993). Available at https://undocs.org/pdf?symbol=en/S/25500.

United Nations, General Assembly Security Council. *Agreement on a Firm and Lasting Peace*. A/51/796 S/1997/114 (February 7, 1997). Available at https://peace maker.un.org/guatemala-firmlastingpeace96.

United Nations Humans Rights Council. *Detailed Findings of the Independent International Factfinding Mission on the Bolivarian Republic of Venezuela*. A/HRC/45/ CRP.11. September 15, 2020. https://www.ohchr.org/documents/hrbodies/hrcouncil/ FFMV/A_HRC_45_CRP.11.pdf.

United Nations Office on Drugs and Crime. *Global Study on Homicide; Homicide Trends, Patterns, and Criminal Justice Responses 2019*, 2019. http://www.unodc.org/documents/data-and-analysis/gsh/Booklet2.pdf.

United States Army Intelligence Agency. "Colombia Army Country Profile." August 9, 1990.

United States Bureau of Citizenship and Immigration Services. "Venezuela: Information on Círculos Bolivarianos." April 30, 2002. https://www.refworld.org/docid/3dec9b4b4.htm.

United States Central Intelligence Agency. *Consequences of a Military Coup in Chile* (1973).

United States Department of State Agency for International Development Office of Public Safety. "Report on the Republic of Colombia: National Police and the Administrative Department of Security." December 1962.

USAF Office of Commercial and Economic Analysis. 2021. https://www.afocea.com.

U.S. Department of Defense, *Summary of the 2018 National Defense Strategy of The United States of America: Sharpening the American Military's Competitive Edge*. Available at https://dod.defense.gov/Portals/1/Documents/pubs/2018-National-Defense-Strategy-Summary.pdf.

U.S. Navy Press Office. "NPS Launches Distance Learning Graduate Certificate in Great Power Competition." September 17, 2020. https://www.navy.mil/Press-Office/News-Stories/Article/2351609/nps-launches-distance-learning-graduate-certificate-in-great-power-competition/.

Valencia Ramírez, Cristóbal. "Venezuela's Bolivarian Revolution: Who Are the Chavistas?" *Latin American Perspectives* 32, no. 3 (2005): 79–97. http://www.jstor.org/stable/30040243.

Vallarino, Raúl. *Mi Nombre es Patria.* Montevideo: Fin de Siglo, 2016.

Van Puyvelde, Damien. *Outsourcing US Intelligence: Contractors and Government Accountability*. Glasgow: Edinburgh University Press.

Vanden, Harry E., and Gary Prevost. *Politics of Latin America: The Power Game*. Seventh edition. New York: Oxford University Press, 2021.

Varas, Augusto, and Fernando Bustamante. *Fuerzas Armadas y Política en Ecuador.* Quito: FLACSO-Ecuador, 1977.

Vargas, Mateus. "Informes da Abin destacam benefício da quarentena e citam subnotificação." *O Estado de São Paulo*, May 31, 2020. https://cutt.ly/VxSXQXq.

Varnoux Garay, Marcelo. "La Seguridad Ciudadana en Bolivia: Entre la Delincuencia y los Motines Policiales." *Diálogo Político* 20, no. 3 (2003).

Vela, Manolo. "De Peras y Olmos: La Reforma de los Servicios de Inteligencia en Guatemala." *Revista de la Secretaría de Análisis Estratégico de la Presidencia de la República* 1, no. 1 (2002): 67–100.

Vela, Manolo. "Dilemas de la Reforma del Sistema de Inteligencia en Guatemala." *Diálogo* 3 (1999).

Velez de Berliner, Maria. "The Middle East and Latin America: Implications for Latin America's Security." In *Routledge Handbook of Latin American Security*, eds. David R. Mares and Arie M. Kacowicz, 313–23. New York: Routledge, 2016.

Vélez Jiménez, Palmira. "Dictaduras, Derechos Humanos, Memoria y Archivos en Latinoamérica. El Caso Paraguayo." In *América: Poder, Conflicto y Política*, coords. Gabriela Dalla Corte Caballero, Ricardo Piqueras Céspedes, and Meritxell Tous Mata. Universidad de Murcia—Asociación Española de Americanistas, 2013. Available at https://dialnet.unirioja.es/descarga/libro/569094.pdf.

Velit, Juan. "Inteligencia Sin Espejismos." Interview by Pablo O'Brien. *Caretas*. May 23, 2002. Available at http://www2.caretas.pe/2002/1722/articulos/inteligencia.phtml.

Vera Lama, Rodrigo. *Sistema de Inteligencia del Estado a la luz del Derecho*. Santiago, Chile: Librotecnia, 2008.

Verdélio, Andreia. "Bolsonaro preside hoje 39ª Reunião do Conselho de Governo." *Agência Brasil*, November 19, 2020. https://agenciabrasil.ebc.com.br/politica/noticia/2020-11/bolsonaro-preside-hoje-39a-reuniao-do-conselho-de-governo.

Verdes-Montenegro Escánez, Francisco J., and Érika M. Rodríguez-Pinzón. "Bukele y las Fuerzas Armadas: Un Tándem que Erosiona los Contrapesos de la Democracia Salvadoreña." In *Pensamiento Propio, Militarización y Seguridad Pública en las Américas*, eds., Thiago Rodrigues, Érika M. Rodríguez-Pinzón, and Ole Wæver, 205–32. CRIES, January–June 2020. Available at http://www.cries.org/wp-content/uploads/2020/08/012-Montenegro.pdf.

Verón, Mariana. "Cristina descabezó la ex SIDE por las internas y la ofensiva judicial." *La Nación*, December 17, 2014. Available at http://edicionimpresa.lanacion.com.ar/la-nacion/20141217/textview.

Vilas, Carlos M. "El Camino hacia la Revolución y la Guerra." In *Observatorio Latinoamericano 9. Dossier El Salvador*, 44–51. Buenos Aires: Instituto de Estudios de América Latina y el Caribe, 2012.

Von Santos, Herard. "El Servicio Territorial como parte del Sistema de Control Social y Territorial del Estado Salvadoreño durante el Conflicto Armado (1972–1992)." *Revista Policía y Seguridad Pública* (2016): 227–94.

Von Santos, Herard. "Estudio Historiográfico sobre los Sistemas de Inteligencia de los Antiguos Cuerpos de Seguridad Pública Salvadoreños." *Revista Policía y Seguridad Pública* 5, no. 2 (2015): 287–350.

Von Santos, Herard. "La Formación en Inteligencia Policial: Análisis de la Oferta Educativa de la ANSP." *Revista Policía y Seguridad Pública* 7, no. 2 (2017): 81–141.

Waldmann, Peter. "¿Protección o Extorsión? Aproximación al Perfil Real de la Policía en América Latina." In *El Estado Anómico. Derecho, Seguridad Pública y Vida Cotidiana en América Latina*, ed., Peter Waldmann, 111–38. Caracas: Nueva Sociedad, 2003.

Wallace, Elisabeth. "The West Indies Federation: Decline and Fall:" *International Journal*, June 25, 2016. https://doi.org/10.1177/002070206201700305.

Webber, Jeffery R. "Bolivia in the Era of Evo Morales." *Latin American Research Review* 45, no. 3 (2010): 248–60.

Weeks, Gregory. "A Preference for Deference: Reforming the Military's Intelligence Role in Argentina, Chile and Peru." *Third World Quarterly* 29, no. 1 (2008): 45–61.

Weld, Kirsten. *Paper Cadavers: The Archives of Dictatorship in Guatemala*. Durham, NC: Duke University Press, 2014.

Wetzling, Thorsten. "Options for More Effective Intelligence Oversight." Stiftung Neue Verantwortung, 2017. https://www.stiftung-nv.de/de/publikation/options -more-effective-intelligence-oversight.

Weyland, Kurt. "Neopopulism and Neoliberalism in Latin America: How Much Affinity?" *Third World Quarterly* 24, no. 6 (2003): 1095–115.

Weyland, Kurt. "Revolution and Reaction." Rocking Our Priors. Accessed January 19, 2021. https://soundcloud.com/user-845572280/revolution-reaction-professor -kurt-weyland.

Weyland, Kurt. "The Rise and Decline of Fujimori's Neopopulist Leadership." In *The Fujimori Legacy: The Rise of Electoral Authoritarianism in Peru*, ed. Julio F. Carrión, 13–38. University Park, PA: Penn State University Press, 2006.

Wickham-Crowley, Timothy. "Two 'Waves' of Guerrilla-Movement Organizing in Latin America, 1956–1990." *Comparative Studies in Society and History* 56, no. 1 (January 2014): 215–42. https://doi.org/10.1017/S0010417513000674.

Wilkinson, Tracy. "Guerrillas Return to Arms in Colombia Complicates U.S. Policy in Latin America." *Los Angeles Times,* September 4, 2019.

Wilson, David B., Roger B. Parks, and Stephen D. Mastrofski. "The Impact of Police Reform on Communities of Trinidad and Tobago." *Journal of Experimental Criminology*, Dordrecht 7, no. 4 (December 2011): 375–405. http://dx.doi.org/10.1007/ s11292-011-9131-y.

Winer, Sonia. *Doctrina de inSeguridad Mundial: Paraguay como Laboratorio de Estados Unidos en la Región.* Buenos Aires: Prometeo Libros, 2015.

Wishart, Eric. *Intelligence Networks and the Tri-Border Area of South America: The Dilemma of Efficiency versus Oversight.* Master's thesis, Naval Postgraduate School, 2002. Available at http://www.dtic.mil/cgi-bin/GetTRDoc?AD=ADA4112 44&Location=U2&doc=GetTRDoc.pdf.

WOLA. *El Estado Cautivo, Crimen Organizado y Derechos Humanos en América Latina.* Washington, DC: Washington Office of Latin America, 2007. Available at https://www.wola.org/sites/default/files/downloadable/Citizen%20Security/past/ el_estado_cautivo%20FINAL.pdf.

WOLA. *La Comisión Internacional contra la Impunidad en Guatemala (CICIG): Un instrumento innovador contra redes criminales y para el fortalecimiento del Estado de derecho.* Washington, DC: Oficina en Washington para Asuntos Latinoamericanos, 2015.

Wolf, Sonja. "El Nexo entre las Maras y el Crimen Organizado." In *Anuario 2012 de Seguridad Regional en América Latina y el Caribe*, eds. Hans Mathieu and Catalina Niño Guarnizo, 252–74. Bogotá: Friedrich Ebert Stiftung en Colombia, 2012.

Yannuzzi, Rick E. 2000 "In-Q-Tel: A New Partnership between the CIA and the Private Sector," CIA, Center for the Study of Intelligence. Available at https://www .cia.gov/library/publications/intelligence-history/in-q-tel.

Yauri-Miranda, Jaseff R. "Principles to Assess Accountability: A Study of Intelligence Agencies in Spain and Brazil." *International Journal of Intelligence and Counter-Intelligence*, 2020. DOI: 10.1080/08850607.2020.1809954.

Ybarra, Gustavo, and Lucas Colonna. "Sigue en vigor la polémica 'ley espía,' *La Nación*, Buenos Aires, May 2, 2005. Available at https://www.lanacion.com.ar/ politica/sigue-en-vigor-la-polemica-ley-espia-nid700765/.

Yore, Fátima Myriam. *La Dominación Stronista: Orígenes y Consolidación. "Seguridad Nacional" y Represión.* Asunción: BASE-IS, 1992.

Young, Gerardo. *Código Stiuso: La SIDE, La Política desde las Cloacas y la Muerte de Nisman.* Buenos Aires: Planeta, 2015.

Young, Gerardo. "Diez Años de Espionaje Nacional y Popular." *La Nación*, July 28, 2013. Available at https://www.lanacion.com.ar/opinion/diez-anos-de-espionaje -nacional-y-popular-nid1604944.

Young, Gerardo. *SIDE: La Argentina Secreta.* Buenos Aires: Planeta, 2006.

Young, Kevin A. "El Salvador's FMLN and the Constraints on Leftist Government." In *Oxford Research Encyclopedia of Latin American Politics*, eds. Harry Vanden and Gary Prevost. New York: Oxford University Press, 2019. DOI: 10.1093/acre fore/9780190228637.013.1768.

Index

Contributors

Florina Cristiana Matei is a lecturer at the Center for Homeland Defense and Security at the United States Naval Postgraduate School, Monterey, California, where she has been a lecturer and research associate since 2003. A native of Romania, she earned her BS in physics (nuclear interactions and elementary particles) at the University of Bucharest, then worked for the Romanian Ministry of Defense as a civilian subject matter expert. She later earned an MA in International Security Affairs and Civil-Military Relations at the Naval Postgraduate School, and her PhD in the War Studies Department at King's College London. A frequent author on security matters, she was coeditor, with Dr. Thomas C. Bruneau, of *The Routledge Handbook of Civil-Military Relations* (2012) and coeditor, with Dr. Carolyn Halladay, of *The Conduct of Intelligence in Democracies: Processes, Practices, Cultures* (2019). Currently serving as co-program chair of the Intelligence Studies Section of the International Studies Association, and associate editor of the *International Journal of Intelligence and Counterintelligence.*

Eduardo E. Estévez is an independent consultant/researcher specializing in intelligence and security, police reforms, and citizen security. He is adjunct professor at the Instituto Universitario de la Policía Federal Argentina (IUPFA), Buenos Aires, Argentina. He served as secretary of analysis and articulation of processes, ministry of security of the Province of Santa Fe (2015–2019). He held key positions in the Ministry of Interior of the Nation, and the Ministry of Security of the Province of Buenos Aires (2000–2015). In the 1990s he served as parliamentary advisor to the National Congress of Argentina. He has authored or coauthored numerous book chapters and articles in peer-reviewed journals on intelligence studies and related issues. He is a contributor to *World Police Encyclopedia* (2006) and *Diccionario Inteligencia y Seguridad* (2013).

Carolyn Halladay is senior lecturer in the National Security Affairs Department at the Naval Postgraduate School (NPS). She also lectures at the NPS Center for Homeland Defense and Security. A historian and a lawyer, Dr. Halladay's academic focus is on contemporary Central Europe, but she has participated in CCMR programs around the world. Before joining the NPS faculty, she was a lecturer in history at Pennsylvania State Erie, The Behrend College. She has also taught history and international relations at the graduate and undergraduate levels at The George Washington University in Washington, DC. Her government service has included working as a historian in the U.S. Department of State and as a federal tax prosecutor in the U.S. Department of Justice, in addition to legal assignments in the offices of general counsel at the U.S. Departments of Defense and Transportation.

CONTRIBUTING AUTHORS

Nicolás Alvarez holds a degree and a post-graduate diploma in political science from the University of the Republic in Uruguay. Furthermore, he has been awarded a diploma of specialization in international security from the University of Santiago de Compostela, Spain. He served as a parliamentary advisor on security, defense, and intelligence subject matters in Uruguay, participating in the drafting of one of the first bills regarding the democratic control of intelligence services. Furthermore, he worked as a researcher at the Faculty of Social Sciences in projects on worldwide drugs problems. He is currently finishing his political science master's thesis.

Jason M. Blazakis is a professor of practice at Middlebury Institute of International Studies, director of its Center on Terrorism, Extremism, and Counterterrorism, and a senior research fellow at the Soufan Center. From 2008 to August 2018, he was director of the State Department's Office of Counterterrorism Finance and Designations. He also worked at State's Bureau of Intelligence and Research and was a domestic intelligence analyst with the Congressional Research Service.

Brendan J. de Brun grew up in Mexico City, Mexico. He attended the United States Air Force Academy, earning a degree in foreign area studies. After graduating and receiving his commission, Major de Brun became a fixed-wing combat search and rescue (CSAR) pilot, deploying across East Africa, South America, and the Middle East. His experience spans both combat and humanitarian operations (the latter both domestic and abroad), and he is currently a foreign area officer (FAO) focused on South America. Major de Brun is currently attending the Naval Postgraduate School in Monterey, California, where he is earning his master's degree in western hemisphere security affairs.

Carlos Humberto Cascante-Segura is a lawyer and professor of history of international relations and foreign policy of Costa Rica and Central America, National University and University of Costa Rica. He holds a master's degree in diplomacy and history from the University of Costa Rica. He is currently a PhD candidate in history at the University of Costa Rica.

Marco Cepik is experienced in three distinct areas of knowledge: international security, intelligence studies, and digital government. He is currently based in Porto Alegre, south of Brazil, as associate professor at the Federal University of Rio Grande do Sul (UFRGS). So far he has published eleven books and more than seventy scientific articles and book chapters in Portuguese, English, and Spanish. Professor Cepik holds a PhD in political science (IUPERJ, 2001). He has been a post-doctoral visiting professor at Oxford University and Naval Post Graduate School (NPS), among other institutions in Latin America, the United States, and Europe.

Richard Elmore is an air force pilot, foreign area officer, and air advisor tasked with advancing security cooperation efforts in the Latin American region. He received his bachelor of science in biology from the United States Air Force Academy, holds a master of aeronautical science from Embry-Riddle University, and recently graduated from the Naval Postgraduate School, receiving a master of arts in security studies (western hemisphere). Currently, he and his family are stationed in the California Bay Area, where Richard is tasked with building Latin American partner nations' air mobility capabilities and furthering shared national objectives.

Germán E. Gallino holds a degree in political science from the National University of La Matanza (UNLam), Argentina. He is a professor of political science and law, UNLam. He is also a researcher at the Center for Science and Thought of the National University of San Martin (UNSAM). He is currently a PhD candidate in social and human sciences at National University of Quilmes (UNQ) focusing on the areas of public security and state intelligence in the context of democratic governments.

Gerardo Hernández-Naranjo has a PhD in social sciences from Colegio de México. He is associate professor and director of the Political Sciences School, University of Costa Rica, San José de Costa Rica. He has coauthored book chapters in *Handbook of Central American Governance* (2014) and *Government Formation and Minister Turnover in Presidential Cabinets: Comparative Analysis in the Americas* (2018).

Marco Vinicio Méndez-Coto has a PhD in international studies from the FLACSO Ecuador. He holds a master's degree in human rights and education for peace from the National University of Costa Rica. He serves as a professor and researcher at the School of International Relations in the field of international politics and strategic and security studies. He obtained a graduate scholarship from the Organization of American States between 2016 and 2018. He has published several papers in academic journals and books related to international politics in Latin America, Costa Rican foreign policy, and human rights. His most recent research analyzes the foreign policy of Latin American small states.

Marcos Pablo Moloeznik has a PhD in law from the University of Alcala, Spain. He is a full-time professor-researcher, Political Sciences Department, Center of Social Sciences and Humanities (CUCSH), University of Guadalajara, Mexico, and national researcher level II, National Researchers System, CONACYT, Mexico. He has authored four books and more than seventy book chapters. He has been a visiting professor at Universität Zu Köln and Freie Universität Berlin; University of Warsaw; University of Buenos Aires, University of El Salvador and National University of Rosario, Argentina; University of Alcala; University of Leiden, Netherlands; and University of Miami and San Diego (United States). He was guest professor at the Advanced Course on International Humanitarian Law at the International Institute of Humanitarian Law (IIHL) of Sanremo (Italy), from 2013 to 2018. He was granted the 2017 William J. Perry Award for Excellence in Security and Defense Education, William J. Perry Center for Hemispheric Defense Studies, National Defense University (United States).

Jacques (Jake) Suyderhoud is a former fighter pilot and a navy foreign area officer specializing in Latin American affairs. He received his bachelor's in international relations from Stanford University and graduated with distinction from the Naval Postgraduate School, earning a master's degree in regional security studies (western hemisphere). During his graduate studies, he received the Louis D. Liskin Award for excellence in regional security studies and for the contributions of his master's thesis, "Designed to Fail: Proportional Representation and Presidentialism in Latin America."

Shane Moran is a U.S. Air Force major. He is the deputy chief of the Military Liaison Office for the Eastern Caribbean and the Organization of Eastern Caribbean States in Bridgetown, Barbados. Major Moran earned a bachelor of science degree in military history at the United States Air Force Academy and a master of arts in western hemisphere security studies from the Naval Postgraduate School. Prior to his current assignment, Major Moran served as a wing executive officer and KC-135 evaluator pilot at Fairchild Air Force Base in Spokane, Washington, and also served on the training and operations staff in Seventh Air Force at Osan Air Base in South Korea.

John "Clay" Oeffinger is a U.S. Air Force major. He is a staff officer in the Theater Security Cooperation Division at Headquarters, Air Forces Southern, located at Davis-Monthan Air Force base in Tucson, Arizona. Major Oeffinger earned his BA in political science from Texas A&M University, College Station, and a, MS in western hemisphere regional security studies from the Naval Postgraduate School. Prior to his current assignment, Major Oeffinger served as a nuclear launch officer at Minot Air Force Base in Minot, North Dakota.

María Alejandra Otamendi is a researcher, National Scientific and Technical Research Council (CONICET), based at Gino Germani Research Institute, University of Buenos Aires (UBA), where she teaches social research methods. She holds a double PhD in sociology from UBA and the School of Advanced Studies in Social Sciences (EHESS) in Paris; a master of science degree in global governance and diplomacy at the University of Oxford, and a degree in sociology at UBA. She is regional editor of *Global Dialogue*, a journal of the International Sociological Association and editorial board member of *URVIO* journal (FLACSO Ecuador). She was in charge of the police training section and adviser at the National Institute of Strategic Security Studies (INEES), Ministry of Security of Argentina. She was a consultant at IADB and UNDP.

Kevin Peters is the chief of the National Threat Evaluation and Reporting (NTER) Program, Partner Engagement, Field Operations Division, Office of Intelligence and Analysis, Department of Homeland Security. He holds a master's degree from the Naval Postgraduate School in Monterey, California.

Victor Ray holds a master of arts in western hemisphere security studies from the Naval Postgraduate School in Monterey, California, and conducted his undergraduate studies at the University of California, Berkeley. He currently lives in Lima, Peru, and is a Latin America foreign area officer in the United States Marine Corps.

Renato Rivera Rhon holds a master's degree in international relations, Institut Barcelona d' Estudis Internationals, IBEI. He is currently finishing his master's thesis in international relations from the FLACSO Ecuador. He served as analyst for coordination of strategic insertion, National Secretariat of Planning and Development of Ecuador.

Fredy Rivera Vélez holds a PhD in social sciences from the National University of Cuyo, Argentina. He has been a tenured professor and researcher since 1999 at FLACSO Ecuador, where he works as a research coordinator. In the Republic of Ecuador, he has served as undersecretary of internal security and political coordination of the police and cults (2008–2010); advisor of international affairs of the Ministerial Cabinet of National Defense, and chair of the board of directors of International Cooperation (2008–2011). He was also the director of the *Latin American Journal of Security Studies* (*URVIO*) and the Latin American Network for Security Analysis and Organized Crime (RELASEDOR).

www.ingramcontent.com/pod-product-compliance
Lightning Source LLC
Chambersburg PA
CBHW021807270326
41932CB00007B/82